DELTA'S
Key to the
Next Generation
TOEFL® Test

Advanced Skill Practice for the iBT

by

Nancy Gallagher

DELTA PUBLISHING COMPANY

DELTA PUBLISHING COMPANY
A Divison of DELTA SYSTEMS CO., INC.
1400 Miller Parkway
McHenry, IL 60050 USA
(800) 323-8270 or (815) 363-3582
www.delta-systems.com

Editor:	Patricia Brenner
Page Layout & Design:	Linda Bruell
Cover Design:	Damon Taylor
Additional Artwork:	Damon Taylor and Kathy Combs
Audio Production:	Jay Kenney and Audio Logic, Inc.

Printed in the United States of America

10 9 8 7 6 5 4 3 2

Text	1-887744-94-0
Audio CD's	1-887744-95-9

CONTENTS

The Next Generation TOEFL® Test

The Test of English as a Foreign Language® (TOEFL®) is a standardized test that measures the English proficiency of students who wish to enter college and university programs in the United States and Canada. The TOEFL is produced and administered by Educational Testing Service, a professional test development organization in Princeton, New Jersey, USA.

The Next Generation TOEFL® Test is the Internet–based test (iBT) introduced worldwide in September 2005. This new version of the test replaces the earlier computer–based TOEFL Test (CBT). The new test has four sections covering the language skills of reading, listening, speaking, and writing. The test is approximately 3½ hours long, with one 10–minute break after the Listening section.

NEXT GENERATION TOEFL® IBT			
Section	**Content**	**Number of Questions**	**Approximate Time**
Reading	3 passages	36–42	60 minutes
Listening	2 conversations 4 lectures	34	60 minutes
Speaking	2 independent tasks 4 integrated–skills tasks	6	20 minutes
Writing	1 integrated–skills task 1 independent task	2	60 minutes

In the Reading section, students read three passages and answer questions about them. In the Listening section, students listen to two conversations and four lectures and answer questions about them. In the Speaking section, students speak in response to two questions about their own experience and four questions about texts that they listen to or read during the test. In the Writing section, students write in response to two questions. One question is about a reading passage and a lecture, and the other question is about a general topic.

The most important differences between the new TOEFL test and previous versions of the test are:

- Note taking is allowed throughout the test.
- Speaking skills are evaluated.
- Some questions involve integrated skills, such as reading–listening–speaking.
- Knowledge of grammar is not tested separately but is tested indirectly in all sections of the test.

The content of the new TOEFL test reflects the language that is used in real academic settings. The content is based on a collection of spoken and written language that Educational Testing Service obtained from educational institutions throughout the United States. The spoken language came from lectures, class discussions, office hours, study groups, and service interactions such as conversations at the library. The written language was collected from textbooks and other course materials.

The Speaking and Writing sections of the test include some tasks that integrate, or combine, language skills. For example, a student might read a passage, listen to a lecture, and then write or speak in response. The integrated–skills tasks reflect how people use language in real life; thus, they give academic programs a more realistic measure of how well prospective students will be able to communicate in an English–speaking environment.

For the most current information about the TOEFL test, including information on test dates and how to register to take the test, visit the official TOEFL Web site at: www.ets.org/toefl.

Scoring on the New Test

TOEFL scores help the admissions staff of colleges and universities to determine if a student's English skills are adequate for enrollment in a specific program of study. There is no single passing score; rather, institutions set their own standards for admission.

The TOEFL score report will show:

- a separate score of 0 to 30 for each of the four language skills;
- a total test score of 0 to 120; and
- a TOEFL CBT score comparison.

In the Reading section, most correct answers will earn 1 raw point each, but some questions are worth 2, 3, or 4 points. In the Listening section, most correct answers will earn 1 raw point, but some questions are worth 2 points. In the Speaking section, each of the six responses will earn a raw score of 1 to 4 points. In the Writing section, the two responses will each earn a raw score of 1 to 5 points. In each section of the test, the total number of raw points earned will be converted to a scaled section score of 0 to 30.

NEXT GENERATION TOEFL® iBT				
Section	Number of Questions	Raw Points per Question	Total Raw Points	Scaled Section Score
Reading	36–42	1–4	42–46	30
Listening	34	1–2	34–36	30
Speaking	6	1–4	24	30
Writing	2	1–5	10	30
			Total Test Score	120

The four section scores will be combined to obtain the total test score, which is on a scale of 0 to 120. The score report will also show a comparison between the total score and a score on the previous version of the test, the TOEFL CBT. For example, a total score of 100 on the Next Generation TOEFL test is equivalent to a score of 250 on the TOEFL CBT.

TOTAL SCORE COMPARISON		
Next Generation TOEFL® iBT	TOEFL® CBT	Paper–based TOEFL® Test
120	300	677
100	250	600
80	213	550
61	173	500
46	133	450

HOW TO USE THIS BOOK

Delta's Key to the Next Generation TOEFL® Test: Advanced Skill Practice for the iBT is a complete test preparation course for high intermediate to advanced learners of English. The course has two objectives: (1) to prepare students to take the TOEFL test, and (2) to build the language skills necessary for success in college and university.

Advanced Skill Practice for the iBT contains 36 skill units and four full–length practice tests, with more than 1,200 test questions that are similar in form and content to those on the real TOEFL test. There is enough material for approximately 15 weeks of study. The book can be used in a number of ways:

- as the primary text in a comprehensive TOEFL test preparation course;
- as the primary or secondary text for courses in reading, listening, speaking, or writing skills; or
- as a resource for independent study, laboratory, or tutoring.

Advanced Skill Practice for the iBT is inspired by cognitive learning theory and designed around how people learn language. Its organizing scheme is the five–part unit composed of *Focus, Do You Know...?, Practice, Extension*, and *Progress*.

 Focus

Each unit opens with an exercise to focus attention, activate prior learning, and help students predict the content. Focus begins with an English text—a reading passage, a conversation, part of a lecture, or an essay paragraph—and challenges the learner to identify a relevant principle. Focus stimulates inductive thinking. These exercises can be done in class or as homework.

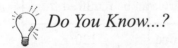 *Do You Know...?*

Do You Know...? provides instruction in one of the four skill areas: reading, listening, speaking, or writing. It defines relevant terms and concepts, explains how the skill will be tested, provides examples, and identifies useful strategies. Do You Know...? can be the subject of classroom lectures and discussions, or it can be studied as homework.

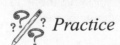 *Practice*

Practice consists of sets of test questions that challenge students to apply their skills. Practice exercises foster ease with TOEFL test form and content and build confidence and skill retention. They can be done in class as individual, pair, or group exercises, or they can be assigned as homework.

 *Extension*

People acquire language through social interaction, and Extension presents ideas for classroom activities that foster cooperation, stimulate discussion, extend skill practice, guide peer review, and link the classroom with the real world. Extension activities are student–centered, and many engage students in finding or creating their own TOEFL–like texts.

 Progress

Because regular assessment is an integral part of skill building, the skills are tested throughout the course. Thirty–four timed quizzes simulate parts of the TOEFL test, with each quiz covering the skills studied in one or more units. Quiz content builds cumulatively, with some quizzes integrating and reviewing several units.

 Tests

Four full–length practice tests contain questions that are similar in form and content to the questions on the new version of the TOEFL test. The tests can be used to review course material and to assess student readiness to take the real TOEFL test.

 Answer Key

The Answer Key provides the correct answers for all Practice exercises and Progress quizzes as well as the four full–length Tests. The Answer Key provides references to relevant units for review and study. The Answer Key can easily be removed from the book.

 Audio Scripts

The Audio Scripts include the transcripts for all listening material in the book. The scripts can be used in several ways in addition to TOEFL test preparation. For example, students can read the conversations aloud or perform them as skits. They can use the conversations and lectures to learn vocabulary and idioms in context. The Audio Scripts can easily be removed from the book.

 Progress Charts

Students can graph their scores for all quizzes and tests on the Progress Charts beginning on page 692. The charts motivate students and encourage them to set goals for achievement. The charts can be removed from the book and included in the student's portfolio of work.

 Audio CDs

The companion set of audio disks is the listening component of the course. The ten disks contain all of the audio texts for the Listening, Speaking, and Writing sections of the book and for the four Tests. In addition to TOEFL test preparation, the recordings can be used for practice in note taking, summarizing, pronunciation, and intonation, as well as the study of vocabulary and idioms in context and English through academic content.

SAMPLE COURSE OUTLINE

	15-week TOEFL® Test Preparation Course 75 hours of instruction		
Week	**Units**	**Topics**	**Quiz or Test**
1	1.1 – 1.2 2.1– 2.2	**Reading:** Facts and Details; Negative Facts **Listening:** Topic and Main Idea; Details	Reading Quiz 1 Listening Quiz 1
2	1.3 2.3	**Reading:** Referents **Listening:** Attitude and Purpose	Reading Quiz 2 Listening Quiz 2 & 3
3	1.4	**Reading:** Vocabulary in Context	Reading Quiz 3 & 4
4	1.5 – 1.6 2.4	**Reading:** Inferences; Purpose **Listening:** Inferences and Predictions	Reading Quiz 5 & 6 Listening Quiz 4 & 5
5	1.7 – 1.8 2.5 – 2.6	**Reading:** Paraphrases; Coherence **Listening:** Categorizing Information; Summarizing a Process	Reading Quiz 7 & 8 Listening Quiz 6
6	1.9 – 1.10	**Reading:** Summarizing Important Ideas; Organizing Information	Reading Quiz 9 & 10 Listening Quiz 7 & 8
7	3.1 – 3.4	**Speaking:** Developing a Topic; Stating and Supporting an Opinion; Speaking Clearly and Coherently; Evaluating Independent Speaking	Speaking Quiz 1, 2 & 3
8	4.1 – 4.4	**Writing:** Connecting Information; Taking Notes; Developing Ideas; Sentence Structure	—
9	3.5 – 3.7 4.5	**Speaking:** Connecting Information; Taking Notes; Developing a Topic **Writing:** Evaluating the Response	Writing Quiz 1, 2 & 3
10	3.8 – 3.10	**Speaking:** Summarizing a Problem; Summarizing Important Ideas; Evaluating Integrated Speaking	Speaking Quiz 4, 5 & 6
11	4.6 – 4.9	**Writing:** Prewriting; Stating and Supporting an Opinion; Writing Coherently; Sentence Variety and Word Choice	Speaking Quiz 7 & 8
12	4.10	**Writing:** Evaluating the Essay	Writing Quiz 4, 5, & 6 Writing Quiz 7 & 8
13 14 15		Review and Evaluation	Test 1 – Test 4

The Reading section of the TOEFL measures your ability to read and understand passages in English. You will be tested on your comprehension of major ideas, important information, vocabulary, and relationships among ideas in the passages. You will be required to:

- identify major ideas and distinguish them from minor ideas;
- verify what information is true and what information is not true or not included in the passage;
- define words and phrases as they are used the passage;
- make inferences about information that is not directly stated;
- identify the author's purpose;
- connect ideas within sentences and among sentences; and
- summarize and organize important ideas from across the passage.

The passages are about subjects that students commonly study in their first and second year of university, such as natural sciences, social sciences, business, and the arts. The language is generally formal and academic rather than informal or conversational. The rhetorical purpose of the passages may be expository, argumentative, historical, or biographical. All of the questions are based on the information in the passage. You do not need special knowledge of the topics to answer the questions.

Students in North American schools are required to do a lot of reading in their courses. Success in college and university depends on being able to read effectively, so reading is an essential academic skill. In an academic program, you will be expected to read extensively, understand important and supporting ideas in the material, and discuss the ideas in class. You will also be required to paraphrase and summarize ideas when you write reports and term papers.

READING SECTION			
Reading Text	**Time Allowed**	**Length of Passage**	**Number of Questions**
Passage 1	20 minutes	600 – 700 words	12 – 14
Passage 2	20 minutes	600 – 700 words	12 – 14
Passage 3	20 minutes	600 – 700 words	12 – 14
Passage 4 & 5*	20 minutes each	600 – 700 words each	12 – 14 each

*There may be five reading passages in some versions of the test.

THE TEST EXPERIENCE

The time allowed for the entire Reading section is 60 minutes. In some versions of the test, it is 100 minutes. The time allowed includes the time that you spend reading the passages and answering the questions.

You may take notes and you may use your notes to help you answer the questions. However, at the end of the test, you must give all of your notes to the test supervisor. Your notes will not be scored.

A few words in the passages, especially technical terms, may be defined in a glossary that is available to you during the test. If a word is highlighted in the text, click on the word to read a definition of it.

There are three types of reading comprehension questions. For each type of question, you will use the mouse to click on an answer or to move text. Some questions will be worth more than one point. These questions have special directions that indicate how many points you can receive.

The computer will give you one question at a time. You will be able to see the passage while you are answering the questions. You may skip questions and return to them later by clicking either the **Back** button or the **Review** button at the top of the screen. The **Back** button will take you to the previous question. The **Review** button will take you to a list of all reading questions on the test. From this list, you may return to any previous question to review or change your answer.

READING SKILLS ON THE TEST

Unit in *Delta's Key*	Skill	Number of Questions (test with 3 passages)
1.1	Understanding Facts and Details	8 – 10
1.2	Identifying Negative Facts	2 – 3
1.3	Locating Referents	2 – 3
1.4	Understanding Vocabulary in Context	8 – 10
1.5	Making Inferences	3
1.6	Determing Purpose	3
1.7	Recognizing Paraphrases	3
1.8	Recognizing Coherence	3
1.9	Summarizing Important Ideas	2 – 3
1.10	Organizing Information	1
	Total Number of Questions	36 – 42

READING PASSAGES AND QUESTIONS

The Reading section contains three passages. In some versions of the test, there may be five passages. Each passage is approximately 600 to 700 words long and is followed by a set of comprehension questions. Here is an example.

ACIDS AND BASES

Acids and bases are substances that form compounds and solutions with an electrical charge. When acids dissolve in water, they donate additional hydrogen ions to the solution. An acid, therefore, is a substance that increases the hydrogen ion concentration of a solution. A base, on the other hand, reduces the hydrogen ion concentration of a solution.

The strength of acids and bases is measured by using a numeric scale known as pH, a measurement that represents the number of hydrogen ions in a solution. pH is measured with a pH meter or with paper strips that have color indicators. The pH scale runs from 0 to 14, with the midpoint at 7. A neutral solution, such as pure water, has a pH of 7.0. A pH value of less than 7.0 denotes an acidic solution, and a value above 7.0 denotes a basic, or alkaline, solution. The pH of a solution declines as the concentration of hydrogen ions increases; the lower the number, the more acidic the solution. For example, a solution with a pH of 4.5 is far more acidic than one with a pH of 6.0. The pH for bases, or alkalis, is above 7.0, and the higher the number, the greater the basicity or alkalinity. A pH of 8.5 is more alkaline than a pH of 7.5.

The internal pH of most living cells is close to 7.0. Most biological fluids measure within the pH range of 6.0 to 8.0. There are a few exceptions, however, including the strongly acidic digestive juice of the human stomach, which has a pH of about 2.0. The chemical processes of living cells are very sensitive to the concentrations of hydrogen ions. Biological fluids resist changes to their pH when acids or bases are introduced because of the presence of buffers, substances that minimize changes in the concentrations of these ions. Buffers in human blood, for example, normally maintain the blood pH very close to 7.4 because a person cannot survive very long if the blood pH drops to 7.0 or rises to 7.8.

Acids and bases are used in food preparation and in industrial processes. They can be very dangerous, causing burns and other injuries to people and animals, as well as damage to the environment, so they must be used properly and handled with care.

Acids are very important substances. They cause lemons to taste sour, they digest food in the stomach, and they dissolve rock to make fertilizer. They also dissolve tooth enamel to form cavities. Vinegar is a weak acid, a dilute solution of acetic acid used in food preservation. Lemon juice, citric acid, is added to foods and beverages to give them a sour flavor. Other acids have agricultural uses, such as hydrochloric acid—also known as muriatic acid—which is used as a fertilizer for acid–loving plants.

Bases, or alkalis, have a bitter taste and a slippery feel. Most hand soaps and commercial products for unclogging drains are highly basic. Household ammonia and lye are bases. Slaked lime, calcium hydroxide, is a base that is used in cements and paints.

Most plants and animals have preferred pH ranges, where they attain their best growth and health. Acid materials can be made less acidic by adding basic materials to them. In the pH management of soil, compounds that are basic—like slaked lime or crushed limestone—are added to the soil to raise its pH. Limestone has a pH of about 8.2, which will lower the acidity of acid soil.

Question Type 1 – Click on One Answer

For this multiple–choice type of question, you will choose the best of four possible answers. You will see:

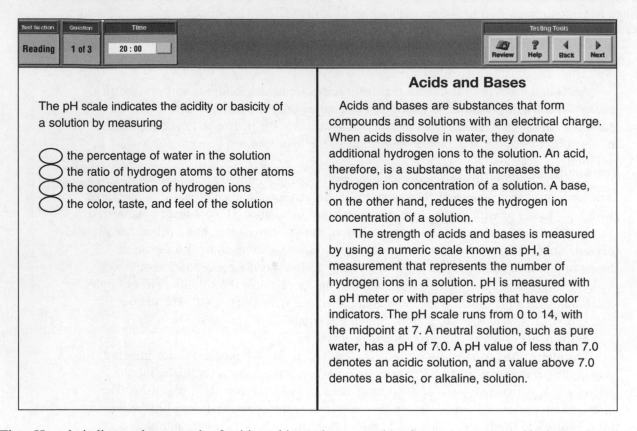

The pH scale indicates the strength of acids and bases by measuring *the concentration of hydrogen ions* in a solution. Therefore, you should click on the oval next to the third answer.

When you click on an oval, the oval will darken. To change your answer, click on a different oval. When you are satisfied that you have chosen the right answer, click on **Next**. The computer will move to the next question.

READING

Question Type 2 – Add a Sentence

For this type of question, you will click on a square to add a sentence to the passage. You will see:

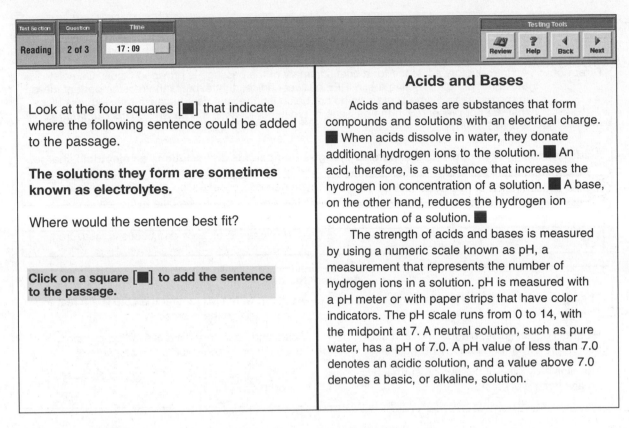

The sentence would fit best at the first square. The paragraph should read:

> Acids and bases are substances that form compounds and solutions with an electrical charge. **The solutions they form are sometimes known as electrolytes.** When acids dissolve in water, they donate additional hydrogen ions to the solution. An acid, therefore, is a substance that increases the hydrogen ion concentration of a solution. A base, on the other hand, reduces the hydrogen ion concentration of a solution.

When you click on a square, the sentence will appear there. To change your answer, click on a different square. The sentence will then appear at this new location. When you are ready to proceed, click on **Next**. The computer will move to the next question.

Question Type 3 – Drag Answer Choices

For this type of question, you will use the mouse to drag text to complete a summary or table. You will see:

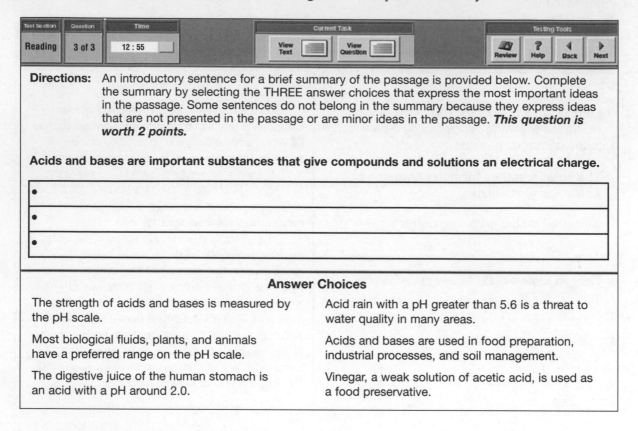

The three most important ideas in the passage are:

> The strength of acids and bases is measured by the pH scale.
> Most biological fluids, plants, and animals have a preferred range on the pH scale.
> Acids and bases are used in food preparation, industrial processes, and soil management.

To complete the summary, move the cursor to the answer choice that you want to move. Click and hold to drag the sentence to the space where it belongs. The sentence will appear in that space. To change an answer, click on it. Then drag your new choice to the correct space.

If you choose all three correct answers, you will receive two points. If you choose two correct answers, you will receive one point. If you choose only one correct answer, or no correct answers, you will receive no points.

STRATEGIES FOR THE READING SECTION

Before the Test

- Read on a variety of topics to build your English vocabulary. Most of the TOEFL reading passages are about topics in the natural sciences, the social sciences, business, and the arts. Read as much as you can in these subject areas, particularly from textbooks, journals, magazines, and newspapers.

- Practice trying to guess the meaning of unfamiliar words from how they are used in context. Use other words in the sentence, your understanding of the passage, and your general knowledge as clues to the meaning of unfamiliar words.

- Become familiar with the various ways that the incorrect answers on the TOEFL may confuse you.

- Become familiar with the various types of questions and how to answer them.

- Become familiar with the testing tools, such as **Next**, **Back**, and **Review**. Practice using the mouse to click on and drag text.

- Your own best strategy: _____

_____

During the Test

- Begin each passage by skimming it. **Skimming** is reading quickly for a general understanding of the topic and organization of the passage. To skim a passage, read the first two or three sentences of the first paragraph, and the first sentence of each paragraph after that. Notice key words and phrases that are repeated throughout the passage.

- Identify exactly what each question wants to know. Does it ask you about…

    - information that is stated in the passage?
    - information that is NOT stated directly in the passage?
    - the meaning of a word?
    - the author's purpose for making a particular statement?
    - the major and minor ideas in the passage?

- When a question asks about specific information, scan the passage to find this information. **Scanning** is looking for specific information: key words and phrases. Sometimes the computer will highlight text to help you scan a specific place in the text.

- In questions about vocabulary, look for context clues in the passage. Use your knowledge of sentence structure, punctuation, word parts, and other ideas in the passage.

- Think carefully about questions that ask you to make an inference. Eliminate answer choices that you cannot reasonably infer from the information in the passage.

- Do not leave any questions unanswered. It is best to answer all questions about one passage before you move on to the next passage.

- Work as quickly as you can. Pay attention to the number of questions and the amount of time you have left. You can review previous questions and change previous answers as long as you have time left.

- If you do not find the correct answer right away, use the *process of elimination*. This means you should omit the choices you know are incorrect. If you can eliminate one or two choices, you will improve your chance of selecting the correct answer. Your score is based on the number of questions you answer correctly, and incorrect answers are not subtracted.

- Your own best strategy: _____

_____

1.1 Understanding Facts and Details

FOCUS

Read the following passage and answer the question:

> In one study, 83 percent of 140 male and female executives in a variety of businesses report having a mentor when they were younger. Generally, they view the mentor–protégé relationship as an important aspect of the initial phase of their careers. Mentors are given credit for teaching protégés the key elements of the job, and for providing a key relationship in the young adult's shift from dependence on parents to complete independence.
>
> Within organizations, protégés are more likely to be promoted, get larger raises, and have more opportunities within a company, law firm, or other group than are young workers who have no mentor. But it is difficult to know whether these advantages arise from the mentoring process itself, since those who are selected as protégés are usually the most strongly motivated or best skilled among the younger workers.
>
> According to the passage, one way in which mentors help protégés is by
>
> ○ giving them credit for excellent work
> ○ encouraging them to aim for executive positions
> ○ teaching them important aspects of the job
> ○ arranging for them to receive a larger salary

The question asks about a **detail** in the passage: one way in which mentors help protégés. The correct answer is *teaching them important aspects of the job*. A key idea in the first paragraph is *Mentors are given credit for teaching protégés the key elements of the job*.

Now answer another question:

> Why is it difficult to know whether certain advantages for a protégé are the result of having a mentor?
>
> ○ Most people chosen as protégés are already highly motivated and skilled.
> ○ Mentors do not have direct control over workers' promotions and salaries.
> ○ Having a mentor is a fairly common experience for junior executives.
> ○ Little research has been done concerning why protégés are successful.

The question asks about a **fact** in the passage. The answer to a *Why*–question will be a reason. The correct answer is both a reason and a fact: *Most people chosen as protégés are already highly motivated and skilled*. What key words provide clues to help you find the answer?

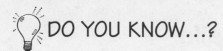

DO YOU KNOW...?

1. A *fact* is a real occurrence, event, or phenomenon—something that happens or has happened. Facts are information that is presented as real and true. Sometimes a fact functions as a supporting detail in a passage.

    A *detail* is a specific bit of information, such as an example, a reason, a statistic, a description, or an illustration. In written English, both facts and details are used to support the thesis or main idea of the work. Facts and details are evidence that make main ideas stronger and more convincing.

2. Fact and detail questions on the TOEFL test your ability to answer questions about information that is stated directly in the passage. Questions about facts and details look like this:

    > According to the passage,   what _____?
    >
    > which _____?
    >
    > why _____?
    >
    > how _____?
    >
    > who _____?
    >
    > where _____?
    >
    > when _____?
    >
    > According to the passage, which of the following statements is true?
    >
    > In paragraph __, what does the author say about _____?
    >
    > What point does the author make about _____?
    >
    > What is the main cause of _____?
    >
    > What reason is given for _____?
    >
    > The author argues that _____.
    >
    > The author mentions _____ as an example of _____.
    >
    > _____ is an example of _____.
    >
    > _____ is a type of _____.
    >
    > Which of the following statements applies to _____?
    >
    > Which statement best describes _____?

3. Three skills that will help you answer fact questions are skimming, scanning, and scrolling.

    Skimming is reading quickly to understand the general message of a passage. Skimming involves looking at key sentences that give you an idea of the passage's major ideas and overall organization. When you skim, your eyes move quickly through the passage, and you do not read every word or every sentence.

    Scanning is looking through a passage to find specific information. The test question usually tells you what kind of information to scan for, such as reasons, examples, causes, effects, or characteristics. Scanning is searching for the facts and details that will help you answer the question.

    Scrolling is moving quickly through text on the computer by using the scroll bar. You must scroll through a passage when it is too long for you to see all of it on the screen at the same time. Scrolling is a useful skill when you skim a passage for overall meaning and when you scan a passage for specific details.

4. Certain expressions are clues that can help you understand the relationships between ideas within sentences and paragraphs. These words and phrases are called *transitions*. Can you add any others to the list below?

FUNCTION	TRANSITIONS		
Illustrate	for example for instance	next to illustrate	such such as
Explain	at this point because	furthermore how	in fact in this case
Give Reasons	as a result of because	because of due to	one reason is since
Show Result	accordingly as a result	consequently otherwise	therefore thus
Compare	both equally important	like the same	similarly similar to
Contrast	although conversely however in contrast	instead nevertheless on the contrary on the other hand	rather unlike whereas while
Add	also another as well as	finally first, second, third… furthermore	moreover not only…but also too
Limit	although but	except for even though	however yet
Emphasize	certainly clearly	indeed in fact	most importantly surely

5. In questions about facts and details, the correct answer may paraphrase information from the passage. To *paraphrase* means to restate the same information by using different words.

The incorrect answer choices may be incorrect because they:

- repeat information from the passage but do not answer the question;
- incorrectly state information or ideas from the passage;
- are inaccurate or untrue according to the passage; or
- are irrelevant or not mentioned in the passage.

6. Here are some examples:

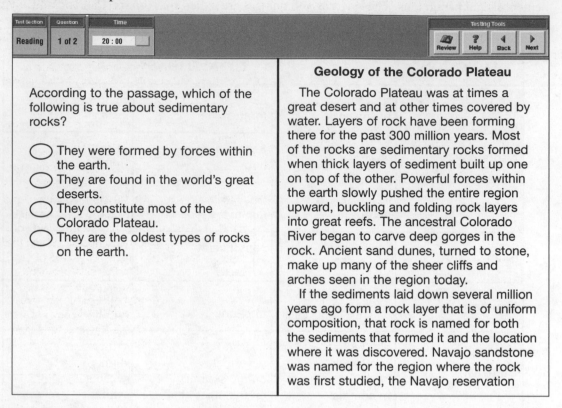

Test Section: **Reading** Question: **1 of 2** Time: **20 : 00**	Testing Tools: Review Help Back Next

According to the passage, which of the following is true about sedimentary rocks?

○ They were formed by forces within the earth.
○ They are found in the world's great deserts.
○ They constitute most of the Colorado Plateau.
○ They are the oldest types of rocks on the earth.

Geology of the Colorado Plateau

The Colorado Plateau was at times a great desert and at other times covered by water. Layers of rock have been forming there for the past 300 million years. Most of the rocks are sedimentary rocks formed when thick layers of sediment built up one on top of the other. Powerful forces within the earth slowly pushed the entire region upward, buckling and folding rock layers into great reefs. The ancestral Colorado River began to carve deep gorges in the rock. Ancient sand dunes, turned to stone, make up many of the sheer cliffs and arches seen in the region today.

If the sediments laid down several million years ago form a rock layer that is of uniform composition, that rock is named for both the sediments that formed it and the location where it was discovered. Navajo sandstone was named for the region where the rock was first studied, the Navajo reservation

The question asks you to identify a fact from the passage. The key phrase *sedimentary rocks* enables you to scan the passage for the needed information. The correct answer is *They constitute most of the Colorado Plateau.* The first paragraph introduces the topic of the Colorado Plateau and also states that *Most of the rocks are sedimentary rocks*—a statement that is paraphrased in the correct answer.

Why are the other three answers incorrect? *They were formed by forces within the earth* repeats information from the passage but does not describe sedimentary rocks. *They are found in the world's great deserts* and *They are the oldest types of rocks on earth* are not mentioned in the passage, so you do not know whether these statements are true or not.

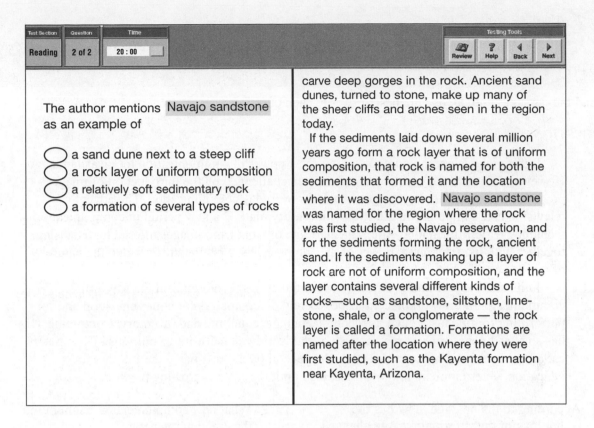

The question is about a detail, *Navajo sandstone*. If you scan the passage, you can find where *Navajo sandstone* is mentioned. Sometimes the computer highlights text to help you scan quickly. If you read the previous sentence, you will see that Navajo sandstone is an example of *a rock layer that is of uniform composition, … named for both the sediments that formed it and the location where it was discovered.* Therefore, the correct answer is *a rock layer of uniform composition.*

Why are the other three answers incorrect? *A sand dune next to a steep cliff* is inaccurate because the author says nothing about Navajo sandstone being next to a steep cliff. *A relatively soft sedimentary rock* is not mentioned in the passage. *A formation of several types of rocks* is untrue because it describes a rock layer that is not of uniform composition.

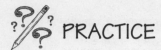

PRACTICE

Exercise 1.1.A

Read the passages and choose the best answer to each question.

QUESTIONS 1–2

Before television and computers, our most powerful communication tool was language. However, the supremacy of language has been challenged by the introduction of images—powerful, realistic, moving images—into our everyday communication. The advent of television and computing in the twentieth century marked a new period in communication technology, the Information Age. The marriage of words and images offered by television, together with the interactive power of the computer, have profoundly affected the nature of our society.

In its short life of half a century, the computer has revolutionized the way we communicate. In the workplace, businesses rely on computers for communication and for performing routine tasks such as record keeping, accounting, and inventory. Computing has spawned new forms of media, such as the worldwide network of millions of computers called the Internet. By the mid–1990s, the general public was using the Internet for education, entertainment, and business, making it the fastest–growing medium today.

1. According to the passage, how has the technology of the Information Age changed our daily communication?

   (A) It helps us learn language more easily.
   (B) It combines language with visual images.
   (C) It improves our ability to think logically.
   (D) It makes routine tasks more interesting.

2. What new communication medium did the computer generate?

   (A) Language
   (B) Television
   (C) Record keeping
   (D) The Internet

QUESTIONS 3–4

It was not until enterprising sea captains imported exotic animals to sell to traveling showmen that words such as *lion* or *polar bear* had much meaning to Americans. In 1789 the first large collection of exotic wild animals was put on permanent exhibit in New York. By the 1830s, most circuses had a collection of animals that generally included elephants, camels, lions, tigers, kangaroos, and apes. These animal shows served as traveling zoos where many Americans saw their first exotic animal. The creatures made such an impression that American English began to acquire new phrases.

To monkey around and *monkey business* are expressions of the early 1800s, and *to make a monkey out of someone* is from 1899, all being terms based on the increasing number of monkeys seen in circuses and zoos. A large or uncouth man was called a *big ape* by 1831, and *gorilla* was used to mean a hairy, tough man by the 1860s and a thug by 1926.

3. According to the passage, what was one effect of traveling animal shows?

  (A) New laws regulated the importation of exotic animals.
  (B) There was an increase in popular forms of entertainment.
  (C) People worked to improve the living conditions of animals.
  (D) American English acquired many new words and phrases.

4. What point does the author make in paragraph 2?

  (A) Monkeys were the most popular animals in circuses and zoos.
  (B) Several expressions reflect an interest in monkeys and apes.
  (C) There are many similarities between monkeys and humans.
  (D) Many words to describe large men are considered vulgar.

QUESTIONS 5–7

The cells of a plant are organized into three tissue systems: dermal, vascular, and ground tissue. Each tissue system is continuous throughout the plant's body. The specific characteristics of each tissue, however, are different in the different organs of the plant.

The dermal tissue system is the "skin" of the plant. The dermal system, or epidermis, is a single layer of cells covering the entire body of the plant. The main function of the epidermis is to protect the plant. The epidermis also has specialized characteristics for the particular organs it covers. For example, the epidermis of leaves and stems has a waxy coating that helps the plant conserve water, and the epidermal cells near the tips of the plant's roots help the plant absorb water and nutrients from the soil.

The second tissue system—the vascular system—is the transportation system for water and nutrients. Vascular tissue also helps to support the plant's structure. The third system—the ground tissue—makes up the bulk of a plant, filling all of the spaces between the dermal and vascular tissue systems. Ground tissue functions in photosynthesis, storage, and support.

5. How are the three tissue systems of a plant similar to each other?

  (A) They all continue throughout the plant's body.
  (B) They all have a protective waxy coating.
  (C) They all consist of a single layer of cells.
  (D) They all perform the same bodily functions.

6. Which of the following statements best describes the plant's epidermis?

  (A) It helps the plant to stand upright.
  (B) It transports water and nutrients.
  (C) It covers the plant's entire body.
  (D) It is found only in young plants.

7. Which type of tissue does a plant's body mainly consist of?

  (A) Dermal
  (B) Vascular
  (C) Epidermis
  (D) Ground

QUESTIONS 8–10

By the decades just before the Civil War of the 1860s, the Southern states had developed an economic culture distinct from that of the North. The economy of the South depended largely on two things: cotton and slave labor. Because of the rising demand for cotton from the mills of England, and the invention of the cotton gin in 1793, the cotton production of the South increased tremendously. In 1790, cotton output had been 9,000 bales a year, but by the 1850s, output had soared to five million bales. In the South, cotton was "king." The most readily available source of labor was the institution of slavery. Thus, cotton and slavery became interdependent, and the South grew more reliant on both.

This was in sharp contrast to the North, where farming was becoming more mechanized and diversified. Northern farmers would boast of improvements in the form of new roads, railways, and machinery, and of the production of a variety of crops. In the South, however, farmers bought laborers instead of equipment, and a man's social status depended on the number of slaves he owned. The economic differences between the two regions would ultimately lead to armed conflict and the social restructuring of the South.

8. Why did the Southern output of cotton greatly increase between 1790 and 1850?

   (A) Southern farmers invested in transportation.
   (B) Mills in England demanded more cotton.
   (C) The South was trying to dominate the North.
   (D) Southern cotton was superior to Northern cotton.

9. What was associated more with the North in the period discussed?

   (A) Farm machinery
   (B) Slave labor
   (C) Military service
   (D) Reliance on one crop

10. The author argues that the Civil War between the North and the South

   (A) was a conflict over control of the cotton trade
   (B) began in 1790 and lasted almost seventy years
   (C) was largely the result of economic differences
   (D) forced the South to produce different crops

Exercise 1.1.B

Read the passages and choose the best answer to each question.

QUESTIONS 1–3

Erik Erikson believed that personality development is a series of turning points, which he described in terms of the tension between desirable qualities and dangers. He emphasized that only when the positive qualities outweigh the dangers does healthy psychosocial development take place.

An important turning point occurs around age six. A child entering school is at a point in development when behavior is dominated by intellectual curiosity and performance. He or she now learns to win recognition by producing things. The child develops a sense of industry. The danger at this stage is that the child may experience feelings of inadequacy or inferiority. If the child is encouraged to make and do things, allowed to finish tasks, and praised for trying, a sense of industry is the result. On the other hand, if the child's efforts are unsuccessful, or if they are criticized or treated as bothersome, a sense of inferiority is the result. For these reasons, Erikson called the period from age six to eleven *Industry vs. Inferiority*.

1. According to Erikson's theory, what desirable quality should develop in a child who is six to eleven years old?

   (A) A liking for school
   (B) A feeling of inadequacy
   (C) An ability to finish tasks
   (D) A sense of industry

2. According to Erikson's theory, what will happen if a child's efforts are criticized?

   (A) The child will dislike his teacher.
   (B) The child will avoid other children.
   (C) The child will try harder to win recognition.
   (D) The child will feel inferior.

3. *Industry vs. Inferiority* is an example of

   (A) the tension between a positive quality and a danger
   (B) a personality disorder in children
   (C) the difference between a child of six and a child of eleven
   (D) an educational strategy

QUESTIONS 4–6

In the storytelling traditions of West Africa, the tiny rabbit appears frequently as a rascal who teases or plays jokes on bigger animals. In one story, Mr. Rabbit tricks Mr. Elephant and Mrs. Whale into a tug of war with each other. Such tales about Mr. Rabbit continue to be part of the oral traditions of the Wollof people of Senegal.

The African–American folktales of the U.S. South also feature a trickster rabbit in the character of Brer Rabbit. In his American incarnation, Brer Rabbit uses his wits to overcome circumstances and even to enact playful revenge on his larger, stronger adversaries, Brer Fox, Brer Wolf, and Brer Bear. Although he is not always successful, Brer Rabbit's efforts make him both a folk hero and a friendly comic figure. Joel Chandler Harris, a journalist in Georgia, had heard old men tell Brer Rabbit tales by the fireside when he was a young boy. Harris wrote down and published many of the stories, popularizing them for the general public.

A folklorist named Alcée Fortier recorded very similar versions of the same stories in southern Louisiana, where the rabbit character was known as Compair Lapin in Creole French. Today, the rabbit enjoys another incarnation as the cartoon character Bugs Bunny— a rascally rabbit who causes trouble, tricks the hunter, and always gets the final word.

4. What trait belongs to the rabbit character in tales of West African origin?

  (A) Storytelling ability
  (B) Very keen eyesight
  (C) Ability to fool others
  (D) Strong, athletic body

5. How did a wide audience of people know about the Brer Rabbit stories?

  (A) They studied the oral traditions of West Africa.
  (B) They heard old men tell the stories by the fireside.
  (C) They read the stories published by a journalist.
  (D) They listened to recordings from southern Louisiana.

6. What do Brer Rabbit, Compair Lapin, and Bugs Bunny have in common?

  (A) All are cartoon characters.
  (B) All play tricks on others.
  (C) All save others from trouble.
  (D) All speak Creole French.

QUESTIONS 7–10

A hot spot is a giant underground caldron of molten rock in one of the world's many volcanically active areas. The steamy geysers, thermal pools, and mud pots of Yellowstone National Park owe their origins to hot spots.

Annually, more than 200 geysers erupt in Yellowstone, making this one of the most interesting places in the world for geologists. Over 100 geysers lie within the Upper Geyser Basin, a one–square–mile area near Old Faithful, the most famous geyser in the world. The Yellowstone hot spot was created around ten million years ago, and the center of the park is still volcanically active, with molten rock only a mile or two beneath the Earth's surface.

When rain and melted snow seep down through tiny cracks in the Earth, the water eventually reaches underground chambers of lava–heated rock. The rock heats the water, and the boiling water and steam often make their way back up to the surface in the form of a geyser, a thermal pool, or a mud pot.

In a geyser, water trapped in an underground chamber heats up beyond the boiling point and forms steam. Since steam takes up 1,500 times more space than water, pressure builds up, eventually forcing the superheated water to burst to the surface as a geyser. A thermal pool is formed when the water from the hot spot reaches the surface before cooling off. If the water does not make it all the way to the surface, steam and gases may dissolve rocks and form a bubbling mud pot instead.

7. Where do hot spots occur?

   (A) In rocky regions near the equator
   (B) Below the ground near active volcanoes
   (C) About a mile above a volcano's crater
   (D) In the center of ancient volcanoes

8. According to the passage, why is Yellowstone National Park an interesting place for geologists?

   (A) There are 100 square miles of hot spots.
   (B) Over 200 geysers erupt there each year.
   (C) There are more than 100 different kinds of geysers.
   (D) More than 200 types of rock are found there.

9. How do hot spots contribute to the formation of geysers?

   (A) Hot spots melt all of the snow falling into a volcano's crater.
   (B) Water is trapped in an underground chamber and cannot escape.
   (C) Hot rocks create boiling water, steam, and pressure underground.
   (D) Water from hot spots rises to the surface before it cools off.

10. When do mud pots form?

   (A) When steam and gases dissolve rocks near the surface
   (B) When underground water exceeds the boiling point
   (C) When snow melts in Yellowstone's geyser basins
   (D) When superheated water bursts to the surface

Exercise 1.1.C

Read the passages and choose the best answer to each question.

QUESTIONS 1–3

Most matter exists as compounds—combinations of atoms or oppositely charged ions of two or more different elements held together in fixed proportions by chemical bonds. Compounds are classified as organic or inorganic. Organic compounds contain atoms of the element carbon, usually combined with itself and with atoms of one or more other elements such as hydrogen, oxygen, nitrogen, sulfur, phosphorus, and chlorine. Many materials important to us—food, vitamins, blood, skin, cotton, wool, paper, oil, plastics—are organic compounds.

Larger and more complex organic compounds, called polymers, consist of a number of basic structural units linked together by chemical bonds. Important organic polymers include carbohydrates, proteins, and nucleic acids. Carbohydrates, such as the complex starches in rice and potato plants, are composed of a number of simple sugar molecules. Proteins are produced in plant and animal cells by the linking of different numbers and sequences of about twenty different structural units known as amino acids. Most animals, including humans, can manufacture about ten of these amino acids in their cells, but the other ten, called essential amino acids, must be obtained from food in order to prevent protein deficiency. Nucleic acids are composed of hundreds to thousands of four different units called nucleotides linked together in different numbers and sequences. DNA and RNA in plant and animal cells are nucleic acids.

1. Which of the following statements applies to all organic compounds?

   (A) They are composed of carbon and one or more other elements.
   (B) They contain atoms of the seven most abundant elements.
   (C) They have stronger chemical bonds than inorganic compounds do.
   (D) They are produced by linking several simple sugar molecules.

2. Carbohydrates, proteins, and nucleic acids are types of

   (A) elements
   (B) inorganic compounds
   (C) polymers
   (D) amino acids

3. Why is it important for humans to obtain some amino acids from food?

   (A) Without certain amino acids, humans store too much fat.
   (B) Organically grown food is the only source of amino acids.
   (C) Sufficient amino acids are necessary for DNA production.
   (D) Humans cells cannot make the ten essential amino acids.

QUESTIONS 4–6

By the 1840s, British North America had developed a vibrant commercial economy based on its abundant natural resources and a growing international trade. Fish, furs, timber, and grains represented over 90 percent of all economic activity. The oldest of the resource commodities, fish, was traditionally associated with Newfoundland and continued to dominate that colony's economy throughout the nineteenth century. The other traditional resource, fur, had a much smaller economic value compared to other resources. However, the fur trade was of tremendous value politically because it provided the means for Great Britain to retain its claim over much of Canada, and also formed the basis of the relationship between the British and the aboriginal peoples.

Timber and grain eventually replaced fish and fur in economic importance. Every province of British North America except Newfoundland was involved in the timber trade. In New Brunswick, the timber industry controlled every aspect of life, and settlement was closely connected to the opening of new timber territory. In the extensive agricultural lands of the St. Lawrence Valley and Upper Canada, wheat quickly became the dominant crop. Wheat met a growing demand abroad and it transported well as either grain or flour.

4. Which resource was the earliest to contribute to the economy of British North America?

   (A) Timber from New Brunswick
   (B) Fur from across Canada
   (C) Fish from Newfoundland
   (D) Wheat from Upper Canada

5. According to the passage, what is the main reason for the importance of the fur trade?

   (A) Fur had more economic value than any other natural resource.
   (B) Fur formed the basis of the local economy everywhere in Canada.
   (C) The fur trade supplied all of the fur needed in Great Britain.
   (D) The fur trade allowed Great Britain to control a large part of Canada.

6. Which statement best describes the British North American economy around 1840?

   (A) Four important resources supported most of the commercial activity.
   (B) The economy was based mainly on the exportation of timber and wheat.
   (C) Economic activity varied greatly from one province to another.
   (D) Great Britain maintained strict control over all aspects of the economy.

QUESTIONS 7–10

The youngest child of a prosperous Midwestern manufacturing family, Dorothy Reed was born in 1874 and educated at home by her grandmother. She graduated from Smith College and in 1896 entered Johns Hopkins Medical School. After receiving her M.D. degree, she worked at Johns Hopkins in the laboratories of two noted medical scientists. Reed's research in pathology established conclusively that Hodgkin's disease, until then thought to be a form of tuberculosis, was a distinct disorder characterized by a specific blood cell, which was named the Reed cell after her.

In 1906, her marriage to Charles Mendenhall took Reed away from the research laboratory. For ten years, she remained at home as the mother of young children before returning to professional life. She became a lecturer in Home Economics at the University of Wisconsin, where her principal concerns were collecting data about maternal and child health and preparing courses for new mothers.

Dorothy Reed Mendenhall's career interests were reshaped by the requirements of marriage. Her passion for research was redirected to public health rather than laboratory science. Late in life, she concluded that she could not imagine life without her husband and sons, but she hoped for a future when marriage would not have to end a career of laboratory research.

7. What was Dorothy Reed's area of research at Johns Hopkins?

(A) Manufacturing
(B) Pathology
(C) Tuberculosis
(D) Maternal health

8. Why did Reed stop working in the research laboratory?

(A) Marriage required that she remain at home.
(B) She became more interested in public health.
(C) Johns Hopkins did not like women doing research.
(D) Her work on Hodgkin's disease was completed.

9. What did Dorothy Reed Mendenhall conclude about marriage?

(A) Marriage inspired her passion for laboratory research.
(B) It was a mistake for her to give up her career for marriage.
(C) Marriage need not keep women from careers in laboratory science.
(D) Women cannot have both a happy marriage and a successful career.

10. Which fact should be included in a biography of Dorothy Reed Mendenhall?

(A) She was the first woman in her family to earn a degree in medicine.
(B) Marriage and motherhood prevented her from resuming her career.
(C) She proved that Hodgkin's disease was characterized by a certain blood cell.
(D) Her career was devoted to finding a cure for tuberculosis in children.

Answers to Exercises 1.1.A through 1.1.C are on page 559.

EXTENSION

1. Outside of class, look in a newspaper, a magazine, or a university textbook. Select a short passage of one to three paragraphs. Make a photocopy and bring it to class. In class, work with a partner. Read the passage and underline the most important ideas. Circle the important facts, details, and examples. With your partner, practice asking each other questions and giving answers about the facts.

2. Outside of class, work with a partner. Look in a magazine or a university textbook. Select a short passage of around 100 words. Write two questions about facts and details in the passage. You do not have to write the answers. For examples of how to write the questions, see the list of questions on page 16. Write the passage and questions on an overhead projector transparency, or make enough copies of the passage and questions for everyone in your class. Your class now has a reading test made entirely by students! As a class, take the test by either writing or discussing answers to the questions. Can you answer all of the questions about each passage by using only the information provided in the passage?

1.2 Identifying Negative Facts

FOCUS

Read the following passage and answer the question:

> Like air and water, soil is also vulnerable to pollution from several sources. One source is the atmosphere, as many harmful air pollutants leach through the soil into groundwater supplies. Another source is hazardous waste, the deadly byproducts of industrial processes, buried in landfills or dumped in fields. One of the most critical soil–quality problems is the increase in concentration of dissolved salts, commonly referred to as salinization. Natural processes or human activities can salinize lands. Irrigation water contains large quantities of salt, and as this water evaporates, it leaves the salt behind, thus contaminating the soil.
>
> All of the following are given as causes of soil pollution EXCEPT
>
> ⃝ the leaching of air pollutants
> ⃝ the decomposition of organic matter
> ⃝ the increasing amount of dissolved salts
> ⃝ the dumping of hazardous waste

The question asks you to identify which *three* causes of soil pollution are mentioned in the passage and which *one* is not mentioned. The correct answer is the one choice that is NOT mentioned in the passage: *the decomposition of organic matter*. All of the other choices are given as causes of soil pollution.

Some TOEFL questions ask about **negative facts**: information that is not given in the passage.

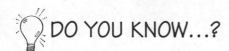DO YOU KNOW...?

1. A **fact** is a real occurrence, event, phenomenon, or other type of information that is presented as true. A **negative fact** is information that is not presented as true. A negative fact may be presented as false, or it may be omitted from the passage.

2. Negative fact questions on the TOEFL test your ability to verify what information is true and what information is not true, or not included, in the passage. Questions about negative facts look like this:

> The passage discusses all of the following EXCEPT _____.
> All of the following are mentioned in the passage EXCEPT _____.
> All of the following describe _____ EXCEPT _____.
> All of the following are examples of _____ EXCEPT _____.
> _____ involves all of the following EXCEPT _____.
> _____ are characterized by all of the following EXCEPT _____.
> According to the passage, all of the following statements are true EXCEPT _____.
> Which of the following is NOT mentioned as _____?
> Which of the following is NOT given as a reason for _____?

3. In questions with the word EXCEPT or NOT, *three* of the answers will be true, and one answer will be either false or not mentioned in the passage. Look for the *one* answer containing information that is:

    ✎ not mentioned in the passage
        or
    ✎ not true according to the passage.

4. ***Scanning*** is a skill that will help you answer negative fact questions. The question and answer choices tell you what information to scan for, such as examples, reasons, causes, effects, or characteristics. Scanning is searching for the specific facts and details that will help you answer the question.

5. Here is an example:

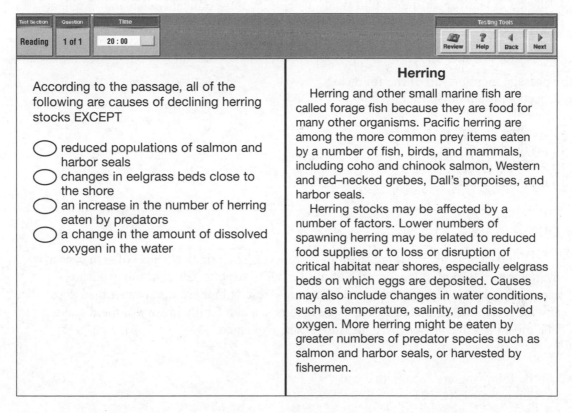

An important word in the question is *EXCEPT*. It tells you to look for the one answer that is *not* given as a cause of declining herring stocks. Begin by scanning the passage for key words from each answer choice. Which answer is *not* a cause of declining herring stocks?

The correct answer is *reduced populations of salmon and harbor seals* because it is not true according to the passage. The passage states: *More herring might be eaten by greater numbers of predator species such as salmon and harbor seals....*

The other three answers are given as causes of declining herring stocks:

Lower numbers of spawning herring may be related to...loss or disruption of critical habitat near shores, especially eelgrass beds on which eggs are deposited.
More herring might be eaten by greater numbers of predator species....
Causes may also include changes in water conditions, such as...dissolved oxygen.

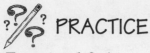 PRACTICE

Exercise 1.2.A

Read the passages and choose the best answer to each question.

QUESTION 1

An important element of drama is that it is a presentation by performers in front of an audience—for example, a ceremony conducted by civic leaders before members of a community. Another aspect is costumes, such as those worn by tribal chiefs who impersonate animals or gods. Moreover, drama involves storytelling—recitation of myths or legends, teaching lessons through stories—to a group of listeners. Sometimes the storyteller imitates the characters in the story by changing his or her voice for different characters.

1. The passage mentions all of the following as aspects of drama EXCEPT

    Ⓐ wearing costumes
    Ⓑ performing before an audience
    Ⓒ writing dialogue for characters
    Ⓓ narrating a story

QUESTION 2

Skin cancer is the most prevalent of all cancers. The principal cause of skin cancer is overexposure to sunlight, according to most medical experts. Chronic sun exposure—especially when it causes sunburn or blistering—results in more skin cancer than does any other risk factor, including exposure to x–rays and a family history of the disease. The most effective preventative measure is sun avoidance.

2. All of the following are factors that can cause skin cancer EXCEPT

    Ⓐ exposure to x–rays
    Ⓑ sun blistering
    Ⓒ family history of skin cancer
    Ⓓ sun avoidance

QUESTIONS 3–4

Laughter is a key to a good life and good health: it can diminish feelings of tension, anger, and sadness. Just as exercise conditions our bodies, frequent laughter can train our bodies to be healthier. When laughter is a regular experience, it lowers blood pressure and boosts brain chemicals that fight pain. It can also reduce stress hormones that increase vulnerability to illness, as well as increase hormones that have been shown to help produce restful sleep. Laughter is like an instant vacation in the way it changes our psychobiology.

To make laughter a regular part of your life, try keeping a humor journal in which you record some of the amusing things that happen to you. Another technique is to create a weekly fun time to look forward to, such as watching a comedy video or having a dinner with friends that features joke telling. Another sure source of laughter is spending time with children and animals.

3. According to the passage, laughter provides all of the following benefits EXCEPT

(A) elevating brain chemicals that prevent pain
(B) increasing the body's vulnerability to illness
(C) promoting a more restful kind of sleep
(D) reducing feelings of stress and anger

4. The author recommends all of the following EXCEPT

(A) playing tricks on family and friends
(B) planning a special fun time every week
(C) enjoying time with pets and children
(D) writing down humorous experiences

QUESTIONS 5–6

About 300 genera and 3,000 species of the *Apiaceae* family exist in the Northern Hemisphere. Nearly a quarter of these genera are native to the United States, with several large genera in the West.

Members of this family are usually aromatic herbs with hollow stems, fern–like leaves, and small flowers in flat–topped or rounded umbels that are further grouped into a compound cluster. The family is important for such foods as carrots, parsnips, and celery and such spices and seasonings as coriander, caraway, anise, parsley, and dill. However, some species are very poisonous.

5. All of the following statements describe the *Apiaceae* family EXCEPT

(A) This family has three thousand species in the Northern Hemisphere.
(B) Plants in this family are native to one–fourth of the United States.
(C) This family includes vegetables, herbs, spices, and poisons.
(D) Most members of this family have small flowers grouped in clusters.

6. All of the following are members of the *Apiaceae* family EXCEPT

(A) parsnips
(B) potatoes
(C) carrots
(D) parsley

QUESTIONS 7–8

Indian filmmaker Satyajit Ray is still regarded by many film critics as one of the world's great directors. Ray's films are known for their compassion, honesty, and quiet dignity. His Apu Trilogy, three films about Bengali life, was hailed as a national epic in the 1950s. The first film, *Pather Panchali*, is the story of a Bengali family's noble struggle against poverty and the heartbreaks of life. It was followed by *Aparajito*, in which the son of the family, Apu, grows to manhood. In the final film, *The World of Apu*, the young man marries, but fails at his life's ambitions, and then, after losing his wife, he wanders across the country for several years before returning home to claim his son.

Satyajit Ray's movies have never been very popular in India itself, but those who appreciate his unobtrusive technique and his compassion for his characters view his films as a poetic record of Indian life.

7. According to the passage, the films of Satyajit Ray are characterized by all of the following EXCEPT

  (A) adventure
  (B) honesty
  (C) compassion
  (D) dignity

8. The third film of the Apu Trilogy deals with all of the following themes EXCEPT

  (A) failure at a major goal
  (B) loss of a spouse
  (C) struggle against poverty
  (D) going home after a long absence

QUESTIONS 9–10

Archaeology is the study of prehistoric and historic cultures through the analysis of material remains. Archaeologists interpret the past from the objects made by past peoples. Often these objects lie buried in the ground, so our image of the archaeologist is of a scientist who is always digging. Archaeological digs include ruins of buildings and monuments, and also objects made by people who often had no written language and therefore no other record of their way of life. Tools, weapons, body ornaments, household furnishings, and items used in religious ceremonies are all examples of artifacts that typically turn up in digs.

Like historians, archaeologists establish the sequence of events that occurred in a given place and time period. But unlike historians, they take on a time span of roughly half a million years. Archaeologists try not only to piece together what happened in a particular setting but also to fit these small pieces into a much bigger picture. They aim to document how big changes occurred in the way peoples exploited their environment and one another.

9. The passage mentions all of the following as studied by archaeologists EXCEPT

   (A) weapons
   (B) religious objects
   (C) diaries
   (D) remains of buildings

10. Archaeologists do all of the following EXCEPT

   (A) plan and design more efficient uses for objects and materials
   (B) determine what took place in a specific place and time period
   (C) dig up the remains of objects that are buried in the ground
   (D) explain how past humans related to others and their environment

Exercise 1.2.B

Read the passages and choose the best answer to each question.

QUESTIONS 1–2

Political parties are necessary in the exercise of democracy in nation states. The enlargement of the electorate—the body of qualified voters—has increased the importance of parties to the point where it is practically impossible for a candidate to get elected without the support of a party organization. This is because the variety of issues facing nation states has complicated the problem of creating an informed electorate that can use its vote responsibly. The job of influencing popular opinion through newspapers, television, the Internet, and other mass media is too complicated and costly for an individual candidate to undertake. Although individual candidates continue to appear at public meetings—to answer questions and shake hands with voters— the influencing of public opinion on a mass scale has become a specialized technique. Building political support on a nation–wide scale carries a high cost, and it requires nationally organized and well–financed parties. Party organizations thus have come to occupy a prominent place in the functioning of democracies.

1. According to the passage, what is one effect of the enlargement of the electorate?

   (A) There are more political parties than ever before.
   (B) Candidates need political parties to get elected.
   (C) Political parties control all forms of mass media.
   (D) It is impossible to have a perfect democracy.

2. All of the following are given as reasons for the necessity of political parties EXCEPT

   (A) Influencing popular opinion through the media is a large and complex job.
   (B) It is difficult to inform voters about the variety of important issues.
   (C) Building nation–wide support is too expensive for individual candidates.
   (D) Voters prefer candidates that express the values of an established party.

QUESTIONS 3–4

Coral reefs are one of the earth's most ancient ecosystems and also the richest, most diverse, and most beautiful ecosystems in any ocean. The huge cities built by corals provide shelter and food for billions of other marine animals. A quarter of all sea creatures depend on coral reefs during some part of their life cycles.

In the past century, the ocean's surface temperature has risen an average of 1.8 degrees Fahrenheit. It has taken only this slight increase in sea–surface temperature to sicken the world's coral reefs. The brilliant blue, purple, green, gold, and pink have begun to disappear as a disease called bleaching drains the color and the life from the reefs. Scientists have reported mass bleaching on reefs in the Caribbean, in southern Japan, in Indonesia, and on the world's largest coral reef, the Great Barrier Reef, where the corals have bleached to a dirty white.

Bleaching has killed more corals than all other causes combined. More than 16 percent of the world's corals have sickened and died from bleaching. Millions of aquatic animals that depend directly or indirectly on corals have died as well—anemones, sponges, mollusks, shrimp, crabs, fish, turtles, and seabirds—making the loss of corals a catastrophe for the natural world.

3. Which of the following is NOT stated about coral reefs?

(A) They are among the oldest ecosystems in the world.
(B) They have caused sea–surface temperatures to rise.
(C) They are brilliantly colored when they are healthy.
(D) They supply shelter for a diversity of marine life.

4. All of the following are effects of the bleaching of coral reefs EXCEPT

(A) fading colors
(B) loss of dependent animals
(C) death of corals
(D) rising water level

QUESTIONS 5–7

What made Native American and European subsistence cycles so different from one another in colonial America had less to do with their use of plants than with their use of animals. Domesticated grazing animals and the plow were the most distinguishing characteristics of European agricultural practices. The Native Americans' relationship to the deer, moose, and beaver they hunted was far different from that of the Europeans to the pigs, cows, sheep, and horses they owned.

Where Natives had contented themselves with burning the woods and concentrating their hunting in the fall and winter months, the English sought a much more total and year–round control over their animals' lives. The effects of that control could be seen in most aspects of New England's rural economy. By the end of the colonial period, the Europeans were responsible for a host of changes in the New England landscape: endless miles of fences, a system of country roads, and new fields covered with grass, clover, and buttercups.

5. What point does the author make about Native Americans and Europeans?

(A) They competed over the same plants and animals.
(B) They both tried to control New England's animals.
(C) They taught each other techniques for hunting animals.
(D) They differed in their attitudes toward animals.

6. European settlers raised all of the following animals EXCEPT

(A) deer
(B) sheep
(C) horses
(D) pigs

7. All of the following were agricultural practices of Europeans in New England EXCEPT

(A) constructing fences
(B) burning the woods
(C) plowing fields
(D) planting grass and clover

QUESTIONS 8–10

Landscape architects design landscapes in residential areas, public parks, and commercial zones. They are hired by many types of organizations, from real estate firms starting new developments to municipalities constructing airports or parks. They usually plan the arrangement of vegetation, walkways, and other natural features of open spaces.

In planning a site, landscape architects first consider the nature and purpose of the project, the funds available, and the proposed elements. Next, they study the site and map such features as the slope of the land, the positions of existing buildings, existing utilities, roads, fences, walkways, and trees. Then, working either as the leader of a design team or in consultation with the project architect or engineer, they draw up plans to develop the site. If the plans are approved, they prepare working drawings to show all existing and proposed features. They outline the methods of constructing features and draw up lists of building materials.

Newcomers to the field usually start as junior drafters, tracing drawings and doing other simple drafting work for architectural, landscape architectural, or engineering firms. After two or three years, they can carry a design through all stages of development. Highly qualified landscape architects may become associates in private firms, but usually those who progress this far open their own offices.

8. Landscape architects do all of the following EXCEPT

(A) design landscapes in residential and commercial zones

(B) decide where to build walkways in public parks

(C) draw or paint scenes from the natural environment

(D) plan the arrangement of vegetation and other natural features

9. All of the following are listed as stages in the landscape design process EXCEPT

(A) thinking about the project's purpose and the funding

(B) building a fence around the construction site

(C) making drawings that include old and new features

(D) preparing lists of building materials and methods

10. How do most landscape architects begin their careers?

(A) They lead the design team of a small landscaping project.

(B) They apply for a position as an associate in a private company.

(C) They do drafting work for an architectural or engineering firm.

(D) They open their own business as a landscape architect.

Answers to Exercise 1.2.A through 1.2.B are on page 559.

 EXTENSION

1. Fact or Opinion? Select a passage from each of the following sources:

   a science textbook   the international page of a newspaper
   a book of essays   the editorial page of a newspaper

   Make enough copies of each passage for everyone in your class. In class, identify statements in the passages that are facts and statements that are opinions. Discuss the following questions:

   a. What is a fact?
   b. Is a fact always true for every person?
   c. What is an opinion?
   d. How do writers use facts and opinions?
   e. How can you distinguish a fact from an opinion?

PROGRESS – 1.1 through 1.2

QUIZ 1   *Time – 15 minutes*

Read the passages and choose the best answer to each question. Answer all questions about a passage on the basis of what is stated or implied in that passage.

EFFECTS OF IONIZING RADIATION

Everyone on Earth is continually exposed to small, relatively harmless amounts of ionizing radiation, known as background radiation, from natural sources such as soil and rock. However, other types of ionizing radiation—x–rays, ultraviolet radiation from the sun, and alpha, beta, and gamma radiation emitted by radioactive isotopes—have the potential to harm the human body. Ionizing radiation has enough energy to remove one or more electrons from the atoms it hits to form positively charged ions that can react with and damage living tissue. Most damage occurs in tissues with rapidly dividing cells, such as the bone marrow, where blood cells are made, and the digestive tract, whose lining must be constantly renewed.

Exposure to ionizing radiation can damage cells in two ways. The first is genetic damage, which alters genes and chromosomes. This can show up as a genetic defect in children or in later generations. The second type of damage is somatic, which causes victims direct harm in the form of burns, miscarriages, eye cataracts, some types of leukemia, or cancers of the bone, thyroid, breast, skin, and lung. Small doses of ionizing radiation over a long period of time cause less damage than the same total dosage given all at once. Exposure to a large dose of ionizing radiation over a short time can be fatal within a few minutes to a few months later.

1. According to the passage, what is one difference between background radiation and other types of ionizing radiation?

   (A) Background radiation is rare in nature, while other types are not.
   (B) Background radiation is less likely to harm the human body.
   (C) Background radiation cannot form positively charged ions.
   (D) Background radiation causes more damage to the environment.

2. What types of tissues are harmed most by ionizing radiation?

   (A) Tissues with cells that divide quickly
   (B) Tissues on the outside surface of the body
   (C) Tissues exposed to background radiation
   (D) Tissues with a large number of chromosomes

3. All of the following are examples of somatic damage EXCEPT

   (A) genetic defects
   (B) eye cataracts
   (C) radiation burns
   (D) lung cancer

4. Which exposure to ionizing radiation causes the most serious damage to humans?

   (A) Continuous exposure to background radiation in the environment
   (B) Small doses of ionizing radiation over a long period of time
   (C) A single dose of a moderate amount of ionizing radiation
   (D) Exposure to a large amount of ionizing radiation in a short period

THE COYOTE

All North American canids have a doglike appearance characterized by a graceful body, long muzzle, erect ears, slender legs, and bushy tail. Most are social animals that travel and hunt in groups or pairs. After years of persecution by humans, the populations of most North American canids, especially wolves and foxes, have decreased greatly. The coyote, however, has thrived alongside humans, increasing in both numbers and range.

Its common name comes from *coyotl*, the term used by Mexico's Nahuatl Indians, and its scientific name, *canis latrans*, means "barking dog." The coyote's vocalizations are varied, but the most distinctive are given at dusk, dawn, or during the night and consist of a series of barks followed by a prolonged howl and ending with short, sharp yaps. This call keeps the band alert to the locations of its members. One voice usually prompts others to join in, resulting in the familiar chorus heard at night throughout the West.

The best runner among the canids, the coyote is able to leap fourteen feet and cruise normally at 25–30 miles per hour. It is a strong swimmer and does not hesitate to enter water after prey. In feeding, the coyote is an opportunist, eating rabbits, mice, ground squirrels, birds, snakes, insects, many kinds of fruit, and carrion—whatever is available. To catch larger prey, such as deer or antelope, the coyote may team up with one or two others, running in relays to tire prey or waiting in ambush while others chase prey toward it. Often a badger serves as involuntary supplier of smaller prey: while it digs for rodents at one end of their burrow, the coyote waits for any that may emerge from an escape hole at the other end.

Predators of the coyote once included the grizzly and black bears, the mountain lion, and the wolf, but their declining populations make them no longer a threat. Man is the major enemy, especially since coyote pelts have become increasingly valuable, yet the coyote population continues to grow, despite efforts at trapping, shooting, and poisoning the animals.

5. According to the passage, the coyote is unlike other North American canids in what way?

  (A) The coyote's body is not graceful.
  (B) The coyote is not hunted by humans.
  (C) The coyote population has not decreased.
  (D) The coyote does not know how to swim.

6. All of the following statements describe the coyote's vocalizations EXCEPT

  (A) Vocalizations communicate the locations of other coyotes.
  (B) The coyote uses its distinctive call to trick and catch prey.
  (C) A group of coyotes will often bark and howl together.
  (D) The coyote's scientific name reflects its manner of vocalizing.

7. According to the passage, the coyote is an opportunist because it

  (A) knows how to avoid being captured
  (B) likes to team up with other coyotes
  (C) has better luck than other predators
  (D) takes advantage of circumstances

8. Which animal sometimes unknowingly helps the coyote catch food?

  (A) Wolf
  (B) Rodent
  (C) Deer
  (D) Badger

9. According to the passage, the chief predator of the coyote is

  (A) the wolf
  (B) the mountain lion
  (C) the human
  (D) the grizzly bear

10. According to the passage, all of the following statements are true EXCEPT

  (A) The coyote is a serious threat to human activities.
  (B) The coyote is a skillful and athletic predator.
  (C) The coyote hunts cooperatively with other coyotes.
  (D) The coyote survives despite persecution by humans.

Answers to Reading Quiz 1 are on page 560.

Record your score on the Progress Chart on page 693.

1.3 Locating Referents

FOCUS

Read the following paragraph:

> When the temperature of hydrogen atoms is raised high enough, a helium atom is formed from four hydrogen atoms. In the center of our sun and other stars, hydrogen is being transformed into helium as hydrogen atoms fuse together to form helium. Fusion is a process in which atomic nuclei collide so fast that they stick together and emit a great deal of energy.

Look at the word they in the passage. What word or phrase could replace *they* and still make sense?

In the passage, *they* refers to things that stick together and emit a great deal of energy. Logic tells you that *they* refers to *atomic nuclei*. You can verify this by putting *atomic nuclei* in place of *they* in the sentence. The sentence will read: *Fusion is a process in which atomic nuclei collide so fast that atomic nuclei stick together and emit a great deal of energy*. The sentence still makes sense in the context of the passage.

Atomic nuclei is the **referent** of *they*. The author uses *they* to avoid unnecessary repetition of *atomic nuclei*.

Now read another paragraph:

> Because human behavior is so complex, research psychologists must concentrate on specific types of behavior and restrict themselves to examining one facet of behavior at a time. Thus, most research reports provide specific information about a particular aspect of behavior. All descriptions of behavior, even those appearing in multi–volume texts, are based on selected information that writers interpret in their own way.

Look at the word those in the passage. What noun could replace *those* and still make sense? If you change *those* to *descriptions*, the sentence will have the same meaning. The sentence will read: *All descriptions of behavior, even descriptions appearing in multi–volume texts, are based on selected information that writers interpret in their own way*.

Descriptions, or *descriptions of behavior*, is the **referent** of *those*. *Those* is used to avoid unnecessary repetition.

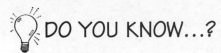

DO YOU KNOW…?

1. **Referents** are words in a passage that other words refer to. Pronouns such as *they* and *those* refer to nouns elsewhere in the passage—these nouns are the referents of the pronouns. The noun referents are the words that the pronouns replace.

    Usually the referent is mentioned before the pronoun in the passage, often immediately before it, but sometimes the referent appears after the pronoun. The referent may be in the same sentence as the pronoun, or it may be in another sentence.

    Words such as *this*, *that*, *many*, and *some* can also have noun referents in a passage. The referent may be in the same sentence as the referring word, or it may be in another sentence.

2. TOEFL questions about referents look like this:

    > The word _____ in the passage refers to _____.
    > The phrase _____ in paragraph __ refers to _____.

3. Some words and phrases that have referents are:

Subject Pronouns	he	she	it	they
Object Pronouns	him	her	it	them
Possessive Adjectives	his	her	its	their
Demonstrative Pronouns	this	that	these	those
Relative Pronouns	who	whom	which	whose
Other Pronouns	all	either	none	the first
	another	a few	one	the last
	any	many	others	the former
	both	most	several	the latter
	each	neither	some	the other

4. Look at some examples of pronouns and referents. The referent for each highlighted word is shown in *italics*.

    Because she was essentially a realist, *Willa Cather* made human nature the subject of her novels.

    The refraction of light by *the moonstone's* internal layers gives it a milky sheen.

    Although *songbirds* have no commercial value, they freely give us their music.

    Driving while intoxicated is illegal, but this is not the only reason to avoid drinking and driving.

    The tallest peak of the Rockies is twice as high as that of the Appalachians.

    The thyroid gland, which is part of the endocrine system, regulates the body's metabolic rate.

Three common herbs are effective remedies for a sore throat: *angelica*, *sage*, and *vervain*; all are available in health food stores.

Electromagnetism is the relationship between *electricity* and *magnetism*; either can be used to produce the other.

Most *daisies* are perennials, but some bloom for only one or two seasons.

Only two *elements* are liquids at normal temperatures; one is mercury and the other is bromine.

5. The referent questions most commonly seen on the TOEFL ask you to locate the referent of a pronoun. However, sometimes you must identify the referent of a specified term or phrase. Look at the highlighted phrase in the following passage:

    Like the gray and fox squirrels, the Eastern chipmunk often feeds on acorns and hickory nuts. Essentially a ground species, this pert rodent does not hesitate to climb large oak trees when the acorns are ripe.

    This pert rodent refers to *the Eastern chipmunk*, which is the subject of the previous sentence.

6. The meaning of the sentence can help you answer referent questions. The function of the pronoun or referring word—for example, whether it is a subject or object—can help you find the correct referent. Grammatical structures are often clues that point to the identity of referents. Sentence structure, logic, and common sense can help you locate referents.

    You can check your answer by putting it in the sentence in place of the pronoun or referring word. If the sentence still makes sense according to the passage, your answer is correct.

7. Here are some examples:

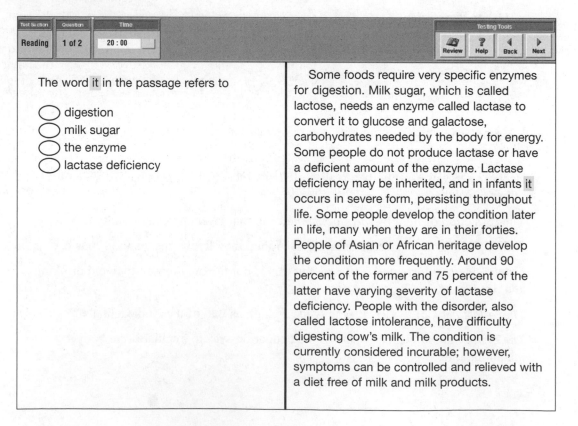

| Test Section | Question | Time | | Testing Tools |
| Reading | 1 of 2 | 20 : 00 | | Review Help Back Next |

The word it in the passage refers to

○ digestion
○ milk sugar
○ the enzyme
○ lactase deficiency

Some foods require very specific enzymes for digestion. Milk sugar, which is called lactose, needs an enzyme called lactase to convert it to glucose and galactose, carbohydrates needed by the body for energy. Some people do not produce lactase or have a deficient amount of the enzyme. Lactase deficiency may be inherited, and in infants it occurs in severe form, persisting throughout life. Some people develop the condition later in life, many when they are in their forties. People of Asian or African heritage develop the condition more frequently. Around 90 percent of the former and 75 percent of the latter have varying severity of lactase deficiency. People with the disorder, also called lactose intolerance, have difficulty digesting cow's milk. The condition is currently considered incurable; however, symptoms can be controlled and relieved with a diet free of milk and milk products.

The referent of *it* is something that occurs in severe form in infants. The subject of the sentence is *Lactase deficiency*. Logic tells you that *it* refers to *lactase deficiency*, which is the correct answer.

You can check the answer by reading the sentence with *lactase deficiency* in place of *it*: *Lactase deficiency may be inherited, and in infants lactase deficiency occurs in severe form, persisting throughout life.*

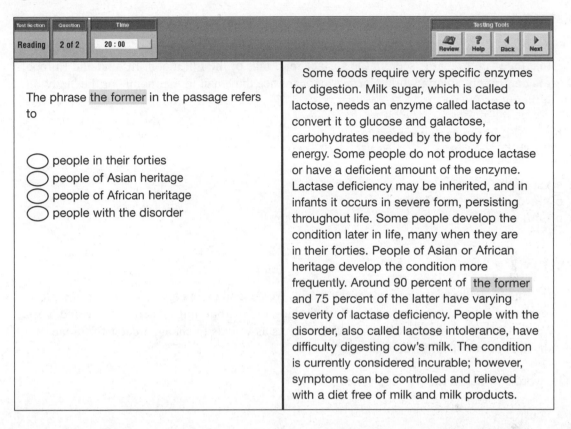

What is the referent of *the former*? In all cases where two things are mentioned, *the former* refers to the first thing, and *the latter* refers to the second thing. In this passage, *the former* refers to *people of Asian heritage* because this phrase is mentioned first in the previous sentence. *The latter* refers to *people of African heritage* because this phrase is mentioned second.

The correct answer is *people of Asian heritage*. You can check this by reading the sentence with *people of Asian heritage* in place of *the former* and *people of African heritage* in place of *the latter*. The passage will read: *People of Asian or African heritage develop the condition more frequently. Around 90 percent of people of Asian heritage and 75 percent of people of African heritage have varying severity of lactase deficiency.*

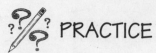 PRACTICE

Exercise 1.3.A

Read the passages and choose the best answer to each question.

QUESTION 1

Passed from generation to generation by word of mouth, every society has a favorite imagined figure that is seen in the surface markings of the full moon. In Asia and Europe, it is commonly a hare, while North Americans see the "man in the moon" or the "lady in the moon."

1. The word it in the passage refers to

   (A) word of mouth
   (B) society
   (C) favorite imagined figure
   (D) full moon

QUESTION 2

Energy is the real currency of the world. We depend on energy to grow our food, to keep us alive, and to warm and cool our bodies and the buildings where we live and work. We also use it to move people and other objects as well as to change matter from one physical or chemical form to another.

2. The word another in the passage refers to

   (A) currency
   (B) energy
   (C) matter
   (D) form

QUESTION 3

Young potential leaders should gain exceptional command, in both writing and speaking, of their own language. In addition, they should have workable knowledge of a second language. Leadership requires strong public speaking skills. Courses in public speaking do not enjoy high status in the academic world today; however, many bright young people are poor speakers, and they must develop their ability in this area.

3. The phrase this area in the passage refers to

   (A) a second language
   (B) leadership
   (C) public speaking
   (D) the academic world

QUESTION 4

At least one central quality of music—rhythmic organization—can exist apart from the ability of people to hear it. Some composers, such as Scriabin, have emphasized the importance of the rhythmic aspect of music by translating their works into rhythmic series of colored forms. Others, such as Stravinsky, have stressed the significance of seeing music performed by an orchestra or a dance troupe. Thus, certain aspects of the musical experience are accessible even to deaf individuals who cannot appreciate its auditory qualities.

4. The word Others in the passage refers to

- (A) people
- (B) composers
- (C) works
- (D) forms

QUESTIONS 5–6

Stratified societies are marked by differences among people that identify them as being "higher" or "lower." The simplest forms of inequality are based on age and sex. For example, old people may have a high or a low position; women may be ranked below men. But in every society there is another form of inequality that ranks families rather than individuals. If a large number of families are similar to each other in education, income, and values, they constitute a social class.

5. The word them in the passage refers to

- (A) societies
- (B) differences
- (C) people
- (D) forms

6. The word they in the passage refers to

- (A) stratified societies
- (B) individuals
- (C) large number of families
- (D) education, income, and values

QUESTIONS 7–8

Most Americans still get married at some point in their lives, but even that group is shrinking. Among current generations of adults—starting with those born in the 1920s—more than 90 percent have married or will marry at some point in their lives. However, based on recent patterns of marriage and mortality, demographers calculate that a growing share of the younger generation is postponing marriage for so long that an unprecedented number will never marry at all. Data on cohabitation and unmarried childbearing suggest that marriage is becoming less relevant to Americans. 2.8 million of the nation's households are unmarried couples, and one–third of them are caring for children, according to the Census Bureau.

7. The word those in the passage refers to

- (A) Americans
- (B) lives
- (C) adults
- (D) 90 percent

8. The word them in the passage refers to

- (A) younger generations
- (B) data
- (C) Americans
- (D) unmarried couples

QUESTIONS 9–10

Pesticides temporarily increase the productivity of crops, until insects develop genetic resistance to them. Traces of chemical pesticides appear in many foods grown on pesticide–treated soils, in the groundwater that many people drink, and in the air we breathe.

The effects of pesticides occur mostly at the cellular level. Certain chemicals selectively inhibit the action of specific enzymes in plant and animal cells. Some are absorbed from an organism's environment and act as metabolic poisons. For example, the agricultural insecticides DDT and parathion are inhibitors of key enzymes in the nervous system of animals.

9. The word them in paragraph 1 refers to

- (A) pesticides
- (B) crops
- (C) insects
- (D) soils

10. The word Some in paragraph 2 refers to

- (A) effects
- (B) chemicals
- (C) enzymes
- (D) cells

Exercise 1.3.B

Read the passages and choose the best answer to each question.

QUESTIONS 1–2

In the final decades of the nineteenth century, the guiding principles for the applied arts were sensitive handcrafting, simplicity, and respect for indigenous designs. These were promoted in books, magazines, newspapers, and art schools of the period. The philosophy encouraged the development of an artistic setting for home life and a substantial role for women in fostering that environment. More women began to study drawing, painting and the creation of art objects—pottery, jewelry, and textiles—and to exhibit their works more often in public. In cultivating the home, women also began to associate more with one another, founding art societies and social–reform clubs that empowered them. Many of the great art museums can trace their origins to that period and those women.

1. The word These in the passage refers to

(A) final decades
(B) guiding principles
(C) applied arts
(D) indigenous designs

2. The word them in the passage refers to

(A) works
(B) women
(C) societies
(D) clubs

QUESTIONS 3–4

The great tulip grower E.H. Krelage of Holland changed forever the way we look at tulips in our gardens. At the world trade fair in Paris in 1889, he introduced his new Darwin tulips, which were planted in brilliant bands of color under the Eiffel Tower and alongside the Seine. In that one brilliant marketing ploy, Krelage changed the tulip from a flower that was carefully and individually displayed to one that was planted in mass beddings of beautiful color.

Gardeners all over the world fell in love with Krelage's tulips, which were tall, strong, and weatherproof. In New York, the public parks of the Bronx blazed with red tulips, as did Golden Gate Park in San Francisco and the St. Louis Botanic Garden. Although the wildly differing climatic zones of North America did not always suit them, tulips have proved to be forgiving plants and have thus remained garden favorites.

3. The word one in paragraph 1 refers to

(A) ploy
(B) tulip
(C) flower
(D) color

4. The word them in paragraph 2 refers to

(A) gardeners
(B) parks
(C) tulips
(D) favorites

QUESTIONS 5–6

The philosophy of existentialism is based on the belief that individual human beings face a meaningless, absurd, and science–oriented world. Individuals must therefore find or construct meaning for their existence and answer their own questions about self–identity and truth. The philosophy of phenomenology is the study of human experience and the interpretation of experience. Phenomenology is a close cousin to existentialism. Both echo many of the themes of earlier philosophies, particularly realism and transcendentalism, and in turn had an effect on other ways of thinking. Existentialism and phenomenology influenced theological and humanist thinkers, such as Martin Buber and Abraham Maslow. The former focused on the I–Thou and teacher–student relationships, while the latter theorized about the hierarchy of human needs and the ultimate need for self–actualization.

5. The word Both in the passage refers to

   (A) self–identity and truth
   (B) phenomenology and existentialism
   (C) human experience and the interpretation of experience
   (D) realism and transcendentalism

6. The phrase the latter in the passage refers to

   (A) existentialism
   (B) phenomenology
   (C) Martin Buber
   (D) Abraham Maslow

QUESTIONS 7–10

Vitamin D increases the efficiency of the intestine to absorb calcium and phosphorus from food in order to mineralize the bones in the body. It also increases the activity of bone cells that make and lay down bone matrix. The bone matrix is like the frame of a building. If the body has adequate amounts of calcium and phosphorus, they are incorporated into the bone matrix, and the result is a strong, healthy skeleton. Our skin can make vitamin D when it is exposed to sunlight. However, most people living in North America do not get enough sunlight in the winter to make adequate amounts of the vitamin.

Young children who do not get enough calcium and vitamin D are unable to properly mineralize the bone matrix. Consequently, when gravity pushes on the skeleton, it causes the typical bowing of the legs seen in a child with the disease called rickets.

In adults, a deficiency in both calcium and vitamin D will increase the risk of bone fracture. Vitamin D is necessary to increase the body's ability to absorb calcium. If the body does not have enough vitamin D, it can absorb only 10 to 15 percent of the calcium it receives. If the bloodstream does not have enough calcium, it will draw it out of the bones, which causes osteoporosis. With osteoporosis, the bones break down as bone cells called osteoclasts dissolve the matrix and release calcium from the bones. A vitamin D deficiency will increase the severity of the disease because it increases the number of holes in the bones.

7. The word they in paragraph 1 refers to

   (A) vitamin D and calcium
   (B) bones
   (C) bone cells
   (D) calcium and phosphorus

8. The word it in paragraph 1 refers to

   (A) skin
   (B) vitamin D
   (C) skeleton
   (D) North America

9. The word it in paragraph 2 refers to

    (A) calcium
    (B) vitamin D
    (C) bone matrix
    (D) gravity

10. The phrase the disease in paragraph 3 refers to

    (A) rickets
    (B) bone fracture
    (C) osteoporosis
    (D) vitamin D deficiency

Answers to Exercises 1.3.A through 1.3.B are on page 561.

 EXTENSION

1. Outside of class, look in a newspaper, a magazine, or a university textbook. Select a short passage of one to three paragraphs. Make a photocopy and bring it to class. In class, work with a partner. Read the passage and circle all pronouns that refer to other words or ideas in the passage. Then identify the referent of each pronoun. Draw a line between each pronoun and its noun referent. Check your answers by reading the sentence aloud, putting the noun in place of each pronoun. Does the sentence make sense? With your partner, discuss why the writer probably chose to use the pronouns.

2. In reading done outside class, select a short passage of no more than 100 words. In the passage, locate pronouns/referring words and their noun referents. Write the passage on an overhead projector transparency, but omit the pronouns and referents. Leave a blank space where each pronoun and referent should be. Below the passage, write the missing words in mixed–up order. Your class must fill in the blanks correctly. Is there only one correct answer for each space?

    Here is an example:

    _____ burn uncontrolled in a forested, wooded, or scrubby area. Forest fires occur chiefly in old growth or second–growth forest. Brush fires are _____ that occur in scrub areas. Fires inject tremendous amounts of microscopic _____ into the atmosphere. _____ may be considered pollutants by people living downwind from a fire, but _____ are essential to the generation of clouds and precipitation.

    ASH PARTICLES   THEY   WILDFIRES   THESE PARTICLES   THOSE

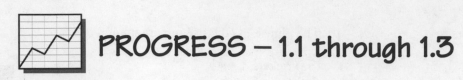

PROGRESS – 1.1 through 1.3

QUIZ 2   *Time – 40 minutes*

Read the passages and choose the best answer to each question. Answer all questions about a passage on the basis of what is stated or implied in that passage.

GERMAN EXPRESSIONISM

The Cabinet of Dr. Caligari, directed by Robert Wiene in 1919, remains the supreme example of expressionistic filmmaking. The film is narrated by a young man who suspects Dr. Caligari, a **mountebank** who is part of a traveling fair, of being responsible for a series of violent crimes. Caligari's instrument of crime is Cesare, a sleepwalker who is under the control of the evil doctor. Cesare captures a young woman, but she escapes, and in the subsequent search for the doctor we learn that he is really the director of a local **insane asylum**, in which the narrator is a patient. The film's expressionistic sets and lighting reflect the narrator's madness. Walls are slanted and windows triangular. Surreal effects of light and shadow are painted directly on the sets. Furniture is distorted and oversized, evoking a nightmare world of insanity. *Dr. Caligari* is a unique film with a secure place in film history.

The so–called expressionistic "street films" dealing with the lives of common people had a great influence on the popular imagination. Director Fritz Lang's *Metropolis* (1926) presents a chilling vision of life in the twenty–first century in which the rich live luxuriously in skyscrapers while the workers toil as slaves below the ground. *Metropolis* is another spectacular exercise in German expressionism, and the screen is filled with stylized shadows, sloping camera angles, and nightmarish underground chambers.

Glossary:

> **mountebank**: a seller of false medicines who attracts customers with lies or tricks
> **insane asylum**: mental hospital

1. According to the passage, the plot of *The Cabinet of Dr. Caligari* is mainly about

   (A) a young man who is responsible for several violent acts
   (B) an evil doctor who uses another man to commit crimes
   (C) a young woman who looks for a doctor to help her
   (D) the terrible conditions in a hospital for the insane

2. The word he in paragraph 1 refers to

   (A) Robert Wiene
   (B) Dr. Caligari
   (C) Cesare
   (D) the narrator

3. How do the walls, windows, and furniture in *The Cabinet of Dr. Caligari* contribute to the film?

   (A) They reveal the doctor's lies and tricks.
   (B) They portray the popular styles of the period.
   (C) They display the director's artistic vision.
   (D) They express the insanity of the narrator.

4. How does the author characterize *Metropolis*?

   (A) A street film about the lives of common people

   (B) A documentary about life in the twenty–first century

   (C) A criticism of unfair working conditions

   (D) An imperfect example of German expressionism

5. All of the following are characteristics of expressionistic film EXCEPT

   (A) surreal effects of light and shadow

   (B) nightmarish imagery

   (C) luxurious sets and furniture

   (D) slanting and distortion

RURAL CANADA

In the 1880s, over three–fourths of Canada's population lived outside urban centers. One view of rural Canada at that time portrays it as a vast wasteland of isolated farm communities. However, a more accurate view shows that rural Canadians had access to considerable information. The postal service was efficient and inexpensive and connected rural Canadians with the outside world. Many farm families received at least one newspaper through the mail, usually within a day of publication. The daily newspapers of the period were more substantial than those of today, and many reproduced precise accounts of court trials and public events. Rural Canadians read magazines and books and held discussions about them at club meetings.

Rural Canadians were also able to get together socially. The local school served other functions besides providing formal education, and school districts were often the only sign of political organization in vast regions of the country. Every community valued its one–room schoolhouse as a meeting place, especially during the winter, when work on the farm was much lighter and people had more time for a variety of social and cultural events. People of all ages got together to sing and play musical instruments, perform skits, and play parlor games.

Between 1880 and 1920, there was a growing exodus from farms to the city, mainly because smaller farms could not afford to modernize their technology and were no longer able to support the entire family. However, most Canadians continued to hold rural values, and artists and writers romanticized the family farm. In the novel *Anne of Green Gables* (1908), Lucy Maud Montgomery wrote about a young woman who strove to reconcile the beauty and peace of the rural landscape with the need to leave it in order to fulfill her ambitions. For large numbers of young Canadians, growing up meant leaving the farm to find work in the city.

6. According to the passage, rural Canada in the 1880s was not an isolated wasteland because

   (A) most farms were close to the city
   (B) education was inexpensive
   (C) the rural population was growing
   (D) information was available to farmers

7. The word those in paragraph 1 refers to

   (A) rural Canadians
   (B) farm families
   (C) daily newspapers
   (D) magazines

8. The word them in paragraph 1 refers to

   (A) court trials
   (B) public events
   (C) rural Canadians
   (D) magazines and books

9. According to the passage, the rural school provided all of the following services EXCEPT

   (A) formal education
   (B) public health clinics
   (C) political organization
   (D) social and cultural events

10. What reason is given for large numbers of people leaving the family farm?

   (A) There was not enough work on the farm during the winter.
   (B) People grew tired of the social isolation of rural life.
   (C) Small farms could no longer support the whole family.
   (D) Modern farm technology was not available in many areas.

11. Which statement best describes the period from 1880 to 1920?

  (A) Literature portrayed a romanticized view of life on the farm.
  (B) More Canadians lived in urban areas than in rural areas.
  (C) Rural communities began to acquire characteristics of the city.
  (D) People gave up their rural values when they moved to the city.

ICE

Two conditions are necessary for the formation of ice: the presence of water and temperatures below freezing. Ice in the atmosphere and on the ground can assume various forms, depending on the conditions under which water is converted to its solid state. Ice that forms in the atmosphere can fall to the ground as snow, sleet, or hail. Snow is an assemblage of ice crystals in the form of flakes; sleet is a collection of frozen raindrops, which are actually ice pellets. Hail consists of rounded or jagged lumps of ice, often in layers like the internal structure of an onion. Ice also forms directly on the ground or on bodies of water. In North America, ice forms in late autumn, winter, and early spring. On very large bodies of water, it may not form until late winter because there must be several months of low temperatures to chill such large amounts of water.

On puddles and small ponds, ice first freezes in a thin layer with definite crystal structure that becomes less apparent as the ice thickens. On lakes large enough to have waves, such as the Great Lakes, the first ice to form is a thin surface layer of slush, sometimes called grease ice, which eventually grows into small floes of pancake ice. If the lake is small enough or the weather cold enough, the floes may freeze together into a fairly solid sheet of pack ice. Pack ice may cover the entire lake or be restricted to areas near the shore.

Because water expands when it freezes, ice is less dense than liquid water and therefore floats rather than sinks in water. As ice floats on the surface of a lake, ocean, or river, it acts as an insulator and is thus important in maintaining the balance of the ecosystem. Without the insulating effect of floating ice sheets, surface water would lose heat more rapidly, and large bodies of water such as the Arctic Ocean and Hudson Bay might freeze up completely.

12. What condition is necessary for water in the atmosphere to change to its solid state?

  (A) A solid cloud cover that absorbs the sun's heat
  (B) A weather forecast for snow, sleet, or hail
  (C) A position directly above a large body of water
  (D) A temperature below water's freezing point

13. Ice that forms in the atmosphere in the form of layered lumps is known as

  (A) snow
  (B) pack ice
  (C) hail
  (D) grease ice

14. All of the following are forms of ice that form on bodies of water EXCEPT

  (A) sleet
  (B) slush
  (C) pancake ice
  (D) pack ice

15. Why does ice form later on very large bodies of water?

  (A) Most large bodies of water are located at low elevations or low latitudes.
  (B) It takes several months of cold temperatures to cool a large body of water.
  (C) Large bodies of water are fed by underground springs of warmer water.
  (D) The waves on large bodies of water prevent the water from freezing quickly.

16. The word it in paragraph 3 refers to

    (A) water
    (B) ice
    (C) surface
    (D) river

17. Which of the following is an effect of the density of ice?

    (A) Ice that forms on large lakes has a greasy consistency.
    (B) Each ice crystal is unique, but all are six–sided structures.
    (C) Pack ice is restricted to areas near the shore of a lake.
    (D) Floating ice sheets prevent bodies of water from losing heat.

THE ROLE OF GOVERNMENT IN THE ECONOMY

Because most people do not volunteer to pay taxes or police their own financial affairs, governments cannot influence economic activity simply by asking people to pollute less, to give money to the poor, or to be innovative. To accomplish these things, governments have to pass laws. Since the early twentieth century, governments of countries with advanced industrial or service economies have been playing an increasing role in economics. This can be seen in the growth of government taxation and spending, in the growing share of national income devoted to income–support payments, and by the enormous increase in the control of economic activity.

The large–scale organization of business, as seen in mass production and distribution, has led to the formation of large–scale organizations—corporations, labor unions, and government structures—that have grown in importance in the past several decades. Their presence and growing dominance have shifted capitalist economies away from traditional market forces and toward government administration of markets.

In the United States, government provides a framework of laws for the conduct of economic activity that attempt to make it serve the public interest. For instance, the individual states and the federal government have passed laws to shield investors against fraud. These laws specify what information has to be disclosed to prospective investors when shares of stocks or bonds are offered for sale. Another important area of law concerns the labor force, such as regulation of work hours, minimum wages, health and safety conditions, child labor, and the rights of workers to form unions, to strike, to demonstrate peacefully, and to bargain collectively through representatives of their own choosing.

In other nations, the ways in which governments intervene in their economies has varied; however, governments everywhere deal with essentially the same issues and participate in economic activity. Even governments that are reluctant to regulate commerce directly have undertaken large–scale projects such as hydroelectric and nuclear energy developments, transportation networks, or expansion of health, education, and other public services.

18. According to the passage, why do governments intervene in economic activity?

(A) People do not willingly regulate their own business affairs.
(B) Governments understand the economy better than anyone else does.
(C) Businesses pay governments to participate in economic activity.
(D) The economy would fail without the help of government.

19. The word This in paragraph 1 refers to

(A) economic activity
(B) asking people to pollute less
(C) the early twentieth century
(D) increasing role in economics

20. According to the passage, how has the growth of large–scale organizations such as corporations and labor unions affected capitalist economies?

(A) It has forced governments to pass laws protecting traditional markets.
(B) It has destroyed capitalism and replaced it with government ownership.
(C) It has led to the increasing role of government in economic activity.
(D) It has caused unfair competition between large and small businesses.

21. In paragraph 3, the author mentions laws to shield investors against fraud as an example of

(A) laws that organize business
(B) laws that serve the public interest
(C) laws that protect the labor force
(D) laws that set the price of stocks

22. The word their in paragraph 3 refers to

    (A) individual states
    (B) laws
    (C) workers
    (D) unions

23. All of the following are given as issues concerning the labor force EXCEPT

    (A) stock ownership
    (B) health and safety
    (C) hours of work
    (D) the right to strike

24. What point does the author make about governments that do not want to regulate business directly?

    (A) They cannot compete effectively with government–controlled economies.
    (B) They have capitalist economies based on traditional market forces.
    (C) They have no laws for protecting the environment and public health.
    (D) They participate in the economy through public projects and services.

25. According to the passage, all of the following are examples of government participation in economic activity EXCEPT

    (A) taxation and spending
    (B) small business ownership
    (C) income–support payments
    (D) transportation networks

Answers to Reading Quiz 2 are on page 561.

Record your score on the Progress Chart on page 693.

1.4 Understanding Vocabulary in Context

FOCUS

Read the following passage and answer the question:

A 1625 map of North America drawn by Henry Briggs is one of the most notorious maps in the history of North American cartography. It was the first printed map to show California as an island. Briggs based his map on information from the 1602 Spanish expedition to the West Coast in search of a safe haven for the Spanish colonial fleets. Briggs also wrote a treatise based on the Spanish account, in which he described California as a "goodly islande." The map and treatise initiated one of the most famous and persistent of all cartographical misconceptions, and California was still being depicted as an island in atlases issued in Amsterdam as late as the 1790s.

What is cartography ?

- ○ geography
- ○ exploration
- ○ printing
- ○ mapmaking

Look at the word cartography in the passage. What other words in the passage help you understand the meaning of this word? Some possible clues are *map*, *drawn*, *history of*, and *printed map*. These clues will help you see that the correct answer is *mapmaking*.

Now answer another question:

The word depicted in the passage is closest in meaning to

- ○ promised
- ○ drawn
- ○ developed
- ○ sought

Some clues to the meaning of depicted are:

…the first printed map to show California as an island.
…California was still being depicted as an island in atlases….

In the passage, *depicted* means shown or drawn. Therefore, the correct answer is *drawn*.

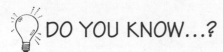
DO YOU KNOW...?

1. The *context* is the setting—the sentence and paragraph—in which a word or phrase appears. The meaning of a word or phrase *in context* is its meaning in the particular sentence and paragraph in which it is used. A single English word can have many different meanings. Its precise meaning always depends on the context in which it is used.

2. TOEFL questions about vocabulary in context look like this:

> The word/phrase _____ in the passage is closest in meaning to _____.
> The word/phrase _____ in the passage means _____.
> The word/phrase _____ in paragraph __ refers to a type of _____.
> What is _____?

3. To understand the meaning of a word in context, you can use different types of *context clues*: your knowledge of structure, punctuation, and the meaning of other words in the same sentence or paragraph. In the reading that you do in class and the real world, there may not always be context clues to help you. However, sometimes you can guess the probable meaning of an unfamiliar word by using your overall understanding of the ideas in a passage as well as your common sense and knowledge of the world.

4. *Structural clues* are one type of context clue. Structural clues are certain words, phrases, and grammatical structures that point to the relationships among the various parts of a sentence. These clues help you understand the meaning of an unfamiliar word by showing how the word relates to other words and ideas in the sentence. The structural clues below can help you understand vocabulary in context.

5. **CLUE:** *BE*

Example	**Explanation**
A supernova *is* a massive star that undergoes a gravitational collapse, then a gigantic explosion, blasting away the outer layers into space.	The meaning of *supernova* is given by the information after the verb *is*. A *supernova* is a massive star that collapses and then explodes.
Everyone faces times when one goal or another has to come first; deciding which goals are most important *is* setting priorities.	The meaning of *priorities* is given by the information before the verb *is*. *Priorities* are the most important goals.

6. **CLUE:** *OR*

Example	**Explanation**
The inclination *or* tilt of the earth's axis with respect to the sun determines the seasons.	The meaning of *inclination* is given by the information after the conjunction *or*. *Inclination* means tilt.
A skyscraper, *or* building more than twenty stories high, is built on a foundation of concrete supported by piles driven into the ground.	The meaning of *skyscraper* is given by the information after the conjunction *or*. A *skyscraper* is a building more than twenty stories high.

7. **Clue: Appositive**

Example

Thermal power stations are designed to pass as much energy as possible from the fuel to the turbines, *machines whose blades are turned by the movement of the steam.*

Explanation

The meaning of *turbines* is given by the appositive, the noun phrase after the comma. *Turbines* are machines with blades that are turned by the movement of the steam.

8. **Clue: Adjective Clause or Phrase**

Example

The sun crosses the equator twice a year at the equinoxes, *when day and night are nearly equal in length.*

Explanation

The meaning of *equinoxes* is given in the adjective clause beginning with *when*. *Equinoxes* are times when day and night are nearly equal in length.

Example

Prescribed fire, *ignited by forest rangers under controlled conditions to restore balance in the forest,* is a safe way to mimic natural fire conditions.

Explanation

The meaning of *prescribed* is given in the adjective phrase beginning with *ignited*. *Prescribed* describes something done under controlled conditions to restore balance.

Example

The radiating surface of the sun is called the photosphere, and just above it is the chromosphere, *which is visible to the naked eye only during total solar eclipses, appearing then to be a pinkish–violet layer.*

Explanation

The meaning of *chromosphere* is given in the adjective clause beginning with *which* and in the adjective phrase beginning with *appearing*. The *chromosphere* is a pinkish–violet layer that is visible to the naked eye only during total solar eclipses.

9. **Clue: List or Series**

Example

Because of their similar teeth, seals and walruses are believed to have evolved from the same ancestral groups as the *weasels, badgers, and other* mustelids.

Explanation

Items in a list or series are related in some way. The meaning of *mustelids* is suggested by the other words in the list: *weasels, badgers, and other*. *Mustelids* are animals like weasels and badgers.

Example

If someone is said to have "a chip on his shoulder," he is angry, pugnacious, sullen, and looking for trouble.

Explanation

The meaning of *pugnacious* is suggested by the other words and phrases in the list: *angry, sullen, and looking for trouble*. *Pugnacious* means inclined to fight.

10. CLUE: EXAMPLE

for example	for instance	like	such as

Example

Several personnel managers complain about the lag of business colleges in eliminating obsolete skills. *For instance*, shorthand is still taught in many secretarial programs although it is rarely used.

Explanation

The meaning of *obsolete* is given by the information after *for instance*. Shorthand is an example of an obsolete skill. *Obsolete* describes something that is no longer useful.

Intangible assets, *such as* a company's recognized name and its goodwill, are neither physical nor financial in nature.

The meaning of *intangible assets* is given by the information after *such as*. A company's name and goodwill are examples of intangible assets. More information is provided after the verb *are*. *Intangible assets* are not physical and not financial.

11. CLUE: CONTRAST

alternatively	different	instead	rather
but	however	nevertheless	unlike
conversely	in contrast	on the contrary	whereas
despite	in spite of	on the other hand	while

Example

Twilight rays are nearly parallel, *but* because of the observer's perspective, they appear to diverge.

Explanation

The meaning of *diverge* is given by *but* and *parallel*. From this, you know that *diverge* is different from *parallel*.

Songbirds are early risers and remain active throughout the day, except during the warmest hours in summer. Owls, *on the other hand*, are primarily nocturnal.

The meaning of *nocturnal* is given by *on the other hand* and *active throughout the day*. From this, you know that *nocturnal* is different from active throughout the day. *Nocturnal* means active at night.

Unlike sun pillars, which are caused by reflection of light, arcs and haloes are caused by refraction of light through ice crystals.

The meaning of *refraction* is given by *unlike* and *reflection*. From this, you know that *refraction* is different from *reflection*.

12. ***Punctuation clues*** are another type of context clue that can help you understand the meaning of unfamiliar words. Punctuation marks often show that one word identifies, renames, or defines another word.

comma	,	parentheses	( )
dash	—	quotation marks	" "
colon	:	brackets	[ ]

Example

Crepuscular rays—alternating bright and dark rays in the sky—appear to radiate from the sun.

Virtually every community college now offers contract education: short–term programs, ranging from a few hours to several days, for employees of specific companies, which pay a share of the cost.

Folate supplementation before and during pregnancy can prevent certain defects of the brain and spine, such as anacephaly (absence of a major part of the brain).

Explanation

The meaning of *crepuscular rays* is given by the information between the dashes. *Crepuscular rays* are alternating bright and dark rays in the sky.

The meaning of *contract education* is given by the information after the colon. *Contract education* is short–term programs for employees of specific companies.

The meaning of *anacephaly* is given by the information inside the parentheses. *Anacephaly* is absence of a major part of the brain.

13. ***Key words*** in a sentence or passage can be context clues. Use the meanings of key words and your understanding of the sentence or paragraph as a whole to help you guess the meaning of an unfamiliar word.

Example

Accessories add interest to a room. They can accent or highlight an area and give a room beauty and personality.

Light output, measured in lumens, depends on the amount of electricity used by a bulb.

Explanation

The meaning of *accessories* is suggested by other words in the sentence: *interest, accent, highlight, beauty,* and *personality*. From these key words, you know that *accessories* are things that improve a room.

The meaning of *lumens* is suggested by other words in the sentence: *light output, measured,* and *electricity*. From these key words, you know that a *lumen* is a unit of measurement of light output.

14. ***Word parts*** are clues that can help you understand the meaning of unfamiliar words. Many English words are made up of parts of older English, Greek, and Latin words. If you know the meanings of some of these word parts, you will have a general understanding of some unfamiliar words, especially in context.

There are three types of word parts: *prefixes, stems,* and *suffixes*. A ***prefix*** is a word beginning. A prefix affects the meaning of a word. A ***stem*** is the basic, underlying form of a word. Groups of words that have the same stem are related in meaning. A ***suffix*** is a word ending. A suffix affects the function of a word, for example, making it a noun or a verb.

Prefix	Stem	Suffix	Word
con	feder	ate	confederate
intro	duc	tion	introduction
syn	chron	ize	synchronize

On the TOEFL, use both context clues and word parts to help you understand the meaning of unfamiliar words and phrases.

15. Study the following lists of common prefixes and stems. Can you add any more examples?

Prefix	Meaning	Examples
ab–	away, from	abolish, abnormal, abstract
ad–	to, toward	advance, admire, adhere
anti–	against	antiwar, antipathy, antibiotic
auto–	self, same	autobiography, autoimmune
bene–, bon–	good	benefit, benevolence, bonus
bi–	two	bilingual, binary, bilateral
co–, com–, con–	with, together	cooperate, compose, convene
contra–, counter–	against	contrary, contradict, counteract
de–	down, from, away	descend, derive, dehydration
dia–	through, across	dialogue, diagram, diagonal
dis–	not, take away	disease, disability, disappear
e–, ec–, ex–	out	emigrate, ecstasy, export
fore–	front, before	forehead, forecast, foreshadow
in–, im–	in, into, on	invade, immigrate, impose
in–, im–, il–, ir–	not	inequality, illegal, irrational
inter–	between	international, intersect
intro–, intra–	within, inside	introspection, intravenous
micro–	small	microchip, microscope
mis–	bad, wrong	misprint, misunderstand
mono–	one	monopoly, monotonous
multi–	many	multiply, multinational
ob–, op–, of–	against, facing	object, opposite, offend
out–	beyond	outlive, outnumber, outspend
over–	too much	overbearing, overcompensate
para–	beside, alongside	parallel, paraphrase, paragraph
post–	after	postwar, posterior, postpone
pre–	before	prepare, prevent, preview
pro–	forward	process, promote, produce
re–	back, again	return, replay, reunite
se–	apart, aside	separate, secede, segregate
sub–, sup–, sus–	below, under, after	subsidize, support, suspend
syn–, sym–, syl–	with, together	synthesis, symbol, syllabus
tele–	far, distant	telephone, telepathy
trans–	across	translate, transmit, transaction
un–	not	unable, unreal, unreasonable
uni–	one	unit, uniform, universe

Stem	Meaning	Examples
–bio–	life	biology, biodiversity, antibiotic
–cap–, –capit–	head, chief	captain, capital, decapitate
–cede–, –ceed–, –cess–	go, move	concede, proceed, success
–chron–	time	chronicle, anachronism
–cred–	believe	credit, incredible, creed
–dic–, –dict–	say, speak	dictator, predict, jurisdiction
–dorm–	sleep	dormant, dormitory
–duc–, –duct–	lead	duct, introduce, reduction
–fact–, –fect–	make, do	factory, manufacture, effect
–fid–, –feder–	trust, faith	confidence, federation
–flect–, –flex–	bend	deflect, reflect, flexible
–geo–	earth	geology, geothermal
–graph–, –gram–	write, draw	graphic, photography, grammar
–hydro–	water	hydroelectric, dehydrate
–log–, –ology–	word, study	logic, catalog, psychology
–luc–, –lum–, –lus–	light	translucent, illuminate, luster
–man–, –manu–	hand	manual, manager, manuscript
–mit–, –miss–	send	transmit, omit, mission
–mob–, –mot–, –mov–	move	automobile, emotion, remove
–mort–	death	mortality, immortal, mortify
–nov–	new	novice, innovation, renovate
–phon–, –son–	sound	microphone, supersonic
–polis–, –polit–	city	metropolis, politics, police
–pon–, –pos–	put, place	postpone, position, deposit
–port–	carry	portable, reporter, import
–rect–	right, straight	correct, rectangle, rectify
–scrib–, –script–	write	describe, script, inscription
–secut–, –sequ–	follow	consecutive, sequence
–spec–, –spect–	look at, see, observe	spectator, spectacle, inspector
–struct–	build	structure, instruct, destructive
–therm–	heat	thermometer, hypothermia
–ven–, –vene–	come	convention, intervene
–ver–	true	verify, conversation, universal
–vid–, –vis–	see	video, visit, invisible
–viv–, –vita–	alive, life	vivid, revive, vitamin
–voc–, –vok–	call, voice	vocal, vocabulary, revoke

16. Here are some TOEFL questions:

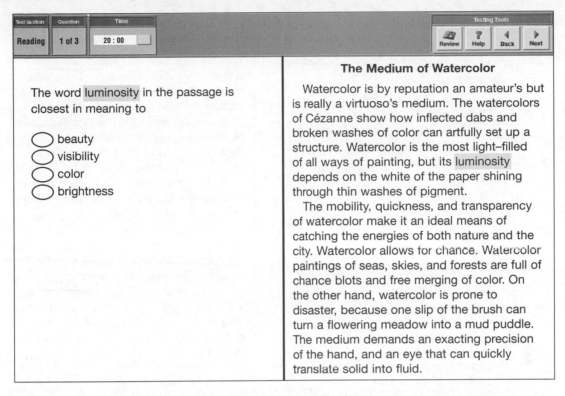

The correct answer is *brightness*. Some context clues in the sentence are *light–filled* and *shining*. Also, *luminosity* contains the stem *–lum–*, which means light.

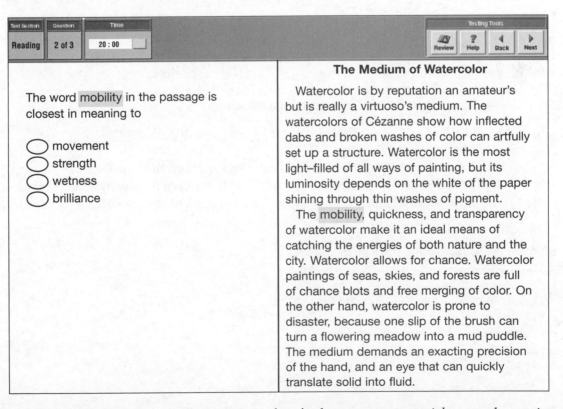

The correct answer is *movement*. Some context clues in the sentence are *quickness* and *energies of both nature and the city*. Also, *mobility* contains the stem *–mob–*, which means move.

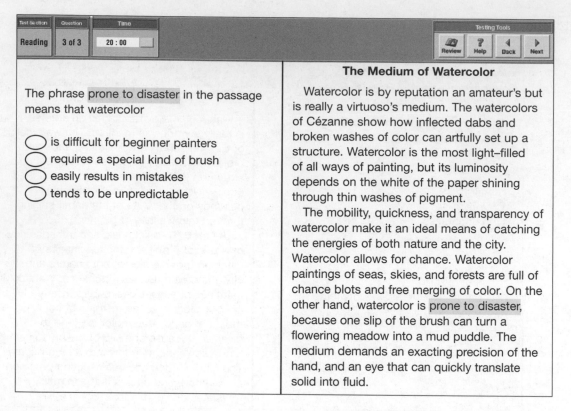

| Test Section | Question | Time | | Testing Tools |
| Reading | 3 of 3 | 20 : 00 | | Review Help Back Next |

The Medium of Watercolor

The phrase prone to disaster in the passage means that watercolor

○ is difficult for beginner painters
○ requires a special kind of brush
○ easily results in mistakes
○ tends to be unpredictable

Watercolor is by reputation an amateur's but is really a virtuoso's medium. The watercolors of Cézanne show how inflected dabs and broken washes of color can artfully set up a structure. Watercolor is the most light–filled of all ways of painting, but its luminosity depends on the white of the paper shining through thin washes of pigment.

The mobility, quickness, and transparency of watercolor make it an ideal means of catching the energies of both nature and the city. Watercolor allows for chance. Watercolor paintings of seas, skies, and forests are full of chance blots and free merging of color. On the other hand, watercolor is prone to disaster, because one slip of the brush can turn a flowering meadow into a mud puddle. The medium demands an exacting precision of the hand, and an eye that can quickly translate solid into fluid.

The correct answer is *easily results in mistakes*. Some context clues in the passage are *chance blots; on the other hand*; and *one slip of the brush can turn a flowering meadow into a mud puddle*.

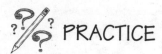 PRACTICE

Exercise 1.4.A

Read the passages and choose the best answer to each question.

QUESTION 1

Although the sensory receptors and brain pathways for taste and smell are independent, the two senses do interact. A great deal of what we consider taste is actually smell. If the sense of smell is obstructed, as by a head cold, the perception of taste is sharply reduced.

1. The word obstructed in the passage is closest in meaning to

(A) involved
(B) increased
(C) developed
(D) blocked

QUESTION 2

A water molecule consists of two hydrogen atoms attached to a single, larger oxygen atom. The angle between the two hydrogen atoms is 120 degrees—the same angle as the angles of a hexagon—which accounts for the characteristic six–sided structure of ice crystals.

2. The phrase accounts for in the passage means

- (A) explains
- (B) decreases
- (C) connects
- (D) summarizes

QUESTION 3

Reports on an organization's projects may fill several major functions at the same time. A report can be used to educate and gain support from key people and groups, to facilitate and inform decision–making about current and future projects, and to provide documentation for the organization's records. The employees who are responsible for preparing the report must have a clear understanding of how the report will be used before they compile it.

3. The word compile in the passage is closest in meaning to

- (A) agree with
- (B) put together
- (C) ask about
- (D) look forward to

QUESTION 4

The evolutionary origins of music are wrapped in mystery. There is ample concrete evidence of musical instruments dating back to the Stone Age and much presumptive evidence about the role of music in organizing work groups, hunting parties, and religious rites. Many scholars suspect that musical and linguistic expression had common origins but then split off from one another several hundred thousand years ago.

4. The phrase split off in the passage is closest in meaning to

- (A) separated
- (B) borrowed
- (C) evolved
- (D) learned

QUESTIONS 5–6

Modern tourism began with the transition from a rural to an industrial society, the rise of the automobile, and the expansion of road and highway systems. Before the Second World War, travel for pleasure was limited to the wealthy, but since then, improved standards of living and the availability of transportation have allowed more people to indulge. In the 1960s, improvements in aircraft technology and the development of commercial jet airlines enabled fast international travel. The tourism industry exploded. Today, airports in nearly every country can accommodate jumbo jets full of tourists seeking exotic destinations.

5. The word indulge in the passage is closest in meaning to

  (A) participate
  (B) migrate
  (C) survive
  (D) change

6. The word exploded in the passage is closest in meaning to

  (A) was competitive
  (B) expanded rapidly
  (C) was expensive
  (D) became dangerous

QUESTIONS 7–8

At the college level, the best preparation for management is a liberal arts education. Individuals who will guide the future of their companies must broaden and deepen their understanding of the world. This means covering the whole range of the liberal arts, from science to literature to mathematics to history. Today's executives must have some grasp of economic realities and the political process, as well as some comprehension of the basic framework within which scientific and technological changes take place. They must gain an understanding of human nature, including its negative aspects, such as the sources of human conflict and the pitfalls of power.

7. The word grasp in the passage is closest in meaning to

  (A) understanding
  (B) communication
  (C) criticism
  (D) prediction

8. The word pitfalls in the passage is closest in meaning to

  (A) benefits
  (B) stages
  (C) causes
  (D) hazards

QUESTIONS 9–10

It is a popular notion that autumn leaves are tinted by freezing temperatures. In truth, the foliage is dulled, not colored, by frost. Red leaves such as maples are brightest when sunny days are followed by cool—but not freezing—nights. Under such conditions, sun–made sugars are trapped in the leaves, where they form the red pigment anthocyanin. Leaves that appear yellow in autumn are no less yellow in spring and summer. However, in spring and summer the yellow pigments—carotenoid and xanthophyll—are masked by the green pigment chlorophyll, which breaks down with the diminishing sunlight of fall.

9. The word foliage in the passage means

(A) season of year
(B) type of chemical
(C) mass of leaves
(D) species of tree

10. The word masked in the passage is closest in meaning to

(A) created
(B) colored
(C) captured
(D) concealed

Exercise 1.4.B

Read the passages and choose the best answer to each question.

QUESTIONS 1–2

Earthshine—the faint light that allows us to see the dark side of the moon when the moon is a thin crescent—is sunlight reflected from the earth to the moon, then back again. Earthshine is variable because the earth's reflectivity changes as large cloud masses come and go. The moon with its earthshine acts as a crude weather satellite by reporting, in a very simple way, the general state of terrestrial cloudiness. Because the amount of light reflected from the earth depends on the amount of cloud cover, the brightness of the dark side of the moon varies.

As the phase of the moon progresses beyond a thin crescent, earthshine fades in a day or two. This is because the amount of sunlit earth available to make earthshine diminishes as the moon orbits the earth. Also, there is the increasing glare of the moon's growing crescent, which causes a loss of visibility by irradiation.

1. The word crude in paragraph 1 is closest in meaning to

(A) false
(B) stormy
(C) random
(D) simple

2. The word glare in paragraph 2 is closest in meaning to

(A) cloud cover
(B) bright light
(C) wave frequency
(D) dark sphere

Questions 3–4

Cool has withstood the fleeting nature of most slang. As a modifier, as a noun, and as a verb, *cool* has been around a long time. Shakespeare used *cool* as a verb, and the word later evolved into other parts of speech. It has been used as an adjective since 1728 to describe large sums of money, as in "worth a cool ten million."

Cool, meaning "excellent" or "first–rate," was popularized in jazz circles, and jazz musicians and jazz lovers still refer to great works as "cool." As long as Miles Davis's classic 1949 album, *Birth of the Cool*, remains one of the best–selling jazz recordings of all time, *cool* will stay cool—it will carry the same weight as it did more than 50 years ago. One reason for the endurance of *cool* is that its meaning continues to evolve. While it meant "wow!" two decades ago, today it is more often used to mean, "That's OK with me," as in "I'm cool with that."

3. The word fleeting in paragraph 1 is closest in meaning to

   (A) temporary
   (B) youthful
   (C) emotional
   (D) popular

4. The phrase carry the same weight in paragraph 2 means

   (A) refer to great music
   (B) refer to a large sum of money
   (C) have the same importance
   (D) have the same meaning

Questions 5–6

The dominant feature on the map of Canada is the two–million–square–mile mass of ancient rock known as the Canadian Shield. The shield sweeps in a great arc around Hudson Bay from far northwest to far northeast, touching the Great Lakes on the south and extending eastward deep into Quebec. The rock of the shield consists mainly of granite and gneiss formed nearly four billion years ago. During the ice ages, huge glaciers advanced and retreated over the region, scouring the surface, removing most of the existing soil, and hollowing out countless lakes.

Clay soils exist in a few areas on the shield's southern edge, but attempts to bring them into agricultural use have been largely unsuccessful. However, the region's mineral wealth has sustained both temporary and permanent settlements during the past century, and more recently, some of its vast potential for hydroelectric power has been tapped.

5. The word scouring in paragraph 1 is closest in meaning to

   (A) freezing
   (B) uplifting
   (C) improving
   (D) scraping

6. The word sustained in paragraph 2 is closest in meaning to

   (A) prevented
   (B) protected
   (C) supported
   (D) ruined

QUESTIONS 7–10

A growing number of companies are finding that small–group discussions allow them to develop healthier ways to think about work. People at all levels of the corporate structure are starting groups that meet weekly or monthly to talk over ways to make workplaces more ethical and just.

Several factors must be present for small–group discussions to be successful. First, it is important to put together the right group. Groups work best when they consist of people who have similar duties, responsibilities, and missions. This does not mean, however, that everyone in the group must think in lockstep.

All participants should agree on the group's purpose. Finding the right subject matter is essential. There are several ways to fuel the discussion: by using the company's mission statement, by finding readings on work and ethics by experts in the topic, or by analyzing specific workplace incidents that have affected the company or others like it.

Finally, the dynamics of the group should be balanced, and the discussion leader must not be allowed to overwhelm the conversation or the agenda. Groups work best when the same person is not always in charge. It is better to rotate the leadership for each meeting and let that leader choose the material for discussion.

7. The phrase talk over in paragraph 1 is closest in meaning to

  (A) demand
  (B) overlook
  (C) explore
  (D) remove

8. The phrase in lockstep in paragraph 2 is closest in meaning to

  (A) alike
  (B) critically
  (C) aloud
  (D) quickly

9. The word fuel in paragraph 3 is closest in meaning to

  (A) categorize
  (B) stimulate
  (C) sequence
  (D) conclude

10. The word overwhelm in paragraph 4 is closest in meaning to

  (A) dominate
  (B) plan
  (C) summarize
  (D) contradict

Exercise 1.4.C

Read the passages and choose the best answer to each question.

QUESTIONS 1–4

There is growing evidence that urbanization has a sharp impact on climate, causing changes that can wreak havoc on precipitation patterns that supply the precious resource of water. The heavy amounts of heat and pollution rising from cities both delay and stimulate the fall of precipitation, depriving some areas of rain while drenching others.

Cities are on average one to ten degrees warmer than surrounding undeveloped areas. Cities also produce large amounts of pollutants called aerosols, gaseous suspensions of dust particles or byproducts from the burning of fossil fuels. Both heat and aerosols change the dynamics of clouds. When hoisted up in the sky, the microscopic particles act as multiple surfaces on which the moisture in clouds can condense as tiny droplets. This can prevent or delay the formation of larger raindrops that fall more easily from the sky, or it can cause the rain to fall in another location.

In California, pollution blows eastward and causes a precipitation shortage of around one trillion gallons a year across the Sierra Nevada mountain range. By contrast, in very humid cities, such as Houston, heat and pollutants seem to invigorate summer storm activity by allowing clouds to build higher and fuller before releasing torrential rains.

1. The phrase wreak havoc on in paragraph 1 means

   (A) disrupt
   (B) omit
   (C) strengthen
   (D) separate

2. The word drenching in paragraph 1 is closest in meaning to

   (A) almost missing
   (B) severely damaging
   (C) thoroughly wetting
   (D) entirely avoiding

3. The word hoisted in paragraph 2 is closest in meaning to

   (A) lifted
   (B) grouped
   (C) returned
   (D) pointed

4. The word torrential in paragraph 3 is closest in meaning to

   (A) unexpected
   (B) warm
   (C) infrequent
   (D) heavy

QUESTIONS 5–10

So much sentimentality is attached to the rose in popular culture that it is difficult to separate the original mythological and folkloric beliefs from the emotional excess that surrounds the flower. Yet if we look into the beliefs, we find that the rose is much more than the mere symbol of romantic love invoked by every minor poet and painter.

One of the rose's most common associations in folklore is with death. The Romans often decked the tombs of the dead with roses; in fact, Roman wills frequently specified that roses were to be planted on the grave. To this day, in Switzerland, cemeteries are known as rose gardens. The Saxons equated the rose with life, and they believed that when a child died, the figure of death could be seen plucking a rose outside the house.

The rose has a long association with female beauty. Shakespeare mentions the rose more frequently than any other flower, often using it as a token of all that is lovely and good. For the Arabs, on the other hand, the rose was a symbol not of feminine but of masculine beauty.

Later the rose became a sign of secrecy and silence. The expression sub rosa, "under the rose," is traced to a Roman belief. During the sixteenth and seventeenth centuries, it was common practice to carve or paint roses on the ceilings of council chambers to emphasize the intention of secrecy.

5. The word sentimentality in paragraph 1 is closest in meaning to

- (A) confusion
- (B) beauty
- (C) feeling
- (D) popularity

6. The word invoked in paragraph 1 is closest in meaning to

- (A) avoided
- (B) called on
- (C) criticized
- (D) taken away

7. The word decked in paragraph 2 is closest in meaning to

- (A) painted
- (B) separated
- (C) decorated
- (D) disguised

8. The word plucking in paragraph 2 is closest in meaning to

- (A) growing
- (B) smelling
- (C) wearing
- (D) picking

9. The word token in paragraph 3 is closest in meaning to

- (A) symbol
- (B) proof
- (C) justification
- (D) contradiction

10. The phrase sub rosa in paragraph 4 means

- (A) romantically
- (B) intentionally
- (C) secretly
- (D) commonly

Exercise 1.4.D

Read the passages and choose the best answer to each question.

QUESTIONS 1–5

In the nineteenth century, Americans were becoming more familiar with European homes and luxuries. When "period" furniture became popular, American furniture factories attempted to duplicate various styles of French and English furniture of the seventeenth and eighteenth centuries. At the same time, designers in England were attempting a return to handicrafts as a means of self–expression. William Morris and other leaders of the English Arts and Crafts movement created home furnishings that celebrated the individuality of the designer.

In the United States, a similar movement soon followed. The American Arts and Crafts—or Craftsman—movement was based not only on individualism but also on a return to simplicity and practicality. Like the Arts and Crafts furniture in England, the Craftsman furniture in America represented a revolt from mass–produced furniture. Makers of Craftsman furniture sought inspiration in human necessity, basing their furniture on a respect for the sturdy and primitive forms that were meant for usefulness alone.

Gustav Stickley, pioneer of the Craftsman movement, believed that average working people wanted furniture that was comfortable to live with and would also be a good investment of money. Stickley felt that any American style in furniture would have to possess the essential qualities of durability, comfort, and convenience. Craftsman furniture was plain and unornamented—made to look as if the common man could build it himself in his own workshop. Locally obtained hardwoods and simple, straight lines were the hallmarks of its construction. The severity of the style departed greatly from the ornate and pretentious factory–made "period" furniture that had dominated in homes up till then.

1. What is "period" furniture?

   Ⓐ Reproductions of earlier styles
   Ⓑ Furniture that is made by hand
   Ⓒ The last pieces made in any style
   Ⓓ Nineteenth–century designer furniture

2. The word revolt in paragraph 2 is closest in meaning to

   Ⓐ style
   Ⓑ benefit
   Ⓒ break
   Ⓓ inspiration

3. The word primitive in paragraph 2 is closest in meaning to

   Ⓐ special
   Ⓑ beautiful
   Ⓒ innovative
   Ⓓ simple

4. The word hallmarks in paragraph 3 is closest in meaning to

   Ⓐ features
   Ⓑ limits
   Ⓒ commands
   Ⓓ plans

5. Which chair most closely resembles a chair in the Craftsman style?

QUESTIONS 6–10

Zora Neale Hurston devoted five years to the collection of rural black folklore in Haiti, the West Indies, and the American South. Her ear for the rhythms of speech and her daring in seeking initiation into many voodoo cults resulted in ethnographic studies such as *Mules and Men*, which conveyed the vitality, movement, and color of rural black culture.

Hurston continued her fieldwork in the Caribbean but eventually followed her most cherished calling, that of fiction writer. *Their Eyes Were Watching God* (1937), a novel about a black woman finding happiness in simple farm life, is now her most famous book, although for thirty years after publication, it was largely unknown, unread, and dismissed by the male literary establishment. In this novel, Hurston gives us a heroic female character, Janie Crawford, who portrays freedom, autonomy, and self–realization, while also being a romantic figure attached to a man. This novel reveals an African American writer struggling with the problem of the hero as woman and the difficulties of giving a woman character such courage and power in 1937.

From the beginning of her career, Hurston was criticized for not writing fiction in the protest tradition. Her conservative views on race relations put her out of touch with the temper of the times. She argued that integration would undermine the strength and values of African American culture. Hurston died in poverty and obscurity in 1960, and it was only afterward that later generations of black and white Americans were to rediscover and revere her celebrations of black culture.

6. The word vitality in paragraph 1 is closest in meaning to

    (A) politics
    (B) energy
    (C) disadvantages
    (D) humor

7. The word calling in paragraph 2 is closest in meaning to

    (A) profession
    (B) example
    (C) character
    (D) description

8. The word autonomy in paragraph 2 is closest in meaning to

    (A) independence
    (B) selfishness
    (C) evil
    (D) romance

9. The phrase out of touch in paragraph 3 means that

    (A) other writers were not interested in race relations
    (B) Hurston ignored the topic of race relations
    (C) Hurston's opinions differed from those of most other people
    (D) there was no contact between Hurston and other writers

10. The word revere in paragraph 3 is closest in meaning to

    (A) imitate
    (B) be amused by
    (C) disagree with
    (D) honor

Answers to Exercises 1.4.A through 1.4.D are on page 562.

EXTENSION

1. With your teacher and classmates, discuss ways to improve your English vocabulary. Answer these questions:

    a. What is the best way to acquire new English vocabulary?
    b. How did you learn in the past?
    c. What method or methods work best for you now?

    (Possible answers: listen to lectures; watch television and movies; have an English–speaking roommate; write down three new words every day; memorize word lists; translate words into your native language; read an English newspaper; read various types of materials; read textbooks in your major field of study.)

    On the board, make a list of the various ways to learn new words. Then, decide which three ways work best for you. Practice these ways to improve your vocabulary!

2. Every week, learn five prefixes and five stems from the charts on pages 67-68. In reading done outside of class, look for examples of words with these prefixes and stems. Bring examples to share in class.

3. Outside of class, look in a magazine, a newspaper, or a university textbook. Find a paragraph in which you have learned a new word. Underline the word. Make four copies of the paragraph to bring to class.

    In class, form groups of four students. In your group, give each classmate a copy of your paragraph. Read each paragraph from your classmates. Work as a team. Look for context clues and word parts that help you understand the meaning of each underlined word. Is the word a noun, a verb, an adjective, or some other part of speech? Write a short definition of each underlined word. Then, look up the word in an English–only dictionary. How close is your group's definition to the dictionary definition?

4. In reading done outside of class, find three sentences, each of which contains a word that is new for you. Bring the sentences to class. Choose one sentence to write on the board, but omit the new word, leaving a blank space where the word should be. Your classmates must think of words that would fit the context of the sentence. How many words would be correct in the sentence? Compare these words with the real missing word.

5. Start a vocabulary notebook to help you prepare for the TOEFL. In the notebook, write new words that you have learned through reading. Include examples of the words used in context. Organize the notebook into word categories. (Possible categories: words by subject area, such as science, business, and the arts; important terms from your major field of study; words with the same prefix or stem; words that are difficult to remember; words that have an interesting sound.)

PROGRESS – 1.4

Quiz 3   *Time – 15 minutes*

Read the passages and choose the best answer to each question. Answer all questions about a passage on the basis of what is stated or implied in that passage.

JOHNNY APPLESEED

In 1801, a 26–year–old man named John Chapman wandered the sparsely populated "western country" that was still two years away from becoming the state of Ohio. Chapman had a simple purpose: wherever he found suitable soil, he planted apple seeds. To the settlers of the Ohio frontier, Chapman became known as Johnny Appleseed, a strange man who wore odd clothes and went barefoot. He was a pacifist in a time of warfare and brutality against the Indians, treating Indians and settlers alike with respect. He killed no animals and was a vegetarian. He even opposed pruning his apple trees because he did not want to cause them pain.

Chapman spent forty years wandering as Johnny Appleseed. Journeying by foot and canoe through Ohio and Indiana, he planted seeds, sold and gave away apple saplings, and exchanged knowledge of medicinal plants with Indians and settlers. He prepared the way for farms and towns by planting apple seeds in clearings along rivers and constructing simple wooden fences to keep animals out of his primitive orchards.

The agricultural development that Chapman anticipated was in fact marching across the eastern half of the continent at an ever–increasing pace. When Chapman started his "apple seeding" in 1801, the population of Ohio was 45,000, and ninety percent of the land was still covered with elm, ash, maple, oak, and hickory trees. By the time of Chapman's death in 1845, the state's population had reached two million, and more than forty percent of the land had been cleared of trees and converted to farms. Not until 1880 did the cutting of trees subside. By then, three–quarters of Ohio had been cleared, and people were becoming aware of the limits of expansion. Only then did they begin to take seriously the tree–loving ideas of Johnny Appleseed, who had become the subject of folk tales.

1. The phrase sparsely populated in paragraph 1 means that

   (A) the area had many resources
   (B) most of the people were young
   (C) few people lived in the region
   (D) the land was undeveloped

2. The word pacifist in paragraph 1 is closest in meaning to

   (A) citizen soldier
   (B) peace advocate
   (C) social scientist
   (D) respected speaker

3. Johnny Appleseed performed all of the following activities EXCEPT

   (A) traveling on foot
   (B) building fences
   (C) giving away meat
   (D) studying medicinal plants

4. The word marching in paragraph 3 is closest in meaning to

   (A) crawling
   (B) advancing
   (C) attacking
   (D) declining

5. The word subside in paragraph 3 is closest in meaning to

- (A) matter
- (B) succeed
- (C) resume
- (D) decrease

THE ORIGIN OF THE UNIVERSE

Astronomers believe that the universe began with a large, dense mass of gas consisting mainly of hydrogen, the simplest of all the naturally occurring chemical elements. The mass of hydrogen was very hot and caused intense light and much expanding motion. As the universe expanded, its light became dimmer, yet even now some of the primeval light may be present.

The original universe underwent a physical transition that gradually differentiated it into galaxies, stars, and planets. As the original mass of gas expanded and cooled, large clouds separated themselves from the parent mass. Gravity played an important role in this mechanism. Matter is subject to gravity, yet matter is also the cause of gravity since it is matter's mass that determines the strength of the gravitational force.

Scientists believe that the original mass of gas in the universe was not completely uniform, and there were some regions that were slightly denser and capable of generating stronger gravitational fields than others. Since gravity tends to pull matter together, the denser regions tended to become even more compact. Thus, small variations in the original mass evolved into denser clouds that gradually separated from the expanding parent mass. From these clouds, the galaxies were formed.

At the end of the first phase of the universe, a great number of huge clouds had become separate entities that could start their own independent evolution. These turbulent clouds—ancient galaxies—contained variations that grew in importance over time. The clouds divided into smaller and smaller "cloudlets" that gravity caused to contract. The increase in pressure from this contraction caused the temperature to rise until the cloudlets began to glow as individual, luminous stars.

6. The word primeval in paragraph 1 is closest in meaning to

- (A) original
- (B) important
- (C) expanding
- (D) beautiful

7. The word transition in paragraph 2 is closest in meaning to

- (A) transaction
- (B) struggle
- (C) combination
- (D) change

8. The word uniform in paragraph 3 is closest in meaning to

- (A) suitable
- (B) unusual
- (C) consistent
- (D) filled

9. The word compact in paragraph 3 is closest in meaning to

- (A) distinct
- (B) dense
- (C) disconnected
- (D) distant

10. The word luminous in paragraph 4 is closest
in meaning to

(A) light–emitting
(B) densely packed
(C) high–pressure
(D) very beautiful

Answers to Reading Quiz 3 are on page 564.

Record your score on the Progress Chart on page 693.

PROGRESS – 1.1 through 1.4

QUIZ 4   *Time – 40 minutes*

Read the passages and choose the best answer to each question. Answer all questions about a passage on the basis of what is stated or implied in that passage.

ROAD BUILDING AND THE AUTOMOBILE

Car registrations in the United States rose from one million in 1913 to ten million in 1923. By 1927, Americans were driving some twenty–six million automobiles, one car for every five people in the country. Automobile sales in the state of Michigan outnumbered those in Great Britain and Ireland combined. For the first time in history, more people lived in cities than on farms, and they were migrating to the city by automobile.

The automobile was every American's idea of freedom, and the construction of hard–surface roads was one of the largest items of government expenditure, often at great cost to everything else. The growth of roads and the automobile industry made cars the lifeblood of the petroleum industry and a major consumer of steel. The automobile caused expansions in outdoor recreation, tourism, and related industries—service stations, roadside restaurants, and motels. After 1945, the automobile industry reached new heights, and new roads led out of the city to the suburbs, where two–car families transported children to new schools and shopping malls.

In 1956 Congress passed the Interstate Highway Act, the peak of a half–century of frenzied road building at government expense and the largest public works program in history. The result was a network of federally subsidized highways connecting major urban centers. The interstate highways stretched American mobility to new distances, and two–hour commutes, traffic jams, polluted cities, and Disneyland became standard features of life. Like almost everything else in the 1950s, the construction of interstate highways was justified as a national defense measure.

The federal government guaranteed the predominance of private transportation. Between 1945 and 1980, 75 percent of federal funds for transportation were spent on highways, while a scant one percent went to buses, trains, or subways. Even before the interstate highway system was built, the American bias was clear, which is why the United States has the world's best road system and nearly its worst public transit system.

1. The word those in paragraph 1 refers to

   (A) car registrations
   (B) automobiles
   (C) people
   (D) automobile sales

2. The phrase the lifeblood in paragraph 2 is closest in meaning to

   (A) a supervisor
   (B) an important part
   (C) an opponent
   (D) a serious threat

3. The word frenzied in paragraph 3 is closest in meaning to

(A) intense
(B) scientific
(C) disorganized
(D) wasteful

4. Which sentence best describes road building in the 1940s and 1950s?

(A) It was the last public works project funded by the federal government.
(B) It cost more money than the government spent on national defense.
(C) It produced a network of highways that favored large cities and suburbs.
(D) It led to an increase in the demand for better public transit systems.

5. The word scant in paragraph 4 is closest in meaning to

(A) more important
(B) barely sufficient
(C) very generous
(D) privately funded

6. According to the passage, the growth in the number of cars had a positive impact on all of the following EXCEPT

(A) tourism
(B) service stations
(C) subway systems
(D) shopping malls

7. According to the passage, the American attitude toward the automobile has resulted in

(A) a preference for private cars over public transportation
(B) loss of farmland and destruction of traditional farm life
(C) an increase in the number of deaths due to car accidents
(D) criticism of the amount of money spent on roads

BIRD SONG

One instance in the animal kingdom with parallels to human music is bird song. Much has recently been discovered about the development of song in birds. Some species are restricted to a single song learned by all individuals, while other species have a range of songs and dialects, depending on environmental stimulation. The most important auditory stimuli for birds are the sounds of other birds, including family or flock members and territorial rivals. For all bird species, there is a prescribed path to development of the final song, beginning with the subsong, passing through plastic song, until the bird achieves the species song or songs. This process is similar to the steps through which young children pass as they first babble and then mimic pieces of the songs they hear around them, although the ultimate output of human singers is much vaster and more varied than even the most impressive bird **repertoire**.

Underlying all **avian** vocal activity is the syrinx, an organ unique to birds that is located at the first major branching of the **windpipe** and is linked to the brain. There are general parallels between the syrinx in birds and the larynx in humans. Both produce sound when air is forced through the windpipe, causing thin membranes to vibrate. However, compared to the human larynx, which uses only about two percent of exhaled air, the syrinx is a far more efficient sound–producing mechanism that can create sound from nearly all the air passing through it.

Possibly the most interesting aspect of bird song from the perspective of human intelligence is its foundation in the central nervous system. Like humans, birds have large brains relative to their body size. Song is a complex activity that young birds must learn, and learning implies that higher–brain activity must be complex in the control of song. This control is associated with two song–control centers in the avian brain. If the links between these centers and the syrinx are interrupted, a bird is unable to produce normal song. Moreover, bird song is one of the few instances in the animal kingdom of a skill that is lateralized; the song–control centers are located in the left side of the avian brain. A lesion there will destroy bird song, while a similar lesion in the right half of the brain will result in much less damage.

Glossary:
    repertoire: stock of songs
    avian: relating to birds
    windpipe: main airway to the lungs; trachea

8. The word range in paragraph 1 is closest in meaning to

    (A) region
    (B) memory
    (C) variety
    (D) system

9. How does the development of song in birds parallel its development in humans?

    (A) Bird song and human music evolved during the same period in history.
    (B) All birds and humans are capable of learning a large number of songs.
    (C) The song repertoire of both birds and humans changes over their lifetime.
    (D) Song development progresses through stages in both birds and humans.

10. The word mimic in paragraph 1 is closest in meaning to

  (A) imitate
  (B) enjoy
  (C) compose
  (D) memorize

11. In what way are the avian syrinx and the human larynx different?

  (A) The syrinx is located near the windpipe, but the larynx is not.
  (B) The syrinx is larger than the larynx relative to body size.
  (C) The syrinx produces a wider variety of sounds than the larynx.
  (D) The syrinx uses much more of the passing air to produce sound.

12. What aspect of bird song suggests the involvement of the brain in the control of song?

  (A) The purpose of song is similar in birds and humans.
  (B) Song is a complex activity that must be learned.
  (C) Birds can produce two separate sounds at the same time.
  (D) Song consists of a wide variety of musical notes.

13. The word lateralized in paragraph 3 is closest in meaning to

  (A) linked to a specific area of the brain
  (B) highly evolved
  (C) shared by all species
  (D) easily damaged or destroyed

14. The word there in paragraph 3 refers to

  (A) the central nervous system
  (B) the syrinx
  (C) the animal kingdom
  (D) the left side of the brain

15. All of the following statements characterize bird song EXCEPT

  (A) Birds learn song mainly by listening to the sounds of other birds.
  (B) Birds are born with the full ability to sing their species song.
  (C) Song is produced in the syrinx, which is linked to the avian brain.
  (D) The central nervous system has the lead role in the control of song.

MACHIAVELLI

Niccolo Machiavelli, an Italian statesman and political philosopher of the early sixteenth century, is considered the founder of modern political thinking. Machiavelli was a product of Renaissance Florence, a city–state that was struggling for expansion and survival among a competing group of similar states. As a public servant and diplomat, Machiavelli came to understand power politics by observing the spectacle around him without any illusions. In 1512, he was briefly imprisoned and then forced to leave public life. He retired to his country estate, where he recorded his reflections on politics. Two of his books would become classics in political theory: *Discourses on the First Ten Books of Livy*, a set of essays on ancient and modern politics, and *The Prince*, a potent little book that would shock readers for centuries.

Machiavelli saw politics as an affair separate from religion and ethics, an activity to be practiced and studied for its own sake. Politics was simply the battle of men in search of power, and since all men were brutal, selfish, and cowardly, politics must follow certain rules. In his most famous work, *The Prince* (1532), Machiavelli described the means by which a leader may gain and maintain power. The ideal prince was the man who had studied his fellow men, both by reading history and by observing the present, and was willing to exploit their weaknesses. Machiavelli thought that his own time was too corrupt to permit any alternative to the Renaissance despots that he saw all around him.

Machiavelli's philosophy arose more from a deeply pessimistic view of human nature than from a lack of moral sense, which many readers criticized in him. He was, and still is, misunderstood to have promoted atheism over religion and criminality over other means of governing. Despite the ruthless connotation of the term "Machiavellian," many of his works, such as the *History of Florence* (1532), express republican principles. Machiavelli's supporters saw him not as a cynic who gloried in evil but as a scientist of politics who saw the world more clearly than others and reported what he saw with lucidity and honesty.

The cultural impact of Machiavelli's philosophy was far–reaching, and negative interpretations have persisted. The dramatic literature of the late sixteenth century, notably the plays of Shakespeare, often featured a villainous but humorous character type known as the Machiavel. The Machiavel character loved evil for its own sake, and this delight in evil made all other motivation unnecessary. The Machiavel had a habit of using humorous monologues to comment on his own wickedness and contempt for goodness. Shakespeare's principal Machiavel characters are the treacherous Iago in *Othello*, the ruthlessly ambitious Edmund in *King Lear*, and the murderous title character in *Richard III*.

16. According to the passage, what was a main influence on Machiavelli's political philosophy?

  (A) The power struggles within and among city–states
  (B) The desire to express his anger for being imprisoned
  (C) The rejection of ancient theories about politics
  (D) The shock and disgust he felt toward political leaders

17. The word illusions in paragraph 1 is closest in meaning to

  (A) conclusions
  (B) false beliefs
  (C) limits
  (D) good intentions

18. What is the subject of *The Prince*?

  (A) The trial and imprisonment of Machiavelli
  (B) The relationship between politics and religion
  (C) The ways that a ruler gains and maintains power
  (D) The history of the political leadership of Florence

19. The word their in paragraph 2 refers to

  (A) religion and ethics
  (B) certain rules
  (C) fellow men
  (D) Renaissance despots

20. The word pessimistic in paragraph 3 is closest in meaning to

  (A) negative
  (B) cautious
  (C) religious
  (D) emotional

21. Machiavelli's political philosophy included all of the following beliefs EXCEPT

  (A) Politics is the power struggle among men who are all brutal and selfish.
  (B) The ideal ruler understands and exploits the weaknesses of others.
  (C) People must organize to fight against evil and corruption in politics.
  (D) Politics should be studied and practiced separately from religion and ethics.

22. According to the author, how has Machiavelli been misunderstood?

  (A) Some people think he was cowardly for retiring from public life.
  (B) Some of his writings seem to support religion, while others oppose it.
  (C) Some of his principles of republican government have been misused.
  (D) Some people interpret his writings as promoting evil in government.

23. The word lucidity in paragraph 3 is closest in meaning to

  (A) distaste
  (B) clarity
  (C) respect
  (D) concern

24. The word monologues in paragraph 4 is closest in meaning to

  (A) speeches
  (B) actions
  (C) noises
  (D) costumes

25. The Machiavel character in drama has all of the following characteristics EXCEPT

  (A) dislike for goodness
  (B) humorous commentary
  (C) enjoyment of evil
  (D) complex motivation

Answers to Reading Quiz 4 are on page 564.

Record your score on the Progress Chart on page 693.

1.5 Making Inferences

 FOCUS

Read the following passage and answer the question:

When Thomas Lincoln took his family across the Ohio River into Indiana in 1816, he was searching for a permanent homestead site. He found it near Little Pigeon Creek on a plot of land he had laid claim to earlier. The family settled down and remained here for fourteen years, and it was here that Thomas's wife, Nancy Hanks, died from "milksick," an illness caused by milk from cattle that had eaten snakeroot leaves.

Today, bronze castings of sill logs and a stone hearth mark the site of the Lincoln cabin. Just beyond this, a reconstruction of the little house contains the clutter of Abraham Lincoln's boyhood home: log table and benches, a trundle bed, spinning wheels, and a fireplace with iron pots. In a shed behind the cabin the tobacco crop is dried. A few horses, sheep, and chickens complete the scene, and interpreters in period dress are at hand to answer questions. Five panels depicting scenes from Abraham Lincoln's life decorate the visitor center. A walkway leads to the small hill where the president's mother is buried, and another path has stones marking important events in Lincoln's early life.

It can be inferred from paragraph 1 that "milksick"

- ⃝ was a common illness on farms
- ⃝ did not affect children
- ⃝ was caused by a poisonous plant
- ⃝ killed both people and cattle

What do you know about "milksick" from the passage? You know that it killed a woman and that it was *caused by milk from cattle that had eaten snakeroot leaves.* You can infer that "milksick" *was caused by a poisonous plant*—the correct answer. The other answer choices cannot be inferred from the passage.

Now answer another question:

Which of the following can be inferred from the passage?

- ⃝ The Lincoln family was originally from Indiana.
- ⃝ Tobacco was the only crop raised on the Lincoln farm.
- ⃝ The Lincoln cabin was constructed of bronze and stone.
- ⃝ The site of the Lincoln homestead is now a museum.

You can infer that *The site of the Lincoln homestead is now a museum*. Some clues are:

Today…mark the site of the Lincoln cabin. …panels depicting scenes…
…a reconstruction of the little house… …the visitor center.
…interpreters in period dress… …stones marking important events…

The other answer choices cannot reasonably be inferred from the passage.

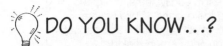 DO YOU KNOW…?

1. An *inference* is a conclusion you can make from the information given in a passage. An inference is an idea that you can reasonably take to be true, based on what the author says. Some inferences can be made from a single sentence. Some inferences are based on a whole paragraph or on the entire passage.

    An inference is a "hidden" idea. To make an inference, you must understand an idea that the author does not state directly. To do this, you must interpret the information that is stated directly. What the author does not state directly and openly, he or she may *imply* or *suggest* by mentioning certain facts and details. When an author implies something, you must *infer* or *conclude* the meaning based on what the author does say.

    When you make inferences, use key words and ideas in the passage and your overall understanding of the author's message, as well as reason, logic, and common sense.

2. TOEFL questions about inferences look like this:

    > What can be inferred about _____?
    > It can be inferred from paragraph __ that _____.
    > Which of the following can be inferred from paragraph __?
    > Which of the following statements is most likely true about _____?
    > What probably occurred after _____?
    > It can be inferred from the passage that the author most likely believes which of the following about _____?
    > Which of the following statements most accurately reflects the author's opinion about _____?

3. In inference questions, an answer choice may be incorrect because it:

    - is not supported by the information stated or implied in the passage;
    - restates information from the passage but does not answer the question;
    - is too general or vague;
    - is inaccurate or untrue according to the passage; or
    - is irrelevant or not mentioned in the passage.

4. Here are some examples:

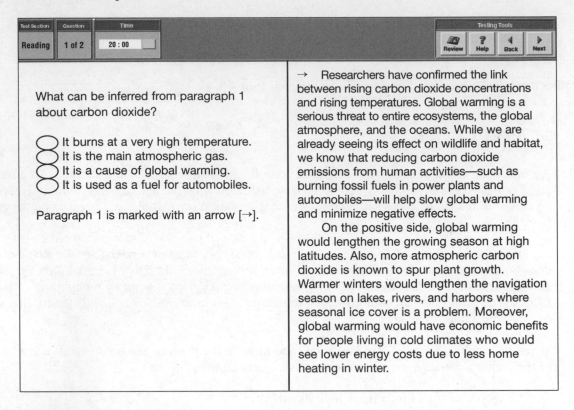

The question asks you to make an inference about carbon dioxide. The correct answer is *It is a cause of global warming*. Some clues in paragraph 1 are:

> …confirmed the link between rising carbon dioxide concentrations and rising temperatures…
> …reducing carbon dioxide emissions…will help slow global warming….

The other answer choices are not supported by the information in the passage. *It burns at a very high temperature* is not mentioned. *It is the main atmospheric gas* is too vague and is not supported by the information given. *It is used as a fuel for automobiles* is inaccurate because carbon dioxide is a product or effect of burning fossil fuels—not a fuel itself.

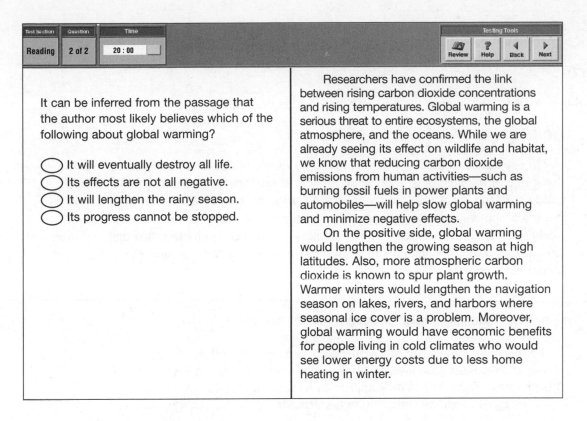

The question requires you to infer what the author probably believes about global warming. You must make this inference based on what the author says. Look at each answer choice and determine if it can reasonably be inferred from the information in the passage. Are there words or ideas in the passage that support the answer?

The author most likely believes *Its effects are not all negative*, and this is the correct answer. Some clues are:

> On the positive side, global warming would....
> Warmer winters would lengthen the navigation season on lakes, rivers, and harbors....
> Moreover, global warming would have economic benefits....

It will eventually destroy all life is not supported by the information in the passage. *It will lengthen the rainy season* is inaccurate; according to the passage, global warming will *lengthen the navigation season*, not the rainy season. *Its progress cannot be stopped* is inaccurate; the author says that *reducing carbon dioxide emissions from human activities...will help slow global warming and minimize negative effects*.

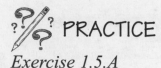 PRACTICE

Exercise 1.5.A

Read the passages and choose the best answer to each question.

QUESTION 1

In classical and medieval times, the study of music shared many features with the discipline of mathematics, such as an interest in proportions, special ratios, and recurring patterns. In the twentieth century, the introduction of twelve–tone music and the widespread use of computers inspired further study into the relationship between musical and mathematical abilities. Musical performances require sensitivity to ratios that are often complex, and to appreciate the operation of rhythms, a performer must have some basic numerical competence.

1. Which of the following can be inferred from the passage?

   (A) The disciplines of music and mathematics originated in classical times.
   (B) People have long been aware of links between music and mathematics.
   (C) Both music and mathematics require an understanding of computers.
   (D) Professional musicians must study mathematics at the university level.

QUESTION 2

Corvids are sociable and tend to form social groups. This is particularly true of rooks, which stay in their flocks all year round. The raven, largest of the corvids, joins a social group as a juvenile, pairing off at around the age of three and mating for life. Courtship can involve such games as pair snow sliding and the synchronized flight test. Corvids can be found all over the world. The adaptability and intelligence of this family have made them extremely successful. For centuries, the raven and the crow have held a special place in the mythology of various cultures.

2. It can be inferred from the passage that corvids are

   (A) a family of birds
   (B) games for children
   (C) members of a sports club
   (D) imaginary beings

QUESTION 3

The input of solar energy supplies 99 percent of the energy needed to heat the earth and all buildings on it. How is this possible? Most people think of solar energy in terms of direct heat from the sun. However, broadly defined, solar energy includes direct energy from the sun as well as a number of indirect forms of energy produced by this direct input. Major indirect forms of solar energy include wind, hydropower, and biomass—solar energy converted to chemical energy in trees, plants, and other organic matter.

3. It can be inferred from the passage that the author most likely believes which of the following about solar energy?

(A) Solar energy is not used as much as it could be used.
(B) It is not possible to develop direct forms of solar energy.
(C) Trees, plants, and organic matter can store solar energy.
(D) The definition of solar energy will continue to change.

QUESTION 4

The reasons for the migration from rural to urban life were exploitation and lack of economic opportunity. The family members who would not inherit a share in the property were exploited by the laws of inheritance. The system was particularly hard on women, who usually did not share in the ownership of the farm and who rarely were paid for their labor. The workday for women was even more demanding than it was for men. Women were responsible for the kitchen garden and the small livestock as well as the care of the family. Unmarried women increasingly left the farm in search of economic opportunity in the factories that processed fish or farm products.

4. It can be inferred from the passage that women under this system

(A) moved from farm to farm in search of work
(B) were paid less than men for the same work
(C) did not acquire property through inheritance
(D) had to get married in order to stay on the farm

QUESTIONS 5–6

One of the most significant elements of age stratification in all cultures is the pattern of experiences connected to marriage and parenting—a pattern that sociologists call the family life cycle. In North America, about 90 percent of adults marry, and the great majority of them have children and thus a family life cycle related to family experiences. When the family's first child is born, the parents embark on a sequence of experiences linked to the child's development—from infancy and toddlerhood, through school age and adolescence, and eventually, to departure from the nest. Each of these periods in the child's life makes a different set of demands on the parents.

5. The phrase embark on in the passage is closest in meaning to

   (A) attempt
   (B) begin
   (C) discuss
   (D) avoid

6. It can be inferred from the passage that the family life cycle

   (A) takes place whether or not people have children
   (B) does not occur in cultures outside of North America
   (C) must be redefined from one generation to the next
   (D) shapes several years in the lives of most adults

QUESTIONS 7–8

Some people believe that odors and fragrances affect the body and mind and are capable of healing anxiety, stress, and other sources of disease. Interest in aromatherapy—and the use of aromatherapy products such as lotions and inhalants—continues to boom. Some popular essential oils and their uses in aromatherapy include lavender and chamomile, which are reputed to ease stress and promote sleep. The scent of jasmine will uplift the mood and reduce depression. Orange eases anxiety and depression and promotes creativity. Peppermint has antibacterial and analgesic qualities, eases mental fatigue, and relieves headaches.

However, aromatherapy is not for everyone. For people who suffer from fragrance sensitivity, asthma, or allergies, aromas like perfumes can prompt disabling health problems, including headaches, dizziness, nausea and vomiting, fatigue, difficulty breathing, difficulty concentrating, flu–like symptoms, and anaphylaxis.

7. It can be inferred that aromatherapy is

   (A) the main use of essential oils from plants
   (B) the use of certain scents to promote health
   (C) not recommended for treating headaches
   (D) not an effective method of curing disease

8. All of the following fragrances are believed to reduce stress EXCEPT

   (A) lavender
   (B) jasmine
   (C) chamomile
   (D) orange

QUESTIONS 9-10

Animal behaviorists believe the orangutan is a cultured ape, able to learn new living habits and to pass them along to the next generation. Some orangutan parents teach their young to use leaves as napkins, while others demonstrate the technique of getting water from a hole by dipping a branch in and then licking the leaves. Orangutans have been observed saying goodnight with the gift of a juicy raspberry. Such social interactions lead researchers to conclude that if orangutans have culture, then the capacity to learn culture is very ancient.

In the evolutionary timeline, orangutans separated from the ancestors of humans many millions of years ago, and they may have had culture before they separated. The discovery of orangutan culture suggests that early primates—including ancestors of humans—might have developed the ability to invent new behaviors, such as tool use, as early as 14 million years ago, approximately 6 million years earlier than once believed.

9. What can be inferred from paragraph 1 about social interactions related to teaching and learning?

  (A) They are behaviors that only orangutans have displayed.
  (B) They are misunderstood by animal behaviorists.
  (C) They indicate similarities between orangutans and other apes.
  (D) They provide evidence that orangutans have culture.

10. Which of the following can be inferred from paragraph 2?

  (A) The ancestors of humans learned culture from orangutans.
  (B) Orangutans were more advanced than most other early primates.
  (C) Primate culture may be older than scientists used to believe.
  (D) Scientists have found orangutan tools that are 6 million years old.

Exercise 1.5.B

Read the passages and choose the best answer to each question.

QUESTIONS 1–2

In the early nineteenth century, most of the Europeans who immigrated to the United States were from northern and western European countries such as England, Germany, France, and Sweden. However, most of the fifteen million Europeans arriving between 1890 and 1914 came from southern and eastern Europe, with the largest numbers coming from Russia, Italy, Greece, Austria–Hungary, and Armenia.

A similar pattern occurred in Canada, where most immigrants were traditionally from England and the United States. After 1890, an increasing number came from eastern Europe, particularly Russia and Ukraine. Many of these headed for the Prairie Provinces. The Doukhobors, a pacifist sect from southern Russia, established communal settlements in Saskatchewan. Together with other immigrants, they arrived in such numbers that in the two decades between the completion of the main railroad network and the outbreak of war in 1914, the population of the prairies had increased from about 150,000 to 1.5 million.

1. Which of the following can be inferred from paragraph 1 about European immigration to the United States in the nineteenth century?

    (A) The sources of immigrants shifted to different parts of Europe.
    (B) Most of the European immigrants could not speak English.
    (C) More immigrants came from Europe than from other continents.
    (D) Northern and western Europeans did not immigrate after 1890.

2. It can be inferred from paragraph 2 that the Doukhobors

    (A) were the largest immigrant group in North America
    (B) also immigrated to the United States
    (C) mainly settled in the Canadian prairies
    (D) helped to build Canada's railroad network

QUESTIONS 3–6

David Smith worked primarily in iron, exploring its possibilities more fully than any other sculptor before or since. To Smith, iron spoke of the power, mobility, and vigor of the industrial age. Smith was born in Indiana in 1906, the descendant of a nineteenth–century blacksmith. His iron sculptures flowed naturally out of the mechanized heart of America, a landscape of railroads and factories. As a child, Smith played on trains and around factories, as well as in nature on hills and near creeks. He originally wanted to be a painter, but after seeing photographs of the metal sculpture of Picasso in an art magazine, he began to realize that iron could be handled as directly as paint.

Many of Smith's sculptures are "totems" that suggest variations on the human figure. They are not large iron dolls, although several have "heads" or "legs." Still, they forcefully convey posture and gesture. Their message flows from the internal relations of the forms and from the impression of tension, spring, and alertness set up by their position in space.

Later in his career, Smith produced two series of sculptures in stainless steel: the *Sentinels* in the 1950s and the *Cubis* in the 1960s. He also began placing his sculptures outdoors, in natural light, where the highly reflective stainless steel could bring sunlight and color into the work. In the late afternoon sun, the steel planes of the *Cubis* reflect a golden color; at other times, they have a blue cast. The mirror–like steel creates an illusion of depth, which responds better to sunshine than it would to the static lighting of a museum.

3. Which of the following can be inferred from paragraph 1 about David Smith's background?

(A) He gained experience while working in a blacksmith factory.
(B) His childhood exposed him to the uses and possibilities of iron.
(C) His early sculptures revealed his desire to be a landscape painter.
(D) He first learned about metals by seeing pictures in a magazine.

4. The word several in paragraph 2 refers to

(A) sculptures
(B) variations
(C) dolls
(D) forms

5. What can be inferred about the *Sentinels* and the *Cubis*?

(A) They are the best–known examples of Smith's "totem" sculptures.
(B) Smith originally intended to use iron instead of stainless steel.
(C) The *Sentinels* are made of blue steel, and the *Cubis* are of gold steel.
(D) They each consist of a number of pieces placed in outdoor settings.

6. It can be inferred from the passage that the author most likely believes which of the following about David Smith's works?

(A) His metal sculptures are more interesting than are those of Picasso.
(B) His sculptures attempt to portray the proportions of the human body.
(C) His pieces capture the power of industry and the beauty of natural light.
(D) His works are best appreciated when viewed all at once in a museum.

QUESTIONS 7–10

Baseball fans love statistics. There is absolutely no doubt about it: baseball is the greatest statistics game there is. Because baseball goes back so far in history, it is embedded in most of the population. Fans really understand a home run, a batting average, and an earned run average—all those basics that have been with baseball throughout its history. The basics have never changed, so people know and love them.

In the last half century, many new statistics have evolved: hitting with runners in scoring position; the percentages of men driven in with runners on second and third base; a pitcher's saves, as opposed to the percentage of times he has the opportunity to make a save. These are the so–called sophisticated statistics.

There is a whole lore of baseball history involving statistics. One "game" is to compare the players of old with the players of today. Many times on talk shows people will say, "Could Sammy Sosa or Alex Rodriguez have played with Ty Cobb or Mickey Cochran or Joe Dimaggio?" What they have to argue with is statistics. They have to go back and examine Dimaggio's years in the big leagues. They look at what he did year by year: he was on average a .300–and some hitter; he drove in so many home runs; he did such–and–such defensively in the outfield. The statistics are all that remain of the career of that star player of the past. So, the statistics are laid out and compared with those of a player of today—this is what makes the game fun.

7. It can be inferred from paragraph 1 that an earned run average is

   (A) a statistic
   (B) difficult to achieve
   (C) a baseball game
   (D) not well known

8. Which of the following can be inferred from paragraph 2?

   (A) Baseball fans invented statistics about fifty years ago.
   (B) Hitting with runners in scoring position is a complex statistic.
   (C) The pitcher is the most sophisticated player on every team.
   (D) There is a limit to the possible number of statistics.

9. Which of the following can be inferred from paragraph 3?

   (A) Baseball players are frequently guests on talk shows.
   (B) Sammy Sosa could have played baseball with Ty Cobb.
   (C) Joe Dimaggio's career inspired new kinds of statistics.
   (D) Ty Cobb and Mickey Cochran were great baseball players.

10. It can be inferred from the passage that the author most likely believes which of the following about baseball statistics?

   (A) Statistics will replace baseball as the greatest game there is.
   (B) Baseball provides a fascinating way to look at statistics.
   (C) Someone is always inventing a better statistics game.
   (D) Statistics are too complex for many baseball fans to understand.

Exercise 1.5.C

Read the passages and choose the best answer to each question.

QUESTIONS 1–4

The human ear contains the organ for hearing and the organ for balance. Both organs involve fluid–filled channels containing hair cells that produce electrochemical impulses when the hairs are stimulated by moving fluid.

The ear can be divided into three regions: outer, middle, and inner. The outer ear collects sound waves and directs them to the eardrum separating the outer ear from the middle ear. The middle ear conducts sound vibrations through three small bones to the inner ear. The inner ear is a network of channels containing fluid that moves in response to sound or movement.

To perform the function of hearing, the ear converts the energy of pressure waves moving through the air into nerve impulses that the brain perceives as sound. Vibrating objects, such as the vocal cords of a speaking person, create waves in the surrounding air. These waves cause the eardrum to vibrate with the same frequency. The three bones of the middle ear amplify and transmit the vibrations to the oval window, a membrane on the surface of the cochlea, the organ of hearing. Vibrations of the oval window produce pressure waves in the fluid inside the cochlea. Hair cells in the cochlea convert the energy of the vibrating fluid into impulses that travel along the auditory nerve to the brain.

The organ for balance is also located in the inner ear. Sensations related to body position are generated much like sensations of sound. Hair cells in the inner ear respond to changes in head position with respect to gravity and movement. Gravity is always pulling down on the hairs, sending a constant series of impulses to the brain. When the position of the head changes—as when the head bends forward—the force on the hair cells changes its output of nerve impulses. The brain then interprets these changes to determine the head's new position.

1. What can be inferred about the organs for hearing and balance?

   Ⓐ Both organs evolved in humans at the same time.
   Ⓑ Both organs send nerve impulses to the brain.
   Ⓒ Both organs contain the same amount of fluid.
   Ⓓ Both organs are located in the ear's middle region.

2. Hearing involves all of the following EXCEPT

   Ⓐ motion of the vocal cords so that they vibrate
   Ⓑ stimulation of hair cells in fluid–filled channels
   Ⓒ amplification of sound vibrations
   Ⓓ conversion of wave energy into nerve impulses

3. It can be inferred from paragraphs 2 and 3 that the cochlea is a part of

   Ⓐ the outer ear
   Ⓑ the eardrum
   Ⓒ the middle ear
   Ⓓ the inner ear

4. What can be inferred from paragraph 4 about gravity?

   Ⓐ Gravity has an essential role in the sense of balance.
   Ⓑ The ear converts gravity into sound waves in the air.
   Ⓒ Gravity is a force that originates in the human ear.
   Ⓓ The organ for hearing is not subject to gravity.

QUESTIONS 5–10

The Pacific Northwest coast of North America is a temperate rain forest, where trees like the red cedar grow straight trunks more than two meters thick at the base and sixty meters high. Western red cedar is often called the canoe cedar because it supplied the native people of the region with the raw material for their seagoing dugout canoes. These extraordinary crafts, as much as twenty meters in length, were fashioned from a single tree trunk and carried as many as forty people on fishing and whaling expeditions into the open ocean.

The Haida people from the Queen Charlotte Islands off British Columbia were noted for their skill in canoe building. After felling a giant tree with controlled burning, the canoe makers split the log into lengthwise sections with stone wedges. They burned away some of the heartwood, leaving a rough but strong cedar shell. They then carved away wood from the inside, keeping the sections below the waterline thickest and heaviest to help keep the canoe upright in stormy seas. To further enhance the canoe's stability, they filled the hull with water and heated it to boiling by dropping in hot stones. This rendered the wood temporarily flexible, so the sides of the hull could be forced apart and held with sturdy wooden thwarts, which served as both cross braces and seats. The canoes were often painted with elaborate designs of cultural significance to the tribe.

The Haida raised canoe building to a high art, designing boats of such beauty and utility that neighboring tribes were willing to exchange quantities of hides, meats, and oils for a Haida canoe. These graceful vessels became the tribe's chief item of export. In their swift and staunch canoes, the first people of the Northwest were able to take full advantage of the riches provided by the sea. With harpoons of yew wood, baited hooks of red cedar, and lines of twisted and braided bark fibers, they fished for cod, sturgeon, and halibut, and hunted whales, seals, and sea otters.

5. The phrase These extraordinary crafts in paragraph 1 refers to

   (A) straight trunks
   (B) native people of the region
   (C) seagoing dugout canoes
   (D) fishing and whaling expeditions

6. Why did the canoe makers keep the sections of the canoe below the waterline thickest and heaviest?

   (A) To prevent the canoe from overturning in rough water
   (B) To shorten the work of carving wood from the inside
   (C) To avoid having to paint the bottom of the canoe
   (D) To make the canoe strong enough to hold forty people

7. Which of the following can be inferred from paragraph 2?

   (A) Carving changed the texture and strength of the wood.
   (B) It took the canoe makers several months to build a canoe.
   (C) The wood was beaten with stone tools to make it flexible.
   (D) Canoes were important cultural artifacts of the Haida.

8. The word staunch in paragraph 3 is closest in meaning to

   (A) silent
   (B) strong
   (C) scented
   (D) severe

9. It can be inferred from paragraph 3 that

   (A) canoes were the Haida's only known art form
   (B) the Haida dominated trade among local tribes
   (C) the people used up all of the natural resources
   (D) trees provided essential tools for obtaining food

10. Which of the following statements can be inferred from the passage?

   (A) The western red cedar thrives in a variety of climates.
   (B) The skill of the Haida canoe makers has never been copied.
   (C) Haida canoes were of great value in the regional economy.
   (D) People no longer use cedar canoes for fishing and whaling.

Answers to Exercises 1.5.A through 1.5.C are on page 565.

 EXTENSION

1. Work in a group of three or four students. Read the passage below, and write a list of statements that can be inferred from the information in the passage. Work for ten minutes. Then, share your inferences with the whole class. Your classmates must determine which information in the passage supports each inference made by your group.

> A distinction between two kinds of intelligence—crystallized and fluid intelligence—has been widely studied by researchers studying adult learning. Crystallized intelligence is heavily dependent on education and experience. It consists of the set of skills and knowledge that we each learn as part of growing up in any culture. It includes such skills as vocabulary, the ability to reason clearly about real–life problems, and the technical skills we learn for our jobs. Crystallized abilities are "exercised" abilities.
>
> Fluid intelligence, in contrast, is thought to be a more "basic" set of abilities, not so dependent on specific education. These are the "unexercised" abilities. Most tests of memory tap fluid intelligence.
>
> Crystallized abilities generally continue to rise over our lifetime, while fluid abilities begin to decline much earlier, beginning perhaps at age 35 or 40.

2. With your teacher and classmates, discuss the difference between facts and inferences. When someone you know makes a statement, how can you tell if it is a fact or an inference? Are facts and inferences ever the same?

3. Select a passage from a newspaper, a magazine or a university textbook. In class, work in a group of three or four students. Read the passage, and write a list of facts in the passage. Then write a list of statements that can be inferred or concluded from the information in the passage. In your classroom, post the passage, your facts, and your inferences where your classmates can read them.

1.6 Determining Purpose

 FOCUS

Read the following passage and answer the question:

> As with most economic issues, economists disagree over the exact causes of inflation. But they do generally agree that a sharp increase in the cost of one essential item is likely to be a contributing factor. When oil prices rose sharply in the mid–1970s, consumers were suddenly hit with higher prices for oil and for many other things. All the companies that used oil—to heat their buildings or run their machines—suddenly had to raise their prices to cover the increased cost of the oil. Anything transported by truck cost more. At the same time, all the consumers who bought oil in the form of gasoline for their cars had to spend a much larger portion of their paychecks on oil. These higher prices were a form of inflation.
>
> Why does the author mention oil prices?
>
> ⃝ To track the increases and decreases in oil prices in a certain period
> ⃝ To explain how companies determine the price of an item
> ⃝ To show how a price increase for one item contributes to inflation
> ⃝ To compare prices paid by consumers with prices paid by companies

The question asks about the author's purpose in mentioning a specific detail, *oil prices*. The correct answer is *To show how a price increase for one item contributes to inflation*. What key words and phrases help you determine this? There are several clues in the passage, especially:

> …the exact causes of inflation.
> …a sharp increase in the cost of one essential item is likely to be a contributing factor.
> …higher prices for oil and for many other things.
> These higher prices were a form of inflation.

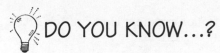 DO YOU KNOW...?

1. The *purpose* of a passage is the reason the author wrote it. The author wants you to understand the topic in a certain way. Every good piece of writing has a purpose. The purpose may be to inform, define, explain, illustrate, compare, criticize, or do something else. The author's purpose is closely related to the main points made about the topic.

    Each part of a passage may have a different purpose. For example, one paragraph may define a concept, another paragraph may give examples to illustrate the concept, and yet another paragraph may compare the concept to other ideas.

2. Many questions on the TOEFL ask about the purpose of a specific detail. Some ask about why the author used a certain word or phrase. Questions about purpose look like this:

    > Why does the author discuss _____?
    >
    > Why does the author mention _____ in paragraph __?
    >
    > Why does the author compare _____ to _____?
    >
    > The author mentions _____ in order to _____.
    >
    > The author discusses _____ in paragraph __ in order to _____.
    >
    > Why does the author order the information by _____?
    >
    > Why does the author use the word _____ in discussing _____?

3. Some purpose words you may see in the answer choices are:

argue	define	illustrate	prove
caution	describe	introduce	show
classify	emphasize	persuade	summarize
compare	explain	point out	support
contrast	give examples	praise	trace
criticize	identify	predict	warn

4. In questions about purpose, an answer choice may be incorrect because it is:

    - too general: a purpose that is beyond the focus of the question;
    - inaccurate: not true or only partly true according to the passage; or
    - irrelevant: not mentioned in the passage or not related to the question.

5. Questions about purpose require you to scan the passage for specific information. Here are some examples:

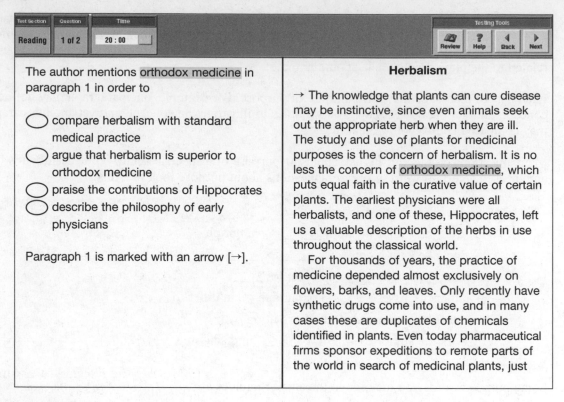

The question asks about the author's purpose in mentioning a specific detail, *orthodox medicine*. The correct answer is to *compare herbalism with standard medical practice*. Some clues in paragraph 1 are:

> …use of plants for medicinal purposes is the concern of herbalism.
> …no less the concern of orthodox medicine, which puts equal faith in…
> The earliest physicians were all herbalists….

Why are the other three answers incorrect? *Argue that herbalism is superior to orthodox medicine* is inaccurate; *praise the contributions of Hippocrates* and *describe the philosophy of early physicians* are too general.

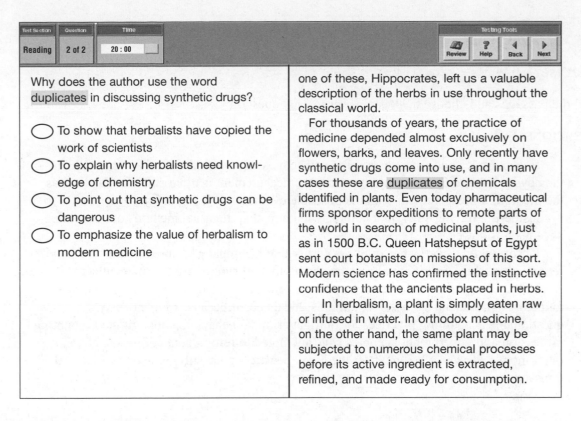

Why does the author use the word duplicates in discussing synthetic drugs?

○ To show that herbalists have copied the work of scientists
○ To explain why herbalists need knowledge of chemistry
○ To point out that synthetic drugs can be dangerous
○ To emphasize the value of herbalism to modern medicine

one of these, Hippocrates, left us a valuable description of the herbs in use throughout the classical world.

For thousands of years, the practice of medicine depended almost exclusively on flowers, barks, and leaves. Only recently have synthetic drugs come into use, and in many cases these are duplicates of chemicals identified in plants. Even today pharmaceutical firms sponsor expeditions to remote parts of the world in search of medicinal plants, just as in 1500 B.C. Queen Hatshepsut of Egypt sent court botanists on missions of this sort. Modern science has confirmed the instinctive confidence that the ancients placed in herbs.

In herbalism, a plant is simply eaten raw or infused in water. In orthodox medicine, on the other hand, the same plant may be subjected to numerous chemical processes before its active ingredient is extracted, refined, and made ready for consumption.

The question asks about the author's purpose in using a specific word, *duplicates*, in discussing synthetic drugs. *Duplicates* means to copy exactly. The correct answer is *To emphasize the value of herbalism to modern medicine*. Some clues in the passage are:

…the practice of medicine depended almost exclusively on…
…these are duplicates of chemicals identified in plants.
Modern science has confirmed the instinctive confidence that the ancients placed in herbs.

Why are the other three answers incorrect? *To show that herbalists have copied the work of scientists* and *To explain why herbalists need knowledge of chemistry* are inaccurate. *To point out that synthetic drugs can be dangerous* is not mentioned in the passage.

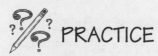 PRACTICE

Exercise 1.6.A

Read the passages and choose the best answer to each question.

QUESTIONS 1–2

In economics and finance, nothing can be measured with the precision possible in the physical sciences. However, approximate measurement is often sufficient as long as the method of measurement remains the same over time. It is important for anyone who is considering buying stock in a company to know that the usual methods of accounting have been followed.

Unfortunately, even when auditors certify that a company has prepared its financial reports properly, they cannot always be certain that all figures are 100 percent accurate. Because a company's books are not open to public scrutiny, it is possible for a company to distort its financial status. Accounting scandals occur because of dishonesty, questionable accounting practices, or outright criminal behavior. Although the accounting profession and government agencies have attempted to reform some of these abuses, the principle of *caveat emptor*—let the buyer beware—must still guide one's financial transactions.

1. Why does the author mention the physical sciences in paragraph 1?

  Ⓐ To point out that financial measurements are not always precise
  Ⓑ To compare the physical sciences unfavorably with other sciences
  Ⓒ To explain why methods of measurement are important in different fields
  Ⓓ To argue that economics and finance should be considered physical sciences

2. Why does the author mention the principle of *caveat emptor* in paragraph 2?

  Ⓐ To recommend that the government review all stock purchases
  Ⓑ To criticize inadequate efforts to stop bad accounting practices
  Ⓒ To argue that buying stock is the best way to make money fast
  Ⓓ To warn potential buyers of the possibility of accounting abuses

QUESTIONS 3–4

Lake Wissanotti, just outside the town of Mariposa, is one of Canada's most popular and enduring fictional places. The lake and town are the setting of Stephen Leacock's masterpiece, *Sunshine Sketches of a Little Town*, a collection of comic sketches and witty observations originally published in 1912. Leacock, one of the founders of Canadian literature, worked for most of his life as a professor of economics. His reputation as a political economist was worldwide, but it is Lake Wissanotti and Mariposa for which he is most remembered today.

Sunshine Sketches is a portrait of small–town Canadian life in the early twentieth century. Mariposa represents a past to be cherished, a pastoral and idyllic town that allows for human folly. If there is any satire, it is immediately bathed in warm sunshine. Although *Sunshine Sketches* has the complexity of a novel, it is more properly defined as a short–story cycle. A vital force is the book's narrator, who is at times intimately close to the comings and goings of Mariposa life, but distant enough to sustain the focus on human folly.

3. Why does the author discuss Stephen Leacock in paragraph 1?

   (A) To give the name of the main character in a book
   (B) To provide biographical information about the author
   (C) To point out a relationship between literature and economics
   (D) To identify the narrator of a book of stories about a town

4. Why does the author use the phrase bathed in warm sunshine in the passage?

   (A) To describe the tone of the book
   (B) To explain the meaning of satire
   (C) To compare a novel and a short story
   (D) To illustrate the theme of human folly

QUESTIONS 5–7

Everyone in a particular society recognizes social roles: father, mother, child, teacher, student, police officer, store clerk, doctor, judge, political leader, and so on. Every culture expects certain types of behavior from people who play certain social roles. Anyone occupying a given position is expected to adopt a specific attitude. A store clerk is expected to take care of customers patiently and politely, and a judge is expected to make wise and fair decisions about laws.

Informal social roles are not always easy to recognize, but can be identified with careful research. They are key indicators of a group's health and happiness. Within the family, one informal role is the family hero, the person who defines integrity and upholds family morality. Others are the family arbitrator, the person who keeps the peace, and the family historian, often a grandparent, who relays valuable cultural information that maintains both the family and the larger society. And finally, there is the family friend, the person who provides comfort and companionship to the family members with emotional needs.

5. Why does the author mention a store clerk and a judge in paragraph 1?

(A) To give examples of people who hold positions of respect
(B) To explain why social roles are important to a society
(C) To illustrate the behavior required of certain social roles
(D) To compare the responsibilities of two different occupations

6. Why does the author use the term key indicators in discussing informal social roles?

(A) To identify the most important type of social role
(B) To explain how to identify informal social roles
(C) To point out that informal roles are unique to families
(D) To emphasize the value of informal roles to a group

7. Which informal social role supports the family by preserving the family's culture?

(A) Friend
(B) Hero
(C) Historian
(D) Arbitrator

QUESTIONS 8–10

The many parts of the earth's atmosphere are linked with the various parts of the earth's surface to produce a whole—the climate system. Different parts of the earth's surface react to the energy of the sun in different ways. For example, ice and snow reflect much of it. Land surfaces absorb solar energy and heat up rapidly. Oceans store the energy without experiencing a significant temperature rise. Thus, the different types of surfaces transfer heat into the atmosphere at different rates.

We can view climate as existing in three domains: space, time, and human perception. In the domain of space, we can study local, regional, and global climates. In time, we can look at the climate for a year, a decade, a millennium, and so forth. Finally, we depend on our perceptions of the data, so we must include our own human perception into our model. Human perception ranges from our personal observations to our public predictions about climate. Human perception must be included if our understanding of climatic processes is to be translated into societal actions. As a society, we make informed choices about how to use the beneficial effects of climate, such as deciding when and where to plant crops. We also make choices about how to minimize the harmful effects of climate—storms, blizzards, and droughts.

8. Why does the author discuss different parts of the earth's surface in paragraph 1?

  (A) To explain why humans live in some parts but not in others
  (B) To show that the entire earth is made of the same materials
  (C) To compare how various surfaces transfer heat into the atmosphere
  (D) To describe changes in the earth's appearance throughout the year

9. According to the author, why must we include human perception in our study of climate?

  (A) We must interpret data and take actions related to climate.
  (B) We must create an interesting model of the climate system.
  (C) We must develop an understanding of our environment.
  (D) We must change our traditional ways of studying climate.

10 Why does the professor mention storms, blizzards, and droughts in paragraph 2?

  (A) To explain why humans are afraid of the unknown
  (B) To show how the atmosphere and the earth are linked
  (C) To give examples of dangerous effects of climate
  (D) To illustrate the effects of human activity on climate

Exercise 1.6.B

Read the passages and choose the best answer to each question.

QUESTIONS 1–3

Several men have been responsible for promoting forestry as a profession. Foremost was Gifford Pinchot, the father of professional forestry in America. He was chief of the Forest Service from 1898 until 1910, working with President Theodore Roosevelt to instigate sound conservation practices in forests. Later he was professor of forestry and founder of the Pinchot School of Forestry at Yale University. Another great forester was Dr. Bernard E. Fernow, the first head of the U.S. Forest Service. He organized the first American school of professional forestry at Cornell University.

The foresters of today, like Pinchot and Fernow in the past, plan and supervise the growth, protection, and utilization of trees. They make maps of forest areas, estimate the amount of standing timber and future growth, and manage timber sales. They also protect the trees from fire, harmful insects, and disease. Some foresters may be responsible for other duties, ranging from wildlife protection and watershed management to the development and supervision of camps, parks, and grazing lands. Others do research, provide information to forest owners and to the general public, and teach in colleges and universities.

1. Why does the author call Gifford Pinchot the father of professional forestry in America?

   (A) To emphasize his contributions to the field
   (B) To describe his family background
   (C) To praise his management skills
   (D) To illustrate his influence on the president

2. Why does the author compare Pinchot and Fernow to the foresters of today?

   (A) To describe different philosophies of forestry management
   (B) To show how the field of forestry has changed in 100 years
   (C) To argue for the expansion of university forestry programs
   (D) To introduce the types of work done by professional foresters

3. All of the following are mentioned in the passage EXCEPT

   (A) what foresters do besides protecting trees
   (B) how to select a good school of forestry
   (C) people who promoted forestry as a career
   (D) management of timber and timber sales

QUESTIONS 4–6

One's style of dress reveals the human obsession with both novelty and tradition. People use clothing to declare their membership in a particular social group; however, the rules for what is acceptable dress for that group may change. In affluent societies, this changing of the rules is the driving force behind fashions. By keeping up with fashions, that is, by changing their clothing style frequently but simultaneously, members of a group both satisfy their desire for novelty and obey the rules, thus demonstrating their membership in the group.

There are some interesting variations regarding individual status. Some people, particularly in the West, consider themselves of such high status that they do not need to display it with their clothing. For example, many wealthy people in the entertainment industry appear in very casual clothes, such as the worn jeans and work boots of a manual laborer. However, it is likely that a subtle but important signal, such as an expensive wristwatch, will prevail over the message of the casual dress. Such an inverted status display is most likely to occur where the person's high status is conveyed in ways other than with clothing, such as having a famous face.

4. According to the author, fashions serve all of the following purposes EXCEPT

(A) satisfying an interest in novelty
(B) signaling a change in personal beliefs
(C) displaying membership in a social group
(D) following traditional rules

5. Why does the author discuss individual status in paragraph 2?

(A) To state that individual status is not important in the West
(B) To argue that individuals need not obey every fashion rule
(C) To contrast the status of entertainers with that of manual laborers
(D) To explain how high status may involve an inverted status display

6. Why does the author mention a wristwatch in paragraph 2?

(A) To give an example of an item that conveys one's actual status
(B) To recommend wearing an expensive wristwatch with casual clothes
(C) To explain why it is not necessary to dress entirely in one style
(D) To show that a wristwatch is an important fashion accessory

QUESTIONS 7–10

The war for independence from Britain was a long and economically costly conflict. The New England fishing industry was temporarily destroyed, and the tobacco colonies in the South were also hard hit. The trade in imports was severely affected, since the war was fought against the country that had previously monopolized the colonies' supply of manufactured goods. The most serious consequences were felt in the cities, whose existence depended on commercial activity. Boston, New York, Philadelphia, and Charleston were all occupied for a time by British troops. Even when the troops had left, British ships lurked in the harbors and continued to disrupt trade.

American income from shipbuilding and commerce declined abruptly, undermining the entire economy of the urban areas. The decline in trade brought a fall in the American standard of living. Unemployed shipwrights, dock laborers, and coopers drifted off to find work on farms and in small villages. Some of them joined the Continental army, or if they were loyal to Britain, they departed with the British forces. The population of New York City declined from 21,000 in 1774 to less than half that number only nine years later in 1783.

The disruptions produced by the fighting of the war, by the loss of established markets for manufactured goods, by the loss of sources of credit, and by the lack of new investment all created a period of economic stagnation that lasted for the next twenty years.

7. Why does the author mention the fishing industry and the tobacco colonies?

   (A) To show how the war for independence affected the economy
   (B) To compare the economic power of two different regions
   (C) To identify the two largest commercial enterprises in America
   (D) To give examples of industries controlled by British forces

8. Why were the effects of the war felt most in the cities?

   (A) Most of the fighting occurred in the cities.
   (B) The British army destroyed most of the cities.
   (C) The cities depended on manufacturing and trade.
   (D) The urban population did not support the war.

9. Why does the author mention the population of New York City in paragraph 2?

   (A) To show that half of New York remained loyal to Britain
   (B) To compare New York with other cities occupied during the war
   (C) To emphasize the great short–term cost of the war for New York
   (D) To illustrate the percentage of homeless people in New York

10. What probably occurred during the years right after the war for independence?

   (A) Development of new shipbuilding technology
   (B) A return to traditional methods of manufacturing
   (C) A shift to an agricultural economy in New York
   (D) Shortages of money and manufactured goods

Answers to Exercises 1.6.A through 1.6.B are on page 566.

 EXTENSION

1. Outside of class, look in a magazine or a university textbook. Select a short passage of two to three paragraphs. Type or photocopy the paragraphs. Make three copies to bring to class. In class, form groups of three students each. In your group, give each classmate a copy of your passage. Individually, read all of your group's passages. For each one, write an answer to these questions:

    a. Why did the author write this?
    b. What is the author's attitude toward the topic?
    c. What is the purpose of each paragraph?
    d. What details in the passage support the author's purpose?
    e. What words does the author use to emphasize points?

When everyone in your group has finished reading and answering the questions for all passages, compare your answers with your classmates' answers. Are the answers similar or different? Work as a team to agree on the best answer to each question.

PROGRESS – 1.5 through 1.6

QUIZ 5   *Time – 15 minutes*

Read the passages and choose the best answer to each question. Answer all questions about a passage on the basis of what is stated or implied in that passage.

FREEZING FOOD

The discovery of freezing has changed our eating habits more than any other related invention. Because many foods contain large amounts of water, they freeze solidly at or just below 32 degrees Fahrenheit. When we lower the temperature to well below the freezing point and prevent air from penetrating the food, we retard the natural process of decay that causes food to spoil. Freezing preserves the flavor and nutrients of food better than any other preservation method. When properly prepared and packed, foods and vegetables can be stored in the freezer for one year.

Most vegetables and some fruits need blanching before they are frozen, and to avoid this step would be an expensive mistake. The result would be a product largely devoid of vitamins and minerals. Proper blanching curtails the enzyme action, which vegetables require during their growth and ripening but which continues after maturation and will lead to decay unless it is almost entirely stopped by blanching. This process is done in two ways, either by plunging vegetables in a large amount of rapidly boiling water for a few minutes or by steaming them. For steam blanching, it is important that timing begin when the water at the bottom of the pot is boiling. Different vegetables require different blanching times, and specified times for each vegetable must be observed. Underblanching is like no blanching at all, and overblanching, while stopping the enzyme action, will produce soggy, discolored vegetables.

1. Why does the author mention 32 degrees Fahrenheit?

   (A) To suggest the storage temperature for most foods
   (B) To identify the freezing point of water
   (C) To state the correct setting for a freezer
   (D) To give the temperature for blanching

2. Why does the author use the term expensive mistake in discussing blanching?

   (A) To state that blanching is expensive but very effective
   (B) To warn that not blanching will harm the food's nutritional value
   (C) To emphasize the importance of blanching only a few items at a time
   (D) To show that many people waste food by blanching improperly

3. What can be inferred about enzyme action in vegetables?

   (A) It eventually causes vegetables to spoil.
   (B) It is a necessary step in the blanching process.
   (C) It stops after the vegetables have ripened.
   (D) It preserves the flavor of frozen vegetables.

4. It can be inferred that underblanched vegetables would

   (A) spoil quickly
   (B) taste like canned vegetables
   (C) lack vitamins and minerals
   (D) be soggy and discolored

EUROPEAN SETTLEMENT OF NORTH AMERICA

The large–scale settlement of North America by Europeans began in the seventeenth century. France took the early lead in the contest for the temperate regions of North America. In 1608, the first permanent French colony was established at Quebec. In 1682, La Salle explored the Mississippi River and claimed the entire river system for France. But despite these early successes, there were never enough French settlers to make French North America a large center of population.

The Dutch under Henry Hudson explored the eastern coast of the continent and claimed a large area, including the river that was named after him. The Dutch colony of New Netherlands started with a few trading posts on the Hudson River, where New York City is now located, and expanded into enterprises in New Jersey, Delaware and Connecticut. The Dutch settlements suffered a lot of competition from the English, and eventually the Dutch governor was forced to surrender all Dutch lands to the English.

England's commercial and political growth at home soon gave it the lead in the colonial race, but this success came only after some early losses, such as the failed colony on Roanoke Island. The first success for England was in 1607 at Jamestown. There were also permanent colonies farther north, in the area known as New England.

The colonies of North America grew dramatically beyond the first settlements at Quebec and Jamestown. Population figures for the seventeenth century show that in 1625 there were around 500 settlers in French Canada and 200 in Dutch settlements, but there were 2,000 in the English colonies. Fifty years later, the English had absorbed the Dutch colonies. By 1700, New France had around 20,000 people, but the English colonies had a quarter of a million.

The European conquest of North America contributed to international conflict. In the seventeenth and eighteenth centuries, the European powers fought several wars in North America. Most of these conflicts were extensions of wars taking place in Europe at the same time, but some were started by the colonists themselves. The conflicts—especially those between England and France—were mostly over commercial interests and signaled the intense rivalry for control of North American land and resources.

5. What can be inferred from paragraph 1 about the French settlement of North America in the seventeenth century?

(A) The French were more successful than any other European nation at the time.
(B) French settlement never extended beyond the original colony at Quebec.
(C) The French settled North America in order to control international trade.
(D) The French colonies had fewer people than did other North American colonies.

6. Why does the author use the word race in paragraph 3?

(A) To emphasize the competition among European groups
(B) To trace the origin of a popular sport in North America
(C) To show that failure comes more quickly than success
(D) To describe the ethnic differences among Europeans

7. What can be inferred about England in the seventeenth century?

(A) England had colonies on every continent.
(B) England was a leading European power.
(C) England had a democratic political system.
(D) England won every war in which it fought.

8. The author discusses population numbers in paragraph 4 in order to

   (A) compare the populations of North America and Europe
   (B) show how humans influenced the natural environment
   (C) explain why Europeans migrated to North America
   (D) illustrate England's growing power in North America

9. What can be inferred from the passage about the relationship between the Dutch and English colonies?

   (A) The Dutch and the English were each other's largest trading partners.
   (B) The Dutch settled in areas where the English had failed earlier.
   (C) The Dutch and the English competed for land, and the English prevailed.
   (D) The Dutch joined forces with the French to fight against the English.

10. According to the passage, why did the European powers fight wars in North America?

    (A) The European powers wanted to conquer the native population.
    (B) There was great competition for control of land and resources.
    (C) The French and English armies wanted to test their new weapons.
    (D) The European nations were trying to spread their political systems.

Answers to Reading Quiz 5 are on page 567.

Record your score on the Progress Chart on page 693.

PROGRESS – 1.1 through 1.6

QUIZ 6

Time – 40 minutes

Read the passages and choose the best answer to each question. Answer all questions about a passage on the basis of what is stated or implied in that passage.

THE QUEEN ANNE HOUSE

The house style that dominated American housing during the 1880s and 1890s was known as Queen Anne, a curious name for an American style. The name was, in fact, a historical accident, originating with fashionable architects in Victorian England who coined it with apparently no reason other than its pleasing sound. The Queen Anne style was loosely based on medieval structures built long before 1702, the beginning year of Queen Anne's reign.

A distinctive characteristic found in most Queen Anne houses is the unusual roof shape— a steeply pitched, hipped central portion with protruding lower front and side extensions that end in gables. It is often possible to spot these distinctive roof forms from several blocks away. Another feature of this style is the detailing, shown in the wood shingle siding cut into fanciful decorative patterns of scallops, curves, diamonds, or triangles. Queen Anne houses are almost always asymmetrical. If you draw an imaginary line down the middle of one, you will see how drastically different the right and left sides are, all the way from ground level to roof peak. A final characteristic is the inviting wraparound porch that includes the front door area and then extends around to either the right or left side of the house.

Queen Anne houses faded from fashion early in the twentieth century as the public's taste shifted toward the more modern Prairie and Craftsman style houses. Today, however, Queen Anne houses are favorite symbols of the past, painstakingly and lovingly restored by old–house buffs and reproduced by builders who give faithful attention to the distinctive shapes and detailing that were first popularized more than one hundred years ago.

1. Why does the author use the word curious in describing the name of an American style?

   (A) The style was invented before Queen Anne's reign.
   (B) The name was accidentally misspelled.
   (C) The style was more popular in Victorian England.
   (D) The name did not originate in America.

2. The word it in paragraph 1 refers to

   (A) style
   (B) name
   (C) accident
   (D) England

3. The word asymmetrical in paragraph 2 is closest in meaning to

   (A) inefficient
   (B) bold
   (C) strange
   (D) unbalanced

4. Which of the following is NOT mentioned as a characteristic feature of Queen Anne houses?

   (A) Decorative windows
   (B) Wood shingle exterior walls
   (C) Large porch
   (D) Steeply pitched roof

5. Which of the following can be inferred from paragraph 2 about the Queen Anne style?

  (A) The Queen Anne style combined several other styles.
  (B) The Queen Anne style had to be built in the city.
  (C) The Queen Anne style was elaborate and ornate.
  (D) The Queen Anne style was not very popular.

6. According to the passage, why did Queen Anne houses go out of style?

  (A) People came to see them as a symbol of the past.
  (B) People started moving to the suburbs and the prairies.
  (C) People were more interested in newer house styles.
  (D) People could no longer afford to build such large houses.

7. The word buffs in paragraph 3 is closest in meaning to

  (A) experts
  (B) sellers
  (C) critics
  (D) painters

SPORTS COMMENTARY

One of the most interesting and distinctive of all uses of language is commentary. An oral reporting of ongoing activity, commentary is used in such public arenas as political ceremonies, parades, funerals, fashion shows, and cooking demonstrations. The most frequently occurring type of commentary may be that connected with sports and games. In sports there are two kinds of commentary, and both are often used for the same sporting event. "Play–by–play" commentary narrates the sports event, while "color–adding" or "color" commentary provides the audience with pre–event background, during–event interpretation, and post–event evaluation. Color commentary is usually conversational in style and can be a dialogue with two or more commentators.

Play–by–play commentary is of interest to linguists because it is unlike other kinds of narrative, which are typically reported in past tense. Play–by–play commentary is reported in present tense. Some examples are "he takes the lead by four" and "she's in position." One linguist characterizes radio play–by–play commentary as "a monologue directed at an unknown, unseen mass audience who voluntarily choose to listen…and provide no feedback to the speaker." It is these characteristics that make this kind of commentary unlike any other type of speech situation.

The chief feature of play–by–play commentary is a highly formulaic style of presentation. There is distinctive grammar not only in the use of the present tense but also in the omission of certain elements of sentence structure. For example, "Smith in close" eliminates the verb, as some newspaper headlines do. Another example is inverted word order, as in "over at third is Johnson." Play–by–play commentary is very fluent, keeping up with the pace of the action. The rate is steady and there is little silence. The structure of the commentary is cyclical, reflecting the way most games consist of recurring sequences of short activities—as in tennis and baseball—or a limited number of activity options—as in the various kinds of football. In racing, the structure is even simpler, with the commentator informing the listener of the varying order of the competitors in a "state of play" summary, which is crucial for listeners or viewers who have just tuned in.

8. The word that in paragraph 1 refers to

   (A) language
   (B) ongoing activity
   (C) commentary
   (D) sporting event

9. Which of the following statements is true of color commentary?

   (A) It narrates the action of the event in real time, using the present tense.
   (B) It is a monologue given to an audience that does not respond to the speaker.
   (C) It is steady and fluent because it must keep up with the action of the event.
   (D) It gives background on the event, and interprets and evaluates the event.

10. How is play–by–play commentary distinct from other types of narrative?

    (A) It is not published in magazines.
    (B) It is not spoken in past tense.
    (C) It involves only one reporter.
    (D) It takes place after the event.

11. Why does the author quote a linguist in paragraph 2?

    (A) To describe the uniqueness of radio play–by–play
    (B) To show how technical sports commentary is
    (C) To give examples of play–by–play commentary
    (D) To criticize past trends in sports commentary

12. All of the following are examples of play–by–play commentary EXCEPT

    (A) "He pitched for Chicago."
    (B) "Junior out of bounds."
    (C) "Straight away it's Owens."
    (D) "He can't make the shot."

13. The word pace in paragraph 3 is closest in meaning to

    (A) plan
    (B) score
    (C) cause
    (D) speed

14. The word crucial in paragraph 3 is closest in meaning to

    (A) fascinating
    (B) important
    (C) confusing
    (D) generous

15. It can be inferred from the passage that the author most likely agrees with which of the following statements about sports commentary?

    (A) Color commentary is more important than play–by–play commentary.
    (B) Sports commentators do not need special knowledge of the sport.
    (C) Commentary enhances the excitement and enjoyment of sports.
    (D) Sports commentators should work hard to improve their grammar.

THE CIRCULATORY SYSTEM OF TREES

Inside the tree's protective outer bark is the circulatory system, consisting of two cellular pipelines that transport water, mineral nutrients, and other organic substances to all living tissues of the tree. One pipeline, called the xylem—or sapwood—transports water and nutrients up from the roots to the leaves. The other, the phloem—or inner bark—carries the downward flow of foodstuffs from the leaves to the branches, trunk, and roots. Between these two pipelines is the vascular cambium, a single–cell layer too thin to be seen by the naked eye. This is the tree's major growth organ, responsible for the outward widening of the trunk, branches, twigs, and roots. During each growing season, the vascular cambium produces new phloem cells on its outer surface and new xylem cells on its inner surface.

Xylem cells in the roots draw water molecules into the tree, taking in hydrogen and oxygen and also carrying chemical nutrients from the soil. The xylem pipeline transports this life–sustaining mixture upward as xylem sap, all the way from the roots to the leaves. Xylem sap flows upward at rates of 15 meters per hour or faster. Xylem veins branch throughout each leaf, bringing xylem sap to thirsty cells. Leaves depend on this delivery system for their water supply because trees lose a tremendous amount of water through transpiration, evaporation of water from air spaces in the leaves. Unless the transpired water is replaced by water transported up from the roots, the leaves will wilt and eventually die.

How a tree manages to lift several liters of water so high into the air against the pull of gravity is an amazing feat of **hydraulics**. Water moves through the tree because it is driven by negative pressure—tension—in the leaves due to the physical properties of water. Transpiration, the evaporation of water from leaves, creates the tension that drives long–distance transport up through the xylem pipeline. Transpiration provides the pull, and the cohesion of water due to hydrogen bonding transmits the pull along the entire length of xylem. Within the xylem cells, water molecules adhere to each other and are pulled upward through the trunk, into the branches, and toward the cells and air spaces of the leaves.

Late in the growing season, xylem cells diminish in size and develop thicker skins, but they retain their capacity to carry water. Over time the innermost xylem cells become clogged with hard or gummy waste products and can no longer transport fluids. A similar situation occurs in the clogging of arteries in the aging human body. However, since the vascular cambium manufactures healthy new xylem cells each year, the death of the old cells does not mean the death of the tree. When they cease to function as living sapwood, the dead xylem cells become part of the central column of heartwood, the supportive structure of the tree.

Glossary:
   hydraulics: the science of the movement of water and other fluids

16. What are the primary components of the tree's circulatory system?

   (A) Water, minerals, and organic substances
   (B) Xylem and phloem
   (C) Leaves, branches, and trunk
   (D) Roots and heartwood

17. The word This in paragraph 1 refers to

   (A) phloem
   (B) inner bark
   (C) vascular cambium
   (D) naked eye

18. It can be inferred from paragraph 1 that the xylem is located

    (A) on the surface of the outer bark
    (B) inside the phloem and the vascular cambium
    (C) next to the inner bark
    (D) between the vascular cambium and the phloem

19. What can be inferred from paragraph 2 about xylem sap?

    (A) It is composed mainly of water.
    (B) It causes water loss by transpiration.
    (C) It gives leaves their green color.
    (D) It is manufactured in the leaves.

20. The word wilt in paragraph 2 is closest in meaning to

    (A) melt
    (B) grow
    (C) swell
    (D) sag

21. Why is the process of transpiration essential to the tree's circulatory system?

    (A) It supplies the hydrogen and oxygen that trees need to live and grow.
    (B) It produces new phloem and xylem in the trunk, branches, and roots.
    (C) It causes the negative pressure that moves water through the xylem.
    (D) It replaces the water vapor that is lost through the leaves' air spaces.

22. The phrase adhere to in paragraph 3 is closest in meaning to

    (A) depend on
    (B) stick to
    (C) warm up
    (D) respond to

23. The word gummy in paragraph 4 is closest in meaning to

    (A) sticky
    (B) liquid
    (C) smelly
    (D) fluffy

24. Why does the author mention arteries in the aging human body in paragraph 4?

    (A) To show that trees and people get the same diseases
    (B) To imply that trees might provide a solution to human problems
    (C) To compare what happens in two aging circulatory systems
    (D) To explain the cause of death in most trees

25. All of the following are functions of the xylem EXCEPT

    (A) transporting food from the leaves to the trunk
    (B) taking in chemical nutrients from the soil
    (C) forming part of the tree's structural support
    (D) moving water upward through the trunk

Answers to Reading Quiz 6 are on page 568.

Record your score on the Progress Chart on page 693.

READING

1.7 Recognizing Paraphrases

FOCUS

Read the following passage and answer the question:

The word "literature" has many meanings. In one sense, when we speak of the literature on a subject, we mean the vast body of research, interpretation, and opinion attached to a particular art or science. Such material has little claim to literary merit; in fact, some of it is barely intelligible to those outside the field. In another sense, we have the campaign literature distributed by political parties. Such "literature" has even less literary or artistic value. However, when we speak of "French literature" or "Russian literature," we mean something quite different. In this sense, literature is a written tradition that preserves a canon of great works defining the identity of a civilization. The literature of a society is available to a large literate public. It sets a standard against which later writers measure their own achievement as they aim to meet, reject, or exceed the literary masters.

Which sentence below best expresses the essential information in the highlighted sentence?

- ⭕ Most people are able to identify their country's greatest works of literature.
- ⭕ Every nation has a collection of writings that are thought of as great books.
- ⭕ Traditional literature must be preserved because it identifies the society's values.
- ⭕ The literature of a society maintains a body of writings that define the society.

The question asks you to identify the answer that most closely conveys the important information in the sentence In this sense, literature is a written tradition that preserves a canon of great works defining the identify of a civilization.

Look at the ideas in each part of the sentence:

In this sense (when we speak of "French literature" or "Russian literature")…

…literature is a written tradition…

…that preserves a canon of great works…

…defining the identity of a civilization.

The correct answer is *The literature of a society maintains a body of writings that define the society* because it paraphrases the essential information in the original sentence.

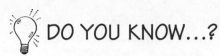

DO YOU KNOW...?

1. A ***paraphrase*** is a restatement of another sentence that gives the same information as the original sentence but in a different way. Paraphrases or restatements may have different sentence structure or use different words. They often use ***synonyms***, words that have the same meaning, or nearly the same meaning, as the words in the original sentence.

   You can identify the paraphrase of a sentence by focusing on the essential information in the original sentence. ***Essential information*** is the most important information in the sentence. It includes the ideas that are basic to the sentence's meaning and necessary in conveying the author's message and purpose.

2. TOEFL questions about paraphrases look like this:

   > Which sentence below best expresses the essential information in the highlighted sentence in the passage? Incorrect choices change the meaning in important ways or leave out essential information.

3. A paraphrase may have different sentence structure, or it may put the clauses in a different order. Here are some examples:

Original Sentence	**Paraphrase**
Despite the social, technical, and functional aspects of building—those that link architecture most closely to history—architecture exists in the realm of the visual arts.	Architecture is one of the visual arts, even though the social, technical, and functional aspects of building link architecture to history.
Most birds have body temperatures between 40 and 42 degrees Celsius, while most mammals have body temperatures between 36 and 38 degrees.	The body temperatures of most mammals are between 36 and 38 degrees Celsius, and those of birds are between 40 and 42 degrees.

4. A paraphrase may use synonyms and other expressions to convey ideas that have the same meaning as those in the original sentence. Here are some examples:

Original Sentence	**Paraphrase**
Generally, most adult human stomachs hold slightly more than four cups of food, but the stomach can expand to accommodate as many as 16 cups.	The stomach of an adult person is usually full when it contains just over four cups of food, but it can stretch to hold up to 16 cups.
The supply of natural ice was an industry unto itself in the late nineteenth century, and refrigeration with ice became more inexpensive and accessible.	Natural ice supply was a separate business in the late nineteenth century, and refrigeration with ice became cheaper and more available.

5. A pronoun or other referring word in the highlighted sentence may refer to something in a previous sentence (see 1.3). The correct paraphrase may use the referent instead of the pronoun. Here are some examples, with pronouns and their referents shown in *italics*:

Original Sentence

Culture consists of the *language, values, norms, and artifacts* that define and unite a society. *These* can be spread from one society to another through culture contact. Some of the most important discoveries, such as fire and the wheel, were made in more than one place and then diffused across cultures.

In 1889, an Austrian physicist named *Ernst Mach created a system of numbers for measuring "supersonic" speeds. This* is why when a plane travels at a speed faster than the speed of sound, its speed is referred to as Mach 1.

Paraphrase

Contact with other cultures is a way of spreading language, values, norms, and artifacts.

A plane moving faster than the speed of sound has a speed of Mach 1, after the inventor of the numbering system.

6. In questions about paraphrases, the incorrect answer choices may be incorrect because they:

- have a different meaning from that of the original sentence;
- are untrue according to the original sentence;
- omit information or ideas that are necessary to the meaning of the original sentence; or
- include information or ideas that are not in the original sentence.

7. Here are some examples:

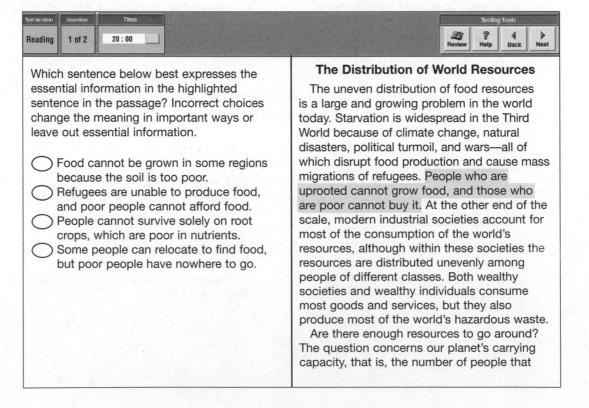

Reading | **1 of 2** | **20 : 00** | Testing Tools: Review, Help, Back, Next

Which sentence below best expresses the essential information in the highlighted sentence in the passage? Incorrect choices change the meaning in important ways or leave out essential information.

○ Food cannot be grown in some regions because the soil is too poor.
○ Refugees are unable to produce food, and poor people cannot afford food.
○ People cannot survive solely on root crops, which are poor in nutrients.
○ Some people can relocate to find food, but poor people have nowhere to go.

The Distribution of World Resources

The uneven distribution of food resources is a large and growing problem in the world today. Starvation is widespread in the Third World because of climate change, natural disasters, political turmoil, and wars—all of which disrupt food production and cause mass migrations of refugees. People who are uprooted cannot grow food, and those who are poor cannot buy it. At the other end of the scale, modern industrial societies account for most of the consumption of the world's resources, although within these societies the resources are distributed unevenly among people of different classes. Both wealthy societies and wealthy individuals consume most goods and services, but they also produce most of the world's hazardous waste.

Are there enough resources to go around? The question concerns our planet's carrying capacity, that is, the number of people that

The question asks you to identify the paraphrase of the highlighted sentence. The correct answer is *Refugees are unable to produce food, and poor people cannot afford food*. Look at the information in the original sentence and how it is paraphrased in the correct answer:

Original Sentence	**Paraphrase**
People who are uprooted cannot grow food	Refugees are unable to produce food
those who are poor cannot buy it	poor people cannot afford food

Why are the other three answers incorrect? *Food cannot be grown in some regions because the soil is too poor* and *People cannot survive solely on root crops, which are poor in nutrients* both have a different meaning from that of original sentence. *Some people can relocate to find food, but poor people have nowhere to go* has a new idea, *poor people have nowhere to go*, which is not in the original sentence.

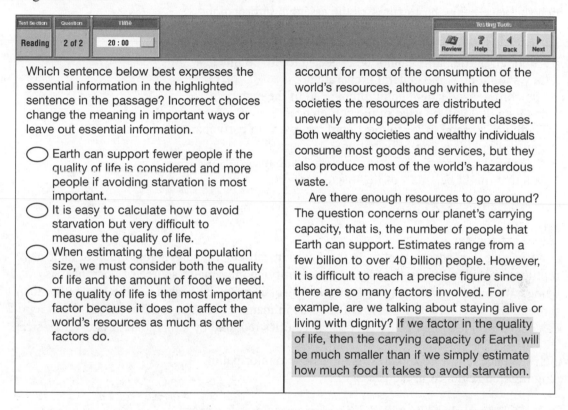

The correct answer is *Earth can support fewer people if the quality of life is considered and more people if avoiding starvation is most important*. Look at the information in the original sentence and how it is paraphrased in the correct answer:

Original Sentence	**Paraphrase**
If we factor in the quality of life	if the quality of life is considered
then the carrying capacity of Earth will be much smaller than	Earth can support fewer people
if we simply estimate how much food it takes to avoid starvation	if avoiding starvation is most important

The other three answers do not accurately express the essential information in the original sentence.

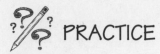 **PRACTICE**

Exercise 1.7.A

Read the passages and choose the best answer to each question.

QUESTION 1

In a typical business conference, associates meet to discuss policy or to solve problems. The average participants do not do much specific preparing; their background and thinking usually formulate their contribution. But it is best if all participants know in advance the purpose of the conference. Some general preparation may be in order, and participants may want to take into the conference materials or data that might be useful if a matter comes up.

1. Which sentence below best expresses the essential information in the highlighted sentence in the passage?

   (A) Although participants cannot be expected to do too much, they should do some general preparation.
   (B) The conference leader should prepare all of the materials and data that will be used in the conference.
   (C) There is a general order to most conferences, with participants contributing ideas and information.
   (D) As general preparation, participants can bring materials or data that might be a part of the discussion.

QUESTION 2

Because they absorb heat from the environment rather than generate much of their own, reptiles are said to be ectotherms, a term identifying their major source of body heat as being external. Ectotherms heat directly with solar energy by basking in the sun, rather than through the metabolic breakdown of food, as in mammals and birds. This means that a reptile can survive on less than 10 percent of the calories required by a mammal of equivalent size.

2. Which sentence below best expresses the essential information in the highlighted sentence in the passage?

   (A) Because a reptile heats with solar energy, it requires less than 10 percent of the calories that a mammal of the same size needs.
   (B) A reptile obtains only 10 percent of its calories from the metabolic breakdown of food; it obtains the rest by basking in the sun.
   (C) Some reptiles and mammals are equal in size, but they require vastly different quantities of calories for survival.
   (D) Reptiles need to spend only 10 percent of their time eating because they do not need as many calories as mammals of equal size.

QUESTION 3

Architecture is concerned with the large–scale manipulation of elements in the dimensions of length, width, and height. These dimensions may apply to a solid, such as the Egyptian pyramids, or to hollow interior spaces, ranging in size and complexity from a domestic room to a vast cathedral. They may also apply to the spaces around and between buildings. Moreover, every building has a physical context in relation to other buildings. Sometimes the designer disregards the context on the assumption that surrounding structures will later be replaced. However, it is more often posterity that destroys the once appropriate original context.

3. Which sentence below best expresses the essential information in the highlighted sentence in the passage?

Ⓐ Some architects do not like other buildings to be too close to the building they are designing.

Ⓑ Most buildings eventually have to be replaced, so the physical context is not very important.

Ⓒ Architects often believe that nearby structures will not always be there, so they ignore them.

Ⓓ Designers should ignore the assumptions of people who plan to destroy the original context.

QUESTION 4

The first great collector of Canadian folk traditions was Marius Barbeau, who oversaw the preservation of thousands of texts in what is now the National Museum of Canada. Fearing that these traditions would disappear unless gathered and catalogued, Barbeau preserved the folklore and folk songs of cultures ranging from rural Quebec to the Tsimshian Indians of British Columbia. These folkways—songs, dialects, legends, tall tales, riddles, and children's rhymes—were all part of Canada's traditional rural experience. They provided evidence of the everyday life of the people that was far richer than that in most other historical texts.

4. Which sentence below best expresses the essential information in the highlighted sentence in the passage?

Ⓐ There is a lot of information in historical texts, but most of it does not deal with real life.

Ⓑ Canada's folkways give us a much better description of daily life than most histories do.

Ⓒ The texts collected by Barbeau reveal that some rural Canadians were richer than others.

Ⓓ The Canadian people provided a lot of materials that illustrate their traditional values.

QUESTION 5

Ruminants—cattle, bison, sheep, goats, deer, antelopes, and giraffes—have a large four–chambered stomach that enables them to digest fibrous plant matter. When a ruminant first swallows a mouthful of grass or leaves, the food enters the stomach's first chamber, the rumen, where bacteria start to break down the cellulose–rich matter and form it into small balls of cud. The ruminant periodically returns the cud to its mouth where it is chewed at length to crush the fibers, making them more accessible to further bacterial action. The ruminant then reswallows the cud, which passes through the other three chambers of the stomach for further digestion.

5. Which sentence below best expresses the essential information in the highlighted sentence in the passage?

- (A) Ruminants eat continuously, spending long periods eating grass and chewing their cud in order to access the nutrients.
- (B) The bacterial action begins when the ruminant puts the cud in its mouth and starts the long process of chewing.
- (C) The ruminant's strong teeth must crush the plant fibers in the cud in order to neutralize the cud's harmful bacteria.
- (D) The cud is sent back to the ruminant's mouth and chewed extensively so that the fibers can be digested more easily.

QUESTION 6

Cities differ from towns in the size, density, and diversity of their population. The city offers a wider variety of goods and services, as well as more extensive employment and cultural opportunities. City life is characterized by impersonal and formal social relationships, greater privacy, and more lifestyle choices—a way of life referred to as urbanism. The urban spirit is sophisticated and dynamic, stimulating the mind through contrasts and encouraging tolerance of differences. However, urbanism is not restricted to city dwellers; it can be considered a trait of all modern societies at a high level of technological development. The urban spirit spreads beyond the city via the mass media: television, movies, CDs, and the Internet.

6. Which sentence below best expresses the essential information in the highlighted sentence in the passage?

- (A) City dwellers do not let urbanism restrict their ability to develop new technology.
- (B) Urbanism characterizes all highly developed societies, not just people who live in cities.
- (C) All modern societies have a sophisticated level of technology; this is the primary goal of urbanism.
- (D) Living in the city limits one's knowledge to only the most advanced technology.

QUESTIONS 7–8

Alligators have no natural predators except humans. In fact, humans drove alligators to near extinction in many of their marsh and swamp habitats in North America. Hunters once killed large numbers of these animals for their meat and soft belly skin, which was used to make shoes, belts, and wallets. Between 1950 and 1960, hunters wiped out 90 percent of the alligators in Louisiana and greatly reduced the alligator population in the Florida Everglades.

In 1967 the federal government placed the American alligator on the endangered species list. In the next decade, protected by hunters and averaging about 40 eggs per nest, the alligator made a strong comeback. It was reclassified from endangered to threatened in Florida, Louisiana, and Texas, where the vast majority of the animals live. As a threatened species, it is still protected from excessive harvesting by hunters; however, limited hunting is allowed in some areas to keep the population from growing too large.

7. Which sentence below best expresses the essential information in the highlighted sentence in paragraph 1?

  Ⓐ It is a fact that humans forced alligators to live in North America's marshes and swamps.
  Ⓑ Many alligators were killed when people built roads and drove cars through their habitats.
  Ⓒ People almost destroyed the native alligator population in many North American environments.
  Ⓓ In North America, humans and alligators rarely choose to live together in the same area.

8. Which sentence below best expresses the essential information in the highlighted sentence in paragraph 2?

  Ⓐ Alligators are still protected, but hunters are allowed to kill a certain number to control their population in some places.
  Ⓑ In order to prevent alligators from growing too large, hunters can harvest adult alligators that exceed a specified size.
  Ⓒ Hunting is restricted to areas where alligators are no longer a threatened species and therefore do not need protection.
  Ⓓ Alligators are more threatened than ever by excessive hunting, and hunters should not be allowed to destroy all of them.

QUESTIONS 9–10

Current archaeological theory holds that the first humans in the Americas were bands of advanced Stone Age people who crossed over from what is now Siberia in Asia sometime between 12 and 30 thousand years ago. Some scientists think that these early humans crossed what is now the Bering Sea on a land bridge, a stretch of glacial ice connecting Asia and North America. Others speculate that they may have crossed that 55–mile–wide channel by boat.

These early humans probably migrated southward along an ice–free corridor. After several thousand years, perhaps at a pace of only ten miles every year, the migrants spread over this new land from Alaska to the tip of South America, a trail over ten thousand miles long. In South America, where the glaciers from the ice age melted first, the migrants took strong root in the fertile soil and warming climate of Patagonia. As the ice receded farther north, civilization in what is now Central America and Mexico began to take shape and flourish.

9. Which sentence below best expresses the essential information in the highlighted sentence in paragraph 1?

   (A) Theories vary widely over how the first humans arrived in the Americas, but most state that it occurred around 30 thousand years ago.
   (B) The best current theory states that between 12 and 30 thousand early humans crossed over from Siberia to North America.
   (C) Human beings originated in Siberia in Asia and later formed into bands that migrated to the Americas during the Stone Age.
   (D) Archaeologists believe that groups of Stone Age humans first came to the Americas from Asia about 12 to 30 thousand years ago.

10. Which sentence below best expresses the essential information in the highlighted sentence in paragraph 2?

   (A) When the glaciers in South America melted, the climate became warmer in Patagonia, helping the people grow strong.
   (B) The favorable conditions in Patagonia attracted migrants from other parts of South America, where there were still glaciers.
   (C) The ice age glaciers melted earliest in South America, where the migrants settled in the warm, fertile region of Patagonia.
   (D) The migrants in Patagonia in South America survived on the root crops that grew well in the fertile soil and warm climate.

Exercise 1.7.B

Read the passages and choose the best answer to each question.

QUESTIONS 1–3

A subculture is a cultural group within the larger society that provides social support to people who differ from the majority in terms of status, race, ethnic background, religion, or other factors. Whenever these differences lead to exclusion or discrimination, subcultures develop as a shield to protect members from the negative attitudes of others. Subcultures unify the group and provide it with values, norms, and a history.

Some subcultures do not experience discrimination yet differ from the mainstream enough to generate a "we" feeling among members and a sense of separateness. Examples include military officers, college students, information technology specialists, social workers, jazz musicians, or any subgroup with its own special language and customs. Subcultures usually have values that are variations on those of the dominant culture. These variations are close enough for the subgroup to remain under the societal umbrella but different enough to reflect the unique experience of subgroup members. In North America today, teenagers are a distinct subculture with a special way of talking and dressing so that insiders can recognize one another while keeping outsiders out.

1. Which sentence below best expresses the essential information in the highlighted sentence in paragraph 1?

   (A) People are excluded from subcultures for various reasons, but especially if they have a negative attitude.
   (B) When some people discriminate against others, it is the responsibility of the majority culture to do something.
   (C) When people are different from others, they may experience negative effects, including discrimination.
   (D) Subcultures form to protect people who differ from the majority when these people face discrimination.

2. All of the following are given as characteristics of subcultures EXCEPT

   (A) a desire to join the dominant culture
   (B) experiences outside those of the mainstream
   (C) special customs and way of talking
   (D) a "we" feeling among members

3. Which sentence below best expresses the essential information in the highlighted sentence in paragraph 2?

   (A) The different experiences of subgroups cause their members to seek protection in the values and customs of their own group.
   (B) Every society is like a large umbrella that covers people from a wide variety of backgrounds and cultures, protecting everyone equally.
   (C) A subculture's values show its separateness yet resemble the majority's values enough to keep the subgroup within the larger society.
   (D) Each group member has experiences that differ from those of all other members and are completely outside those of the mainstream.

QUESTIONS 4–6

The cerebral cortex of the human brain is divided into two hemispheres that are linked by a thick band of fibers called the corpus callosum. Each hemisphere has four discrete lobes, and researchers have identified a number of functional areas within each lobe. The left hemisphere has areas for controlling speech, language, and calculation, while the right hemisphere controls creative ability and spatial perception. This centering of functions in specific areas of the brain is known as lateralization.

Much of our knowledge about brain lateralization comes from studies of "split–brain" patients, people with a damaged corpus callosum. In one experiment, a subject holding a key in his left hand, with both eyes open, was able to name it as a key. However, when the subject's eyes were covered, he could use the key to open a lock, but was unable to name it as a key. The center for speech is in the left hemisphere, but sensory information from the left hand crosses over and enters the right side of the brain. Without the corpus callosum to function as a switchboard between the two sides of the brain, the subject's knowledge of the size, texture, and function of the key could not be transferred from the right to the left hemisphere. The link between sensory input and spoken response was disconnected.

4. Which sentence below best expresses the essential information in the highlighted sentence in paragraph 1?

   (A) Each half of the brain consists of four types of tissues that are identified by their size and location.
   (B) The brain's two hemispheres each have four separate parts, and each part controls several functions.
   (C) There are a number of functional centers in the brain, and these can be divided into four main groups.
   (D) Research has shown that the brain controls four basic functions, each with a number of variations.

5. According to the passage, what is one effect of a damaged corpus callosum?

   (A) Functions from one side of the brain are transferred to the other side.
   (B) People with their eyes open cannot see an object held in the left hand.
   (C) The connection between sensory input and spoken response is broken.
   (D) Creative ability and spatial perception are greatly diminished.

6. Which sentence below best expresses the essential information in the highlighted sentence in paragraph 2?

   (A) Information about the key could not travel from one side of the brain to the other because the corpus callosum did not provide the link.
   (B) Some people are born without a corpus callosum, so they cannot exchange knowledge between the two hemispheres of the brain.
   (C) Both sides of the brain control knowledge of familiar objects, and the corpus callosum functions as a key to that knowledge.
   (D) The corpus callosum acts like a computer keyboard in the way that it takes information from the hands and enters it into the brain.

QUESTIONS 7–10

Organic compost (partially decomposed organic matter) requires four basic elements: carbon, nitrogen, air, and water. The carbon comes from dead organic matter, such as dried leaves, straw, and wood chips. The nitrogen comes from fresh or green materials, such as vegetative kitchen waste, untreated grass clippings, and animal manure. Fungi, bacteria, and other microorganisms use the carbon for energy and the nitrogen to grow and reproduce. The microorganisms secrete enzymes that break down the cells of the dead vegetation and animal matter. These enzymes are the glue that cements the soil particles into larger, coarser grains. Coarse soil crumbles easily, which aerates the soil and allows it to absorb moisture efficiently. This partially digested mixture is compost.

Compost is a stage of decay in which most of the organic matter has been broken down, but it may still be possible to identify individual parts such as leaves and twigs. The final phase of decay is called humus—a dark, sticky, nutrient–rich substance in which the original materials can no longer be distinguished. Although the terms "compost" and "humus" are often used interchangeably, they are not synonymous.

7. Which sentence below best expresses the essential information in the highlighted sentence in paragraph 1?

(A) Enzymes from the microorganisms break apart when they come into contact with organic matter.
(B) Nonliving plant and animal matter is digested when microorganisms produce certain enzymes.
(C) Vegetation and animal matter contain enzymes that hinder the growth of dangerous microorganisms.
(D) Microorganisms invade the cells of plants and animals, eventually causing the death of the host.

8. The word cements in paragraph 1 is closest in meaning to

(A) lifts
(B) freezes
(C) sorts
(D) combines

9. It can be inferred from paragraph 1 that organic compost

(A) is less expensive than other types of compost
(B) relies on the digestive processes of microorganisms
(C) is based on the belief that everything in nature changes
(D) requires about a year before it can be used in the soil

10. Which sentence below best expresses the essential information in the highlighted sentence in paragraph 2?

(A) Compost and humus are different substances, but people sometimes confuse the two words.
(B) It is often possible to change compost into humus, but you cannot change humus into compost.
(C) "Compost" used to be a synonym for "humus," but the meaning of both words has changed over time.
(D) Some people think that compost eventually becomes humus, but actually the reverse is true.

Answers to Exercises 1.7.A through 1.7.B are on page 569.

EXTENSION

1. Outside of class, look in a magazine or a university textbook. Select a short passage of one to three paragraphs. In class, work with a partner. Identify the nouns and verbs in each selected passage. Then, use a dictionary, synonym finder, or thesaurus to find as many synonyms as possible for the nouns and verbs you have identified. Names and other proper nouns will not have synonyms. Also, be aware that not every synonym will be appropriate for the context of your passage, and some synonyms will be more appropriate than others. If you are not sure whether a synonym is correct in the context, ask your teacher.

2. In reading done outside class, select a short passage of no more than 100 words. Write a paraphrase of the passage by restating each sentence in a different way, using different words. You may also combine ideas from more than one sentence into one sentence. To extend this activity further, bring the original passage and your paraphrase to class. Exchange your original passage with a partner's. Next, write a paraphrase of this new passage while your partner paraphrases the original passage from you. When you are both finished writing, compare the two paraphrases for each original passage. Do both paraphrases contain the same essential information as the original?

3. Outside of class, select a short passage of no more than 100 words. Make a copy of the passage for each student in your class, or write the passage on an overhead projector transparency. Choose one sentence from the passage and restate it in a different way, using different words. In class, write the paraphrased sentence on the board or the overhead projector. Your class must read the passage and the paraphrased sentence and determine which sentence in the original passage is being paraphrased. Does your paraphrase include all of the essential information from the original sentence?

1.8 Recognizing Coherence

 FOCUS

Read the sentences below. Put them in order. Which sentence should come first? Beside each sentence, write 1, 2, or 3 to show the correct order:

____ The trunk's inner core consists of vertically oriented cells that are closely packed together in parallel rows.

____ Millions upon millions of such cells form the heartwood—the nonliving central pillar on which the living tree hoists itself skyward.

____ The most distinguishing characteristic of a mature tree is its self–supporting woody spine, or trunk.

The most logical order, from top to bottom, is: 2, 3, 1. Now look at the sentences in a paragraph:

> ■ The most distinguishing characteristic of a mature tree is its self–supporting woody spine, or trunk. ■ The trunk's inner core consists of vertically oriented cells that are closely packed together in parallel rows. ■ Millions upon millions of such cells form the heartwood—the nonliving central pillar on which the living tree hoists itself skyward. ■

Now read the following sentence, which can be added to the above paragraph.

All trees share certain growth characteristics that distinguish them from other members of the plant kingdom.

Where would the sentence best fit? Choose the square [■] where the sentence could be added.

The sentence would best fit at the first square. Now read the paragraph with the sentence added in the correct place. Notice how each sentence leads into the next sentence, helping the paragraph flow smoothly.

> **All trees share certain growth characteristics that distinguish them from other members of the plant kingdom.** The most distinguishing characteristic of a mature tree is its self–supporting woody spine, or trunk. The trunk's inner core consists of vertically oriented cells that are closely packed together in parallel rows. Millions upon millions of such cells form the heartwood—the nonliving central pillar on which the living tree hoists itself skyward.

All of the sentences in the paragraph flow smoothly and logically. This logical order gives the paragraph *coherence*.

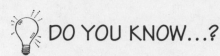

DO YOU KNOW...?

1. *Coherence* is the quality of unity and order among the parts of a written passage. If a passage is *coherent*, there are logical and orderly connections among the ideas within sentences and among the sentences within paragraphs. There are also orderly connections among the various paragraphs. Coherent writing makes sense. It is easy to understand because all of its parts fit together and flow logically one after another.

2. Coherence questions on the TOEFL test your ability to identify where a sentence can be added to a passage. Questions about coherence look like this:

   > Look at the four squares [■] that indicate where the following sentence could be added to the passage.
   >
   > **(Sentence)**
   >
   > Where would the sentence best fit?
   >
   > Click on a square [■] to add the sentence to the passage.

3. On the TOEFL, the squares in the passage indicate answer choices. When you click on a square, the sentence will appear in that place. You can then read the passage with the added sentence and check to see if this is the best place to put the sentence. You can try putting the sentence at any square until you are satisfied that the passage reads logically and coherently.

4. Your understanding of the organization and purpose of the passage, and your knowledge of transitions and reference words, will help you determine where to add the sentence to the passage. You can also determine where *not* to add the sentence by identifying places where adding it would interrupt the logical connection between ideas in consecutive sentences.

5. Certain words and phrases called *transitions* are clues to coherence because they connect ideas and control the order of sentences. Transitions identify relationships of ideas in sentences and in paragraphs. Some commonly used transitions are:

Addition	Contrast	Example	Cause/Result
also	although	for example	because
another	however	for instance	consequently
other	in contrast	including	therefore
first, second…	while	such as	thus

   For a longer list of transitions, see the table on page 17.

6. Transitions show the relationship between consecutive sentences. Look at this example:

   > Akira Kurosawa's masterful works burst on the international film scene in the 1950s with the sound of fireworks and epic battles. *In contrast*, the quiet dignity and unobtrusive techniques of Satyajit Ray's films also placed him among the world's great directors.

   In contrast is a transition that makes a logical connection between the two sentences. The transition determines the order of the sentences because it introduces the information in the second sentence as a contrast to the information in the first sentence.

7. Coherence is related to the author's purpose. Look at this example:

> *Two reasons* for government regulation of industry stand out. *First*, economists have traditionally stressed the importance of containing market power. A *second reason* is that the regulators are captured by the regulated.

The transitions *two reasons*, *first*, and *second reason* tell you that the author's purpose is to list reasons. Beware that adding a sentence between any of these sentences might interrupt the logical flow, unless the added sentence would further develop an idea in one of the sentences.

8. Pronouns and other reference words are clues to coherence. Look at this example:

> The brain of a computer is its central processing unit. In the case of a microcomputer, *this* is a chip called the microprocessor. *It* is connected to the other units by groups of wires along which binary code signals pass.

The pronoun *this* refers to *central processing unit* in the previous sentence. The pronoun *It* refers back to *microprocessor*. The use of pronouns and referents is linked to the order of the sentences. Beware that adding a sentence between any of these sentences might interrupt the logical connection between a pronoun and its referent.

9. In questions about coherence, an answer choice may be incorrect because adding the sentence there would:

- interrupt the logical flow of ideas in consecutive sentences;
- interfere with the correct use of transitions;
- interrupt the logical connection between a pronoun and its referent; or
- separate two sentences that should be consecutive in the passage.

10. Here are some examples:

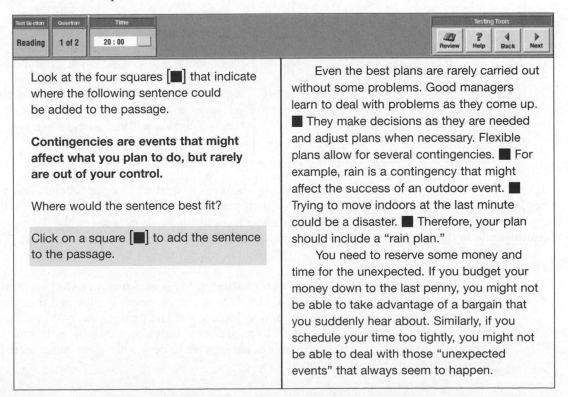

The added sentence defines the term *contingencies*. The author first mentions this term in the sentence *Flexible plans allow for several contingencies*. The next sentence gives an example of a contingency: *For example, rain is a contingency that might affect the success of an outdoor event*. The logical order is to introduce the new term, define it, and then give an example to illustrate it. Therefore, the sentence best fits at the second square. The passage should read:

> Even the best plans are rarely carried out without some problems. Good managers learn to deal with problems as they come up. They make decisions as they are needed and adjust plans when necessary. Flexible plans allow for several contingencies. **Contingencies are events that might affect what you plan to do, but rarely are out of your control.** For example, rain is a contingency that might affect the success of an outdoor event. Trying to move indoors at the last minute could be a disaster. Therefore, your plan should include a "rain plan."

Adding the sentence at any of the other squares would make a less coherent paragraph because it would interrupt the logical flow of ideas between the sentences.

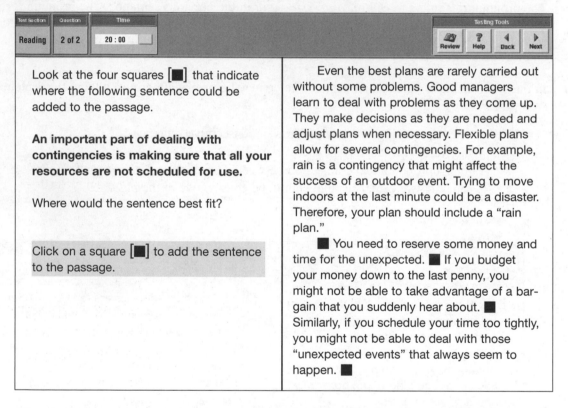

The added sentence introduces the idea of having resources to deal with contingencies. The sentence best fits at the first square, where it serves as the introductory sentence of the paragraph. *An important part of dealing with contingencies* also serves as a transition between the definition of contingency in the first paragraph and the additional information in the second paragraph. The passage should read:

> **An important part of dealing with contingencies is making sure that all your resources are not scheduled for use.** You need to reserve some money and time for the unexpected. If you budget your money down to the last penny, you might not be able to take advantage of a bargain that you suddenly hear about. Similarly, if you schedule your time too tightly, you might not be able to deal with those "unexpected events" that always seem to happen.

Adding the sentence at any of the other squares would interrupt the smooth flow of ideas between the sentences.

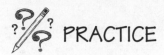 PRACTICE

Exercise 1.8.A

Read the passages and choose the best answer to each question.

1. Look at the four squares, **A**, **B**, **C**, and **D**, which indicate where the following sentence could be added to the passage. Where would the sentence best fit?

   Most of them like to talk, especially in front of a group.

   Kindergartners are quite skillful with language. **A** Providing a "sharing time" gives children a natural opportunity for talking. However, many will need help in becoming good listeners. **B** Some sort of rotation scheme is usually necessary to divide talking opportunities between the talkative and silent extremes. **C** Teachers can provide activities or experinces for less confident children to talk about, such as a field trip, a book, or a film. **D**

2. Look at the four squares, **A**, **B**, **C**, and **D**, which indicate where the following sentence could be added to the passage. Where would the sentence best fit?

   However, the ground surface is spongy and wet to the touch.

   Bogs are a distinctive type of wetland. **A** They appear relatively dry, with only small amounts of shallow water visible. **B** The surface material is largely sphagnum moss or other organic matter rather than mineral soil. **C** Bogs are usually characterized by evergreen trees and shrubs and are underlain by deep peat deposits. **D** Bogs will develop in former glacial lakes by the gradual accumulation of organic matter falling from beneath a floating mat of vegetation advancing out over the water.

3. Look at the four squares, **A**, **B**, **C**, and **D**, which indicate where the following sentence could be added to the passage. Where would the sentence best fit?

   The narrower leaves of trees like willows and mimosa provide a dappled shade, which may be more beneficial to lawns and garden plants.

   While all living things need sunlight, too much of it can be oppressive, even damaging. **A** Any overheated dog or cat can appreciate the relief provided by a mature shade tree on a sunny day. **B** The densest foliage, and so the densest shade, is found under the broad leaves of deciduous trees like oaks and maples. **C** By cooling the surrounding air, the shade from trees reduces the demand for air conditioning in nearby homes. **D** This translates into reduced emissions of carbon dioxide from oil– or coal–fired electrical generators.

4. Look at the four squares, **A**, **B**, **C**, and **D**, which indicate where the following sentence could be added to the passage. Where would the sentence best fit?

This is due to the beating of the double reed through which the air travels as it leaves the player's mouth.

The highest of the standard orchestral instruments, the flute is unlike the other woodwinds because it is held across the player's mouth. **A** The air inside is set in vibration by the action of the airstream against the edge of the hole. **B** The flute has no reed, so its tone is pure and creamy. **C** In contrast, the oboe has a rasping, "sawtooth" configuration to its sound when played loud. **D** However, the oboe can produce a quiet and gentle sound when called for, and it can even approximate the human voice.

5. Look at the four squares, **A**, **B**, **C**, and **D**, which indicate where the following sentence could be added to the passage. Where would the sentence best fit?

It is the only method available for obtaining a variety of colors in bamboo.

For centuries, bamboo has provided building materials for Eastern cultures. Now it is becoming more popular and available in the West, particularly as a substitute for expensive hardwood flooring. **A** As a flooring material, natural honey–colored bamboo is more stable than carbonized bamboo. **B** Carbonizing is a technique of steaming and pressurizing the bamboo to introduce carbon fibers that darken the original material. **C** However, it lowers the hardness factor, making the darker bamboo more susceptible to damage. **D**

6. Look at the four squares, **A**, **B**, **C**, and **D**, which indicate where the following sentence could be added to the passage. Where would the sentence best fit?

No one can be made better off without making someone else worse off.

An economy is efficient if there is no way of reorganizing production and distribution to improve everyone's satisfaction. Economists call such a state *allocative efficiency*. **A** When people come to a market with goods they have produced, they trade their goods for those of others. **B** Every completed trade raises the satisfaction of both sides. **C** When all of the beneficial trades have been completed, no one can find another trade to improve his situation. **D** Under such conditions, the economy has attained allocative efficiency.

7. Look at the four squares, **A**, **B**, **C**, and **D**, which indicate where the following sentence could be added to the passage. Where would the sentence best fit?

Researchers found that high–pitched notes made people think of bright colors, while low tones brought dark colors to mind.

For people with a condition called *synesthesia*, sound is directly linked to the sense of sight, and they experience sounds by seeing them as colors. **A** However, different sounds sometimes remind everyone of different colors. **B** In one study, students were asked to relate colors to different tones of music. **C** White, yellow, and pink were associated with tones in the 4,000–Hz range; blue and green were associated with tones in the 1,000–Hz range; and brown, gray, and black were associated with tones in the 200–Hz range. **D**

8. Look at the four squares, **A**, **B**, **C**, and **D**, which indicate where the following sentence could be added to the passage. Where would the sentence best fit?

This irritation is caused by viruses or bacteria, exposure to tobacco smoke, or air pollution.

Bronchitis is an inflammation of the bronchial tubes in the lungs. **A** It often appears after a cold or an upper respiratory infection that does not heal completely. It also may accompany childhood infections such as measles, whooping cough, and typhoid fever. **B** The inflamed bronchial tubes secrete a sticky mucus called sputum. It is difficult for the tiny hairs on the bronchi to clear out this sputum. **C** The cough that comes with bronchitis is the body's attempt to eliminate it. **D** Other symptoms include discomfort or tightness in the chest, low fever, sore throat, and sometimes wheezing. Severe cases of bronchitis may lead to pneumonia.

9. Look at the four squares, **A**, **B**, **C**, and **D**, which indicate where the following sentence could be added to the passage. Where would the sentence best fit?

Courses included Far Eastern, Spanish, and Native American dances as well as basic ballet.

Among the modern dance innovators of the early twentieth century was Ruth St. Denis, whose dances were lush and graceful, tinged with exoticism and mysticism. **A** St. Denis was particularly expert in the manipulation of draperies and veils so that the moving fabrics seemed like magical extensions of her own body. **B** St. Denis's 1914 marriage to dancer–choreographer Ted Shawn resulted in a wedding of names, Denishawn, which first became a school and then a dance company. **C** Denishawn drew its inspiration and derived its curriculum from a variety of ethnic sources. **D** The touring Denishawn company might offer on a single program a Hindu dance, a rhythmic interpretation of concert music, a romantic duet, a hula, and a demonstration of the latest ballroom craze.

10. Look at the four squares, **A**, **B**, **C**, and **D**, which indicate where the following sentence could be added to the passage. Where would the sentence best fit?

Both biological and chemical oceanographers are trying to make ocean life and industrial progress compatible so marine ecosystems will not be endangered.

A Within the field of oceanography, the major areas stressed are physical, biological, chemical, geological, engineering, and technological. However, each of these areas is interdependent of the others. Both physical oceanographers and ocean engineers are involved in harnessing the energies of the ocean to fill the demand for electrical power. **B** Even if oceanographers have an area of major interest, they are consistently forced to take a more interdisciplinary view of their work because the various sciences overlap. **C** Oceanographers of different backgrounds depend on each other to further their own research. **D** A conference of marine scientists might include discussions of plate tectonics, effects of offshore mining on fisheries, effects of climate change on marine life, technology for deep–sea exploration, and other related topics.

Exercise 1.8.B

Read the passages and choose the best answer to each question.

QUESTIONS 1–3

The 2,000–year–old complex of mounds occupying thirteen acres on the banks of the Scioto River in southwestern Ohio is one of the most important sites of the Hopewell Indian culture. Their mound construction was especially intensive in this area. It offers evidence that this society flourished in the Ohio Valley for five hundred years.

The 23 mounds are spaciously placed but with no overall pattern. Archaeologists have determined that the complex—called Mound City—was apparently both a village and a burial site. Numerous artifacts have been found in excavations of the burial mounds. They include shell beads, bear and shark teeth, pottery, and ear spools of copper and silver. A number of pipes found in one mound—probably belonging to a chief or priest—are remarkable for their exquisite workmanship and stylized realism in the likenesses of animals and birds: wildcat, beaver, great blue heron, and raven.

1. The word flourished in paragraph 1 is closest in meaning to

   (A) suffered
   (B) fished
   (C) lived
   (D) competed

2. The word They in paragraph 2 refers to

   (A) archaeologists
   (B) artifacts
   (C) excavations
   (D) mounds

3. Look at the four squares, **A**, **B**, **C**, and **D**, which indicate where the following sentence could be added to the passage. Where would the sentence best fit?

The quantity and type of burial objects in particular mounds indicates the status and occupation of the deceased.

The 23 mounds are spaciously placed but with no overall pattern. Archaeologists have determined that the complex—called Mound City—was apparently both a village and a burial site. **A** Numerous artifacts have been found in excavations of the burial mounds. **B** They include shell beads, bear and shark teeth, pottery, and ear spools of copper and silver. **C** A number of pipes found in one mound—probably belonging to a chief or priest—are remarkable for their exquisite workmanship and stylized realism in the likenesses of animals and birds: wildcat, beaver, great blue heron, and raven. **D**

QUESTIONS 4–6

Although some fish appear capable of swimming at extremely high speeds, most fish, such as trout and minnows, can actually swim only about ten body lengths per second. Translated into kilometers per hour, it means that a 30–centimeter trout can swim only about 10.4 kilometers per hour. Generally speaking, the larger the fish the faster it can swim.

We can understand how fish swim by studying the motion of a very flexible fish such as an eel. The movement is **serpentine**, with **undulations** moving backward along the body by alternate contraction of the muscles on either side of the eel's body. While the undulations move backward, the bending of the body pushes sideways against the water, producing a reactive force that is directed forward at an angle. The movement has two components: thrust and lateral force. Thrust is used to propel the fish forward, and lateral force tends to make the fish's head deviate from the course in the same direction as the tail. This side–to–side head movement is very obvious in a swimming eel, but fish with large, rigid heads have enough surface resistance to minimize the lateral movement.

Glossary:
> **serpentine:** like a snake
> **undulation:** wavelike motion

4. It can be inferred from paragraph 1 that a 60–centimeter fish can swim

   (A) at extremely high speeds
   (B) faster than a 30–centimeter fish
   (C) only about 10.4 kilometers per hour
   (D) fast enough to catch an eel

5. Which sentence below best expresses the essential information in the highlighted sentence in the passage? Incorrect choices change the meaning in important ways or leave out essential information.

   (A) The fish uses thrust when moving forward, and lateral force when moving backward or sideways.
   (B) Both force and lateral thrust are needed for the fish to maintain its intended course.
   (C) Thrust can be seen in the fish's head, while lateral force is seen in both its head and its tail.
   (D) Thrust pushes the fish forward, and lateral force pushes both its head and its tail to the same side.

6. Look at the four squares, **A**, **B**, **C**, and **D**, which indicate where the following sentence could be added to the passage. Where would the sentence best fit?

> **The front end of the body bends less than the back end, so each undulation increases in size as it travels along the body.**

We can understand how fish swim by studying the motion of a very flexible fish such as an eel. **A** The movement is serpentine, with undulations moving backward along the body by alternate contraction of the muscles on either side of the eel's body. **B** While the undulations move backward, the bending of the body pushes sideways against the water, producing a reactive force that is directed forward at an angle. **C** The movement has two components: thrust and lateral force. **D** Thrust is used to propel the fish forward, and lateral force tends to make the fish's head deviate from the course in the same direction as the tail. This side–to–side head movement is very obvious in a swimming eel, but fish with large, rigid heads have enough surface resistance to minimize the lateral movement.

QUESTIONS 7–10

Both the Greeks and the Romans minted coins. The Romans called the place where coins were made and stored by the Latin word *moneta*, the ancestor of the English word *money*. Even after coins were developed, however, the world was still a long way away from our current system of money. Each city made its own coins, with no common way of exchanging one type for another. Gradually, traders worked out different rates of exchange.

Another complication lay in the fact that for thousands of years, most people did not use money for important purchases. Although the wealthier classes used money for major transactions, ordinary people continued to barter for most things in their daily lives. For example, workers would be paid in food, clothing, and shelter, rather than in money. Farmers would grow food and make items for themselves, trading the tiny surplus for whatever they could not make or grow.

Paper money had a lot of advantages: it was lighter and easier to carry. It was also a lot cheaper to make. The development of paper money meant that people had grasped the difference between money as a symbol and money as something that was worth only the actual cost of the paper and ink in making a bill. The first known use of paper money was in China, around the year 1300. The first use of paper money in Europe was in Sweden in the 1600s, a time of extensive international trade and exploration. Because paper money made trade easier and more efficient, its use quickly caught on throughout the world.

7. The word another in paragraph 1 refers to

(A) place where coins were made
(B) city
(C) type of coin
(D) rate of exchange

8. Look at the four squares, **A**, **B**, **C**, and **D**, which indicate where the following sentence could be added to the passage. Where would the sentence best fit?

However, this was a long, slow process that often developed differently, depending on the individual trader.

Both the Greeks and the Romans minted coins. The Romans called the place where coins were made and stored by the Latin word *moneta*, the ancestor of the English word *money*. **A** Even after coins were developed, however, the world was still a long way away from our current system of money. **B** Each city made its own coins, with no common way of exchanging one type for another. **C** Gradually, traders worked out different rates of exchange. **D**

9. Which sentence below best expresses the essential information in the highlighted sentence in the passage? Incorrect choices change the meaning in important ways or leave out essential information.

(A) Because the majority of people did not have much money, they had to use other methods of exchange.

(B) Rich people used money for important purchases, but common people traded goods and services directly.

(C) The daily life of the rich and the poor differed mainly in the amount of money that was available to them.

(D) The wealthier classes had more control over how they used their money than did members of the lower classes

10. Look at the four squares, **A**, **B**, **C**, and **D**, which indicate where the following sentence could be added to the passage. Where would the sentence best fit?

As trade became an ever more important part of the world economy, people began to use paper money as well as coins.

A Paper money had a lot of advantages: it was lighter and easier to carry. **B** It was also a lot cheaper to make. **C** The development of paper money meant that people had grasped the difference between money as a symbol and money as something that was worth only the actual cost of the paper and ink in making a bill. The first known use of paper money was in China, around the year 1300. **D** The first use of paper money in Europe was in Sweden in the 1600s, a time of extensive international trade and exploration. Because paper money made trade easier and more efficient, its use quickly caught on throughout the world.

Answers to Exercises 1.8.A through 1.8.B are on page 570.

 EXTENSION

1. Outside of class, look in a newspaper, a magazine, or a university textbook. Select a short passage of one to three paragraphs. Make a photocopy and bring it to class. In class, work with a partner. Read the passage and underline the transitions, pronouns, and other key words and phrases that help make the passage coherent.

2. Outside of class, select a paragraph of four to six sentences from a magazine or a university textbook. Copy out the sentences in the form of a list. Now, *mix up the order of the sentences*. In class, write the list of sentences in the mixed–up, incorrect order on the board or an overhead projector transparency. As a class, put the sentences into a coherent order as a paragraph. What words and phrases are clues to coherence? What makes the order of sentences logical? Is there more than one possible order for the sentences? Does changing the order of sentences change the meaning of the paragraph?

3. Outside of class, select a paragraph of four to six sentences from a magazine or university textbook. Copy out the paragraph on an overhead projector transparency, *but omit one sentence*. Write the omitted sentence in a separate box above or below the paragraph. In class, work in pairs or small groups to determine where the omitted sentence would best fit in the paragraph. Compare your answer with the answers of other students and with the original passage.

PROGRESS – 1.7 through 1.8

QUIZ 7   *Time – 20 minutes*

Read the passages and choose the best answer to each question. Answer all questions about a passage on the basis of what is stated or implied in that passage.

HISTORY OF LANGUAGE

In evolutionary history, the development of language set humans apart from the rest of the animal kingdom. Spoken language originated when early humans began to string grunts and squeals together to form a sound–meaning system. Language provided humans with the tools to create ideas and then to communicate these ideas to other people.

As human knowledge and civilization expanded, a system that stored information became necessary. The first writing systems used pictures to represent objects. These early systems were successful in recording concrete details concerning trade and taxes, but they could not convey abstract ideas and emotions. Between 800 and 500 B.C., the ancient Greeks began to use a phonetic alphabet that used symbols to represent sounds, with each sound making up part of a word. Thus, written language became a means of mass communication.

The expansion of humanity from an oral society to one that also used the written word for communication was a defining point in human civilization. Early oral cultures required a tribal mentality with histories defined by family or clan perspectives, but writing allowed a broader, global perspective to emerge.

1. Which sentence below best expresses the essential information in the highlighted sentence in paragraph 1? Incorrect choices change the meaning in important ways or leave out essential information.

   (A) Humans evolved as the most powerful species after they developed language.
   (B) The creation of human language has its origins in the language of animals.
   (C) The emergence of language distinguished early humans from other animals.
   (D) Humans and animals developed completely different systems of communication.

2. Look at the four squares, **A**, **B**, **C**, and **D**, which indicate where the following sentence could be added to the passage. Where would the sentence best fit?

   Before written language evolved, there was no way of permanently recording language.

   A As human knowledge and civilization expanded, a system that stored information became necessary. The first writing systems used pictures to represent objects. **B** These early systems were successful in recording concrete details concerning trade and taxes, but they could not convey abstract ideas and emotions. **C** Between 800 and 500 B.C., the ancient Greeks began to use a phonetic alphabet that used symbols to represent sounds, with each sound making up part of a word. **D** Thus, written language became a means of mass communication.

3. Which sentence below best expresses the essential information in the highlighted sentence in paragraph 3? Incorrect choices change the meaning in important ways or leave out essential information.

(A) Civilization changed a great deal when humans rejected oral communication in favor of more complex systems of communication.

(B) Human societies were not able to define themselves until they developed written language.

(C) The power of language is humanity's most basic characteristic because language provides new tools of communication.

(D) An important development in human history occurred when writing was added to speaking as a form of communication.

PAIN

Virtually all animals experience pain. Pain is a distress call from the body signaling some damaging stimulus or internal disorder. It is one of the most important sensations because it is translated into a negative reaction, such as withdrawal from danger. Rare individuals who are born without the ability to feel pain may die from such conditions as a ruptured appendix because they are unaware of the danger.

Pain receptors are unspecialized nerve fiber endings that respond to a variety of stimuli signaling real or possible damage to tissues. Some groups of pain receptors respond to specific classes of chemicals released from damaged or inflamed tissue. When pain fibers respond to peptides released by injured cells, this is called slow pain. Fast pain responses—for example, a pinprick or hot or cold stimuli—are a more direct response of the nerve endings to mechanical or thermal stimuli.

There is no pain center in the **cerebral cortex**. However, discrete areas have been located in the brain stem where pain messages from various parts of the body terminate. These areas contain two kinds of small peptides, endorphins and enkephalins, which have activity similar to morphine or opium. When these peptides are released, they bind with specific opiate receptors in the midbrain, decreasing the perception of pain.

Glossary:
   cerebral cortex: part of the brain that controls high–level functions such as thought and sensation

4. Which sentence below best expresses the essential information in the highlighted sentence in paragraph 1? Incorrect choices change the meaning in important ways or leave out essential information.

(A) Escaping from danger is a negative reaction, but it is the most important thing an individual learns.

(B) The ability to sense pain is extremely important because pain signals the body to respond to a threat.

(C) Experiencing pain is one type of reaction to a negative stimulus; another type is avoiding danger.

(D) We experience a lot of sensations, and the most important ones are translated into appropriate actions.

5. Look at the four squares, **A**, **B**, **C**, and **D**, which indicate where the following sentence could be added to the passage. Where would the sentence best fit?

They respond to stimuli such as changes in temperature and pressure, and movement of the tissue.

    Pain receptors are unspecialized nerve fiber endings that respond to a variety of stimuli signaling real or possible damage to tissues. **A** Some groups of pain receptors respond to specific classes of chemicals released from damaged or inflamed tissue. **B** When pain fibers respond to peptides released by injured cells, this is called slow pain. **C** Fast pain responses—for example, a pinprick or hot or cold stimuli—are a more direct response of the nerve endings to mechanical or thermal stimuli. **D**

6. Look at the four squares, **A**, **B**, **C**, and **D**, which indicate where the following sentence could be added to the passage. Where would the sentence best fit?

Thus, they are considered the body's own natural painkillers.

    There is no pain center in the brain's cerebral cortex. **A** However, discrete areas have been located in the brain stem where pain messages from various parts of the body terminate. **B** These areas contain two kinds of small peptides, endorphins and enkephalins, which have activity similar to morphine or opium. **C** When these peptides are released, they bind with specific opiate receptors in the midbrain, decreasing the perception of pain. **D**

PRESTIGE

Prestige refers to a person's social standing—the level of respect that other people are willing to show. A person with high prestige is honored or esteemed by other people, while a person with low prestige is disrespected or marginalized. Prestige is a valued resource for people at all levels of a society, and this can be seen among inner–city youth, where to disrespect or "diss" someone has negative consequences. Exactly what qualities are respected will vary from one society to another.

In the United States, the top–status occupations are the professions—physicians, lawyers, professors, and clergy—requiring many years of education and training. At the other end of the hierarchy, the lowest prestige is associated with occupations requiring little formal education—for example, bus drivers, sanitation workers, and janitors. Prestige is linked to income, but there are exceptions, such as college professors, who have high prestige but relatively low salaries compared to physicians and lawyers. Conversely, some low–prestige workers receive high union wages and benefits. Criminals are often well rewarded with income and respect in their communities, while politicians—many of whom are wealthy—are frequently less respected than occupations such as secretary and bank teller.

7. Which sentence below best expresses the essential information in the highlighted sentence in paragraph 1? Incorrect choices change the meaning in important ways or leave out essential information.

  (A) The most valuable resource in any society is prestige, but young people who disrespect others reject this.
  (B) People at all social levels value prestige, and to disrespect another is punished, for example, among urban youth.
  (C) The disrespectful behavior of some young people shows that prestige is not valued equally throughout a society.
  (D) There are serious consequences when teenagers from the inner city do not show respect for other groups.

8. Look at the four squares, **A**, **B**, **C**, and **D**, which indicate where the following sentence could be added to the passage. Where would the sentence best fit?

  Some societies honor wisdom and old age; others value warriors or youth.

  Prestige refers to a person's social standing—the level of respect that other people are willing to show. **A** A person with high prestige is honored or esteemed by other people, while a person with low prestige is disrespected or marginalized. **B** Prestige is a valued resource for people at all levels of a society, and this can be seen among inner–city youth, where to disrespect or "diss" someone has negative consequences. **C** Exactly what qualities are respected will vary from one society to another. **D**

9. Which sentence below best expresses the essential information in the highlighted sentence in paragraph 2? Incorrect choices change the meaning in important ways or leave out essential information.

(A) If an occupation has high prestige, then it usually has a high income; college professors, physicians, and lawyers are good examples.

(B) Occupational status depends on income, although there is a wide range of income levels in occupations such as college professor.

(C) The fact that college professors have high prestige but relatively low incomes is an exception to the rule that prestige and income are related.

(D) It is unfair for college professors to have low salaries compared to other high–prestige professions that have high salaries.

10. Look at the four squares, **A**, **B**, **C**, and **D**, which indicate where the following sentence could be added to the passage. Where would the sentence best fit?

In postindustrial societies, prestige is linked to occupational status, although income is also important.

   A In the United States, the top–status occupations are the professions—physicians, lawyers, professors, and clergy—requiring many years of education and training. **B** At the other end of the hierarchy, the lowest prestige is associated with occupations requiring little formal education—for example, bus drivers, sanitation workers, and janitors. Prestige is linked to income, but there are exceptions, such as college professors, who have high prestige but relatively low salaries compared to physicians and lawyers. **C** Conversely, some low–prestige workers receive high union wages and benefits. **D** Criminals are often well rewarded with income and respect in their communities, while politicians—many of whom are wealthy—are frequently less respected than occupations such as secretary and bank teller.

Answers to Reading Quiz 7 are on page 570.

Record your score on the Progress Chart on page 693.

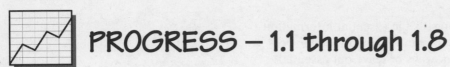

PROGRESS – 1.1 through 1.8

QUIZ 8   *Time – 40 minutes*

Read the passages and choose the best answer to each question. Answer all questions about a passage on the basis of what is stated or implied in that passage.

THE LONGHOUSE

The people of the longhouse lived in fortified villages in elevated areas that were easy to defend and were located near a water supply. Twenty–foot palisades surrounded a group of longhouses and acted as a defensive wall that also kept forest animals from foraging within the village. The longhouse was the typical housing unit within the stockade. A number of families were housed within each longhouse, which varied in size from 20 by 16 feet to huge multiple family structures of 60 by 18 feet. In the more populous villages, longhouses could be more than 300 feet long. The longhouse was more than just a shelter; it was the basic unit upon which the entire society was constructed.

In building the longhouse, a row of forked poles was placed in the ground, between four and five feet apart. Cross poles were lashed to the forked uprights to form an arched roof. Slender poles or rafters were then secured to the roof frame, and traverse poles were added to further strengthen the overhead structure. Large pieces of bark were then tied to the frame. An outer set of poles kept the bark in place on the sides and roof. Smoke holes were built into the roof at about twenty–foot intervals. Two families shared the stone–lined hearth beneath each smoke hole.

At each end of the longhouse was a door with a covering of animal hide or hinged bark that could be lifted up for entering and exiting. Along each inside wall were bunks that served as beds at night and benches in the day. Corn, dried fish, and other foods hung from overhead. The dwelling was compartmentalized to accommodate each family. At the front of the longhouse, over the door, carved images of clan symbols represented the families living there.

1. The word palisades in paragraph 1 is closest in meaning to

   (A) roads
   (B) fences
   (C) bridges
   (D) ponds

2. The author discusses the dimensions of longhouses in paragraph 1 in order to

   (A) describe the village's strong defenses
   (B) illustrate the importance of certain families
   (C) explain why rivalry occurred between families
   (D) show that villages varied in population

3. Which sentence below best expresses the essential information in the highlighted sentence in paragraph 1? Incorrect choices change the meaning in important ways or leave out essential information.

   (A) The largest longhouses could provide shelter to everyone who was a member of the society.
   (B) The longhouse was basically a shelter that also served important functions related to the defense of the village.
   (C) Everyone in the society had a role in building the longhouse because a variety of construction skills were needed.
   (D) The longhouse not only provided housing for families but also formed the foundation of the whole society.

4. The frame of a longhouse was constructed of

   (A) tree bark
   (B) animal hide
   (C) wooden poles
   (D) flat stones

5. The word dwelling in paragraph 3 refers to

   (A) longhouse
   (B) door
   (C) corn
   (D) dried fish

6. According to the passage, all of the following statements are true EXCEPT

   (A) Each longhouse was a separate village.
   (B) People cooked and stored food in a longhouse.
   (C) The longhouse was like an apartment building.
   (D) The people of the longhouse belonged to clans.

7. Look at the four squares, **A**, **B**, **C**, and **D**, which indicate where the following sentence could be added to the passage. Where would the sentence best fit?

   Elm, ash, cedar, fir, or spruce trees were the usual sources of bark.

   In building the longhouse, a row of forked poles was placed in the ground, between four and five feet apart. Cross poles were lashed to the forked uprights to form an arched roof. **A** Slender poles or rafters were then secured to the roof frame, and traverse poles were added to further strengthen the overhead structure. **B** Large pieces of bark were then tied to the frame. **C** An outer set of poles kept the bark in place on the sides and roof. Smoke holes were built into the roof at about twenty–foot intervals. **D** Two families shared the stone–lined hearth beneath each smoke hole.

LANGSTON HUGHES

Among the many talented African American writers connected with the Harlem Renaissance of the 1920s and 1930s, Langston Hughes was the most popular in his time. His two most important achievements were the incorporation of the rhythms of black music into his poetry and the creation of an authentic black folk speaker in the character of Jesse B. Semple. Through both poetry and storytelling, Hughes captured in written form the dominant oral and improvisatory traditions of black culture.

Langston Hughes was born in Missouri in 1902. He began to write poetry in high school and later attended Columbia University in New York. After one year at university, Hughes commenced a nomadic life in the United States and Europe. He shipped out as a merchant marine and worked in a Paris nightclub, all the while writing and publishing poetry. His prolific literary career was launched in 1926 with the publication of his first book, *The Weary Blues*, a collection of poems on African American themes set to rhythms from jazz and blues. His first novel appeared in 1930, and from that point on Hughes was known as "the bard of Harlem."

In the activist 1930s, Hughes was a public figure. He worked as a journalist, published works in several media, and founded African American theaters in New York, Chicago, and Los Angeles. Hughes's concern with race, mainly in an urban setting, is evident in his poetry, plays, screenplays, novels, and short stories. His poetry includes lyrics about black life and black pride as well as poems of racial protest. His major prose writings are those concerned with the character Jesse B. Semple, a shrewd but supposedly ignorant Harlem resident nicknamed Simple. Simple was a wise fool, an honest man who saw through sham and spoke plainly. The Simple stories were originally published as newspaper sketches and later collected in five book volumes.

By the 1960s, readers preferred themes that reflected the struggles of the times, and Hughes's writings were overshadowed by those of a younger generation of black poets. However, in more recent decades, scholars and readers have rediscovered Hughes and regard him as a major literary and social influence. His poetry and stories remain an enduring legacy of the Harlem Renaissance, and for this reason his position in the American canon is secure.

8. It can be inferred from paragraph 1 that the Harlem Renaissance is the name of

   (A) a university
   (B) a literary movement
   (C) a newspaper
   (D) a book of poems

9. The word prolific in paragraph 2 is closest in meaning to

   (A) surprising
   (B) transitory
   (C) mature
   (D) productive

10. What is significant about *The Weary Blues*?

    (A) It expressed themes of protest and unrest.
    (B) Hughes wrote it when he was in high school.
    (C) It put the rhythms of black music into poetry.
    (D) Hughes performed it in a Paris nightclub.

11. According to the passage, Langston Hughes did all of the following EXCEPT

    (A) teach university courses
    (B) write novels and screenplays
    (C) start theater companies
    (D) set poetry to jazz and blues

12. The word sham in paragraph 3 is closest in meaning to

    (A) falsehood
    (B) the media
    (C) blindness
    (D) literature

13. The word those in paragraph 4 refers to

    (A) readers
    (B) themes
    (C) struggles
    (D) writings

14. Which sentence below best expresses the essential information in the highlighted sentence in paragraph 4? Incorrect choices change the meaning in important ways or leave out essential information.

    (A) The writings of Hughes, although still well known, are not as relevant today as they were at the time of the Harlem Renaissance.
    (B) Hughes attained prominence in American literature because his writings represent the accomplishments of the Harlem Renaissance.
    (C) Today Hughes is most remembered for the humorous poetry and stories that made Americans feel secure in the 1930s.
    (D) Americans like the old–style rhythms of Hughes's poems and stories, and this is why a musical composition was dedicated to him.

15. Look at the four squares, **A**, **B**, **C**, and **D**, which indicate where the following sentence could be added to the passage. Where would the sentence best fit?

    The success of this book helped finance Hughes's further education at Lincoln University in Pennsylvania.

    Langston Hughes was born in Missouri in 1902. He began to write poetry in high school and later attended Columbia University in New York. **A** After one year at university, Hughes commenced a nomadic life in the United States and Europe. **B** He shipped out as a merchant marine and worked in a Paris nightclub, all the while writing and publishing poetry. **C** His prolific literary career was launched in 1926 with the publication of his first book, *The Weary Blues*, a collection of poems on African American themes set to rhythms from jazz and blues. **D** His first novel appeared in 1930, and from that point on Hughes was known as "the bard of Harlem."

COASTS AND SHORES

The terms "coast" and "shore" are often used interchangeably, but there are actually differences between them. One difference is that "coast" applies only to oceans, but "shore" can apply to other bodies of water as well. A shore is the zone at the edge of an ocean, lake, or river that is subject to the regular action of tides, waves, and currents. The shore is the area between the high–water mark and the low–water mark, and thus every part of it is sometimes underwater. The shifting line where the shore meets the water is called the shoreline. An ocean shore extends seaward to the edge of the continental shelf—the submerged edge of the continental block—or to the beginning of the continental slope, which extends down into deep water.

A coast is the land just inland from the shore, beyond the usual reach of high water. On the shore side, the boundary of the coast—the coastline—may be either a cliff face or a line marking the inland limit of tidewater. On the landward side, the boundary is usually the edge of a highland or some other kind of terrain distinct from the shore; however, some coastal boundaries have no clear distinction. Many coasts are sea bottoms uplifted by earthquakes to become dry land, so they may show some features of shores, even though the sea never reaches them.

In areas where river valleys meet the sea along a rocky coast, bays are likely to occur. The direction of the structural "grain" of the coastal rock affects the shape of the coastline. If the grain is mostly parallel to the coast, as along the Oregon coast, the mouths of few rivers will indent the coastline because river valleys tend to follow the grain. Such coastlines—called Pacific type—are likely to be smooth, straight, or gently curving. On the other hand, if the grain of the rock is at an angle to the coast, as in Maine and Norway, many more valleys will reach the coastline, forming closely spaced bays. Such coastlines are of the Atlantic type.

Coasts and shores are areas of continuous change. Like all other terrain, coasts and shores are subject to the processes of weathering, erosion, deposition, and tectonic activity. Unlike other terrain, shores are also subject to the daily action of tides, waves, and currents. These forces erode rocky shores and transport sand and debris from place to place, depleting some beaches and building up others. During storms, waves crash against sea cliffs, weakening them and creating rockfalls and landslides. Storm waves batter beaches and—especially at high tide—rush beyond them, sweeping away docks, roads, and buildings. Over time, coastal processes change as tectonic activity raises, lowers, and disrupts the terrain and the sea bottoms near shores. Coastal processes are also affected by changes in sea level due to melting glaciers and changes in the density and temperature of ocean water.

16. Why does the author discuss the terms "coast" and "shore" in paragraph 1?

    (A) To show how each term has changed over time
    (B) To describe how a coast can change into a shore
    (C) To clarify the distinctions between the two terms
    (D) To explain why more people use the term "coast"

17. The word submerged in paragraph 1 is closest in meaning to

    (A) moveable
    (B) irregular
    (C) steep
    (D) underwater

18. All of the following statements accurately describe coasts and shores EXCEPT

  (A) A shore is the area at the water's edge, and a coast is the land next to the shore.
  (B) A coast extends to the continental shelf; a shore extends inland to a highland.
  (C) Only oceans have coasts, but lakes, rivers, and oceans all have shores.
  (D) A coast is beyond the high–water mark, but a shore is at times underwater.

19. According to the passage, why do many coasts have characteristics of shores?

  (A) "Coast" and "shore" are the same thing.
  (B) Both coasts and shores are shaped by tides.
  (C) Many coasts are former sea bottoms.
  (D) Shorelines move inland because of erosion.

20. It can be inferred from paragraph 3 that the Oregon coast is

  (A) relatively straight
  (B) lined with cliffs
  (C) very rainy
  (D) indented with bays

21. Which of the following is given as a cause of the different shapes of Pacific and Atlantic type coastlines?

  (A) A difference in direction of the structural "grain" of coastal rock
  (B) Different rates of erosion caused by tides, waves, and currents
  (C) A difference in the frequency of offshore tectonic activity
  (D) Differences in population and the amount of developed land

22. Which sentence below best expresses the essential information in the highlighted sentence in paragraph 4? Incorrect choices change the meaning in important ways or leave out essential information.

  (A) The forces of erosion improve the appearance and comfort of some beaches, while completely destroying others.
  (B) Some shores are very rocky, and others have beautiful sandy beaches that encourage people to move there.
  (C) Tides, waves, and currents wear away shores in some places and deposit sand and rock elsewhere along the shore.
  (D) Because of powerful natural forces that erode shores, it is impossible to predict which beaches are safe to build on.

23. The word them in paragraph 4 refers to

  (A) beaches
  (B) storms
  (C) waves
  (D) cliffs

24. The word batter in paragraph 4 is closest in meaning to

  (A) create
  (B) strike
  (C) improve
  (D) avoid

25. Look at the four squares, **A**, **B**, **C**, and **D**, which indicate where the following sentence could be added to the passage. Where would the sentence best fit?

The straightness or irregularity of a coastline depends on the processes that have shaped it.

A In areas where river valleys meet the sea along a rocky coast, bays are likely to occur. The direction of the structural "grain" of the coastal rock affects the shape of the coastline. **B** If the grain is mostly parallel to the coast, as along the Oregon coast, the mouths of few rivers will indent the coastline because river valleys tend to follow the grain. **C** Such coastlines—called Pacific type—are likely to be smooth, straight, or gently curving. **D** On the other hand, if the grain of the rock is at an angle to the coast, as in Maine and Norway, many more valleys will reach the coastline, forming closely spaced bays. Such coastlines are of the Atlantic type.

Answers to Reading Quiz 8 are on page 571.

Record your score on the Progress Chart on page 693.

1.9 Summarizing Important Ideas

FOCUS

Read the following passage:

> Several companies are classified as small businesses, including gift shops, cafés, video stores, self–service laundries, and shoe repair shops. Franchise operations such as fast food restaurants and gas stations may also be small businesses. Real estate is often a small business, and consultants in various fields run their own small businesses from an office in their home.
>
> The three most common types of small businesses are sole proprietorships, partnerships, and corporations. In a sole proprietorship, one person—the proprietor— owns the business. In a partnership, two or more people own the business together. In both sole proprietorships and partnerships, the owners keep the company's profits, but they are also liable for the company's debts. In the third type of business, the corporation, the owners are usually the officers, and they cannot be held personally responsible for the firm's debts.

Which sentences below are important ideas in the passage? Check all of the sentences that are major ideas.

___ A variety of businesses are considered to be small businesses.
___ Video stores and fast food franchises are expanding elements in the service economy.
___ Sole proprietorships, partnerships, and corporations are the three main types of small businesses.
___ A sole proprietorship has one owner.
___ A corporation's owners are not responsible for the company's debts.

The two most important ideas in the passage are:

> A variety of businesses are considered to be small businesses.
> Sole proprietorships, partnerships, and corporations are the three main types of small businesses.

The other sentences either are about something that is not mentioned or are minor ideas in the passage.

 DO YOU KNOW...?

1. To **summarize** is to state the major ideas from a passage in a shorter form. A **summary** is a brief report of the most important ideas and information in the passage. A summary does not include minor ideas or supporting details.

2. TOEFL questions about summarizing ideas have special directions. The questions look like this:

> An introductory sentence for a brief summary of the passage is provided below. Complete the summary by selecting the THREE answer choices that express the most important ideas in the passage. Some sentences do not belong in the summary because they express ideas that are not presented in the passage or are minor ideas in the passage. *This question is worth 2 points.*

3. In this type of question, you use the computer mouse to drag answer choices to the summary table. The summary table fills the computer screen, but you can return to the passage while you are answering the question. You may take notes and you may use your notes to help you answer the question.

4. The summary question is worth 2 points, and it is possible to receive partial credit. If you choose all three correct answers, you earn 2 points. If you choose two correct answers, you earn 1 point. If you choose only one correct answer, or no correct answers, you receive no credit for the question.

5. The reading skill of skimming will help you summarize the important information in the passage. ***Skimming*** is reading through the passage quickly to understand its overall meaning, purpose, and organization.

6. In questions about summarizing information, the incorrect answer choices may be incorrect because they:

   ⟿ are minor ideas or supporting details instead of major ideas;
   ⟿ are inaccurate or untrue according to the passage; or
   ⟿ are irrelevant or not mentioned in the passage.

7. Here is an example:

THE HISTORY OF THE PIANO

As early as the twelfth century, there was an instrument consisting of a flat, rectangular wooden box of strings that players struck with sticks. Its name, "dulcimer," came from a Latin term meaning "sweet song." In the late seventeenth century, a harpsichord maker in Florence was seeking ways to vary the volume of plucked harpsichord strings. He remembered the dulcimer's ability to vary its volume according to the force of the strike, so he experimented on his harpsichords. He eventually built an instrument that could indeed play both softly and loudly ("piano" and "forte"), giving it the name "pianoforte," which was later shortened to "piano."

Over the next century, piano construction was constantly improving. To preserve the strings, the piano's hammers were covered in a soft material—usually leather—which imparted a dull sound in the low and middle registers. Improvements accelerated as concert halls grew in size and composers became more demanding. By 1800, it was clear that composers preferred the piano to the harpsichord for its greater power and wider range of expression. Beethoven's sonatas, written between 1783 and 1822, illustrate not only his compositional development but also the ever–greater refinements available on the piano, including its widening range of notes.

In domestic settings, the piano was proving popular, but smaller rooms required instruments that took up less space. The so–called "square piano" needed less room, while the "giraffe piano" needed even less floor space but much height because it resembled a grand piano stood on end. The first upright "parlor piano" was made in Germany around 1770, and this became the chief means of providing home musical entertainment up till the early decades of the twentieth century, when the gramophone replaced it.

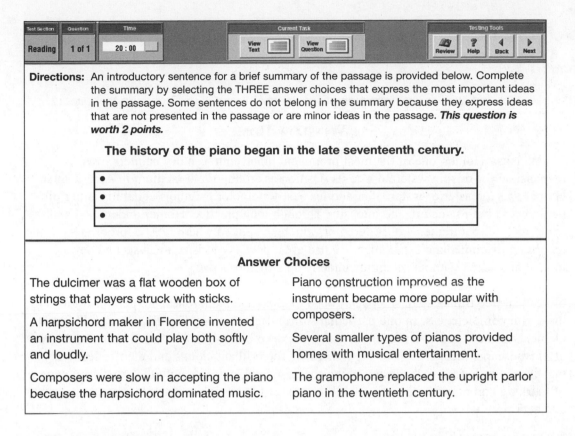

A summary includes only the major ideas and most important information in a passage. Therefore, the correct answers are:

> A harpsichord maker in Florence invented an instrument that could play both softly and loudly.
> Piano construction improved as the instrument became more popular with composers.
> Several smaller types of pianos provided homes with musical entertainment.

Some key information in the passage is:

> …a harpsichord maker in Florence…built an instrument that could indeed play both softly and loudly….
> Improvements accelerated as…composers became more demanding. By 1800, it was clear that composers preferred the piano….
> In domestic settings, the piano was proving popular, but smaller rooms required instruments that took up less space. …"square piano"…"giraffe piano"… "parlor piano"….

Why are the other three answers incorrect? *The dulcimer was a flat wooden box of strings that players struck with sticks* is a minor idea. *Composers were slow in accepting the piano because the harpsichord dominated music* is not mentioned in the passage. *The gramophone replaced the upright parlor piano in the twentieth century* is a minor idea.

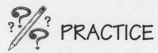 PRACTICE

Exercise 1.9.A

Read the passages and answer each question based on what is stated or implied in that passage.

WINSLOW HOMER

Winslow Homer, one of the most prominent nineteenth–century painters, was responsible for raising watercolor to its position as an important medium in American art. Homer was a master of watercolor, and his best watercolor paintings equal his larger oil paintings in both structure and intensity. Through long practice, Homer understood and exploited the requirements of watercolor, which he applied where most appropriate—to the recording of immediate experience. He had great powers of visual analysis and never looked at a scene without seeing its underlying structure.

Some of Homer's watercolors of the Adirondack woods, with their complicated weaving of vertical tree trunks against a background of deep autumnal tones, are demonstrations of masterful completeness. In one particular Adirondack painting, *The Blue Boat* (1892), all elements come together with perfect unity: the deep blue of the boat's hull, the green and gold landscape, the alertness of the fishermen, the brilliant clouds and their reflections on the water. Furthermore, its design unites the structural elements with the artist's enjoyment of marking and coloring the paper—all are blended as though in a single moment of vision and action.

1–2. An introductory sentence for a brief summary of the passage is provided below. Complete the summary by selecting the THREE answer choices that express the most important ideas in the passage. Some sentences do not belong in the summary because they express ideas that are not presented in the passage or are minor ideas in the passage. ***This question is worth 2 points.***

The painter Winslow Homer made watercolor an important medium in American art.
•
•
•

Answer Choices

(A) Homer was a master of watercolor and used it to record immediate experience.

(B) Homer is best known for his dramatic oil paintings of seascapes.

(C) His understanding of structure is shown in watercolors of masterful completeness.

(D) Winslow Homer was born in Massachusetts in 1836.

(E) *The Blue Boat* is a watercolor painting of fishermen in a boat on the water.

(F) Homer's Adirondack watercolors combine structural elements and color in perfect unity.

MORAINES

The term *moraine* refers to the rock debris carried or deposited by a glacier. The term applies to the debris moved along within the glacier or on its surface, the debris left behind after the glacier melts, and the landforms made up of these debris deposits. The debris transported by a glacier is produced either by erosion of the rock beneath the glacier or by erosion on the slopes rising above the surface of the glacier. Material eroded by the glacier is carried primarily at the base of the glacier and along the outer margins of the glacier.

While rivers sort transported rock according to size, a glacier transports its material like a factory conveyer belt, moving the largest blocks and the finest dust next to each other at the same rate of movement over the same distance. Thus, moraine debris remains unsorted both during its transport and after it has been deposited. This unsorted glacial material is called drift. Some moraines are composed only of coarse material and large boulders, while others contain large quantities of finer–grained material such as silt and clay.

Once the glacial ice has retreated, the moraine deposits are left exposed on the land surface. The various landforms—moraines—indicate the position of the debris within or on the glacier during the glacier's movement. Their shape and composition also provide information about the shape, mass, and ice flow of the glacier.

3–4. An introductory sentence for a brief summary of the passage is provided below. Complete the summary by selecting the THREE answer choices that express the most important ideas in the passage. Some sentences do not belong in the summary because they express ideas that are not presented in the passage or are minor ideas in the passage. *This question is worth 2 points.*

A moraine is the rock debris carried or deposited by a glacier.
•
•
•

Answer Choices

(A) The mapping of moraines is an important part of fieldwork in the study of glaciers.

(B) Glaciers transport debris from the erosion of rock below the glacier or from the slopes above the glacier.

(C) Rivers sort rocks according to size while the rocks are being transported.

(D) We can compare the movement of a glacier to that of a factory conveyer belt.

(E) Moraine debris may include large and small rocks that remain unsorted both during and after transport.

(F) After a glacier melts, the moraine deposits remain as various landforms that are also called moraines.

CULTURAL EVOLUTION

The history of life is the story of biological evolution on a changing planet, and at no time has change ever been as rapid as in the age of humans. The evolution of humans and their culture has had enormous consequences, making humans a new force in the history of life.

Cultural evolution has occurred in stages, beginning with the nomads who hunted and gathered food on the African grasslands two million years ago. These hunter–gatherers made tools, organized communal activities, and divided labor. Next came the development of agriculture in several parts of the world 10 to 15 thousand years ago. Agriculture led to permanent settlements, the first cities, and trade among societies. An important cultural leap was the Industrial Revolution, which began in the eighteenth century. Since then, new technology has escalated exponentially, and so has the human impact on the planet.

Throughout this cultural evolution, from simple hunter–gatherers to high–tech societies, humans have not changed much biologically. Our knowledge is stored not in our genes but in the product of thousands of years of human experience. Cultural evolution has enabled us to defy our physical limitations and shortcut biological evolution. We no longer have to wait to adapt to our environment through natural selection; we simply change the environment to meet our needs. We are the dominant species of life and bring environmental change wherever we go.

5–6. An introductory sentence for a brief summary of the passage is provided below. Complete the summary by selecting the THREE answer choices that express the most important ideas in the passage. Some sentences do not belong in the summary because they express ideas that are not presented in the passage or are minor ideas in the passage. ***This question is worth 2 points.***

Cultural evolution has made humans a new force in the history of life.
•
•
•

Answer Choices

(A) Biological evolution is the most important force in the history of life.

(B) There have been several stages in the evolution of human culture.

(C) The development of agriculture 10 to 15 thousand years ago resulted in permanent settlements, the first cities, and trade.

(D) Human technology has advanced rapidly, increasing the human role in environmental change.

(E) Cultural evolution has allowed humans to change their environment, thus avoiding the need for biological evolution.

(F) Humans are changing the world faster than many other species can adapt.

SHAKESPEARE'S ROMANCES

Shakespeare's late comedies—including *Cymbeline*, *The Tempest* and *The Winter's Tale*—are classified as romances. They are based on a tradition of romantic literature going back at least to ancient Greece, in which the central theme of love serves as the trigger for extraordinary adventures. Love is subjected to abnormal strains, often involving separation, jealousy, and other elements of tragedy. There are also fantastic journeys to exotic lands, and absurd coincidences and mistaken identities that complicate the plot, but everything is resolved in the traditional happy ending of comedy.

All of Shakespeare's romances share a number of these classical themes, such as the theme of separation and reunion of loved ones, particularly family members. Daughters are separated from parents, and wives from husbands, in *Cymbeline* and *The Winter's Tale*. Sons are separated from fathers in *The Winter's Tale* and *The Tempest*. The related idea of exile also occurs, with the banished characters—usually rulers or future rulers—restored to their rightful position at the end of the play. The theme of jealousy is prominent, with the conclusion that love requires patience in times of adversity. The characters are frequently subjected to long journeys, many involving shipwrecks. Magical developments arise and supernatural beings appear, most notably in *The Tempest*, in which the leading character is a sorcerer.

7–8. An introductory sentence for a brief summary of the passage is provided below. Complete the summary by selecting the THREE answer choices that express the most important ideas in the passage. Some sentences do not belong in the summary because they express ideas that are not presented in the passage or are minor ideas in the passage. *This question is worth 2 points.*

Shakespeare's late comedies are considered romances because they are based on an older romantic tradition.
•
•
•

Answer Choices

(A) The main theme of love provides the characters with remarkable adventures in strange lands.

(B) The romances involve many elements of tragedy but have the traditional happy ending of comedy.

(C) Shakespeare's romances are less well known than his comedies, tragedies, and history plays.

(D) *Cymbeline*, *The Tempest* and *The Winter's Tale* are examples of Shakespeare's romances.

(E) In many of the plays, love is subjected to jealousy and separation but ultimately to resolution and reunion.

(F) The romances often feature shipwrecks that separate characters from family members and lovers.

WATER LOSS

Metabolic activities require a constant supply of certain materials such as water, oxygen, and salts, and cells must replace these materials by withdrawing them from the environment. Humans lose water by evaporation from respiratory and body surfaces and must replenish such losses by drinking water, by obtaining water from food, and by retaining metabolic water formed in cells by oxidation of foods, especially carbohydrates.

Humans obtain half of their total water requirement by drinking. With enough water to drink, the human body can withstand extremely high temperatures while preventing a rise in body temperature. When the surrounding air temperature rises, the body's internal environment responds to this change by the evaporative cooling method of sweating. The ability to keep cool in this way was impressively demonstrated in the eighteenth century by a British scientist who stayed for 45 minutes in a room heated to 260 degrees Fahrenheit (126 degrees Celsius). He survived uninjured and his body temperature did not rise because he continuously drank water and sweated. A steak he had brought into the room with him, however, was thoroughly cooked.

Sweating rates may exceed three liters of water per hour under such conditions and cannot be tolerated unless the lost water is replaced. Without water to drink, the body will continue to sweat and lose water. When the water deficit exceeds 10 percent of the body weight, collapse occurs, and when the water deficit reaches about 15 to 20 percent, death occurs.

9–10. An introductory sentence for a brief summary of the passage is provided below. Complete the summary by selecting the THREE answer choices that express the most important ideas in the passage. Some sentences do not belong in the summary because they express ideas that are not presented in the passage or are minor ideas in the passage. *This question is worth 2 points.*

The human body needs a constant supply of water for metabolism.
•
•
•

Answer Choices

(A) Water lost through evaporation from respiratory and body surfaces must be replaced.

(B) Water is an important product of the oxidation of carbohydrates.

(C) Given water to drink, humans can tolerate high temperatures by using the cooling method of sweating.

(D) A scientist remained in a 260–degree room for 45 minutes, which was long enough to cook a steak.

(E) Unless water is replaced by drinking, continuous sweating will eventually lead to collapse and death.

(F) No human has ever survived more than two days in a desert without water.

Exercise 1.9.B

Read the passages and answer each question based on what is stated or implied in that passage.

MATHEMATICIANS

Like a painter or a poet, a mathematician is a creator of patterns, but mathematical patterns are made with ideas rather than paint or words. Mathematicians are motivated by the belief that they may be able to create a pattern that is entirely new, one that changes forever the way that others think about the mathematical order. Mathematics allows great speculative freedom, and mathematicians can create any kind of system they want. However, in the end, every mathematical theory must be relevant to physical reality, either directly or by importance to the body of mathematics.

Mathematicians have an exceptional ability to manage long chains of reasoning. They routinely develop theories from very simple contexts and then apply them to very complex ones. For example, they may develop a formula for the movement of an ameba and then try to apply it to successive levels of the animal kingdom, concluding with a theory of human walking.

An extended chain of reasoning may be intuitive, and many mathematicians report that they sense a solution long before they have worked out each step in detail. However, even when guided by intuition, they must eventually work out the solution in exact detail if they are to convince others of its validity. They must demonstrate the solution without any errors or omissions in definition or in line of reasoning. In fact, errors of omission (forgetting a step) or of commission (making some assumption that is untrue) can destroy the value of a mathematical contribution. The mathematician must be rigorous: no fact can be accepted unless it has been proved by steps conforming to universally accepted principles.

At the center of mathematical talent lies the ability to recognize significant problems and then to solve them. One source of delight for mathematicians is finding the solution to a problem that has long been considered insoluble. Other accomplishments are inventing a new field of mathematics and discovering links between otherwise separate fields of mathematics.

1. Which sentence below best expresses the essential information in the highlighted sentence in paragraph 1? Incorrect choices change the meaning in important ways or leave out essential information.

   (A) Mathematicians are more creative than ordinary people in the ways that they think about patterns and order.

   (B) Motivation is less important to mathematicians than the belief in their own ability to change other people.

   (C) Mathematicians use their creative talent to motivate other people to look for new ways to solve important problems.

   (D) The idea of establishing a completely new way of understanding mathematics is what motivates mathematicians.

2. According to the passage, why must mathematicians be able to manage long chains of reasoning?

   (A) A solution must be demonstrated in detail to convince others of its validity.

   (B) Mathematicians enjoy creating complex solutions to simple problems.

   (C) There are often no computer programs that are able to solve the problem.

   (D) Mathematical problems involve abstract ideas that are difficult to explain.

3. The word insoluble in paragraph 4 is closest in meaning to

  (A) irrelevant to reality
  (B) not mathematical
  (C) impossible to solve
  (D) not interesting to others

4–5. An introductory sentence for a brief summary of the passage is provided below. Complete the summary by selecting the THREE answer choices that express the most important ideas in the passage. Some sentences do not belong in the summary because they express ideas that are not presented in the passage or are minor ideas in the passage. *This question is worth 2 points.*

The work of mathematicians involves several skills and abilities.
•
•
•

Answer Choices

(A) Mathematicians share many characteristics with painters and poets.

(B) Mathematicians must be able to recognize significant problems and find relevant solutions to them.

(C) The ability to handle long chains of reasoning is essential in developing complex theories.

(D) Mathematicians often have to explain mathematical concepts in simple terms to people from other fields.

(E) Mathematicians must be rigorous in demonstrating solutions in precise detail with no errors in definition or reasoning.

(F) The ability to find links between separate fields of mathematics is a test of mathematical talent.

WHITE–COLLAR CRIME

A variety of illegal acts committed by people in the course of their employment, for their own personal gain, are collectively known as white–collar crime. Embezzlement, theft, and trading securities on the basis of insider information are common forms of white–collar crime. The majority of cases involve low–level employees who steal because they are under temporary financial stress. Many plan to put the money back as soon as possible but may never do so. Their crimes are usually never discovered because the amounts of money are small, no one notices the loss, and law enforcement agencies have few resources for investigating this type of crime.

However, there are some very large cases of white–collar crime, such as multimillion–dollar stock market or banking scams that take years to discover and are extremely difficult and expensive to prosecute. In the 1980s, hundreds of executives of American savings and loan associations took advantage of a change in the law that allowed them to make unsecured loans to friends and relatives—which they then did, in the amount of $500 billion in unpaid debt. Only a few of those executives were prosecuted, and little of the money was recovered. American taxpayers ultimately covered the amount at a cost of about $4,000 per person.

White–collar crime is not confined to the business sector. Government employment, especially at the city level, also provides opportunities to line one's pockets. For example, building inspectors accept bribes and kickbacks, auctioneers rig sales of seized property, and full–time employees receive welfare payments.

Although white–collar crime is less violent than street crime, it involves far more money and harm to the public than crimes committed by street criminals. It is likely that there are more criminals in the office suites than in the streets, yet the nature of white–collar crime makes it difficult to uncover the offenses and pursue the offenders. As the economy shifts from manufacturing to services and electronic commerce, opportunities for white–collar crime will multiply, while the technology needed to stop such crimes will lag behind.

6. Why does the author mention savings and loan associations in paragraph 2?

  (A) To compare stock market scams with savings and loan scams
  (B) To give an example of a very large case of white–collar crime
  (C) To argue in favor of changing the law to restrict unsecured loans
  (D) To explain why American taxpayers do not trust the government

7. The phrase line one's pockets in paragraph 3 means

  (A) bribe officials
  (B) advance one's career
  (C) take money illegally
  (D) hide one's crimes

8. Which sentence below best expresses the essential information in the highlighted sentence in paragraph 4? Incorrect choices change the meaning in important ways or leave out essential information.

  (A) White–collar criminals may be more numerous than street criminals but are difficult to catch because the crimes often go unnoticed.
  (B) It is easier to solve crimes that take place in the office than to solve crimes that occur in the streets, but street crimes are more serious.
  (C) White–collar crime is very similar to street crime, although street crime gets more attention because it is more offensive.
  (D) It takes a very long time to discover white–collar crime and identify the criminals, but street crimes are solved relatively quickly.

9–10. An introductory sentence for a brief summary of the passage is provided below. Complete the summary by selecting the THREE answer choices that express the most important ideas in the passage. Some sentences do not belong in the summary because they express ideas that are not presented in the passage or are minor ideas in the passage. ***This question is worth 2 points.***

White–collar crime refers to illegal acts committed by people in the course of their employment.
•
•
•

Answer Choices

(A) Most white–collar crime involves low–level employees who take small amounts of money and are never found out.

(B) Examples of white–collar crime are embezzlement and trading securities on the basis of insider information.

(C) White–collar crime occurs in both business and government, causing great harm to the public.

(D) Some employees commit white–collar crime by destroying documents and making false statements.

(E) In the 1980s, a change in the law allowed executives to make unsecured loans to friends and relatives.

(F) The nature of white–collar crime makes it difficult to discover and expensive to prosecute.

Exercise 1.9.C

Read the passages and answer each question based on what is stated or implied in that passage.

SOCIAL BEHAVIOR IN ANIMALS

Social behavior is communication that permits a group of animals of the same species to become organized cooperatively. Social behavior includes any interaction that is a consequence of one animal's response to another of its own species, such as an individual fighting to defend a territory. However, not all **aggregations** of animals are social. Clusters of moths attracted to a light at night or trout gathering in the coolest pool of a stream are groupings of animals responding to environmental signals. Social aggregations, on the other hand, depend on signals from the animals themselves, which stay together and do things together by influencing one another.

Social animals are not all social to the same degree. Some species cooperate only long enough to achieve reproduction, while others—such as geese and beavers—form strong pair bonds that last a lifetime. The most persistent social bonds usually form between mothers and their young. For birds and mammals, these bonds usually end when the young can fly, swim, or run, and find enough food to support themselves.

One obvious benefit of social organization is defense—both passive and active—from predators. Musk oxen that form a passive defensive circle when threatened by a pack of wolves are much less vulnerable than an individual facing the wolves alone. A breeding colony of gulls practices active defense when they, alerted by the alarm calls of a few, attack a predator as a group. Such a collective attack will discourage a predator more effectively than individual attacks. Members of a town of prairie dogs cooperate by warning each other with a special bark when a predator is nearby. Thus, every individual in a social organization benefits from the eyes, ears, and noses of all other members of the group. Other advantages of social organization include cooperation in hunting for food, huddling for protection from severe weather, and the potential for transmitting information that is useful to the society.

Glossary:
    aggregation: gathering; group

1. Why does the author mention moths and trout in paragraph 1?

    (A) To show how social behavior benefits each individual in a group
    (B) To point out the role of the environment in social organization
    (C) To give examples of groupings that do not represent social behavior
    (D) To explain how not all social behavior has the same purpose

2. All of the following are examples of social behavior EXCEPT

    (A) a bird fighting to defend its territory
    (B) a group of turtles sunning on a log
    (C) musk oxen forming a defensive circle
    (D) a pack of wolves hunting together

3. The word huddling in paragraph 3 is closest in meaning to

    (A) gathering
    (B) hiding
    (C) escaping
    (D) searching

4–5. An introductory sentence for a brief summary of the passage is provided below. Complete the summary by selecting the THREE answer choices that express the most important ideas in the passage. Some sentences do not belong in the summary because they express ideas that are not presented in the passage or are minor ideas in the passage. *This question is worth 2 points.*

Social behavior allows animals of the same species to organize cooperatively.
•
•
•

Answer Choices

(A) Social behavior is defined as any beneficial grouping of animals of the same species.

(B) Any exchange resulting from the response of one animal to another of the same species is social behavior.

(C) The most important social bond occurs between mother animals and their young.

(D) Members of a group influence one another in different degrees and for various reasons.

(E) Living together provides many benefits, including the defense of the group from danger.

(F) Prairie dogs are organized into social units that alert each other when danger threatens.

THE PRODUCTION OF COFFEE

All great coffee comes from the same tree, *Coffea arabica*. The distinguishing taste of coffee is a product of the climate, air, and soil in which it is grown. The perfect climate for coffee production exists between the latitudes of 25 degrees north and 25 degrees south of the equator. The coffee plant is particular about temperature, and changes of more than 20 degrees in twenty–four hours, or temperatures of over 70 degrees Fahrenheit, tend to have harmful effects on production. In general, coffee trees are comfortable where people are. If people feel too cold or hot, especially during flowering and fruit development, the trees are not likely to do well.

Altitude is an important factor, and most coffee–producing countries grade their coffees according to the altitude at which they were grown. The best–tasting coffees are grown at between five and eight thousand feet in elevation, in the thin air and rocky soil of places such as the mountain ridges of Central America and Africa.

Coffee trees require certain nutrients to produce beans in economically viable quantities; thus, soil chemistry is carefully watched in commercial operations. A soil rich in nitrogen, phosphorus, and potassium will yield a coffee more complex in character. Nitrogen in soil gives rise to coffee's sparkling acidity; potassium produces fuller–bodied coffees; and phosphorus, while having no bearing on coffee in the final cup, helps the tree to develop a healthy root system. Generally, the more balanced the soil, the better the coffee.

Caring for the coffee tree is critical to the character of the final product. Stock for new coffee trees is usually grown from seeds produced by trees already growing on the farm. After the seeds germinate, the seedlings are transferred to nursery beds, which are typically kept under mesh netting that filters out direct sunlight. Young seedlings grow slowly, are very delicate, and require careful replanting. The transfer from nursery to plantation is a critical part of the process, and a seedling that is mishandled at this stage may die after it is replanted. Most varieties take at least three years before they begin producing fruit.

6. It can be inferred that the best coffee would come from which region?

   Ⓐ A mountainous region close to the equator
   Ⓑ A region with a large coffee–drinking population
   Ⓒ A coastal region with a moderate amount of rainfall
   Ⓓ A region with an average temperature of 70 degrees F

7. The word bearing in paragraph 3 is closest in meaning to

   Ⓐ opinion
   Ⓑ influence
   Ⓒ stress
   Ⓓ dependence

8. Which sentence below best expresses the essential information in the highlighted sentence in paragraph 4? Incorrect choices change the meaning in important ways or leave out essential information.

   Ⓐ Coffee trees require a large amount of care because they are delicate.
   Ⓑ The most important step in coffee production is selecting the stock.
   Ⓒ People care more about the taste of coffee than the appearance of the tree.
   Ⓓ The quality of the finished coffee depends on the care given to the tree.

9–10. An introductory sentence for a brief summary of the passage is provided below. Complete the summary by selecting the THREE answer choices that express the most important ideas in the passage. Some sentences do not belong in the summary because they express ideas that are not presented in the passage or are minor ideas in the passage. *This question is worth 2 points.*

Several factors are important in the production of high–quality coffee.
•
•
•

Answer Choices

Ⓐ Coffee is best grown in climates within specific latitudes and at certain altitudes.
Ⓑ Coffee is graded according to the altitude at which it is grown.
Ⓒ Some people prefer rich, full–bodied coffees, while others like coffees that taste clean and crisp.

Ⓓ The best commercial coffee is grown in soil containing a balance of essential chemical nutrients.
Ⓔ A special kind of mesh netting filters out direct sunlight over nursery beds.
Ⓕ Coffee growers must carefully cultivate the coffee plant through all stages of its life.

Answers to Exercises 1.9.A through 1.9.C are on page 572.

How to score Multiple-Point Questions		
Points Possible	**Answers Correct**	**Points Earned**
2 points	3	2
	2	1
	0 – 1	0

 EXTENSION

1. With your teacher and classmates, discuss situations in which writing summaries is important. On the board, write a list of as many situations as you can think of. (Possible situations: college research papers; letters to parents; monthly reports for the company where you work; personal diary.)

    Make another list of situations in which reading summaries is important. What types of summaries have you read recently? Find examples of different kinds of summaries to bring to class, such as a summary in a research paper, a summary at the end of a chapter in a textbook, and the executive summary of a business report.

2. In reading done outside class, select a short passage of one to three paragraphs. Make three photocopies and bring them to class. In class, work in a group of three students. Work as a team to identify key words and sentences that provide clues to the major ideas in each passage. Write a brief summary of each passage. Include only the ideas and information that are essential for a general understanding of each passage. Each summary should have no more than four sentences.

1.10 Organizing Information

FOCUS

Read the following passage:

> Human diseases can be classified according to their effect and duration. An acute disease is an illness such as measles, influenza, or typhoid fever, from which the victim either recovers or dies in a relatively short time. Many acute diseases are also transmissible, which means they are caused by living organisms such as bacteria and viruses and can be spread from one person to another by air, water, or food.
>
> Chronic diseases, on the other hand, develop slowly and last for a long time, sometimes for a lifetime. Examples include cardiovascular disorders, most cancers, diabetes, emphysema, alcoholism, and malnutrition. Although a chronic disease may go into remission, it may flare up periodically (malaria), become progressively worse (cancers and cardiovascular disorders), or disappear with age (childhood asthma).
>
> One hundred years ago, two of the major causes of death in North America were epidemics of influenza and intestinal infections—short–term acute diseases that struck young and old alike and ran quickly through the population. In contrast, the leading causes of death today are chronic illnesses, the types of heart disease and cancer that take a long time to develop and get progressively worse.

The passage compares two types of diseases: acute and chronic. Put the following sentences in the correct column below.

They take a long time to develop.
The victim recovers or dies quickly.
They are major causes of death today.
Measles and influenza are examples.
They run quickly through a population.
The victim gets progressively worse.

Acute diseases	Chronic diseases

The question asks you to organize information from across the whole passage. The correctly organized information is:

Acute diseases	Chronic diseases
The victim recovers or dies quickly.	*They take a long time to develop.*
Measles and influenza are examples.	*They are major causes of death today.*
They run quickly through a population.	*The victim gets progressively worse.*

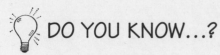 DO YOU KNOW...?

1. The organization of a passage is closely linked with its function. The **organization** of a passage is how the author presents ideas and information to meet a specific purpose. Recognizing the organization of a text is an important reading skill because it deepens your understanding of the material and increases your ability to remember it.

   Some reading passages on the TOEFL are organized according to these functions:

   - to compare or contrast things or ideas;
   - to describe different parts of something; or
   - to present alternative arguments.

2. On the TOEFL, you must demonstrate your ability to understand the function of a passage by organizing information from across the entire passage. You will be asked to organize information into categories, classes, divisions, or types.

   The questions about organizing information have special directions. The questions look like this:

   > Select the appropriate sentences from the answer choices and match them to the type of _____ that they describe. TWO of the answer choices will NOT be used. **This question is worth 3 points.**

3. You must identify the correct items in the list of answer choices and put them in the correct box in the table. The table fills the computer screen, but you can return to the passage while you are answering the question. You may take notes and you may use your notes to help you answer the question.

4. The question is worth either 3 or 4 points, depending on the number of answer choices given. It is possible to receive partial credit. You must put at least some of the answer choices in the correct place to earn credit. Here is how the points are earned:

Points Possible	Answers Correct	Points Earned
3 points	5	3
	4	2
	3	1
	0 – 2	0
4 points	7	4
	6	3
	5	2
	4	1
	0 – 3	0

5. The reading skill of scanning will help you check your answers to questions about organizing information. **Scanning** is searching the passage for specific information. If your answers are correct, they should be easy to confirm by scanning the passage to locate relevant information.

6. The correct answers summarize information from across the whole passage. To *summarize* means to state the essential information in a shorter form. The correct answers represent major ideas and important supporting information in the passage.

7. Two of the answer choices will be incorrect for either category in the table. An answer choice may be incorrect because it is:

    ⟿ inaccurate or untrue according to the passage; or
    ⟿ irrelevant or not mentioned in the passage.

8. Here is an example:

ENERGY QUALITY

Energy is the power to do work or to cause a heat transfer between two objects. Energy varies in its quality, that is, its ability to perform useful work. High–quality energy is organized or concentrated and has great ability to do useful work. Some high–quality forms of energy are electricity, coal, gasoline, concentrated sunlight, high–temperature heat, and nuclei of uranium–235. Conversely, low–quality energy is disorganized or dilute and has little ability to do useful work. An example is the low–temperature heat in the air around us or in a river, lake, or ocean. Heat is so widely dispersed in the ocean that we cannot use it to move objects or to heat objects to high temperatures.

Scientists have repeatedly demonstrated that in any conversion of energy from one form to another, there is always a decrease in energy quality or the amount of useful energy. This law of energy quality degradation is known as the second law of thermodynamics. It is a fundamental scientific law that in any conversion of energy from one form to another, some of the initial energy input is always degraded to lower–quality, less useful energy, usually low–temperature heat that flows into the environment. This low–quality energy is so disordered and dispersed that it is unable to perform useful work.

Select the appropriate phrases from the answer choices and match them to the type of energy that they illustrate. TWO of the answer choices will NOT be used. *This question is worth 3 points.*

Drag your answer choices to the spaces where they belong. To remove an answer, click on it.

Answer Choices	Type of Energy
Concentrated sunlight	**High–quality**
Heat stored in the ocean	•
Psychological energy	•
Energy with great ability to do work	•
High–temperature heat	**Low–quality**
Energy that is disorganized	•
Conversion of energy	•

The passage contrasts high–quality and low–quality energy. The correct answers are:

Answer Choices	Type of Energy
	High–quality
	• Concentrated sunlight
Psychological energy	• Energy with great ability to do work
	• High–temperature heat
	Low–quality
	• Heat stored in the ocean
Conversion of energy	• Energy that is disorganized

Some key information about high–quality energy is:

> High–quality energy is organized or concentrated and has great ability to do useful work. Some high–quality forms of energy are…concentrated sunlight, high–temperature heat….

Some key information about low–quality energy is:

> Heat is so widely dispersed in the ocean….
> This low–quality energy is so disordered and dispersed that it is unable to perform useful work.

Psychological energy is incorrect because it is not mentioned in the passage. *Conversion of energy* is incorrect because it is neither high–quality nor low–quality energy but rather the changing of energy from one form to another.

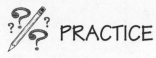 PRACTICE

Exercise 1.10.A

Read the passages and answer each question based on what is stated or implied in that passage.

THE ENLIGHTENMENT AND ROMANTICISM

The Romantic Movement in music and literature was a reaction against the Enlightenment philosophy that had dominated much of the eighteenth century. Enlightenment ideals held that human society could reach perfection through rational thought, while Romantic philosophy reveled in the beauty and unpredictable power of Nature. The Enlightenment gloried in civilization and believed in princely rule of a benevolent kind. Romanticism believed in democracy and the common people, reviving folk traditions, ballads, and medieval sagas that made heroes of rural characters. Artistically, the Enlightenment condemned excess and dictated that the discipline of formal structure was beneficial to artistic expression. Romanticism, on the other hand, celebrated emotions and the senses, believing that the emotional demands of a particular work should dictate its form. While the Enlightenment believed in a generally positive approach to life and the abandonment of superstition, Romanticism found inspiration in death as an "other kingdom" and in the supernatural; hence, literature developed a "Gothic" streak that eventually found its way into music.

1–3. Select the appropriate sentences from the answer choices and match them to the philosophy that they illustrate. TWO of the answer choices will NOT be used. ***This question is worth 3 points.***

Answer Choices	Philosophy
(A) There is value in emotions, the senses, and the power of Nature.	**Enlightenment**
(B) The discipline of formal structure benefits artistic expression.	•
(C) Death and the supernatural are sources of inspiration.	•
(D) Artistic values are more important than social themes.	**Romanticism**
(E) Human society can reach perfection through rational thought.	•
(F) Folk traditions are important because common people are heroes.	•
(G) Symbols and patterns of images convey artistic meaning.	•

VALLEY FLOORS

The floor of a river valley develops in one of two ways: as a rock–floored valley bottom or as an accumulation valley floor. A rock–floored valley is formed by a stream that no longer incises by cutting downward but rather erodes laterally in a course that winds from side to side across the valley floor. In a rock–floored valley, the valley slopes are undercut and steepened by the sideways erosion. The floor of the river channel lies in the bedrock, and on either side of the channel it is covered by only a thin layer of gravel and sand. As the stream swings across the valley floor, it deposits material on the insides of the bends in the channel.

The second type of valley bottom, the accumulation floor, cannot easily be distinguished from a rock–floored valley on its surface. An accumulation valley floor is created by the continuous deposition of gravel and sand in an existing incised valley where the accumulation of material has replaced the cutting action. Both the channel floor and the floodplain—the part of the valley floor flooded frequently at high water—are composed entirely of these gravel and sand deposits. An accumulation floor is much less resistant to erosion than a rock floor since the gravel and sand of its channel bed have already been transported and may easily be removed during the next flood.

4–6. Select the appropriate sentences from the answer choices and match them to the type of valley floor that they describe. TWO of the answer choices will NOT be used. ***This question is worth 3 points.***

Answer Choices	Type of Valley Floor
(A) The river channel flows directly over the bedrock.	**Rock Floor**
(B) The top layer of rock is more resistant to erosion than the underlying rock.	•
(C) Deposits of gravel and sand accumulate on the valley floor.	•
(D) The river swings from side to side, leaving material on the insides of bends in the channel.	•
(E) Sand and rock accumulate parallel to the coast but separated from it by a channel.	**Accumulation Floor**
(F) The sideways erosion of the river undercuts and steepens the valley slopes.	•
(G) The channel floor and the floodplain are made entirely of gravel and sand deposits.	•

ANIMALS AND PLANTS

We can distinguish animals from plants by looking at their contrasting modes of nutrition. Unlike plants, animals cannot manufacture their own food. Animals cannot construct organic molecules from inorganic chemicals as plants can during photosynthesis. Animals must take pre–formed organic molecules into their bodies. Most animals do this by ingestion—that is, by eating other organisms or organic material. Animals store their food reserves as glycogen, whereas plants store their food as starch.

Animal cells lack the cell walls that characterize plant cells, and animal cells have unique types of junctions between them. In most animals, cells are successively organized into tissues, organs, and organ systems. Animals have two types of tissues that plants do not have. The first is nervous tissue, for the conduction of electrical impulses, and the other is muscle tissue, for movement. Nerves and muscles, which control active behavior, are unique to animals.

Animal life began in the Precambrian seas with the evolution of multi–cellular forms that lived by eating other organisms. This new way of life led to an evolutionary explosion of diverse forms. Early animals populated the seas, fresh water, and eventually the land. The diversity of animal life on Earth today is the result of over half a billion years of evolution from those first ancestors that consumed other life forms.

7–10. Select the appropriate sentences from the answer choices and match them to the form of life that they describe. TWO of the answer choices will NOT be used. ***This question is worth 4 points.***

Answer Choices	Form of Life
(A) They are not able to manufacture their own food.	**Plants**
(B) They construct organic molecules from inorganic chemicals.	•
(C) They have the ability to survive on another planet.	•
(D) Nerves and muscles control their active behavior.	•
(E) They evolved from multi–cellular forms that ate other organisms.	
(F) They store their food reserves as starch.	**Animals**
(G) They have evolved very little over one billion years.	•
(H) They have neither nervous tissue nor muscle tissue.	•
(I) Their cells do not have walls.	•

Exercise 1.10.B

Read the passages and answer each question based on what is stated or implied in that passage.

COMMERCIAL ARCHITECTURE OF THE NINETEENTH CENTURY

Arcades were built in Paris as early as 1799 and in London in 1816, but these were primarily arched passages through buildings to connect institutions. American arcades, by contrast, were not just passages to some other destination but the entire focus of large commercial blocks, and were, in effect, prototypical shopping malls. The Providence Arcade (1829) in Rhode Island's capital illustrates the American transformation of the arcade into a temple of shopping. The Arcade's pitched glass roof sheltered a large open space surrounded by tiered shops. The Arcade was set at the edge of Providence's business district, making it a focal point for future growth. On the two street sides, six huge granite columns modeled on a Greek temple dominated the building's facades.

Nineteenth–century urban Americans flocked to another ancestor of the contemporary shopping mall, the department store, a controlled indoor world where an array of goods were organized under a single management. The origins of the department store were in Cincinnati, where in 1829, a new kind of building was dedicated to trade, business, and culture. This building, called the Bazaar, featured a four–story rotunda beneath a huge dome that meant to unite multiple functions under one symbolic roof. Unfortunately, however, the Bazaar was short–lived. A more successful commercial and architectural prototype was the department store known as the Marble Palace, which opened in New York in 1846. Monumental in style, the building's impressive facade of Corinthian columns, with large plate glass display windows between them, easily lured in the city's wealthy customers.

1–3. Select the appropriate sentences from the answer choices and match them to the type of building that they describe. TWO of the answer choices will NOT be used. ***This question is worth 3 points.***

Answer Choices	Type of Building
(A) It is a passage under or through a building to connect streets.	**Arcade**
(B) A glass roof encloses an area lined with vertical rows of shops.	•
(C) A wide variety of goods are organized under one management.	•
(D) It is designed to be the entire focus of a large commercial block.	
(E) The earliest example had a four–story rotunda under a large dome.	**Department Store**
(F) It specializes in selling a single category of high–quality good.	•
(G) Its large display windows are designed to attract customers.	•
	•

RESEARCH DESIGNS

In the fields of psychology and sociology, a crucial decision for researchers is which research design to use. When the subject of the study is how people change or develop over time, two designs are frequently used: the cross–sectional design and the longitudinal design.

Cross–sectional studies look at a cross–section of subjects and compare their responses. The essential characteristics of the design are that it includes groups of subjects at different age levels, and that each subject is tested or interviewed only once. For example, researchers may give a memory test to adults in their twenties through seventies, select the youngest group as a standard, and then compare each older group to that norm. Cross–sectional studies are relatively quick to do and can provide information about possible age differences. However, they do not reveal anything about individual change over time, since each subject is tested only once.

Longitudinal studies differ from cross–sectional studies because they test or interview the same subjects over time and therefore allow us to look at consistency or change within the same individual. The typical procedure is to select a relatively small group of subjects who are all about the same age at the beginning of the study and then look at them repeatedly over a period of time. Short–term longitudinal studies cover several years and are common in research on both children and adults. Long–term longitudinal studies follow subjects from childhood into adulthood, from early to middle adulthood, or from middle adulthood to old age. One advantage of longitudinal studies is that any changes found are real changes, not just age–group differences.

4–6. Select the appropriate sentences from the answer choices and match them to the research design that they describe. TWO of the answer choices will NOT be used. *This question is worth 3 points.*

Answer Choices

(A) A group of subjects of the same age is tested repeatedly over a long period.

(B) Researchers examine an existing relationship between two groups of subjects.

(C) This design allows researchers to study human behavior indirectly.

(D) Researchers test or interview each subject only one time.

(E) This type of study may reveal differences that are not just age–group differences.

(F) Researchers can study consistency or change within the same individual.

(G) This design can tell us about possible differences among various age groups.

Research Design

Cross–sectional
-
-

Longitudinal
-
-
-

PROXIMATE AND ULTIMATE CAUSATION

Behavioral biologists ask two basic types of questions about animal behavior: how animals behave and why they behave as they do. The "how" questions seek to understand the proximate or immediate causes underlying a behavior at a particular time and place. For example, a biologist might want to explain the singing of a male white–throated sparrow in the spring in terms of hormonal or neural mechanisms. Such physiological causes of behavior are proximate factors. Alternatively, another biologist might ask what purpose singing serves the sparrow, and then attempt to understand events in the evolution of birds that led to springtime singing. These are "why" questions that focus on ultimate causation, the evolutionary origin and purpose of behavior. These two types of questions are very independent approaches to behavior.

Questions about proximate causation examine how animals perform their various functions at the molecular, cellular, organismal, and population levels. The biological sciences that address proximate causes are known as experimental sciences because they use the experimental method of: (1) predicting how a system will respond to a disturbance, (2) making the disturbance, and (3) comparing the observed results with the predictions. Researchers repeat the experimental conditions many times to eliminate chance results that might lead to false conclusions.

Questions about ultimate causation ask what produced biological systems and their distinctive properties through evolutionary time. The sciences dealing with ultimate causes are known as evolutionary sciences, and they mainly use the comparative method rather than experimentation. Researchers compare characteristics of molecular biology, cell biology, anatomy, development, and ecology among related species to identify patterns of variation.

7. Which sentence below best expresses the essential information in the highlighted sentence in paragraph 1? Incorrect choices change the meaning in important ways or leave out essential information.

  (A) All questions asked by behavioral biologists fall into two basic categories.
  (B) Proximate and ultimate causation are distinct ways of thinking about behavior.
  (C) "Why" questions and questions about ultimate causes require very different methods.
  (D) Behavioral biologists must think very independently about important questions.

8–10. Select the appropriate sentences from the answer choices and match them to the type of cause that they describe. TWO of the answer choices will NOT be used. *This question is worth 3 points.*

Answer Choices

Ⓐ Researchers want to know about the evolutionary origin and purpose of behavior.

Ⓑ Behavioral biologists use the experimental method to answer a question.

Ⓒ A scientist wants to know how a male sparrow produces its springtime song.

Ⓓ Some animal behaviors are random and serve no beneficial function.

Ⓔ Scientists compare characteristics of related species to identify similarities and differences.

Ⓕ Researchers disagree over the reason for a particular behavior.

Ⓖ A behavior at a specific time and place has an immediate, underlying cause.

Type of Cause

Proximate
·
·
·

Ultimate
·
·

Answers to Exercises 1.10.A through 1.10.B are on page 573.

How to Score Multiple–Point Questions		
Points Possible	**Answers Correct**	**Points Earned**
3 points	5	3
	4	2
	3	1
	0 – 2	0
4 points	7	4
	6	3
	5	2
	4	1
	0 – 3	0

 EXTENSION

1. Outside of class, select an article from a magazine or journal or part of a chapter from a university textbook. Do the following activity as an individual or small–group exercise, making as many photocopies of the article as necessary.

   Read the article and think about its organization and purpose. Answer the following questions:

   a. What is the function of the article? Why did the author write it?
   b. How are the ideas and information organized?
   c. What is the purpose of each paragraph or division?
   d. What are the major ideas and most important information in the article?

   Make a table or chart of the article. Show the article's major divisions and the most important ideas and information in each division.

PROGRESS – 1.9 through 1.10

QUIZ 9

Time – 20 minutes

Read the passages and choose the best answer to each question. Answer all questions about a passage on the basis of what is stated or implied in that passage.

LIFE EXPECTANCY

The greatest **demographic** story of the twentieth century was the enormous increase in life expectancy, the average number of years a person can expect to live. In most modern societies, life expectancy rose dramatically, from about 47 years in 1900 to about 76 years in 2000. This does not mean, however, that people suddenly died on their forty–seventh birthday in 1900. It means that if half of the people born in 1900 died in childhood and the rest lived 95 years, the average age at death was around 47. The data for 1900 reflect high infant and childhood mortality rates. At that time, surviving the first fifteen years of life was the key to living to old age. Over the century, several factors increased life expectancy, most notably improvements in public health, such as pasteurized milk, sewers, and indoor plumbing. Advances in medical practice, including the use of antibiotics and vaccinations for childhood illnesses, made it increasingly likely that infants would reach adulthood.

On the one hand, increased life expectancy is a sign of societal well being; on the other hand, an aging population poses its own set of problems. Large numbers of elderly, many with chronic diseases, become a burden on the health care system and on their families. In societies where care of the elderly is a family responsibility, adult children caring for aging parents experience great personal and financial stress.

Glossary:
> **demographic:** relating to demography, the study of human populations

1–2. An introductory sentence for a brief summary of the passage is provided below. Complete the summary by selecting the THREE answer choices that express the most important ideas in the passage. Some sentences do not belong in the summary because they express ideas that are not presented in the passage or are minor ideas in the passage. ***This question is worth 2 points.***

Life expectancy in modern societies has increased dramatically.
•
•
•

Answer Choices

(A) Around half of the population died on their forty–seventh birthday in 1900.

(B) The average number of years a person could expect to live rose from 47 to 76 in only a century.

(C) The leading causes of death in 1900 were epidemic diseases.

(D) Mortality rate is the number of deaths in a period as a proportion of the entire population.

(E) Improvements in public health and medical practices significantly raised life expectancy.

(F) An aging population increases the stress on a society's health care system and on families.

ARTISTS' USE OF OIL AND ACRYLIC PAINTS

The oil technique for painting on canvas is superior to other methods mainly because of its great flexibility and ease of manipulation, as well as the wide range of effects that can be produced. Colors do not change to any great extent on drying, which means that the color the artist puts down is, with only slight variation, the color desired in the finished work. The artist is free to combine transparent and opaque effects in the same painting. However, the principal defect of oil painting is the darkening of the oil over time, but this may be reduced by using the highest quality materials.

The most widely used artists' colors based on the synthetic resins are made by dispersing pigment in acrylic emulsion. Acrylic paints are thinned with water, but when they dry, the resin particles coalesce to form a tough film that is impervious to water. Acrylic colors may be made mat or glossy and can imitate most of the effects of other water–based colors. They are a boon to painters with a high rate of production because a painting can be completed in one session that might have taken days in oil because of the drying time required between layers of paint.

Acrylic colors are not a complete substitute for oil paints, and artists whose styles require the special manipulative properties of oil colors—including delicacy in handling or smoothly blended tones—find that these possibilities are the exclusive properties of oils. Although painting in acrylics has certain advantages over painting in oils, the latter remains the standard because the majority of painters find that its advantages outweigh its defects and that in optical quality oil paints surpass all others.

3–5. Select the appropriate sentences from the answer choices and match them to the type of paint that they describe. TWO of the answer choices will NOT be used. ***This question is worth 3 points.***

Answer Choices	Type of Paint
(A) They appear transparent on paper.	**Oil Paints**
(B) The colors can be thinned with water.	•
(C) They allow for smoothly blended tones.	•
(D) The paints are applied to wet plaster.	•
(E) They are the preferred paints among artists.	**Acrylic Paints**
(F) They have a relatively fast drying time.	•
(G) The colors will eventually darken.	•

WORLD CLIMATIC PATTERNS

Climate is the general pattern of atmospheric conditions, seasonal variations, and weather extremes in a region over a period of decades. One major factor determining the uneven patterns of world climates is the variation in the amount of solar energy striking different parts of the earth. The amount of incoming solar energy reaching the earth's surface varies with latitude, the distance north or south from the equator. Air in the **troposphere** is heated more at the equator (zero latitude), where the sun is almost directly overhead, than at the high–latitude poles, where the sun is lower in the sky and strikes the earth at a low angle.

The large input of heat at and near the equator warms large masses of air. These warm masses rise and spread northward and southward, carrying heat from the equator toward the poles. At the poles, the warm air becomes cool and falls to the earth. These cool air masses then flow back toward the equator near ground level to fill the space left by rising warm air masses. This general air circulation pattern in the troposphere results in warm average temperatures near the equator, cold average temperatures near the poles, and moderate average temperatures at the middle latitudes.

The larger input of solar energy near the equator evaporates huge amounts of water from the earth's surface into the troposphere. As the warm, humid air rises, it cools rapidly and loses most of its moisture as rain near the equator. The abundant rainfall and the constant warm temperatures near the equator create the world's tropical rain forests.

Two major factors cause seasonal changes in climate. One is the earth's annual orbit around the sun; the other is the earth's daily rotation around its tilted axis, the imaginary line connecting the two poles. When the North Pole leans toward the sun, the sun's rays strike the Northern Hemisphere more directly per unit of area, bringing summer to the northern half of the earth. At the same time, the South Pole is tilted away from the sun; thus, winter conditions prevail throughout the Southern Hemisphere. As the earth makes its annual rotation around the sun, these conditions shift and cause a change of seasons.

As the earth spins around its axis, the general air circulation pattern between the equator and each pole breaks into three separate belts of moving air, or prevailing surface winds, which affect the distribution of precipitation over the earth.

Glossary:
    troposphere: the lowest region of the earth's atmosphere

6–7. An introductory sentence for a brief summary of the passage is provided below. Complete the summary by selecting the THREE answer choices that express the most important ideas in the passage. Some sentences do not belong in the summary because they express ideas that are not presented in the passage or are minor ideas in the passage. ***This question is worth 2 points.***

Several factors influence the earth's climatic patterns.
•
•
•

Answer Choices

(A) The variation in the amount of solar energy reaching different parts of the earth has a great influence on global climate.

(B) Warm air flows from the equator toward both poles, where it cools and then flows back toward the equator, creating a general air circulation.

(C) The moisture–holding capacity of air, humidity, increases when air is warmed and decreases when it is cooled.

(D) The consistently warm temperatures and heavy rainfall near the equator result in tropical rain forests.

(E) The earth's annual circling of the sun and its daily spinning around its axis cause its seasonal changes in climate.

(F) The chemical content of the troposphere is another factor determining the earth's average temperatures and thus its climates.

READING

8–10. Select the appropriate sentences from the answer choices and match them to the location that they describe. TWO of the answer choices will NOT be used. *This question is worth 3 points.*

Answer Choices

(A) Solar energy strikes the earth at a low angle.
(B) Average annual temperatures are moderate.
(C) The large input of solar energy heats great masses of air.
(D) A large quantity of water evaporates into the atmosphere.
(E) Warm air cools and sinks to the earth's surface.
(F) The sun is almost directly overhead.
(G) There are three belts of prevailing surface winds.

Location

At the Equator

•
•
•

At the Poles

•
•

Answers to Reading Quiz 9 are on page 574.

Record your score on the Progress Chart on page 693.

How to Score Multiple–Point Questions		
Points Possible	**Answers Correct**	**Points Earned**
2 points	3	2
	2	1
	0 – 1	0
3 points	5	3
	4	2
	3	1
	0 – 2	0
4 points	7	4
	6	3
	5	2
	4	1
	0 – 3	0

PROGRESS – 1.1 through 1.10

QUIZ 10   *Time – 40 minutes*

Read the passages and choose the best answer to each question. Answer all questions about a passage on the basis of what is stated or implied in that passage.

BLACK HOLES

Nothing in the history of modern astronomy has excited as much speculation as the object, or event, known as a black hole. Black holes have provided endless imaginative fodder for science fiction writers and endless theoretical fodder for astrophysicists. They are one of the more exotic manifestations of the theory of general relativity, and their fascination lies in the way their tremendous gravity affects nearby space and time.

A black hole is very simple in structure: it has a surface—the event horizon—and a center—the singularity. Everything else is gravity. The standard model for the formation of a black hole involves the collapse of a large star. The imaginary spherical surface surrounding the collapsed star is the event horizon—an artificial boundary in space that marks a point of no return. Outside the event horizon, gravity is strong but finite, and it is possible for objects to break free of its pull. However, once within the event horizon, an object would need to travel faster than light to escape.

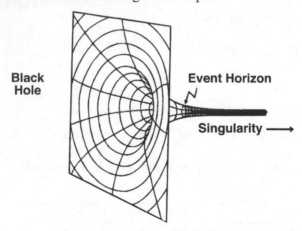

For extremely massive stars, the exclusion principle—the resistance between the molecular particles within the star as they are compressed—will not be strong enough to offset the gravity generated by the star's own mass. The star's increasing density will overwhelm the exclusion principle. What follows is runaway gravitational collapse. With no internal force to stop it, the star will simply continue to collapse in on itself. Once a collapsing star has contracted through its event horizon, nothing can stop it from collapsing further until its entire mass is crushed down to a single point—a point of infinite density and zero volume—the singularity.

The star now disappears from the perceivable universe, like a cartoon character that jumps into a hole and pulls the hole in after him. What this process leaves behind is a different kind of hole—a profound disturbance in space–time, a region where gravity is so intense that nothing can escape from it. Any object falling within the boundary of a black hole has no choice but to move inward toward the singularity and disappear from our universe forever. Moreover, a black hole can never be plugged up or filled in with matter; the more matter that is poured into a black hole, the bigger it gets.

What would happen to objects, such as astronauts, as they vanished into a black hole? Physicists have been amusing themselves with this question for years, and most believe that the intense gravitational forces would rip apart the astronauts long before they were crushed at the singularity. Theoretically, any astronauts who managed to survive the passage would encounter some very strange things. For instance, they would experience acute time distortion, which would enable them to know, in a few brief seconds, the entire future of the universe.

Inside a black hole, space and time are so warped that the distance from the event horizon to the singularity is not a distance in space in the normal sense that we can measure in kilometers. Instead, it becomes a distance in time. The time it takes to reach the singularity from the event horizon—as measured by someone falling in—is proportional to the mass of the black hole.

The only way that astronauts would know whether they had crossed the event horizon would be if they tried to halt their fall and climb out again by firing their engines enough to push themselves back from the center of the hole. However, because of the time warp, if the astronauts tried to do this, they would reach the singularity faster than if they had left their engines off. Moreover, since they could get no farther once they had reached the singularity, this point would mark the end of time itself.

1. The word fodder in paragraph 1 is closest in meaning to

    (A) material
    (B) stories
    (C) support
    (D) problems

2. What happens to an object that falls within the event horizon of a black hole?

    (A) The object changes shape until it is spherical.
    (B) The object is pushed from the hole at the speed of light.
    (C) The object cannot escape the black hole's gravity.
    (D) The object explodes into particles that drift into space.

3. The opposing force between the molecular particles inside a star is called

    (A) general relativity
    (B) the exclusion principle
    (C) infinite density
    (D) the singularity

4. The word runaway in paragraph 3 is closest in meaning to

    (A) frequent
    (B) long–term
    (C) uncontrolled
    (D) slow–paced

5. Why does the author mention a cartoon character in paragraph 4?

    (A) To illustrate the complete disappearance of a collapsing star
    (B) To warn of the danger of being sucked into a black hole
    (C) To point out a humorous phenomenon in astrophysics
    (D) To announce the creation of a cartoon about black holes

6. Which sentence below best expresses the essential information in the highlighted sentence in paragraph 4? Incorrect choices change the meaning in important ways or leave out essential information.

   (A) The collapse of a star creates a black hole, a distortion of space and time with gravity strong enough to pull in any nearby object.

   (B) Several different kinds of black holes exist, but the most powerful are those that result in an interchange of space and time.

   (C) Behind every black hole is a different type of hole that is even more disturbing to our current beliefs about gravity, space, and time.

   (D) The process of black hole formation occurs only in regions of space where gravity is the predominant physical force.

7. Astronauts who fell into a black hole would probably experience all of the following EXCEPT

   (A) distortion of space and time
   (B) traveling faster than light
   (C) knowledge of the universe
   (D) strong gravitational forces

8. What can be inferred from paragraph 6 about the distance between the event horizon and the singularity?

   (A) The distance increases and decreases continuously.
   (B) The distance is more than several trillion kilometers.
   (C) The distance cannot be traveled in less than a year.
   (D) The distance is related to the size of the black hole.

9. The phrase this point in paragraph 7 in refers to

   (A) the event horizon
   (B) firing their engines
   (C) the time warp
   (D) the singularity

10. Look at the four squares, **A**, **B**, **C**, and **D**, which indicate where the following sentence could be added to the passage. Where would the sentence best fit?

   A few believe that the astronauts would explode in a flash of gamma rays as they approached the singularity.

   What would happen to objects, such as astronauts, as they vanished into a black hole? **A** Physicists have been amusing themselves with this question for years, and most believe that the intense gravitational forces would rip apart the astronauts long before they were crushed at the singularity. **B** Theoretically, any astronauts who managed to survive the passage would encounter some very strange things. **C** For instance, they would experience acute time distortion, which would enable them to know, in a few brief seconds, the entire future of the universe. **D**

11–12. An introductory sentence for a brief summary of the passage is provided below. Complete the summary by selecting the THREE answer choices that express the most important ideas in the passage. Some sentences do not belong in the summary because they express ideas that are not presented in the passage or are minor ideas in the passage. *This question is worth 2 points.*

Black holes fascinate us because of the effect they have on space and time.
•
•
•

Answer Choices

(A) Black holes are thought to form when a large star collapses inward on itself to a point of infinite density and zero volume.

(B) Both scientists and science fiction writers have developed theories and written accounts of black holes.

(C) A black hole consists of a surface called the event horizon, a strong gravitational force, and a center called the singularity.

(D) Depending on a star's mass, it may evolve into a white dwarf, collapse into a black hole, or explode as a supernova.

(E) Astronauts can escape a black hole only if they fire their engines before they get too close to the singularity.

(F) An object falling within the event horizon will be pulled inward and experience a time warp as it approaches the singularity.

THEORIES OF EXPERIENCE AND EDUCATION

Two American philosophers, William James and John Dewey, developed very influential theories about how we think and learn. Both believed that the truth of any idea is a function of its usefulness and that experience is central to learning.

William James (1842–1910) was a philosopher and psychologist who believed that truth is not absolute and unchangeable; rather, it is made in actual, real–life events. In a person's life, there are experiences that have meaning and truth for that person. Truth cannot be separated from experience, and in order to understand truth, we have to study experience itself. Thus, for James, human experience should be the primary subject of study, and he called upon thinkers to concentrate on experience instead of essences, abstractions, or universal laws.

James focused on what he called the "stream" of experience, the sequential course of events in our lives. He believed that human consciousness is a stream of thoughts and feelings, and that this stream of consciousness is always going on, whether we are awake or asleep. The stream consists of very complex waves of bodily sensations, desires and aversions, memories of past experiences, and determinations of the will. One wave dissolves into another gradually, like the ripples of water in a river.

In James's theory, thought and experience are connected. Incoming waves of thought flow in next to outgoing waves of previous experience and thus become associated with each other. An incoming thought is "workable" only if it is meaningful and can be associated with something already in the person's mind. James's theory supports later theories of associative learning, which assert that new learning involves activating previous learning to find "hooks" on which to hang new information.

The theories of John Dewey (1859–1952), philosopher and educator, have had a tremendous impact on generations of thinkers. Dewey viewed life as a continuously reconstructive process, with experience and knowledge building on each other. He believed that learning is more than the amassing and retention of information; learning is learning how to think. Thinking is not something abstract; it is a living process that starts when old habits meet new situations.

For Dewey, experience cannot be separated from nature because all experience is rooted in nature. Nature is what we experience: air, stones, plants, diseases, pleasure, and suffering. Dewey believed that experience is an interaction between what a person already knows and the person's present situation. Previous knowledge of nature interacts with the present environment, and together they lead to new knowledge that in turn will influence future experience.

Dewey asserted that experience is central to education; however, experience cannot be equated with education because all experiences are not necessarily educative. Experience is educative only when it contributes to the growth of the individual. It can be miseducative if it distorts the growth of further experience. It is the quality of experience that matters. Thus, productive experience is both the means and the goal of education.

Dewey felt that education should be problem–centered and interdisciplinary rather than subject–centered and fragmented. The methods and curricula of education must make the child's growth the central concern. Furthermore, truly progressive education must involve the participation of the learner in directing the learning experience.

13. Which sentence below best expresses the essential information in the highlighted sentence in paragraph 2? Incorrect choices change the meaning in important ways or leave out essential information.

(A) We can comprehend what truth is only if we separate truth from experience and study each individually.

(B) The truth of any experience cannot be understood unless it is compared with past experiences.

(C) It is more important to learn from personal experience than to study philosophy to understand truth.

(D) We must study experience to know the meaning of truth because the two are necessarily connected.

14. The word sequential in paragraph 3 is closest in meaning to

(A) continuous
(B) apparent
(C) conscious
(D) interesting

15. Why does the author mention a river in paragraph 3?

(A) To describe how thoughts and feelings flow into each other

(B) To compare the processes of falling asleep and waking up

(C) To emphasize the complexity of bodily sensations

(D) To show that truth is not absolute and unchangeable

16. The word it in paragraph 4 refers to

(A) James's theory
(B) previous experience
(C) incoming thought
(D) the person's mind

17. The word reconstructive in paragraph 5 is closest in meaning to

(A) exciting
(B) creative
(C) unifying
(D) aimless

18. According to John Dewey, the interplay between a person's previous knowledge and present situation is

(A) truth
(B) consciousness
(C) education
(D) experience

19. All of the following ideas are part of Dewey's theory of experience and education EXCEPT

(A) Knowledge and experience interact.
(B) Present experience affects future experience.
(C) Every experience is educative.
(D) Experience should develop the individual.

20. According to Dewey, progressive education should include

(A) both positive and negative experiences
(B) an emphasis on specific core subjects
(C) complete rejection of traditional methods
(D) the active participation of the student

21. It can be inferred from the passage that William James and John Dewey would probably agree on which of the following statements?

(A) The truth of an idea is something that all people can agree upon.

(B) Our life experiences are a very important part of our education.

(C) To be truly educated, we must have our own theory of experience.

(D) The quantity of experience is more important than the quality.

22. Look at the four squares, **A**, **B**, **C**, and **D**, which indicate where the following sentence could be added to the passage. Where would the sentence best fit?

The incoming thoughts will come to resemble the outgoing thoughts, even though the two have never been experienced together before.

In James's theory, thought and experience are connected. **A** Incoming waves of thought flow in next to outgoing waves of previous experience and thus become associated with each other. **B** An incoming thought is "workable" only if it is meaningful and can be associated with something already in the person's mind. **C** James's theory supports later theories of associative learning, which assert that new learning involves activating previous learning to find "hooks" on which to hang new information. **D**

23–25. Select the appropriate sentences from the answer choices and match them to the correct philosopher. TWO of the answer choices will NOT be used. *This question is worth 3 points.*

Answer Choices

(A) Learning is not merely the storing of information; it is learning how to think.

(B) Truth is absolute and unchangeable because it is based on universal laws of nature.

(C) Human consciousness is a stream of experiences, sensations, thoughts, and feelings.

(D) Education should be problem–centered and interdisciplinary, and it should provide productive experience.

(E) A new thought is workable when it is associated with previous experience or learning.

(F) Experience and knowledge grow upon and influence each other in an ongoing process.

(G) The goal of education should be the development of the child's ability to think abstractly.

Philosopher

William James

•

•

John Dewey

•

•

•

Answers to Reading Quiz 10 are on page 574.

Record your score on the Progress Chart on page 693.

How to Score Multiple–Point Questions		
Points Possible	**Answers Correct**	**Points Earned**
2 points	3	2
	2	1
	0 – 1	0
3 points	5	3
	4	2
	3	1
	0 – 2	0
4 points	7	4
	6	3
	5	2
	4	1
	0 – 3	0

The Listening section of the TOEFL measures your ability to understand conversations and lectures in English. You will be tested on your comprehension of the general ideas and supporting details of the conversations and lectures. You will also be asked to identify a speaker's purpose in making a particular statement, and a speaker's attitude toward a particular topic.

LISTENING SECTION		
Type of Audio Text	Length of Audio Text	Number of Questions
Conversation 1	2 – 3 minutes	5
Conversation 2	2 – 3 minutes	5
Lecture 1	3 – 5 minutes	6
Lecture 2	3 – 5 minutes	6
Lecture 3	3 – 5 minutes	6
Lecture 4	3 – 5 minutes	6
Extra Audio Texts*	2 – 5 minutes each	5 – 6 each

*There may be an extra conversation and two extra lectures in some versions of the test.

Some of the listening topics are non–academic and informal, and they reflect typical experiences of college and university students. Some of the topics are academic and come from various fields of study in the natural sciences, the social sciences, the arts, and business. All of the questions are based on what the speakers state or imply. You do not need special knowledge of the topics to answer the questions.

THE TEST EXPERIENCE

The entire Listening section takes approximately 40 to 60 minutes to complete. This includes the time that you spend listening to the directions, listening to the conversations and lectures, and answering the comprehension questions.

You will use headphones to listen to the conversations and lectures. You can change the volume of the sound at any time during the test. You may take notes on paper while you are listening. You may use your notes to help you answer the questions. However, at the end of the test, you must give all of your notes to the test supervisor. Your notes will not be scored.

You will hear each conversation and lecture only one time. The two conversations and four lectures may be presented in any order. After each conversation or lecture, you will answer five or six comprehension questions. You will both *hear* and *see* and the questions on the screen.

There are six types of questions. For each type of question, you will use the mouse to click on one or more answers or to move text. Some of the questions have special directions, which appear in a gray box on the screen. Some questions may be worth more than one point. These questions have special directions that indicate how many points you can receive.

You must answer each question before you can go on to the next question. You can change your answer as many times as you like—until you click on **OK**. When you click on **OK**, the computer will go to the next question. You cannot go back to previous questions. Once you have left a question, you cannot return to it.

You can take as much time as you need to answer each question. However, you should work as quickly as possible because there is a time limit for the whole Listening section. A clock at the top of the screen shows how much time is left. The clock counts down only during your response time; it does not count down while you are listening to the conversations, lectures, and questions.

LISTENING SKILLS ON THE TEST

Unit in *Delta's Key*	Skill	Number of Questions (test with 6 texts)
2.1	Identifying the Topic and Main Idea	4 – 6
2.2	Listening for Details	8 – 12
2.3	Determining Attitude and Purpose	8 – 12
2.4	Making Inferences and Predictions	4 – 8
2.5	Categorizing Information	1 – 2
2.6	Summarizing a Process	1 – 2
	Total Number of Questions	34

CONVERSATIONS

The Listening section contains two conversations, which may appear in any sequence with the lectures. In some versions of the test, there may be three conversations. Each conversation is two to three minutes long and is followed by a set of comprehension questions.

Here is an example. While you are listening, you will see a picture of the speakers:

(Narrator)   Listen to a conversation between a student and a professor.
(Woman)   Excuse me, Dr. Gupta. May I speak with you?
(Professor) Sure. What can I do for you?
(Woman)   I'm... uh... I'd like to change the topic of my paper. I was planning to write about trade, but I thought of something more interesting.
(Professor) Oh...?
(Woman)   I was thinking... my friend introduced me to her grandparents, who came from Japan around seventy years ago. They're really interesting people, and we talked for a long time. So I got the idea it might be good to write about them... I mean, about Japanese immigration and the stories of people who came here from Japan. I could interview my friend's grandparents and their friends. Is that OK?
(Professor) Yes, I'd say that's a good research topic. But, in addition to the interview data, you'll want to be sure you have some historical facts. Focus on the history, and use the interviews to illustrate the history.
(Woman)   I... um... I found some books on the *Issei* and the *Nisei*. Is that what you mean?
(Professor) That's a good place to start. You should also check out cultural organizations, like the Japanese American Historical Society. I'm sure many of these organizations have Web pages. You may find links to other useful information.
(Woman)   Sure, sure, of course I'll do that. So... uh... it's all right to change my topic?
(Professor) Certainly. And let me know how it's going.
(Woman)   I sure will. Thanks, Dr. Gupta.

Then you will hear the first question. You will see the question and four possible answers:

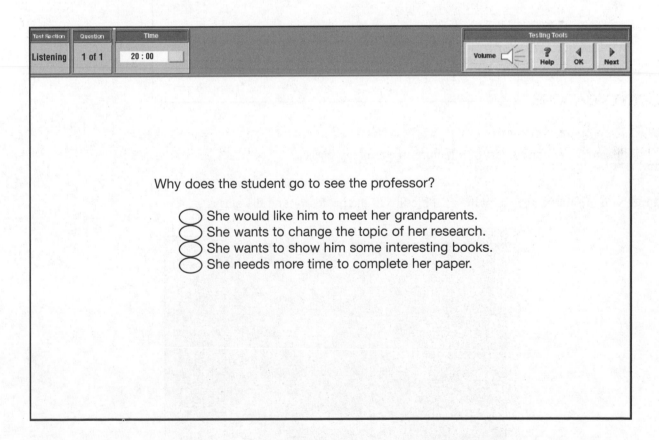

Why does the student go to see the professor?

○ She would like him to meet her grandparents.
○ She wants to change the topic of her research.
○ She wants to show him some interesting books.
○ She needs more time to complete her paper.

The best answer to the question *Why does the student go to see the professor?* is *She wants to change the topic of her research*. Therefore, you should click on the oval next to that answer.

When you click on an oval, the oval will darken. To change your answer, click on a different oval. When you are satisfied that you have chosen the correct answer, click on **Next**. Then click on **OK**. The computer will move to the next question.

LECTURES

The Listening section contains four academic lectures, which may appear in any sequence with the conversations. In some versions of the test, there may be six lectures. Each lecture is approximately three to five minutes long and is followed by a set of comprehension questions.

Here is an example.

Geology

(Narrator)   Listen to part of a lecture in a geology class.

While you are listening, you will see a picture of the professor and the class:

(Professor) After the water drains from a cave, a new kind of growth may begin. Delicate straws grow from the ceiling. Twisted fingers protrude from the walls and floor. Smooth mounds appear in pools. All of these amazing formations are called speleothems. They sometimes grow in sandstone and lava–tube caves, but most commonly we see them in limestone caves.

Among the most interesting speleothems are stalactites and stalagmites. People always want to know: how do you keep straight… which is a stalactite and which is a stalagmite? There's an easy way to remember. "Stalactite" is spelled with a "c" and it hangs from the ceiling. "Stalagmite" is spelled with a "g" and it grows up from the ground.

You may also see other pictures:

(Professor) Both stalactites and stalagmites begin with a drop of water on a cave ceiling. The ground–water seeping into the cave contains carbon dioxide from the atmosphere or the soil, as well as dissolved limestone that it picked up from the layers of rock above the cave.

As a drop of water hangs from the ceiling, a tiny amount of carbon dioxide escapes—just like bubbles from a can of soda pop. Now the water drop can't carry much dissolved lime-stone, and a tiny ring of stone called dripstone forms around its outside edges. The drop of water hangs for a moment, then it falls.

Each drop of water adds another layer as it trickles down through the growing ring of drip-stone. Eventually, the dripstone forms a slender tube. These slender, hollow tubes are called tubular stalactites, or—because they look like straws—soda–straw stalactites. They're very fragile. As they grow, their own weight may cause them to break off and fall to the floor. Soda straws can grow into conical stalactites as dripstone builds up on the outside. Stalactites don't grow very quickly… on average, only about a half–inch in a hundred years.

The dripping water that hits the floor still contains some dissolved limestone. The impact of the water hitting the floor causes it to break into droplets, releasing the excess carbon dioxide. Then limestone crystals start to grow upward, forming stalagmites… starting with tiny finger–like structures, and eventually forming large, rounded domes up to ten meters tall and ten meters in diameter.

At the end of the lecture, you will see:

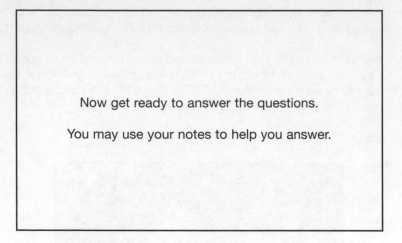

Now get ready to answer the questions.

You may use your notes to help you answer.

There are six different types of listening comprehension questions. However, you may not see all six types after every lecture.

Question Type 1 – Click on One Answer

For this multiple–choice type of question, you will choose the best of four possible answers. You will see:

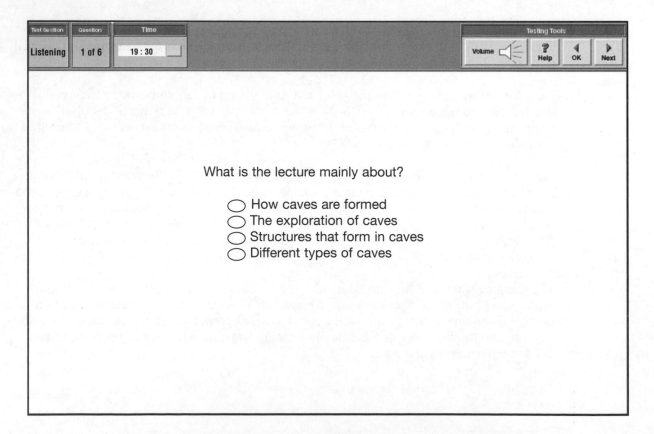

What is the lecture mainly about?

- How caves are formed
- The exploration of caves
- Structures that form in caves
- Different types of caves

The topic of the lecture is *Structures that form in caves*. Therefore, you should click on the oval next to the third answer.

When you click on an oval, the oval will darken. To change your answer, click on a different oval. When you are satisfied that you have chosen the correct answer, click on **Next**. Then click on **OK**. The computer will move to the next question.

Question Type 2 – Click on Two Answers

For this type of question, you will click on two answers. You will click on boxes instead of ovals. You will see:

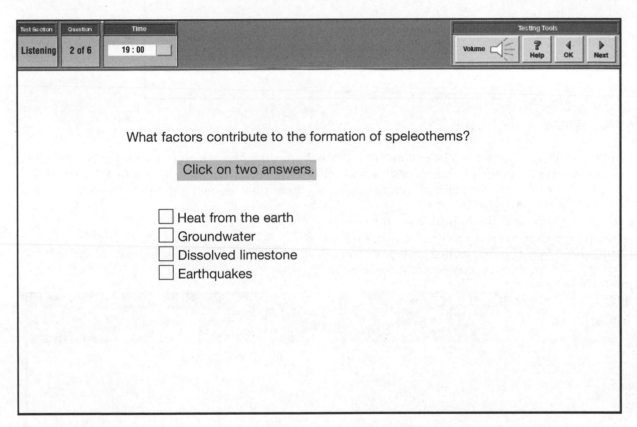

The professor says:

> Both stalactites and stalagmites begin with a drop of water on a cave ceiling. The groundwater seeping into the cave contains carbon dioxide from the atmosphere or the soil, as well as dissolved limestone that it picked up from the layers of rock above the cave.

Therefore, you should click on the boxes next to *Groundwater* and *Dissolved limestone*.

When you click on a box, an X will appear in it. To change an answer, click on a different box.

You must choose both correct answers to receive credit for answering the question correctly.

Question Type 3 – Listen Again to Part of the Text

For this type of question, you will hear part of the audio again. You will hear and see:

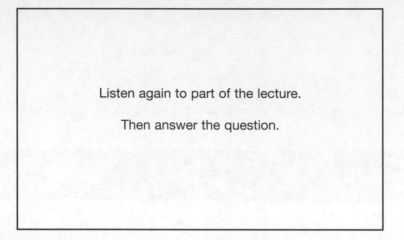

Listen again to part of the lecture.

Then answer the question.

Then you will hear:

(Professor) People always want to know: how do you keep straight… which is a stalactite and which is a stalagmite? There's an easy way to remember. "Stalactite" is spelled with a "c" and it hangs from the ceiling. "Stalagmite" is spelled with a "g" and it grows up from the ground.

(Narrator) Why does the professor say this:

(Professor) "Stalactite" is spelled with a "c" and it hangs from the ceiling. "Stalagmite" is spelled with a "g" and it grows up from the ground.

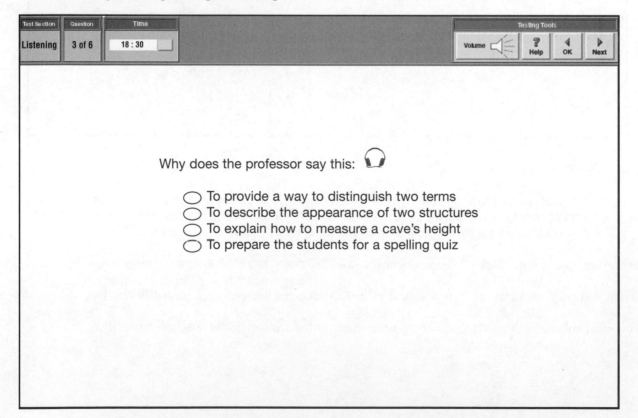

Why does the professor say this:

○ To provide a way to distinguish two terms
○ To describe the appearance of two structures
○ To explain how to measure a cave's height
○ To prepare the students for a spelling quiz

When you see the symbol 🎧 next to a question, it means that part of the question will not appear on the screen. However, you will hear part of the lecture again, so you must listen carefully. The computer will replay something that the professor says in the lecture.

The professor says:

> People always want to know: how do you keep straight… which is a stalactite and which is a stalagmite? There's an easy way to remember.

Then the professor discusses the spelling of stalactite and stalagmite. The correct answer is *To provide a way to distinguish two terms*. Therefore, you should click on the oval next to the first answer.

Question Type 4 – Click on a Picture

For this type of question, you will click on a picture or part of a picture. You will see:

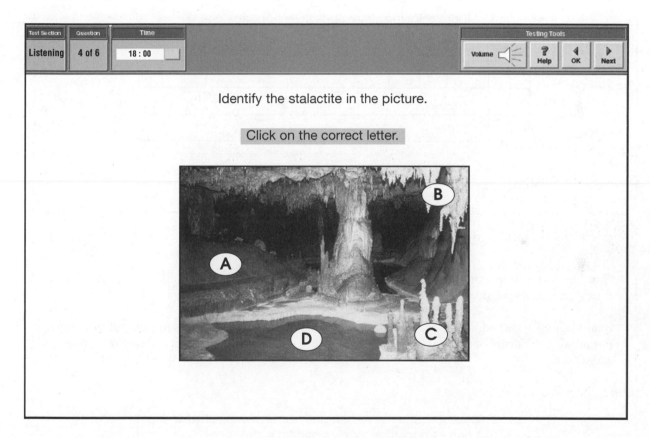

The professor says:

> "Stalactite" is spelled with a "c" and it hangs from the ceiling.

The stalactite is at ⬭B in the picture. Therefore, you should click on ⬭B.

When you click on a letter, the letter will highlight. To change your answer, click on a different letter.

Question Type 5 – Drag Answer Choices

For this type of question, you will use the mouse to drag text to complete a list, table, or summary. You will see:

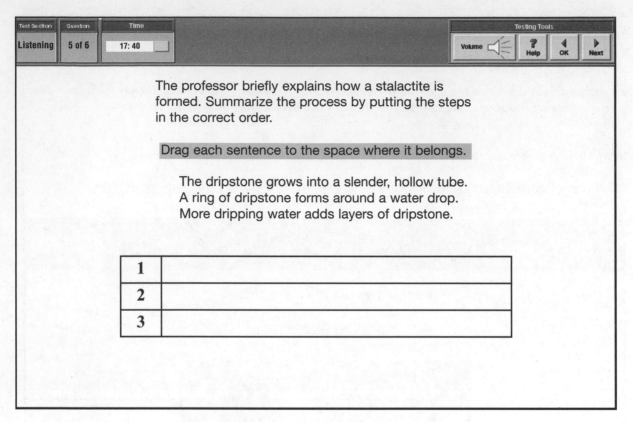

The professor says:

Now the water drop can't carry much dissolved limestone, and a tiny ring of stone called dripstone forms around its outside edges....

Each drop of water adds another layer as it trickles down through the growing ring of dripstone. Eventually, the dripstone forms a slender tube. These slender, hollow tubes are called tubular stalactites....

Therefore, the correct order is:

1	A ring of dripstone forms around a water drop.
2	More dripping water adds layers of dripstone.
3	The dripstone grows into a slender, hollow tube.

Move the cursor to the answer choice that you want to move. Click and hold to drag the text to the space where it belongs. The text will appear in that space. To change an answer, click on it. Then drag your new answer choice to the space. You must put all of the answer choices in the correct space to receive credit for answering the question correctly.

Question Type 6 – Click on a Table

For this type of question, you will click on boxes in a table. You will see:

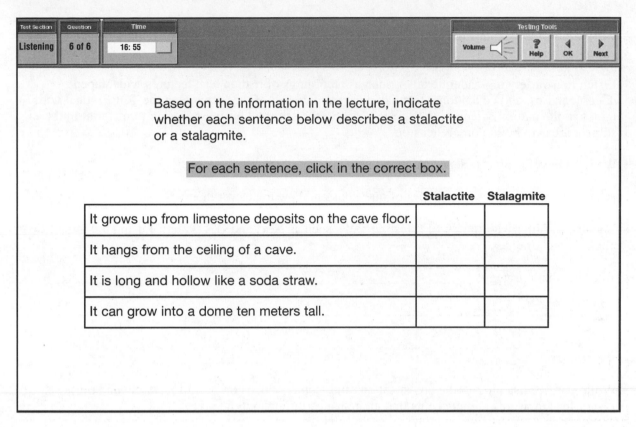

The professor says:

"Stalactite"… hangs from the ceiling. "Stalagmite"… grows up from the ground.

These slender, hollow tubes are called… because they look like straws—soda–straw stalactites.

Then limestone crystals start to grow upward, forming stalagmites… eventually forming large, rounded domes up to ten meters tall….

Therefore, the correct answers are:

	Stalactite	Stalagmite
It grows up from limestone deposits on the cave floor.		✓
It hangs from the ceiling of a cave.	✓	
It is long and hollow like a soda straw.	✓	
It can grow into a dome ten meters tall.		✓

When you click on a box, a ✓ will appear in it. You must click on one box in each row. To change an answer, click on a different box in the same row. You must put all of the ✓s in the correct space to receive credit for answering the question correctly.

STRATEGIES FOR THE LISTENING SECTION

Before the Test

- Work on building your vocabulary. Use the conversations and lectures in this book to become familiar with the level of vocabulary on the TOEFL.

- Listen to a variety of academic talks, such as recordings of real college lectures, videotaped documentaries, and educational television programs. Most of the lectures on the TOEFL deal with topics in the natural sciences, the social sciences, the arts, and business. Listen to material in these subject areas to build comprehension.

- Work on developing efficient note–taking skills.

- Become familiar with the six types of questions and how to answer them.

- Become familiar with the TOEFL testing tools, such as **Next** and **OK**. Practice using the mouse to click on and drag text.

- Your own best strategy: _____

_____

During the Test

- While you are listening to the conversations and lectures, focus on overall meaning and purpose. Listen for key words and concepts that are repeated throughout the piece.

- When you take notes, write down only essential terms and concepts. Do not allow your writing to detract from your listening.

- Work as quickly as possible. Although you can control the amount of time you spend answering each question, there is a time limit for answering the total number of questions in the Listening section.

- For multiple choice questions, use the ***process of elimination***. This means that if you do not find the correct answer right away, omit the choices you know are incorrect. If you can eliminate one or two choices, you will improve your chance of selecting the correct answer.

- Click on **OK** only when you are certain you are ready to go on to the next question. After you click on **OK**, you cannot return to the previous question.

- Your own best strategy: _____

_____

212   DELTA'S KEY TO THE NEXT GENERATION TOEFL® TEST

2.1 Identifying the Topic and Main Idea

FOCUS

Disk 1, Track 1

What is the subject of the conversation?

○ A political organization
○ A course reading list
○ A physical science class
○ A summer school program

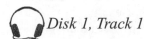*Stop*

The subject of the conversation is the most general answer to the question *What are the people talking about?*

The speakers use several key words and phrases:

Dr. Perry's class	check the computer	substantial amount of reading
Political Science	summer session	print out a copy
book list	Here…found	few minutes

The man asks about the book list for Dr. Perry's Introduction to Political Science class, and the woman offers to print out a copy for him. Therefore, the correct answer is *A course reading list*.

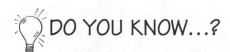DO YOU KNOW…?

1. The *topic* is the general subject of the conversation or lecture. The topic is the most general answer to the question *What are the speakers talking about?*

   TOEFL questions about the topic sound like this:

   What is the subject of the conversation?
   What is the topic of the discussion?
   What are the students discussing?
   What is the man's problem?
   What problem does the woman have?
   What is the professor mainly discussing?
   What is the lecture mainly about?
   What is the main topic of the talk?
   What aspect of _____ does the professor mainly discuss?

2. Key words and phrases can help you identify the topic of the conversation or lecture. Sometimes speakers emphasize key words and phrases. Sometimes speakers use the same key words more than once. Listen for words and phrases that are stressed or repeated by the speakers.

   Key words are usually **content words**: nouns, verbs, adjectives, and adverbs. Content words can help you identify the topic and general message.

3. Listen again to the recording for the Focus exercise. Listen for key words and phrases that the speakers emphasize and repeat. Listen for key content words: nouns, verbs, adjectives, and adverbs.

Disk 1, Track 1

    W: Good afternoon. May I help you?

    M: Hello. I'm thinking of taking <u>Dr. Perry's class</u> this summer—<u>Intro to Political Science</u>. And I was wondering… uh… is there a… do you happen to have a <u>book list for that class</u>?

    W: I can <u>check the computer</u> to see if she submitted it yet.

    M: Thanks. I'd appreciate it.

    W: Did you say Introduction to Political Science?

    M: Yes. For <u>summer session</u>.

    W: <u>Here</u> it is, I <u>found</u> it. Oh… and it sure looks like a <u>substantial</u> amount of <u>reading</u>!

    M: Really? Is it <u>long</u>?

    W: Would you like me to <u>print</u> out a <u>copy</u> for you?

    M: Yeah, that would be great!

    W: All right. This will only take a <u>few minutes</u>.

    M: Thank you. I really appreciate it.

Stop

---

4. The **main idea** is the general message of the conversation or lecture. The main idea is what is important about the topic, according to the speakers. Key words and phrases can help you identify what the speakers think is important about the topic. In a longer piece, there may be two or more major ideas that together form the general message.

   TOEFL questions about the main idea sound like this:

   > What is the speaker's main point?
   > What is the main idea of the lecture?

5. The **organization** of a talk or lecture is the order in which the speaker presents information. The organization is usually related to the speaker's main point and purpose. A good speaker organizes the information so that it best supports the main idea.

TOEFL questions about organization sound like this:

How does the speaker organize the information that he presents?
Which of the following best describes the organization of the lecture?
How does the professor develop the topic?
How does the professor help the student?
How does the instructor clarify her point about _____?

6. Some examples of organization are:

Classify or categorize information	Give instructions
Describe causes and effects	Narrate an event
Describe uses	Show differences between ideas
Explain causes	Show similarities between things
Explain reasons	Summarize a process
Give examples	Trace the history or development

7. In questions about the topic and main idea, an answer choice may be incorrect because it is:

 too general: an idea that is beyond the focus of the conversation or lecture;
 too specific: a supporting detail instead of a main idea;
 inaccurate: not true, or only partly true, according to the speakers; or
 irrelevant: about something that the speakers do not mention.

When you answer questions about the topic and main idea, think about the overall message of the conversation or lecture. Try not to *overthink* this type of question; it is often best to trust your first impression.

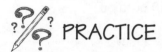 PRACTICE

Exercise 2.1.A

Listen to the recording. Choose the best answer to each question. To make this practice more like the real test, cover the questions and answers during each conversation and lecture. When you hear each question, uncover that question and answers.

 Disk 1, Track 2

1. What is the woman's problem?

  (A) She does not have enough time to finish writing her paper.
  (B) She is concerned about receiving a poor grade in history.
  (C) She is confused by her professor's response to her paper.
  (D) She does not think her professor graded her paper fairly.

2. What is the conversation mainly about?

  (A) A place that is special
  (B) Problems with families
  (C) Plans for a school vacation
  (D) A popular beach resort

3. What is the woman mainly discussing?

  (A) Her courses in child development
  (B) Her internship at a children's agency
  (C) How to look for a job after graduation
  (D) How to organize a political campaign

4. What problem does the man have?

    (A) He has difficulty remembering some terms.
    (B) He is not skilled at climbing trees.
    (C) He will not be able to take the botany quiz.
    (D) He can't decide which botany course to take.

5. How does the woman help the man?

    (A) She shows him how to put words in alphabetical order.
    (B) She tells him that memorization is not a good way to study.
    (C) She gives him a list of names beginning with "P" and "X".
    (D) She suggests that he imagine a tree with key letters on it.

 Stop

Exercise 2.1.B

Listen to the recording. Choose the best answer to each question. To make this practice more like the real test, cover the questions and answers during each conversation and lecture. When you hear each question, uncover that question and answers.

 Disk 1, Track 3

1. What is the talk mainly about?

    (A) The best places to park on campus
    (B) Services of the Safety and Security Office
    (C) The increasing need for campus security
    (D) Reporting criminal incidents on campus

2. What is the topic of the lecture?

    (A) Traditions of American Indian cultures
    (B) How religion, art, and culture are related
    (C) Different ways to view American culture
    (D) The vision quest of the Plains tribes

3. Which of the following best describes the organization of the talk?

    (A) Reasons to buy property–liability insurance
    (B) Instructions for buying life insurance
    (C) A classification of insurance
    (D) A history of insurance

4. What is the lecture mainly about?

    (A) How ancient rivers created deserts
    (B) How scientists work in the desert
    (C) How to walk on sand dunes
    (D) How sand dunes shift position

5. What is the lecture mainly about?

    (A) Research in pain management
    (B) The benefits of exercise
    (C) Why people have faith in doctors
    (D) The chemistry of the human brain

 Stop

Exercise 2.1.C

Listen to the recording. Choose the best answer to each question. To make this practice more like the real test, cover the questions and answers during each conversation and lecture. When you hear each question, uncover that question and answers.

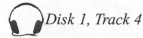 *Disk 1, Track 4*

1. What is the speaker's main point?

   Ⓐ Attitudes toward aging can affect how long a person lives.
   Ⓑ People have difficulty learning new skills as they get older.
   Ⓒ Young adults generally have a negative view of older adults.
   Ⓓ People are now living longer than they did in the past.

2. What is the speaker mainly discussing?

   Ⓐ Popular bachelor's degree programs
   Ⓑ The art and science of engineering
   Ⓒ Educational programs for engineers
   Ⓓ How engineers contribute to society

3. How does the speaker organize the information that he presents?

   Ⓐ By comparing the benefits of various engineering specialties
   Ⓑ By outlining the steps for applying to engineering school
   Ⓒ By tracing the development of the engineering profession
   Ⓓ By giving examples of undergraduate and graduate programs

4. What aspect of RSI does the instructor mainly discuss?

   Ⓐ Similarities to other illnesses
   Ⓑ Causes and effects
   Ⓒ Reasons for its rapid growth
   Ⓓ Available treatments

5. How does the instructor develop the topic of RSI?

   Ⓐ She compares treatments for RSI.
   Ⓑ She explains how to avoid RSI.
   Ⓒ She discusses recent research on RSI.
   Ⓓ She describes symptoms of RSI.

 Stop

Answers to Exercises 2.1.A through 2.1.C are on page 576.

EXTENSION

1. Listen again to the conversations and lectures in Exercises 2.1.A through 2.1.C (Disk 1, Tracks 2 through 4). While you are listening, write down key content words: nouns, verbs, adjectives, and adverbs. Don't try to write down everything. Write down only the words and phrases that are keys to understanding the overall message. Compare the words that you wrote down with those that your classmates wrote down. Which words and phrases are the most important for understanding the message?

2. With a classmate, discuss why the incorrect answer choices in Exercises 2.1.A through 2.1.C are incorrect. Are the answers wrong because they are:

   - too general: beyond the focus of the conversation or lecture?
   - too specific: supporting detail instead of main idea?
   - inaccurate: not true, or only partly true, according to the speakers?
   - irrelevant: about something that the speakers do not mention?

3. Listen again to the conversations in Exercise 2.1.A (Disk 1, Track 2). With your classmates, discuss the meaning of the underlined expressions in the script below. In what other situations might these expressions be used?

How's it going?	Hi, Kelsey! <u>How's it going</u>?
get (something) back	I just <u>got my history paper back</u>….
You'd better	<u>You'd better</u> go talk to him.
find out	You need to <u>find out</u> what he's thinking.
hang out	I'm going to Mexico to <u>hang out</u> on the beach!
How about you?	Four of us will be staying at a resort…. <u>How about you?</u>
not mind	But, I <u>don't mind</u>. It's my turn.
(one's) turn.	It's <u>my turn</u>. He's done so much for me in the past.
do an internship	I'll be <u>doing an internship</u> instead.
sounds like	That <u>sounds like</u> a great experience because….
if only I could	I guess so, <u>if only I could</u> remember the difference between….
get it straight	I can't seem to <u>get it straight</u> on which one….

4. Make a short audio recording from the radio or television. Record two or three minutes of a speech, documentary, or educational program. Bring your tape to class. Play the tape for your classmates. Then, discuss the recording with the class. Identify the topic and important ideas from the piece. What key words and phrases help you to identify the topic and what is important about it?

2.2 Listening for Details

 FOCUS

 Disk 1, Track 5

---

1. At what decibel level does the risk of hearing loss begin?

    ○ 60 decibels
    ○ 90 decibels
    ○ 125 decibels
    ○ 140 decibels

2. Which sounds could contribute to hearing loss?

    Click on two answers.

    ☐ A conversation at close range
    ☐ A rock band at close range
    ☐ A jet engine at close range
    ☐ A vacuum cleaner at close range

 Stop

Question 1 asks you to identify the decibel level at which the risk of hearing loss begins. The professor says:

> The danger zone—the risk of injury—begins at around 90. Continual exposure to sounds above 90 decibels can damage your hearing.

Therefore, the correct answer is *90 decibels*.

Question 2 asks you to identify the sounds that could contribute to hearing loss. For this question, there are two correct answers. The professor says:

> Lots of everyday noises are bad for us in the long run. For example…. A rock band at close range is 125 decibels. A jet engine at close range is one of the worst culprits at an ear–busting 140 decibels.

The correct answers are *A rock band at close range* and *A jet engine at close range*.

These two questions ask about some important details in the talk. The details support the main idea that long–term exposure to noise can cause hearing loss. What other details can you recall from the talk?

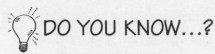

DO YOU KNOW...?

1. **Details** are specific bits of information, such as facts, descriptions, definitions, reasons, and examples. Detail questions on the TOEFL involve facts as they are stated by the speakers. Detail questions ask you to recall specific information from the conversation or lecture, but do not require you to make inferences (see 2.4).

   TOEFL questions about details sound like this:

   > What does the woman want to know?
   > What does the man suggest the woman do?
   > What happened to _____?
   > What reason is given for _____?
   > What does the professor say about _____?
   > How does the speaker describe _____?
   > How does the professor emphasize her point about _____?
   > According to the professor, _____?
   > What _____?
   > What type _____?
   > Who _____?
   > Where _____?
   > When _____?
   > Which _____?
   > How _____?
   > Why _____?

2. Some questions ask you to select a picture or part of a picture:

   > Which picture _____?
   > Select the drawing that shows _____.
   > Select the diagram that represents _____.
   > Identify the part of the picture that represents _____.
   > Which area of the diagram illustrates _____?

3. Some questions ask about specific terms:

   > What is a _____?
   > In this conversation, what does _____ mean?
   > According to the speaker, what does _____ mean?
   > How does the professor define _____?

4. Listen again to the recording for the Focus exercise. Listen for important details and content words.

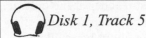 *Disk 1, Track 5*

Long–term underline exposure to noise can lead to underline loss of hearing. The relative loudness of sounds is underline measured in underline decibels. Just to give you an idea of what this means, the sound of a underline whisper is underline 30 decibels, while a underline normal conversation is 60 decibels. The noise a underline vacuum cleaner makes is around 85 decibels.

The underline danger zone—the risk of injury—begins at around underline 90. Continual exposure to sounds above 90 decibels can underline damage your hearing. underline Loud noises—especially when they come at you underline every day—all this noise can underline damage the delicate hair cells in your inner ear. Lots of everyday noises are underline bad for us in the long run. For example, a underline car horn sounds at around underline 100 decibels. A underline rock band at close range is underline 125 decibels. A underline jet engine at close range is one of the underline worst culprits at an ear–busting underline 140 decibels.

The underline first thing to go is your underline high–frequency hearing, where you detect the consonant sounds in words. That's why a person with hearing loss can hear voices, but has underline trouble understanding what's being said.

 Stop

5. In questions about details, an answer choice may be incorrect because it:

- repeats some of the speakers' words but has a different message;
- uses words that sound similar to the speakers' words;
- is incorrect or inaccurate, according to the speakers; or
- is about something that the speakers do not mention.

Remember, you can answer all of the questions based on the information you hear in the conversations and lectures. You do not need special knowledge of the topics to answer the questions correctly.

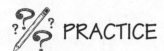 PRACTICE

Exercise 2.2.A

Listen to the recording. Choose the best answer to each question. To make this practice more like the real test, cover the questions and answers during each conversation and lecture. When you hear each question, uncover that question and answers.

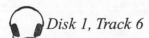 *Disk 1, Track 6*

1. What does the woman suggest the man do?

- (A) Look at the posted job openings
- (B) Call for information about a job
- (C) Make an appointment with a counselor
- (D) Apply for a job in the student center

2. What type of job does the man want?

- (A) A job that pays well
- (B) A job that will let him study
- (C) A job in his field of interest
- (D) A job as a counselor

3. What does the woman agree to do?

   (A) Donate some books to the library
   (B) Meet the man outside the library
   (C) Volunteer to work as a cashier
   (D) Buy books at the annual book sale

4. How are book sale workers compensated?

   (A) They take any ten books that they want.
   (B) They are paid ten dollars an hour in cash.
   (C) They receive a set of encyclopedias.
   (D) They get credit to buy books at the sale.

5. When will the woman arrive at the book sale?

   (A) 10:00 a.m.
   (B) 12:00 p.m.
   (C) 3:00 p.m.
   (D) 6:00 p.m.

6. Why does the woman like her class with Professor Hahn?

   (A) Professor Hahn is a well–known scientist.
   (B) The assignments and lectures are valuable.
   (C) The students solve practical problems in class.
   (D) Political science is the woman's favorite subject.

7. What does the man say about Professor Hahn?

   (A) She is the best teacher at the college.
   (B) She tries to amuse her students.
   (C) She cares a lot about her students.
   (D) She expects her students to work hard.

8. What does the professor want the woman to do?

   (A) Help him write a paper
   (B) Arrange some articles
   (C) Look up information
   (D) Organize a research study

9. What is the subject of the professor's research?

   (A) Animal behavior
   (B) Journal writing
   (C) Time management
   (D) Child psychology

10. When will the woman do the work?

   (A) That afternoon
   (B) The next day
   (C) The day after tomorrow
   (D) The following week

 Stop

Exercise 2.2.B

Listen to the recording. Choose the best answer to each question. To make this practice more like the real test, cover the questions and answers during each conversation and lecture. When you hear each question, uncover that question and answers.

Disk 1, Track 7

1. When did the hunting season take place?

   (A) In spring and summer
   (B) In summer and early fall
   (C) From fall until midwinter
   (D) From midwinter until spring

2. What animals did the northwoods tribes hunt?

   Click on two answers.

   A Lion
   B Eagle
   C Deer
   D Moose

3. According to the man, how did women participate in hunting?

(A) Managing the camps
(B) Snaring small animals
(C) Searching for game
(D) Making the bows and arrows

4. Which activities did women control?

Click on two answers.

[A] Fishing
[B] Clan leadership
[C] Education
[D] Agriculture

5. According to the professor, what factors are important in choosing a career in the arts?

Click on two answers.

[A] Wealth
[B] Talent
[C] Luck
[D] Experience

6. According to the professor, why does a career in the arts require a special calling?

(A) Public tastes in art change frequently.
(B) Employment in the arts can be uncertain.
(C) Art schools are expensive and difficult.
(D) Artistic talent cannot be measured fairly.

7. How does the professor suggest one get started in a career in the arts?

(A) Ask a famous artist for a letter of recommendation.
(B) Look at the job advertisements in the newspaper.
(C) Do part–time or volunteer work in one's chosen art.
(D) Apply for a scholarship to a prestigious art school.

8. According to the instructor, what is the first step in preparing a speech?

(A) Choose a topic that your teacher will like.
(B) Realize the speech's importance to you.
(C) Develop your ideas with examples.
(D) Read a book about preparing a speech.

9. What examples of purpose are mentioned in the discussion?

Click on two answers.

[A] To inform others about your subject
[B] To describe an interesting experience
[C] To make your audience laugh
[D] To explain how to do something

10. What does the instructor want the students to do next?

(A) Practice their speeches in small groups
(B) Write down ideas that they think of
(C) Choose from a list of possible topics
(D) Brainstorm ways to entertain the class

 Stop

Exercise 2.2.C

Listen to the recording. Choose the best answer to each question. To make this practice more like the real test, cover the questions and answers during each conversation and lecture. When you hear each question, uncover that question and answers.

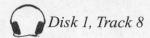 *Disk 1, Track 8*

1. What is the main topic of the talk?

    (A) Types of winds over the sea
    (B) Characteristics of the sea breeze
    (C) How sea breezes help sailors
    (D) Coastal temperature changes

2. Select the diagram that represents the sea breeze.

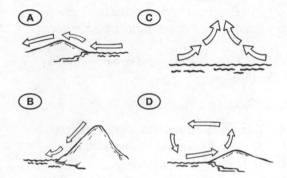

3. Identify the part of the diagram that shows the sea breeze's return flow.

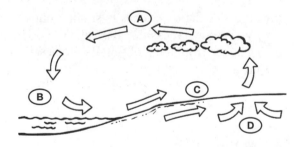

4. What topics does the speaker discuss?

    Click on two answers.

    A Popular horn players in history
    B How a horn's sound is produced
    C The horn as a jazz instrument
    D Early uses of the horn

5. When did the horn become a standard part of the orchestra?

    (A) In the Middle Ages
    (B) In the fourteenth century
    (C) In the eighteenth century
    (D) In the nineteenth century

6. How does the professor develop the topic of tsunamis?

    Click on two answers.

    A By comparing tsunamis and floods
    B By describing causes of tsunamis
    C By sharing his experience of a tsunami
    D By giving examples of tsunamis

7. Why is the term "tidal wave" inaccurate for a tsunami?

    (A) Tides cause only the worst tsunamis.
    (B) Tsunamis occur only at high tide.
    (C) Waves do not have enough force to kill.
    (D) Tsunamis are not related to tides.

8. What causes tsunamis?

    Click on two answers.

    A Movement of the ocean floor
    B Heavy precipitation
    C Undersea earthquakes
    D The moon's gravity

9. What point does the professor make about the eruption of the volcano Krakatoa?

    (A) People could see the eruption from as far away as Hawaii.
    (B) A tsunami following the eruption killed thousands of people.
    (C) Krakatoa erupts more frequently than any other volcano.
    (D) The eruption caused thousands of fishing boats to sink.

10. What is true of the tsunami that struck Japan in 1896?

    (A) It was caused by an undersea earthquake.
    (B) It occurred while people were sleeping.
    (C) It followed a series of volcanic eruptions.
    (D) It was first reported by fisherman at sea.

 Stop

Exercise 2.2.D

Listen to the recording. Choose the best answer to each question. To make this practice more like the real test, cover the questions and answers during each conversation and lecture. When you hear each question, uncover that question and answers.

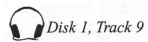 *Disk 1, Track 9*

1. What are the students discussing?

    (A) Terms from a lecture
    (B) Questions on a test
    (C) Property rights
    (D) Topics for a term paper

2. What does "primogeniture" mean?

    (A) A state in which the ruler owns all property
    (B) Dividing property among several children
    (C) A system of inheritance by the firstborn son
    (D) Paying property taxes to the state

3. According to the professor, why do many small businesses fail?

    (A) They do not demand hard work from their employees.
    (B) They do not expand into large businesses.
    (C) They have poor–quality products and services.
    (D) They lack the financial reserves to absorb losses.

4. According to the professor, what is essential for success as a small business owner?

    (A) A master's degree in business
    (B) Friends in positions of power
    (C) A large amount of credit
    (D) Good management skills

5. What are two responsibilities of a store owner?

    Click on two answers.

    [A] Buying the store building
    [B] Keeping track of inventory
    [C] Promoting the store's products
    [D] Inventing new products

6. What does the woman want to discuss with the teaching assistant?

    (A) Trouble that happened in class last week
    (B) A friend she met on a field trip
    (C) Something she saw when she was hiking
    (D) A problem with one of her classmates

7. Where did the woman meet the young man who had a problem?

    (A) In high school
    (B) In biology class
    (C) On a mountain road
    (D) On a desert trail

8. What help did the young man receive?

    Click on two answers.

    [A] The woman gave him water.
    [B] A doctor repaired his leg.
    [C] The ranger showed him a map.
    [D] His teacher brought him food.

9. Why did the young man experience muscle cramps?

- (A) His muscles were weak from too little exercise.
- (B) The cells in his muscles did not have enough oxygen.
- (C) He injured his leg muscle when he fell on a rock.
- (D) An excessive amount of salt collected in the muscles.

10. What point does the teaching assistant make about what the woman saw?

- (A) The woman recognized biology in real life.
- (B) The woman saw two foolish young men.
- (C) The woman should try to forget what she saw.
- (D) The woman will see more interesting things.

 Stop

Exercise 2.2.E

Listen to the recording. Choose the best answer to each question. To make this practice more like the real test, cover the questions and answers during each conversation and lecture. When you hear each question, uncover that question and answers.

 Disk 1, Track 10

1. What is a pigment?

- (A) A chemical used for cleaning painting equipment
- (B) A cover to protect paintings from the effects of sunlight
- (C) A substance that gives its color to another material
- (D) A synthetic fabric that is suitable for painting on

2. According to the instructor, what characteristic should a pigment have?

- (A) Ability to be applied at any temperature
- (B) Ability to dry quickly after application
- (C) No loss of strength when dissolved
- (D) No harmful reaction with other pigments

3. How are pigments generally classified?

- (A) By origin
- (B) By texture
- (C) By color
- (D) By quality

4. Which natural pigment did the Romans obtain from a shellfish?

- (A) Raw umber
- (B) Indigo
- (C) Tyrian purple
- (D) Ochre

5. According to the instructor, why are synthetic pigments superior to natural pigments?

Click on two answers.

- [A] They last for a longer time.
- [B] They have a smoother surface.
- [C] They are less expensive.
- [D] They provide stronger, brighter colors.

6. What aspect of volcanoes does the professor mainly discuss?

- (A) Substances produced by volcanoes
- (B) Different types of volcanoes
- (C) The formation of shield volcanoes
- (D) Volcanoes of Hawaii and Iceland

7. Identify the types of substances that erupt from volcanoes.

Click on two answers.

A Hot gases
B Liquefied rock
C Ice cones
D Yellow stone

8. Select the picture that is most like a shield volcano.

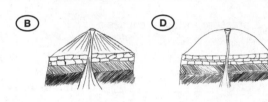

9. Select the picture that is most like a caldera.

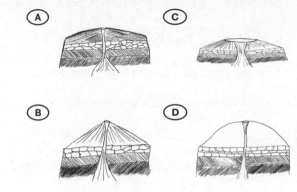

10. Which type of volcano is associated with the geysers in Yellowstone National Park?

Ⓐ Caldera
Ⓑ Shield
Ⓒ Cinder cone
Ⓓ Bomb

 Stop

Answers to Exercises 2.2.A through 2.2.E are on page 576.

 EXTENSION

1. Listen again to the conversations in Exercise 2.2.A (Disk 1, Track 6). With your classmates, discuss the meaning of the underlined expressions in the script below. In what other situations might these expressions be used?

check out	You should <u>check out</u> the job board in the student center.
spare time	…I need the money but I don't have a lot of <u>spare time</u>.
free	If you're <u>free</u> in the afternoon…
help out	…why not volunteer to <u>help</u> us <u>out</u>?
I guess I could	<u>I guess I could</u> spare a few hours.
put (one's) name down	I can <u>put your name down</u> then?
make (someone do something)	She really <u>makes us think</u>. And she really <u>makes you work</u> in her class!
figure out	I'm starting to <u>figure</u> things <u>out</u> as a result of this class.
go through	These are all journal articles that I need to <u>go through</u> for my research.
deal with	Most are about primate behavior, but a few <u>deal with</u> other mammals or birds….

2. Listen again to the first lecture in Exercise 2.2.C. As you listen, write the correct words on the blank lines in the script below. Check your answers with the audio script on page 619.

🎧 *Disk 1, Track 8*

Listen to part of a talk in a geography class.

Now we'll turn our attention to a _____ of local wind known as the sea

_____. The sea breeze is the _____, most widespread, and most persistent

of _____ winds. The sea breeze _____ from the heating of land and

_____ along a coastline in near–_____ conditions.

The more rapid _____ of the land during the _____ results in the

development of a _____ gradient across the coast. This _____ to ascent

over the land and _____ over the sea. Thus, a pressure gradient causes a

_____ of air from sea to land.

At the _____ time as the breeze flows from _____ to land, there is

a return flow _____ up, from land to sea. The airflow forms a _____ pattern,

from sea to land, _____, and back out to sea. The flow _____ through the

day, and by the middle of the _____, may extend several _____ inland.

At _____, the situation is _____ and the flow is from the

_____ land to the warmer sea, as a _____ breeze.

🎧 *Stop*

3. Listen again to the first lecture in Exercise 2.2.E. As you listen, write the correct words on the blank lines in the script below. Check your answers with the audio script on page 621.

🎧 *Disk 1, Track 10*

Listen to a talk in an _____ class. The instructor is talking about _____.

Whether you're working with oil, tempera, or _____, it's the pigment that gives

the paint its _____. A pigment can either be _____ with another material or

applied over its _____ in a thin layer. When a pigment is _____ or ground

in a liquid vehicle to form _____, it does not dissolve but remains _____ in

the liquid.

A paint pigment should be a _____, finely divided powder. It should withstand the action of _____ without changing color. A pigment should not exert a harmful _____ reaction upon the medium, or upon other color _____ it is mixed with.

Generally, _____ are classified according to their _____, either natural or _____. Natural inorganic pigments, also known as _____ pigments, include the native "earths" such as ochre—_____ iron oxide—and raw umber—_____ iron oxide. Natural organic pigments come from _____ and animal sources. Some examples are indigo, from the indigo _____, and Tyrian purple, the imperial _____ the Romans prepared from a _____ native to the Mediterranean.

Today, many pigments are _____ varieties of traditional inorganic and _____ pigments. Synthetic organic pigments provide _____ of unmatched intensity and tinting _____. The synthetic counterparts of the _____ and red earths are more _____ and, if well prepared, are _____ in all other respects to the _____ products. Inorganic synthetic colors made with the aid of strong _____ are generally the most _____ for all uses. In contrast, pigments from _____ sources are less permanent than the average synthetic _____.

🎧 *Stop*

4. Listen again to each lecture in Exercise 2.2.E (Disk 1, Track 10). Imagine that you are in class, listening to the professor speak. While you are listening, take notes about the important ideas and details. Do not try to write down every word or memorize the lecture. After each lecture, use your notes and your own words to (1) write a short summary, and (2) orally summarize the main ideas of the lecture.

5. Look in a newspaper, a magazine, or a textbook. Find a short passage of two or three paragraphs and bring it to class. In class, form groups of four students. Read your passage to the students in your group. When you are finished, your classmates must report the details that they heard. One student writes the details as a list. Then, working together, write questions about the details.

Use these question words:

What _____?	Where _____?	Why _____?
Who _____?	When _____?	How _____?

PROGRESS – 2.1 through 2.2

QUIZ 1   *Time – approximately 10 minutes*

Listen to the recording. Choose the best answer to each question. To make this practice more like the real test, cover the questions and answers during each conversation and lecture. When you hear the first question for each set, uncover the questions and answers.

🎧 *Disk 1, Track 11*

1. What is the discussion mainly about?

   Ⓐ The computerized workplace
   Ⓑ Health dangers in the workplace
   Ⓒ How to arrange office furniture
   Ⓓ Disorders of the neck and back

2. What does the instructor recommend for relieving eyestrain?

   Ⓐ Turn off the computer for 30 minutes.
   Ⓑ Look at objects that are far away.
   Ⓒ Adjust the level of the room lights.
   Ⓓ Wash the eyes with warm water.

3. According to the discussion, why is it important to have the right chair?

   Ⓐ Your chair is the best place to take a nap.
   Ⓑ The right chair will impress your boss.
   Ⓒ The chair's color affects your level of stress.
   Ⓓ The right chair can help you avoid back pain.

4. According to the instructor, what health problem is associated with copy machines?

   Ⓐ Eyestrain
   Ⓑ Neck pain
   Ⓒ Skin rash
   Ⓓ Back pain

5. Where in the workplace might ozone be a problem?

   Ⓐ At a computer terminal
   Ⓑ On the elevator
   Ⓒ Near the copy machines
   Ⓓ In the parking lot

6. What aspect of perspective does the instructor mainly discuss?

- (A) Professions that use perspective drawings
- (B) The function of perspective in abstract drawing
- (C) Changes in the theory of perspective
- (D) Principles of perspective and related concepts

7. According to the instructor, which fields require an understanding of perspective?

Click on two answers.

- [A] Architecture
- [B] Marketing
- [C] Railroad engineering
- [D] Industrial design

8. Select the drawing that illustrates the concept of perspective.

9. Identify the part of the drawing that represents the vanishing point.

10. What does the instructor advise the students to do?

- (A) Take an advanced course in perspective drawing
- (B) Draw only objects that represent the real world
- (C) Sketch eye level and vanishing points in every drawing
- (D) Do several quick sketches before beginning to draw

 Stop

Answers to Listening Quiz 1 are on page 578.

Record your score on the Progress Chart on page 694.

2.3 Determining Attitude and Purpose

FOCUS

Disk 2, Track 1

---

1. Why does the student go to see her adviser?

   ○ She needs a tutor for her psychology course.
   ○ She has decided to change her field of study.
   ○ She wants to talk about a terrible accident.
   ○ She needs advice about running a business.

2. What is the student's attitude toward the school counselors that she observed?

   ○ She is shocked by their terrible work.
   ○ She is surprised that they work so hard.
   ○ She does not think they are necessary.
   ○ She is inspired by their good work.

 Stop

Question 1 asks you to identify the woman's purpose for starting the conversation. The woman says:

> I wanted to talk about the school psychology program. I've been thinking about this for a while, and I've decided to change my major to counseling.

The woman plans to change her major field of study to counseling. The correct answer is *She has decided to change her field of study.*

Question 2 asks you to identify the woman's attitude about the counselors at the school where the woman is a tutor. The woman says:

> …I'm just so impressed with what the counselors are doing there.

> I had a chance to observe some of the counselors talking to the kids, helping them deal with the tragedy. They—the counselors, that is—they were so, so… they were really amazing. It really got me thinking about… how to help people heal. I started thinking, "This is something I'd like to do."

The woman is impressed by the work of the counselors in helping the children. The experience of observing the counselors has contributed to the woman's decision to change her major to counseling. The correct answer is *She is inspired by their good work.*

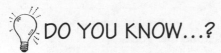 DO YOU KNOW...?

1. The *purpose* of a conversation or lecture is its function, the main reason why the conversation or lecture takes place. In conversations, a speaker's purpose is related to the topic of the conversation, the relationship between the speakers, and the context in which the speakers meet.

    In TOEFL conversations, questions about purpose sound like this:

    > Why does the student go to see the professor?
    > What is the man's problem?
    > Why is the woman concerned?
    > What is the purpose of the conversation?

2. The purpose of a talk or lecture is related to the main idea. Questions about purpose sound like this:

    > What is the purpose of the talk?
    > What is the main purpose of the lecture?
    > What is the speaker's main purpose?

3. Some purpose questions focus on only part of the conversation or lecture. These questions ask about the function of a specific phrase or sentence:

    > Why does the student say _____?
    > Why does the professor mention _____?
    > Why does the instructor talk about _____?
    > Why does the speaker tell a story about _____?
    > Why does the professor ask the class about _____?

4. Sometimes you will be allowed to listen again to part of the conversation or lecture. Then you will hear a question about the speaker's purpose. Here is an example:

    > Listen again to part of the lecture. Then answer the question.
    > (You hear part of the lecture again.)
    > Why does the professor say this:

5. Some examples of purpose are:

To ask for advice	To emphasize importance
To answer a question	To explain causes and effects
To compare two or more things	To give examples
To complain about something	To give reasons
To define a term	To introduce a new concept
To describe a process	To recommend a course of action

6. Sometimes a speaker states his or her purpose directly:

    "I need advice about my paper."
    "I'm concerned about my grade for this class."
    "I'm applying to graduate school, and I was wondering if you'd write me a letter of recommendation."

However, often speakers do not state their purpose directly; rather, they communicate purpose indirectly. Intonation can often help you understand the meaning behind the words.

7. The *attitude* of a speaker is the speaker's thoughts or feelings about something that is being discussed. For example, the speaker's attitude may be one of like, dislike, interest, boredom, surprise, or anxiety. Usually, the speaker conveys his or her attitude indirectly, so you must listen carefully to the speaker's intonation. Listen to key words and phrases that the speaker emphasizes in a certain manner to convey their true meaning.

   TOEFL questions about attitude sound like this:

   > What is the student's attitude toward _____?
   > What is the speaker's opinion of _____?
   > What does the professor think of _____?
   > What is the professor's point of view concerning _____?

8. Listen again to the recording for the Focus exercise. Listen for key words, phrases, and intonation that help you determine the purpose of the conversation and the attitude of the woman.

 Disk 2, Track 1

W: Hi, Greg. Um…do you <u>have a minute</u>?

M: Nicole. Hello. I have… uh… about twenty minutes. Come in and sit down.

W: Thanks. I <u>wanted to talk</u> about the <u>school psychology program</u>. I've been thinking about this for a while, and I've decided to <u>change my major</u> to counseling.

M: Really? It's quite a <u>change</u> from being an accountant to being a counselor!

W: I know. It's funny, isn't it? All my life I thought I wanted to run my own business someday. But this year I've been working as a volunteer tutor—at Garfield Elementary—and I'm just so <u>impressed</u> with what the <u>counselors</u> are doing there.

M: Did you say Garfield?

W: Yes, where those kids in the <u>accident</u> went to school. That was <u>terrible</u>, that accident. It was such a <u>shock</u> to the whole <u>school</u>. But it was <u>eye opening</u> for me. I had a <u>chance to observe</u> some of the <u>counselors talking to the kids</u>, <u>helping them</u> deal with the <u>tragedy</u>. They—the counselors, that is—they were so, so… they were <u>really amazing</u>. It really <u>got me thinking</u> about… about how to make… how to <u>help people heal</u>. I started thinking, "This is <u>something I'd like to do</u>."

 Stop

---

9. In questions about attitude and purpose, an answer choice may be incorrect because it:

   - repeats some of the speaker's words but has a different message;
   - uses words that sound similar to the speaker's words;
   - is incorrect or inaccurate, according to the speakers; or
   - is about something that the speakers do not mention.

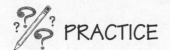

PRACTICE

Exercise 2.3.A

Listen to the recording. Choose the best answer to each question. To make this practice more like the real test, cover the questions and answers during each conversation and lecture. When you hear each question, uncover that question and answers.

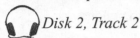 *Disk 2, Track 2*

1. Why does the student go to see his professor?

   (A) He is transferring to a school in Oklahoma.
   (B) He must leave school for a family emergency.
   (C) He wants to discuss his term paper.
   (D) He needs to have surgery.

2. What is required for an Incomplete?

   (A) Completing the work within a certain time
   (B) Writing an additional term paper
   (C) Paying a fee of sixty dollars
   (D) Enrolling in a special make–up course

3. What is the purpose of the conversation?

   (A) The man wants permission to bring food to class.
   (B) The man is applying for a job as cafeteria cashier.
   (C) The man was overcharged and is requesting a refund.
   (D) The man would like a different meal arrangement.

4. Why does the woman say this:

   (A) To complain about the cafeteria breakfast
   (B) To criticize the man's poor eating habits
   (C) To emphasize the importance of breakfast
   (D) To show that she is a morning person

5. Why does the woman tell the man about Plan C?

   (A) To list the special diets that are available
   (B) To give him another choice of meal plan
   (C) To recommend a different place to eat
   (D) To explain the benefits of each meal plan

6. Why does the student speak to the professor?

   (A) She wants to take a quiz that she missed.
   (B) She would like to discuss her grade.
   (C) She is having difficulty in the class.
   (D) She must miss class the following day.

7. What does the professor suggest the student do?

   (A) Read the chapter over again
   (B) Study harder for the next quiz
   (C) Write about what she learned
   (D) Try not to be absent from class

8. What are the speakers mainly discussing?

   (A) A field trip
   (B) A reading assignment
   (C) A guest speaker
   (D) A term paper

9. Why does the man say this:

   (A) To emphasize the professor's qualifications
   (B) To state a desire to read the professor's books
   (C) To predict that the seminar attendance will be high
   (D) To imply that the seminar needs improvement

10. What is the man's opinion of the assignment?

    (A) The assignment will improve their public speaking skills.
    (B) The assignment will help them meet people in their field.
    (C) The assignment is more difficult than he had expected.
    (D) The assignment has taken too much of their time.

 Stop

Exercise 2.3.B

Listen to the recording. Choose the best answer to each question. To make this practice more like the real test, cover the questions and answers during each conversation and lecture. When you hear each question, uncover that question and answers.

 Disk 2, Track 3

1. What is the main purpose of the discussion?

   (A) The professor is giving a writing assignment.
   (B) The class is evaluating last week's assignment.
   (C) The professor is changing the reading assignment.
   (D) The class is summarizing the assigned readings.

2. What is the woman's attitude toward the assignment?

   (A) She is confused by it.
   (B) She likes it very much.
   (C) She thinks it is too difficult.
   (D) She finds it boring.

3. What is the main purpose of the talk?

   (A) To contrast Native American and European concepts of resources
   (B) To explain why Native Americans valued personal alliances
   (C) To list the commodities found in the New England environment
   (D) To show that the European economic system originated in New England

4. What does the professor say about the Native Americans' use of resources?

   (A) They traded resources with the European colonists.
   (B) They used resources to show wealth and social status.
   (C) They used resources mainly for economic subsistence.
   (D) They viewed resources as commodities to buy and sell.

5. Listen again to part of the discussion. Then answer the question.

   Why does the professor say this:

   (A) To state that the Native Americans were very poor
   (B) To show similarities between economic systems
   (C) To explain differences in wealth among people
   (D) To define the Native American concept of wealth

6. Why does the professor say this:

   (A) To illustrate the colonists' view of commodities
   (B) To emphasize the scarcity of resources in New England
   (C) To suggest that the colonists did not use many resources
   (D) To describe the growth of the New England economy

7. What is the purpose of the talk?

   (A) To imagine life without culture
   (B) To compare various cultures
   (C) To explain cultural differences
   (D) To define what culture is

8. Why does the professor mention student culture?

   (A) To illustrate how culture involves shared ideas and behaviors
   (B) To encourage students to think critically about their culture
   (C) To compare the student culture of the past and the present
   (D) To give students ideas for conducting their own research

9. What is the woman's attitude toward student culture?

- (A) She enjoys being a part of it.
- (B) She is frustrated by all the work.
- (C) She thinks it is similar to a club.
- (D) She doesn't understand its rules.

10. What does the professor think of comparing a culture to a club?

- (A) A culture is exactly the same as a club.
- (B) The comparison is imperfect.
- (C) It is easier to define a culture than a club.
- (D) Clubs are important in most cultures.

 Stop

Exercise 2.3.C

Listen to the recording. Choose the best answer to each question. To make this practice more like the real test, cover the questions and answers during each conversation and lecture. When you hear each question, uncover that question and answers.

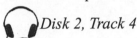 *Disk 2, Track 4*

1. What is the main purpose of the talk?

- (A) To list qualities of effective managers
- (B) To explain why workers criticize management
- (C) To describe negative effects of stress
- (D) To discuss ways of dealing with stress

2. What is the professor's opinion of rest?

- (A) Too much rest can have negative results.
- (B) Activity and exercise are forms of rest.
- (C) Managers should allow rest time for workers.
- (D) Few people know the real meaning of rest.

3. What is the purpose of the lecture?

- (A) To compare clinical diagnosis and treatment
- (B) To describe how psychologists diagnose problems
- (C) To support the use of psychological testing
- (D) To diagnose the problems of students

4. How do clinical psychologists diagnose a client's problems?

   Click on two answers.

- [A] Psychic readings
- [B] Psychological tests
- [C] Interviews
- [D] Personal letters

5. Why does the professor discuss taking a client's case history?

- (A) To show that a client's past behavior assists in diagnosis
- (B) To compare the case histories of various clients
- (C) To explain why some clients lie and some tell the truth
- (D) To entertain the students with stories of unusual clients

6. According to the professor, why are personality tests useful?

- (A) They are short and easy to administer.
- (B) They allow clients to diagnose their own problems.
- (C) They give the psychologist data for publication.
- (D) They reveal feelings the client cannot talk about.

7. What is the main purpose of the talk?

  (A) To describe the migration of bats
  (B) To promote an appreciation of bats
  (C) To give advice about contact with bats
  (D) To explain how to care for young bats

8. Why does the speaker say this:

  (A) To describe the reproductive behavior of bats
  (B) To show similarities between bats and mosquitoes
  (C) To give an example of how bats benefit us
  (D) To warn students about dangerous insects

9. How can you prevent bats from entering your house?

  (A) By blocking every opening
  (B) By planting bushes near the doors
  (C) By training your dog to hunt bats
  (D) By using poison to kill the bats

10. Why does the speaker recommend getting medical advice if you come in physical contact with a bat?

  (A) Bats are needed for medical research.
  (B) Contact with humans is unhealthy for bats.
  (C) Bats' sharp teeth can cause a painful bite.
  (D) The bat might be carrying a fatal disease.

 Stop

Exercise 2.3.D

Listen to the recording. Choose the best answer to each question. To make this practice more like the real test, cover the questions and answers during each conversation and lecture. When you hear each question, uncover that question and answers.

Disk 2, Track 5

1. According to the professor, why do most people welcome laughter?

  (A) People like to learn new ways to communicate.
  (B) Laughter releases stress and gives pleasure.
  (C) Humans enjoy several kinds of entertainment.
  (D) Laughter can express every human emotion.

2. Why does the professor say this:

  (A) To give examples of stress that is carefully controlled
  (B) To show that children like to pretend they are flying
  (C) To describe how children respond when they are afraid
  (D) To give parents advice about child development

3. Which of the following is a universal characteristic of situations where people laugh?

  (A) Confusion about what is happening
  (B) Injury to someone who is a stranger
  (C) Ability to remember a funny name
  (D) Shock or stress in a safe situation

4. Why does the professor talk about social rules and conventions?

  (A) To suggest that many rules for comedians are not effective
  (B) To find out what students think about rules and conventions
  (C) To show that humor is a safe way to bring about social change
  (D) To explain why people enjoy telling stories that are not true

5. Listen again to part of the lecture. Then answer the question.

   Why does the professor say this:

   Ⓐ To show how humor can be understood across cultures
   Ⓑ To emphasize the importance of humor in managing anxiety
   Ⓒ To explain why humans are the only animals that laugh
   Ⓓ To remind students that the world is a dangerous place

6. How does the instructor develop the topic of roadside beautification?

   Ⓐ By comparing two different approaches to the topic
   Ⓑ By criticizing past efforts at roadside beautification
   Ⓒ By discussing an example of a beautification project
   Ⓓ By describing recent research in flower horticulture

7. Why does the professor quote botanist Catherine Parr Traill?

   Ⓐ To provide an intellectual context for the issue
   Ⓑ To criticize agricultural development policies
   Ⓒ To praise the botanist's accomplishments
   Ⓓ To remind the class of a reading assignment

8. Why does the professor mention the Adopt–a–Highway programs that began in the 1960s?

   Ⓐ To explain why early beautification projects failed
   Ⓑ To encourage students to volunteer for highway cleanup
   Ⓒ To recommend an increase in funding for the programs
   Ⓓ To trace the history of roadside beautification efforts

9. Why does the professor say this:

   Ⓐ To suggest a change in the seed mixture
   Ⓑ To illustrate the success of the plantings
   Ⓒ To argue for more wildflower research
   Ⓓ To emphasize the short growing season

10. What does the professor think of partnerships between government and private citizens?

    Ⓐ They have been shown to work successfully.
    Ⓑ They rely too much on private donations.
    Ⓒ They are the best way to get anything done.
    Ⓓ They can cause damage to the economy.

 Stop

Answers to Exercises 2.3.A through 2.3.D are on page 578.

EXTENSION

1. Listen again to the conversations in Exercise 2.3.A (Disk 2, Track 2). With your classmates, discuss the meaning of the underlined expressions in the script below. In what other situations might these expressions be used?

take an Incomplete	I was wondering if I could <u>take an Incomplete</u> for your class.
make up	…you would have six weeks to <u>make up</u> the term paper….
take care of	…why don't we <u>take care of</u> it right now?
take turns	We <u>take turns</u> bringing doughnuts or bagels to have at the break.
sounds like	Oh, really? Hmm. That <u>sounds like</u> a good deal.
have to	My daughter was sick yesterday, and I <u>had to</u> stay home with her.
get out of	…the most important thing you <u>got out of</u> the chapter.
turn out	This assignment…has <u>turned out</u> to be harder than I thought.

2. The conversations in Exercise 2.3.A (Disk 2, Track 2) mention the following aspects of North American university life:

a grade of Incomplete	a meal plan	a sabbatical
a term paper	a make–up test	a seminar
a final exam	a one–page report	a guest speaker

With your classmates, discuss whether these are part of university life in your country. Which of the items are present at the school where you are currently studying?

3. Listen again to the three discussions in Exercise 2.3.B (Disk 2, Track 3). Imagine that you are one of the students in each discussion. In your own words, write a brief summary of each discussion. The following expressions may be useful:

Today my professor talked about…	I asked…
We discussed…	What I wanted to know was…
Then she asked…	I made a comment about…
My professor explained how…	I described…

4. Listen again to the first lecture in Exercise 2.3.C. As you listen, write the correct words on the blank lines in the script below. Check your answers with the audio script on page 624.

🎧 *Disk 2, Track 4*

Listen to part of a talk in a business management class.

Management _____ a great deal of energy and _____—more than most _____ care to make. One _____ that affects managers and _____ their capacity to provide leadership is _____. Stress has lots of causes—work _____, criticism from workers—and can have _____ health effects, including loss of _____.

It's a fact: _____ have to deal with stress. Some _____ it by making time to be by themselves. Most have some _____ place or pastime—a beach to _____ on, maybe a stream to _____ in, or a game to play with the _____. It's important to have some form of _____ and relaxation—creating art, working with your _____, gardening, playing _____—the list goes on. Rest doesn't _____ mean inactivity. For some people, _____ is rest.

🎧 *Stop*

5. Listen again to the first lecture in Exercise 2.3.D. As you listen, write the correct words on the blank lines in the script below. Check your answers with the audio script on page 625.

🎧 *Disk 2, Track 5*

Listen to part of a lecture in an anthropology class. The professor is discussing _____ and laughter.

Being amused is a _____ we're all familiar with, but what exactly is a _____ of humor? Well, it's something very _____, and yet we communicate it to others by _____. Laughter is a universal human _____. All normal human beings can _____. Children as young as one _____ old will laugh. People often laugh _____, and people laugh _____ and more frequently when other _____ around them are also laughing. Every _____ knows this, and research has confirmed it.

_____, laughter is an involuntary tensing of the _____ muscles, followed by a rapid inhalation and exhalation of _____—a mechanism that _____ tension. For most people, a good laugh is _____—and worth looking for—because it brings _____ and relief.

_____ adults everywhere in the world _____ making their children laugh. Adults make playful _____ on their children, tickling, _____, and even pretending to _____ them. Adults will throw small children up in the air and _____ them again. This causes the child to experience mild _____, but in a secure setting because the stress is carefully _____ by the parent. And when the child laughs, it's a _____ that he or she has successfully dealt with mild _____ of insecurity. This teaches the child about the _____ and fears that are part of human _____, and which every human eventually has to _____ with. This element of shock in an otherwise _____ situation is a universal characteristic of situations where people _____.

Our sense of humor allows us to tell _____ about situations we haven't _____ firsthand. We call these little stories "_____." We tell jokes to show our _____ with the society we live in, especially its... well, its _____. Social rules and conventions provide us with a _____ of situations that we can turn into _____. And the things we joke about—the _____ and rules we live by—are sort of _____ areas in our society, they're _____ where we can see the _____ for change. Humor gives us the _____ to think about changing the rules. Making _____ and laughing are safe ways to _____ our social rules and conventions. Therefore, comedians—whether they _____ it or not—are agents of _____ change.

The ability to laugh is a _____ part of being human. People who _____ together—or laugh at each other's jokes—feel _____ to each other. Laughter creates a sense of _____. Humor can also help us _____ with anxieties that we can't _____. Failure, fear, pain, and _____—they're all real to us, as they are to no other _____ on Earth. And without a _____ of humor, it would be difficult for us to _____ with everything we that know about the _____.

 Stop

DELTA'S KEY TO THE NEXT GENERATION TOEFL® TEST

6. Listen again to each lecture in Exercise 2.3.D (Disk 2, Track 5). Imagine that you are in class, listening to the professor speak. While you are listening, take notes about the important ideas and details. Do not try to write down every word or memorize the lecture. After each lecture, use your notes and your own words to (1) write a short summary, and (2) orally summarize the main ideas of the lecture.

7. Think about the last time you spoke to one of the following people:

adviser	mechanic	roommate
best friend	neighbor	school staff person
co–worker	parent	supervisor
librarian	professor	tutor

Why did you speak to that person? What was the purpose of your conversation? Write down two or three things that you and the other person said. With a classmate, write a dialogue. Then act out the conversation for the rest of the class. Your classmates must determine the purpose of the conversation.

8. With a classmate, discuss what you would say to your professor if you wanted to do the following things. What words and expressions would you use?

Make an appointment	Request more time to complete an assignment
Get help with an assignment	Discuss a grade that you think is unfair
Make up work that you missed	Ask for a letter of recommendation

PROGRESS – 2.1 through 2.3

QUIZ 2   *Time – approximately 10 minutes*

Listen to the recording. Choose the best answer to each question. To make this practice more like the real test, cover the questions and answers during each conversation and lecture. When you hear the first question for each set, uncover the questions and answers.

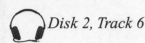 *Disk 2, Track 6*

1. What are the students discussing?

   Ⓐ A lecture that they will attend next week
   Ⓑ Topics to review for an upcoming test
   Ⓒ Their vacation in the mountains
   Ⓓ A report that they are working on

2. Listen again to part of the conversation. Then answer the question.

   Why does the man say this:

   Ⓐ To invite the woman to join him at hockey practice
   Ⓑ To inform the woman that he has only a little time now
   Ⓒ To let the woman know that she worries too much
   Ⓓ To suggest a different topic for their presentation

3. What types of data will the students use in their presentation?

   Click on two answers.

   Ⓐ The history of eruptions in the area
   Ⓑ Photographs that the man took
   Ⓒ A series of pictures of the mountain
   Ⓓ A videotaped interview with a geologist

4. What is the man's opinion of the photographs?

   Ⓐ They are the best photographs he has ever taken.
   Ⓑ They are nice, but they do not support their topic.
   Ⓒ They show the mountain's changes very well.
   Ⓓ They would be better if they were in color.

5. According to the man, why is a bulge forming on the mountain?

   Ⓐ Geologists disagree over the cause of the bulge.
   Ⓑ Wind and water are wearing away the mountain's face.
   Ⓒ There has been a rapid increase in the amount of snowfall.
   Ⓓ Magma is pushing upward from below the earth's surface.

6. What is the main purpose of the talk?

   (A) To describe some of the functions of banks
   (B) To explain why banks charge interest on loans
   (C) To compare banks with other financial institutions
   (D) To outline the history of bank failures

7. For what reasons do individuals take out bank loans?

   Click on two answers.

   [A] To build a housing complex
   [B] To do medical research
   [C] To pay for education
   [D] To purchase a home

8. How do banks make a profit?

   (A) Banks pay fewer taxes than other businesses.
   (B) Banks sell ideas and products to the government.
   (C) Banks collect more interest than they pay out.
   (D) Banks lend money only to large corporations.

9. Why does the professor say this:

   (A) To encourage students to close their bank accounts
   (B) To show that banks are the safest place to store money
   (C) To recommend more government regulation of banks
   (D) To explain how bank failures have occurred

10. Why were banks closed during the Great Depression of the 1930s?

    (A) The government encouraged people to spend more money.
    (B) Banks could not afford to let people withdraw all their money.
    (C) The president was experimenting with a new system of banking.
    (D) Bank managers needed time to hire and train more employees.

 Stop

Answers to Listening Quiz 2 are on page 580.

Record your score on the Progress Chart on page 694.

PROGRESS – 2.1 through 2.3

Quiz 3   *Time – approximately 10 minutes*

Listen to the recording. Choose the best answer to each question. To make this practice more like the real test, cover the questions and answers during each conversation and lecture. When you hear the first question for each set, uncover the questions and answers.

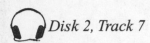 *Disk 2, Track 7*

1. Why does the student speak to his professor?

   (A) He needs help in preparing for the midterm exam.
   (B) He wants advice about how to organize his paper.
   (C) He is concerned about his grade for the course.
   (D) He wants permission for his brother to visit class.

2. What reason does the student give for not completing his assignments?

   (A) He had difficulty understanding the assignments.
   (B) He has spent a lot of time helping a family member.
   (C) He forgot the schedule for turning in assignments.
   (D) He had to work extra hours at his bio–research job.

3. When were the assignments due?

   (A) October 1 and 13
   (B) October 2 and 3
   (C) October 4 and 30
   (D) October 21 and 30

4. What point does the professor make about the student's work?

   (A) His work is the worst in the class.
   (B) His work was better in the past.
   (C) His work will improve if he studies.
   (D) His work should be his top concern.

5. Why does the student say this:

   (A) To help his professor better understand his problem
   (B) To convince his professor that he will complete the work
   (C) To show his professor that he is not worried about his grade
   (D) To state that he will turn in all assignments the next day

6. What is the main idea of the lecture?

- (A) Television research is an interesting field.
- (B) Advertising is effective in selling products.
- (C) Television promotes a culture of consumerism.
- (D) The television industry should be regulated.

7. According to the professor, why do researchers study television?

- (A) To learn about the types of programs
- (B) To understand the culture of the society
- (C) To decide which programs to export
- (D) To measure how well it sells products

8. According to the professor, why do advertisers have control over television programming?

- (A) Advertisers have the best ideas about what viewers want.
- (B) The television industry depends on money from advertisers.
- (C) The government permits advertisers to vote for programs.
- (D) Most television stations are owned by large corporations.

9. Listen again to part of the lecture. Then answer the question.

Why does the professor say this:

- (A) To argue that television images of life lack depth and meaning
- (B) To warn students not to spend more money than they can afford
- (C) To show that television programs can contribute to personal growth
- (D) To recommend that students watch only high–quality programs

10. What is the professor's opinion of television?

- (A) Television is the best way to advertise products and services.
- (B) Television has had a mostly negative effect on society.
- (C) Television has been unfairly criticized by intellectuals.
- (D) Television deserves credit for creating an affluent society.

 Stop

Answers to Listening Quiz 3 are on page 580.

Record your score on the Progress Chart on page 694.

2.4 Making Inferences and Predictions

 FOCUS

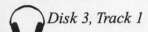 *Disk 3, Track 1*

---

1. What does the professor imply about the student's paper?

   ◯ It contains grammatical errors.
   ◯ It does not meet the assignment.
   ◯ It deals with a strange topic.
   ◯ It needs a stronger ending.

2. What will the student probably do?

   ◯ Write about a different topic
   ◯ Rewrite the conclusion
   ◯ Correct the sentence errors
   ◯ Make the introduction longer

 Stop

Question 1 asks you to determine the professor's message to the student about her paper. The professor says:

> …I can't tell where you're going with it.

> You start out strong… The middle part, too…that's very engaging… But after that… well, I'm lost. What does it all mean? It just gets a little vague.

> Well, it's a little too open. You need to tie it all together… leave your reader with one clear thought….

The professor does not directly state what he means. Rather, he implies his meaning. The professor implies that the student's paper lacks a strong ending. Therefore, the correct answer is *It needs a stronger ending*.

Question 2 asks you to predict what the student will do. The student says:

> Do you mean my conclusion's not clear?

> Oh well, I see. Um… maybe I'd better work on that part some more.

The professor implies that the student's paper needs a stronger ending, so the student will probably rewrite that part. The correct answer is *Rewrite the conclusion*.

In each question, you can infer the correct answer from what the speakers say. The other answers are incorrect because you cannot reasonably infer them from the conversation.

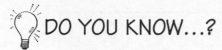

DO YOU KNOW...?

1. An *inference* is a conclusion that you make when something is not directly stated. An inference is a "hidden" idea. To make an inference, you must interpret a message that is not stated directly. When a speaker *implies* or *suggests* something, you must *infer* the meaning. You infer the meaning from the information that the speaker gives. You infer the message behind the speaker's words.

2. TOEFL questions about inferences sound like this:

> What can be inferred about _____?
> What does the speaker imply about _____?
> What is probably true about _____?
> What can be concluded about _____?
> What can be inferred from the talk?
> How does the student probably feel?

3. A *prediction* is a type of inference in which you determine what will probably happen in the future. You make a prediction when you know what a speaker will probably do in the future, based on what he or she says.

   For example, when someone says…

   > "I'd better see a dentist about my toothache"

   …you can reasonably predict that he or she will make an appointment with a dentist.

   When a student says…

   > "I have a lot of material to review for my chemistry test tomorrow"

   …you can predict that the student will probably study for the test.

4. TOEFL questions about predictions sound like this:

> What will the woman probably do?
> What will the student probably do next?
> What will probably happen next?
> What will the professor probably discuss next?
> What will the next lecture probably be about?

5. To make inferences and predictions, use key ideas and your overall understanding of the topic and context, as well as logic and common sense.

   Listen again to the recording for the Focus exercise. Look at the script on page 250. Listen for key words and phrases that help you infer the professor's meaning and predict what the student will do.

Disk 3, Track 1

W: Professor Elliott, did you <u>read the draft of my paper</u> yet?

M: Why hello, Amy. Uh, yes, I did read it. As a matter of fact, I wanted to talk to you about it. I'm glad you stopped by. I think I have your paper... here we go, I have it right here.

W: Is there <u>something wrong with it</u>?

M: No, not terribly, but... <u>I can't tell where you're going</u> with it.

W: Oh. I'm not sure I understand.

M: <u>Let me put it like this</u>. You <u>start out strong</u>. In fact, your introduction is done quite well. You really get your teacher interested in technology and society and how they're related and all. <u>The middle part</u>, too—where you interview the engineer—that, that's <u>very engaging</u>. Lots of good and original ideas. <u>But after that</u>... well, <u>I'm lost</u>. What does it all mean? It just <u>gets a little vague</u>.

W: Oh, I think I see what you mean. Do you mean my <u>conclusion's not clear</u>?

M: Well, it's <u>a little too open</u>. You need to <u>tie it all together</u>... leave your reader with <u>one clear thought</u>, one new way of thinking about technology.

W: Oh well, I see. Um... maybe <u>I'd better work on that part some more</u>. I really appreciate your comments. This helps me a lot. Thanks, Professor Elliott.

M: My pleasure. Any time.

Stop

6. Some questions ask you to identify a paraphrase of something that a speaker says. A ***paraphrase*** is the restatement of a message in different words. To ***paraphrase*** is to say the same thing in another way. A paraphrase has the same general meaning as the original message.

TOEFL questions about paraphrases sound like this:

> What does the professor mean by this statement:
>
> What does the student mean when she says this:
>
> What does the professor imply when he says this:
>
> Select the sentence that best expresses how the student probably feels.

For example, when a student says to another student...

> "What? I don't know...are you sure that's right? I thought the TA said first we need to calculate the present value of an asset"

...you can infer that the student probably means:

> "I disagree with your solution to the problem."

7. Some questions ask you to make a generalization based on what a speaker says. A ***generalization*** is a type of inference in which you make a general statement about the information that you hear. To ***generalize*** is to state a general principle or to draw a general conclusion about information.

TOEFL questions involving generalization sound like this:

> Would the professor most likely agree or disagree with each statement below?
>
> Based on the information in the talk, indicate whether each statement below describes _____.
>
> Based on the information in the lecture, indicate whether each statement below reflects the ideas of _____.

For example, here is part of a lecture:

> The philosophy of pragmatism, which has had a tremendous influence on American education, holds that the meaning and truth of any idea is a function of its practical outcome. Knowledge that is useful has value. Pragmatists believe there's a vital relationship between experience and knowledge, and so we need to interact with both our natural environment and our society. The pragmatist thinks that education should focus on solving problems. It should involve experimentation. Education is a process—it's continuous experiment—a continuous process where experience and knowledge build on each other.

Here is a sample question:

> Based on the information in the lecture, indicate whether each statement below reflects the philosophy of pragmatism.

For each sentence, click in the correct box.

	Yes	No
Ideas with a practical use are important to society.	✓	
Students should believe the ideas of their teachers.		✓
Experience is central to learning.	✓	

You should click in the "Yes" column next to *Ideas with a practical use are important to society* and *Experience is central to learning* because these statements reflect what the professor says and can be supported by the information in the lecture. You should click in the "No" column next to *Students should believe the ideas of their teachers* because you cannot conclude this from what the professor says.

8. In questions about inferences and predictions, an answer choice may be incorrect because it:

   - is not supported by what the speakers state or imply;
   - cannot reasonably be concluded from what the speakers say;
   - repeats some of the speakers' words but has a different message;
   - is incorrect or inaccurate, according to the speakers; or
   - is about something that the speakers do not mention.

Remember, you can answer all of the questions based on the information you hear in the conversations and lectures. You can infer the correct answer from what the speakers say.

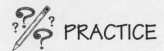 PRACTICE

Exercise 2.4.A

Listen to the recording. Choose the best answer to each question. To make this practice more like the real test, cover the questions and answers during each conversation and lecture. When you hear each question, uncover that question and answers.

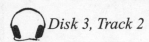 *Disk 3, Track 2*

1. Why does the student go to see his adviser?

    (A) To enroll in her geometry class next quarter
    (B) To discuss an assignment for his history class
    (C) To get extra help with a difficult problem
    (D) To obtain advice about dropping a class

2. What will the student probably do?

    (A) Make up a geometry test
    (B) Transfer to another school
    (C) Not continue in his history class
    (D) Not enroll in classes next quarter

3. What is the man's problem?

    (A) He can't afford to be a full–time student.
    (B) There is an unpaid charge on his account.
    (C) His charge account is no longer valid.
    (D) All of the courses he needs are closed.

4. What will the man probably do?

    (A) Pay his roommate to fix the shower door
    (B) Have an argument with his roommate
    (C) Speak to someone in the accounting office
    (D) Try to register for next quarter in person

5. Why does the student go to see her professor?

    (A) There was a problem with her registration.
    (B) She will miss the beginning of the summer term.
    (C) She wants advice about joining a study group.
    (D) She would like to discuss her research project.

6. What does the professor imply?

    (A) It is not acceptable to miss class time.
    (B) The first day of class has been changed.
    (C) Students are required to take the course.
    (D) The summer course has been canceled.

7. What will the student probably do?

    (A) Take the course during the fall
    (B) Make up the work she misses
    (C) Join an available study group
    (D) Cancel her trip to Vancouver

8. What are the students mainly discussing?

    (A) Problems with parking on campus
    (B) Off–campus apartments for students
    (C) Free bus transportation to campus
    (D) Ways for students to manage money

9. What can be inferred about the woman?

    (A) She does not own a car.
    (B) She has a roommate.
    (C) She is not married.
    (D) She has a job off campus.

10. What will the man probably do?

    (A) Transfer to a different university
    (B) Look for a less expensive car
    (C) Move to a building for married students
    (D) Find out more about the apartments

 Stop

Exercise 2.4.B

Listen to the recording. Choose the best answer to each question. To make this practice more like the real test, cover the questions and answers during each conversation and lecture. When you hear each question, uncover that question and answers.

 Disk 3, Track 3

1. What does the instructor imply about composition?

   (A) Composition in painting is similar to composition in writing.
   (B) Composition is less important than shape, tone, and color.
   (C) Composition must be complex in order to be interesting.
   (D) Composition is the only concept that artists must understand.

2. Would the instructor most likely agree or disagree with each statement below?

   For each sentence, click in the correct box.

	Agree	Disagree
A composition must contain numerous subjects to be interesting.		
If a picture is too crowded, it does not possess the element of unity.		
A successful composition conveys a single, clear message.		

3. What is the main purpose of the talk?

   (A) To explain why people become scientists
   (B) To describe different scientific disciplines
   (C) To persuade students to become biologists
   (D) To introduce students to the course

4. According to the professor, why is biology the most demanding of all sciences?

   Click on two answers.
   [A] Biology studies complex living systems.
   [B] Biology deals with controversial issues.
   [C] Biology requires knowledge of other sciences.
   [D] Biology cannot answer every question about life.

5. What does the professor imply about scientists?

   (A) Scientists are motivated to save the environment.
   (B) Scientists are more intelligent than artists.
   (C) Scientists are fascinated by scientific technology.
   (D) Scientists are enthusiastic in their study of nature.

6. What is probably true about the students in this course?

   (A) They are students at a community college.
   (B) They plan to apply to medical school.
   (C) They are pursuing various fields of study.
   (D) They have never taken a science course before.

7. What do plant hormones do?

   (A) Regulate the plant's temperature
   (B) Transport water through the plant
   (C) Stimulate responses in cells and tissues
   (D) Make the plant unattractive to animals

8. Which picture illustrates phototropism?

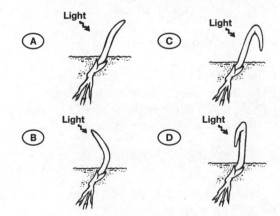

9. Which grass seedlings would probably NOT bend toward light?

    Click on two answers.

    [A] Seedling in a moist ecosystem
    [B] Seedling with the tip cut off
    [C] Seedling wearing a black cap
    [D] Seedling with multiple shoots

10. What can be inferred about the tip of a plant's stem?

    (A) It stops growing once the plant produces real leaves.
    (B) It plays an important role in temperature control.
    (C) It can be removed with no influence on the plant.
    (D) It produces a hormone that affects the stem's growth.

 Stop

Exercise 2.4.C

Listen to the recording. Choose the best answer to each question. To make this practice more like the real test, cover the questions and answers during each conversation and lecture. When you hear each question, uncover that question and answers.

 Disk 3, Track 4

1. What is the man's problem?

    (A) He will not have time to finish his paper.
    (B) He is confused by cultural differences.
    (C) He cannot think of a topic for his paper.
    (D) He thinks the assignment is too artificial.

2. What will the man probably do?

    (A) Describe his hometown culture
    (B) Move to a different community
    (C) Ask his professor for more time
    (D) Write about culture shock

3. Why does the professor say this: 🎧

    (A) She will not be in class the next day.
    (B) The student has to drop out of school.
    (C) There was a death in the student's family.
    (D) The coursework is very difficult.

4. What will the student probably do next?

    (A) Arrange to take the test next week
    (B) Apply for a job in the office
    (C) Look for a tutor to help him study
    (D) Change the time of his appointment

5. What is the man's problem?

    (A) The university bookstore does not have a book he needs.
    (B) He just bought more books than he is able to read.
    (C) The books that he needs are a strain on his finances.
    (D) The third edition of the chemistry book is not available.

6. What can be inferred about the man?

    (A) He finds science courses very difficult.
    (B) He lives in the Pioneer District.
    (C) He enjoys studying with the woman.
    (D) He is taking a chemistry course.

7. What will the man probably do?

    (A) Look for a cheaper copy of the chemistry book
    (B) Return all of the books to the university bookstore
    (C) Buy a different edition of the chemistry book
    (D) Complain to the university about the cost of books

8. What does the man imply about the medication?

  (A) It may be dangerous if taken incorrectly.
  (B) It is the least expensive allergy medication.
  (C) It should be available only by prescription.
  (D) It is an effective remedy for many illnesses.

9. Listen again to part of the conversation. Then answer the question.

  Select the sentence that best expresses how the woman probably feels.

  (A) "I don't like other people telling me what to do."
  (B) "I'm concerned about taking this medicine before the test."
  (C) "I appreciate your thoughtful advice about the dangers."
  (D) "I don't understand your instructions about the drug."

10. What will the woman probably do?

  (A) Complain to the manager of the pharmacy
  (B) Go back to the nurse for additional advice
  (C) Buy a different medicine and hope it works
  (D) Take the medicine a few hours before the test

 Stop

Exercise 2.4.D

Listen to the recording. Choose the best answer to each question. To make this practice more like the real test, cover the questions and answers during each conversation and lecture. When you hear each question, uncover that question and answers.

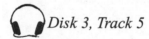 *Disk 3, Track 5*

1. What problem does the man have?

  (A) He is failing in his biology class.
  (B) He owes a fee for his lab section.
  (C) His attendance in class has been poor.
  (D) He cannot afford to pay all his fees.

2. What will the man probably do next?

  (A) Change his biology lab section
  (B) Show the woman his tuition bill
  (C) Go to the cashier's office
  (D) Pay for his biology textbooks

3. What are the students discussing?

  (A) Houses
  (B) Fruit
  (C) Birds
  (D) Stars

4. What can be inferred about starlings?

  Click on two answers.

  [A] They live in rural and urban areas.
  [B] They are a problem for fruit growers.
  [C] They have a beautiful song.
  [D] They are killed for their feathers.

5. Why does the student want to leave a message for Dr. Owada?

- (A) He would like to apply for a job.
- (B) He needs to discuss his grade.
- (C) He will not attend class today.
- (D) He wants to record her lecture.

6. What does the secretary imply about Dr. Owada?

- (A) Dr. Owada will be absent until the next day.
- (B) Dr. Owada does not like students to call her.
- (C) Dr. Owada is visiting Professor Strong's class.
- (D) Dr. Owada answers her mail every morning.

7. What will the student probably do?

- (A) Return to the office after class
- (B) Change his schedule of classes
- (C) Write a note to his professor
- (D) Miss the lecture by Professor Strong

8. What are the people discussing?

- (A) A textbook
- (B) A college course
- (C) A television series
- (D) A government agency

9. What can be inferred about the United States in the nineteenth century?

- (A) There were few large cities.
- (B) A great natural disaster occurred.
- (C) Baltimore was founded.
- (D) The population grew rapidly.

10. What can be inferred about New York City?

Click on two answers.

- [A] It was originally five cities.
- [B] It used to be part of Baltimore.
- [C] It is a progressive city.
- [D] It has a borough called Brooklyn.

 Stop

Exercise 2.4.E

Listen to the recording. Choose the best answer to each question. To make this practice more like the real test, cover the questions and answers during each conversation and lecture. When you hear each question, uncover that question and answers.

 Disk 3, Track 6

1. What can be inferred about the course in which the talk is given?

- (A) It is a course for graduate students.
- (B) It is a course that many students fail.
- (C) It is the most popular science course.
- (D) It is a general course in life science.

2. What does the professor imply about the videotape?

- (A) It cannot be checked out of the library.
- (B) It covers material that will be on the next test.
- (C) It will be shown on television later that week.
- (D) It contains examples of the professor's research.

3. For which course would the talk be most appropriate?

    (A) Classical Europe
    (B) Global Economics
    (C) Music History
    (D) American Literature

4. What does the instructor imply about the style of music known as the blues?

    (A) It originated in Chicago in the 1920s.
    (B) It contributed to European classical music.
    (C) It changed and developed over time.
    (D) It made many musicians wealthy.

5. According to the instructor, why is the song "St. Louis Blues" significant?

    (A) It combined elements of different musical styles.
    (B) It was the first song ever to be recorded.
    (C) It gave its name to the decade of the 1920s.
    (D) It was never accepted by classical musicians.

6. Based on the information in the talk, indicate whether each statement below accurately describes jazz.

    For each sentence, click in the correct box.

	Yes	No
Jazz was one of the most popular styles of music in the 1920s.		
Jazz originated in the electric style of blues from Chicago.		
Jazz includes sounds from folk, popular, and classical music.		

7. What is the main purpose of the lecture?

    (A) To compare land animals and sea animals
    (B) To explain why fish are excellent swimmers
    (C) To describe how various sea animals move
    (D) To review material that will be on a test

8. Select the drawing of the creature that is probably the fastest swimmer.

9. Listen again to part of the lecture. Then answer the question.

    What is probably true about whales and dolphins?

    (A) They can swim faster than most fish.
    (B) They move their tails as land mammals do.
    (C) They swim to great depths underwater.
    (D) They would prefer to live on land.

10. What can be inferred about creatures that live on the bottom of the ocean?

    (A) They swim fast to catch food.
    (B) They are less than one foot long.
    (C) They have flattened fins and tails.
    (D) They move slowly and fluidly.

 Stop

Answers to Exercises 2.4.A through 2.4.E are on page 581.

 EXTENSION

1. Listen again to the conversations in Exercise 2.4.A (Disk 3, Track 2). With your classmates, discuss the meaning of the underlined expressions in the script below. In what other situations might these expressions be used?

a hard time	…I'm having <u>a hard time</u> keeping up in geometry.
keep up	…I'm having a hard time <u>keeping up</u> in geometry.
drop a class	…why not <u>drop</u> your <u>history class</u>?
catch up	If I drop history, maybe then I'll be able to <u>catch up</u> in geometry.
run into	I <u>ran into</u> a problem when I tried to register by telephone.
clear it up	You'd better go to the accounting office and try to <u>clear it up</u>.
make sure	I'd better <u>make sure</u> my roommate pays for the damage.
make up	Could I… um… <u>make up</u> the work when I get back?
can't afford	Summer session is only six weeks, and you <u>can't afford</u> to get a late start.
see (someone) around	I haven't <u>seen you around</u> lately.
look into	Maybe I'll <u>look into</u> that.
Why not?	<u>Why not?</u> The apartments are nice and spacious….

2. Listen again to the conversations in Exercise 2.4.C (Disk 3, Track 4). With your classmates, discuss the meaning of the underlined expressions in the script below. In what other situations might these expressions be used?

come up with	I'm having trouble <u>coming up with</u> a good idea.
What about	<u>What about</u> the culture of your family?
grow up	I <u>grew up</u> in a small town….
Bingo!	<u>Bingo!</u> Write about the culture of the orchard community.
pass away	My great aunt <u>passed away</u> and her funeral is tomorrow.
make–ups	Eric handles all <u>make–ups</u>. He's the instructional aide….
stop by	Can you <u>stop by</u> the office today…?
out of sight	Science books are always <u>out of sight</u>.
not a bad idea	That's <u>not a bad idea</u>. Where did you say that was again?
drive (someone) crazy	I've been having sneezing fits, and it's <u>driving me crazy</u>.
It doesn't matter	<u>It doesn't matter</u>. Hmm… capsules, I guess.
knock (someone) out	Do you have anything else that's effective but won't <u>knock me out</u>?

3. Listen again to the conversations in Exercise 2.4.D (Disk 3, Track 5). With your classmates, discuss the meaning of the underlined expressions in the script below. In what other situations might these expressions be used?

show up	The fee probably didn't <u>show up</u> on your bill because….
I'm afraid	<u>I'm afraid</u> you'll have to pay it at the cashier's office.
take care of	OK, I'd better <u>take care of</u> it right away.
let (someone) know	Thanks for <u>letting me know</u>.
write down	Well, maybe you're right. We'd better <u>write it down</u> anyway.
put a question mark by	I'll <u>put a question mark by</u> it.
miss	Oh, it's too bad I'll <u>miss</u> that. He's a great speaker.
catch	Did anyone happen to <u>catch</u> "The American Metropolis"…?

4. Listen again to the first lecture in Exercise 2.4.B. As you listen, write the correct words on the blank lines in the script below. Check your answers with the audio script on page 629.

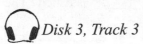 *Disk 3, Track 3*

Listen to an art instructor talk about composition.

Composition is the _____ of shapes and forms into a _____—an expressive whole. The elements of composition—_____, shape, tone, and _____—need to be well–arranged, need to be _____. They need to be coherent… just like the _____ and phrases and sentences in a piece of _____.

All paintings have a compositional _____. Successful paintings sort of suggest the _____ dimension, the sense that the _____ goes beyond the picture frame. A picture's _____—which includes the shapes, _____ and colors—is linked to what the _____ has to say. The artist's message is strongest when it's _____. A composition is better if it says one thing _____ than if it tries to say too many things. A _____ composition is sort of fussy and splintered and _____ unity. Even a painting of a _____ object needs thoughtful composition so the _____ of the object is present in every _____.

 Stop

5. Listen again to the first lecture in Exercise 2.4.E. As you listen, write the correct words on the blank lines in the script below. Check your answers with the audio script on page 632.

Disk 3, Track 6

Listen to part of a talk in a science class.

As you _____ from our previous discussion, the _____ of life is organized into metabolic _____. Next year, in your organic chemistry _____, you'll go into this—into metabolism—in more depth. Since this is an _____ course, you need only a general _____ of the process for now.

There's a wonderful _____ I'd like you to know about that will help you _____ for the test next week. It's part of the "Transformations" series that was on _____ about a year ago. The episode you should _____ is called "The Industry of a _____." I strongly urge you to see it. I believe our _____ has more than one copy.

It shows lots of _____—the many ways that cells use _____ for metabolism. For example, it shows how _____ in the "headlight" of a certain _____—how these bacteria take the energy stored in _____ and convert it into light, in a _____ called bioluminescence. You should all try to see this program before next _____. I highly recommend it. In fact, you can expect to see examples from it on the _____.

Stop

6. Listen again to each lecture in Exercise 2.4.E (Disk 3, Track 6). Imagine that you are in class, listening to the professor speak. While you are listening, take notes about the important ideas and details. Do not try to write down every word or memorize the lecture. After each lecture, use your notes and your own words to (1) write a short summary, and (2) orally summarize the main ideas of the lecture.

7. Obtain an audio recording of a real university lecture. In class, listen to a four–minute section of the tape. While you are listening, take notes about the information that you hear. Take notes about (1) topics and main ideas, and (2) details and facts. Form groups of three or four students. Compare your notes with those of the students in your group. Then, with your group, write a list of statements that you can infer, conclude, or generalize from the information. What is the probable purpose of the lecture? Who is the probable audience? Is it easy or difficult to make inferences? Why?

PROGRESS – 2.1 through 2.4

Quiz 4   *Time – approximately 10 minutes*

Listen to the recording. Choose the best answer to each question. To make this practice more like the real test, cover the questions and answers during each conversation and lecture. When you hear the first question for each set, uncover the questions and answers.

 Disk 3, Track 7

1. What is the conversation mainly about?

   (A) A job opening in the computer lab
   (B) An interesting television program
   (C) An application for a scholarship
   (D) An opportunity at a television station

2. Why does the man want to get the internship?

   Click on two answers.

   [A] He will earn a high internship wage.
   [B] He would like television work in the future.
   [C] He likes the other people who work there.
   [D] He will gain production experience.

3. Listen again to part of the conversation. Then answer the question.

   Select the sentence that best expresses how the man probably feels.

   (A) "I'm the most qualified person for the job."
   (B) "I wish I knew people who could help me."
   (C) "I'm not confident about getting the internship."
   (D) "I'm worried that my work will be criticized."

4. Why does the woman tell a story about her friend?

   (A) To reassure the man about his chance of getting the position
   (B) To find out if the man would like to meet her friend
   (C) To encourage the man to apply for a different internship
   (D) To impress the man with her political connections

5. What does the man want the woman to do?

   (A) Give him an internship application
   (B) Help him with an assignment
   (C) Watch a television program
   (D) Write a letter of recommendation

6. What is the discussion mainly about?

   (A) Hiking safely in bear habitat
   (B) Why bears are aggressive
   (C) Training bears to trust humans
   (D) Ways to predict bear behavior

7. What does the naturalist think of bear bells?

   (A) They are not effective in keeping away bears.
   (B) They destroy the peace and quiet of the woods.
   (C) They sound like the language of bears.
   (D) They trick bears into thinking you are a bear.

8. Listen again to part of the discussion. Then answer the question.

   Why does the naturalist say this:

   (A) To explain why certain trails have become overused
   (B) To list the resources that bears need to survive
   (C) To warn that bears may not notice you in certain conditions
   (D) To recommend the most interesting places to observe bears

9. What can be inferred about the behavior of bears?

   (A) Bears may respond to people suddenly.
   (B) Bears growl fiercely before they attack.
   (C) Bears like to socialize in large groups.
   (D) Bear behavior is very predictable.

10. Which situations should hikers avoid?

    Click on two answers.

    [A] Carrying bear bells
    [B] Approaching a bear
    [C] Shouting at a bear
    [D] Hiking when it is dark

 Stop

Answers to Listening Quiz 4 are on page 583.

Record your score on the Progress Chart on page 694.

PROGRESS – 2.1 through 2.4

Quiz 5   *Time – approximately 10 minutes*

Listen to the recording. Choose the best answer to each question. To make this practice more like the real test, cover the questions and answers during each conversation and lecture. When you hear the first question for each set, uncover the questions and answers.

 Disk 3, Track 8

1. What is the discussion mainly about?

   (A) Science as a process of discovery
   (B) How science and technology are connected
   (C) Ways that technology has harmed society
   (D) Responsibilities of scientists to society

2. What does the electron microscope provide an example of?

   (A) How technology applies scientific knowledge
   (B) How inventions improve our standard of living
   (C) How governments control science and technology
   (D) How science can advance without technology

3. Why does the professor mention tools, pottery, and musical instruments?

   (A) To compare past technology with current technology
   (B) To list inventions that scientists helped to design
   (C) To show that art and science are not separate activities
   (D) To give examples of technology that came before science

4. Listen again to part of the discussion. Then answer the question.

   What does the professor mean by this statement:

   (A) Technology has created powerful weapons.
   (B) Technology can cure every human problem.
   (C) Technology has both helped and harmed us.
   (D) Technology cannot exist without science.

5. Why does one of the students plan to get a master's degree in public policy?

   (A) He wants to convince the government to support technology.
   (B) He believes scientists should inform people about technology.
   (C) He would like to teach in a graduate school of technology.
   (D) He thinks technology has caused more damage than good.

6. What is the talk mainly about?

    Click on two answers.

   A Forestry as a profession
   B Different forest ecosystems
   C Where foresters work
   D Job openings in forestry

7. What can be inferred about the profession of forestry?

   A It is a broad field requiring diverse skills.
   B It has donated land to the government.
   C It hires over 700 new employees each year.
   D It requires a master's degree in biology.

8. Why does the student say this:

   A He would like the forester to recommend places to camp and hike.
   B He wants to understand how national parks and forests are different.
   C He wants to share his personal experiences with the class.
   D He doesn't think camping should be allowed in national forests.

9. Listen again to part of the talk. Then answer the question.

   What can be inferred about national parks?

   A National parks administer their own schools of forestry.
   B National parks have more employees than national forests.
   C National parks do not allow hiking and recreation.
   D National parks do not supply commercial wood products.

10. Listen again to part of the talk. Then answer the question.

   Why does the forester say this:

   A To encourage students to major in forestry management
   B To impress students with his knowledge of biology
   C To show that foresters and biologists have shared interests
   D To discuss controversial policies of the national parks

Stop

Answers to Listening Quiz 5 are on page 583.

Record your score on the Progress Chart on page 694.

2.5 Categorizing Information

FOCUS

 Disk 4, Track 1

Match each biome with the correct description.

Drag each answer choice to the correct box.

Taiga	Arctic tundra	Alpine tundra
Northern limit for plant growth	High mountaintop with strong winds	Evergreen forests with snow

---

 Stop

The speaker describes three types of biomes: taiga, arctic tundra, and alpine tundra. The speaker says:

> The taiga—also known as boreal or evergreen forest—is a broad band across North America, Europe, and Asia. Winters are long and cold…. Precipitation here is mostly in the form of snow.
>
> …the arctic tundra here, which extends northward from the taiga…. The tundra is the northern-most… uh… limit… for plants to grow.
>
> …alpine tundra, a biome found on high mountaintops…. Here, above the tree line, strong winds and cold temperatures create plant communities similar to those of the arctic tundra.

This question asks you to categorize information by matching the name of each biome with the correct description. The correctly matched items are:

Northern limit for plant growth	High mountaintop with strong winds	Evergreen forests with snow
Arctic tundra	*Alpine tundra*	*Taiga*

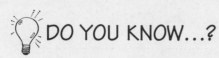

DO YOU KNOW…?

1. A *category* is a general class of things or ideas. To *categorize* information is to put it into categories, classes, divisions, or types.

    TOEFL questions about categorizing sound like this:

    > Match each term with the correct definition.
    > Match each type of _____ with the correct description.
    > Which _____ is associated with each _____?
    > Based on the speaker's description, classify the following _____.
    > Based on the information in the talk, indicate whether each phrase below describes _____ or _____.

2. Questions about categorizing have special directions. Here is an example:

    Match each animal with the correct classification.

    Drag each answer choice to the correct box.

Frog	Lizard	Eel

Fish	Amphibian	Reptile

    In this type of question, you use the computer mouse to drag words or phrases to the correct place in the table. You must match all of the items correctly to answer the question correctly. The correctly matched items are:

Fish	Amphibian	Reptile
Eel	*Frog*	*Lizard*

3. Here is another example:

    Indicate whether each animal below is a fish or an amphibian.

    For each animal, click in the correct box.

	Fish	Amphibian
Frog		✓
Shark	✓	
Eel	✓	
Toad		✓

    In this type of question, you click in one box in each row of the table. When you click in a box, a ✓ will appear there. The correct answers are shown above.

4. Some questions are worth more than one point. Here is an example:

> Sensations—and the perceptions they evoke in the brain—begin with the sensory receptors. There are several types of sensory receptors. One way of looking at them is in terms of the energy stimulus they respond to. Mechanoreceptors, for example, detect stimuli like touch, pressure, motion, and sound—all forms of mechanical energy. The hair cell is a common type of mechanoreceptor that detects motion. Some sensory receptors respond to chemicals. Chemoreceptors—like taste and smell receptors—respond to groups of related chemicals, which we often define as sweet, sour, salt, or bitter. Another type of sensory receptor—electromagnetic— detects various forms of electromagnetic energy: light, electricity, and magnetism. Electromagnetic receptors that detect visible light are often organized into eyes. Some animals—rattlesnakes, for example—have extremely sensitive infrared receptors that can detect the body heat of prey standing out against a colder background.

Based on the information in the lecture, indicate whether each sentence below describes mechanoreceptors, chemoreceptors, or electromagnetic receptors.

For each sentence, click in the correct box. This question is worth 2 points.

	Mechanoreceptors	Chemoreceptors	Electromagnetic receptors
They can detect sweet and sour tastes.		✓	
They help snakes locate the body heat of prey.			✓
The hair cell is an example that detects motion.	✓		
They detect electricity and magnetism.			✓

In this type of question, you click in one box in each row of the table. When you click in a box, a ✓ will appear there. The correct answers are shown above.

This question is worth 2 points, and it is possible to receive partial credit. If you choose all four correct answers, you earn 2 points. If you choose three correct answers, you earn 1 point. If you choose two or fewer correct answers, you receive no credit for the question.

5. On the TOEFL, questions about categorizing information may seem more difficult than the examples in this book. This is because on the real test:

  ↝ you will not see the table during the lecture, and
  ↝ you will not hear the question until after the lecture.

However, on the real test, you may take notes while you are listening to the lecture. If you hear a speaker discuss types, classes, or categories of something, you may want to take notes about characteristics and examples of each category.

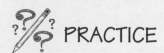

PRACTICE

Exercise 2.5.A

Listen to the recording. Choose the best answer to each question. To make this practice more like the real test, cover the questions and answers during each conversation and lecture. When you hear each question, uncover that question and answers.

 Disk 4, Track 2

1. Match each type of drum with the correct picture.

   Drag each answer choice to the correct box.

   (A) Tubular   (B) Vessel   (C) Frame

2. Which creatures have lived in each cave zone?

   Drag each answer choice to the correct box.

   (A) Shrimp   (B) Bats   (C) Early humans

Entrance zone	Twilight zone	Dark zone

3. Indicate whether each item below characterizes the dark zone of a cave.

   For each phrase, click in the correct box.

	Yes	No
Warm temperatures		
Blind animals		
Few air currents		
Green plants		

4. Indicate whether each phrase below describes an extravert or an introvert.

   For each phrase, click in the correct box.

	Extravert	Introvert
Prefers looking outward to the world		
Prefers learning in private, individual ways		
Has a variety of interests		
Has fewer interests, but on a deeper level		

5. What type of assignment would an introverted student probably prefer?

   (A) Reflective journal writing
   (B) Competitive team game
   (C) Large group discussion
   (D) Humorous performance

6. What is the main purpose of the talk?

   (A) To list major economic problems
   (B) To discuss some effects of inflation
   (C) To explain why bread prices increase
   (D) To classify the types of inflation

7. Why does the instructor talk about a loaf of bread?

   (A) To complain about the price of bread
   (B) To illustrate the effect of price changes
   (C) To compare bread with other foods
   (D) To explain social and political turmoil

8. What happens when prices go up but salaries remain the same?

  (A) The government will regulate the economy.
  (B) People will save money rather than spend it.
  (C) Workers might lose their jobs if they complain.
  (D) People must work longer to buy the same things.

9–10. Based on the information in the talk, indicate whether each sentence below describes moderate inflation, galloping inflation, or hyperinflation.

For each sentence, click in the correct box. This question is worth 2 points.

	Moderate inflation	Galloping inflation	Hyper–inflation
People try to get rid of their currency.			
Incomes and relative prices rise slightly.			
Inflation occurs at a rate of 100 percent in a year.			
There is social and political disorder.			

 Stop

Exercise 2.5.B

Listen to the recording. Choose the best answer to each question. To make this practice more like the real test, cover the questions and answers during each conversation and lecture. When you hear each question, uncover that question and answers.

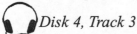 *Disk 4, Track 3*

1. What is the purpose of the talk?

  (A) To train new college administrators
  (B) To recommend becoming a specialist
  (C) To assist students in career planning
  (D) To suggest places to look for a job

2. According to the speaker, which people are likely to be specialists?

Click on two answers.

  [A] Engineers
  [B] Managers
  [C] Writers
  [D] Accountants

3. Based on the information in the talk, indicate whether each characteristic below more accurately describes a specialist or a generalist.

For each phrase, click in the correct box.

	Specialist	Generalist
Skilled in directing other people		
Concerned with tools and techniques		
Trained in a technical or professional field		
Must be able to make overall judgments		

4. According to the speaker, why are generalists needed in administrative positions?

   (A) Generalists have a better education than specialists.
   (B) Generalists are skilled in leadership and coordination.
   (C) Generalists prefer the higher salaries of administrators.
   (D) Generalists receive advanced training in technology.

5. What can be inferred from the talk?

   (A) Specialists are more intelligent than generalists.
   (B) The speaker was educated as a generalist.
   (C) Government workers are usually specialists.
   (D) Both specialists and generalists can find jobs.

6. How does the instructor organize the information that she presents?

   (A) She explains the scientific method of classifying leaves.
   (B) She discusses the annual growth of a wildflower's leaves.
   (C) She compares leaf arrangements of flowers, shrubs, and trees.
   (D) She describes each leaf arrangement and gives an example.

7. Select the drawing that best shows the alternate leaf arrangement.

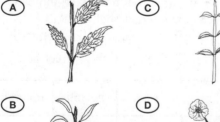

8-9. Based on the information in the talk, indicate whether each sentence below describes the alternate, opposite, or basal leaf arrangement.

> For each sentence, click in the correct box. This question is worth 2 points.

	Alternate	Opposite	Basal
The plant's leaves are paired on the opposite sides of the stem.			
All the plant's leaves are at ground level.			
Each leaf is attached at a different level on the stem.			
The leaves are attached at the same level on the stem, but on different sides.			

10. What will the students probably do next?

    (A) Bring flowers to class
    (B) Look at flower samples
    (C) Count a flower's leaves
    (D) Draw pictures of flowers

 Stop

Answers to Exercises 2.5.A through 2.5.B are on page 584.

How to score Multiple-Point Questions		
Points Possible	**Answers Correct**	**Points Earned**
2 points	4	2
	3	1
	0 – 2	0

 EXTENSION

1. Work in a group of three students. Choose one of the topics from the list below.

Agriculture	Fields of Study	Movies
Animals	Forms of Government	Music
Cities	Industries	Technology

Brainstorm ideas about your topic. Divide the topic into various categories. Choose three categories to focus on. For each category, think of an example, description, or characteristic. Write a few sentences about each category. Then choose someone in your group who will read the sentences to the whole class. The class listens to each group's "lecture" and takes notes. After each lecture, you and your classmates must (1) identify the categories, and (2) list key details about each category.

LISTENING

2.6 Summarizing a Process

 FOCUS

 Disk 4, Track 4

> The professor explains how a film is made. Summarize the process by putting the steps in the correct order.
>
> Drag each sentence to the space where it belongs.
>
> The director supervises the camera work.
> The editor cuts and reorders the film.
> The script is developed into a storyboard.
> The producer and the director plan the film.
>
> | 1 | |
> |---|---|
> | 2 | |
> | 3 | |
> | 4 | |

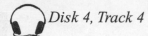 *Stop*

The professor summarizes the process of making a film. The professor says:

> The producer hires a director to make the creative decisions. The producer and the director work together to plan the film.
>
> They hire writers to develop a script for the film. Then, from the script comes the storyboard, an important step in the planning.
>
> Then comes the production, when the filming takes place. …the director and crew concentrate on getting the perfect camera shot.
>
> After the filming is done…. This is the post–production phase, and includes editing the film. The editor's job is to cut up the various film sequences and then put them together in the right order….

The correct order is:

1	*The producer and the director plan the film.*
2	*The script is developed into a storyboard.*
3	*The director supervises the camera work.*
4	*The editor cuts and reorders the film.*

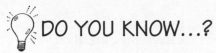

DO YOU KNOW...?

1. A ***process*** is a series of steps or actions that take place over time. A process ends with a result or a product.

   Some examples of processes are:

How to take a photograph	How to write a research paper
How a computer works	What happens during a thunderstorm
How a plant grows	How television was invented

2. A ***summary*** is a brief report of major points or important events. ***Summarizing a process*** is briefly stating the main steps of the process in the correct order. On the TOEFL, you will hear a speaker describe a process, and then you will answer a question that involves a summary of the process.

3. TOEFL questions about summarizing a process sound like this:

   > The professor briefly explains how _____. Summarize the process by putting the steps in the correct order.
   > The speaker describes a sequence of events. Put the events in the correct order.
   > The professor briefly describes the process of _____. Determine whether the sentences below are steps in the process.

4. Questions about summarizing a process have special directions. Here is an example:

   > One product of a thunderstorm is the onset of a hailstorm. Inside the clouds, violent air drafts cause water droplets to become supercooled. At zero degrees, the water droplets turn to ice crystals if there's also a catalyst present, in the form of tiny particles of solid matter. Ice forms around the particles, and supercooled water continues to coat them. They grow into rounded icy masses, becoming hailstones when they reach a diameter of 5 millimeters. Hailstones hit the ground with a loud rattle when they hit buildings and roads. Think of a hailstorm as a giant pummeling machine. It can be the most damaging part of a thunderstorm because of the damage it causes to crops.

   The professor describes how a hailstorm develops. Summarize the process by putting the steps in the correct order.

   Drag each sentence to the space where it belongs.

   Water freezes around particles of solid matter.
   Hailstones strike the ground with force.
   Rounded icy particles grow into hailstones.
   Water droplets in a cloud become supercooled.

In this type of question, you use the computer mouse to drag sentences to the correct place in the table. You must put all of the sentences in the correct order to answer the question correctly. The correct order is:

1	*Water droplets in a cloud become supercooled.*
2	*Water freezes around particles of solid matter.*
3	*Rounded icy particles grow into hailstones.*
4	*Hailstones strike the ground with force.*

5. Here is another example:

> The instructor briefly explains how a hailstorm develops.
> Indicate whether each sentence below is a step in the process.

> For each sentence, click in the correct box.

	Yes	No
Water droplets in a cloud become supercooled.	✓	
Water droplets freeze when they hit the ground.		✓
Rounded icy particles grow into hailstones.	✓	
Ice re–crystallizes by melting and refreezing.		✓

In this type of question, you click in one box in each row of the table. When you click in a box, a ✓ will appear there. The correct answers are shown above.

6. On the TOEFL, questions about summarizing a process may seem more difficult than the examples in this book. This is because on the real test:

- ➤ you will not see the table during the lecture, and
- ➤ you will not hear the question until after the lecture.

However, on the real test, you may take notes while you are listening to the lecture. If you hear a speaker discuss a process, you may want to take notes about what happens at each step in the process.

PRACTICE

Exercise 2.6.A

Listen to the recording. Choose the best answer to each question. To make this practice more like the real test, cover the questions and answers during each conversation and lecture. When you hear each question, uncover that question and answers.

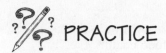 *Disk 4, Track 5*

1. What is the purpose of the talk?

   Ⓐ To compare a chair with a violin
   Ⓑ To compare two techniques of drawing
   Ⓒ To explain how to draw with pen and ink
   Ⓓ To explain why drawing with a pen is difficult

2. The instructor briefly explains how to draw the subject. Indicate whether each sentence below is a step in the process.

   For each sentence, click in the correct box.

	Yes	No
Draw the outline of the violin.		
Take a photograph of the subject.		
Study the subject for a few minutes.		
Rub the violin strings with a bow.		

3. According to the professor, why is it important to control an avalanche when it is small?

   Ⓐ A small avalanche requires fewer technicians.
   Ⓑ A small avalanche is easy to videotape.
   Ⓒ A large avalanche has several types of snow.
   Ⓓ A large avalanche can bury the highway.

4. What are the natural causes of an avalanche?

   Click on two answers.

   Ⓐ The weight of the snow
   Ⓑ The slope of the road
   Ⓒ The pull of gravity
   Ⓓ The size of the gun

5. The professor explains how a controlled avalanche is achieved. Summarize the process by putting the steps in the correct order.

   Drag each sentence to the space where it belongs.

   Ⓐ All traffic is removed from the highway.
   Ⓑ Large guns fire shells into the snow slopes.
   Ⓒ A team decides when the snow will slide.
   Ⓓ Shock waves cause the snow to slide.

1	
2	
3	
4	

6. The professor explains what happens during the salmon's run. Indicate whether each sentence below is a step in the process.

   For each sentence, click in the correct box.

	Yes	No
Salmon compete with eagles for food.		
Young fry swim downstream in rivers.		
Adult salmon migrate home to spawn.		
Salmon die from pollution in rivers.		

7. How do salmon find their way to their home stream?

   Click on two answers.

   Ⓐ By following other fish
   Ⓑ By seeing the sun's position
   Ⓒ By listening for waterfalls
   Ⓓ By smelling the water

8. Listen again to part of the discussion. Then answer the question.

Why does the student say this:

- Ⓐ She saw one large fish eat many smaller fish.
- Ⓑ She felt sick after seeing dead fish in the river.
- Ⓒ The sight of leaping salmon amazed her.
- Ⓓ There were more salmon than she could count.

9. According to the professor, why are salmon an important link in the food chain?

- Ⓐ They eat small fish that make other animals sick.
- Ⓑ They move vegetation downstream to the sea.
- Ⓒ They produce more eggs than they need.
- Ⓓ They carry nutrients from the ocean to streams.

10. What can be concluded from this statement:

- Ⓐ Baby salmon eat the bodies of dead salmon.
- Ⓑ Several natural food sources are endangered.
- Ⓒ Salmon eat a variety of other life forms.
- Ⓓ An adult salmon reproduces several times.

 Stop

Exercise 2.6.B

Listen to the recording. Choose the best answer to each question. To make this practice more like the real test, cover the questions and answers during each conversation and lecture. When you hear each question, uncover that question and answers.

 Disk 4, Track 6

1. Which of the following best describes the organization of the lecture?

- Ⓐ A list of causes and effects
- Ⓑ A comparison of two things
- Ⓒ A definition with examples
- Ⓓ A description of a process

2. What must be present for photosynthesis to begin?

Click on two answers.

- Ⓐ Carbon dioxide
- Ⓑ Nitrogen
- Ⓒ Water
- Ⓓ Glucose

3. The professor briefly explains what happens during photosynthesis. Indicate whether each sentence below is a step in the process.

For each sentence, click in the correct box.

	Yes	No
Chlorophyll absorbs light from the sun.		
The leaves take in water and carbon dioxide.		
The plant pushes roots through the soil.		
Hydrogen combines with carbon dioxide.		

4. According to the professor, why are psychologists interested in developing laws?

   (A) To raise the status of psychology as a serious science
   (B) To be able to make predictions about human behavior
   (C) To permit scientists to experiment with human subjects
   (D) To help students understand the art of psychology

5. According to the professor, what assumption do psychologists make?

   (A) There are patterns to human behavior.
   (B) There are few laws that can be proven.
   (C) People like to participate in experiments.
   (D) People obey only the laws they agree with.

6. Which behavior illustrates the Law of Effect?

   (A) A boy notices a stray cat while he is walking to school.
   (B) A boy stops pulling a cat's tail when the cat bites him.
   (C) A boy forgets where he put a gift from his grandmother.
   (D) A boy teaches his grandmother how to use a computer.

7. The professor explains how psychologists develop laws. Summarize the process by putting the steps in the correct order.

   Drag each sentence to the space where it belongs.

   (A) State the law.
   (B) Conduct an experiment.
   (C) Make a hypothesis.
   (D) Repeat the experiment.

1	
2	
3	
4	

8. According to the professor, which type of vegetation grows in marshes?

   (A) Shrubs
   (B) Grasses
   (C) Vegetables
   (D) Trees

9. The professor briefly describes a biological process that occurs in a marsh. Indicate whether each sentence below is a step in the process.

   For each sentence, click in the correct box.

	Yes	No
Dead plants and animals contribute energy to the food chain.		
Acids from decaying vegetation turn the water brown.		
The marsh is drained for agricultural development.		
Bacteria and fungi break down organic matter in the water.		

10. Why have so many wetlands been destroyed?

    Click on two answers.

    A Wetlands have no ecological importance.
    B People could not eat plants from wetlands.
    C Wetlands were thought to cause disease.
    D Land was needed for agriculture.

 Stop

Answers to Exercises 2.6.A through 2.6.B are on page 585.

 EXTENSION

1. Work in a group of three students. Choose one of the processes from the list below.

How to apply for university admission	How to install software on a laptop
How to bake bread	How to make soup
How to check the oil in a car	How to plant seeds
How to conduct a simple experiment	How to send a package to another country
How to give a dog a bath	How to use an automatic teller machine

Think about the steps in the process. Write them down in a list. What is the best order? Now, try to limit the number of steps to the four most important ones. Then choose someone in your group who will read the process to the whole class. The class listens to each group's process and takes notes. After each "lecture," you and your classmates must (1) write a short summary of the process, or (2) orally summarize the process.

PROGRESS – 2.5 through 2.6

QUIZ 6   *Time – approximately 10 minutes*

Listen to the recording. Choose the best answer to each question. To make this practice more like the real test, cover the questions and answers during each conversation and lecture. When you hear the first question for each set, uncover the questions and answers.

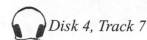 *Disk 4, Track 7*

1. According to the professor, what characterizes the ocean's upper zone?

   Click on two answers.

   A Plant life
   B Pollution
   C Cold water
   D Sunlight

2. The professor briefly describes the ocean's food chain. Indicate whether each sentence below is a step in the process.

   For each sentence, click in the correct box.

	Yes	No
Large fish regulate their body temperature.		
Animal plankton eats plant plankton.		
Microscopic plants grow in sunlit water.		
Large schools of fish feed on plankton.		

3. How does the professor describe each layer of the ocean's waters?

   Drag each answer choice to the correct box.

   A Completely dark
   B Clear and bright
   C Dimly lit

Top	Middle	Bottom

4. What tasks does the worker bee perform?

   Click on two answers.

   A Laying the eggs
   B Stinging the queen
   C Defending the colony
   D Gathering the food

5. The professor describes the stages of a worker bee's development. Summarize the process by putting the events in the correct order.

   Drag each sentence to the space where it belongs.

   A The egg hatches into a larva.
   B The larva enters the pupa state.
   C The adult worker emerges.
   D The egg is placed in the worker cell.

1	
2	
3	
4	

6. What segment of the bee's body contains the feature necessary for each activity?

   Drag each sentence to the space where it belongs.

   A Head   B Thorax   C Abdomen

Stinging	Working	Flying

7. What topics does the speaker discuss?

   Click on two answers.

   A Recipes for baking bread
   B Where bread originated
   C Grains that are grown today
   D How people harvest cereal

8. The speaker traces the history of bread.
   Indicate whether each sentence below
   describes an event in the history.

   For each sentence, click in the correct box.

	Yes	No
People discover that yeast makes bread rise.		
Beer is commonly used in making bread.		
Primitive bread is made on heated stones.		
The Egyptians invent the art of baking.		

9. Why did people stamp their bread with the family name?

   A To make it more attractive than other loaves
   B To advertise the baking skill of their family
   C To identify their bread in a communal bakery
   D To encourage customers to buy their bread

10. Based on the information in the talk, indicate whether each
    phrase below describes wheat or oats.

    For each phrase, click in the correct box.

	Wheat	Oats
Mainly fed to cattle		
Used to make bread and pasta		
Rich in a protein called gluten		

 Stop

Answers to Listening Quiz 6 are on page 586.

Record your score on the Progress Chart on page 694.

PROGRESS – 2.1 through 2.6

QUIZ 7

Time – approximately 10 minutes

Listen to the recording. Choose the best answer to each question. To make this practice more like the real test, cover the questions and answers during each conversation and lecture. When you hear the first question for each set, uncover the questions and answers.

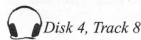 *Disk 4, Track 8*

1. Why is improvisation difficult to define?

   Click on two answers.

   [A] There are several kinds of improvisation.
   [B] People disagree about what improvisation is.
   [C] No musicians have recorded improvisation.
   [D] The dictionary does not define improvisation.

2. How does the professor develop the topic of improvisation?

   (A) By analyzing improvisation in classical music
   (B) By giving the correct definition of improvisation
   (C) By discussing the history of improvisation
   (D) By demonstrating improvisation on the organ

3. Who first improvised when playing music?

   (A) Jazz musicians
   (B) Italian organists
   (C) Prehistoric people
   (D) Military bandsmen

4. Based on the information in the discussion, indicate whether each phrase below describes prehistoric humans or jazz musicians.

   For each phrase, click in the correct box.

	Prehistoric humans	Jazz musicians
Made music for work, play, and war		
Combined their own music with stock melodies		
Used music as a force to show relationships		
Improvised on the music of other bands		

5. What does the professor imply about early jazz improvisation?

   (A) It copied the music of ancient people.
   (B) It was an entirely new way to make music.
   (C) It changed the nature of popular music.
   (D) It was developed by trained musicians.

6. What is the main idea of the lecture?

- (A) Children do not care much about the feelings of other people.
- (B) Children need guidance in developing their social skills.
- (C) Children become more egocentric when they are teenagers.
- (D) Children go through stages of mental and social development.

7. At what age is a child least able to recognize the thoughts of other people?

- (A) Four
- (B) Eight
- (C) Twelve
- (D) Fifteen

8. Listen again to part of the lecture. Then answer the question.

   Why does the professor say this:

- (A) To explain why children are sometimes rude to other people
- (B) To illustrate how children must experience directly to understand
- (C) To give examples of enjoyable classroom activities for children
- (D) To challenge a conventional theory about abstract thinking

9. What can be inferred about children in the multiple role–taking stage?

- (A) They know that different social roles require certain behavior.
- (B) They prefer taking roles that younger children will admire.
- (C) They understand that every person has only one social role.
- (D) They know how to amuse their classmates by role playing.

10. The professor briefly explains the stages of social development in children. Indicate whether each sentence below is a stage in the process.

For each sentence, click in the correct box.

	Yes	No
The child understands actions as others see them.		
The child prefers large crayons and paint brushes.		
The child is interested in learning about nature.		
The child can judge actions as they affect all people.		

🎧 *Stop*

Answers to Listening Quiz 7 are on page 587.

Record your score on the Progress Chart on page 694.

PROGRESS – 2.1 through 2.6

Time – approximately 10 minutes

Listen to the recording. Choose the best answer to each question. To make this practice more like the real test, cover the questions and answers during each conversation and lecture. When you hear the first question for each set, uncover the questions and answers.

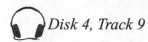 *Disk 4, Track 9*

1. Why does the woman go to see her professor?

   (A) To find out how her project will be graded
   (B) To discuss a problem she has with her boss
   (C) To talk about ideas for her project
   (D) To ask for more time to finish her project

2. When is the project plan due?

   (A) The following day
   (B) The next week
   (C) At the end of the month
   (D) On the first of next month

3. Listen again to part of the conversation. Then answer the question.

   Select the sentence that best expresses how the woman probably feels.

   (A) "I'm sorry to disagree with you."
   (B) "I don't understand the assignment."
   (C) "I like what I'm learning in this class."
   (D) "I'm concerned about my grade."

4. What topics will the woman write about?

   Click on two answers.

   A An economic development organization
   B Why all women should have an education
   C How an organization promotes social change
   D A group of women company presidents

5. What information will the woman include in her project?

   For each phrase, click in the correct box.

	Include	Not include
Photographs of art		
Information from a Web site		
An interview with her boss		
A product catalog		

6. Which picture represents a mesa?

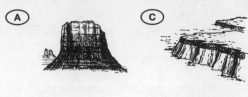

Ⓐ

Ⓒ

Ⓑ

Ⓓ

7. What reasons are given for the erosion of a mesa?

Click on two answers.

Ⓐ The rock on the sides is softer than that on the top.

Ⓑ Strong earthquakes frequently shake the region.

Ⓒ Plants dissolve the cements in the surface rock.

Ⓓ The force of water cuts away the softer rock.

8. Listen again to part of the talk. Then answer the question.

Why does the professor say this: 🎧

Ⓐ To show similarities between spires and sand

Ⓑ To describe the appearance of spires

Ⓒ To identify the material on the classroom floor

Ⓓ To warn students not to step on rocks

9. The professor briefly explains how erosion changes landforms. Summarize the process by putting the stages in the correct order.

Drag each sentence to the space where it belongs.

Ⓐ Soft stone is washed away, leaving a spire.

Ⓑ The rocks break down into pebbles and sand.

Ⓒ Water cuts a mesa into smaller landforms.

Ⓓ A spire is reduced and falls to the ground.

1	
2	
3	
4	

10. What can be concluded about erosion?

Ⓐ Erosion was discovered by Spanish explorers.

Ⓑ Erosion continually changes the shape of rock.

Ⓒ Erosion occurs only in the presence of water.

Ⓓ Erosion is a topic of scientific debate.

 Stop

Answers to Listening Quiz 8 are on page 587.

Record your score on the Progress Chart on page 694.

PART 3 – SPEAKING

The Speaking section measures your ability to speak in English about a variety of topics. There are six questions in this section. All of the questions are about topics that are appropriate for international students. You do not need special knowledge of any subject to respond to the questions.

The first two questions are independent speaking tasks in which you will speak from your own personal knowledge and experience. The next two questions are integrated–skills tasks in which you will read a passage, listen to a conversation or lecture, and then speak in response to a question about what you have read and heard. The last two questions are integrated–skills tasks in which you will listen to a conversation or lecture, and then speak in response to a question about it.

SPEAKING SECTION

Question	Reading Time	Listening Time	Preparation Time	Speaking Time
Independent Task 1	—	—	15 seconds	45 seconds
Independent Task 2	—	—	15 seconds	45 seconds
Integrated Task 1	45 seconds	1 – 2 minutes	30 seconds	60 seconds
Integrated Task 2	45 seconds	1 – 2 minutes	30 seconds	60 seconds
Integrated Task 3	—	1 – 2 minutes	20 seconds	60 seconds
Integrated Task 4	—	1 – 2 minutes	20 seconds	60 seconds

THE TEST EXPERIENCE

The entire Speaking section takes approximately 20 minutes to complete. This includes the time that you spend reading the directions, reading the passages, listening to the conversations and lectures, preparing your responses, and recording your responses. For the integrated–skills tasks, you will use headphones to listen to the conversations and lectures. You will be able to change the volume of the sound.

You may take notes on paper, and you may use your notes to help you respond to the tasks. However, at the end of the test you must give all of your notes to the test supervisor. Your notes will not be scored; only what you say during the recording time will be scored.

For each speaking task, you will both hear and see the question. You will have time to prepare your response before you begin speaking. A clock shows how much preparation time you have left. When the preparation time is up, you will hear a beep. The beep is your signal that the recording time will begin immediately.

You will answer the questions by speaking into a microphone. You have 45 or 60 seconds to record each response. A clock shows how much recording time you have left. When the response time is up, the computer will take you to the next question.

INDEPENDENT SPEAKING TASKS

There are two independent speaking tasks on the test. Each task measures your ability to speak in response to a question about a familiar topic. You must use your own knowledge and experience to develop your ideas.

In your responses, you must demonstrate your ability to:

- state and support an opinion;
- develop points with appropriate details and explanation;
- express ideas coherently; and
- make yourself understood by speaking clearly and fluently.

Two qualified evaluators will listen to each of your responses. They will assign to each a score on a scale of 1 to 4, with 4 being the highest score possible. You will receive a score of 0 if you do not respond to the given question. Your scores on the independent speaking tasks will be combined with your scores on the integrated speaking tasks. The total number of points you earn for all six speaking questions will be converted to a Speaking section score of 0 to 30.

Here is an example of an independent speaking task:

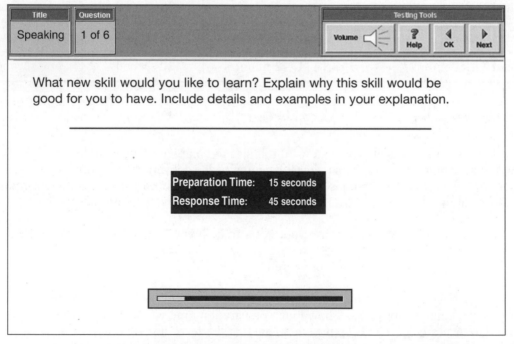

During the preparation time and the response time, the clock will count down the seconds remaining. When the time is up, the computer will begin the next question.

INTEGRATED SPEAKING TASKS

There are four integrated–skills speaking tasks on the test. Each task measures your ability to understand key information from one or more sources and to speak in response to a question about this information. The sources include reading passages, conversations, and lectures. The reading passages will be timed, and you will hear each conversation and lecture only one time. You may take notes and you may use them to help you answer the questions. You must determine what information in the sources is relevant to the question.

In your responses, you must demonstrate your ability to:

- convey relevant information from one or two sources;
- develop points with appropriate details and explanation;
- express ideas coherently; and
- make yourself understood by speaking clearly and fluently.

Two qualified evaluators will listen to each of your responses. They will assign to each a score on a scale of 1 to 4, with 4 being the highest score possible. You will receive a score of 0 if you do not respond to the given question. Your scores on the integrated speaking tasks will be combined with your scores on the independent speaking tasks. The total number of points you earn for all six speaking questions will be converted to a Speaking section score of 0 to 30.

There are two different types of integrated–skills speaking tasks: reading–listening–speaking and listening–speaking.

Task Type 1 – Reading–Listening–Speaking

For this type of task, you will read a short passage, listen to a conversation or lecture, and then speak in response to a question about what you have read and heard. After the question appears, you will have 30 seconds to prepare your response and 60 seconds (1 minute) to speak.

First, you have 45 seconds to read a passage. Here is an example:

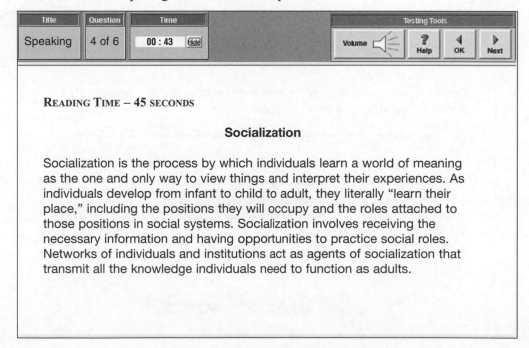

Title	Question	Time		Testing Tools
Speaking	4 of 6	00 : 43 Hide		Volume ? Help ◀ OK ▶ Next

READING TIME – 45 SECONDS

Socialization

Socialization is the process by which individuals learn a world of meaning as the one and only way to view things and interpret their experiences. As individuals develop from infant to child to adult, they literally "learn their place," including the positions they will occupy and the roles attached to those positions in social systems. Socialization involves receiving the necessary information and having opportunities to practice social roles. Networks of individuals and institutions act as agents of socialization that transmit all the knowledge individuals need to function as adults.

After 45 seconds have passed, the passage will disappear from the screen, and you will not see it again. You will then listen to a conversation or lecture about the same topic. While you are listening, you will see a picture of the speaker or speakers:

(Narrator)   Now listen to part of a talk in a sociology class.

(Professor) Agents of socialization are the people and institutions that teach you about the culture you live in, including its rules. The first agents of socialization are your parents or other adults who take care of you when you're a baby. Your parents give you the first important lessons in how to behave in society.

When you're a teenager, your peers—your friends and classmates—are agents of socialization. Your peers support you and help you grow up and out of your family's nest. Your parents and peers are important in different ways. Your parents give you guidance on long–term goals, like career choice, but your peers are more likely to influence your immediate lifestyle choices, like how you dress and what you do for fun.

And since you spend so many years in school under the guidance of teachers, teachers are also agents of socialization. Teachers give you knowledge and also serve as models for responsible adulthood. Institutions—like clubs and religious organizations—are also agents of socialization. So are the mass media—television, magazines, popular music, and the Internet.

Then you will both *hear* and *see* the speaking question:

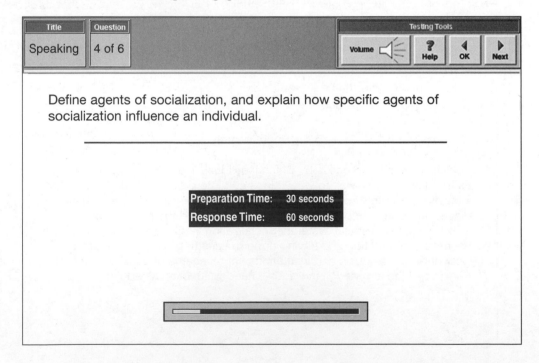

Title	Question		Testing Tools			
Speaking	4 of 6		Volume	? Help	◀ OK	▶ Next

Define agents of socialization, and explain how specific agents of socialization influence an individual.

Preparation Time:	30 seconds
Response Time:	60 seconds

During the preparation time and the response time, the clock will count down the seconds remaining. When the time is up, the computer will begin the next question.

Task Type 2 – Listening–Speaking

For this type of task, you will listen to a conversation or lecture and then speak in response to a question about it. The listening part is one to two minutes long. After the question appears, you will have 20 seconds to prepare your response and 60 seconds (1 minute) to speak.

Here is an example. While you are listening, you will see a picture of the speaker or speakers:

(Narrator)   Listen to part of a conversation between two students.

(Man)   How do you like living in the campus apartments?
(Woman)   Well … it's OK. I mean, I like the apartment, but my roommate is kind of a problem. Sometimes she uses my things without asking—mostly little things, like paper and toothpaste, but once it was my favorite sweater. And she never cleans the bathroom when it's her turn.
(Man)   Have you sat down with her and had a good talk about these things?
(Woman)   Maybe if I saw her more often. The problem is, she's hardly ever home.
(Man)   Try leaving her a note.
(Woman)   I did, but it didn't help.
(Man)   Isn't there an apartment manager, someone who will help you sort out problems like this? I don't know … like set up a meeting with your roommate?
(Woman)   I didn't know the manager does that kind of thing. I guess I could find out.
(Man)   And if that doesn't work … if talking it over doesn't help, then you should probably just move out, find another place. There's always someone looking for a roommate.

Then you will both *hear* and *see* the speaking question:

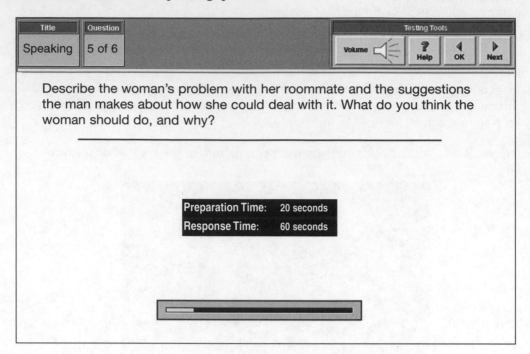

During the preparation time and the response time, the clock will count down the seconds remaining. When the time is up, the computer will begin the next question.

STRATEGIES FOR THE SPEAKING SECTION

Before the Test

- Work on building your spoken vocabulary. Practice using transitions—connecting words and expressions—to make your speech more fluent and coherent.

- Work to improve your pronunciation. Pay special attention to stress and intonation.

- Record your voice, and listen to the recording. Ask yourself this question: *Will other people understand what I am saying?*

- Listen to a variety of recorded materials that use academic English, such as university lectures, documentaries, and in–depth radio news programs. Practice taking notes as you listen. Practice summarizing in your own words the information that you hear.

- Your own best strategy: _____

_____

During the Test – Independent Tasks

- Use the preparation time wisely. Read the question carefully and note everything that it asks you to do. Think about what you want to convey in a simple, organized way. Write down a simple plan of a few key details or examples that you want to include.

- During the recording time, speak clearly into the microphone. Pronounce words carefully, especially important content words. Speak at a normal speed—not too fast and not too slow. Keep the structure of your sentences fairly simple. Use appropriate transitions, such as *first, second, next, also, finally,* and *most importantly.*

- Watch how much time you have left. Pace yourself so you are able to say everything you want to say.

- Your own best strategy: _____

During the Test – Integrated Tasks

- While you are reading the short passages, focus on the topic and general message. Do not try to memorize every detail.

- While you are listening to the conversations and lectures, focus on major ideas. Listen for key words and concepts that the speakers emphasize or repeat.

- Take notes only about the information that will be important to remember: key points, examples, and reasons. Do not try to write down everything you hear. Do not allow your writing to detract from your listening.

- Use the preparation time wisely. Read the question carefully and note everything that it asks you to do. Do not try to write a response. Review your notes, and concentrate on what you will say. Plan to state and support two or three points.

- During the recording time, respond to each part of the question. Use key ideas and relevant details from the conversation or lecture to support your points.

- Speak clearly into the microphone. Pronounce words carefully, especially important content words. Speak at a normal speed—not too fast and not too slow. Keep the structure of your sentences fairly simple. Use appropriate transitions to make your speech more fluent and coherent. Use the vocabulary that you are familiar with.

- Pace yourself so you have enough time to cover all of your points. Watch how much time you have left. If you finish answering but still have recording time left, you may add a brief conclusion or summary of your points.

- Your own best strategy: _____

3.1 Independent Speaking: Developing a Topic

 FOCUS

Imagine you are having a conversation with an older friend who advises you about many important things. Your friend asks you the following question:

> What new skill would you like to learn? Explain why this skill would be good for you to have.

How would you respond to this question? Check all of the things that you would do:

____ Take a few seconds to think about what you will say.

____ Change the subject and talk about something else.

____ Describe all of the skills that you already have.

____ Choose one new skill that you would like to have.

____ Think of two or three ways that this skill would help you.

When faced with a serious question like this, it is wise to take a few seconds to think. Thinking will allow you to make a choice and to organize your thoughts.

It is not a good idea to change the subject and talk about something else, nor to describe all of the skills you already have. Neither of these actions would satisfy your friend with a direct answer.

Your friend has asked you to (1) name a skill that you would like to learn, and (2) explain why you would choose to learn this skill. The best way to respond is to answer directly. Choose one new skill you would like to have. Think of two or three reasons for learning this skill—these reasons will support your choice.

 DO YOU KNOW...?

1. The first two speaking questions are independent speaking tasks in which you will state, explain, and support your opinion about a familiar topic. You must use your own personal knowledge and experience to develop the topic. In the first of these tasks, you will be asked to choose a relevant person, place, object, or event. You will present your opinion about this person, place, object, or event, and provide details that support your choice.

2. After the speaking question is presented, you will have 15 seconds to prepare your response and 45 seconds to speak. You will record your response by speaking into a microphone. Your response will be evaluated on how well you speak and on how well you develop the topic.

3. Use the preparation time to choose the information that you want to convey about the topic. For example, if the question asks you to describe a person that you admire, the first thing to do is choose a person to talk about. Then, plan at least two points that you want to make about that person. Think of examples, reasons, and other details that will develop your points. Here is an example:

> Describe a person that you admire. Explain why you admire this person. Include details and examples to support your explanation.

Task	Describe a person that you admire.
Opinion	I admire my grandfather.
Supporting Points and Details (why you admire your grandfather)	• two jobs to support family • railroad worker • night clerk in hotel • interesting stories • family history • people he met at work • funny

4. You have 45 seconds to record your response. This is enough time to answer the question effectively. It is enough time to state your opinion about the topic and develop it with examples, explanation, and personal experience. Forty–five seconds is enough time to make at least six or seven statements.

5. Here is an example of an independent speaking task and a student's response:

> What new skill would you like to learn? Explain why this skill would be good for you to have. Include details and examples in your explanation.

"I would like to learn how to play the guitar. Now I can't play a musical instrument, so this would be a new skill for me. It would be a good skill to have because I could take my guitar to parties and play music for my friends. Also, I could join a band and play songs with other musicians. Maybe I could make money that way, but the main reason is I enjoy music and want to understand it better."

The student's response is successful because it clearly states an opinion:

"I would like to learn how to play the guitar."

The response gives appropriate reasons for this choice:

"...I could take my guitar to parties and play music for my friends."
"...I could join a band and play songs with other musicians."
"...I could make money that way..."
"...the main reason is I enjoy music and want to understand it better."

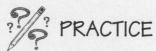 PRACTICE

Exercise 3.1.A

For each independent speaking question below, allow 15 seconds to prepare your response and 45 seconds to speak. Record your response on a cassette.

Preparation Time – 15 seconds
Response Time – 45 seconds

1. What was your favorite toy when you were a child? Describe this toy and explain why it was important to you. Include details and examples to support your explanation.

2. What famous person would you like to visit for one hour? Explain why you would like to meet this person and what you would talk about. Include details and examples in your explanation.

3. Describe a place where you go for rest and relaxation. Explain why it is a good place for you to relax. Include details and examples in your explanation.

4. What event in your life made you very happy? Explain what happened to you, and why you felt so happy. Include details and examples in your explanation.

5. Describe an object that is very special in your life. Explain why this object is important to you. Include details and examples in your explanation.

6. What important lesson have you learned from a family member? Explain the significance of this lesson in your life. Include details and examples in your explanation.

Answers to Exercise 3.1.A will vary.

 EXTENSION

1. With your teacher and classmates, discuss the characteristics of a good speaker. On the board, write the names of good speakers that you know. They can be famous people or people that you know personally. Next to each name, list the qualities that make that person a good speaker. Which qualities on your list will be important when you take the TOEFL?

2. Share and discuss your recorded response to one of the speaking questions in Exercise 3.1.A. Work in a group of three or four students. Listen to each student's recorded response. Discuss each student's response by answering the following questions:

   a. Does the speaker present an opinion about the given topic? What is the speaker's opinion?
   b. What points does the speaker make to support this opinion?
   c. What specific details, examples, or reasons develop the speaker's ideas?
   d. Does the response answer the question effectively? Why or why not?

   Make suggestions that will help each student improve in the future.

3.2 Independent Speaking:
Stating and Supporting a Position

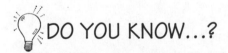 FOCUS

Imagine you are having a discussion with some of your friends. You are all students, and you are discussing the following question:

> Sometimes students have to write papers. Sometimes they have to give oral presentations. Which activity do you think is better for students, and why? Include details and examples in your explanation.

How would you respond to this question? How would you expect other students to respond? If one of your friends had an opinion that differed from yours, would you want to know your friend's reasons for holding that opinion?

We all have opinions about things that affect us. We have reasons for holding our opinions. We express our opinions at times, and we explain why we hold these opinions.

Sometimes we face choices in life. Sometimes we must decide which of two activities is better. Making such choices involves evaluating the two activities and having reasons for choosing one over the other.

One speaking question on the TOEFL requires you to choose between two possible options. In this question, you must state your choice and support that choice with examples and explanation.

DO YOU KNOW...?

1. The first two speaking questions are independent speaking tasks in which you will state, explain, and support your opinion about a familiar topic. In the second of these tasks, you will be presented with two possible actions or situations. You must choose which position you prefer and explain the reasons for your choice. You must state your opinion clearly and support it with appropriate details.

2. You have 15 seconds to prepare your response. Use the preparation time to choose a position on the topic and to plan at least two supporting points that you will make. Think about how best to develop your points. What examples from your own knowledge and experience will explain your position? Think about what you will say, and in what order you will say it.

3. You have 45 seconds to record your response. This is enough time to answer the question effectively. It is enough time to state your position and support it with examples and explanation. It is enough time to make six or more complete statements.

4. Your response will be evaluated on how well you speak and on how well you support your position. The evaluators who listen to your response are not interested in *which* position you choose but rather in *how* you support your choice. Do not be concerned about whether the evaluators will agree with your position. Be concerned about whether you state your position clearly and support it with appropriate reasons and examples.

5. Here is an example of an independent speaking task:

> Sometimes students have to write papers. Sometimes they have to give oral presentations. Which activity do you think is better for students, and why? Include details and examples in your explanation.

Here is one position on the topic:

Task	Choose which is better: writing papers or giving oral presentations.
Opinion	Writing papers is better for students.

Supporting Points and Details (why writing papers is better)	• need strong writing skills
	  • reading and writing
	  • prepare for exams
	
	• show understanding
	  • more time to explain
	  • think deeply

STUDENT'S RESPONSE

"I think writing papers is better for students. We need to develop strong writing skills. We go to school mainly to learn reading and writing, so we need a lot of practice. Examinations require a lot of writing, so writing papers is good preparation. Also, I think writing is a better way to show that I understand. When I write a paper, I can think deeply because I have more time to explain my ideas."

Here is a different position on the topic:

Task	Choose which is better: writing papers or giving oral presentations.
Opinion	Giving oral presentations is better for students.

Supporting Points and Details (why giving oral presentations is better)	• easier
	  • less time to prepare
	  • interesting for other students
	
	• important job skill
	  • confidence

STUDENT'S RESPONSE

"Students have to write papers and give oral presentations. I think oral presentations are better because they are easier and take less time to prepare. Another reason is oral presentations are interesting for other students who are listening. Finally, many jobs require oral presentations, so students can learn an important skill and develop confidence in speaking to a group."

Both students have responded to the question effectively. Both state their position clearly and support their position with appropriate examples and reasons.

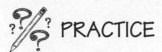 PRACTICE

Exercise 3.2.A

For each independent speaking question below, allow 15 seconds to prepare your response and 45 seconds to speak. Record your response on a cassette.

Preparation Time – 15 seconds
Response Time – 45 seconds

1. Some people eat their main meal of the day around noon. Others have their main meal in the evening. What time of day do you think is better, and why? Include details and examples in your explanation.

2. Some people take one long vacation each year. Others take several short vacations. Which do you prefer and why? Include details and examples in your explanation.

3. Some people like going to large parties where there are many people they don't know. Other people prefer small parties with a few close friends. Which type of party do you prefer and why? Include details and examples in your explanation.

4. Some high schools require students to wear uniforms. Others allow students to wear clothing of their own choice. Which situation do you think is better and why? Include details and examples in your explanation.

5. Some people like going to concerts to hear music played live. Others prefer listening to recorded music. Which musical experience do you think is better, and why? Include details and examples in your explanation.

6. Some people get up early in the morning and go to bed early at night. Others get up late in the morning and stay up until late at night. Which do you think is better and why? Include details and examples in your explanation.

Answers to Exercise 3.2.A will vary.

SPEAKING

 EXTENSION

1. With your teacher and classmates, discuss situations when you must choose between two options. For example, you may have to choose whether to live in a dormitory on campus or in an apartment off campus. Write a list of situations on the board. Next to each situation, write two possible choices. Now, conduct an oral exercise in which the teacher or a student selects one of the situations. Other students take turns stating which of the two choices they prefer and giving at least two reasons for their choice.

2. Share and discuss your recorded response to one of the speaking questions in Exercise 3.2.A. Work in a group of three or four students. Listen to each student's recorded response. Discuss each student's response by answering the following questions:

   a. Does the speaker present an opinion about the given topic? What is the speaker's opinion?
   b. What points does the speaker make to support this opinion?
   c. What specific details, examples, or reasons develop the speaker's ideas?
   d. Does the response answer the question effectively? Why or why not?

   Make suggestions that will help each student improve in the future.

3.3 Speaking Clearly and Coherently

 FOCUS

Look at the following independent speaking task and a student's response to it:

> Describe a person that you admire. Explain why you admire this person. Include details
> and examples to support your explanation.

> "I admire Nelson Mandela for several reasons. First, he is an excellent speaker, and
> his ideas inspire many people. Second, he spent over twenty years in jail as a political
> prisoner. However, that experience didn't stop his dream. Third, he became the president
> of South Africa when he was seventy years old. I admire Nelson Mandela because he
> was a strong leader for his country at a time of change."

Which of the following statements apply to the student's response? Check all of the statements that are true:

____ The student's opinion is difficult to understand.
____ Each sentence conveys a complete thought.
____ The student uses some words incorrectly.
____ Each point is developed with appropriate details.
____ The student expresses ideas coherently.

Without taking the student's pronunciation into account, most people would think the student has provided
a clear and coherent response. The student's opinion is clearly stated at the beginning:

> "I admire Nelson Mandela for several reasons."

The student then clearly states three reasons:

> "First, he is an excellent speaker, and his ideas inspire many people."
> "Second, he spent over twenty years in jail as a political prisoner. However, that
> experience didn't stop his dream."
> "Third, he became the president of South Africa when he was seventy years old."

Each sentence conveys a complete thought, and each point is developed with appropriate details. The
student expresses ideas coherently. The transitions *first*, *second*, and *third* help to make the student's points
clear and coherent.

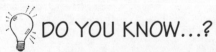 DO YOU KNOW...?

1. Two trained evaluators will listen to your responses to the independent speaking tasks. They will
    rate your speaking on how well you:

    ↪ state and support an opinion;
    ↪ develop points with appropriate details and explanation;
    ↪ express ideas coherently; and
    ↪ make yourself understood by speaking clearly and fluently.

2. To convey your opinion, you must speak clearly and coherently. Think of your listeners and try to make your response easy for them to understand. Your speech will be easier to understand if:

   - each sentence conveys a complete thought;
   - your sentence structure is fairly simple;
   - you use vocabulary correctly;
   - you pronounce words clearly and correctly; and
   - you speak at a normal speed.

3. Your response will be easier to understand if your speech is coherent. **Coherence** is the quality of order in speech. When speech is coherent, it is more likely that listeners will understand the message. The following *transitions* will help you convey examples and reasons coherently.

Give Examples		
for example	one example	also
such as	another example	in addition
Give Reasons		
because	one reason	first, second, third…
so (that)	another reason	finally

4. Your response will be easier to understand if you speak in phrases. This means grouping words into idea units—according to their meaning and connection to each other. For example, look at this sentence:

   "I admire Nelson Mandela because he was a strong leader for his country at a time of change."

   This sentence is easier to understand if it is spoken in phrases, like this:

   "I admire / Nelson Mandela / because he was / a strong leader / for his country / at a time / of change."

5. Your response will be easier to understand if you pronounce words clearly and correctly, especially key transitions and *content words*: nouns, verbs, and adjectives that convey important information. Use voice stress to emphasize key words.

   "I admire **Nelson Mandela** for **several reasons**. **First**, he is an **excellent speaker**, and his ideas **inspire** many people. **Second**, he spent over **twenty years** in **jail** as a **political prisoner**. However, that experience **didn't stop** his **dream**. **Third**, he became the **president** of **South Africa** when he was **seventy** years old. I **admire** Nelson Mandela because he was a **strong leader** for his country at a **time** of **change**."

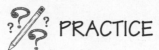 PRACTICE

Exercise 3.3.A

For each independent speaking question below, allow 15 seconds to prepare your response and 45 seconds to speak. Record your response on a cassette.

Preparation Time – 15 seconds
Response Time – 45 seconds

1. How do you like to spend your leisure time? Choose a leisure activity and explain why you like to do it. Include details and examples in your explanation.

2. Some students like to take classes early in the morning. Others prefer having classes later in the day. Which time of day is better for you and why? Include details and examples in your explanation.

3. What type of animal would you like to have, either as a pet or for some other reason? Choose an animal and explain why you would like to own this type of animal. Include details and examples in your explanation.

4. Some people plan every detail of their vacation in advance. Others prefer to leave most details flexible or open to chance. Which do you think is better and why? Include details and examples in your explanation.

5. What place or landmark in your country do you recommend that other people visit? Explain why you think people should go there. Include details and examples to support your explanation.

6. Some people like to eat most of their meals with other people. Others prefer eating most of their meals alone. Which do you prefer and why? Include details and examples in your explanation.

Answers to Exercise 3.3.A will vary.

 EXTENSION

1. Share and discuss your recorded response to one of the speaking questions in Exercise 3.3.A. Work in a group of three or four students. Listen to each student's recorded response. Discuss each student's response by answering the following questions:

    a. Does the speaker clearly state an opinion about the topic? What is the speaker's opinion? Is the opinion supported?
    b. What examples, explanation, or other details are included? Do they successfully develop the topic?
    c. Can the response be easily understood? Why or why not?
    d. Is the response coherent? Why or why not?
    e. Does the response answer the question effectively? Why or why not?

Make suggestions that will help each student improve in the future.

3.4 Evaluating Independent Speaking

FOCUS

If you ask someone for information, what do you want to hear? What does a speaker do to make you understand? What makes a speaker a good communicator?

Circle **T** if the statement is true. Circle **F** if the statement is false.

T	**F**	A good communicator listens and responds to what I am asking.
T	**F**	I understand better if the speaker uses a strong, clear voice.
T	**F**	It's better if the speaker uses big words and complex sentences.
T	**F**	Good speakers pronounce words distinctly and correctly.
T	**F**	It's easier to understand if the speaker gives numerous details.
T	**F**	A good communicator conveys more information by talking fast.
T	**F**	A good speaker avoids saying "um" or "ah" too many times.

Which statements are true? If you circled **T** for these sentences...

A good communicator listens and responds to what I am asking.
I understand better if the speaker uses a strong, clear voice.
Good speakers pronounce words distinctly and correctly.
A good speaker avoids saying "um" or "ah" too many times.

...you would find that most people agree with you.

Good speakers make themselves understood to their listeners. They speak to be understood. They provide all of the information that is requested. They speak in a clear voice, and they pronounce important words distinctly. They avoid saying "um" and "ah." Good speakers do not force their listeners to work hard to understand them.

 DO YOU KNOW...?

1. When you take the TOEFL, two trained evaluators will listen to your response to each independent speaking question. They will evaluate your speech and assign a score of 1 to 4, with 4 the highest score possible. Each response will be judged on your ability to state and support an opinion on a familiar topic and on the clarity and coherence of your speech.

2. The evaluators will use criteria similar to those in the following table as they score your responses.

INDEPENDENT SPEAKING TASK
Description of Score Levels

4	**A response at this level** ↝ effectively addresses the task and is generally well developed and coherent; and ↝ demonstrates effective use of grammar and vocabulary, but may contain minor language errors that do not interfere with meaning; and ↝ demonstrates clear, fluid speech with high overall intelligibility, but may contain minor problems with pronunciation or intonation.
3	**A response at this level** ↝ conveys ideas and information relevant to the task, but overall development is somewhat limited, and connections among ideas are sometimes unclear; and ↝ demonstrates somewhat effective use of grammar and vocabulary, but may contain language errors that do not seriously interfere with meaning; and ↝ demonstrates generally clear, somewhat fluid speech, but may contain minor problems with pronunciation, intonation, or pacing and may occasionally require some listener effort.
2	**A response at this level** ↝ is related to the task, although the development of ideas is limited, and connections among ideas are unclear; or ↝ demonstrates a limited range and control of grammar and vocabulary; or ↝ demonstrates some clear speech, but contains problems with pronunciation, intonation, or pacing and may require significant listener effort.
1	**A response at this level** ↝ fails to provide much relevant content because ideas that are expressed are inaccurate, limited, or vague; or ↝ demonstrates a limited control of grammar and vocabulary that severely limits expression of ideas and connections among ideas; or ↝ demonstrates fragmented speech with frequent pauses and consistent problems with pronunciation and intonation that obscure meaning and require great listener effort.
0	**A response at this level** ↝ is not related to the topic; or ↝ is absent.

SPEAKING

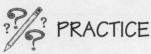

PRACTICE

Exercise 3.4.A

For each independent speaking question below, allow 15 seconds to prepare your response and 45 seconds to speak. Record your response on a cassette.

Preparation Time – 15 seconds
Response Time – 45 seconds

1. Describe a place that you consider to be beautiful. Explain why certain qualities of this place make it beautiful. Include details and examples to support your explanation.

2. Some people relax by staying home. Others relax by going out. Which type of relaxation is better for you and why? Include details and examples in your explanation.

3. Describe an occasion when you were surprised. What happened to you, and why did you feel surprised? Include details and examples in your explanation.

4. Some students prepare for tests by studying alone. Others prepare for tests by studying with other students or a tutor. Which study method do you think is better, and why? Include details and examples in your explanation.

5. What type of home would you like to live in? Describe the characteristics of such a home, and explain why you would like to live there. Include details and examples in your explanation.

6. Some people exercise early in the morning. Others exercise in the afternoon or evening. Which time of day do you think is better for exercising and why? Include details and examples to support your explanation.

Answers to Exercise 3.4.A will vary.

EXTENSION

1. Study the descriptions of the four score levels on page 303. Make sure you understand the description for each level. Check your understanding of the meaning of these words and phrases:

addresses the task	fluid speech	pacing
coherent	intelligibility	listener effort
minor	intonation	vague
interfere	limited	fragmented speech

2. Review your recorded responses to the integrated speaking questions in units 3.1 through 3.4. Evaluate each response according to the descriptions of the four levels on page 303. What score would your responses receive? What are the areas of strength in your speaking? What are your most serious problems? What can you do to improve your speaking and earn a high score for the independent speaking questions on the TOEFL?

PROGRESS – 3.1 through 3.4

QUIZ 1

Time – approximately 5 minutes

There are two questions in this quiz. Use your own personal knowledge and experience to answer each question. After you hear the question, you have 15 seconds to prepare your response and 45 seconds to speak. Record your response to each question on a cassette. Each response will earn a score of 1, 2, 3, or 4, with 4 the highest score. Add the two scores to obtain your total score.

QUESTION 1

 Disk 5, Track 1

> What is the most interesting class you have ever taken? Explain the aspects of the class that made it interesting. Include details and examples in your explanation.

 Stop

Preparation Time – 15 seconds
Response Time – 45 seconds

QUESTION 2

 Disk 5, Track 2

> Some people like to read classic works of literature. Others prefer watching film versions of the same stories. Which do you prefer and why? Include details and examples in your explanation.

 Stop

Preparation Time – 15 seconds
Response Time – 45 seconds

Record your total score on the Progress Chart on page 695.

PROGRESS – 3.1 through 3.4

QUIZ 2   *Time – approximately 5 minutes*

There are two questions in this quiz. Use your own personal knowledge and experience to answer each question. After you hear the question, you have 15 seconds to prepare your response and 45 seconds to speak. Record your response to each question on a cassette. Each response will earn a score of 1, 2, 3, or 4, with 4 the highest score. Add the two scores to obtain your total score.

QUESTION 1

 Disk 5, Track 3

> Describe a city or town where you have lived. Explain why this place is either a good place or not a good place to live. Include details and examples in your explanation.

 Stop

Preparation Time – 15 seconds
Response Time – 45 seconds

QUESTION 2

 Disk 5, Track 4

> Some students take one long examination at the end of a course. Others have several shorter tests throughout the course. Which situation do you think is better for students, and why? Include details and examples in your explanation.

 Stop

Preparation Time – 15 seconds
Response Time – 45 seconds

Record your total score on the Progress Chart on page 695.

PROGRESS – 3.1 through 3.4

QUIZ 3   *Time – approximately 5 minutes*

There are two questions in this quiz. Use your own personal knowledge and experience to answer each question. After you hear the question, you have 15 seconds to prepare your response and 45 seconds to speak. Record your response to each question on a cassette. Each response will earn a score of 1, 2, 3, or 4, with 4 the highest score. Add the two scores to obtain your total score.

QUESTION 1

 Disk 5, Track 5

> Describe your idea of the perfect job. Explain why this job would be appealing to you. Include details and examples in your explanation.

 Stop

Preparation Time – 15 seconds
Response Time – 45 seconds

QUESTION 2

 Disk 5, Track 6

> Some people like taking their vacation in a city. Others prefer spending their vacation in the countryside. Which do you prefer and why? Include details and examples in your explanation.

 Stop

Preparation Time – 15 seconds
Response Time – 45 seconds

Record your total score on the Progress Chart on page 695.

3.5 Integrated Speaking: Connecting Information from Two Sources

 FOCUS

Imagine you are attending a university, and you see the following notice posted on a campus bulletin board:

NOTICE OF VOTE ON CAMPUS FOOD SERVICE

　　　Students are encouraged to vote on the university's proposal to change the food service on campus. Students should vote for which of two options they prefer. Option 1 would expand the main cafeteria in the Student Center, including the addition of more food choices and more dining space; this option would also close the two snack bars on campus. Option 2 would close the cafeteria in the Student Center but would maintain the two snack bars, and would add five food service areas across campus, including two cafes, a deli, a barbecue grill, and a fine dining room.

How would you respond to the notice? Check all of the things that you would do.

　　____ Ignore the notice.
　　____ Discuss the two food service options with your friends.
　　____ Write to the university president about the food service.
　　____ Listen to various opinions about the options.
　　____ Decide which of the two options you prefer.

Some students would ignore the notice. However, students who regularly eat on campus would probably discuss the two options with their friends. They would listen to various opinions about the options before they decide which of the two options they prefer.

One type of speaking question on the TOEFL deals with similar topics of campus–related interest. In the integrated reading–listening–speaking task, you will read a short passage, listen to one or two speakers discussing the topic, and then speak about what you have just read and heard.

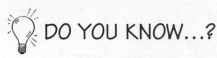 DO YOU KNOW...?

1. The first two integrated speaking tasks involve the three language skills of reading, listening, and speaking. In each reading–listening–speaking task you will:

    - read a short passage of around 100 words about either a campus situation or an academic topic;
    - listen to a short conversation or lecture about the same topic; and
    - speak in response to a question about information in the two sources.

2. You have 45 seconds to read the passage. Then the passage will disappear from the screen, and you will not see it again. You will see a picture of the speakers as you listen to the conversation or lecture. After that, you will see and hear the speaking question. The question requires you to connect information from the conversation or lecture with information from the reading. It does not ask for your opinion on the topic.

3. The reading passage provides general background information on the topic. The conversation or lecture is from one to two minutes long. The conversation or lecture does not merely repeat information from the reading passage; rather, it develops and expands on the reading in some way. For example, a speaker may:

    - express an opinion about the topic of the reading;
    - offer a different view or explanation of the reading; or
    - illustrate a general point in the reading with a specific example.

4. After the speaking question is presented, you have 30 seconds to prepare your response and 60 seconds to speak. You will record your response by speaking into a microphone. Your response will be evaluated on how well you speak and on how well you convey relevant information from the two sources to answer the question.

5. Here is an example of an integrated reading–listening–speaking task:

READING *(Time – 45 seconds)*

NOTICE OF VOTE ON CAMPUS FOOD SERVICE

Students are encouraged to vote on the university's proposal to change the food service on campus. Students should vote for which of two options they prefer. Option 1 would expand the main cafeteria in the Student Center, including the addition of more food choices and more dining space; this option would also close the two snack bars on campus. Option 2 would close the cafeteria in the Student Center but would maintain the two snack bars, and would add five food service areas across campus, including two cafes, a deli, a barbecue grill, and a fine dining room.

SPEAKING

LISTENING AND SPEAKING

 Disk 5, Track 7

(Narrator)

Now listen to two students as they discuss the campus food service.

W: Have you voted on the food service yet?
M: No, but I intend to. I'm going to vote for the second option.
W: That's the one that closes the main cafeteria, isn't it?
M: Right.
W: But the main cafeteria is in the Student Center. That's where everyone goes at lunchtime. Doesn't it make sense to have food there?
M: But it's always so crowded in there at lunchtime. You have to wait a long time in the food line. And there are never enough places to sit.
W: That's true, but they say they'll add more tables.
M: There aren't enough bike racks outside either. I have no place to put my bike. Most of the time I eat at one of the snack bars. Besides, I like the idea of having several smaller eating places all over campus. That seems a lot more convenient, since we have classes all over campus anyway. It also means less crowding, and you don't have to wait as long to get your food. More food choices, too—I kind of like the idea of barbecue on campus.
W: Yeah, that does sound good, doesn't it?

(Narrator)

The man expresses his opinion about the campus food service. State his opinion and explain the reasons he gives for holding that opinion.

 Stop

Preparation Time – 30 seconds
Response Time – 60 seconds

6.   The above task requires you to do two things: (1) state the man's opinion about the campus food service, and (2) explain the reasons he gives for holding that opinion. To respond to the question completely and effectively, you must connect information from the conversation and the reading.

The key points in the reading and conversation are:

- Option 1 for the campus food service would expand the main cafeteria and close the snack bars.
- The man does not like Option 1 because he thinks the cafeteria is too crowded, there is a long wait for food, there are not enough places to sit, and there are not enough bike racks outside.
- Option 2 would close the main cafeteria but would add several more food service areas across campus.
- The man plans to vote for Option 2 because he likes the idea of several smaller eating places all over campus. He believes this will be more convenient and less crowded, and there will be more food choices.

Here is a successful response by a student:

> "The man's opinion about the campus food service is that Option 2 is better. The man likes this option because it adds several more places to get food. He will not vote for Option 1 because he doesn't like the cafeteria. The cafeteria is too crowded and there is no place to put his bike. He prefers having many places to eat on campus because this will be less crowded and more convenient. Also, there will be more food choices, such as barbecue."

 PRACTICE

Exercise 3.5.A

Read the passage and then listen to the recording. To make this practice more like the real test, cover the passage and question while you are listening. You may take notes, and you may use your notes to help you answer the question. After you hear the question, you have 30 seconds to prepare your response and 60 seconds to speak. Record your response on a cassette.

Reading Time – 45 seconds

TRAINING COURSE FOR TUTORS

Western University announces a new course in the practice of professional tutoring. The course combines a discussion class with practical experience in either the Math Center or the Writing Center. In the discussion class, students will explore tutoring theories, examine the role of the peer tutor, and develop effective tutoring practices. In their practical experience, students will observe peer tutoring and advance to supervised tutoring. Students who are considering graduate school in related fields will benefit from this course. Enrollment is limited to 40 and requires the signature of an academic adviser.

Now cover the passage and question. Listen to the recording. When you hear the question, uncover the question and begin preparing your response.

 Disk 5, Track 8

> The woman expresses her opinion about the training course for tutors. State her opinion and explain the reasons she gives for holding that opinion.

 Stop

Preparation Time – 30 seconds
Response Time – 60 seconds

Exercise 3.5.B

Read the passage and then listen to the recording. To make this practice more like the real test, cover the passage and question while you are listening. You may take notes, and you may use your notes to help you answer the question. After you hear the question, you have 30 seconds to prepare your response and 60 seconds to speak. Record your response on a cassette.

Reading Time – 45 seconds

PROPOSAL TO CHANGE THE PHYSICAL EDUCATION REQUIREMENT

The college is considering a proposal from the dean's office that would increase the physical education requirement of the core curriculum from one course to two courses. If approved by a vote of the administration, the new requirement will become effective in the fall semester. At the same time, the college will offer several new physical education courses, including martial arts, dance, and team sports. Students are invited to express their views on the proposed change at a meeting in Room 100 of the Administration Building at 2:00 this Friday.

Now cover the passage and question. Listen to the recording. When you hear the question, uncover the question and begin preparing your response.

 Disk 5, Track 9

> The man expresses his opinion about the physical education requirement. State his opinion and explain the reasons he gives for holding that opinion.

 Stop

Preparation Time – 30 seconds
Response Time – 60 seconds

Exercise 3.5.C

Read the passage and then listen to the recording. To make this practice more like the real test, cover the passage and question while you are listening. You may take notes, and you may use your notes to help you answer the question. After you hear the question, you have 30 seconds to prepare your response and 60 seconds to speak. Record your response on a cassette.

Reading Time – 45 seconds

COMMUNITY COURSE IN THEATER

Members of the community are invited to join students in the Baxter College Theater Arts program in a fully staged college theater production. In this course, you will learn theory, methods, and an analysis of theater production in acting or technical theater. You will assist with scenery construction and costumes, box office procedures, and lighting and sound systems during the production of a play. The instructor has extensive experience in the performing arts and is director of the college's Theater Arts program. This course is not open to full–time or part–time students of Baxter College.

Now cover the passage and question. Listen to the recording. When you hear the question, uncover the question and begin preparing your response.

 Disk 5, Track 10

> The man expresses his opinion about the theater course. State his opinion and explain the reasons he gives for holding that opinion.

 Stop

Preparation Time – 30 seconds
Response Time – 60 seconds

Exercise 3.5.D

Read the passage and then listen to the recording. To make this practice more like the real test, cover the passage and question while you are listening. You may take notes, and you may use your notes to help you answer the question. After you hear the question, you have 30 seconds to prepare your response and 60 seconds to speak. Record your response on a cassette.

Reading Time – 45 seconds

CHILDCARE ON CAMPUS

Students can use an on–campus childcare center for children from 12 months to 6 years. Hours of operation are 6:45 a.m. to 9:00 p.m., Monday through Thursday, and 6:45 a.m. to 6:00 p.m., Friday. The Child Care Center is conveniently located near the main classroom buildings and the library. The Center offers safe playrooms, an outdoor playground, trained staff, and a safe and caring environment. Full–time students have priority to enroll their children at the center. For enrollment and rate information, call 305–1144. Space is limited, so we recommend that you enroll your children early.

Now cover the passage and question. Listen to the recording. When you hear the question, uncover the question and begin preparing your response.

 Disk 5, Track 11

> The woman expresses her opinion on the on–campus childcare. State her opinion and explain the reasons she gives for holding that opinion.

 Stop

Preparation Time – 30 seconds
Response Time – 60 seconds

Key points for Exercises 3.5.A through 3.5.D are on page 588.

 EXTENSION

1. Share and discuss your recorded response to one of the speaking questions in Exercises 3.5.A through 3.5.D. Work in a group of three or four students. Listen to each student's recorded response. Discuss each student's response by answering the following questions:

    a. What information from the conversation and the reading does the response include? Is the information accurate?
    b. Can the response be easily understood? Why or why not?
    c. Does the response answer the question effectively? Why or why not?

    Make suggestions that will help each student improve in the future.

3.6 Integrated Speaking: Taking Notes

 FOCUS

Read the following passage:

> ### FUNGI AND PLANT DISEASE
>
> Of all the organisms responsible for diseases in plants, fungi cause the most problems. Although a fungus is technically a small plant, it cannot make its own food and therefore survives by being a parasite—living off other plant hosts. A common fungus, southern blight, affects many vegetables, including tomatoes and potatoes. It appears as a fuzzy white growth on the plant's stem near soil level. When the plant is infected with the blight, it wilts and then dies. The fungus may spread to the soil, where it can survive for years.

Now listen to part of a lecture on this topic in a botany class. What information from the lecture will be important to remember? Write down information that you think is important.

 Disk 5, Track 12

_____

_____

_____

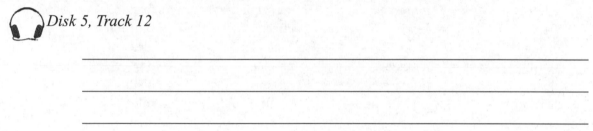 *Stop*

Some important words and phrases you may have heard are:

fungus can survive	six centimeters of soil
control disease	wash off tools
remove and destroy	cleanup

While listening to a lecture, your most important task is to note and record essential information. When you take notes, concentrate on terms, concepts, examples, and other details that you think will be important to remember.

?/? DO YOU KNOW...?

1. **Taking notes**, or **note taking**, is writing down key information that you hear. Note taking is an essential academic skill. During your university experience, you will take notes to help you remember important information from lectures and class discussions.

2. When you take the TOEFL, the test supervisor will give you paper to write on. You may take notes, and you may use your notes to help you answer the speaking questions. Your notes will not be scored. Only what you say into the microphone will be scored.

3. You will not know the question until after the conversation or lecture. While you are listening, focus on the major ideas and take notes about them. Do not try to write down everything. Limit your note taking to examples, reasons, and other details that you think will be useful to remember. Do not allow your writing to detract from your listening.

4. Sometimes a speaker emphasizes certain words or repeats certain ideas. Listen for information that a speaker emphasizes or repeats. A speaker may use certain expressions to identify important ideas. For example, the speaker may state that something is *important to know* or *necessary to keep in mind*. Listen for what follows, and take notes about this information.

5. A speaker may use the following words to point to important information:

one	essential	cause	characteristic
another	important	consequence	feature
first	key	effect	function
second	main	example	idea
third	necessary	problem	point
next	primary	reason	quality
finally	significant	result	role

6. Here is an example of an integrated reading–listening–speaking task:

READING

FUNGI AND PLANT DISEASE

Of all the organisms responsible for diseases in plants, fungi cause the most problems. Although a fungus is technically a small plant, it cannot make its own food and therefore survives by being a parasite—living off other plant hosts. A common fungus, southern blight, affects many vegetables, including tomatoes and potatoes. It appears as a fuzzy white growth on the plant's stem near soil level. When the plant is infected with the blight, it wilts and then dies. The fungus may spread to the soil, where it can survive for years.

LISTENING AND SPEAKING

Disk 5, Track 13

(Narrator)

Now listen to part of a lecture in a botany class.

(Professor)

Because a fungus can survive for years in the soil, the best way to control such a disease is to remove and destroy the infected plants, as well as six centimeters of soil around them. Avoid spreading disease by washing off your tools and your shoes when you go from an infected area to a healthy part of your garden. At the end of the gardening season, do a complete cleanup.

You can also keep disease away by rotating crops. Crop rotation can be effective in preventing soil–borne disease, especially when the disease is caused by a fungus that likes specific plants. For example, the fungus that causes southern blight is attracted to tomatoes. Once this fungus is present, it will thrive in the soil from year to year, attacking the tomato plants.

With crop rotation, you don't grow the same plant in the same place for at least three consecutive years. So, for example, if you grow tomatoes one year, the next year you shouldn't plant tomatoes in the same place. By planting something else the second and third years, any tomato–loving fungus that survived the winter wouldn't have any tomato plants to feed on. With three years between planting tomatoes, the fungus will die off from lack of a host plant.

(Narrator)

Explain ways that a gardener can control plant disease caused by a fungus, and explain why these methods work.

Stop

Preparation Time – 30 seconds
Response Time – 60 seconds

7. Here are the notes that two students took during the sample lecture. Add other words and phrases that you think are important to remember about the lecture.

STUDENT 1	**STUDENT 2**
fungus – soil – years	control fungus
destroy plants, soil around	remove 6 cm soil
wash tools, shoes	crop rotation
specific – tomato blight	fungus cause disease
crop rotation –	soil – year to year
tomatoes	3 year
don't plant same place	1 tomato
sev. yrs betw. –	2 other plant
fungus die off	3 " "
	fungus die – lack host

For examples of responses to this speaking question, see page 325.

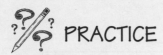 PRACTICE

Exercise 3.6.A

Read the passage and then listen to the recording. To make this practice more like the real test, cover the passage and question while you are listening. You may take notes, and you may use your notes to help you answer the question. After you hear the question, you have 30 seconds to prepare your response and 60 seconds to speak. Record your response on a cassette.

Reading Time – 45 seconds

EMOTIONAL INTELLIGENCE

Emotional intelligence consists of self–awareness, self–control, self–motivation, enthusiasm, and social ability. People with emotional intelligence understand their feelings and manage them in ways that are positive and helpful. They make decisions about life— what job to pursue, what direction to take, and whom to marry—with greater confidence and skill than people with low or no emotional intelligence. Their people skills make them more likely to succeed at relationships, cooperation, and leadership, and less likely to engage in risky or criminal behavior.

Now cover the passage and question. Listen to the recording. When you hear the question, uncover the question and begin preparing your response.

Disk 5, Track 14

> The professor discusses a study on emotional intelligence. Explain how emotional intelligence affects the experiences of young people like those in the study.

Stop

Preparation Time – 30 seconds
Response Time – 60 seconds

Exercise 3.6.B

Read the passage and then listen to the recording. To make this practice more like the real test, cover the passage and question while you are listening. You may take notes, and you may use your notes to help you answer the question. After you hear the question, you have 30 seconds to prepare your response and 60 seconds to speak. Record your response on a cassette.

Reading Time – 45 seconds

BOYCOTTS

Boycotts are a form of nonviolent protest, the practice of applying power to achieve sociopolitical goals, without the use of physical force. People who participate in a boycott refuse to buy, sell, or otherwise trade with an individual or business that they believe to be doing something morally wrong. The purpose of a boycott is to call attention to a wrong and to punish those responsible for the wrong. Usually, the punishment is economic, but sometimes it brings shame to the offenders. When a boycott is long–term and widespread, it can be a factor in causing social change.

Now cover the passage and question. Listen to the recording. When you hear the question, uncover the question and begin preparing your response.

 Disk 5, Track 15

> Explain what happens during a boycott, and explain the causes and effects of the boycotts discussed in the lecture.

 Stop

Preparation Time – 30 seconds
Response Time – 60 seconds

Exercise 3.6.C

Read the passage and then listen to the recording. To make this practice more like the real test, cover the passage and question while you are listening. You may take notes, and you may use your notes to help you answer the question. After you hear the question, you have 30 seconds to prepare your response and 60 seconds to speak. Record your response on a cassette.

Reading Time – 45 seconds

SOCIAL ROLES

In sociological terms, every person has a position in a social system. One person may have a number of positions because he or she belongs to various social systems, such as home, school, workplace, and community. The behavior attached to each position is called a social role. A person in a particular social role will follow the script for that role; for example, the role of student requires one to study. Each role in a social system is related to other roles in the system. Relationships such as student and teacher, supervisor and staff, and husband and wife are known as role partners.

Now cover the passage and question. Listen to the recording. When you hear the question, uncover the question and begin preparing your response.

 Disk 5, Track 16

> Explain the concept of role conflict, and explain when and why a person experiences role conflict.

 Stop

Preparation Time – 30 seconds
Response Time – 60 seconds

Exercise 3.6.D

Read the passage and then listen to the recording. To make this practice more like the real test, cover the passage and question while you are listening. You may take notes, and you may use your notes to help you answer the question. After you hear the question, you have 30 seconds to prepare your response and 60 seconds to speak. Record your response on a cassette.

Reading Time – 45 seconds

SPATIAL MEMORY

An important survival skill of animals is their ability to remember and recognize objects in the environment. Animals use their spatial memory to assemble a list of paths that lead to various goals. For an animal, navigating by a series of landmarks is a simple but quite effective procedure. An animal basically learns from experience that turning right at the rock and then left at the tall tree leads to home. Some animals can recognize a landmark from several different directions, making it possible to find their way to a familiar goal even when approaching from an unfamiliar direction.

Now cover the passage and question. Listen to the recording. When you hear the question, uncover the question and begin preparing your response.

Disk 5, Track 17

> Explain how the skill of spatial memory influences the behavior of specific animals.

Stop

Preparation Time – 30 seconds
Response Time – 60 seconds

Key points for Exercises 3.6.A through 3.6.D are on page 589.

 EXTENSION

1. Share and discuss your recorded response to one of the speaking questions in Exercises 3.6.A through 3.6.D. Work in a group of three or four students. Listen to each student's recorded response. Discuss each student's response by answering the following questions:

    a. What key points from the lecture does the response convey?
    b. What examples, explanation, or other details does the response include? Do these details accurately convey information from the lecture?
    c. Can the response be easily understood? Why or why not?
    d. Does the response answer the question effectively? Why or why not?

    Make suggestions that will help each student improve in the future.

2. As you listen to the conversations and lectures for units 3.7 through 3.10, take notes about the main idea, key points, and important details. Use the format shown below. Do not try to write down every word that you hear. Train your listening to focus on the essential information.

    Main idea/problem: _____

    Key points: _____ Details: _____

    _____ _____

    _____ _____

    _____ _____

3. Obtain permission to make a tape recording of a real college or university lecture. (Topics in history, anthropology, sociology, and psychology are good choices.) Bring your tape to class. In class, everyone listens to two minutes of the recording. While listening, everyone takes notes about the important information in the lecture. Don't try to write down everything. Write only the key words and phrases that you think are important to remember.

    Then break into groups of three or four students each. Compare your notes with the notes taken by the other students in your group. Listen again to the same two–minute recording. In your group, try to agree on the key points of the lecture. Choose a student to read your group's list of key points to the whole class.

3.7 Integrated Speaking: Developing a Topic

 FOCUS

Listen to part of a lecture in a botany class:

 Disk 5, Track 18

 Stop

In the lecture, the professor makes the point that crop rotation can help control plant disease caused by a fungus. How is this point developed?

The professor develops the point with examples, facts, and explanation:

- ✎ Crop rotation can be effective against a fungus that likes specific plants, such as southern blight.
- ✎ Crop rotation means not growing the same plant in the same place in consecutive years.
- ✎ With crop rotation, the fungus will die off from lack of a host plant.

For each integrated speaking question on the TOEFL, you will listen to a conversation or lecture. You must listen for the major points and for details that support these points. You must take good notes about this key information because you will be required to speak about it.

 DO YOU KNOW...?

1. You have 60 seconds (1 minute) to speak in response to each of the two integrated reading–listening–speaking questions. Your responses should include key information from the conversation or lecture and the reading that will answer the question completely.

2. The reading–listening–speaking tasks do not ask for your opinion about the topic. For these tasks, your opinion is irrelevant and should not be included in your responses. Your responses should be based on only what you have just read and heard.

3. Each reading–listening–speaking task requires you to do more than one thing. For example, it may ask you to (1) state an opinion expressed in a conversation, and (2) summarize the reasons the speaker gives to support that opinion. Or it may ask you to (1) describe something a professor discusses, and (2) explain how this relates to information in the reading. You must address each part of the question.

4. Two trained evaluators will listen to your responses. They will rate your speaking on how well you:

    - convey relevant information from two sources;
    - develop points with appropriate details and explanation;
    - express ideas coherently; and
    - make yourself understood by speaking clearly.

5. For each reading–listening–speaking task, you have 30 seconds to prepare your response. Read the question carefully. Review your notes and select information from the conversation or lecture that you can use to answer the question. Think about the important ideas you want to convey. Plan to make two or three points, and choose relevant details to develop these points. Think about what you will say.

6. You have 60 seconds to record your response. This is enough time to address all parts of the question. Speak at a natural speed—as if you were talking to your parents or a teacher. Do not try to rush. Watch the countdown clock. If you plan to make three points, you have approximately 20 seconds to state and develop each point.

7. Your response will be evaluated on the coherence of your speech. *Coherence* is the quality of order in speech. Speech is coherent when sentences flow naturally, one after the other, following a logical order. Coherent speech is generally easy for listeners to understand. The following words and expressions will help you express yourself coherently.

Introduce Key Points from the Two Sources

The man's opinion is that
The woman believes that
According to the lecture,
The professor made the point that
The reading stated that

Give Examples

for example	one example is	also
such as	another example is	in addition

Give Reasons

because	one reason is	first, second, third…
since	another reason is	next
so that	most importantly	finally

---

8. Your response will be evaluated on well you make yourself understood. Your speech will be easier to understand if:

    - each sentence conveys a complete thought;
    - your sentence structure is fairly simple;
    - you use vocabulary correctly;
    - you pronounce words clearly and correctly; and
    - you speak at a normal speed.

9. Here is an example of an integrated reading–listening–speaking task:

READING

FUNGI AND PLANT DISEASE

Of all the organisms responsible for diseases in plants, fungi cause the most problems. Although a fungus is technically a small plant, it cannot make its own food and therefore survives by being a parasite—living off other plant hosts. A common fungus, southern blight, affects many vegetables, including tomatoes and potatoes. It appears as a fuzzy white growth on the plant's stem near soil level. When the plant is infected with the blight, it wilts and then dies. The fungus may spread to the soil, where it can survive for years.

LISTENING AND SPEAKING

 Disk 5, Track 13

Explain ways that a gardener can control plant disease caused by a fungus, and explain why these methods work.

 Stop

10. The key points in the above reading and lecture are:

- A fungus survives by living off other plant hosts.
- A fungus can survive in the soil for several years.
- The best way to control a fungus is to remove and destroy the infected plants and six centimeters of soil around them.
- Washing off tools and shoes can control disease caused by a fungus.
- Crop rotation can control disease caused by a fungus because the fungus will die off from lack of a host plant.

RESPONSE BY STUDENT 1

"A gardener can control plant disease caused by a fungus. One way is to destroy sick plants and also destroy the soil around plants. This method works because a fungus lives in the soil. Another way is to wash tools and shoes. This will avoid spreading the disease. Another way is to use crop rotation for a tomato blight. Don't plant tomatoes in the same place every year. This method works because the fungus will die off. The reason is there are no tomato plants to eat."

RESPONSE BY STUDENT 2

"A fungus kills plants because it lives in the soil. You can control fungus by removing infected plants and six centimeters of the soil. Also, crop rotation can control plant disease caused by a fungus. The fungus lives in soil year to year, so crop rotation is three years. For example, plant tomatoes in the first year. In the second and third year, plant other plants. Crop rotation causes the fungus to die because it lacks a host plant."

Both students have responded to the question effectively. Both convey relevant points from the two sources, develop these points with appropriate details, and express their ideas coherently.

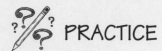

PRACTICE

Exercise 3.7.A

Read the passage and then listen to the recording. To make this practice more like the real test, cover the passage and question while you are listening. You may take notes, and you may use your notes to help you answer the question. After you hear the question, you have 30 seconds to prepare your response and 60 seconds to speak. Record your response on a cassette.

Reading Time – 45 seconds

On–campus Housing

Most first–year students live on campus, and virtually all of them have one or more roommates. Living on campus has many advantages, with varying accommodations available through the Housing Office. On–campus housing includes four apartment buildings and eight dormitories. With living units ranging from one–, two–, and four–bedroom apartments, to single and double dormitory rooms, students are close to classrooms and other campus facilities. The university also offers "specialty dorms" designated by academic major; these are good ways to meet people with interests similar to yours.

Now cover the passage and question. Listen to the recording. When you hear the question, uncover the question and begin preparing your response.

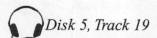 *Disk 5, Track 19*

> The man expresses his opinion about the woman's desire to live on campus. State his opinion and explain the reasons he gives for holding that opinion.

 Stop

Preparation Time – 30 seconds
Response Time – 60 seconds

Exercise 3.7.B

Read the passage and then listen to the recording. To make this practice more like the real test, cover the passage and question while you are listening. You may take notes, and you may use your notes to help you answer the question. After you hear the question, you have 30 seconds to prepare your response and 60 seconds to speak. Record your response on a cassette.

Reading Time – 45 seconds

DEPRESSION

When a person is overwhelmed by an emotional crisis and cannot cope with daily life, he or she may be suffering from depression. Depression ranges in severity but affects approximately 20 percent of adults. Symptoms include feelings of hopelessness, sadness, and despair; loss of interest and pleasure in things; weight loss or weight gain; difficulty falling asleep or sleeping more than usual; lack of motivation; and loss of energy. In cases of mild or situational depression, the symptoms usually decline with a change of scenery or routine, or once the problem that caused the depression disappears.

Now cover the passage and question. Listen to the recording. When you hear the question, uncover the question and begin preparing your response.

 Disk 5, Track 20

> Describe the form of depression discussed in the lecture, explaining its causes, symptoms, and treatment.

 Stop

Preparation Time – 30 seconds
Response Time – 60 seconds

Exercise 3.7.C

Read the passage and then listen to the recording. To make this practice more like the real test, cover the passage and question while you are listening. You may take notes, and you may use your notes to help you answer the question. After you hear the question, you have 30 seconds to prepare your response and 60 seconds to speak. Record your response on a cassette.

Reading Time – 45 seconds

THE PROGRAM SEMINAR

The program seminar is the primary mode of instruction for students at Central College. A program of study might involve 80 students and four faculty members, but most of class time is spent in small group discussions—the seminar. Seminar content centers on a theme or issue relevant to the program. For students, the close interaction with faculty and fellow students provides perspective through differing viewpoints, and depth through concentrated group effort. Students learn to express themselves and to work cooperatively—two traits that our graduates have found particularly helpful in their lives and careers.

Now cover the passage and question. Listen to the recording. When you hear the question, uncover the question and begin preparing your response.

 Disk 5, Track 21

> The woman expresses her opinion about seminars. State her opinion and explain the reasons she gives for holding that opinion.

 Stop

Preparation Time – 30 seconds
Response Time – 60 seconds

Exercise 3.7.D

Read the passage and then listen to the recording. To make this practice more like the real test, cover the passage and question while you are listening. You may take notes, and you may use your notes to help you answer the question. After you hear the question, you have 30 seconds to prepare your response and 60 seconds to speak. Record your response on a cassette.

Reading Time – 45 seconds

ABSTRACT EXPRESSIONISM

Abstract expressionism was a movement in painting that emerged in New York City in the 1940s and attained prominence in American art in the following decade. It emphasized personal expression, freedom from accepted artistic values, attention to surface qualities of paint such as brushstroke and texture, and the use of huge canvases. Abstract expressionism valued the act of painting itself, including the accidents that happen while painting. For this reason, it is sometimes also called action painting. The movement influenced many later schools of art, especially in the use of color and material.

Now cover the passage and question. Listen to the recording. When you hear the question, uncover the question and begin preparing your response.

 Disk 5, Track 22

> The professor describes the painting style of Jackson Pollock. Explain how Pollock's style made him a leading artist of the movement called abstract expressionism.

 Stop

Preparation Time – 30 seconds
Response Time – 60 seconds

Key points for Exercises 3.7.A through 3.7.D are on page 589.

EXTENSION

1. Share and discuss your recorded response to one of the speaking questions in Exercises 3.7.A through 3.7.D. Work in a group of three or four students. Listen to each student's recorded response. Discuss each student's response by answering the following questions:

    a. What key points does the speaker make in the response? Do these points accurately convey information from the conversation/lecture and reading?
    b. What examples, explanation, or other details from the conversation/lecture are included? Do they successfully develop the speaker's points?
    c. Can the response be easily understood? Why or why not?
    d. Is the response coherent? Why or why not?
    e. Does the response answer the question effectively? Why or why not?

    Make suggestions that will help each student improve in the future.

2. Choose one of the reading passages from Exercises 3.7.A through 3.7.D as the topic of a small group discussion. Work in a group of three or four students. Read the passage and then talk about it in your group for five minutes. What did you already know about the topic? What is your opinion of the topic? Do you have any personal knowledge or experience of the topic? Do you know of any similar concepts or examples? At the end of five minutes, allow five more minutes to summarize three or four points that your group made about the topic. Write down these points, and choose a member of your group to present them to the whole class.

3.8 Integrated Speaking: Summarizing a Problem and Solutions

 FOCUS

Listen to a conversation between two students:

 Disk 5, Track 23

 Stop

What is the topic of the conversation? _____

What problem does the woman have? _____

What does the man suggest the woman do? _____

_____

What do you think of the man's suggestions? _____

What do you think the woman should do? _____

Why do you think she should do that? _____

One type of speaking question on the TOEFL will have a similar discussion of a problem and solutions. You will listen to a conversation and then speak about what you have heard. You will describe the problem and talk about possible solutions, including your own opinion on how to solve the problem.

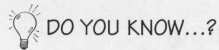 DO YOU KNOW...?

1. Two of the integrated speaking tasks on the TOEFL involve the two language skills of listening and speaking. In the first listening–speaking task you will:

    ✎ listen to a short conversation in which the speakers discuss a problem and solutions;
    ✎ summarize the situation that the speakers discuss; and
    ✎ state your opinion about the solution to the problem.

2. A ***summary*** is a brief report of the important ideas. To ***summarize*** is to state the major ideas from the conversation in a shorter form. In the first listening–speaking task, the major ideas will concern a problem and suggestions for how to solve it. Listen for a description of the problem. Listen for possible solutions to the problem. Take notes about the problem and suggested solutions.

3. Speakers may use the following expressions to point out problems and possible solutions.

    Describe Problems

The problem is _____.	I can't figure out _____.
I need help with _____.	I'd like to _____ but _____.
I'm having trouble _____.	If I _____, then I can't _____.

    Suggest Solutions

You need to _____.	Here's what you could do.
You could _____.	One thing you can do is _____.
You should _____.	The best thing to do would be _____.
You'd better _____.	If you _____, it might _____.
Try _____.	If I were you, I'd _____.
Couldn't you _____?	Why don't you _____?

4. For the listening–speaking task, you have 20 seconds to prepare your response. Read the question carefully. Review the notes you took while listening. Select information from the conversation that you can use to answer the question. Think about what you will say.

5. Two trained evaluators will listen to your response. They will rate your speaking on how well you:

    ✎ convey relevant information from the conversation;
    ✎ state and support your opinion about the problem;
    ✎ express ideas coherently; and
    ✎ make yourself understood by speaking clearly.

6. Your response will be easier to understand if each sentence conveys a complete thought. Keep the structure of your sentences fairly simple. Use transitions to connect ideas and make your speech more coherent. Use the vocabulary that you are familiar with.

7. Your response will be easier to understand if you speak in phrases. This means grouping words together into idea units. For example, look at this sentence:

    "However, her landlord said she can't have a pet, but the woman wants to keep the cat."

    This sentence is easier to understand if it is spoken in phrases, like this:

    "However, / her landlord said / she can't have a pet, / but the woman wants / to keep the cat."

8. Listen again to the sample conversation. Listen for key words and expressions that identify the problem and possible solutions:

 Disk 5, Track 24

(Narrator)

Listen to a conversation between two students.

W: Say, Lenny, do you <u>know anyone who wants a cat</u>?
M: A <u>cat</u>? No. <u>Why</u>?
W: Well, this poor little cat showed up outside my apartment one day. He was hungry and cold, so I gave him some cheese, and now he's still hanging around. My landlord found out and said <u>I have to get rid of it</u> because <u>pets aren't allowed</u>.
M: <u>You shouldn't be feeding it</u>. If you stop giving it food, it will go away.
W: I know, I know, but he's so hungry. I like the cat, and I want him to have a good home. Actually, I'd like to keep him myself.
M: Well, if that's the case, then <u>you'd better look for another apartment</u>—one that allows pets.
W: I hate to do that. My apartment is so close to campus.
M: <u>Why don't you give the cat to your mother</u>? She likes animals.
W: My mother already has two cats, so I don't know...
M: Well, <u>you'd better do something fast</u>, or your landlord will throw you out.

(Narrator)

Describe the woman's problem and the suggestions the man makes about how to solve it. What do you think the woman should do, and why?

 Stop

Preparation Time – 20 seconds
Response Time – 60 seconds

---

9. The above task requires you to do four things: (1) describe the woman's problem, (2) describe the man's suggestions about what to do, (3) state your opinion about what the woman should do, and (4) explain why you think the woman should do that.

    The key points in the conversation are:

    - The woman's problem is that she has found a cat but cannot keep it because pets are not allowed in her apartment.
    - The man suggests that she stop feeding the cat so it will go away.
    - The man suggests that she look for an apartment that allows pets.
    - The man suggests that she give the cat to her mother.

    Here is a successful response by a student:

    "The woman has a problem. It's a cat that is hungry. However, her landlord said she can't have a pet, but the woman wants to keep the cat. The man makes one suggestion to look for another apartment. The man also suggests she give the cat to her mother. However, her mother already has two cats, so it's a problem. I think the woman should ask her mother please take care of the cat. The reason is she can visit the cat, and later she can look for an apartment."

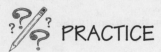 PRACTICE

Exercise 3.8.A

Listen to the recording for each question below. To make this practice more like the real test, cover the question while you are listening. You may take notes, and you may use your notes to help you answer the question. When you hear the question, uncover the question and begin preparing your response. You have 20 seconds to prepare and 60 seconds to speak. Record your response on a cassette.

QUESTION 1

 Disk 5, Track 25

> Describe the man's problem and the suggestions the woman makes about what he should do. What do you think the man should do, and why?

 Stop

Preparation Time – 20 seconds
Response Time – 60 seconds

QUESTION 2

 Disk 5, Track 26

> Describe the woman's problem and the suggestions her adviser makes about how to solve it. What do you think the woman should do, and why?

 Stop

Preparation Time – 20 seconds
Response Time – 60 seconds

QUESTION 3

 Disk 5, Track 27

> Describe the man's problem and the suggestions the woman makes about how he should deal with it. What do you think the man should do, and why?

 Stop

Preparation Time – 20 seconds
Response Time – 60 seconds

Question 4

Disk 5, Track 28

> The students discuss two possible solutions to the woman's problem. Describe the problem. Then state which of the two solutions you prefer and explain why.

Stop

Preparation Time – 20 seconds
Response Time – 60 seconds

Question 5

Disk 5, Track 29

> Describe the man's situation and the suggestions his professor makes about what he should do. What do you think the man should do, and why?

Stop

Preparation Time – 20 seconds
Response Time – 60 seconds

Key points for Exercise 3.8.A are on page 590.

 EXTENSION

1. Listen again to the conversations in Exercise 3.8.A. As you listen, fill in the missing information on the blank lines in the script below. Do not try to write down every word. Take brief notes that will help you remember only the key information. Check your answers with the audio script on page 647.

CONVERSATION 1

🎧 *Disk 5, Track 25*

W: Is something wrong with _____?

M: Oh, not really, it's just that _____.

W: What happened to it?

M: It's _____.

W: Well, you'd better _____.

Are you free right now?

M: Yes, for a little while.

W: Well, come on then. I'll walk over there with you. I'm already heading that way.

M: I can't _____.

W: Baseball practice! You shouldn't _____.

M: I know, but I can't afford to _____. I've missed a

lot already, and _____.

W: You need to _____.

And _____.

M: There isn't anything else to do at my job.

W: Well, then you'd better _____.

M: I know, I know.

🎧 *Stop*

CONVERSATION 2

🎧 *Disk 5, Track 26*

W: I need help with _____.

M: OK. What can I do for you?

W: I still need to _____, but _____

_____.

M: Hmm. I see what you mean. You've already got a full schedule. Why don't you

_____?

W: Because I'll be _____.

M: Hmm. Well … you could _____. There are lots of

_____, in both Winter and Spring Quarters.

W: An evening course … ugh … I _____.

M: Well, with your schedule, this may be your only choice. Another possibility, of course, is

_____. Will you be around

this summer?

W: I hope to _____, and then _____. So this is

kind of a problem for me.

 Stop

CONVERSATION 3

 Disk 5, Track 27

W: How are your classes going?

M: All right mostly, that is, except for _____. The class

is fine, but _____.

W: That's not good. You need to _____. You can't

_____. You need to _____

_____. He has to take responsibility

for his part of the project.

M: That's for sure. He's hard to get a hold of, too. I've left several messages on his answering

machine.

W: You'd better _____. Maybe

_____.

M: It's kind of late for that. Besides, _____

_____.

W: You never know. Maybe you could _____. But I would

_____.

 Stop

CONVERSATION 4

Disk 5, Track 28

M: Hi, Nicole. How's it going?

W: My classes are going well. _____.

M: What's wrong with your _____?

W: I'm not sure, exactly. It just _____. It gave me a lot of

trouble this morning. It _____

_____. I need to have it checked out, but

_____.

M: You could _____. They have

_____

_____.

W: But I'm not _____.

M: Check it out anyway. Maybe you don't have to be _____

_____. Just tell them you're a student.

W: Well, maybe.

M: Another place you could try is _____. People

sometimes advertise services like this. Maybe you can _____

_____.

W: Hmm. Maybe. Thanks for the tips.

M: No problem. Good luck.

Stop

CONVERSATION 5

Disk 5, Track 29

M: Professor Fisher, I'm _____, so I'll

_____. I was wondering if _____.

W: Well, you know my policy is not to _____. If you

_____, then you can try to _____

_____. But ... haven't you already _____?

M: Um ... yeah, I _____ a few weeks ago.

W: Then try not to _____, and try to do well on it too. Your test scores so far have not been strong. You could be _____ _____.

M: Do you mean I might _____?

W: At this point, you need to _____. Why don't you _____, or _____ _____?

M: Well, I guess I could. But, to tell the truth, I don't have _____ _____.

W: Then, in that case, you need to _____ _____. If you're too busy to _____, you should _____.

 Stop

2. Share and discuss your recorded response to one of the speaking questions in Exercise 3.8.A. Work in a group of three or four students. Listen to each student's recorded response. Discuss each student's response by answering the following questions:

   a. Does the response accurately convey information from the conversation about the problem and solutions?
   b. Does the speaker state an opinion about the solution to the problem? What is the speaker's opinion? What reason is given for this opinion?
   c. Can the response be easily understood? Why or why not?
   d. Is the response coherent? Why or why not?
   e. Does the response answer the question effectively? Why or why not?

Make suggestions that will help each student improve in the future.

3.9 Integrated Speaking: Summarizing Important Ideas

FOCUS

Imagine you have just listened to a lecture in a world history class. The professor spoke about mass migrations of people in the nineteenth century. While you were listening, you took notes on the key points. Now a teaching assistant writes the following question on the board and wants you to respond orally:

> Using points and examples from the lecture, describe the mass migrations of people in the nineteenth century, and explain why these migrations occurred.

You are given 20 seconds to prepare your response before you begin to speak. How would you use this preparation time?

____ Close your eyes and relax for a few seconds.

____ Panic and forget everything that you heard in the lecture.

____ Write a response that you will read aloud.

____ Plan to answer only the first part of the question.

____ Review your notes and think about what you will say.

Is it a good idea to close your eyes and relax? We all need to relax, but taking a break during your preparation time is probably not a good choice. Also, if you have enough practice with this type of activity, you will not panic and forget everything you just heard.

Should you write your response, and then read it aloud? You do not have enough time to do this. No one can write that fast. Should you plan to answer only one part of the question and hope that will be good enough? Definitely not—doing that would make your response incomplete. The task requires you to do two things: (1) describe mass migrations, and (2) explain why they occurred.

The best way to use your preparation time is to review your notes and think about what you will say. Think about what the professor said about mass migrations. Scan your notes for ideas and details that will help you describe mass migrations and explain why they occurred. Organize your thoughts and get ready to speak.

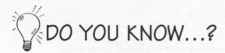

DO YOU KNOW...?

1. Two of the integrated speaking tasks involve the two language skills of listening and speaking. In the second listening–speaking task you will:

   - listen to a short lecture about an academic topic; and
   - summarize the important information in the lecture.

2. A *summary* is a brief report of the important points. The question will require you to *summarize*, to explain the major ideas and important supporting information from the lecture. For this task, your opinion is irrelevant and should not be included in your response. Your response should be based only on the information in the lecture.

3. You will not know what the speaking question is until after you have listened to the lecture. However, you can expect that the question will ask about key ideas. While you are listening to the lecture, focus on the ideas that you think are most important, and take notes about them. Do not try to write down everything. Limit your notes to key ideas and a few important details.

4. You have 20 seconds to prepare your response. Read the question carefully. Review your notes and select information from the lecture that you can use to answer the question. Plan to make two or three points. Choose relevant details to develop your points. Think about what you will say.

5. You have 60 seconds to record your response. This is enough time to address all parts of the question. Speak at a natural speed, and watch the countdown clock. If you plan to make three points, you have approximately 20 seconds to state and develop each point.

6. There is no single correct answer to the question. There are several ways to answer the question successfully. An effective response will:

   - convey relevant information from the lecture;
   - develop points with appropriate details and explanation;
   - express ideas coherently; and
   - be easy for listeners to understand.

7. Your response will be easier to understand if you pronounce words clearly and correctly, especially key *content words* from the lecture. Use voice stress to emphasize the key content words—nouns, verbs, and adjectives—that supply relevant information.

   > "There were *several reasons* for the *mass migrations*. *One* reason was the new types of *transportation*, such as the *railroad* and *steamship*. *Another* reason was the people could get *free land*, for example, in the *United States* and *Canada*."

8. Here is an example of an integrated listening–speaking task:

 Disk 5, Track 30

(Narrator)

Listen to part of a lecture in a world history class. The professor is talking about mass migrations of people.

(Professor)

   In the nineteenth century, there were several periods when large numbers of people moved from one place to another around the world. In many cases, people moved to another continent. These mass migrations were on a much larger scale than any previous migrations in history. One major movement was from Europe to the Americas, Australia, and Africa. This migration of Europeans involved around 60 million people over one hundred years. Another mass migration was from Russia to Siberia and Central Asia. Another was from China, India, and Japan to Southeast Asia.

   These large movements of people were made possible by the new cheap and fast means of transportation, specifically railroads and steamships. Another important factor was the rapid growth in banking and capital, by which large investors financed a lot of the settlement. In some places, immigrants were given free land and other benefits if they settled there. This is what encouraged a lot of people—both immigrant and native–born—to move westward in the United States and Canada. Thus, most regions of the U.S. and Canada were populated by the end of the nineteenth century.

   The majority of the people in these mass migrations came from the lower social and economic classes of society. The immigrants were motivated mainly by the hope of a better life for themselves and their children. Since most of the immigrants were unskilled workers, their main contribution to their new countries was the labor they supplied. It was the hard work and high hopes of the immigrants that contributed to the economic growth of their new countries.

(Narrator)

Using points and examples from the lecture, describe the mass migrations of people in the nineteenth century, and explain why these migrations occurred.

 Stop

   Preparation Time – 20 seconds
   Response Time – 60 seconds

---

9. The above task requires you to do two things: (1) describe the mass migrations of people in the nineteenth century, and (2) explain why these migrations occurred.

The key points in the lecture are:

- People moved from one part of the world to another on a much larger scale than they had during any previous migrations.
- The mass migrations occurred because of new cheap and fast means of transportation.
- The migrations occurred because large investors financed a lot of the settlement and gave immigrants free land.
- Most immigrants were motivated mainly by the hope of a better life for themselves and their children.

Here is a successful response by a student:

"Mass migrations of people occurred in the nineteenth century. Many people moved from Europe to other countries, also from China and Japan to other countries. There were several reasons for the mass migrations. One reason was the new types of transportation, such as the railroad and steamship. Another reason was the people could get free land, for example, in the United States and Canada. Also, the people wanted a better life for their children, so they moved to another country. They worked hard to have a better life and build their new country."

 PRACTICE

Exercise 3.9.A

Listen to the recording for each question below. To make this practice more like the real test, cover the question while you are listening. You may take notes, and you may use your notes to help you answer the question. When you hear the question, uncover the question and begin preparing your response. You have 20 seconds to prepare and 60 seconds to speak. Record your response on a cassette.

QUESTION 1

 Disk 5, Track 31

> Using points and examples from the talk, describe the duties of different types of managers in large hotels.

 Stop

Preparation Time – 20 seconds
Response Time – 60 seconds

QUESTION 2

Disk 5, Track 32

Using points and examples from the lecture, explain how two features of the earth's surface influence climate.

Stop

Preparation Time – 20 seconds
Response Time – 60 seconds

QUESTION 3

Disk 5, Track 33

Using points and examples from the talk, describe traditional beliefs about trees, and explain why people have thought of trees as special.

Stop

Preparation Time – 20 seconds
Response Time – 60 seconds

QUESTION 4

Disk 5, Track 34

Using points and details from the talk, describe the physical differences that animals had to adapt to when they moved from water to land.

Stop

Preparation Time – 20 seconds
Response Time – 60 seconds

Question 5

 Disk 5, Track 35

> Using points and details from the lecture, describe the Flatiron Building and explain how it got its name.

 Stop

Preparation Time – 20 seconds
Response Time – 60 seconds

Key points for Exercise 3.9.A are on page 590.

EXTENSION

1. Listen again to the sample lecture. As you listen, fill in the missing information on the blank lines in the script below. Do not try to write down every word. Take brief notes that will help you remember only the key information. Check your answers with the audio script on page 648.

Disk 5, Track 30

Listen to part of a talk in a world history class. The professor is talking about _____

_____.

   In the nineteenth century, there were several periods when large numbers of people _____

_____

_____. These

mass migrations were _____.

One major movement was _____. This

migration of Europeans involved around _____. Another

mass migration was _____. Another was

_____.

   These large movements of people were made possible by _____

_____. Another

important factor was _____

_____. In some

places, immigrants were _____. This is what

encouraged a lot of people—both immigrant and native–born—_____

_____

_____.

   The majority of the people in these mass migrations came from _____

_____. The

immigrants were motivated mainly by _____

_____.

Since most of the immigrants were unskilled workers, _____

_____

_____.

Stop

2. Share and discuss your recorded response to one of the speaking questions in Exercise 3.9.A. Work in a group of three or four students. Listen to each student's recorded response. Discuss each student's response by answering the following questions:

   a. Does the response accurately summarize the major ideas from the lecture?
   b. Does the response include relevant supporting details and explanation from the lecture?
   c. Is the response coherent? Why or why not?
   d. Can the response be easily understood? Why or why not?
   e. Does the response answer the question effectively? Why or why not?

   Make suggestions that will help each student improve in the future.

3. Obtain permission to make a tape recording of a real college or university lecture. (Topics in history, anthropology, sociology, and psychology are good choices.) Bring your tape to class. In class, everyone listens to two minutes of the recording. While listening, everyone takes notes about the important information in the lecture. Don't try to write down everything. Write only the key information that you think is important to remember.

   Then break into groups of three or four students each. Compare your notes with the notes taken by the other students in your group. Listen again to the same two–minute recording. In your group, summarize the key points of the lecture. Choose a student from your group to present your summary to the whole class.

SPEAKING

3.10 Evaluating Integrated Speaking

🔍 FOCUS

Lee and Robin are two students who take the TOEFL. For one of the integrated speaking questions, this is how each student performs:

Lee...

- ✎ discusses ideas from the lecture accurately and appropriately.

- ✎ speaks continuously and in complete sentences.

- ✎ mispronounces some words.

- ✎ uses some words inaccurately.

Robin...

- ✎ accurately conveys information from the lecture, but omits an important idea.

- ✎ pauses a few times and says "uh" before continuing.

- ✎ pronounces English like a native speaker.

- ✎ uses a large vocabulary correctly.

What kind of score will Lee and Robin receive? Will one student receive a higher score than the other? How would you rate their speaking?

In fact, both Lee and Robin will probably receive a high score—3 or 4—for their speaking. Although each student makes a few mistakes or omissions, they generally perform well.

On the TOEFL, your speaking does not have to be perfect. A few small mistakes will not necessarily lower your score. If your response communicates ideas accurately and appropriately, if it fulfills the task, and if your evaluators can easily understand you, then your response will receive a favorable score.

💡 DO YOU KNOW...?

1. When you take the TOEFL, two trained evaluators will listen to your response to each integrated speaking question. They will evaluate your speech and assign a score of 1 to 4, with 4 the highest score possible. Each response will be judged on the clarity and coherence of your speech as well as your ability to answer the question by presenting relevant information from the listening and reading texts.

2. The evaluators will use criteria similar to those in the following table as they score your responses.

INTEGRATED SPEAKING TASK
Description of Score Levels

4	**A response at this level** ↝ effectively addresses the task by conveying relevant information and appropriate details from the listening and reading texts; and ↝ demonstrates a coherent expression of ideas, with appropriate grammar and vocabulary, but may contain some minor language errors; and ↝ demonstrates clear, fluid speech with high overall intelligibility, but may contain minor problems with pronunciation or intonation.
3	**A response at this level** ↝ conveys information relevant to the task, but shows some incompleteness, inaccuracy, or lack of detail; and ↝ demonstrates a fairly coherent expression of ideas, but may contain some errors in grammar or vocabulary that do not seriously interfere with meaning; and ↝ demonstrates generally clear, somewhat fluid speech, but may contain minor problems with pronunciation, intonation, or pacing and may occasionally require some listener effort.
2	**A response at this level** ↝ conveys some relevant information but omits key ideas, shows limited development, or shows misunderstanding of key ideas; or ↝ demonstrates a limited expression of ideas, inaccurate or unclear connections among ideas, or limited or inaccurate grammar and vocabulary; or ↝ demonstrates some clear speech, but contains problems with pronunciation, intonation, or pacing and may require significant listener effort.
1	**A response at this level** ↝ fails to provide much relevant content because ideas that are expressed are inaccurate, limited, or vague; or ↝ demonstrates a limited control of grammar and vocabulary that severely limits expression of ideas and connections among ideas; or ↝ demonstrates fragmented speech with frequent pauses and consistent problems with pronunciation and intonation that obscure meaning and require great listener effort.
0	**A response at this level** ↝ is not related to the topic; or ↝ is absent.

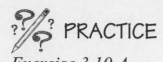 PRACTICE

Exercise 3.10.A

Read the passage and listen to the recording of the lecture and question. Then read the text of a student's response.

Reading Time – 45 seconds

SOCIALIZATION

Socialization is the process by which individuals learn a world of meaning as the one and only way to view things and interpret their experiences. As individuals develop from infant to child to adult, they literally "learn their place," including the positions they will occupy and the roles attached to those positions in social systems. Socialization involves receiving the necessary information and having opportunities to practice social roles. Networks of individuals and institutions act as agents of socialization that transmit all the knowledge individuals need to function as adults.

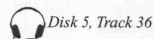 *Disk 5, Track 36*

> Define agents of socialization, and explain how specific agents of socialization influence an individual.

 Stop

STUDENT'S RESPONSE

"Agents of socialization are people, for example, your parents, who teach you how to live. Parents take care of you and teach the correct way to behave. Parents are very important because they help you make the right choices in life. Also, your peers are important agents because they are your friends. Your friends influence you, for example, how you dress. Also, teachers are important because they teach you knowledge. Television and the Internet—they also influence an individual and teach socialization."

Now answer the following questions. Discuss your answers with your teacher and classmates.

1. What key points does the student make in the response? Does the response accurately convey information from the lecture and reading?

2. What examples, reasons, or other details from the lecture are included?

3. What transitions and other expressions make the speech coherent and easy to follow?

4. Does the response answer the question effectively?

5. Evaluate the response according to the descriptions of the four levels on page 349. If the student speaks clearly and generally uses good pronunciation, what score should the response receive?

Exercise 3.10.B

Listen to the recording of the conversation and question. Then read the text of a student's response.

Disk 5, Track 37

> Describe the woman's problem with her roommate and the suggestions the man makes about how she could deal with it. What do you think the woman should do, and why?

Stop

STUDENT'S RESPONSE

"The woman has a problem with her roommate because her roommate uses her things but doesn't ask for permission. Also, her roommate doesn't clean the bathroom. So the woman is not happy about the situation. The man suggests the woman discuss the problem with her roommate. He suggests the apartment manager can help. Another suggestion is to find another apartment. I think the woman should find another apartment. I think this because I had the same problem. It's a better way to solve the problem when you move out and get a new roommate."

Now answer the following questions. Discuss your answers with your teacher and classmates.

1. Does the response accurately convey information from the conversation about the problem and solutions?

2. What examples and reasons from the conversation are included?

3. Does the student's response state an opinion about the solution to the problem? What is the student's opinion? What reason is given for this opinion?

4. What transitions and other expressions make the speech coherent and easy to follow?

5. Does the response answer the question effectively?

6. Evaluate the response according to the descriptions of the four levels on page 349. If the student speaks clearly and generally uses good pronunciation, what score should the response receive?

Answers to Exercise 3.10.A and 3.10.B are on page 591.

EXTENSION

1. Study the descriptions of the four score levels on page 349. Make sure you understand the description for each level. Check your understanding of the meaning of these words and phrases:

addresses the task	incompleteness	listener effort
coherent	inaccuracy	key ideas
fluid speech	lack of detail	vague
intelligibility	pacing	fragmented speech

2. Review your recorded responses to the integrated speaking questions in units 3.5 through 3.9. Evaluate each response according to the descriptions of the four levels on page 349. What score would your responses receive? What are the areas of strength in your speaking? What are your most serious problems? What can you do to improve your speaking and earn a high score for the integrated speaking questions on the TOEFL?

PROGRESS – 3.5 through 3.10

Quiz 4   *Time – approximately 15 minutes*

There are four questions in this quiz. You may take notes, and you may use your notes to help you answer the questions. Record your response to each question on a cassette. Each response will earn a score of 1, 2, 3, or 4, with 4 the highest score. Add the four scores to obtain your total score.

QUESTION 1

In this question, you will read a short passage about a campus situation, listen to a conversation, and then speak in response to a question about what you have read and heard. After you hear the question, you have 30 seconds to prepare your response and 60 seconds to speak.

Reading Time – 45 seconds

NOTICE OF FREE CAREER WORKSHOP

Taylor University invites all students and prospective students to take part in a free career workshop and resource fair, on Saturday, February 10. The purpose of the daylong event is to provide resources to students who want to pursue careers in business, health services, or community development. Dr. Janis Morris, past president of the college, will give the opening address. The resource fair will provide information on employment in the region and educational programs at the university. Employers and career counselors will answer questions.

Now cover the passage and question. Listen to the recording. When you hear the question, uncover the question and begin preparing your response.

 Disk 5, Track 38

> The man expresses his opinion about the career workshop. State his opinion and explain the reasons he gives for holding that opinion.

 Stop

Preparation Time – 30 seconds
Response Time – 60 seconds

QUESTION 2

In this question, you will read a short passage on an academic subject, listen to a lecture on the same topic, and then speak in response to a question about what you have read and heard. After you hear the question, you have 30 seconds to prepare your response and 60 seconds to speak.

Reading Time – 45 seconds

SLEEP AND LEARNING

Scientists have long hypothesized that sleep has an impact on learning. People learn better if they learn smaller bits of information over a period of days rather than if they learn a large amount all at once. Periods of sleep between sessions of learning will help people retain what they learn. Sleep has at least two separate effects on learning: sleep consolidates memories, protecting them against later interference or loss, and it also appears to recover or restore memories. Brain activity during sleep promotes higher–level types of learning, such as the ability to learn language.

Now cover the passage and question. Listen to the recording. When you hear the question, uncover the question and begin preparing your response.

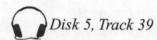 *Disk 5, Track 39*

The professor describes a study about the effects of sleep. Explain how the study supports the connections between sleep and learning.

 Stop

Preparation Time – 30 seconds
Response Time – 60 seconds

DELTA'S KEY TO THE NEXT GENERATION TOEFL® TEST

QUESTION 3

In this question, you will listen to a conversation. You will then be asked to talk about the information in the conversation and to give your opinion about the ideas presented. To make this practice more like the real test, cover the question during the conversation. After you hear the question, you have 20 seconds to prepare your response and 60 seconds to speak.

 Disk 5, Track 40

> The students discuss possible solutions to the woman's problem. Describe the problem. Then state which of the solutions you prefer and explain why.

 Stop

Preparation Time – 20 seconds
Response Time – 60 seconds

QUESTION 4

In this question, you will listen to part of a lecture. You will then be asked to summarize important information from the lecture. To make this practice more like the real test, cover the question during the lecture. After you hear the question, you have 20 seconds to prepare your response and 60 seconds to speak.

 Disk 5, Track 41

> Using points and examples from the talk, describe the uses of gestures and facial expressions in human communication.

 Stop

Preparation Time – 20 seconds
Response Time – 60 seconds

Key points for Speaking Quiz 4 are on page 591.

Record your total score on the Progress Chart on page 695.

PROGRESS – 3.5 through 3.10

Quiz 5

Time – approximately 15 minutes

There are four questions in this quiz. You may take notes, and you may use your notes to help you answer the questions. Record your response to each question on a cassette. Each response will earn a score of 1, 2, 3, or 4, with 4 the highest score. Add the four scores to obtain your total score.

QUESTION 1

In this question, you will read a short passage about a campus situation, listen to a conversation, and then speak in response to a question about what you have read and heard. After you hear the question, you have 30 seconds to prepare your response and 60 seconds to speak.

Reading Time – 45 seconds

BASIC COLLEGE WRITING

The objective of this course is to write effective college essays that integrate assigned readings, class discussions, and the writer's knowledge and experience. Students will produce a total of six essays. Each week, students will have two hours of lecture and discussion, two hours in a writing workshop, and one hour in a peer feedback group. In the feedback group, students will read and respond to each other's writing. The course will help students prepare for future study and/or careers in writing, humanities, literature, and teaching.

Now cover the passage and question. Listen to the recording. When you hear the question, uncover the question and begin preparing your response.

 Disk 5, Track 42

> The man expresses his opinion about the peer feedback group. State his opinion and explain the reasons he gives for holding that opinion.

 Stop

Preparation Time – 30 seconds
Response Time – 60 seconds

QUESTION 2

In this question, you will read a short passage on an academic subject, listen to a lecture on the same topic, and then speak in response to a question about what you have read and heard. After you hear the question, you have 30 seconds to prepare your response and 60 seconds to speak.

Reading Time – 45 seconds

COHORTS

Social scientists use the term "cohort" to describe a group of individuals who were born within a narrow band of years. "Cohort flow" describes the movement through history of people who are members of the same cohort. Members of the same cohort share certain historical and cultural influences since they experience major events at the same age. The life experiences of one cohort will be different from those of another cohort, simply because society changes continuously in terms of educational opportunities, occupational openings, and other factors.

Now cover the passage and question. Listen to the recording. When you hear the question, uncover the question and begin preparing your response.

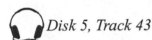 *Disk 5, Track 43*

> Describe the effect of historical events on different cohorts, and explain how the Great
> Depression influenced two cohorts that were close in age.

 Stop

Preparation Time – 30 seconds
Response Time – 60 seconds

QUESTION 3

In this question, you will listen to a conversation. You will then be asked to talk about the information in the conversation and to give your opinion about the ideas presented. To make this practice more like the real test, cover the question during the conversation. After you hear the question, you have 20 seconds to prepare your response and 60 seconds to speak.

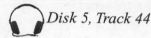*Disk 5, Track 44*

> Describe the woman's problem and the two suggestions the man makes about how to deal with it. What do you think the woman should do, and why?

Stop

Preparation Time – 20 seconds
Response Time – 60 seconds

QUESTION 4

In this question, you will listen to part of a lecture. You will then be asked to summarize important information from the lecture. To make this practice more like the real test, cover the question during the lecture. After you hear the question, you have 20 seconds to prepare your response and 60 seconds to speak.

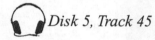*Disk 5, Track 45*

> Using points and examples from the talk, describe two types of organizational charts, and explain what they reveal about an organization.

Stop

Preparation Time – 20 seconds
Response Time – 60 seconds

Key points for Speaking Quiz 5 are on page 591.

Record your total score on the Progress Chart on page 695.

PROGRESS – 3.5 through 3.10

QUIZ 6   *Time – approximately 15 minutes*

There are four questions in this quiz. You may take notes, and you may use your notes to help you answer the questions. Record your response to each question on a cassette. Each response will earn a score of 1, 2, 3, or 4, with 4 the highest score. Add the four scores to obtain your total score.

QUESTION 1

In this question, you will read a short passage about a campus situation, listen to a conversation, and then speak in response to a question about what you have read and heard. After you hear the question, you have 30 seconds to prepare your response and 60 seconds to speak.

Reading Time – 45 seconds

VOLUNTEERS NEEDED FOR CONFERENCE

Students are needed to work as volunteers during the university's 2–day conference on global warming, April 6–7. Volunteer positions are available to set up conference rooms, assist guest speakers, and work at the information booth. Volunteers are asked to work a 2–hour shift on the day before the conference or on either day during the conference. In return, volunteers receive a free conference T–shirt and admission to the reception for guest speakers on April 7. To volunteer, go to the planning meeting on March 15 or talk to Steve in the Environmental Studies office.

Now cover the passage and question. Listen to the recording. When you hear the question, uncover the question and begin preparing your response.

 Disk 5, Track 46

> The woman expresses her opinion about volunteering for the conference. State her opinion and explain the reasons she gives for holding that opinion.

 Stop

Preparation Time – 30 seconds
Response Time – 60 seconds

QUESTION 2

In this question, you will read a short passage on an academic subject, listen to a lecture on the same topic, and then speak in response to a question about what you have read and heard. After you hear the question, you have 30 seconds to prepare your response and 60 seconds to speak.

Reading Time – 45 seconds

THE CHASE FILM

During the silent film era, filmmakers looked for original stories that they could tell expressively in the new medium of film. This was easiest if the story was simple to tell and simple for the audience to follow. These conditions were ideally fulfilled by the chase film, which flourished internationally in the years 1903 to 1913. All that filmmakers needed to do was to establish some offense—a theft, an insult, or a boy's naughty behavior—and then launch a humorous chase after the offender. The chase could be extended for several minutes, through any number of successive scenes and situations.

Now cover the passage and question. Listen to the recording. When you hear the question, uncover the question and begin preparing your response.

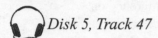 *Disk 5, Track 47*

Describe two variations on the chase film, and explain why the chase film was significant in the history of film.

 Stop

Preparation Time – 30 seconds
Response Time – 60 seconds

QUESTION 3

In this question, you will listen to a conversation. You will then be asked to talk about the information in the conversation and to give your opinion about the ideas presented. To make this practice more like the real test, cover the question during the conversation. After you hear the question, you have 20 seconds to prepare your response and 60 seconds to speak.

 Disk 5, Track 48

> Describe the man's problem and the suggestions his adviser makes about what to do. What do you think the man should do, and why?

 Stop

Preparation Time – 20 seconds
Response Time – 60 seconds

QUESTION 4

In this question, you will listen to part of a lecture. You will then be asked to summarize important information from the lecture. To make this practice more like the real test, cover the question during the lecture. After you hear the question, you have 20 seconds to prepare your response and 60 seconds to speak.

 Disk 5, Track 49

> Using points and examples from the talk, explain how immunization works and how vaccines were developed against various diseases.

 Stop

Preparation Time – 20 seconds
Response Time – 60 seconds

Key points for Speaking Quiz 6 are on page 592.

Record your total score on the Progress Chart on page 695.

PROGRESS – 3.1 through 3.10

QUIZ 7   *Time – approximately 20 minutes*

There are six questions in this quiz. You may take notes, and you may use your notes to help you answer the questions. Record your response to each question on a cassette. Each response will earn a score of 1, 2, 3, or 4, with 4 the highest score. Add the six scores to obtain your total score.

For questions 1 and 2, you will speak in response to a question about a familiar topic. Use your own personal knowledge and experience to answer each question. After you hear the question, you have 15 seconds to prepare your response and 45 seconds to speak.

QUESTION 1

 Disk 6, Track 1

> What book have you read that you would recommend to others? Explain why you think other people should read this book. Include details and examples to support your explanation.

 Stop

Preparation Time – 15 seconds
Response Time – 45 seconds

QUESTION 2

 Disk 6, Track 2

> Some people have a few favorite foods that they eat most of the time. Others are always trying new dishes and styles of cooking. Which do you prefer and why? Include details and examples in your explanation.

 Stop

Preparation Time – 15 seconds
Response Time – 45 seconds

QUESTION 3

In this question, you will read a short passage about a campus situation, listen to a conversation, and then speak in response to a question about what you have read and heard. After you hear the question, you have 30 seconds to prepare your response and 60 seconds to speak.

Reading Time – 45 seconds

PROPOSAL TO LIMIT STUDENT COURSE LOAD

The dean's office has proposed placing a limit on the number of credit hours for which students are allowed to register in a term. Currently, there is no limit on how many credits a student may pursue in a single semester. The proposal would impose a maximum course load per semester of 20 credit hours, with 12 to 20 credit hours indicating full–time status. This proposal comes in response to an increase in the number of students with heavy loads who either withdraw from courses or do not complete courses. The dean will speak about the proposal on Wednesday at 12:30 p.m. in Lecture Hall 2.

Now cover the passage and question. Listen to the recording. When you hear the question, uncover the question and begin preparing your response.

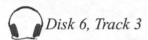 *Disk 6, Track 3*

The woman expresses her opinion about the proposal. State her opinion and explain the reasons she gives for holding that opinion.

 Stop

Preparation Time – 30 seconds
Response Time – 60 seconds

QUESTION 4

In this question, you will read a short passage on an academic subject, listen to a lecture on the same topic, and then speak in response to a question about what you have read and heard. After you hear the question, you have 30 seconds to prepare your response and 60 seconds to speak.

Reading Time – 45 seconds

CHEMICALS IN THE ATMOSPHERE

When a volcano erupts, debris and gases move up through the atmosphere. Volcanic substances in the lower atmosphere wash out fairly quickly, but chemicals reaching the upper atmosphere spread around the world. They undergo chemical reactions that produce a dark haze of sulfuric acid droplets. This haze reflects incoming sunlight and cools the underlying atmosphere, thereby changing the climate. The effect of a single volcanic eruption can last for several years. Scientists believe that the smoke from wildfires may have a similar effect on the chemistry of the atmosphere.

Now cover the passage and question. Listen to the recording. When you hear the question, uncover the question and begin preparing your response.

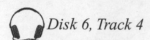 *Disk 6, Track 4*

Explain how forest fires are related to climate change, and compare this to the effect of volcanic eruptions.

 Stop

Preparation Time – 30 seconds
Response Time – 60 seconds

QUESTION 5

In this question, you will listen to a conversation. You will then be asked to talk about the information in the conversation and to give your opinion about the ideas presented. To make this practice more like the real test, cover the question during the conversation. After you hear the question, you have 20 seconds to prepare your response and 60 seconds to speak.

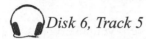 *Disk 6, Track 5*

> Describe the man's problem and the two suggestions the professor makes about how to solve it. What do you think the man should do, and why?

 Stop

Preparation Time – 20 seconds
Response Time – 60 seconds

QUESTION 6

In this question, you will listen to part of a lecture. You will then be asked to summarize important information from the lecture. To make this practice more like the real test, cover the question during the lecture. After you hear the question, you have 20 seconds to prepare your response and 60 seconds to speak.

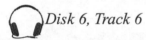 *Disk 6, Track 6*

> Using points and examples from the lecture, explain the three main ways that manufacturers sell goods to consumers.

 Stop

Preparation Time – 20 seconds
Response Time – 60 seconds

Key points for Speaking Quiz 7 are on page 592.

Record your total score on the Progress Chart on page 695.

PROGRESS – 3.1 through 3.10

Quiz 8

Time – approximately 20 minutes

There are six questions in this quiz. You may take notes, and you may use your notes to help you answer the questions. Record your response to each question on a cassette. Each response will earn a score of 1, 2, 3, or 4, with 4 the highest score. Add the six scores to obtain your total score.

For questions 1 and 2, you will speak in response to a question about a familiar topic. Use your own personal knowledge and experience to answer each question. After you hear the question, you have 15 seconds to prepare your response and 45 seconds to speak.

QUESTION 1

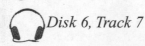 *Disk 6, Track 7*

> What is the best gift you have ever received? Describe this gift and explain its importance to you. Include details and examples in your explanation.

 Stop

Preparation Time – 15 seconds
Response Time – 45 seconds

QUESTION 2

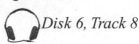 *Disk 6, Track 8*

> Some students like to study for a long period of hours at a time. Others divide their study time into many shorter sessions. Which method do you think is better for studying and why? Include details and examples in your explanation.

 Stop

Preparation Time – 15 seconds
Response Time – 45 seconds

QUESTION 3

In this question, you will read a short passage about a campus situation, listen to a conversation, and then speak in response to a question about what you have read and heard. After you hear the question, you have 30 seconds to prepare your response and 60 seconds to speak.

Reading Time – 45 seconds

SCHOLARSHIP PROGRAMS

A variety of scholarship programs at Middleton College enable deserving students to attend college and lessen their financial burden. Most scholarships are available only for full–time students. Scholarships are generally awarded to prospective students who have excelled in their previous studies or made distinguished contributions in their community or other work. A separate application is required for each scholarship applied for. Scholarship applications are due in the Financial Aid Office by May 1 for the academic year beginning the following September.

Now cover the passage and question. Listen to the recording. When you hear the question, uncover the question and begin preparing your response.

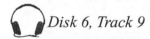*Disk 6, Track 9*

> The counselor expresses his views on scholarship applications. State his views and explain the reasons he gives for holding them.

Stop

Preparation Time – 30 seconds
Response Time – 60 seconds

QUESTION 4

In this question, you will read a short passage on an academic subject, listen to a lecture on the same topic, and then speak in response to a question about what you have read and heard. After you hear the question, you have 30 seconds to prepare your response and 60 seconds to speak.

Reading Time – 45 seconds

CROWDS

Crowds are temporary gatherings of people who share a common focus and an awareness of one another. A crowd is more than a loose collection of individuals but not as structured as an authentic group. A casual crowd, such as the chance coming together of witnesses to an accident, is the most temporary kind of gathering. In a casual crowd, people look to one another for information and clues as to how to respond. In contrast, a conventional crowd is a gathering of people who are bound by the rules or conventions of their particular setting, such as the crowd at a concert, religious service, or political event.

Now cover the passage and question. Listen to the recording. When you hear the question, uncover the question and begin preparing your response.

Disk 6, Track 10

> Describe the emergent quality of crowd behavior, and explain why some crowds behave in certain ways.

Stop

Preparation Time – 30 seconds
Response Time – 60 seconds

QUESTION 5

In this question, you will listen to a conversation. You will then be asked to talk about the information in the conversation and to give your opinion about the ideas presented. To make this practice more like the real test, cover the question during the conversation. After you hear the question, you have 20 seconds to prepare your response and 60 seconds to speak.

 Disk 6, Track 11

> Describe the woman's situation and the suggestions the man makes about how to manage it. What do you think the woman should do, and why?

 Stop

Preparation Time – 20 seconds
Response Time – 60 seconds

QUESTION 6

In this question, you will listen to part of a lecture. You will then be asked to summarize important information from the lecture. To make this practice more like the real test, cover the question during the lecture. After you hear the question, you have 20 seconds to prepare your response and 60 seconds to speak.

 Disk 6, Track 12

> Using points and examples from the lecture, explain how various abiotic factors in ecosystems affect plants and animals.

 Stop

Preparation Time – 20 seconds
Response Time – 60 seconds

Key points for Speaking Quiz 8 are on page 593.

Record your total score on the Progress Chart on page 695.

PART 4 – WRITING

The Writing section of the TOEFL measures your ability to plan and write responses to questions in essay format. You must be able to select and convey relevant information, organize and support ideas, and demonstrate that you can use English effectively.

There are two questions in the Writing section. The first question is an integrated reading–listening–writing task, in which you will read a short passage, listen to a short lecture, and then write a response based on what you have read and heard. The second question is an independent writing task, in which you will write a response based on your own opinion and experience. Both writing questions are about topics that are appropriate for international students. You do not need special knowledge of any subject to respond to the questions.

WRITING SECTION

Question	Reading Time	Listening Time	Writing Time
Integrated task	3 minutes	2–3 minutes	20 minutes
Independent task	—	—	30 minutes

THE TEST EXPERIENCE

The entire Writing section takes approximately one hour to complete. This includes the time that you spend reading the directions, reading the passage, listening to the lecture, and writing your responses to both questions. A clock at the top of the screen shows how much writing time is left for each question. For the integrated writing task, you will use headphones to listen to the lecture. You will be able to change the volume of the sound. The clock does not count down while you are listening to the lecture.

You may take notes on paper during both writing tasks, and you may use your notes to help you write your responses. However, at the end of the test you must give all of your notes to the test supervisor. Your notes will not be scored; only what you type on the computer will be scored.

You must type your responses to both writing questions in the typing box on the computer screen. You will not be allowed to write your responses by hand.

THE INTEGRATED WRITING TASK

The integrated–skills writing task measures your ability to understand key ideas from an academic reading passage and a short lecture, and to write a response to a question about them. You must determine what information in the lecture relates in some way to information in the reading. Then you must organize and compose a response in standard written English.

In your response, you must demonstrate your ability to:

- organize ideas effectively in answering the question;
- draw requested connections between the lecture and the reading;
- develop ideas with appropriate examples and explanation;
- display unity and coherence; and
- use English words and sentences effectively.

Your response is expected to have about 150 to 225 words. It will be read by two qualified evaluators who will score it on a scale of 1 to 5, with 5 being the highest score possible. You will receive a score of 0 if you do not write a response, do not write about the given question, or do not write in English. Your score on the integrated writing task will be combined with your score on the independent writing task. The total number of points you earn for both writing questions will be converted to a Writing section score of 0 to 30.

First, you have three minutes to read a passage that is 250 to 300 words long. Here is an example:

The discovery of penicillin and other antibiotic drugs is the most dramatic medical development of the twentieth century. These new drugs quickly became known as "wonder drugs" because they saved so many lives that were threatened by major forms of infection. The research that led to their development rested on the belief that chemicals could be found that would destroy specific microorganisms without injuring the human body at the same time. Advances in chemistry and in the knowledge of bacteria quickened the discovery of such chemicals.

In 1933, the first of the sulfa drugs, prontosil, was tested clinically on humans and was found to cure blood infections that would otherwise have been fatal. In 1941, the first successful human tests of penicillin were conducted on cases of streptococcus infections. The discovery of penicillin laid the foundation for even more powerful weapons against specific diseases. Within the next decade, researchers identified some 200 antibiotic substances that were effective against one or another type of bacteria. One of the most important was streptomycin, found to be potent against tuberculosis and other infections that were not affected by penicillin.

Antibiotics gave the medical profession powerful tools that could directly fight a very wide range of specific diseases. They made possible the survival of patients during and after surgery. No longer was it necessary to depend largely on the body's own immune system to fight off major infections; these infections could be attacked directly with drugs. Among the most spectacular effects of antibiotics were reductions in the number of deaths from pneumonia and tuberculosis.

Then the passage will disappear temporarily while you listen to a short lecture on the same topic. The passage will reappear later and be available to you during the writing time.

While you are listening, you will see a picture of the professor and the class:

(Narrator) Now listen to part of a lecture in a biology class.

(Professor) As soon as we developed antibiotics, new strains of bacteria appeared that were resistant to some or all of the drugs. Hospitals started using antibiotics regularly in the 1950s, but resistance started appearing within a few years. Today, one–third of the patients in hospitals are on antibiotics, but antibiotic resistance is increasing the danger of hospital infections—to the point where people are almost safer staying home than going to a hospital.

In the forties, penicillin really was a wonder drug. Back then, you could give a patient with bacterial pneumonia ten thousand units of penicillin four times a day and cure the disease. Today, you could give 24 million units of penicillin a day, but the patient might still die. Why? Well, in a way, bacteria are smarter than us. They evolve to counteract any drug we attack them with. A lot of bacteria are now completely resistant to penicillin.

Bacteria can evolve very effective weapons against antibiotics. Some of them develop enzymes to match every antibiotic we throw at them. All these weapons and counter–weapons match one another—just like the weapons in real military warfare. So, no matter what antibiotic we use, the bacteria will come up with a way to make it useless.

How does this happen? Well, if you douse a colony of bacteria with an antibiotic, the colony will be killed—that is, all except for a few cells. A few cells will survive because they carry a resistance gene for that particular antibiotic. The surviving cells quickly multiply, and they pass along this lucky gene to their offspring. And soon you have a new strain of bacteria that's resistant to that drug.

One consequence of antibiotic resistance is the reappearance of tuberculosis as a major illness. Twenty years ago, doctors thought tuberculosis was a defeated disease. Since then, however, new cases of tuberculosis have increased by 20 percent. And several strains of the disease are resistant to any drug we can attack them with.

(Narrator) Summarize the main points made in the lecture, explaining how they differ from points made in the reading.

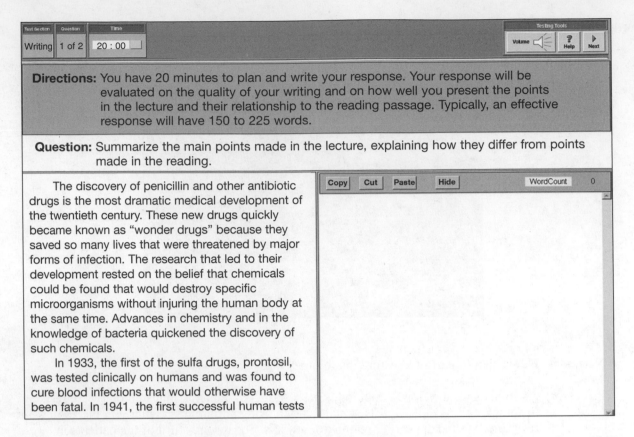

After the lecture, you will both *hear* and *see* the writing question. Then you have 20 minutes to plan, write, and revise your response. The reading passage is available during this time. You may use your notes from the lecture to help you write your response.

As you type, the computer will show your word count—how many words you have written. An effective response usually has approximately 150 to 225 words.

THE INDEPENDENT WRITING TASK

The independent writing task measures your ability to write an essay in response to a given topic. You must be able to generate and organize ideas, to develop and support these ideas, and to compose in standard written English.

In your essay, you must demonstrate your ability to:

- organize ideas effectively in answering the question;
- state and support an opinion;
- develop ideas with appropriate reasons, examples, and personal experience;
- display unity and coherence; and
- use English words and sentences effectively.

Your essay will be read by two qualified evaluators who will score it on a scale of 1 to 5, with 5 being the highest score possible. You will receive a score of 0 if you do not write an essay, do not write about the assigned topic, or do not write in English. Your score on the independent writing task will be combined with your score on the integrated writing task. The total number of points you earn for both writing questions will be converted to a Writing section score of 0 to 30.

Here is an example of an independent writing task:

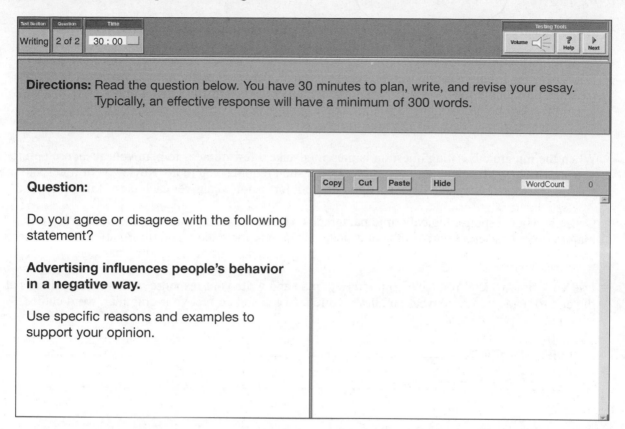

STRATEGIES FOR THE WRITING SECTION

Before the Test

- Listen to a variety of recorded materials that use academic English, such as university lectures, documentaries, educational television programs, and in–depth radio news programs. Practice taking notes as you listen.

- Work on building your vocabulary. Practice using transitions—connecting words and expressions— to make your writing more coherent.

- Become familiar with the types of writing questions that appear on the TOEFL.

- Become familiar with the English keyboard, and practice typing on it.

- Become familiar with the TOEFL testing tools, such as **Copy**, **Cut**, and **Paste**. Practice using these keys to move text and make corrections.

- Your own best strategy: _____

_____

During the Test—Integrated Task

- While you are reading the passage, think about its general message and organization. Notice key words and phrases that appear throughout the passage.

- While you are listening to the lecture, focus on major ideas. Listen for terms and concepts that are repeated throughout the lecture. Take notes only about the information that will be important to remember: key points, examples, and reasons. Do not try to write down everything you hear. Do not allow your writing to detract from your listening.

- When the integrated writing question is presented, take a few minutes to plan your response before you start writing. Think about everything the question requires you to do. Review your notes and the reading passage. Select and organize appropriate information to answer each part of the question.

- Organize your response logically into paragraphs. Generally, each paragraph should develop one major point. Answer all parts of the question, using appropriate ideas and information from the lecture and reading. Use your own words. Do not just copy sentences from the reading passage.

- Use your time wisely. You have 20 minutes to plan and write your response. Allow a few minutes at the end to read and revise what you have written. Check and correct your grammar, word choice, spelling, and punctuation.

- Your own best strategy: _____

_____

During the Test—Independent Task

- When the independent writing question is presented, take a few minutes to plan your essay before you start writing. Read the question carefully and make sure you understand everything it asks you to do. Organize your ideas by making an outline.

- Write only about the given topic. Clearly state your opinion about the topic. Support all of your points with evidence: examples, facts, reasons, personal experiences, and other details.

- Use grammatical structures and vocabulary that you are familiar with. Use transitions to make your sentences and paragraphs coherent.

- Use your time wisely. You have 30 minutes to plan and write your essay. Allow a few minutes at the end to read and revise what you have written. Check and correct your grammar, word choice, spelling, and punctuation.

- Do not be concerned about whether the essay readers will agree with your opinion. Be concerned about whether your essay states your opinion clearly, supports your opinion with appropriate details, shows organization and development, and uses appropriate sentence structure and vocabulary.

- Your own best strategy: _____

_____

4.1 Integrated Writing: Connecting Information from Two Sources

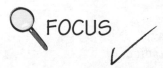

FOCUS

Imagine you are in enrolled in a university course that is studying the world's water resources. Your professor has assigned reading for homework as preparation for the lecture on the following day. What do you expect from this assignment? Check all of the statements that could be true.

____ The reading will be a waste of time, so you do not have to do it.

____ The reading will give background information for the next day's lecture.

____ The professor's lecture will be about a completely different topic.

____ The lecture will provide an example to illustrate a point in the reading.

____ The lecture will offer a view of the topic that differs from that in the reading.

____ You will show that you understand the information in the reading and lecture.

You can expect that the reading will give background information about the topic that will be discussed in class the next day. You can expect that the professor will discuss the reading and elaborate on it—perhaps by providing an example to illustrate a point or by offering a different view of the same topic. You can also expect that you will eventually have to show that you understand the material in the reading and the lecture. You will do this by connecting information from the two sources.

This type of activity is common in university study: you will read course material, listen to a professor talk about the material, and then demonstrate that you understand the material. This type of activity also occurs on the TOEFL in the form of the integrated reading–listening–writing task.

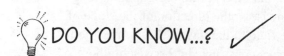

DO YOU KNOW...?

1. The TOEFL integrated writing task involves the three language skills of reading, listening, and writing. In the integrated writing task, you will:

    ➤ read a short passage of 250 to 300 words about an academic topic;

    ➤ listen to part of a lecture about the same topic; and

    ➤ write a response to a question about information from the lecture and the reading.

2. You have 20 minutes to plan and write your response to the integrated writing question. Your response will be evaluated on the quality of your writing and on how well you convey the key points in the lecture and their relationship to information in the reading.

3. The reading passage provides general background information on the lecture topic. The lecture portion is two to three minutes long. The lecture will not merely repeat information from the reading passage; rather, it will develop and expand on the reading in some way. For example, the lecture may contradict or refute ideas in the reading; it may provide a different view or explanation; or it may illustrate a general point in the reading with a specific example.

4. The writing question asks you to summarize the key points or describe the main idea of the lecture. The writing question is more about the lecture than the reading, but it requires you to draw a connection between the two. Among the possible types of connections between the two texts, you might be asked to explain how:

- ideas in the lecture agree or disagree with ideas in the reading;
- the lecture presents a different view of the reading topic;
- the lecture explains causes or effects of something in the reading;
- information in the lecture supports or illustrates points in the reading; or
- points in the lecture contradict, refute, depart from, or cast doubt on points in the reading.

5. Here is an example of an integrated writing task:

READING *(Time – 3 minutes)*

Irrigation, the artificial watering of land for agriculture, uses water from a number of sources: direct rainfall, direct streamflow, water stored in lakes and reservoirs, high–quality groundwater, brackish surface water, and even seawater. Water for irrigation is diverted from rivers and lakes or pumped underground. Different crops have different irrigation requirements, so there are many forms of irrigation and types of irrigation technology.

Various methods of surface irrigation deliver water to a field directly from a canal, well, or ditch. The surface technique of flooding large fields is widely used because of low capital costs and long tradition. Furrow irrigation, practiced since ancient times, involves digging numerous U– or V–shaped open furrows through irrigated land and introducing water into them from a channel at the top of a field. As with other surface techniques, water collects into ponds on the field. In surface–pipe irrigation, the water is piped to the field and distributed via sprinklers or smaller pipes.

Border irrigation is a type of surface irrigation that involves flooding land in long parallel strips separated by earth banks built lengthwise in the direction of the slope of the land. Water flows from the highest point in the field to the lowest. Basin irrigation is similar to border irrigation but includes earth banks constructed crosswise to those used for border irrigation, dividing a field into a series of basins that can be separately irrigated.

LISTENING AND WRITING

Disk 6, Track 13

(Narrator)

Now listen to part of a lecture on the same topic.

(Professor)

One thing that really concerns water resource analysts is how much water agriculture uses. Agriculture uses a lot of water, more than all other water–using sectors of society. One of our greatest concerns is the very high use of water by irrigation. This is because, in most cases, the water used for irrigation can't be used afterward for other purposes, such as water supply for homes or industry.

Some forms of irrigation use water more efficiently than others. The efficiency of water use varies by region, crop, agricultural practice, and technology. The least efficient types of irrigation are the surface methods. Your reading really didn't go into this, but think of how much water it takes for a traditional surface method like field flooding. It takes a lot of water to flood a field. The water collects into ponds or basins, but then most of it either evaporates into the air or passes down through the soil into groundwater. This means that, in lots of places, less than half of all the water applied to a field is actually used by the crop. The rest is lost to evaporation or to groundwater. All of the flooding methods generally waste a lot of water—water that could otherwise be used for other purposes.

Fortunately, there are several irrigation technologies that are more efficient than the poorly controlled and highly wasteful flooding methods. They range from sprinkler systems to drip irrigation. In sprinkler systems, water is sprayed over crops, and this provides an even distribution of water. New precision sprinkler technologies have greatly improved our ability to deliver water exactly when and where it's needed. However, sprinkler systems are also a form of surface irrigation, and just as in other surface methods, some of the water is still lost to evaporation.

(Narrator)

Summarize the points made in the lecture, explaining how they cast doubt on points made in the reading.

Stop

The task requires you to do two things: (1) summarize the key points from the lecture, and (2) explain how they cast doubt on points made in the reading. To respond to the question completely, you have to connect information from the lecture and the reading.

The key points from the lecture are:

- Irrigation uses a lot of water that cannot be used later for other purposes
- Surface methods of irrigation are the least efficient methods.
- The surface method of field flooding wastes a lot of water.
- With field flooding, most of the water evaporates or passes into groundwater.
- Sprinkler systems are more efficient than flooding, but some water is still lost.

Generally, the points made in the lecture cast doubt on the information in the reading, which does not address the wastefulness and lack of efficiency of surface irrigation.

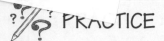

...sponse should answer the question by using relevant information from the lecture and ...An effective response would include all or most of the key ideas from the lecture and ...orrectly to information in the reading.

...es of responses to this writing question, see page 392.

PRACTICE

Exercise 4.1.A

Read the passage and then listen to the recording. To make this practice more like the real test, cover the passage and question during the lecture. Listen for important information. Take notes about examples or reasons that will help you remember the key points. When you hear the question, uncover the passage and question. Then allow 20 minutes to plan and write a response.

Reading Time – 3 minutes

> The transparent front part of the human eye is a five–layer structure called the cornea. The cornea is dense and even in thickness, projecting like a dome beyond the white of the eye and protecting the iris and pupil.
>
> A clear cornea is necessary for clear vision, and an injury to the cornea can pose a long–term problem. A corneal injury may lead to an ulcer, or it may leave a small area of scar tissue after it heals. The location of the injury or ulcer and the remaining scar tissue will determine whether or not there may be vision problems. The area around the edge of the cornea is not terribly important for good vision; however, if an ulcer forms at the center of the cornea, the scar tissue it leaves behind could interfere with vision. If a large ulcer occurs in the center of the cornea, it may be necessary to replace the cornea surgically in a procedure called corneal grafting, in which corneal tissue is transplanted from one human eye to another.
>
> Symptoms of a corneal injury include eye pain, sensitivity to light, bloodshot eyes, a feeling that something is in the eye, blurred vision, and possibly a white spot on the cornea. The term keratitis is used to describe a corneal inflammation in which the outermost cells on the surface of the cornea die. With keratitis, the eyes are sensitive to light and they hurt, water, and become bloodshot. In severe cases, vision may be impaired.
>
> To diagnose a corneal injury or ulcer, a physician will place a few drops of special liquid in the eye, turn the lights out, and shine a light on the eye while looking at the cornea through a special microscope called a slit lamp. If the surface of the cornea is broken anywhere, it will show up as a bright blue–green area.

Now cover the passage and question. Listen to the recording. When you hear the question, uncover the passage and question and begin your response.

 Disk 6, Track 14

> Describe the causes and consequences of corneal injuries and ulcers, and explain how these problems are treated.

 Stop

Exercise 4.1.B

Read the passage and then listen to the recording. To make this practice more like the real test, cover the passage and question during the lecture. Listen for important information. Take notes about examples or reasons that will help you remember the key points. When you hear the question, uncover the passage and question. Then allow 20 minutes to plan and write a response.

Reading Time – 3 minutes

Pruning is cutting off dead or living branches of a tree to improve the tree's health, structure, or growth. A tree will be more vigorous with a few healthy branches than with many weak ones. The best time to prune is in late winter or early spring, when deciduous trees are free of foliage and the arrangement of branches is visible.

Trees are pruned for the following reasons:
- to remove diseased, dead, or broken branches;
- to remove a branch that rubs against another;
- to enhance the natural shape and beauty of the tree;
- to eliminate wild growth and shoots that sprout directly from the roots;
- to hold the tree within bounds;
- to ensure production of larger flowers or fruits.

A few principles should be kept in mind when deciding where to make the cuts. Heavy pruning on top, or topping, causes leaves and branches to grow. Cutting back the tips of new growth forces the development of side branching. Crowded branches never develop to full size; large branches compete with small branches, and the small ones become targets for disease and breakage and should therefore be removed.

Young trees need leaves to make the food they need for growth, so too many branches should not be cut off in one season. After a mature tree reaches the desirable shape, pruning should be done only to remove broken or diseased branches and to thin occasionally. Branches that might come into contact with a building or power line should be pruned. If branches are cut when small and during cool weather, the wounds will heal more quickly.

Now cover the passage and question. Listen to the recording. When you hear the question, uncover the passage and question and begin your response.

 Disk 6, Track 15

Summarize the points made in the talk, explaining how they depart from good pruning practices.

 Stop

Key points for Exercises 4.1.A through 4.1.B are on page 593.

 EXTENSION

1. With your teacher and classmates, discuss situations in which it is necessary to write about information from different types of sources. On the board, write a list of as many situations as you can think of. (Possible situations: research papers; open–book tests; business reports.) What types of sources might be used for each writing situation?

2. Share and discuss your response to the writing question in Exercise 4.1.A or 4.1.B. Work in a group of three students. Make copies of your response, and give a copy to everyone in your group. Read and discuss each student's writing. Answer the following questions about each:

    a. What important points from the lecture does the response convey?
    b. What examples and explanation does the response include?
    c. Does the response answer the question effectively?

Make suggestions that will help each student improve in the future.

4.2 Integrated Writing: Taking Notes

 FOCUS

Listen to part of a university lecture. While you are listening, write down some words and phrases from the lecture that you think are important.

🎧 *Disk 6, Track 16*

_____

_____

_____

🎧 *Stop*

You probably could write down only a few things. It would be impossible to write down everything the professor said. Some important words and phrases you may have heard are:

water	agriculture	a lot
concerns	very high use	irrigation
can't be used	homes	industry

While listening to a lecture, your most important task is to listen carefully for important information. When you take notes, focus on key words and phrases that will be important to remember. Limit your notes to terms, concepts, examples, and reasons that help you understand the major points the speaker is making.

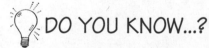 DO YOU KNOW...?

1. **Taking notes**, or **note taking**, is writing down key words and information that you hear. Note taking is an essential academic skill. During your university experience, you have to take notes to help you remember important ideas and details from lectures and class discussions. You have to study and understand the information in your notes. You have to explain this information when you take written examinations.

2. When you take the TOEFL, the test supervisor will give you paper to write on. You may take notes, and you may use your notes to help you answer the integrated writing question. Your notes will not be scored. Only what you type on the computer will be scored.

3. The integrated writing question asks you to summarize key ideas from the lecture and relate them to ideas in the reading passage. You will not know what the writing question is until after the lecture. While you are listening to the lecture, focus on the ideas that you think are most important, and take notes about them. Do not try to write down everything. Limit your note taking to examples and reasons that illustrate the speaker's points. Do not allow your writing to detract from your listening.

4. Sometimes a speaker emphasizes certain words or repeats certain ideas throughout the lecture. Listen for key words that the speaker emphasizes or repeats. Sometimes a speaker uses certain expressions to call your attention to important information. For example, the speaker may say:

There are three types/kinds/groups/classes of _____.

The key feature of _____ is _____.

The main role of _____ is _____.

One function of _____ is _____.

Another example is _____.

The main reason for this is _____.

This is primarily because _____.

First, _____.

Second, _____.

Most importantly, _____.

_____ has the advantage of _____ .

_____ is interesting because _____.

_____ is defined as _____.

A related concept is _____.

If the speaker emphasizes or repeats certain terms, or if the speaker calls your attention to important ideas, take notes about these terms and ideas.

5. Listen again to the sample lecture. Listen for key words and ideas that the professor emphasizes or repeats. Look at the following notes taken by two different students. Add other words and phrases that you think are important to remember about the lecture.

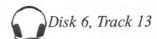 *Disk 6, Track 13*

STUDENT 1	STUDENT 2
water – high use – irrigation	agricul. use of water
can't use other purpose	very high
efficiency	water supply home industry
lot – flood a field	surface method
evaporate, or pass down to	lot of water flood
ground <u>waste</u>	flooding waste a lot
sprinkl system	1/2 by crop
surface – lost to evap.	technology – ? more efficient
	sprinkler = spray crop
	surface meth

 Stop

For examples of responses to this lecture, see page 392.

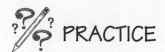 PRACTICE

Exercise 4.2.A

Read the passage and then listen to the recording. To make this practice more like the real test, cover the passage and question during the lecture. Listen for important information. Take notes about examples or reasons that will help you remember the key points. When you hear the question, uncover the passage and question. Then allow 20 minutes to plan and write a response.

Reading Time – 3 minutes

> The International style is the name given to the functionalist style of architecture that evolved in Europe and the United States shortly before the First World War and prevailed during most of the twentieth century. The International style is characterized by an emphasis on function and rejection of traditional decoration. It is also known as the Bauhaus style because it was refined at the famous German design school, the Bauhaus, during the 1920s. The directors of the Bauhaus, Walter Gropius and Ludwig Mies van der Rohe, reduced the urban building to a basic framework of steel, a skin of glass, and an open interior in which "curtain walls" could be moved around to suit the purposes of the user. Supporters of the Bauhaus idiom promoted a utilitarian simplicity in such phrases as "form follows function" and "less is more."
>
> The International style inspired both architects and ordinary citizens, and greatly influenced the mid–century building boom in the United States, particularly in New York. The beauty and simplicity of the Bauhaus idiom was evident in New York structures such as the Rockefeller Center complex. Perhaps the best known New York example is the office building of the United Nations Secretariat, completed in 1952. A Swiss–born architect known as Le Corbusier led the international group of architects that designed it. The UN Secretariat is a slab only 72 feet thick, but its blue–tinted glass walls are 287 feet wide by 544 feet high. The building has a simplicity and elegance worthy of the most prominent international organization, the United Nations. The sleek utilitarian beauty of the International style succeeded in reshaping the city, making it one of the most successful architectural movements in history.

Now cover the passage and question. Listen to the recording. When you hear the question, uncover the passage and question and begin your response.

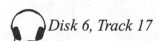 *Disk 6, Track 17*

> Summarize the points made in the lecture, explaining how they agree or disagree with points made in the reading.

 Stop

Exercise 4.2.B

Read the passage and then listen to the recording. To make this practice more like the real test, cover the passage and question during the lecture. Listen for important information. Take notes about examples or reasons that will help you remember the key points. When you hear the question, uncover the passage and question. Then allow 20 minutes to plan and write a response.

Reading Time – 3 minutes

Geothermal energy is derived from the heat contained within the earth. In some places the heat is so intense that it melts mantle rock to create liquid magma. Geologists believe that the ultimate source of geothermal energy is radioactive decay occurring deep within the planet. A renewable energy resource, geothermal heat is produced primarily when water descends from the earth's surface and meets hot magma rising toward it. Some of this geothermal water circulates back up through faults and cracks in the earth's crust and reaches the surface as hot springs or geysers. However, most geothermal water remains deep underground, trapped in cracks and porous rock.

In most regions of the world, geothermal heat reaches the earth's surface in a very diffuse state, having lost much of its energy potential. However, in some areas, including significant portions of western North America, geothermal reservoirs exist close to the surface and are thus easily tapped for power generation. Geographic regions that possess well–developed geothermal systems are located in geologically active areas. Such favored regions with continuous, concentrated heat flow to the surface include Iceland, New Zealand, Japan, and the Philippines.

Tapping geothermal heat can generate electricity without harmful emissions. In geothermal power plants, heat from the earth provides the physical force that spins turbine blades to generate electricity. Thus, energy from the earth itself will likely play an important part in the renewable energy equation of the twenty–first century.

Now cover the passage and question. Listen to the recording. When you hear the question, uncover the passage and question and begin your response.

 Disk 6, Track 18

Describe past and present uses of geothermal energy, and explain why some regions have better potential than others for developing geothermal systems.

 Stop

Key points for Exercises 4.2.A through 4.2.B are on page 593.

EXTENSION

1. Share and discuss your response to the writing question in Exercise 4.2.A or 4.2.B. Work in a group of three students. Make copies of your response, and give a copy to everyone in your group. Read and discuss each student's writing. Answer the following questions about each:

    a. What important points from the lecture does the response convey?
    b. What examples and explanation does the response include?
    c. Does the response answer the question effectively?

    Make suggestions that will help each student improve in the future.

2. Obtain permission to make a tape recording of a real college or university lecture. (Topics in history, anthropology, sociology, and psychology are good choices.) Bring your tape to class. In class, everyone listens to three minutes of the recording. While listening, everyone takes notes about the important information in the lecture. Don't try to write down everything. Write only the key words and phrases that you think are important to remember.

    Then break into groups of three or four students each. Compare your notes with the notes taken by the other students in your group. Listen again to the same three-minute recording. In your group, try to agree on the key points of the lecture. Write a summary of the lecture. Choose a student to read your group's summary to the whole class.

WRITING

4.3 Integrated Writing: Developing Ideas

 FOCUS

Imagine you are enrolled in a university course that is studying the world's water resources. Your class has read an article about irrigation, and your professor has given a lecture on the same topic. Now your professor passes out a sheet of paper and announces that it is an "open–book" quiz. Here is the quiz:

Directions:	You have 20 minutes to plan and write your response. You may use your lecture notes and the article about irrigation. The length of your response should be about 150 to 225 words.
Question:	Summarize the facts about the use of water for irrigation, explaining why some irrigation methods are not efficient in using water.

What would you do? Check all of the things that you would do:

____ Just start writing 150 words as quickly as possible.

____ Read the question carefully and think about what it wants you to do.

____ Review the notes you took during the lecture.

____ Write about a different topic related to irrigation.

____ Plan what facts to present, and in what order.

____ Select three points and write a paragraph about each.

____ Develop your ideas with examples and reasons.

Is it a good idea to just start writing as quickly as you can? Very few people can do that and have good results. It is better to read the question carefully and think about what it wants you to do.

Should you review the notes you took during the lecture? Of course! Should you write about a different but related topic? Probably not, if you want a good score on the quiz. If you do that, your response will not answer the question.

Should you plan what facts to present, and in what order? Definitely yes! Should you select three points and write a paragraph about each? Good idea! Should you develop your ideas with examples and reasons? Absolutely!

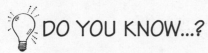
DO YOU KNOW...?

1. Responding to a question in essay format is an academic skill that you will use frequently during your university experience. You will write answers to essay questions when you take examinations. Your writing will demonstrate how well you understand information that you read in your textbooks and hear your professors discuss in lectures.

2. You have 20 minutes to plan, write, and revise your response to the integrated writing task. Your response should include the key information from the lecture and the reading that will answer the question completely.

3. You must type your response on the computer keyboard. Do not write your entire response on paper and then try to type it into the computer; you will not have enough time to do this. Organize your notes on paper, and plan your response. Then type your response directly into the typing box on the screen.

4. The integrated writing task does not ask for your opinion about the topic. For this task, your opinion is irrelevant and should not be included in your response. Your response should be based only on what you hear in the lecture and read in the passage. Usually, your response will include a summary of the major ideas from the lecture.

5. The integrated writing task requires you to do more than one thing. For example, it may ask you to (1) summarize key points from the lecture, and (2) explain how these points relate to information in the reading. You must answer each part of the question.

6. Two trained evaluators will read your response. They will rate your writing on how well you:

   ↝ organize ideas effectively in answering the question;
   ↝ draw requested connections between the lecture and the reading;
   ↝ develop ideas with appropriate examples and explanation; and
   ↝ display unity and coherence.

7. The best way to approach the integrated writing question is PLAN—WRITE—REVISE.

PLAN	Plan what information to present, and in what order.
WRITE	Write a separate paragraph to develop each major point. Support each point with information from the lecture and reading.
REVISE	Allow time to correct grammar and vocabulary errors.

8. Planning the response starts with reading the question carefully. Planning involves reviewing your notes from the lecture and selecting information that you can use to answer the question. It involves scanning the reading passage for key terms and other useful information. Planning concludes with deciding the most effective order to present the information.

9. Your response will be evaluated on its organization, so you should present the information in a logical order. Each paragraph should convey one major point and support it with relevant details or explanation. State the point clearly in the first sentence of the paragraph. All other sentences in the paragraph should provide examples, reasons, or other details to develop the point. Use your time wisely. It is better to develop all of your points with minimum detail than to have an incomplete answer because you spent too much time on the first point.

10. Here is a general plan for organizing your response to the integrated writing task:

INTEGRATED WRITING TASK
General Plan

Paragraph 1	First key point from the lecture
	• Examples from the lecture
	• Explanation or connection to the reading
Paragraph 2	Second key point from the lecture
	• Examples from the lecture
	• Explanation or connection to the reading
Paragraph 3	Third key point from the lecture
	• Examples from the lecture
	• Explanation or connection to the reading

11. Your response should be clearly organized into paragraphs. You can indicate the division into paragraphs in either of two ways:

   - indent the first line of each paragraph; or
   - leave a blank space between paragraphs.

12. *Coherence* is the quality of unity and order in a piece of writing. Writing is coherent when all of the ideas are connected logically. The following *transitions* and other expressions will help you express relationships between ideas and give your writing unity and coherence.

Introduce Key Points

According to the lecture,

The reading stated that

The professor made the point that

The lecture supports/illustrates the idea that

The lecture contradicts/refutes the idea that

Introduce Examples or Reasons

because	for example	one example is
first	for instance	such as

Add Examples or Reasons

also	furthermore	next
another example is	in addition	second, third...

Show Contrast between Ideas

although	in contrast	on the contrary
but	is contrary to	on the other hand
however	is the opposite of	while

13. There is no single correct answer to the integrated writing question. There are several ways to answer the question effectively. A successful response is usually between 150 and 225 words long. A longer response is not always better than a shorter response. It is better to write a shorter response that answers the question completely than to write a longer response that has many errors or does not answer the question completely.

14. Read the passage and listen to the lecture and question. Then read the responses written by two different students:

READING

> Irrigation, the artificial watering of land for agriculture, uses water from a number of sources: direct rainfall, direct streamflow, water stored in lakes and reservoirs, high–quality groundwater, brackish surface water, and even seawater. Water for irrigation is diverted from rivers and lakes or pumped underground. Different crops have different irrigation requirements, so there are many forms of irrigation and types of irrigation technology.
>
> Various methods of surface irrigation deliver water to a field directly from a canal, well, or ditch. The surface technique of flooding large fields is widely used because of low capital costs and long tradition. Furrow irrigation, practiced since ancient times, involves digging numerous U– or V–shaped open furrows through irrigated land and introducing water into them from a channel at the top of a field. As with other surface techniques, water collects into ponds on the field. In surface–pipe irrigation, the water is piped to the field and distributed via sprinklers or smaller pipes.
>
> Border irrigation is a type of surface irrigation that involves flooding land in long parallel strips separated by earth banks built lengthwise in the direction of the slope of the land. Water flows from the highest point in the field to the lowest. Basin irrigation is similar to border irrigation but includes earth banks constructed crosswise to those used for border irrigation, dividing a field into a series of basins that can be separately irrigated.

LISTENING

 Disk 6, Track 13

WRITING

> Summarize the points made in the lecture, explaining how they cast doubt on points made in the reading.

 Stop

RESPONSE BY STUDENT 1

Irrigation, the artificial watering of land for agriculture, has a high use of water. Water for irrigation comes from several sources, such as direct rainfall, rivers, lakes, and reservoirs. Some irrigation methods use a lot of water, such as flooding large fields. According to the reading, flooding is widely used because of low cost and long tradition. However, the lecture casts doubt on this point by stating that surface methods are not efficient.

The water that is used for irrigation can't be used for other purposes. With surface irrigation, some of the water goes to the plants; however, a lot of water evaporates or passes down into the ground. This wastes a lot of water because the water is not available for other purposes such as drinking.

The surface method of flooding large fields requires a lot of water. Some of the water evaporates when it collects into ponds on the field. Sprinkler systems are a more efficient type of surface irrigation, but they also lose water to evaporation.

RESPONSE BY STUDENT 2

The professor made the point that the use of water for irrigation is very high. In general, agriculture uses a lot of water, and the water for irrigation cannot be used for other purposes. For example, it cannot be the water supply for homes and industry. The reading does not discuss this point.

Another important point is that some irrigation methods are not efficient in using water. For example, surface methods of irrigation use a lot of water. Surface methods deliver water to a field directly from a canal, well, or ditch. Examples are flooding, border irrigation, and basin irrigation. Surface methods are not efficient because they waste a lot of water. For example, the surface technique of flooding large fields requires a large amount of water. However, half of the water is used by the crop, and the rest is lost to evaporation. In general, surface methods of irrigation are not efficient, but the reading does not discuss this point.

Finally, the professor stated that some technology is more efficient than flooding. An example is the sprinkler method, which sprays crops with water. However, sprinklers are a surface method, and some water is wasted. In general, the professor discusses problems with surface irrigation that the reading does not include.

Both students have written an effective response to the question. What transitions and other expressions are used to make their writing coherent? What examples and reasons are used to develop key points?

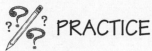

PRACTICE

Exercise 4.3.A

Read the passage and then listen to the recording. To make this practice more like the real test, cover the passage and question during the lecture. Listen for important information. Take notes about examples or reasons that will help you remember the key points. When you hear the question, uncover the passage and question. Then allow 20 minutes to plan and write a response.

Reading Time – 3 minutes

Most work organizations are still characterized by extreme division of labor in which tasks are divided into distinct parts, each part to be performed by an individual worker. In manufacturing, the assembly line is the ultimate in efficient labor, with each worker performing the same set of actions over and over again. In this way, workers themselves become like a machine part, dehumanized and alienated. Alienation is a sense of powerlessness, of being cut off from one's labor and from other workers. Alienation can also occur in office occupations, where most employees perform only a few specialized tasks.

However, despite the routine dullness of most jobs, the majority of workers are generally satisfied with their current jobs, although they are not totally enthusiastic. The most satisfying jobs are those with a high level of autonomy, in which employees can make their own decisions about the pacing and sequence of work with minimal supervision. Job autonomy is most often found in high–pay and high–prestige occupations. In jobs in the middle or lower levels of pay and prestige, workers generally have less autonomy. The lower the occupational status, the more heavily supervised the workers are, and the fewer decisions they can make on their own. Still, when workers are asked what is very important when taking their current job, they tend to list social and personal features of the workplace, such as co–workers and skills utilized, and family–related factors, such as health insurance and family leave. Traditional economic incentives such as pay and promotions are near the bottom of the list.

Now cover the passage and question. Listen to the recording. When you hear the question, uncover the passage and question and begin your response.

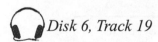 *Disk 6, Track 19*

> Summarize the points the professor made in the talk, explaining how they support points made in the reading.

 Stop

WRITING

Exercise 4.3.B

Read the passage and then listen to the recording. To make this practice more like the real test, cover the passage and question during the lecture. Listen for important information. Take notes about examples or reasons that will help you remember the key points. When you hear the question, uncover the passage and question. Then allow 20 minutes to plan and write a response.

Reading Time – 3 minutes

In the late eighteenth century, an Austrian physician named Franz Joseph Gall observed a relationship between certain mental characteristics and the shapes of people's heads. Gall founded the discipline called phrenology, which is based on the idea that variations in the human skull reflect differences in the size and the shape of the human brain. According to phrenology, different areas of the brain serve separate and distinct functions; therefore, by carefully examining the size and shape of an individual's skull, an expert can determine the strengths, weaknesses, and peculiarities of the person's character and intellect.

Devoting most of his life to a detailed study of the nervous system, Gall showed that the brain's white matter consists of nerve fibers. He also initiated the theory of localization— the belief that the various mental processes are centered in specific parts of the brain. Gall claimed that humans had several different forms of power for each mental process. He developed a list of "organs" of the mind that featured 37 different mental powers. Among these powers were emotional faculties such as secretiveness and the capability for love; sentiments such as hope, reverence, and self–esteem; and reflective and perceptual powers, including aptitude for language, musical ability, and sensitivity to visual properties such as shape and color.

The simple doctrine of phrenology achieved great popularity in Europe and the United States during the early nineteenth century. Many leading scientists of the period supported its basic principles and attempted to advance it as a science. The doctrine also appealed to the general public since everyone could "play the game" of reading skulls.

Now cover the passage and question. Listen to the recording. When you hear the question, uncover the passage and question and begin your response.

Disk 6, Track 20

Summarize the points made in the lecture, explaining how they either support or refute points made in the reading.

Stop

Exercise 4.3.C

Read the passage and then listen to the recording. To make this practice more like the real test, cover the passage and question during the lecture. Listen for important information. Take notes about examples or reasons that will help you remember the key points. When you hear the question, uncover the passage and question. Then allow 20 minutes to plan and write a response.

Reading Time – 3 minutes

At the dawn of cinema in the 1890s, audiences were fascinated by everyday actions caught on film: a train pulling into the station, a family eating breakfast, and soldiers marching in a parade. Then the French filmmaker Georges Méliès demonstrated that films could do far more than merely record everyday life. Méliès, a professional magician and theater operator, decided that the new medium could be used effectively in his magic act. After much experimentation with a moving–picture camera, he realized that film could be manipulated in countless ways. In time, he developed such new techniques as the fade–out, overlap dissolve, stop action, superimposition, double exposure, fast and slow motion, animation, and a host of other devices that he used with invention and wit.

Méliès transformed the cinema into a storytelling medium. At a time when most filmmakers were content to photograph the real world, Méliès was creating his own fantasy world. In his specially built studio near Paris, he produced more than a thousand films between 1896 and 1914. They ranged from brief shorts that were one minute long to much longer films that ran for twenty minutes. The longer films included *Cinderella* (1899) and *A Trip to the Moon* (1902).

Very popular in their day, the trick films of Méliès were shown, often without his permission, all over Europe and North America starting around 1900. At that time, the films were regarded as charming and witty, and Méliès was respected as the first artist of cinema. Although primitive by today's standards, the films of Méliès revealed the cinema's unique and almost limitless possibilities for trickery and special effects— possibilities that continue to evolve with today's computer technology.

Now cover the passage and question. Listen to the recording. When you hear the question, uncover the passage and question and begin your response.

 Disk 6, Track 21

> Summarize the points made in the talk, explaining how they illustrate points made in the reading.

 Stop

Key points for Exercises 4.3.A through 4.3.C are on page 594.

 EXTENSION

1. Share and discuss your response to one of the writing questions in Exercises 4.3.A through 4.3.C. Work in a group of three students. Make copies of your response, and give a copy to everyone in your group. Read and discuss each student's writing. Answer the following questions about each:

    a. How is the response organized?
    b. What key points does the writer convey?
    c. How does the writer support and develop each point?
    d. What transitions and expressions make the writing coherent?
    e. Does the response answer the question effectively?

    Make suggestions that will help each student improve in the future.

4.4 Checking Sentence Structure

FOCUS

Read the following paragraph from a student's response to an integrated writing question:

> Some method of irrigation not efficient. For example, flooding a field with water. The water it collects on the field in a pond then evaporate or passing into groundwater. So waste a lot of water. Sprinkler system spray water on crops, this is better than flooding however they also waste water. Because use a lot of water they waste. Generally speaking, surface method of irrigation are not efficient in using water.

The student's response contains many errors in sentence structure. Some errors obscure meaning, making the writer's message unclear. Can you identify the errors?

Now read the same paragraph without errors.

> Some methods of irrigation are not efficient. One example is flooding a field with water. The water collects on the field in a pond and then evaporates or passes into groundwater, which wastes a lot of water. Sprinkler systems spray water on crops, which is better than flooding; however, they also waste water. Generally speaking, surface methods of irrigation are not efficient in using water.

On the TOEFL, a response to the integrated writing task can have a few minor language errors and still earn a high score—if the errors do not obscure meaning. However, if the response has too many errors that make the meaning unclear, the result will be a lower score.

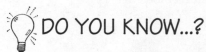DO YOU KNOW...?

1. You have 20 minutes to plan, write, and revise your response to the integrated writing task. Allow a few minutes at the end to check and correct your sentence grammar, vocabulary, and spelling.

2. Your response will be evaluated on how well you use English words and sentences to convey important ideas from the lecture and the reading. Use only grammatical structures that you know well. It is better to keep most of your sentences fairly simple than to write a lot of long, complicated sentences that might confuse your readers. Use appropriate vocabulary: your own words and key words from the lecture. Do not just copy sentences from the reading passage.

3. Every sentence must have at least one subject and one verb. A sentence can have one or more clauses, but the clauses must be joined correctly with either a semicolon (;) or a comma and a conjunction. The verb must agree in number with its subject. Pronouns must agree in number with the nouns they replace. Avoid the following sentence problems:

PROBLEM: INCOMPLETE SENTENCE (FRAGMENT)

Incorrect	**Correct**
Because Earth is our home.	Because Earth is our home, we need to protect our natural resources.
For example, television and computers.	For example, television and computers have impacted family life.

PROBLEM: RUN–ON SENTENCE (INCORRECTLY JOINED CLAUSES)

Incorrect	**Correct**
Most movies were only one minute long one director put several short films together to make longer movies.	Most movies were only one minute long; however, one director put several short films together to make longer movies.
Surface irrigation wastes a lot of water, this water cannot be used for other purposes.	Surface irrigation wastes a lot of water, and this water cannot be used for other purposes.

PROBLEM: DUPLICATE SUBJECT

Incorrect	**Correct**
Private companies they should spend more money to clean up pollution.	Private companies should spend more money to clean up pollution.
The professor she stated that we need to develop more efficient methods of irrigation.	The professor stated that we need to develop more efficient methods of irrigation.

PROBLEM: INCORRECT VERB FORM

Incorrect	**Correct**
An injury to the cornea leading to an ulcer or a scar.	An injury to the cornea may lead to an ulcer or a scar.
Only half of the water actually be used by the crops.	Only half of the water actually is used by the crops.

PROBLEM: NO SUBJECT–VERB AGREEMENT

Incorrect
The unity of all parts are the main feature
of this style.

Correct
The unity of all parts is the main feature
of this style.

Incorrect
One idea is that the size of the brain
indicate a person's intelligence.

Correct
One idea is that the size of the brain
indicates a person's intelligence.

PROBLEM: NO PRONOUN AGREEMENT

Incorrect
The best way to prevent an eye injury is
to prevent them from happening.

Correct
The best way to prevent an eye injury is
to prevent it from happening.

Incorrect
Gall was a physician which developed the
science of phrenology.

Correct
Gall was a physician who developed the
science of phrenology.

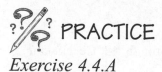 PRACTICE

Exercise 4.4.A

Check the sentence structure of the following paragraphs. Cross out errors and write corrections above them. There may be more than one way to correct an error.

1.

The speaker talk about a maple tree that was topping. This not a good pruning practice.
Because topping cause a lot of damage to trees. The first reason was topping cause leaves
and branches grew fast. The growth rate of a tree speed up when they are topping. Branches
became crowded and dangerous could crush a car. Another reason, topping remove too many
leaves, which the tree's food source. The tree will starve also more likely to infected by disease.
Topping cause a lot of stress for the tree therefore not good pruning practice.

2.

In the past, people use geothermal energy in several ways. For example, hot springs for
bathing, treating disease, and heating buildings. Different tribes in North America they call hot
springs places of peace, everybody could share the hot water for bathing. In European history,
the Romans they also use the water of hot springs for their healing power. For example, eye
and skin diseases. Geothermal energy was also heat homes in Rome and other places who are
geologically active.

3.

The professor made many points about the motivation and needs of workers they support

points made in the reading. First, the professor say the small work group important for workers

about 3 to 15 people with one leader. The work group fill needs of workers the reason is they

can participate and a sense of respect. The small work group also give workers the ability for

make decisions. This point agreed with the reading it said the most satisfying jobs are those with

a high level of autonomy this gave workers a voice can make their own decisions.

Corrected paragraphs for Exercise 4.4.A are on page 594.

 EXTENSION

1. Review the response you wrote to one of the writing questions in units 4.1 through 4.3. Check your sentences for correct grammar and usage. Ask yourself the following questions:

    a. Are all of my sentences complete?
    b. Does every sentence have a correctly formed subject and verb?
    c. Are all subjects and verbs in agreement?
    d. Are there any run–on sentences that need correcting?
    e. Do all pronouns agree with the nouns they replace?
    f. Are there any misspelled words that need correcting?
    g. What improvements can I make to clarify meaning?

2. Share and discuss your response to one of the writing questions in units 4.1 through 4.3. Work in a group of three students. Make copies of your response, and give a copy to everyone in your group. Read and discuss each student's writing. Answer the following questions about each:

    a. Does the response accurately convey key ideas from the lecture?
    b. What transitions and expressions make the writing coherent?
    c. Are all of the sentences complete?
    d. Does every sentence have a correctly formed subject and verb?
    e. Are there any sentences in which the meaning is unclear? If so, what makes it unclear?
    f. Does the response answer the question effectively?
    g. What improvements would you make?

Make suggestions that will help each student earn a high score on the integrated writing task.

4.5 Evaluating the Response

 FOCUS

What are the characteristics of good writing? What is it that successful writers do?

Circle **T** if the statement is true. Circle **F** if the statement is false.

T	**F**	Good writers do not always answer the question that is given.
T	**F**	The best writers support key ideas with relevant details and examples.
T	**F**	An explanation is successful even when the key points are missing.
T	**F**	Writing is more interesting if the reader must guess what it means.
T	**F**	Successful writers make their meaning clear with the right words.
T	**F**	Good writing is easy to read because the information is organized.

Which statements are true? If you circled **T** for these sentences...

The best writers support key ideas with relevant details and examples.
Successful writers make their meaning clear with the right words.
Good writing is easy to read because the information is organized.

...you would find that most people agree with you.

Good writers make themselves understood to their readers. They state key ideas clearly and give appropriate supporting details. They provide all of the information that is necessary to fulfill the writing task. Good writers use the right words to make their meaning clear. Their writing is easy to understand because the information is organized into logical paragraphs and grammatical sentences.

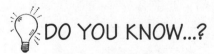 DO YOU KNOW...?

1. When you take the TOEFL, two trained evaluators will read your response to the integrated writing task. They will evaluate it and assign a score of 1 to 5, with 5 the highest score possible. Your response will be judged on the quality of your writing and on how well and how completely you answer the question by presenting key points from the lecture and relating them to information in the reading passage.

2. The evaluators will use criteria similar to those in the following table as they score your writing.

WRITING

INTEGRATED WRITING TASK
Description of Score Levels

5	**A response at this level** ↝ effectively addresses the task by conveying relevant information from the lecture; and ↝ accurately relates key information from the lecture to information in the reading; and ↝ is well organized and coherent; and ↝ contains appropriate grammar and vocabulary, with only occasional minor language errors.
4	**A response at this level** ↝ generally conveys relevant information from the lecture, but may have minor omissions; and ↝ is generally good in relating information from the lecture to information in the reading, but may have minor inaccuracies or vagueness of some content or connections among ideas; and ↝ is generally well organized; and ↝ contains appropriate grammar and vocabulary, but may have noticeable minor language errors or occasional lack of clarity.
3	**A response at this level** ↝ contains some relevant information from the lecture, but may omit one key point; or ↝ conveys some connections between the lecture and the reading, but some content or connections among ideas may be incomplete, inaccurate, or vague; or ↝ contains errors in grammar or usage that result in vagueness of some content or connections among ideas.
2	**A response at this level** ↝ contains some relevant information from the lecture, but may have significant omissions or inaccuracies of key points; or ↝ omits or largely misrepresents the connections between the lecture and the reading; or ↝ contains language errors that obscure meaning of key ideas or connections among ideas.
1	**A response at this level** ↝ contains little or no relevant content from the lecture; or ↝ fails to connect points from the lecture and reading; or ↝ contains language errors that greatly obscure meaning; or ↝ is too brief to allow evaluation of writing proficiency.
0	**A response at this level** ↝ only copies sentences from the reading; or ↝ is not related to the given topic; or ↝ is written in a language other than English; or ↝ is blank.

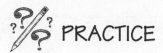 PRACTICE

Exercise 4.5.A

Read the passage and then listen to the recording. Read the integrated writing question and the five responses that follow. Evaluate each response according to the descriptions of the five levels on page 402. Assign each response a score of 5, 4, 3, 2 or 1.

Reading Time – 3 minutes

The discovery of penicillin and other antibiotic drugs is the most dramatic medical development of the twentieth century. These new drugs quickly became known as "wonder drugs" because they saved so many lives that were threatened by major forms of infection. The research that led to their development rested on the belief that chemicals could be found that would destroy specific microorganisms without injuring the human body at the same time. Advances in chemistry and in the knowledge of bacteria quickened the discovery of such chemicals.

In 1933, the first of the sulfa drugs, prontosil, was tested clinically on humans and was found to cure blood infections that would otherwise have been fatal. In 1941, the first successful human tests of penicillin were conducted on cases of streptococcus infections. The discovery of penicillin laid the foundation for even more powerful weapons against specific diseases. Within the next decade, researchers identified some 200 antibiotic substances that were effective against one or another type of bacteria. One of the most important was streptomycin, found to be potent against tuberculosis and other infections that were not affected by penicillin.

Antibiotics gave the medical profession powerful tools that could directly fight a very wide range of specific diseases. They made possible the survival of patients during and after surgery. No longer was it necessary to depend largely on the body's own immune system to fight off major infections; these infections could be attacked directly with drugs. Among the most spectacular effects of antibiotics were reductions in the number of deaths from pneumonia and tuberculosis.

 Disk 6, Track 22

Summarize the main points made in the lecture, explaining how they differ from points made in the reading.

 Stop

Response A   Score: _____

The lecture discusses the resistance of bacteria to antibiotics, which differs from the main idea in the reading that antibiotics are "wonder drugs." When antibiotics were developed in the 1940s, they were successful in curing many diseases. However, bacteria quickly became resistant to some drugs. Today, many people in hospital take antibiotics, but there is the serious danger of hospital infections. Penicillin used to cure diseases such as pneumonia, but today people might still die because bacteria are resistant to the drug.

Bacteria develop resistance to antibiotics because they evolve weapons against the drugs. They can evolve strategies to fight any drug we give them. This situation is similar to the weapons of two armies use in a war. When you treat a disease with an antibiotic, it will kill the bacteria. However, a few cells will survive. Soon the new type of bacteria will appear, and resistant to the antibiotic. Therefore, we should not consider antibiotics as wonder drugs because the bacteria also have strong weapons.

One result of antibiotic resistance is the increase in new cases of tuberculosis. Doctors used to believe that antibiotics were powerful weapons against diseases such as tuberculosis. However, today several types are resistant to antibiotics, so it is a new and serious problem. This is another reason why antibiotics are not wonder drugs.

Response B   Score: _____

I will describe how the resistance of bacteria to antibiotics. First, it's big problem in the hospitals. Hospitals used antibiotics in 1950, but resistance appearing a problem. The reason is danger of hospital infection is very bad so people had better stay home a hospital.

Second, penicillin was a wonder drug in 1940. You gave a man in hospital 10,000 penicillin and he cured the disease. But today you give 24 penicillin but he might die. The reason is bacteria smart so very difficult treat pnemunia and other disease in a hospital. Several people die – because the reason is the resistance of the bacteria to antibiotics.

Third, how does this happen is you dose a colony of bacteria with an antibiotic. The colony killed except a few cells. This is a dangerous problem in a hospital because people may die. Doctors think tuberculosos was a defeated disease but the increase is by 20%.

The changes the view of antibiotics as 'wonder drugs' by resistance of bacteria to antibiotics. It's a big problem today and doctors can't find drugs to cure the disease such as tuberculoses. Penicillin and other antibiotic drugs were wonder drugs in 1940—so it's necessary to have a different view of antibiotics today.

Response C   Score: _____

I discuss a biology professor talk about antibiotics. These new drugs as wonder drugs saving many lifes many people who very sick the diseases. Professor he describe penicilin as wonder drug it causing many people well after sick. The discovery of penicillin and other antibiotic drugs is the most dramatic medical development of the twenteth century quickly become known as 'wonder drugs. Antibiotics gave the medical profession powerful tools that could fight a very wide range of specific diseases. Professor he gave example the antibiotics make the survival of patients. For example, blood infections, pneumonia and tuberculosis. As a result, reductions in the number of death.

Response D   Score: _____

In general, the lecture contradicts the idea that antibiotics are "wonder drugs" as the reading states. On the contrary, antibiotics are not wonder drugs because the resistance of bacteria to antibiotics.

According to the reading, the discovery of penicillin and other antitiotic drugs saved many lives that were threatened by dangerous diseases such a penumonia and tuberculosis. In the twentieth century, penicillin was first a wonder drug because it can cure streptocossus infections. Furthermore, streptomycin found to be potent against tuberculosis. However, the lecture made the point that this is not true in the present. Today tuberculosis is a major illness again because the new strain of bacteria is resistant to antibiotics.

According to the lecture, bacteria have developed effective weapons against some drugs, for example, penicillin. They evolve to counteract antibiotics. It happens when a few cells of bacteria survive because they have the resistance gene. Then new strains of bacteria appeared. After that, antiboitics may attack but they do not kill all disease infections. This serious problem today is the resistance of bacteria to antibiotics.

In the past, antibiotic drugs could attack and kill diseases, but this is not true today. Therefore, it is necessary to develop new wonder drugs to fight disease.

Response E   Score: _____

The resistance of bacteria to antiobiotics changes the view of wonder drugs. One example is penicillin. It is wonder drug in 1941, when the first successful human tests of penicillin. The discovery of penicillin the foundation for even more powerful drugs, for example, antiobiotics. Another example is streptomycin, found against tuberculosis and other infections that were not affected by penicillin.

The resistance of bacteria to antiobiotics to some of the drugs. First example is pnemonia. In the past penicillin cure him, however today he still die. Second example is tuberculosis. The most effects of antibiotics were reductions in the number of deaths, however, since tuberculosis increase 20 precent deaths. It describes the resistance of bacteria to antiobiotics. In the past, it was no problem, however, today it is serious problem. It's changes the view of antiobitics as wonder drugs which saved so many lives. Because today people can still die.

Answers to Exercise 4.5.A are on page 594.

EXTENSION

1. Study the descriptions of the five score levels on page 402. Make sure you understand the description for each level. Check your understanding of the meaning of these words and phrases:

effectively addresses	minor omissions	significant omissions
accurately relates	inaccuracies	misrepresents
coherent	vagueness	obscure meaning
occasional	lack of clarity	writing proficiency

2. Review the five responses in Exercise 4.5.A. In each response, identify the following:

    a. What key points from the lecture does the response convey?
    b. What examples and explanation does the response include?
    c. What transitions and expressions make the writing coherent?
    d. What errors in sentence structure make the meaning unclear?
    e. What errors in word form make the meaning unclear?

    With your teacher and classmates, discuss ways to correct errors that obscure meaning.

3. Review the responses you wrote to the writing questions in units 4.1 through 4.3. Evaluate each response according to the descriptions of the five levels on page 402. What are the areas of strength in your writing? What are your most serious problems? What can you do to improve your writing and earn a high score on the integrated writing task on the TOEFL?

PROGRESS – 4.1 through 4.5

QUIZ 1

Time – approximately 30 minutes

Read the passage and then listen to the recording. You may take notes, and you may use your notes to help you write your response. When you hear the question, uncover the passage and question. Then allow 20 minutes to plan and write your response. Your response will earn a score of 1, 2, 3, 4, or 5, with 5 the highest score.

Reading Time – 3 minutes

Evidence that some animals possess self–awareness comes from a series of experiments in which apes appear to recognize themselves in mirrors. When chimpanzees were first exposed to a mirror they would react to their image as if it were another chimpanzee, with vocalizations and threatening gestures. Eventually, however, they appeared to progress from viewing the image as another chimp to viewing it as themselves. They would stand before the mirror and groom themselves, make faces, and stick out their tongues. Sometimes they just used the mirror to explore parts of their bodies they normally could not see, such as their backs and the insides of their mouths. These results imply that chimpanzees are self–aware because they have a concept of self and are able to recognize the image in the mirror as their own.

One study tried to test more systematically the mirror–recognition ability of chimpanzees by using a procedure called the "mark test." For ten days, chimpanzees were exposed to a mirror. On the eleventh day, they were given a sleeping drug, and researchers marked one eyebrow and one ear on each animal with a bright red dye. The chimpanzees were then watched to see what they would do when they woke up and noticed the red mark. First the chimps were placed in their cage without the mirror. On average, they touched the marked areas only once during a half–hour. Then the mirror was brought in, and the chimpanzees on average touched the marked spots seven times in a half–hour. Some of them touched the marked spots while they looked at their image in the mirror, and then sniffed or examined their fingers. The researchers concluded that the chimpanzees recognized the red mark as being on their own bodies.

Now cover the passage and question. Listen to the recording. When you hear the question, uncover the passage and question and begin your response.

 Disk 6, Track 23

> Summarize the points made in the talk, explaining how they cast doubt on points made in the reading.

 Stop

Writing Time – 20 minutes

Key points for Writing Quiz 1 are on page 595.

Record your score on the Progress Chart on page 696.

WRITING

PROGRESS – 4.1 through 4.5

QUIZ 2   *Time – approximately 30 minutes*

Read the passage and then listen to the recording. You may take notes, and you may use your notes to help you write your response. When you hear the question, uncover the passage and question. Then allow 20 minutes to plan and write your response. Your response will earn a score of 1, 2, 3, 4, or 5, with 5 the highest score.

Reading Time – 3 minutes

Humans have used the windmill to harness wind power for thousands of years. However, it was not until the nineteenth century that windmills possessed the features that made them efficient in the same way as modern wind turbine blades. The windmill was refined when its heavy, inefficient wooden blades were replaced with lighter, faster steel blades around 1870. Over the next century, more than six million small windmills were built in the western United States, where they pumped ground water for livestock and provided the domestic water supply for families living on remote ranches. The first large windmill to produce electricity was a multi–blade design with a 12–kilowatt capability, built in 1888.

Today, wind power is a promising, clean, safe, and environmentally friendly energy resource that can serve as an alternative to electricity generated by fossil fuels such as coal, oil, and natural gas. In 1999, wind–generated electricity exceeded 10,000 megawatts globally, which amounts to approximately 16 billion kilowatt–hours of electricity. This is more than enough to serve five medium–sized cities with a population of 350,000 each.

Wind–generated electricity is projected to be one of the developing world's most important sources of energy, and it also has potential for industrialized nations. Wind power could provide 20 percent of the electricity in the United States, with turbines installed on less than one percent of the nation's land area. Within that area, less than five percent of the land would be occupied by wind equipment; the remaining 95 percent could continue to be used for farming or ranching.

Now cover the passage and question. Listen to the recording. When you hear the question, uncover the passage and question and begin your response.

 Disk 6, Track 24

> Summarize the advantages and disadvantages of wind power discussed in the lecture, explaining how they agree with or depart from points made in the reading.

 Stop

Writing Time – 20 minutes

Key points for Writing Quiz 2 are on page 595.

Record your score on the Progress Chart on page 696.

PROGRESS – 4.1 through 4.5

QUIZ 3   *Time – approximately 30 minutes*

Read the passage and then listen to the recording. You may take notes, and you may use your notes to help you write your response. When you hear the question, uncover the passage and question. Then allow 20 minutes to plan and write your response. Your response will earn a score of 1, 2, 3, 4, or 5, with 5 the highest score.

Reading Time – 3 minutes

Thomas Malthus was an English economist, sociologist, and pioneer in modern population study. He was one of the first writers to analyze the relationship between population and the economy. In 1798 Malthus published *An Essay on the Principles of Population*, warning about the effects of rapid population growth on human well–being. He asserted that poverty and suffering are unavoidable because population increases faster than the means of subsistence.

Malthus suggested that human rates of reproduction are so great that if all the offspring survived, the population would double every generation. This rapid growth causes a constant struggle for existence and competition for food and other means of survival. Besides a limited food supply, the only negative checks on population growth are disease, famine, and war.

The Malthusian theory of population growth states that there is a universal tendency for human population—unless checked—to grow at a geometric rate. This means that population increases at a rate of 1, 2, 4, 8, 16, and so on. However, food production tends to increase at an arithmetic rate, 1, 2, 3, 4, 5..., because the amount of land is fixed while labor input keeps growing. Per capita food production (the amount of food for each person) would thus decline over time, thereby limiting population growth. The theory relies on the economic law that an increasing population working on a fixed amount of land would reduce per capita output and incomes to the bare subsistence level. The Malthusian theory influenced classical economists and was later adapted by neo–Malthusian economists in the 1970s.

Now cover the passage and question. Listen to the recording. When you hear the question, uncover the passage and question and begin your response.

 Disk 6, Track 25

> Summarize the points made in the lecture, explaining how they contradict points made in the reading.

 Stop

Writing Time – 20 minutes

Key points for Writing Quiz 3 are on page 595.

Record your score on the Progress Chart on page 696.

4.6 Independent Writing: Prewriting

FOCUS

Imagine you are taking an essay examination, and you see the following question:

> Do you agree or disagree with the following statement?
> **Teachers are responsible for motivating students to learn.**
> Use specific reasons and examples to support your opinion.

What would you do to answer this question? Check all of the things that you would do:

____ Just start writing as quickly as you can.

____ Think about everything the question asks you to do.

____ Write about a topic that you think is more interesting.

____ Decide whether you agree or disagree with the given statement.

____ Try to guess the opinion of the person who will grade the essay.

____ Make a list of your favorite teachers.

____ Organize your thoughts in the form of an outline.

Most people cannot just start writing quickly and produce a good essay, so that is not a good idea. It is better to start by thinking about everything the question asks you to do.

Writing about a different topic, even a more interesting one, is not a good idea. On the TOEFL, your essay will receive a score of zero if you do not write about the assigned topic. For this question, you must either agree or disagree with the given statement. Do you believe it is true that teachers are responsible for motivating students to learn? Or do you believe it is not true? Your position on the topic will be the main idea of your essay.

Some students think their opinion must agree with the opinion of the person who will grade the essay. This is not true. On the TOEFL, you should not be concerned about whether the essay readers will agree with your opinion. Rather, you should be concerned about whether the essay readers will understand your opinion because it is stated clearly and is well supported with specific reasons and examples.

Should you make a list of your favorite teachers? Maybe. Some of your own teachers might be good examples to help you support your position. Should you organize your thoughts in the form of an outline? Yes, because this will help you write a better, more organized essay.

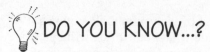 DO YOU KNOW...?

1. The TOEFL independent writing task requires you to write an essay in response to a given topic. You must be able to generate and organize ideas, and to develop and support these ideas in essay format. You have 30 minutes to plan, write, and revise your essay. Your essay will be evaluated on how effectively it:

   - addresses the topic and task (answers the question);
   - shows organization and development; and
   - supports a thesis or opinion about the topic.

2. An *essay* is a written work that contains three or more paragraphs. The function of an essay is to communicate to a reader an opinion about a topic and to provide information that supports or defends this opinion. An essay has three parts: introduction, body, and conclusion.

Parts of an Essay	
Introduction	The *introduction* is the first paragraph of the essay. The introductory paragraph tells your readers what the essay is about. It restates the question in your own words and expresses the main idea, which is called the *thesis* or *thesis statement*. The thesis statement is often the last sentence of the introductory paragraph.
Body	The *body* is the center of the essay. Each body paragraph contains one *supporting point* that develops the thesis. The body paragraphs are sometimes called *developmental paragraphs*. They contain specific examples, reasons, and other details that support the thesis. Your essay for the independent writing task will probably contain two to four body paragraphs.
Conclusion	The *conclusion* is the last paragraph of the essay. The concluding paragraph can restate your thesis, summarize your points, or make a recommendation. The conclusion completes the essay.

3. *Prewriting* is the planning that you do before you start writing your essay. Prewriting includes:

   - reading and thinking about the question;
   - brainstorming and making notes on paper;
   - deciding what your thesis or main idea will be; and
   - writing an outline of your essay.

4. *Brainstorming* is quickly generating ideas—examples, reasons, personal experiences, and other details—in the form of notes, a list, or a diagram. Brainstorming is thinking on paper. It is writing down as many ideas as possible in a short amount of time.

5. In the independent writing task, your *thesis* will be your opinion about the topic that is assigned in the question. For example, your thesis may:

   - state that you agree with a given statement; or
   - state that you disagree with a given statement; or
   - state which of two positions you hold on a given issue.

WRITING

6. An *outline* is a simple plan of your essay. Sometimes it is a short list of your points. Sometimes it is a diagram of each paragraph. Before you write your outline, decide what your thesis will be. Then choose ideas from your brainstorming that will support this position. Choose two to four of your best examples or reasons and discard the rest. Decide the most effective order for arranging these ideas, and write your outline. Your outline should be short. It does not have to be written in complete sentences, but the ideas should be in an order that makes sense.

7. Here is an example of an independent writing task and a student's brainstorming, thesis, and outline:

> Do you agree or disagree with the following statement?
> **Teachers are responsible for motivating students to learn.**
> Use specific reasons and examples to support your opinion.

Brainstorming

Disagree—Student is responsible, not teacher
- learning before & after school – no teacher
- <u>self–motivated</u>
- S not motivated, T can't help
- Parents are responsible
- People <u>naturally</u> want to learn
- my teacher – grade 5
- work/<u>whole life</u>
- learning – <u>no teacher</u>

Outline

- Natural love of learning
- Learning during whole life
- Develop self–motivation

Thesis

Although many people believe it is the teacher's responsibility to motivate students to learn, students will not learn much unless they are self–motivated.

8. Here is another example:

> Some people like to spend their leisure time doing activities with a lot of people. Others prefer to spend their leisure in quiet ways by themselves or with one other person. Which do you prefer? Use specific reasons and examples to support your answer.

Brainstorming

<u>Activities with people</u>
        reason – desk job, alone (computer)
active things/play <u>tennis</u> & <u>basketball</u>
        good for exercise, health
        social
        time with friends/go <u>bowling</u>
college <u>basketball</u> team
enjoy – <u>rafting</u>/teamwork important
        safety
develop important skills

Outline

1. Intro

2. Enjoyment and exercise:
        bowling
        tennis

3. Teamwork:
        basketball
        rafting

Thesis

Since I work mainly by myself in my job as a computer specialist, I prefer leisure activities with other people that provide enjoyment, exercise, and teamwork.

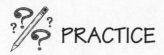 PRACTICE

Exercise 4.6.A

For each writing question below, plan how you will write an essay that will:

- answer the question;
- show organization and development; and
- support a thesis.

Brainstorm and make any notes that will help you plan an essay. Write an outline and thesis statement for each topic. In this exercise, you do not have to write the essay. Focus on writing a good thesis and outline in five minutes.

Time – 5 minutes each

1. Do you agree or disagree with the following statement?
   Children should not have to work or help with household tasks; their only responsibility should be to study.
   Use specific reasons and examples to support your opinion.

2. Some people argue for a broad university education in which students learn about many different subjects. Others argue for a specialized university education in which students learn only about a specific field of study. Which position do you agree with? Use specific reasons and examples to support your opinion.

3. Do you agree or disagree with the following statement?
   You should not believe everything that you read in the newspaper.
   Use specific reasons and examples to support your opinion.

Answers to Exercise 4.6.A will vary.

WRITING

EXTENSION

1. Choose one outline and thesis statement that you wrote for Exercise 4.6.A. Work in a group of three students. Make copies of your outline and thesis, and give a copy to everyone in your group. Read and discuss each student's paper. Answer the following questions about each:

    a. Will the finished essay answer the question?
    b. Will the finished essay show organization and development?
    c. Will the finished essay support the thesis?

    Make suggestions that will help each student improve in the future.

2. Choose one outline and thesis statement that you wrote for Exercise 4.6.A and complete the essay. Allow 25 minutes to write the essay. Then share and discuss your essay in a group of three students. Make copies of your outline, thesis, and essay, and give a copy to everyone in your group. Read and discuss each student's paper. Answer the following questions about each:

    a. Does the essay answer the question?
    b. Does the essay show organization and development?
    c. Does the essay support the thesis?

    Make suggestions that will help each student improve in the future.

4.7 Independent Writing: Stating and Supporting an Opinion

 FOCUS

Read the following essay question and the first paragraph of a student's response:

> Some people think that government should spend as much money as possible on developing space technology for the exploration of the moon and other planets. Others think that this money should be spent on solving the basic problems of society on Earth. Which view do you agree with? Use specific reasons and examples to support your answer.

> Society is often divided on major issues involving government spending. One group believes that we should spend as much money as possible on space exploration, while another group thinks that we should spend this money on solving basic social problems on Earth. I believe there are stronger reasons for spending on space technology because this leads to knowledge that will benefit society on Earth.

Think about each sentence in the paragraph. What does each sentence do?

The first sentence introduces the general topic of the essay: how the government should spend money.

> Society is often divided on major issues involving government spending.

The next sentence restates the question in the writer's own words.

> One group believes that we should spend as much money as possible on space exploration, while another group thinks that we should spend this money on solving basic social problems on Earth.

 The last sentence states the writer's opinion. This is the ***thesis statement***, the main idea of the essay. The rest of the essay must support this idea.

> I believe there are stronger reasons for spending on space technology because this leads to knowledge that will benefit society on Earth.

 DO YOU KNOW...?

1. On the TOEFL, you have 30 minutes to plan, write, and revise your response to the independent writing question. Your response should address the writing task by clearly stating and supporting your opinion about the topic.

2. You must type your essay on the computer keyboard. Do not write your entire essay on paper and then try to type it into the computer; you will not have enough time to do this. Organize your notes on paper, and write an outline. Then type your response directly into the typing box on the screen.

3. The independent writing question requires you to do more than one thing. For example, it may ask you to (1) state your position on a given topic, and (2) support this position with specific reasons and examples. You must answer all parts of the question.

4. Two trained evaluators will read your essay. They will rate your writing on how well you:

- organize ideas effectively in answering the question;
- state and support an opinion; and
- develop ideas with appropriate reasons, examples, and personal experience.

5. A very important part of the question is *Use specific reasons and examples to support your opinion*. The readers who rate your essay are *not* interested in what your opinion is, but they *are* interested in how you support your opinion with appropriate ideas and details.

6. The best way to approach the independent writing task is to use your time wisely to plan, write, and revise your essay.

PLAN	5 minutes	• Decide what your thesis will be. • Plan what information to present, and in what order.
WRITE	20 minutes	• Write a separate paragraph to develop each major point. • Each point should directly support your thesis.
REVISE	5 minutes	• Allow time to correct grammar and vocabulary errors.

7. A well–organized essay has an introduction, a body, and a conclusion. The introduction communicates your opinion about the topic. The body contains supporting ideas that develop your opinion. The conclusion completes the essay.

8. The ***introduction*** is the first paragraph of an essay. The introduction tells your readers what the essay is about. It focuses on the topic and expresses your ***thesis***, which is sometimes called the ***controlling idea***. The thesis is an essential part of your essay because it expresses your opinion about the topic.

9. The thesis is often stated in the last sentence of the introductory paragraph. The thesis statement may preview the points you will make in the body of your essay, in the same order in which they will be discussed. Previewing your supporting points will help your readers know how your essay will be organized.

10. A good introduction contains three or four sentences.

Sentence 1	• introduces the general topic of your essay.
Sentence 2	• focuses on the question; • may restate the question in your own words.
Sentences 3 – 4	• states your thesis; • may preview your supporting points in the order in which you will discuss them.

11. The *body* of the essay consists of the middle paragraphs, which are sometimes called *developmental paragraphs* because they contain ideas that develop the thesis. Each body paragraph should have a *topic sentence* that expresses the main point of the paragraph. The topic sentence of the paragraph should also directly support the thesis; for this reason, it is called a *supporting point*. The rest of the sentences in the paragraph should give appropriate examples, reasons, facts, personal experiences, or other *supporting details*.

✓ 12. Your essay for the independent writing task will probably contain two to four body paragraphs. Each body paragraph should contain four or more sentences.

Sentence 1	• is the topic sentence that states the main idea of the paragraph; • supports the thesis of the essay.
Sentences 2 – 4	• provide specific examples, reasons, or other details that support the topic sentence.
Other Sentences	• provide additional details that support the topic sentence.

✓ 13. The *conclusion* is the last paragraph of an essay. The conclusion is often very short and may contain only one or two sentences. The conclusion should leave your readers with a feeling of completion. It can do one or more of the following:

- restate your thesis in different words (paraphrase);
- summarize your supporting points;
- draw a conclusion;
- make a prediction; or
- make a recommendation.

14. Here is an example of an independent writing task and a student's essay:

> Some people think that government should spend as much money as possible on developing space technology for the exploration of the moon and other planets. Others think that this money should be spent on solving the basic problems of society on Earth. Which view do you agree with? Use specific reasons and examples to support your answer.

STUDENT'S ESSAY   Word count: 271

　　Society is often divided on major issues involving government spending. One group believes that we should spend as much money as possible on space exploration, while another group thinks that we should spend this money on solving basic social problems on Earth. I believe there are stronger reasons for spending on space technology because this leads to knowledge that will benefit society on Earth.

　　Spending money on space technology can lead to better ways to produce food and clothing. Space travel requires special ways to preserve and store food for a long journey. Scientists also work on ways to grow vegetables and fruits in space so that astronauts can have fresh food. Scientists must develop new types of clothing made from new materials. Many of these new methods of food and clothing production also benefit people on Earth.

WRITING

Space exploration has led to important developments in communications technology. One of the first government projects in space technology was for satellite communications. Today, this technology benefits everyone who uses satellite television or telephones.

The most important reason for spending money on space technology is that it promotes international cooperation. When the governments of several different countries work together on space projects, there is better communication between countries. The international space station is a good example of international cooperation that benefits everyone on Earth. Not only does it lead to scientific progress, but it also promotes international understanding.

In conclusion, several developments in space technology have already helped society on Earth. If we spend money on space programs, we may discover even greater knowledge that will improve our life and promote world peace.

The student has chosen the position that government should spend as much money as possible on developing space technology. The thesis is stated in the last sentence of the introduction:

I believe there are stronger reasons for spending on space technology because this leads to knowledge that will benefit society on Earth.

The student makes three supporting points. Each supporting point is the topic sentence of one of the body paragraphs. Each body paragraph develops its topic sentence with examples and reasons. Each body paragraph therefore supports and develops the thesis of the essay:

Supporting Point / Topic Sentence	Supporting Details
Spending money on space technology can lead to better ways to produce food and clothing.	ways to preserve and store food; ways to grow vegetables and fruits; new types of clothing
Space exploration has led to important developments in communications technology.	satellite communications; television; telephones
The most important reason for spending money on space technology is that it promotes international cooperation.	better communication between countries; international space station

In the conclusion, the student restates the thesis:

In conclusion, several developments in space technology have already helped society on Earth.

The student also makes a prediction:

If we spend money on space programs, we may discover even greater knowledge that will improve our life and promote world peace.

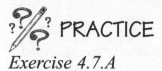 PRACTICE

Exercise 4.7.A

Read the following independent writing question and a student's essay:

> Do you agree or disagree with the following statement?
> **The best things in life do not cost money.**
> Use specific reasons and examples to support your opinion.

WRITING

Many of our favorite activities require us to spend money. Some important things in life, such as getting a good education and buying a home, cost a lot of money. However, it does not cost money to experience the best things in life: enjoying nature and being with our friends and family.

We can relax and enjoy the beauty of nature without spending money. Walking in the park, looking at the colorful leaves, and watching the snow falling are good ways to relax. Listening to the beautiful songs of birds does not cost money, but it can make us feel peaceful. Also, we can enjoy nature by having a garden. When I was a child, I helped my grandmother in her vegetable garden. We pulled up carrots and ate them, and we watched the butterflies and birds. I have many beautiful memories of sunshine and happiness in my grandmother's garden.

It does not cost money to spend time with our friends and family. We can visit friends and have a good time by talking and laughing. Sometimes we need a little money to go to a movie. However, our time together is more important than the money that we spend. We can do a lot of things that are free. For example, we can go to the library. When I was little, I used to walk to the library with my mother and sister every week to borrow books. When we got home, we sat on the porch and read to each other. Many of our best memories result from these simple things.

Money is necessary in our lives, but having a lot of money does not always lead to happiness. The most important things in life do not require a lot of money. If we learn to enjoy simple things, we will have many wonderful memories, and our memories are entirely free.

Now answer the following questions. Discuss your answers with your teacher and classmates.

1. How many parts does the question have? What does each part ask you to do?

2. Does the essay address all parts of the question?

3. How is the essay organized?

4. What does the writer do in the introduction?

5. What is the thesis or main idea of the essay?

6. How does the writer support the thesis?

7. What is the topic sentence of each body paragraph?

8. What specific examples, reasons, and other details does the writer give? What is their purpose?

9. What does the writer do in the conclusion?

10. Does the essay effectively address the topic and task? Why or why not?

Answers to Exercise 4.7.A are on page 595.

Exercise 4.7.B

Your teacher will assign one of the following essay questions. Read the question carefully, and then plan and write a response. To make this practice more like the real test, allow 30 minutes to complete the essay. Use your time like this:

      5 minutes – to brainstorm and write an outline;
      20 minutes – to write the introduction, body, and conclusion; and
      5 minutes – to check your essay and make corrections.

1. Do you agree or disagree with the following statement?
   A student must like a teacher in order to learn from the teacher.
   Use specific reasons and examples to support your opinion.

2. Do you agree or disagree with the following statement?
   Youth is wasted on the young.
   Use specific reasons and examples to support your opinion.

3. Do you agree or disagree with the following statement?
   We should pay attention to the opinions of famous people.
   Use specific reasons and examples to support your opinion.

4. Some people think that teachers and education professionals should make all of the important decisions about what subjects are taught in schools. Others think that business and industry professionals should make all of the major decisions. Which view do you agree with? Use specific reasons and examples to support your opinion.

5. Do you agree or disagree with the following statement?
   In any society, the contributions of scientists and engineers are more important than the contributions of artists and writers.
   Use specific reasons and examples to support your opinion.

6. Some students prefer to live on campus in a dormitory. Others prefer to live in an apartment or house off campus. Which do you prefer? Use specific reasons and examples to support your opinion.

Answers to Exercise 4.7.B will vary.

EXTENSION

1. Share and discuss the essay that you wrote for Exercise 4.7.B. Work in a group of three students. Make copies of your essay, and give a copy to everyone in your group. Read and discuss each student's essay. Answer the following questions about each:

   a. How is the essay organized?
   b. What does the writer do in the introduction?
   c. What is the thesis or main idea of the essay?
   d. What is the topic sentence of each body paragraph?
   e. What supporting details does the writer give?
   f. What does the writer do in the conclusion?

   Make suggestions that will help each student improve in the future.

4.8 Writing Coherently

 FOCUS

Read the following essay question and a paragraph from the body of a student's essay:

> Do you agree or disagree with the following statement?
> **The things we learn from our friends are more important than what we learn from our family.**
> Use specific reasons and examples to support your opinion.

> While my friends have taught me to enjoy my life, my family has taught me to be strong. My friends have taught me how to feel independent. They have encouraged me to be myself, to have a lot of fun, and to find happiness in life. On the other hand, my mother has taught me to be independent in a very different way. When I was a child, she gave me advice such as "Fight your own battles." She said that so I would be strong because she could not always protect me. Sometimes this was very difficult for me when I wanted my mother to help me, even though I knew her advice was important.

This paragraph is easy to read and understand. What makes it so? Check all of the statements that are true:

___ All of the sentences in the paragraph are simple.

___ The topic sentence is stated clearly at the beginning.

___ The sentences are written in a logical order.

___ All of the ideas in the paragraph support the topic sentence.

___ The writer uses appropriate transitions to connect ideas.

All of the statements are true except the first one. All of the sentences in the paragraph are *not* simple, but they *are* easy to understand. This is because the topic sentence is stated clearly at the beginning, the sentences are written in a logical order, and all of the ideas in the paragraph support the topic sentence. Moreover, the writer uses appropriate transitions to connect ideas.

The paragraph is well organized and coherent. When a piece of writing is **coherent**, it is easy for readers to understand.

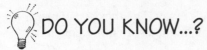

DO YOU KNOW...?

1. Two trained evaluators will read your essay. They will rate your writing on how well you:

    - organize ideas effectively in answering the question; and
    - display unity and coherence.

2. A well–organized essay has an introduction, a body, and a conclusion. Each body paragraph contains one major point that is developed with examples, reasons, and other supporting details. Each body paragraph supports the thesis of the essay. When all of the ideas and information in the essay support the thesis, the essay is said to have *unity*.

3. The body paragraphs should be arranged in the order that will best support the thesis. This is why having an outline is important. Sometimes the body paragraphs are best arranged from the most important point to the least important point. Sometimes it is more effective to put the most important point last, just before the conclusion. Sometimes the points are previewed in the introduction. When the body paragraphs are arranged effectively and logically, the essay is said to have *coherence*.

4. An essay is *coherent* when all of the ideas within paragraphs and between paragraphs are connected logically. The following *transitions* will help you express relationships between ideas and give your essay unity and coherence.

FUNCTION	TRANSITIONS		
Introduce examples or reasons	because first	for example for instance	one reason is such as
Add examples or reasons	also and another example is as well as	finally furthermore in addition moreover	next not only…but also second, third… similarily
Show contrast between ideas	although but by contrast even though however	in contrast instead on the contrary on the one hand… on the other hand	nevertheless rather though while yet
Emphasize or show importance	clearly certainly indeed	in fact moreover most importantly	the best example the most important surely
Make a conclusion	consequently in conclusion	in short in summary	therefore thus

5. Here is an example of an independent writing question and a student's essay. The thesis statement appears in bold text in the introduction. Notice how the transitions make the essay more coherent and easier to understand:

Do you agree or disagree with the following statement?
The things we learn from our friends are more important than what we learn from our family.
Use specific reasons and examples to support your opinion.

STUDENT'S ESSAY   Word count: 340

When I think about the lessons I have learned in my life, I find many similarities in what I learned from my friends and from my family. There are also differences. Both kinds of lessons have been very important to me. *However*, when I consider them carefully, **I know that the lessons from my family are more important**.

While my friends have taught me to enjoy my life, my family has taught me to be strong. My friends have taught me how to feel independent. They have encouraged me to be myself, to have a lot of fun, *and* to find happiness in life. *On the other hand*, my mother has taught me to be independent in a very different way. When I was a child, she gave me advice *such as* "Fight your own battles." She said that so I would be strong *because* she could not always protect me. Sometimes this was very difficult for me when I wanted my mother to help me, *even though* I knew her advice was important.

Furthermore, my family has taught me compassion and forgiveness. My younger brother taught me these qualities. I will never forget that once I was cruel to him *because* I was angry. My brother was afraid of the dark, *but* I turned off the lights to scare him. He was only six years old, *and* he was afraid and cried. *But* later he asked me to read a book to him until he fell asleep. It was his way to forgive me. I can never forget how my little brother taught me how to forgive.

I believe that our family teaches us the most important things *because* the lessons from family last longer. My family has taught me to be independent and strong, *and* this will help me during my whole life. *Moreover*, they have taught me how to forgive, which is necessary for getting along with other people. *In short*, the lessons from my family were not always enjoyable, *yet* they are deeper in my heart.

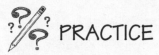 **PRACTICE**

Exercise 4.8.A

Read the following independent writing question and a student's essay:

> Some people learn by reading about things. Others learn by doing things. Which of these methods of learning is better for you? Use specific reasons and examples to support your choice.

There are a lot of different ways for people to learn new things. People can learn by reading, or they can learn by doing things. For some people, learning is better either one way or the other. I prefer to learn by doing things because when I do something myself it becomes more real than when I read about it.

I learned how to ride a bicycle and drive a car by experience. I rode a bicycle when I was six years old. Because I could not read about it, I had to get on the bicycle and use my feet and hands. I could also learn from my mistake when I fell off my bicycle. Similarly, I earned to drive a car by doing it. Although I had to study a driving manual and take a test on a computer, I could not learn driving well until I practiced driving in a car.

Learning mathematics is another example of learning by doing things. When I was in sixth grade, my teacher made the students measure our classroom. We measured the length and width of the room. Therefore, we learned how to calculate the area of our classroom or any other room. This experience made mathematics become real for me.

Finally, I learned how to use a computer by doing it. I tried to read the computer manual, but this was difficult for me because the book was very complex. I learned more when I sat at the keyboard and tried using several keys. Of course, my teacher explained some things about the computer. However, I could learn best when I experienced it.

It is true that I have to learn some things by reading, such as history and literature. Reading gives me important knowledge. However, for most skills that I need for my life, such as driving a car and using a computer, I must experience using them in order to learn the skills well. Therefore, I prefer to learn through action.

Now answer the following questions. Discuss your answers with your teacher and classmates.

1. What does the question ask you to do?

2. What does the writer do in the introduction?

3. What is the thesis or main idea of the essay?

4. How is the essay organized?

5. What is the topic sentence of each body paragraph?

6. Does the essay have unity? Why or why not?

7. What transitions help give the essay coherence?

8. Does the essay effectively address the topic and task? Why or why not?

Answers to Exercise 4.8.A are on page 595.

Exercise 4.8.B

Your teacher will assign one of the following essay questions. Read the question carefully, and then plan and write a response. To make this practice more like the real test, allow 30 minutes to complete the essay. Use your time like this:

- 5 minutes – to brainstorm and write an outline;
- 20 minutes – to write the introduction, body, and conclusion; and
- 5 minutes – to check your essay and make corrections.

1. Do you agree or disagree with the following statement?
    All high school students should be required to have three years of studying a foreign language.
    Use specific reasons and examples to support your opinion.

2. Do you agree or disagree with the following statement?
    The automobile is destroying our quality of life.
    Use specific reasons and examples to support your opinion.

3. Some people like to be the leader of a group. Others like to be a member of a group in which another person is the leader. Which do you prefer? Use specific reasons and examples to support your answer.

4. Do you agree or disagree with this statement?
    Employers should be required to provide smoking areas for their employees who smoke cigarettes.
    Use specific reasons and examples to support your opinion.

5. Some students prefer to study at a large university that has several thousand students. Other students prefer studying at a small school that has only a few hundred students. Which of these two types of schools do you prefer? Use specific reasons and examples to support your answer.

6. Do you agree or disagree with the following statement?
    The use of electronic mail (e–mail) makes people become better writers.
    Use specific reasons and examples to support your opinion.

Answers to Exercise 4.8.B will vary.

 EXTENSION

1. Share and discuss the essay that you wrote for Exercise 4.8.B. Work in a group of three students. Make copies of your essay, and give a copy to everyone in your group. Read and discuss each student's essay. Answer the following questions about each:

    a. What is the thesis or main idea of the essay?
    b. Is the essay easy to understand? Why or why not?
    c. What supporting points does the writer make?
    d. What supporting details does the writer give?
    e. Does the essay have unity and coherence? Why or why not?
    f. What transitions does the writer use? Are they used correctly?

    Make suggestions that will help each student improve in the future.

4.9 Checking Sentence Variety and Word Choice

 FOCUS

Read the following essay question and a paragraph from a student's essay:

Do you agree or disagree with the following statement?
You will not learn much about life if you are always comfortable.
Use specific reasons and examples to support your opinion.

> Children must learning about life in a comfortable place. If a child is no safe, the child can't learn nothing. I wanna have children in the future. My duty is for keep my children safety and protection from bad experiences. I gonna give my children food, clothes, and other stuffs. Because my child is comfortable, they will learn alot of things about life. On the contrary, I disagree with the statement.

The writer makes several errors in word choice. Can you identify them? Underline words and phrases that are incorrect or confusing.

Look at these words and phrases in the paragraph. How many did you underline?

must learning	is for keep	stuffs
no safe	safety	Because my child is
can't learn nothing	protection	alot
wanna	I gonna	On the contrary

Now read the same paragraph without errors.

> Children must learn about life in a comfortable place. If a child is not safe, the child can't learn anything. I want to have children in the future. My duty will be to keep my children safe and protect them from bad experiences. I am going to give my children food, clothes, and other things. If my children are comfortable, they will learn a lot of things about life. Therefore, I disagree with the statement.

On the TOEFL, an essay can have a few language errors and still earn a high score—if the errors are minor and do not obscure meaning. However, frequent or serious errors in word choice will result in a lower score.

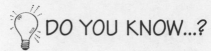

DO YOU KNOW...?

1. On the TOEFL, you have 30 minutes to plan, write, and revise your response to the independent writing task. Allow around 5 minutes at the end to check and correct your sentence structure, sentence variety, word choice, and spelling.

2. Two trained evaluators will read your essay. They will rate your writing on how well you:

    - display unity and coherence; and
    - use English words and sentences effectively.

3. Your essay will be easier to read, more interesting, and more effective if you:

    - use a variety of short and long sentences;
    - avoid common sentence errors; and
    - use appropriate word choice and word forms.

4. Your essay should contain a variety of short and long sentences. If a sentence has more than one clause, the clauses must be joined correctly with a conjunction, subordinator, or conjunctive adverb.

Conjunctions				
and	but	or	so	yet
Subordinators				
although	if	since	unless	where
because	just as	though	when	while
Conjunctive Adverbs				
as a result	furthermore	in addition	moreover	therefore
consequently	however	instead	similarly	thus

5. There are several ways to combine two or more short sentences into one long sentence. Here are some examples:

Short	Living off campus is exciting. Living off campus is more independent. I prefer the convenience of living on campus.
Long	Living off campus is exciting *and* more independent, *but* I prefer the convenience of living on campus.
Short	Teachers are important for motivating children. Parents are even more important.
Long	*Although* teachers are important for motivating children, parents are even more important.
Short	Athletes are such great entertainers. People like to watch athletes play.
Long	*Since* athletes are such great entertainers, people like to watch them play.
Short	Children should grow up in the country. Children can know nature.
Long	Children should grow up in the country, *where* they can know nature.

Short	You are always comfortable. You will never have to struggle. You will not learn much about life.
Long	*If* you are always comfortable, you will never have to struggle; *as a result*, you will not learn much about life.

Short	Students are responsible for their own learning. Students should be self–motivated.
Long	Students are responsible for their own learning, *so* they should be self–motivated.
Long	*Because* students are responsible for their own learning, they should be self–motivated.
Long	Students are responsible for their own learning; *therefore*, they should be self–motivated.

Short	Some people like living in a rural area. I prefer the urban lifestyle.
Long	Some people like living in a rural area, *but* I prefer the urban lifestyle.
Long	*While* some people like living in a rural area, I prefer the urban lifestyle.
Long	Some people like living in a rural area; *however*, I prefer the urban lifestyle.

6. Inappropriate word choice and incorrect word forms may obscure meaning, making your essay difficult to understand. It is best to use vocabulary you are familiar with, but avoid slang and other words that are too informal for an academic essay.

Inappropriate	Parents have to get kids food and other stuff.
Appropriate	Parents have to provide children with food and other necessities.

Inappropriate	Join a hobby club helping you make new friends.
Appropriate	Joining a hobby club will help you make new friends.

Inappropriate	People driving more careful the children are walking to school.
Appropriate	People should drive more carefully when children are walking to school.

Inappropriate	I'm gonna go for a job in broadcast communications.
Appropriate	I am going to look for a job in broadcast communications.

Inappropriate	Competitive sports are totally cool.
Appropriate	Competitive sports benefit us in several important ways.

7. Some words that are useful in writing academic essays are:

although	contribute	essential	issue	probably
benefit	controversy	examine	necessary	provide
cause	dilemma	influence	neither	solution
consequence	effect	instead	prefer	view

WRITING

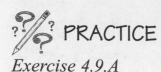 PRACTICE

Exercise 4.9.A

Read the following paragraphs. Check sentence structure, sentence variety, and word choice. Make any corrections that will improve the paragraphs. There may be more than one way to correct an error.

1.

I decide not to get married two years ago. I could finish my university studies. My father he wanted me to get married. My parents they allow me decide. I had married, I have to stay in my husband's home. Because in my culture, married woman, she has a duty to her husband, it's our tradition. I choose finishing my degree instead. I will to be a graduate student in Toronto. I will earning my master's degree in business economics.

2.

I prefer students should have several short vacations throughout the year instead to one long vacation. Students work hardly and need a brake often. Students in my country have several short holidays while every seasons. On the contrast, American students have one long vacation in a summer. I read a paper say that American students forgetting what they learned because the long vacation. This why I belief several short vacations is good than one long vacation.

3.

There are many advantage in having friends that different to me. Such as my friend who is from Turkey learns me alot about his culture. His family is so big and my family is not big. As a result, I like to go to his house to visiting his family. I enjoy the good food. I enjoy the talking because is really cool and interesting. Other friend is an artist. My friend makes pictures and does other arts. It's really cool. In conclusion, my artist friend is not alike me, I learn good things about art from him.

Exercise 4.9.B

Read the following independent writing question and a student's essay. Check sentence structure, sentence variety, and word choice. Make any corrections that will improve the essay. There may be more than one way to correct an error.

Some people prefer occupations in which they work primarily with machines. Others prefer occupations in which they work mainly with people. Which type of occupation do you prefer? Use specific reasons and examples to support your opinion.

Occupations are mainly two kinds. Some occupations require your work primarily with machines. Other need working with other people. My job is working with machines, especial computers, so I prefer this kind.

Computers are important in the society. I am a computer programmer at a medical university. I like to solving the problems of medical record system. Computer has improved business, research, educational, and many the field of study. Many occupations require specialization in computers. People need specialization training. It's in area of computer operations.

On the other hand, some occupations work mainly with people. It's also neccesary for my job. Because I work a team with two other people. Therefore we must help each one. We solve the problems.

In conclusion, I prefer to working with machines. Because machines need people to operate. In addition, machines improve peoples life. Many occupations need specialization, such as computer programmer. But also need ability for communication to other people. Therefore I believe to work with both machines and people are best kind of job.

Corrections for Exercises 4.9.A and 4.9.B are on page 596.

Exercise 4.9.C

Your teacher will assign one of the following essay questions. Read the question carefully, and then plan and write a response. To make this practice more like the real test, allow 30 minutes to complete the essay. Use your time like this:

> ✎ 5 minutes – to brainstorm and write an outline;
> ✎ 20 minutes – to write the introduction, body, and conclusion; and
> ✎ 5 minutes – to check your essay and make corrections.

1. Do you agree or disagree with the following statement?
   You can learn a lot about people by the clothes they wear.
   Use specific reasons and examples to support your opinion.

2. Some people prefer working for a very large company that has several hundred employees. Others prefer working for a small company where they know all of their co–workers. Which do you prefer? Use specific reasons and examples to support your opinion.

3. Do you agree or disagree with the following statement?
   Leaders must pay attention to the advice and opinions of other people.
   Use specific reasons and examples to support your opinion.

4. Do you agree or disagree with the following statement?
   Every child should be raised in a home with two parents.
   Use specific reasons and examples to support your opinion.

5. Some people believe that in high school, boys should be in classes with only boys, and girls should be in classes with only girls. Other people believe that high school classes should be coeducational, with students of both genders studying together. Which view do you agree with? Use specific reasons and examples to support your opinion.

6. Do you agree or disagree with the following statement?
   Technological progress has made us lazy.
   Use specific reasons and examples to support your opinion.

Answers to Exercise 4.9.C will vary.

EXTENSION

1. Review the essay you wrote for one of the essay questions in units 4.7 through 4.9. Check your sentence structure, sentence variety, and vocabulary. Ask yourself the following questions:

    a. Are all of my sentences complete, with correctly formed subjects and verbs?
    b. Are there any grammar errors that need correcting?
    c. Does my essay have a variety of short and long sentences?
    d. Does my essay use appropriate word choice and correct word forms?
    e. Are there any misspelled words that need correcting?
    f. What changes can I make to improve the essay?

2. Share and discuss your essay for one of the essay questions in units 4.7 through 4.9. Work in a group of three students. Make copies of your essay, and give a copy to everyone in your group. Read and discuss each student's essay. Answer the following questions about each:

    a. Is the essay easy to read and understand? Why or why not?
    b. Does the essay have unity and coherence? Why or why not?
    c. Are there any sentences in which the meaning is unclear? If so, what makes them unclear?
    d. Does the essay have a variety of short and long sentences?
    e. Does the essay use appropriate word choice and correct word forms?
    f. What improvements would you make?

Make suggestions that will help each student earn a high score on the independent writing task.

4.10 Evaluating the Essay

FOCUS

Read the following independent writing question and a student's essay:

> Do you agree or disagree with the following statement?
> **Students learn more in large lecture classes than in small discussion classes.**
> Use specific reasons and examples to support your answer.

Students can learn in both large lecture classes and small discussion classes. Large classes are often taught by famous lecturer, and this gives prestige to a university. Students can learn alot from a famous sceintist or writer. However, I beleive that students learn more in small discussion classes because they can practice skills that need in their profession.

First, a small class allows students to improve their speaking skills. Students give alot of oral reports, and they discuss ideas deeply with their instructor and classmates. They express their own opinions and learn about classmate's opinions. Class discussions will give students confidence in speaking to a group, that is a skill required in many professions. Therefore, small classes give useful practice.

Second, a small class is like a work situation. Many professions require people work in teams to solve problems and making decisions. A small class give students valuable practice in teamwork. In a small class, students responsible for participation, just as in a team in a work situation.

Finally, students can get more help from the instructor in a small class. Usually, it is not possible in a large class, students can not ask quetions. However, in a small class, students can ask questions and get better help from the instructor, whose like a boss or older relative.

In summary, both large and small classes have benefits, but students can learn more useful skills in a small class. Therefore, I recommend small classes for students who want experience for their profession.

How would you rate the various aspects of the essay? Check the appropriate space between WEAK and STRONG:

Organization	WEAK __ __ __ __ __	STRONG
Thesis and support	WEAK __ __ __ __ __	STRONG
Unity and coherence	WEAK __ __ __ __ __	STRONG
Grammar and vocabulary	WEAK __ __ __ __ __	STRONG

On the TOEFL, this essay would probably receive a fairly high score. It is generally well organized and is developed with appropriate details. It is written coherently with appropriate use of transitions. However, the essay is a bit short and has some noticeable minor errors in grammar, vocabulary, and spelling.

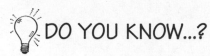 DO YOU KNOW...?

1. Two trained evaluators will read your essay. They will evaluate it and assign a score of 1 to 5, with 5 the highest score possible. Your essay will be judged on the quality of your writing and on how well you state and support your opinion. This includes the organization and development of your ideas and the appropriateness of the language you use to express your ideas.

2. The evaluators will use criteria similar to those in the following table as they score your essay.

INDEPENDENT WRITING TASK Description of Score Levels	
5	**A essay at this level** ➤ effectively addresses the task by clearly stating an opinion; and ➤ is well organized and well developed with appropriate examples, reasons, or details; and ➤ displays unity and coherence; and ➤ uses language effectively, with sentence variety and appropriate word choice and only occasional minor language errors.
4	**A essay at this level** ➤ addresses the task well, but some points may not be fully supported; and ➤ is generally well organized and sufficiently developed with examples, reasons, or details; and ➤ displays unity and coherence, but may have some redundancy or lack of clarity; and ➤ contains sentence variety and a range of vocabulary, but may have noticeable minor language errors that do not interfere with meaning.
3	**A essay at this level** ➤ addresses the task with some development and some appropriate supporting details; or ➤ displays unity and coherence, but connections among ideas may be occasionally unclear; or ➤ is inconsistent in using language effectively, with errors in grammar and vocabulary that occasionally obscure meaning; or ➤ contains an accurate but limited range of sentence structures and vocabulary.
2	**A essay at this level** ➤ displays limited development in response to the task, with inappropriate or insufficient supporting details; or ➤ contains inadequate organization or connections among ideas; or ➤ contains an accumulation of errors in grammar and usage.
1	**A essay at this level** ➤ is flawed by serious disorganization or underdevelopment; or ➤ contains little or no detail, or details that are irrelevant to the task; or ➤ contains serious and frequent errors in grammar and usage.
0	**A essay at this level** ➤ is not related to the given topic; or ➤ is written in a language other than English; or ➤ is blank.

WRITING

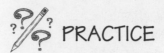 PRACTICE

Exercise 4.10.A

Read the independent writing question and the five essays that follow. Evaluate each essay according to the descriptions of the five levels on page 435. Assign each response a score of 5, 4, 3, 2 or 1.

> Do you agree or disagree with the following statement?
> **Advertising influences people's behavior in a negative way.**
> Use specific reasons and examples to support your opinion.

Response A   Score: _____

　　People see a lot of advertising in newspapers and magazines, on signs, and on television. Today people even see ads in the movie theater! All of this advertising influences people's behavior in a negative way. It influences how people spend their money, how they look at themselves, and how they communicate with other people.

　　Advertising influences how people spend their money. People sometimes buy things they can't afford or don't need. I read a story of a family that bought a computer for their children, but they were living in a tent. They didn't even have electricity for the computer. People spend too much because they have to be better than everyone else. In my country, weddings are a big industry, and families spend too much money because of advertising. This is a negative influence of advertising.

　　Advertising affects how people view themselves. Sometimes it makes people feel bad if they can't buy something. For example, a lot of sports and movie stars advertise shoes, clothes, and so on. Children see this on television and pressure their parents to buy it. There are a lot of crimes because teenagers kill to get designer jackets. Advertising makes them feel like they are nobody without designer clothes. Also, teenagers start to smoke because they think this looks cool. Moreover, some girls want to be thin like girls in the ads.

　　Finally, advertising changes people's communication. I hear a lot of little children saying the phrases they hear on television. They also sing the songs from the commercials. Also, advertising influences spelling. I have seen "night" spelled like "nite." Therefore, advertising has a negative effects on the ways that people speak and write English.

　　Advertising has a lot of good points. It is a way to sell things in a capitalist country. However, there are also a lot of bad influences on people's behavior because of advertising.

Response B   Score: _____

　　Advertising is a large part of our culture, so of course advertising influences people's behavior. But I disagree with the statement, advertising influences behavior in a negative way. On the contrary, I think the effect of advertising is positive for society.

　　One effect of advertising is a way for people to learn about new products to buy. We learn about new types of products and service by seeing it on television. For example, I learned about a special price for a travel to Florida from advertising on television. This had a positive effect on my behavior because I could enjoyed a beautiful week in Florida. Other things I learned are a new restaurant of health food, a movie, and places for automobile service. All these advertising had a positive effect of helping me have a better life.

Another effect of advertising is a way to compare the prices and the quality of service. This is a positive because we can think carefully before we buy something. Also, we can save money. We can find a better quality. So advertising has a positive effect of critical thinking and making smarter shoppers.

Also, another positive effect of advertising is a way to get ideas for living more interesting life. We learn many interesting ideas from television advertising and also in magazines. For example, I read magazines and see intresting ideas to decorate my apartment in advertising. Also, I learn about new kinds of food and places to visit. So advertising has a positive effect of helping me, not a negative influence on my behavior.

Of course, some advertising influence behavior in a negative way, such as smoking. But I think the general influence on people's behavior is positive. Advertising helps people learn about products, compare the prices, and to get interesting ideas for better life.

Response C   Score: _____

We can see advertising in many places. For example, on TV also on buildings, magazines and junk mail. The purpose of advertising is showing people to buy things. We can't avoid a negative way for advertising even we are educated. Many advertising is a lie so we don't always know it's true. It's a negative behavior for people tell a lie in advertising. But it's too bad because people don't know and buy things even it's a lie. This is illegal in many countries. We had better to find the answer to the problem.

I used to watch TV and saw many advertising on TV. I saw lot of negative behavior. Many TV shows are very stupid advertising. Sometimes is a lie, animals don't talk. Advertising – it's good but some is a lie and not real. But still people's belief, and so it's a problem.

Response D   Score: _____

Advertising influences people's behavior in a negative way. I disagree with the statement. The statement is not true.

Sometimes advertising is very interesting. I am interesting by the ads on the bus and train. Some advertising is beautiful art and it's not negative influence, it's very creativity. The advertising industry gives jobs to artists and writers. My two cousins and his friend they have a job in advertising company where draw pictures and design posters. Some posters on the bus and train where many people can see the posters. My cousin he studied at art college and his degree in commercial art. He got a job where make advertising posters. On the other hand, some advertising on television gives jobs to actors and musicians. Sometimes famous actors they make ad for television advertising, then later get a job in movies and so on. Some actor he doesn't act, he uses voice narration on the television ads. I can hear the voice of some famous actors in the advertising, it's not negative influence. The advertising industry has jobs for many people, it's the reason I disagree with the statement. Also, I am interesting by the ads on clothing, such as T–shirts and caps. These pictures they are very beautiful by artists. Some ads in the print media, newspaper and magazine, also, they are very good. My second cousin sometime she designs ads for the print media.

Response E   Score: _____

People influenced by the world around them. Advertising has many ways influencing people's behavior. I agree with the statement. Most the influences of advertising are negative. I will discuss advertising on television and Internet.

Advertising on television is too much. Every hour has too many comercials. Advertising is for cars, lifestyle, cloths, liquer, diamonds, and many other things. People don't need all these things. These things are espensive, so influence is negative. People want too many things. They see the comercial on television. They want rich lifestyle. So they spend too much money can't afford.

Some advertising is for medicine and drugs such as asprin. People need some medicine. However, they take too many drugs don't need them. Some advertising is for food, such as pizza, cookies, candy, coke, and beer. People need food to live. However, many people get very fat. They eat too much junk food. Therefore, advertising is mainly a negative influence. Advertising cause people spend too much money. Moreover, people eat too much junk food. It's bad for health.

Also, people influenced by the Internet advertising. It's too much! Every kind of picture and spam on email – it's too much comercial on Internet. In the past, Internet was for study and learning. But now Internet is mainly way for sell things. People see advertising. They want too many things. It's a pity. It's mainly influences people's behavior in a negative way. Moreover, some Internet advertising is false.

Answers to Exercise 4.10.A are on page 596.

EXTENSION

1. Study the descriptions of the five score levels on page 435. Make sure you understand the description for each level. Check your understanding of the meaning of these words and phrases:

effectively addresses	redundancy	limited range
unity	lack of clarity	limited development
coherence	range of vocabulary	accumulation of errors
minor language errors	obscure meaning	usage

2. Review the essays you wrote for the writing questions in units 4.6 through 4.9. Evaluate each essay according to the descriptions of the five levels on page 435. What are the areas of strength in your writing? What are your most serious problems? How can you improve your writing to earn a high score on the independent writing task?

PROGRESS – 4.6 through 4.10

QUIZ 4   *Time – 30 minutes*

Read the question below and make any notes that will help you plan your response. Then begin typing your essay. You have 30 minutes to plan, write, and revise your essay. Your essay will earn a score of 1, 2, 3, 4, or 5, with 5 the highest score.

Do you agree or disagree with the following statement?
It is more important for students to read books about real events than it is for them to read novels.
Use specific reasons and examples to support your opinion.

Writing Time – 30 minutes

Record your score on the Progress Chart on page 696.

WRITING

PROGRESS – 4.6 through 4.10

Quiz 5   *Time – 30 minutes*

Read the question below and make any notes that will help you plan your response. Then begin typing your essay. You have 30 minutes to plan, write, and revise your essay. Your essay will earn a score of 1, 2, 3, 4, or 5, with 5 the highest score.

> Some people want to have a job where they can make or do things with their hands. Other people prefer having a job where they can work with their heads and think. Which type of job do you prefer? Use specific reasons and examples to support your answer.

Writing Time – 30 minutes

Record your score on the Progress Chart on page 696.

PROGRESS – 4.6 through 4.10

Quiz 6

Read the question below and make any notes that will help you plan your response. Then begin typing your essay. You have 30 minutes to plan, write, and revise your essay. Your essay will earn a score of 1, 2, 3, 4, or 5, with 5 the highest score.

> Do you agree or disagree with the following statement?
> **Solitude, spending time alone, is one of our best teachers.**
> Use specific reasons and examples to support your opinion.

Writing Time – 30 minutes

Record your score on the Progress Chart on page 696.

WRITING

PROGRESS – 4.1 through 4.10

Quiz 7

Time – approximately 60 minutes

There are two questions in this quiz. Question 1 is an integrated reading–listening–writing task. Question 2 is an independent writing task. Your response to each task will earn a score of 1, 2, 3, 4, or 5, with 5 the highest score. Add the two scores to obtain your total score.

QUESTION 1

Read the passage and then listen to the recording. To make this practice more like the real test, cover the passage and question during the lecture. You may take notes, and you may use your notes to help you write your response. When you hear the question, uncover the passage and question. Then allow 20 minutes to plan and write your response.

Reading Time – 3 minutes

In the nineteenth century, when photography was still a relatively new art form, "Pictorialists" were photographers who strove to give their photographs, or "pictures," a resemblance to paintings. Pictorialists wanted their images to evoke the artistic character of oil paintings. Today when we speak of pictorial photography, we mean photographs that stand on their own as valuable works of art, not photographs that imitate paintings.

A pictorial photograph is usually of a still, or fairly still, subject. If a person is included in the shot, he or she is there as part of the composition, and not as a portrait central to the picture. Photographs that evoke an emotional response in the viewer are often classified as pictorial. A pictorial shot often relies on a beautiful lighting effect and attention to detail as well as concern for the overall composition.

In both painting and photography, composition refers to the organization of forms and colors within the frame of the picture. Photographers inherited theories of composition from painters and other visual artists. In the nineteenth century, when young men and women studied painting, they learned the "rules" of composition. These rules were not established by the great masters, who understood and applied composition instinctively. Rather, it was art teachers who formulated the rules after examining the world's great paintings. From these paintings, art teachers extracted a number of factors that occurred frequently in great works. These rules of composition are better described as guidelines and can be quite helpful to the beginning photographer. Generally, composition includes such elements as balance, placement, color, and detail.

Now cover the passage and question. Listen to the recording. When you hear the question, uncover the passage and question and begin your response.

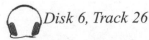

Disk 6, Track 26

> Summarize the points made by the instructor, explaining how they illustrate points made in the reading.

Stop

Writing Time – 20 minutes

QUESTION 2

Read the question below and make any notes that will help you plan your response. Then begin typing your essay. You have 30 minutes to plan, write, and revise your essay.

> Some students like to work in groups with other students when doing assignments and projects. Other students prefer to work independently. Which do you prefer? Use specific reasons and examples to support your answer.

Writing Time – 30 minutes

Key points for Writing Quiz 7 are on page 596.

Record your total score on the Progress Chart on page 696.

PROGRESS – 4.1 through 4.10

QUIZ 8   *Time – approximately 60 minutes*

There are two questions in this quiz. Question 1 is an integrated reading–listening–writing task. Question 2 is an independent writing task. Your response to each task will earn a score of 1, 2, 3, 4, or 5, with 5 the highest score. Add the two scores to obtain your total score.

QUESTION 1

Read the passage and then listen to the recording. To make this practice more like the real test, cover the passage and question during the lecture. You may take notes, and you may use your notes to help you write your response. When you hear the question, uncover the passage and question. Then allow 20 minutes to plan and write your response.

Reading Time – 3 minutes

Sexism is the sum total of society's shared attitudes and assumptions that require people to follow certain "rules" about how they should act, think, and feel, based on their gender. From a very early age, boys and girls are taught these gender "rules" through social conditioning. Children learn their culture's gender rules mainly from the adults in their lives, but also from media images and the toys they are given to play with.

The majority of toys used in preschools and kindergartens, and the toys given to children by adults, are tools that condition children to learn gender roles and accept these roles as normal. Clearly separate classes of toys exist for girls and boys. Girls are given stuffed animals, dolls, dress–up kits, toy houses, and kitchen sets, while boys are given action or violence–oriented toys. Girls' toys condition girls to sit and play quietly and accept things the way they are. Boys' toys, in contrast, teach boys to take things apart, put things together, and move things around—in other words, to have an impact on the environment. The colors used in these gender–specific toys enhance this social conditioning. Toys for girls come in soft colors such as pink, white, lavender, and light blue, while boys' toys are bold orange, yellow, blue, gray, black, and white.

Toy manufacturers market by gender, and their advertising literature emphasizes that boys love action play with trucks, robots, action figures, and machines. By contrast, toymakers assume that girls are more interested in fashion, beauty, and the home, presumably because girls do not like action play. The division by gender extends to television commercials. Research shows that commercials with only boys feature settings away from home, while ads with only girls are more likely to be set in the home.

Now cover the passage and question. Listen to the recording. When you hear the question, uncover the passage and question and begin your response.

 Disk 6, Track 27

> Summarize the points made in the talk, explaining how they agree or disagree with points made in the reading.

 Stop

Writing Time – 20 minutes

QUESTION 2

Read the question below and make any notes that will help you plan your response. Then begin typing your essay. You have 30 minutes to plan, write, and revise your essay.

Do you agree or disagree with the following statement?
Television has had a mostly positive effect on society.
Use specific reasons and examples to support your opinion.

Writing Time – 30 minutes

Key points for Writing Quiz 8 are on page 596.

Record your total score on the Progress Chart on page 696.

READING SECTION DIRECTIONS

The Reading section measures your ability to read and understand passages in English. You will read three passages and answer questions about them.

For most questions, you will choose the one best answer of four possible answers. These questions are worth one point each. The last question in each set is worth more than one point. The directions for this question indicate how many points you can receive.

Some passages have one or more words in bold type. For these bolded words, you will see a definition or explanation in a glossary at the end of the passage.

Answer all questions about a passage on the basis of what is stated or implied in that passage.

You have 60 minutes to read the passages and answer all of the questions. Allow approximately 20 minutes to work on each passage.

THE ART OF THEATER

The means by which an art form presents its message is referred to as the medium. Thus, sound produced by instruments or human voices is the medium of music. Paint on canvas or paper is the medium of painting. For literature, the medium is written language. For theater, it is a story performed by actors on a stage.

Drama is sometimes seen as a branch of literature because plays, like literature, are often printed in book form. However, there is an important difference between the two forms. Unlike a novel, a play is written to be performed, and the script of a play is not a finished work; it is an outline for a performance. The physical production of the play—the scenery, lighting, and costumes—will affect the performance, and so will the actors. How the actors interpret their roles greatly influences the play's effect on the audience.

The basic encounter in theater is between the performers and the audience. This is a special type of encounter because the performers are playing other people, characters. Moreover, the characters are part of a human story that has been written by a dramatist. This combination of elements distinguishes theater from other art forms.

Theater has several other distinctive characteristics. First, the subject matter of theater is always human beings. Second, theater is universal—there is an impulse toward creating theater in all societies. Third, theater is transitory in nature—a play is an event that occurs through time. Finally, theater is set apart by its basic elements: audience, performers, director, dramatist, purpose, viewpoint, and setting.

Human beings and human concerns are always the subject matter of drama, even when the performers play animals, objects, or abstract ideas. In the medieval play *Everyman*, some of the roles are abstract ideas such as Beauty, Knowledge, and Strength. The central character is Everyman, a human character, and the subject is death arriving before we want it to come—a theme that is universal to humans. The focus of drama is on human beings, even though different human concerns have been emphasized in different plays.

In view of the human–centered quality of theater, it is not surprising that the impulse toward theater is universal. The urge to create drama has existed wherever human society has developed: in Europe, Asia, Africa, Australia, and the Americas. In every culture recorded in history or studied by anthropologists, we find rituals, ceremonies, and celebrations that include elements of theater. At various times, these ceremonies and stories developed into a separate realm of theater. In Greece, a fully developed theater emerged almost 2,500 years ago. In India, theater became well–established around 2,000 years ago. Wherever theater has become a separate art form, it has had certain essential qualities: a story—the play—is presented by one group—the performers—to another group—the audience.

One special quality of a theater performance is its immediacy. In the theater, we live in the perpetual present tense. Theater is a transitory art. A performance changes from moment to moment, and each moment is a direct, immediate adventure for the audience. The transitory nature of theater is a quality it shares with music and dance, and sets it apart from literature and the visual arts. A novel or a painting is a fixed object; it exists as a finished product. The performing arts, on the other hand, are not objects but events. Theater occurs through time; it is an experience created by a series of sights, sounds, and impressions.

1. How does the art of theater convey its message?

   (A) An instrument or voice produces sound.
   (B) A camera converts light to images on film.
   (C) People perform a story for another group.
   (D) A person writes a story for others to read.

2. The author discusses literature in paragraph 2 in order to illustrate what point?

   (A) Literature and drama are both written forms of communication.
   (B) Reading a novel and attending a play are different experiences.
   (C) Both novelists and dramatists use an outline to organize ideas.
   (D) Many actors prefer roles from classic works of literature.

3. Which sentence below best expresses the essential information in the highlighted sentence in paragraph 3? Incorrect choices change the meaning in important ways or leave out essential information.

   (A) A play's scenery, lighting, and costumes contribute to the message of the play.
   (B) Theater is the only art form that mixes more than one medium in a single work of art.
   (C) A successful dramatist knows how to blend purpose, viewpoint, and theme into a unique performance.
   (D) Theater is a distinct art form by the way it joins characters and audience in the telling of a story.

4. Why does the author mention *Everyman* in paragraph 5?

   (A) To show that the definition of theater has evolved over time
   (B) To give an example of a play in which abstract ideas are characters
   (C) To compare the importance of beauty, knowledge, and strength
   (D) To illustrate the universal human desire to create theater

5. The word theme in paragraph 5 refers to

   (A) performers playing animals, objects, or ideas
   (B) death arriving before we want it to come
   (C) beauty, knowledge, and strength
   (D) Everyman as a central character

6. The word urge in paragraph 6 is closest in meaning to

   (A) money
   (B) education
   (C) motivation
   (D) patience

7. The word realm in paragraph 6 is closest in meaning to

   (A) form
   (B) ritual
   (C) science
   (D) tool

8. Which of the following can be inferred from paragraph 6 about the development of theater?

   (A) In every human society, theater appeared before other forms of art.
   (B) Theater could not have developed without the support of political leaders.
   (C) People created theater as a way to promote peace between rival groups.
   (D) Theater emerged as a distinct art form at different times around the world.

9. The word transitory in paragraph 7 is closest in meaning to

   (A) temporary
   (B) beautiful
   (C) surprising
   (D) expressive

10. How is theater similar to the other performing arts?

    (A) It is based on works of literature.
    (B) It exists as a finished product.
    (C) It is an event that occurs through time.
    (D) It is presented the same way every time.

11. According to the passage, all of the following are true of theater EXCEPT

- (A) The impulse toward theater is universal.
- (B) The medium of theater is written language.
- (C) Theater is a distinct form of art.
- (D) The focus of theater is always human.

12. Look at the four squares, **A**, **B**, **C**, and **D**, which indicate where the following sentence could be added to the passage. Where would the sentence best fit?

Thus, theater is a shared event, an experience that includes both those who perform and those who observe.

In view of the human–centered quality of theater, it is not surprising that the impulse toward theater is universal. **A** The urge to create drama has existed wherever human society has developed: in Europe, Asia, Africa, Australia, and the Americas. In every culture recorded in history or studied by anthropologists, we find rituals, ceremonies, and celebrations that include elements of theater. **B** At various times, these ceremonies and stories developed into a separate realm of theater. In Greece, a fully developed theater emerged almost 2,500 years ago. In India, theater became well–established around 2,000 years ago. **C** Wherever theater has become a separate art form, it has had certain essential qualities: a story—the play—is presented by one group—the performers—to another group—the audience. **D**

13–14. An introductory sentence for a brief summary of the passage is provided below. Complete the summary by selecting the THREE answer choices that express the most important ideas in the passage. Some sentences do not belong in the summary because they express ideas that are not presented in the passage or are minor ideas in the passage. *This question is worth 2 points.*

Several qualities distinguish theater from other forms of art.
•
•
•

Answer Choices

(A) Theater is a form of literature because we can read plays in books.

(B) Theater requires a human story, performers, and an audience.

(C) An actor must change his voice to play certain characters.

(D) The tendency toward creating theater occurs in all human societies.

(E) Theater developed as a separate art very early in Greece and India.

(F) Each theater performance is an immediate yet transitory experience.

CLOUD FORMATION

Water vapor is an invisible gas, but its **condensation** and **deposition** products—water droplets and ice crystals—are visible to us as clouds. A cloud is an **aggregate** of tiny water droplets or ice crystals suspended in the atmosphere above the earth's surface, the visible indication of condensation and deposition of water vapor within the atmosphere.

Laboratory studies have demonstrated that in clean air—air free of dust and other particles—condensation or deposition of water vapor requires supersaturated conditions, that is, a relative humidity greater than 100 percent. When humid air is cooled, usually by **convection**, unequal heating of the ground surface creates rising air currents. As the air ascends, it expands and cools. Eventually it reaches its dew point, the temperature at which the invisible water vapor in the air condenses into a collection of water droplets. From the ground, we see these tiny particles as a cloud. If the droplets continue to acquire moisture and grow large enough, they fall from the cloud as rain.

Clouds occur in a wide variety of forms because they are shaped by many processes operating in the atmosphere. In fact, monitoring changes in clouds and cloud cover often will provide clues about future weather. British naturalist Luke Howard was among the first to devise a system for grouping clouds. Formulated in 1803, the essentials of Howard's classification scheme are still in use today. Contemporary weather forecasters still divide clouds into two main groups: heaped clouds, resulting from rising unstable air currents; and layered clouds, resulting from stable air.

Clouds are also classified according to their appearance, their altitude, and by whether or not they produce precipitation. Based on appearance, the simplest distinction is among cumulus, stratus, and cirrus clouds. Cumulus clouds occur as heaps or puffs, stratus clouds are layered, and cirrus clouds look like threads. Based on altitude, the most common clouds in the troposphere are grouped into four families: low clouds, middle clouds, high clouds, and clouds exhibiting vertical development. Low, middle, and high clouds are produced by gentle uplift of air over broad areas. Those with vertical development generally cover smaller areas and are associated with much more vigorous uplift.

Cumulus clouds are dense, white, heaped clouds capped with a cauliflower–like dome created by convection. Low–level cumulus clouds are detached from one another and generally have well–defined bases. Their outlines are sharp, and they often develop vertically in the form of rising puffs, mounds, domes, or towers. The sunlit parts are brilliant white; the base is relatively dark and roughly horizontal.

Stratus, or layered, clouds grow from top to bottom in wide sheets, or strata, with minimal vertical and extended horizontal dimensions. These clouds spread laterally to form layers that sometimes cover the entire sky, to the horizon and beyond, like a formless blanket. The air is stable, with little or no convection present.

While cumulus and stratus clouds generally form at low or middle altitudes, a third type of cloud forms at high altitudes. Cirrus clouds are detached clouds that take the form of delicate white filaments, strands, or hooks. These clouds can be seen at close hand from the window of a jet plane flying above 25,000 feet. When viewed from the ground, bands of threadlike cirrus clouds often seem to emerge from a single point on the western horizon and spread across the entire sky. Cirrus clouds are composed almost exclusively of ice crystals. Their fibrous appearance results from the wind "stretching" streamers of falling ice particles into feathery strands called "mares' tails." Snow crystals may fall from thicker, darker cirrus clouds, but they usually evaporate in the drier air below the cloud.

Glossary: **condensation:** the changing of a gas to a liquid
deposition: the act of laying, placing, or depositing
aggregate: total of many parts; mixture
convection: the transfer of heat in a gas or a liquid by the movement of air currents

15. The word suspended in paragraph 1 is closest in meaning to

- (A) hanging
- (B) freezing
- (C) dripping
- (D) hiding

16. Which sentence below best expresses the essential information in the highlighted sentence in paragraph 2? Incorrect choices change the meaning in important ways or leave out essential information.

- (A) Scientists have been able to stimulate the formation of clouds in the laboratory with a success rate of 100 percent.
- (B) If the air contains no dust particles, water vapor will condense and create extremely humid weather conditions.
- (C) Research shows that the formation of clouds in clean air depends on a relative humidity of over 100 percent.
- (D) A relative humidity of more than 100 percent can occur only when the air is clean and dust–free.

17. What happens at the dew point?

- (A) Cool air starts to fall.
- (B) The ground becomes warmer.
- (C) Rain change to snow.
- (D) Water vapor condenses.

18. Why does the author mention Luke Howard in paragraph 3?

- (A) To identify the inventor of our system for classifying clouds
- (B) To give an example of an idea that was not accepted at first
- (C) To name the first scientist who could predict the weather
- (D) To describe the biography of a famous British naturalist

19. The word Those in paragraph 4 refers to

- (A) threads
- (B) clouds
- (C) families
- (D) areas

20. Cumulus clouds are characterized by all of the following EXCEPT

- (A) horizontal base
- (B) dome–like top
- (C) stable air
- (D) low altitude

21. The word sharp in paragraph 5 is closest in meaning to

- (A) distinct
- (B) frozen
- (C) invisible
- (D) straight

22. It can be inferred from the passage that stratus clouds

- (A) are sometimes very difficult to identify
- (B) are likely to produce precipitation
- (C) form layers above other clouds in the sky
- (D) differ from cumulus clouds in appearance

23. Click on the drawing below that most closely resembles cirrus clouds.

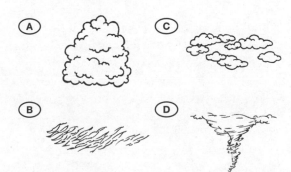

24. The word fibrous in paragraph 7 is closest
in meaning to

- Ⓐ dark
- Ⓑ layered
- Ⓒ threadlike
- Ⓓ changing

25. Look at the four squares, **A**, **B**, **C**, and **D**, which indicate where the following sentence could be added to the passage. Where would the sentence best fit?

These strands often warn of the approach of a warm front signaling the advance of a storm system.

While cumulus and stratus clouds generally form at low or middle altitudes, a third type of cloud forms at high altitudes. **A** Cirrus clouds are detached clouds that take the form of delicate white filaments, strands, or hooks. These clouds can be seen at close hand from the window of a jet plane flying above 25,000 feet. **B** When viewed from the ground, bands of threadlike cirrus clouds often seem to emerge from a single point on the western horizon and spread across the entire sky. Cirrus clouds are composed almost exclusively of ice crystals. **C** Their fibrous appearance results from the wind "stretching" streamers of falling ice particles into feathery strands called "mares' tails." **D** Snow crystals may fall from thicker, darker cirrus clouds, but they usually evaporate in the drier air below the cloud.

26–28. Select the appropriate sentences from the answer choices and match them to the type of clouds that they describe. TWO of the answer choices will NOT be used. ***This question is worth 3 points.***

Answer Choices

(A) These clouds form when the air is stable and no convection occurs.

(B) They form when water droplets acquire moisture and grow very large.

(C) They often develop vertically in the shape of domes, mounds, or towers.

(D) This type of cloud forms at altitudes at least 25,000 feet above the earth.

(E) Rising, unstable air currents lead to the formation of this type of cloud.

(F) They can spread out like a blanket covering the whole sky.

(G) These clouds have a fluffy white top and a flatter, darker bottom.

Type of Clouds

Heaped Clouds

-
-
-

Layered Clouds

-
-

THE ATLANTIC COD FISHERY

Off the northeastern shore of North America, from the island of Newfoundland in Canada south to New England in the United States, there is a series of shallow areas called banks. Several large banks off Newfoundland are together called the Grand Banks, huge shoals on the edge of the North American continental shelf, where the warm waters of the Gulf Stream meet the cold waters of the Labrador Current. As the currents brush each other, they stir up minerals from the ocean floor, providing nutrients for plankton and tiny shrimp–like creatures called krill, which feed on the plankton. Herring and other small fish rise to the surface to eat the krill. Groundfish, such as the Atlantic cod, live in the ocean's bottom layer, congregating in the shallow waters where they prey on krill and small fish. This rich environment has produced cod by the millions and once had a greater density of cod than anywhere else on Earth.

Beginning in the eleventh century, boats from the ports of northwestern Europe arrived to fish the Grand Banks. For the next eight centuries, the entire Newfoundland economy was based on Europeans arriving, catching fish for a few months in the summer, and then taking fish back to European markets. Cod laid out to dry on wooden "flakes" was a common sight in the fishing villages dotting the coast. Settlers in the region used to think the only sea creature worth talking about was cod, and in the local speech the word "fish" became synonymous with cod. Newfoundland's national dish was a pudding whose main ingredient was cod.

By the nineteenth century, the Newfoundland fishery was largely controlled by merchants based in the capital at St. John's. They marketed the catch supplied by the fishers working out of more than 600 villages around the long coastline. In return, the merchants provided fishing equipment, clothing, and all the food that could not be grown in the island's thin, rocky soil. This system kept the fishers in a continuous state of debt and dependence on the merchants.

Until the twentieth century, fishers believed in the cod's ability to replenish itself and thought that overfishing was impossible. However, Newfoundland's cod fishery began to show signs of trouble during the 1930s, when cod failed to support the fishers and thousands were unemployed. The slump lasted for the next few decades. Then, when an international agreement in 1977 established the 200–mile offshore fishing limit, the Canadian government decided to build up the modern Grand Banks fleet and make fishing a viable economic base for Newfoundland again. All of Newfoundland's seafood companies were merged into one conglomerate. By the 1980s, the conglomerate was prospering, and cod were commanding excellent prices in the market. Consequently, there was a significant increase in the number of fishers and fish–processing plant workers.

However, while the offshore fishery was prospering, the inshore fishermen found their catches dropping off. In 1992 the Canadian government responded by closing the Grand Banks to groundfishing. Newfoundland's cod fishing and processing industries were shut down in a bid to let the vanishing stocks recover. The moratorium was extended in 1994, when all of the Atlantic cod fisheries in Canada were closed, except for one in Nova Scotia, and strict quotas were placed on other species of groundfish. Canada's cod fishing industry collapsed, and around 40,000 fishers and other industry workers were put out of work.

Atlantic cod stocks had once been so plentiful that early explorers joked about walking on the backs of the teeming fish. Today, cod stocks are at historically low levels and show no signs of imminent recovery, even after drastic conservation measures and severely limited fishing. Fishermen often blame the diminishing stocks on seals, which prey on cod and other species, but scientists believe that decades of overfishing are to blame. Studies on fish populations have shown that cod disappeared from Newfoundland at the same time that stocks started rebuilding in Norway, raising the possibility that the cod had migrated. Still, no one can predict whether and when the cod will return to the Grand Banks.

29. The word shoals in paragraph 1 is closest in meaning to

(A) shallows
(B) currents
(C) mountains
(D) islands

30. What physical process occurs in the region of the Grand Banks?

(A) Underwater hot springs heat the water.
(B) Warm and cold currents come together.
(C) Nutrient–rich water flows in from rivers.
(D) Tides transport plankton and small fish.

31. Which sentence below best expresses the essential information in the highlighted sentence in paragraph 1? Incorrect choices change the meaning in important ways or leave out essential information.

(A) Millions of cod come to the Grand Banks every year to feed on the abundant supplies of herring and other small fish.
(B) The Grand Banks used to have the world's largest concentration of cod because of favorable natural conditions.
(C) The Grand Banks is the only place on Earth where cod are known to come together in extremely large groups.
(D) The environmental resources of the Grand Banks have made many people wealthy from cod fishing.

32. The phrase the region in paragraph 2 refers to

(A) New England
(B) northwestern Europe
(C) the Grand Banks
(D) Newfoundland

33. Why does the author mention Newfoundland's national dish in paragraph 2?

(A) To encourage the development of tourism in Newfoundland
(B) To describe the daily life of people in Newfoundland
(C) To stress the economic and cultural significance of cod
(D) To show that Newfoundland used to be a separate country

34. All of the following statements characterized Newfoundland's cod fishery in the past EXCEPT

(A) Fishers were dependent on merchants in the capital.
(B) Cod were the foundation of the island's economy.
(C) Fishers competed with farmers for natural resources.
(D) Cod were placed on wooden "flakes" for drying.

35. The word replenish in paragraph 4 is closest in meaning to

(A) defend
(B) repair
(C) restock
(D) improve

36. What event first signaled the overfishing of the Atlantic cod?

(A) The failure of cod to support thousands of fishers in the 1930s
(B) The merging of seafood companies into one huge conglomerate
(C) An increase in the number of fishers and fish–processing plants
(D) The government moratorium on cod fishing during the 1990s

37. Why did the Canadian government decide to build up the Grand Banks fishing fleet?

    (A) The 200–mile limit was seen as an economic opportunity.
    (B) There had not been enough boats to handle all the fish.
    (C) The shipbuilding sector of the economy was in a slump.
    (D) Canada faced stiff competition from other fishing nations.

38. The word commanding in paragraph 4 is closest in meaning to

    (A) suggesting
    (B) missing
    (C) defying
    (D) receiving

39. It can be inferred from paragraph 6 that the author most likely believes which of the following about the future of the Atlantic cod fishery?

    (A) The fishery will improve if the government lifts the fishing ban.
    (B) It may be a long time before cod stocks recover from overfishing.
    (C) The center of the Atlantic cod fishery will shift to Norway.
    (D) The cod will return to the Grand Banks if seal hunting is allowed.

40. Look at the four squares, **A**, **B**, **C**, and **D**, which indicate where the following sentence could be added to the passage. Where would the sentence best fit?

    They suspected this was because the offshore draggers were taking so many cod that the fish did not have a chance to migrate inshore to reproduce.

    However, while the offshore fishery was prospering, the inshore fishermen found their catches dropping off. **A** In 1992 the Canadian government responded by closing the Grand Banks to groundfishing. **B** Newfoundland's cod fishing and processing industries were shut down in a bid to let the vanishing stocks recover. **C** The moratorium was extended in 1994, when all of the Atlantic cod fisheries in Canada were closed, except for one in Nova Scotia, and strict quotas were placed on other species of groundfish. **D** Canada's cod fishing industry collapsed, and around 40,000 fishers and other industry workers were put out of work.

41–42. An introductory sentence for a brief summary of the passage is provided below. Complete the summary by selecting the THREE answer choices that express the most important ideas in the passage. Some sentences do not belong in the summary because they express ideas that are not presented in the passage or are minor ideas in the passage. *This question is worth 2 points.*

The Atlantic cod fishery has shaped Newfoundland's economy for centuries.
•
•
•

Answer Choices

(A) Atlantic cod stocks were once plentiful in the rich environment around the Grand Banks.

(B) The Atlantic cod is a groundfish that preys on herring and small fish that eat krill.

(C) Cod fishing was so successful that few people considered the possibility of overfishing until fish stocks fell.

(D) The Canadian government tried to diversify Newfoundland's economy in the 1980s.

(E) Despite severe limits on fishing, cod stocks remain at low levels and show few signs of recovery.

(F) Newfoundland exports millions of dollars worth of crab and other shellfish every year.

Answers to Test 1 – Reading are on page 597.

Record your score on the Progress Chart on page 697.

How to Score Multiple–Point Questions		
Points Possible	**Answers Correct**	**Points Earned**
2 points	3	2
	2	1
	0 – 1	0
3 points	5	3
	4	2
	3	1
	0 – 2	0
4 points	7	4
	6	3
	5	2
	4	1
	0 – 3	0

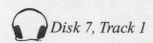
LISTENING SECTION DIRECTIONS

The Listening section measures your ability to understand conversations and lectures in English. You will hear each conversation and lecture only one time. After each conversation or lecture, you will hear some questions about it. Answer all questions based on what the speakers state or imply.

You may take notes while you listen. You may use your notes to help you answer the questions.

Most questions have four possible answers. In some questions, you will see this icon: 🎧. This means that you will hear, but not see, part of the question.

Some questions have special directions, which appear in a gray box. Most questions are worth one point. If a question is worth more than one point, special directions will indicate how many points you can receive.

You have approximately 40 minutes to complete the Listening section. This includes the time for listening to the conversations and lectures and for answering the questions.

To make this practice more like the real test, cover the questions and answers during each conversation and lecture. When you hear the first question, uncover the questions and answers.

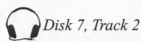 *Disk 7, Track 2*

1. What is the purpose of the conversation?

   (A) The man is interviewing the woman for a job in the office.
   (B) The woman wants to enroll in the communications program.
   (C) The man wants to discuss a change in the course schedule.
   (D) The woman is requesting an interview with the dean.

2. Why does the man say this:

   (A) To express regret that the dean is not available
   (B) To state that the dean cannot change his schedule
   (C) To let the woman know the dean is very busy
   (D) To apologize for the dean's confusing behavior

3. Why does the woman want to meet with the dean?

   (A) To learn about his ideas and vision
   (B) To ask for a letter of recommendation
   (C) To request a change in the school calendar
   (D) To tell him that she enjoyed his lecture

4. What can be inferred about the dean?

   (A) He is in his office two days a week.
   (B) He has been dean for only a short time.
   (C) He generally does not give interviews.
   (D) He is an excellent public speaker.

5. When will the meeting with the dean take place?

   (A) The next day
   (B) The next week
   (C) In two weeks
   (D) In three weeks

 Disk 7, Track 3

6. What are the students mainly discussing?

   (A) Various costs that businesses face
   (B) The concept of opportunity cost
   (C) The rising costs of owning a business
   (D) Differences between economics and accounting

7. How does the man help the woman understand a concept that she finds difficult?

   (A) He illustrates the concept with an example.
   (B) He makes a list of terms for her to study.
   (C) He asks her to explain a similar concept.
   (D) He reads a passage from their textbook.

8. Listen again to part of the conversation. Then answer the question.

   Why does the man ask this:

   (A) To find out how much money the woman made
   (B) To evaluate the food at a restaurant
   (C) To suggest that the profit is less than it seems
   (D) To express his concerns about owning a business

9. According to the man, how does an economist's view of costs differ from that of an accountant?

   (A) An economist's definition of costs never changes.
   (B) An economist uses a computer to calculate costs.
   (C) An economist tries to lessen the effect of costs.
   (D) An economist looks at a broader range of costs.

10. What can be inferred about the true cost of a college education?

    (A) It includes the cost of lost income.
    (B) It is more than the woman can afford.
    (C) It is not as expensive as it appears.
    (D) It continues to increase each year.

11. According to the professor, how did the cycle of volcanic eruptions begin?

  (A) Several earthquakes and avalanches occurred.
  (B) A cloud of ash traveled around the world.
  (C) The volcano erupted suddenly without warning.
  (D) Magma poured out of the top of the mountain.

12. Why does the professor say this: 🎧

  (A) To tell of his own experience of watching the mountain
  (B) To explain why the events were a surprise to geologists
  (C) To show that the eruptions interested a lot of people
  (D) To criticize the media for interfering with the scientists

13. Listen again to part of the lecture. Then answer the question.

  What does the professor mean when he says this: 🎧

  (A) It had been a long time since the previous eruption of St. Helens.
  (B) The public suddenly lost interest in watching the eruptions.
  (C) Scientists took a few days off before continuing their work.
  (D) The small eruptions paused briefly just before the major eruption.

14. The professor explains what happened when Mount St. Helens erupted. Indicate whether each sentence below was part of the event.

  For each sentence, click in the correct box.

	Yes	No
An earthquake caused a huge landslide.		
The mountain gained sixty feet in height.		
Ash and steam rose from the mountain.		
The mountain's side and top exploded.		

15. What were some effects of the eruption?

  Click on two answers.

  A Geologists were criticized for failing to predict it.
  B Large numbers of animals and people were killed.
  C The ash cloud affected weather around the world.
  D Tourists were afraid to visit the Cascade Range.

16. What can be concluded about Mount St. Helens?

  (A) It is a harmless inactive volcano.
  (B) It is no longer of interest to geologists.
  (C) It is the largest volcano in the world.
  (D) It is likely to erupt in the future.

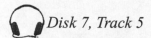
Disk 7, Track 5

17. According to the speaker, what did European explorers notice as they sailed toward the shores of North America?

Ⓐ The strength of the wind
Ⓑ The density of the forests
Ⓒ The fragrance of the trees
Ⓓ The Native American villages

18. According to the speaker, why was pine sap a valuable commodity?

Ⓐ It could make wooden ships waterproof.
Ⓑ It was an effective cure for headaches.
Ⓒ It provided an aromatic spice for food.
Ⓓ It was a good material for starting fires.

19. How was the flowering dogwood used?

Ⓐ As a flavoring for candy and soft drinks
Ⓑ As a spring tonic for pioneer children
Ⓒ As a treatment for fevers and malaria
Ⓓ As an ingredient in soaps and perfumes

20. Why does the speaker say this:

Ⓐ She is demonstrating how to brew tea.
Ⓑ She needs someone to help her lift a heavy tree.
Ⓒ She wants the students to smell a piece of wood.
Ⓓ She is giving a recipe for a medicinal tonic.

21. Why was sassafras once considered a wonder tree?

Ⓐ Its fragrance was the sweetest of any American tree.
Ⓑ Its sap could be made into a tar to seal wooden ships.
Ⓒ It provided more board timber than any other tree.
Ⓓ It was thought to be a cure for almost every disease.

22. Listen again to part of the talk. Then answer the question.

What does the speaker imply about sassafras?

Ⓐ It is probably not harmful to humans.
Ⓑ It is no longer a legal medicine.
Ⓒ It is too expensive for most people.
Ⓓ It is available only in drugstores.

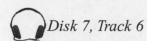
Disk 7, Track 6

23. What aspect of Plato's philosophy does the professor mainly discuss?

   (A) Plato's teachings about culture
   (B) Plato's rules for good government
   (C) Plato's effect on other philosophies
   (D) Plato's views on education

24. Why does the professor mention the mathematical concept of 2 + 2 = 4?

   (A) To compare philosophy and mathematics
   (B) To give an example of a lasting truth
   (C) To show the simplicity of Plato's philosophy
   (D) To discover which students like mathematics

25. What do idealists believe about higher–level thinking?

   Click on two answers.

   [A] It develops a person's character.
   [B] It makes all people equal.
   [C] It benefits the whole society.
   [D] It gives teachers too much power.

26. Listen again to part of the discussion. Then answer the question.

   What is the woman's attitude toward the idealist view of education?

   (A) She thinks it does not give students useful knowledge.
   (B) She finds it complex and difficult to understand.
   (C) She disagrees with its emphasis on truth.
   (D) She considers it the most liberal system of education.

27. Listen again to part of the discussion. Then answer the question.

   What does the professor mean when he says this: 🎧

   (A) Idealism has been criticized unfairly.
   (B) Idealism changes how people think.
   (C) Idealism has diminished in influence.
   (D) Idealism remains the only true philosophy.

28. According to the professor, what do critics say about idealism?

   (A) It gives students immoral ideas about learning.
   (B) It discourages student creativity and questioning.
   (C) It is overly concerned with economic development.
   (D) Its focus on abstract thinking is unfair to many students.

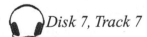
Disk 7, Track 7

29. How does the field of physics define "work"?

   (A) Work is the research done by physicists in a laboratory.
   (B) Work is the change in speed of a falling object.
   (C) Work is the amount of energy in the solar system.
   (D) Work is the ability to move an object.

30. Listen again to part of the lecture. Then answer the question.

   Why does the professor talk about a plow?

   (A) To describe recent improvements in agricultural technology
   (B) To explain what happens when a moving object meets resistance
   (C) To show that a plow is the least efficient piece of farm equipment
   (D) To give reasons for the failure of agriculture in some areas

31. Based on the information in the lecture, indicate whether each statement below reflects the first law of thermodynamics.

    For each sentence, click in the correct box.

	Yes	No
Electricity can be converted to heat or light.		
The amount of energy in any system stays the same.		
Nuclear energy is regulated by international law.		

32. Which two sentences illustrate the conversion of energy from one form to another?

    Click on two answers.

    [A] A car changes the chemical energy in gasoline to motion.

    [B] A tractor engine stops when the fuel tank is empty.

    [C] An electric stove converts electricity to heat energy.

    [D] A light bulb burns out after being on for one hundred hours.

33. Listen again to part of the lecture. Then answer the question.

    Why does the professor say this:

    (A) To support the idea of giving food aid to needy people

    (B) To explain why organisms must create their own energy

    (C) To recommend the development of new energy sources

    (D) To show that both machines and living things need energy

34. What can be inferred about the energy in the earth as a whole system?

    (A) The system gradually gains energy in the form of heat.

    (B) If there is no sunlight, the earth makes its own energy.

    (C) No new energy is created, and no energy is destroyed.

    (D) Plants contribute more energy than animals contribute.

 Stop

Answers to Test 1 – Listening are on page 598.

Record your score on the Progress Chart on page 697.

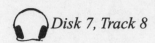

Disk 7, Track 8

SPEAKING SECTION DIRECTIONS

The Speaking section measures your ability to speak in English about a variety of topics. There are six questions in this section. Record your response to each question on a cassette.

Questions 1 and 2 are independent speaking tasks in which you will speak about familiar topics. Your responses will be scored on your ability to speak clearly and coherently about the topics.

Questions 3 and 4 are integrated tasks in which you will read a passage, listen to a conversation or lecture, and then speak in response to a question about what you have read and heard. You will need to combine relevant information from the two sources to answer the question completely. Your responses will be scored on your ability to speak clearly and coherently and on your ability to accurately convey information about what you read and heard.

Questions 5 and 6 are integrated tasks in which you will listen to part of a conversation or lecture, and then speak in response to a question about what you have heard. Your responses will be scored on your ability to speak clearly and coherently and on your ability to accurately convey information about what you heard.

You will hear each conversation and lecture only one time. You may take notes while you listen. You may use your notes to help you answer the questions.

Stop

For questions 1 and 2, you will speak in response to a question about a familiar topic. Use your own personal knowledge and experience to answer each question. After you hear the question, you have 15 seconds to prepare your response and 45 seconds to speak.

QUESTION 1

Disk 7, Track 9

> What game do you enjoy playing? Describe the game, and explain why you like to play it. Include details and examples in your explanation.

Stop

Preparation Time – 15 seconds
Response Time – 45 seconds

QUESTION 2

Disk 7, Track 10

> Some people drive their own car to school or work. Others ride a bus, train, or other form of public transportation. Which do you think is better and why? Include details and examples in your explanation.

Stop

Preparation Time – 15 seconds
Response Time – 45 seconds

TEST 1

QUESTION 3

In this question, you will read a short passage about a campus situation, listen to a conversation, and then speak in response to a question about what you have read and heard. After you hear the question, you have 30 seconds to prepare your response and 60 seconds to speak.

Reading Time – 45 seconds

DISTANCE EDUCATION COURSES

Distance education courses at Valley Community College are regularly scheduled classes that must be completed by the end of the quarter. All online courses are taught by college faculty in conjunction with the related academic departments. Students will be required to participate in a "virtual classroom" online, conduct research, and complete assignments. Students must have daily access to a personal computer with word processing software and connection to the Internet. Students should expect to spend approximately 12–15 hours a week for any online course.

Now cover the passage and question. Listen to the recording. When you hear the question, uncover the question and begin preparing your response.

 Disk 7, Track 11

> The adviser expresses her opinion about online courses. State her opinion and explain the reasons she gives for holding that opinion.

 Stop

Preparation Time – 30 seconds
Response Time – 60 seconds

QUESTION 4

In this question, you will read a short passage on an academic subject, listen to a lecture on the same topic, and then speak in response to a question about what you have read and heard. After you hear the question, you have 30 seconds to prepare your response and 60 seconds to speak.

Reading Time – 45 seconds

CULTURE

Culture consists of the beliefs, values, rituals, texts, and symbols of a society. An important element of culture is the rules—or norms—that regulate behavior and maintain social order. Some norms tell us how we should behave—for example, obey authority and treat others with respect. Some norms are traditions or customs, such as clothing styles. Other norms cover matters of morality, such as courtship behavior or showing respect to ancestors. The most essential norms cover activities that are central to the well being of the whole society; these rules are established as laws, both written and unwritten.

Now cover the passage and question. Listen to the recording. When you hear the question, uncover the question and begin preparing your response.

 Disk 7, Track 12

> Explain how corporations are similar to any other culture, and explain how corporate culture varies in different companies.

 Stop

Preparation Time – 30 seconds
Response Time – 60 seconds

QUESTION 5

In this question, you will listen to a conversation. You will then be asked to talk about the information in the conversation and to give your opinion about the ideas presented. To make this practice more like the real test, cover the question during the conversation. After you hear the question, you have 20 seconds to prepare your response and 60 seconds to speak.

Disk 7, Track 13

> Describe the man's problem and the suggestions the woman makes about how to solve it. What do you think the man should do, and why?

Stop

Preparation Time – 20 seconds
Response Time – 60 seconds

QUESTION 6

In this question, you will listen to part of a lecture. You will then be asked to summarize important information from the lecture. To make this practice more like the real test, cover the question during the lecture. After you hear the question, you have 20 seconds to prepare your response and 60 seconds to speak.

Disk 7, Track 14

> Using points and examples from the lecture, explain why some ocean water is clear and why some water is a certain color.

Stop

Preparation Time – 20 seconds
Response Time – 60 seconds

Key points for Test 1 – Speaking are on page 600.

Each response earns a score of 1, 2, 3, or 4.

Record your total score on the Progress Chart on page 697.

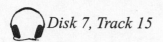 *Disk 7, Track 15*

WRITING SECTION DIRECTIONS

The Writing section measures your ability to use writing to communicate in an academic environment. There are two writing questions.

Question 1 is an integrated writing task. You will read a passage, listen to a lecture, and then answer a question based on what you have read and heard. You have 20 minutes to plan and write your response.

Question 2 is an independent writing task. You will answer a question based on your own knowledge and experience. You have 30 minutes to plan and write your response.

 Stop

QUESTION 1

For this task, you will write a response to a question about a reading passage and a short lecture. The question does not ask you to express your personal opinion.

Read the passage and then listen to the recording. To make this practice more like the real test, cover the passage and question during the lecture. You may take notes, and you may use your notes to help you write your response. When you hear the question, uncover the passage and question. Then allow 20 minutes to plan and write your response.

Typically, an effective response will have 150 to 225 words. Your response will be evaluated on the quality of your writing and on the completeness and accuracy of the content.

Reading Time – 3 minutes

Humans have always traveled across the earth. Early hunting–gathering nomads migrated in search of resources to sustain themselves. Later, after the spread of civilization, people of various religions made pilgrimages on foot or horseback, which led to the growth of wayside inns. Traders journeyed throughout Europe, North Africa, and the Middle East in search of perfumes, spices and other goods. Vikings traveled across vast seas in search of fish, timber, and other natural resources. Europeans explored Africa and the Americas, conquering other civilizations and establishing colonies. These activities—religious pilgrimages, the growth of trade, conquest and colonization—all stimulated the growth of tourism.

While the earliest "tourists" traveled in search of resources, later tourists took trips for cultural, educational, and scientific purposes. During the seventeenth century, the young members of Europe's wealthy classes took "grand tours" through Europe to expand their cultural horizons, and to learn about languages, theater, music, and art. In the nineteenth century, naturalists like Charles Darwin studied animal and plant species in exotic places and contributed greatly to an interest in traveling for scientific advancement. In the early twentieth century, naturalist John Muir began to write about his wanderings through the southern United States, Alaska, and India, and his writings continue to inspire people to observe and preserve the natural world. Other travel heroes, such as Ernest Hemingway, wrote of their African expeditions to hunt big game, exposing people to the possibilities of journeying to faraway lands for adventure.

Now cover the passage and question. Listen to the recording. When you hear the question, uncover the passage and question and begin your response.

 Disk 7, Track 16

> Summarize the points made in the lecture, and explain how they are similar to or different from points made in the reading.

 Stop

Writing Time – 20 minutes

QUESTION 2

For this task, you will write an essay in response to a question that asks you to express, explain, and support your opinion on a topic. You have 30 minutes to plan, write, and revise your essay.

Typically, an effective essay will have a minimum of 300 words. Your essay will be evaluated on the quality of your writing, including the organization and development of your ideas and the quality and accuracy of the language you use to express your ideas.

Read the question below and make any notes that will help you plan your response. Then begin typing your essay.

> Do you agree or disagree with the following statement?
> **Subjects such as art, music, and drama should be a part of every child's basic education.**
> Use specific reasons and examples to support your opinion.

Writing Time – 30 minutes

Key points for Test 1 – Writing are on page 600.

Each response earns a score of 1, 2, 3, 4 or 5.

Record your total score on the Progress Chart on page 697.

READING SECTION DIRECTIONS

The Reading section measures your ability to read and understand passages in English. You will read three passages and answer questions about them.

For most questions, you will choose the one best answer of four possible answers. These questions are worth one point each. The last question in each set is worth more than one point. The directions for this question indicate how many points you can receive.

Some passages have one or more words in bold type. For these bolded words, you will see a definition or explanation in a glossary at the end of the passage.

Answer all questions about a passage on the basis of what is stated or implied in that passage.

You have 60 minutes to read the passages and answer all of the questions. Allow approximately 20 minutes to work on each passage.

THE UNDERGROUND RAILROAD

Slavery was legal for over 200 years in some parts of North America, particularly the southern states of the United States, where the plantation system of agriculture depended on the labor of slaves, most of whom came from Africa. Slaves had no rights or freedoms because they were thought of as property. From the time of its origin, slavery had opponents. The abolitionist movement began in the 1600s when the Quakers in Pennsylvania objected to slavery on moral grounds and wanted to abolish the institution.

In 1793, Canada passed a law abolishing slavery and declared that any escaped slaves who came to Canada would be free citizens. Slavery was already illegal in most northern states; however, slaves captured there by slave hunters could be returned to slavery in the South. Canada refused to return runaway slaves or to allow American slave hunters into the country. It is estimated that more than 30,000 runaway slaves immigrated to Canada and settled in the Great Lakes region between 1830 and 1865.

The American antislavery movement was at the height of its activity during the 1800s, when abolitionists developed the Underground Railroad, a loosely organized system whereby runaway slaves were passed from safe house to safe house as they fled northwards to free states or Canada. The term was first used in the 1830s and came from an Ohio clergyman who said, "They who took passage on it disappeared from public view as if they had really gone to ground." Because the Underground Railroad was so secret, few records exist that would reveal the true number of people who traveled it to freedom. The most active routes on the railroad were in Ohio, Indiana, and western Pennsylvania.

Runaway slaves usually traveled alone or in small groups. Most were young men between the ages of 16 and 35. The fugitives hid in wagons under loads of hay or potatoes, or in furniture and boxes in steamers and on rafts. They traveled on foot through swamps and woods, moving only a few miles each night, using the North Star as a compass. Sometimes they moved in broad daylight. Boys disguised themselves as girls, and girls dressed as boys. In one well–known incident, twenty–eight slaves escaped by walking in a funeral procession from Kentucky to Ohio.

The "railroad" developed its own language. The "trains" were the large farm wagons that could conceal and carry a number of people. The "tracks" were the backcountry roads that were used to elude the slave hunters. The "stations" were the homes and hiding places where the slaves were fed and cared for as they moved north. The "agents" were the people who planned the escape routes. The "conductors" were the fearless men and women who led the slaves toward freedom. The "passengers" were the slaves who dared to run away and break for liberty. Passengers paid no fare and conductors received no pay.

The most daring conductor was Harriet Tubman, a former slave who dedicated her life to helping other runaways. Tubman made 19 trips into the South to guide 300 relatives, friends, and strangers to freedom. She was wanted dead or alive in the South, but she was never captured and never lost a passenger. A determined worker, she carried a gun for protection and a supply of drugs to quiet the crying babies in her rescue parties.

A number of white people joined the effort, including Indiana banker Levi Coffin and his wife Catherine, who hid runaways in their home, a "station" conveniently located on three main escape routes to Canada. People could be hidden there for several weeks, recovering their strength and waiting until it was safe to continue on their journey. Levi Coffin was called the "president of the Underground Railroad" because he helped as many as 3,000 slaves to escape.

The people who worked on the railroad were breaking the law. Although the escape network was never as successful or as well organized as Southerners thought, the few thousand slaves who made their way to freedom in this way each year had a symbolic significance out of proportion to their actual numbers. The Underground Railroad continued operating until slavery in the United States was finally abolished in 1865.

1. The word abolish in paragraph 1 is closest in meaning to

- (A) defend
- (B) end
- (C) legalize
- (D) expand

2. Why did thousands of runaway slaves immigrate to Canada?

- (A) They preferred the climate of the Great Lakes region.
- (B) Working conditions for slaves were better in Canada.
- (C) Canada had no laws restricting immigration.
- (D) Former slaves could live as free citizens in Canada.

3. The phrase The term in paragraph 3 refers to

- (A) antislavery movement
- (B) abolitionist
- (C) Underground Railroad
- (D) free state

4. Which sentence below best expresses the essential information in the highlighted sentence in paragraph 3? Incorrect choices change the meaning in important ways or leave out essential information.

- (A) The Underground Railroad kept secret records in which all of the passengers and trips were documented.
- (B) Few people understood why the Underground Railroad would not reveal how many people chose to travel in this way.
- (C) The Underground Railroad's records were not accurate, so the true number of travelers is difficult to estimate.
- (D) We do not know exactly how many slaves escaped on the Underground Railroad because it was a secret organization.

5. The word fugitives in paragraph 4 is closest in meaning to

- (A) leaders
- (B) old men
- (C) runaways
- (D) brave ones

6. All of the following are mentioned as methods of escape on the Underground Railroad EXCEPT

- (A) hiding in a hay wagon
- (B) wearing a disguise
- (C) riding in a railcar
- (D) walking in a procession

7. The author discusses the language of the Underground Railroad in paragraph 5 in order to

- (A) trace the history of American English words
- (B) illustrate the secret nature of the escape network
- (C) point out that some words have more than one meaning
- (D) compare the Underground Railroad to other railways

8. The word elude in paragraph 5 is closest in meaning to

- (A) avoid
- (B) follow
- (C) find
- (D) assist

9. Which of the following statements is true about passengers on the Underground Railroad?

- (A) Their destination was in the northern states or Canada.
- (B) They were not allowed to make stops during the journey.
- (C) Their babies were disguised to look like baggage.
- (D) They paid the conductors at the end of the journey.

10. Why was Harriet Tubman wanted dead or alive in the South?

    (A) She was a criminal who carried a gun and sold drugs.

    (B) She refused to return the runaway slaves that she captured.

    (C) She was an escaped slave who led others to freedom.

    (D) She became the president of the Underground Railroad.

11. It can be inferred from paragraph 8 that the author most likely believes which of the following about the Underground Railroad?

    (A) The people who worked on the railroad should have been arrested.

    (B) The railroad was unsuccessful because it could not help every slave.

    (C) Southerners did not know about the railroad until after it closed.

    (D) The railroad represented a psychological victory for abolitionists.

12. Look at the four squares, **A**, **B**, **C**, and **D**, which indicate where the following sentence could be added to the passage. Where would the sentence best fit?

Women and children also escaped, but they were more easily captured.

    Runaway slaves usually traveled alone or in small groups. Most were young men between the ages of 16 and 35. **A** The fugitives hid in wagons under loads of hay or potatoes, or in furniture and boxes in steamers and on rafts. **B** They traveled on foot through swamps and woods, moving only a few miles each night, using the North Star as a compass. Sometimes they moved in broad daylight. **C** Boys disguised themselves as girls, and girls dressed as boys. In one well–known incident, twenty–eight slaves escaped by walking in a funeral procession from Kentucky to Ohio. **D**

13–14. An introductory sentence for a brief summary of the passage is provided below. Complete the summary by selecting the THREE answer choices that express the most important ideas in the passage. Some sentences do not belong in the summary because they express ideas that are not presented in the passage or are minor ideas in the passage. *This question is worth 2 points.*

The Underground Railroad was a secret network that helped thousands of people escape slavery.
•
•
•

Answer Choices

(A) Most slaves were captured in West Africa and transported to North America on slave ships.

(B) The railroad was part of the American abolitionist movement that opposed slavery for moral reasons.

(C) Slaves that were captured in the North could be returned to slavery in the South.

(D) The railroad was a loosely organized system that provided guides, hiding places, and food to runaway slaves.

(E) "Conductors" and "agents" led "passengers" north to free states and Canada.

(F) The president of the Underground Railroad was an Indiana banker named Levi Coffin.

FACTORS THAT INFLUENCE TIDES

Tides are a natural phenomenon involving the alternating rise and fall in the earth's large bodies of water caused by the gravitational pull of the moon and the sun. The combination of these two variable forces produces the complex recurrent cycle of the tides. Tides may occur in both oceans and seas, to a limited extent in large lakes, the atmosphere, and, to a very minute degree, in the earth itself.

The force that generates tides results from the interaction of two forces: the centrifugal force produced by the revolution of the earth around the center–of–gravity of the earth–moon system; and the gravitational attraction of the moon acting upon the earth's waters. Although the moon is only 238,852 miles from the earth, compared with the sun's much greater distance of 92,956,000 miles, the moon's closer distance outranks its much smaller mass, and thus the moon's tide–raising force is more than twice that of the sun.

The tide–generating forces of the moon and sun cause a maximum accumulation of the waters of the oceans at two opposite positions on the earth's surface. At the same time, compensating amounts of water are drawn from all points 90 degrees away from these tidal bulges. As the earth rotates, a sequence of two high tides and two low tides is produced each day. Successive high tides occur on an average of 12.4 hours apart. High tide at any given location occurs when the moon is overhead and low tide when it is at either horizon.

The highest and lowest levels of high tide, called spring tide and neap tide, each occur twice in every lunar month of about 27.5 days. A spring tide occurs at the new moon and at the full moon, when the moon and earth are lined up with the sun, and thus the moon's pull is reinforced by the sun's pull. At spring tide, the difference between high and low tides is the greatest. A neap tide, the lowest level of high tide, occurs when the sun–to–earth direction is at right angles to the moon–to–earth direction. When this happens, the gravitational forces of the moon and sun counteract each other; thus, the moon's pull is at minimum strength, and the difference between high and low tides is the least. Spring and neap tides at any given location have a range of about 20 percent more or less, respectively, than the average high tide.

The vertical range of tides—the difference between high and low—varies according to the size, surface shape, and bottom topography of the basin in which tidal movement occurs. In the open water of the central Pacific, the range is no more than about a foot; in the relatively small, shallow North Sea, it is about 12 feet. Along the narrow channel of the Bay of Fundy in Nova Scotia, the difference between high and low tides may reach 45 feet under spring tide conditions—the world's widest tidal range. At New Orleans, which is at the mouth of the Mississippi River, the periodic rise and fall of the tides varies with the river's stage, being about ten inches at low stage and zero at high. In every case, actual high or low tide can vary considerably from the average.

Several factors affect tidal ranges, including abrupt changes in atmospheric pressure or prolonged periods of extreme high or low pressure. They are also influenced by the density and volume of seawater, variations in ocean–current velocities, earthquakes, and the growing or shrinking of the world's glaciers. In fact, any of these factors alone can alter sea level. The greater and more rapid the change of water level, the greater the erosive effect of the tidal action, and thus in the amount of material transported and deposited on the shore.

15. The word recurrent in paragraph 1 is closest in meaning to

   (A) repeating
   (B) mysterious
   (C) simultaneous
   (D) interrupted

16. According to the passage, the force that generates tides on the earth is

   (A) the gravitational pull of the earth's core
   (B) the same force that generates tides on the moon
   (C) abrupt changes in atmospheric pressure
   (D) a combination of gravity and centrifugal force

17. According to the passage, the moon

   (A) has a greater mass than the sun
   (B) is farther from the earth than the sun
   (C) has a gravitational pull toward the sun
   (D) affects tides more than the sun does

18. The word bulges in paragraph 3 is closest in meaning to

   (A) currents
   (B) ridges
   (C) increases
   (D) waves

19. What can be inferred from paragraph 3 about tides in different places on the earth?

   (A) High tide occurs at every location on the earth at the same time.
   (B) When it is high tide in some places, it is low tide in other places.
   (C) Some places have two high tides each day, but others have only one.
   (D) The time between high and low tides is the same in different places.

20. A spring tide occurs at the time of the lunar month when

   (A) the moon's gravitational pull is at its strongest
   (B) the moon appears as a crescent or half–circle
   (C) the sun does not exert any gravitational force
   (D) the difference between high and low tides is the least

21. The word counteract in paragraph 4 is closest in meaning to

   (A) enhance
   (B) signal
   (C) oppose
   (D) avoid

22. Which sentence below best expresses the essential information in the highlighted sentence in paragraph 4? Incorrect choices change the meaning in important ways or leave out essential information.

   (A) Spring tides are 20 percent more, and neap tides 20 percent less, than the average high tide in a particular place.
   (B) There has been a 20 percent change in the number of spring tides and neap tides that occur at certain locations.
   (C) If the location of a spring tide is known, then a neap tide in the same location will be 20 percent less.
   (D) 20 percent of both spring tides and neap tides always occur in the same location.

23. The author mentions the Bay of Fundy in paragraph 5 in order to

   (A) compare the Bay of Fundy with larger bodies of water
   (B) explain why a narrow channel is dangerous to ships
   (C) give the most extreme example of a tidal range
   (D) show how rivers can affect the rise and fall of tides

24. The word prolonged in paragraph 6 is closest in meaning to

    (A) extended
    (B) surprising
    (C) predicted
    (D) dangerous

25. All of the following are mentioned as influences on the vertical range of tides EXCEPT

    (A) the size and shape of the body of water
    (B) sudden changes in atmospheric pressure
    (C) increasing levels of pollution in the oceans
    (D) changes in the size of the world's glaciers

26. Look at the four squares, **A**, **B**, **C**, and **D**, which indicate where the following sentence could be added to the passage. Where would the sentence best fit?

Storm surges, such as the heaping up of ocean water by hurricane winds, are yet another factor.

    Several factors affect tidal ranges, including abrupt changes in atmospheric pressure or prolonged periods of extreme high or low pressure. **A** They are also influenced by the density and volume of seawater, variations in ocean–current velocities, earthquakes, and the growing or shrinking of the world's glaciers. **B** In fact, any of these factors alone can alter sea level. **C** The greater and more rapid the change of water level, the greater the erosive effect of the tidal action, and thus in the amount of material transported and deposited on the shore. **D**

27–28. An introductory sentence for a brief summary of the passage is provided below. Complete the summary by selecting the THREE answer choices that express the most important ideas in the passage. Some sentences do not belong in the summary because they express ideas that are not presented in the passage or are minor ideas in the passage. ***This question is worth 2 points.***

Many factors influence the phenomenon of tides, the alternating rise and fall in the earth's large bodies of water.
•
•
•

Answer Choices

(A) Tides occur in the earth's atmosphere and also in the earth itself.

(B) Scientists have been studying the moon's influence on tides for several centuries.

(C) The gravitational forces of the moon and the sun together produce the cycle of the tides.

(D) The level of high tide varies throughout the lunar month.

(E) The stage of the Mississippi River determines the level of tides at New Orleans.

(F) The character of the basin and various environmental conditions affect the vertical range of tides.

MARY COLTER AND FRANK LLOYD WRIGHT

In the early twentieth century, the thrust in American architecture was toward a style rooted in the American landscape and based on American rather than European forms. Two architects who worked independently yet simultaneously at endorsing an American architecture were Mary Colter (1869–1958) and Frank Lloyd Wright (1867–1959). Both developed regional styles that paralleled the regionalism seen in the other visual arts. Colter created a uniquely Southwestern idiom incorporating desert landscapes with Native American arts; Wright and his followers in Chicago developed the Prairie style of domestic architecure that reflected the natural landscape of the Midwest.

Mary Colter's hotels and national park buildings are rooted so masterfully in the history of the Southwest that they seem to be genuine pieces of that history. Her magnificent Watchtower, overlooking the Grand Canyon in Arizona, was built to suggest an ancient Native American ruin preserved for the delight of the present–day traveler.

Colter was a lifelong student of art history, natural history, and human civilization. Her well–rounded artistic talents empowered her to work historical references into buildings constructed with modern methods and materials. She preferred to use materials **indigenous** to the region, such as Kaibab limestone and yellow pine. She took great stock in materials and setting, gathering many of her materials on–site and incorporating them in their natural state into her projects. She treated building and site as integral halves of a single composition and merged them seamlessly. Her Lookout Studio, for example, appears to rise straight from the rim of the Grand Canyon because its layering of stonework matches the texture, pattern, and color of the canyon wall below it.

When Colter designed the Watchtower, she wanted the building to be a part of its environment while also enhancing the view of the surrounding desert and the canyon and river below. She decided to recreate a Native American watchtower because it would provide the necessary height while assuming the appearance of a prehistoric building. Colter was familiar with the architectural remains of ancient villages scattered about the Southwest and was especially fascinated by the stone towers—round, square, and oval monoliths. The ancient Round Tower at Mesa Verde became the direct inspiration for the form and proportions of the Watchtower. The Twin Towers ruin at Hovenweep, whose stone was closer to that available at the Grand Canyon, was the model for the Watchtower's masonry. The Watchtower is perhaps the best example of Colter's integration of history, architecture, and landscape in a unified work of art.

Like Mary Colter, Frank Lloyd Wright believed that architecture was an extension of the natural environment. Wright was appalled by much of what he saw in the industrialized world. He was not fond of cities, and although he designed office buildings and museums, his favorite commissions were for homes, usually in the country. Wright is associated with the Prairie style of residential architecture, whose emphasis on horizontal elements reflected the prairie landscapes of the Midwest. Most Prairie–style homes have one or two stories and are built of brick or timber covered with stucco. The eaves of the low–pitched roof extend well beyond the walls, enhancing the structure's horizontality.

Wright's own studio–residence in Wisconsin was completely integrated with the surrounding landscape. He nestled his house in the brow of a hill and gave it the name Taliesin, which means "shining brow" in Welsh. Every element of the design corresponded to the surounding landscape. The yellow stone came from a quarry a mile away, so Taliesin looked like the outcroppings on the local hills. The exterior wood was the color of gray tree trunks. The stucco walls above the stone had the same tawny color as the sandbanks in the river below.

Wright's most famous house, Falling Water, was built right over a waterfall in Pennsylvania. The house blends harmoniously with its surroundings, yet it departs from the Prairie philosophy of being a completely integrated extension of the natural landscape.

Glossary:
indigenous: originating or growing in an area; native

29. The word thrust in paragraph 1 is closest in meaning to

   (A) movement
   (B) criticism
   (C) accident
   (D) education

30. According to the passage, both Mary Colter and Frank Lloyd Wright designed buildings that

   (A) reflected the history of the region
   (B) emphasized the architect's individuality
   (C) relied on the assistance of other artists
   (D) blended into the natural environment

31. The author mentions Kaibab limestone and yellow pine in paragraph 3 as examples of

   (A) materials with high artistic value
   (B) references to art history and natural history
   (C) materials that are native to the Southwest
   (D) traditional materials that are now scarce

32. Which sentence below best expresses the essential information in the highlighted sentence in paragraph 3? Incorrect choices change the meaning in important ways or leave out essential information.

   (A) Colter valued materials and location, so she blended into her works many natural materials collected from the building site.
   (B) Because Colter used various types of materials, it was often difficult to combine them in a way that would look natural.
   (C) Colter bought stock in corporations that made building materials and delivered them directly to the project site.
   (D) Materials and setting were equally important to Colter, who was very skilled at choosing the right materials for the job.

33. The word them in paragraph 3 refers to

   (A) modern methods and materials
   (B) her projects
   (C) building and site
   (D) texture, pattern, and color

34. What was the main inspiration for Mary Colter's design of the Watchtower?

   (A) The beautiful views of the American Southwest
   (B) The ancient Round Tower at Mesa Verde
   (C) The colorful stone cliffs of the Grand Canyon
   (D) Architectural remains of masonry homes

35. What can be inferred from the passage about the Watchtower?

   (A) The Watchtower was the only building Colter designed at the Grand Canyon.
   (B) The Watchtower's purpose was to help people appreciate the desert scenery.
   (C) Colter used landscape design to enhance the beauty of the Watchtower.
   (D) The Watchtower's success inspired other architects to design tall buildings.

36. All of the following characterize the Prairie style of architecture EXCEPT

   (A) a concern for the surrounding landscape
   (B) a direct reference to the region's history
   (C) an emphasis on horizontal elements
   (D) a low roof that extends beyond the walls

37. The word nestled in paragraph 6 is closest in meaning to

   (A) set comfortably
   (B) built daringly
   (C) painted brightly
   (D) buried deeply

38. Why does the author mention Falling Water in paragraph 7?

    (A) To criticize Wright's most famous house design
    (B) To provide the best illustration of the Prairie style
    (C) To give an example of an artistic use of a waterfall
    (D) To show that Wright did not work in just one style

39. Look at the four squares, **A**, **B**, **C**, and **D**, which indicate where the following sentence could be added to the passage. Where would the sentence best fit?

Taliesin's rough stone facades and low–slung roofs blurred the distinction between the manmade and the natural.

Wright's own studio–residence in Wisconsin was completely integrated with the surrounding landscape. **A** He nestled his house in the brow of a hill and gave it the name Taliesin, which means "shining brow" in Welsh. **B** Every element of the design corresponded to the surrounding landscape. The yellow stone came from a quarry a mile away, so Taliesin looked like the outcroppings on the local hills. **C** The exterior wood was the color of gray tree trunks. **D** The stucco walls above the stone had the same tawny color as the sandbanks in the river below.

40–42. Select the appropriate sentences from the answer choices and match them to the architect to which they refer. TWO of the answer choices will NOT be used. ***This question is worth 3 points.***

Answer Choices	Architect
(A) Others followed the architect in developing a style that would suit the landscape of the prairies.	**Mary Colter**
(B) The architect improved the designs of famous architects of the past.	•
(C) The architect developed a style integrating the history and landscape of the American Southwest.	• •
(D) The architect preferred designing country residences.	
(E) Native American culture provided the architect with ideas and inspiration.	**Frank Lloyd Wright**
(F) The architect worked exclusively with modern materials and methods.	• •
(G) The architect designed structures that would blend into the desert environment.	

Answers to Test 2 – Reading are on page 601.

Record your score on the Progress Chart on page 697.

How to Score Multiple–Point Questions		
Points Possible	**Answers Correct**	**Points Earned**
2 points	3	2
	2	1
	0 – 1	0
3 points	5	3
	4	2
	3	1
	0 – 2	0
4 points	7	4
	6	3
	5	2
	4	1
	0 – 3	0

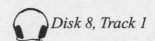
Disk 8, Track 1

LISTENING SECTION DIRECTIONS

The Listening section measures your ability to understand conversations and lectures in English. You will hear each conversation and lecture only one time. After each conversation or lecture, you will hear some questions about it. Answer all questions based on what the speakers state or imply.

You may take notes while you listen. You may use your notes to help you answer the questions.

Most questions have four possible answers. In some questions, you will see this icon: 🎧. This means that you will hear, but not see, part of the question.

Some questions have special directions, which appear in a gray box. Most questions are worth one point. If a question is worth more than one point, special directions will indicate how many points you can receive.

You have approximately 40 minutes to complete the Listening section. This includes the time for listening to the conversations and lectures and for answering the questions.

To make this practice more like the real test, cover the questions and answers during each conversation and lecture. When you hear the first question, uncover the questions and answers.

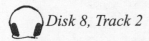 *Disk 8, Track 2*

1. What are the students mainly discussing?

   (A) The classes that they are taking
   (B) The theater program at their school
   (C) The woman's interest in an internship
   (D) The man's experience in a law firm

2. What does the woman like about theater?

   (A) The chance to meet interesting people
   (B) The opportunity to improve her acting
   (C) The efficiency of theater management
   (D) The entire atmosphere of theater

3. What is the woman's opinion of her own acting ability?

   (A) She thinks she needs more acting experience.
   (B) She is excited about learning new acting skills.
   (C) She thinks she is not very skilled at acting.
   (D) She thinks she is better at acting than directing.

4. Why does the man say this:

   (A) To state what he likes about the theater
   (B) To learn more about the woman's interests
   (C) To imply that the woman should be a director
   (D) To compliment the woman on her abilities

5. What does the man suggest the woman do?

   Click on two answers.

   [A] Talk to her adviser
   [B] Observe the director
   [C] Take an acting class
   [D] Write to the theater

 *Disk 8, Track 3*

6. Why does the student go to see the professor?

   (A) He needs advice about a problem with his house.
   (B) He wants to discuss an idea for a paper.
   (C) He is confused about an article that he read.
   (D) He would like to enroll in her geology course.

7. What topic is the man mainly interested in?

   (A) Some houses that are sliding
   (B) Effects of groundwater removal
   (C) How to build a sturdy home
   (D) Why a famous tower is leaning

8. Why does the student say this:

   (A) He would like to visit the Leaning Tower of Pisa.
   (B) He thinks the local slide may have a similar cause.
   (C) He wants to work as an engineer in tall buildings.
   (D) He needs information that he missed due to absence.

9. According to the professor, where are mudslides most common?

   (A) 30 feet beneath the earth's surface
   (B) On slopes of 27 to 45 degrees
   (C) In places where frozen ground melts
   (D) In the San Joaquin Valley of California

10. What will the man probably include in his research?

Click on two answers.

[A] An article about groundwater removal
[B] A visit to a leaning tower
[C] A study of the area's geology
[D] A search for other mudslides in the area

 Disk 8, Track 4

11. What aspects of flowers does the class mainly discuss?

Click on two answers.

[A] The evolution of flowers
[B] The organs of a flower
[C] The composite family of flowers
[D] The uses of flowers in art

12. Which part of the flower attracts insects and birds?

(A) Sepals
(B) Petals
(C) Stamens
(D) Carpels

13. Listen again to part of the discussion. Then answer the question.

Why does the professor say this:

(A) To remind the student that his lab report is due today
(B) To apologize for giving the student incorrect information
(C) To announce that the location of the lab has moved
(D) To imply that the student will see examples in the lab

14. Select the drawing that is most likely a member of the composite family.

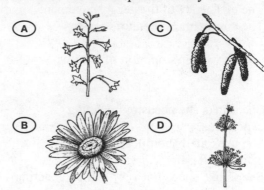

15. Based on the information in the discussion, indicate whether each statement below is true or not true.

For each sentence, click in the correct box.

	True	Not true
Incomplete flowers do not have all four basic flower organs.		
The sunflower has one large symmetrical flower on its stalk.		
All varieties of the English daisy are white with a yellow center.		
The arrangement of flowers on the stalk can help identify the plant's family.		

16. According to the professor, how did the daisy get its name?

(A) Its central disk resembles the human eye.
(B) Its flowers open at dawn, the "day's eye."
(C) It blooms for only one day each year.
(D) It was named for an Anglo–Saxon chief.

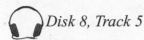 *Disk 8, Track 5*

17. What is the main idea of the lecture?

   Ⓐ Every human society is interested in sports.
   Ⓑ Rules were developed to make sports fair.
   Ⓒ Sports contain many elements of hunting.
   Ⓓ Complex cultures have violent sports.

18. Listen again to part of the discussion. Then answer the question.

   Why does the professor say this:

   Ⓐ To find out if the student did her homework
   Ⓑ To contradict the student's answer
   Ⓒ To learn about what food the student likes
   Ⓓ To encourage the student to elaborate

19. According to the professor, why did the ancient Romans build the Coliseum?

   Ⓐ To make the hunt an entertainment for spectators
   Ⓑ To compete with other cities in sports architecture
   Ⓒ To put Rome at the center of Olympic sports
   Ⓓ To shock and offend the enemies of Rome

20. What point does the professor make about track and field sports?

   Ⓐ They were performed in the Coliseum of Rome.
   Ⓑ They are shocking because an animal is killed.
   Ⓒ They are the most popular sporting events today.
   Ⓓ They involve skills originally used by hunters.

21. Which sports contain a symbolic element of the kill?

   Click on two answers.

   Ⓐ Fencing
   Ⓑ Running
   Ⓒ Baseball
   Ⓓ Boxing

22. What does the professor imply about the negative element of sports?

   Ⓐ People prefer sports with a strong negative element.
   Ⓑ The concept of sportsmanship makes sports less negative.
   Ⓒ Today, only blood sports contain a negative element.
   Ⓓ Sports will become even more negative in the future.

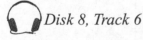 *Disk 8, Track 6*

23. What is the talk mainly about?

   Ⓐ Epidemics around the world
   Ⓑ Why diseases change over time
   Ⓒ How epidemiologists gather data
   Ⓓ Experimental studies of diseases

24. What factors do epidemiologists study?
   Click on two answers.

   Ⓐ What causes outbreaks of a disease
   Ⓑ Different names for the same disease
   Ⓒ How diseases spread through populations
   Ⓓ Stages in the treatment of a disease

25–26. Based on the information in the talk, indicate whether each sentence below describes descriptive, observational, or experimental epidemiology.

For each sentence, click in the correct box. This question is worth 2 points.

	Descriptive	Observational	Experimental
Statistics are used to describe the trend of a disease over time.			
Researchers intervene to test a hypothesis about cause and effect.			
Researchers examine the eating habits of sick and well people.			
A treatment group is compared with a non–treatment group.			

27. Why do epidemiologists often study two groups of people?

(A) To learn why some people get a disease and others do not

(B) To compare different people's attitudes toward work

(C) To explain why some people take better care of themselves

(D) To understand cultural differences in approaches to disease

28. Listen again to part of the talk. Then answer the question.

Why does the speaker talk about her own work?

(A) To show how one organization uses various approaches to epidemiology

(B) To describe her organization's efforts to discover a cure for AIDS

(C) To inform the students that she prefers doing research to giving lectures

(D) To encourage students to work at her organization after they graduate

Disk 8, Track 7

29. What is playing by ear?

(A) Listening to music through ear phones

(B) Playing an instrument that is held up to the ear

(C) Paying attention to what the teacher says

(D) Learning to play music without reading notation

30. Listen again to part of the talk. Then answer the question.

Why does the professor ask this:

(A) To suggest that all children should study music

(B) To introduce the main point he wants to make

(C) To find out if everyone in class can read music

(D) To review material for an examination

31. According to the professor, when should children learn to read musical notation?

    Click on two answers.

    [A] When they first learn how to play an instrument
    [B] When a group of children play music together
    [C] When the music is too complex to learn by ear
    [D] When they are ready to play in front of an audience

32. According to the professor, why should a music teacher play the score for a child the first time?

    (A) To demonstrate how the printed notes translate into music
    (B) To suggest that the score can be played in different styles
    (C) To allow the child to memorize the score by listening
    (D) To show the child that the teacher is an excellent player

33. According to the professor, what is the natural order for children to learn music?

    Drag each sentence to the space where it belongs.

    (A) Learn how to read standard notation.
    (B) Learn how to play the instrument by ear.
    (C) Learn how to play by chord symbols.

1	
2	
3	

34. What does the professor imply about the three methods of playing music?

    (A) Each method is appropriate for some students.
    (B) There is no reason to learn all three methods.
    (C) The best method is playing by standard notation.
    (D) Students should use the teacher's favorite method.

 Stop

Answers to Test 2 – Listening are on page 602.

Record your score on the Progress Chart on page 697.

How to Score Multiple–Point Questions		
Points Possible	Answers Correct	Points Earned
2 points	4	2
	3	1
	0 – 2	0

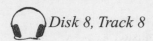 *Disk 8, Track 8*

SPEAKING SECTION DIRECTIONS

The Speaking section measures your ability to speak in English about a variety of topics. There are six questions in this section. Record your response to each question on a cassette.

Questions 1 and 2 are independent speaking tasks in which you will speak about familiar topics. Your responses will be scored on your ability to speak clearly and coherently about the topics.

Questions 3 and 4 are integrated tasks in which you will read a passage, listen to a conversation or lecture, and then speak in response to a question about what you have read and heard. You will need to combine relevant information from the two sources to answer the question completely. Your responses will be scored on your ability to speak clearly and coherently and on your ability to accurately convey information about what you read and heard.

Questions 5 and 6 are integrated tasks in which you will listen to part of a conversation or lecture, and then speak in response to a question about what you have heard. Your responses will be scored on your ability to speak clearly and coherently and on your ability to accurately convey information about what you heard.

You will hear each conversation and lecture only one time. You may take notes while you listen. You may use your notes to help you answer the questions.

 Stop

For questions 1 and 2, you will speak in response to a question about a familiar topic. Use your own personal knowledge and experience to answer each question. After you hear the question, you have 15 seconds to prepare your response and 45 seconds to speak.

QUESTION 1

 Disk 8, Track 9

> Describe a person who has influenced you in an important way. Explain why this person has had an effect on your life. Include details and examples in your explanation.

 Stop

Preparation Time – 15 seconds
Response Time – 45 seconds

QUESTION 2

 Disk 8, Track 10

> Some people get most of their news from the radio or television. Others read the newspaper. Which source of news do you think is better and why? Include details and examples in your explanation.

 Stop

Preparation Time – 15 seconds
Response Time – 45 seconds

QUESTION 3

In this question, you will read a short passage about a campus situation, listen to a conversation, and then speak in response to a question about what you have read and heard. After you hear the question, you have 30 seconds to prepare your response and 60 seconds to speak.

Reading Time – 45 seconds

ATTENDANCE POLICY

Students are expected to attend all classes for which they are registered, including the first class session. Classes for which attendance is mandatory from the first session will be so noted in the class schedule. Instructors may set an attendance policy for each class, and it is the student's responsibility to know and comply with individual class attendance policies. Students who fail to comply with the established attendance policy for the class forfeit the right to continue in class and will be subject to an administrative withdrawal.

Now cover the passage and question. Listen to the recording. When you hear the question, uncover the question and begin preparing your response.

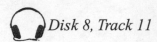 *Disk 8, Track 11*

The woman expresses her opinion about the attendance policy. State her opinion and explain the reasons she gives for holding that opinion.

 Stop

Preparation Time – 30 seconds
Response Time – 60 seconds

QUESTION 4

In this question, you will read a short passage on an academic subject, listen to a lecture on the same topic, and then speak in response to a question about what you have read and heard. After you hear the question, you have 30 seconds to prepare your response and 60 seconds to speak.

Reading Time – 45 seconds

PARTICIPANT OBSERVATION

To study real–life behaviors, social scientists have to get out in the field and take notes, and they have to do it systematically. A favorite method for many researchers is participant observation. In participant observation, the researcher becomes part of the group under study. This method is often used to study groups that are not easy to observe from the outside, such as street gangs or farm laborers. In some studies, no one knows the researcher's identity. However, this is controversial because observing people without their knowledge, or recording their comments without their permission, is not always considered ethical.

Now cover the passage and question. Listen to the recording. When you hear the question, uncover the question and begin preparing your response.

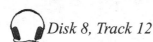 *Disk 8, Track 12*

> Explain the ethical problem in the participant observation study discussed in the lecture. State what the researcher did to solve the problem, and explain why this was acceptable.

 Stop

Preparation Time – 30 seconds
Response Time – 60 seconds

QUESTION 5

In this question, you will listen to a conversation. You will then be asked to talk about the information in the conversation and to give your opinion about the ideas presented. To make this practice more like the real test, cover the question during the conversation. After you hear the question, you have 20 seconds to prepare your response and 60 seconds to speak.

 Disk 8, Track 13

> Describe the man's problem and the suggestions the woman makes about what he should do. What do you think the man should do, and why?

 Stop

Preparation Time – 20 seconds
Response Time – 60 seconds

QUESTION 6

In this question, you will listen to part of a lecture. You will then be asked to summarize important information from the lecture. To make this practice more like the real test, cover the question during the lecture. After you hear the question, you have 20 seconds to prepare your response and 60 seconds to speak.

 Disk 8, Track 14

> Using points and examples from the talk, explain the two types of competition in bird populations. Then explain how population size and competition are related.

 Stop

Preparation Time – 20 seconds
Response Time – 60 seconds

Key points for Test 2 – Speaking are on page 604.

Each response earns a score of 1, 2, 3 or 4.

Record your total score on the Progress Chart on page 697.

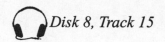 *Disk 8, Track 15*

WRITING SECTION DIRECTIONS

The Writing section measures your ability to use writing to communicate in an academic environment. There are two writing questions.

Question 1 is an integrated writing task. You will read a passage, listen to a lecture, and then answer a question based on what you have read and heard. You have 20 minutes to plan and write your response.

Question 2 is an independent writing task. You will answer a question based on your own knowledge and experience. You have 30 minutes to plan and write your response.

 Stop

QUESTION 1

For this task, you will write a response to a question about a reading passage and a short lecture. The question does not ask you to express your personal opinion.

Read the passage and then listen to the recording. To make this practice more like the real test, cover the passage and question during the lecture. You may take notes, and you may use your notes to help you write your response. When you hear the question, uncover the passage and question. Then allow 20 minutes to plan and write your response.

Typically, an effective response will have 150 to 225 words. Your response will be evaluated on the quality of your writing and on the completeness and accuracy of the content.

Reading Time – 3 minutes

Research data show that multi–age play groups are common in simple societies made up of communities with fewer than 1,500 people. In contrast, complex industrial societies are more likely to have same–age peer groups that are made up of children who are equal in age.

In most of the world's traditional, non–Western cultures, children play in groups with others of different ages. Multi–age play groups consist of six or more children of both genders, ranging in age from late infancy to adolescence. In multi–age groups, younger children have the opportunity to learn language, survival skills, and games from children ahead of them in the process of development. The older children get experience in teaching what they know and a chance to feel important and responsible.

In Western culture, on the other hand, parents and teachers generally believe that it is best for children to study and play with other children of the same age. Thus, same–age peer groups are the norm for children both in and out of school, and at all ages, including infancy. Peers play an important positive role in children's socialization because peers are both equals and competitors. In childhood and adolescence, peers are usually friends, and peer groups build friendship, tolerance, and cooperation. Peers are status equals in terms of power; they can tease and tolerate each other without the intervention of adults. With peers, children create worlds of meaning in which they become active agents in their own socialization. Same–age peer groups promote cooperation and group identity. They also promote the learning of competitive strategies that are healthy and necessary for survival in a competitive society.

Now cover the passage and question. Listen to the recording. When you hear the question, uncover the passage and question and begin your response.

 Disk 8, Track 16

> Summarize the points made by the professor about same–age peer groups, explaining how they cast doubt on points made in the reading.

 Stop

Writing Time – 20 minutes

QUESTION 2

For this task, you will write an essay in response to a question that asks you to express, explain, and support your opinion on a topic. You have 30 minutes to plan, write, and revise your essay.

Typically, an effective essay will have a minimum of 300 words. Your essay will be evaluated on the quality of your writing, including the organization and development of your ideas and the quality and accuracy of the language you use to express your ideas.

Read the question below and make any notes that will help you plan your response. Then begin typing your essay.

> Do you agree or disagree with the following statement?
> **There are times when lying is acceptable.**
> Use specific reasons and examples to support your opinion.

Writing Time – 30 minutes

Key points for Test 2 – Writing are on page 605.

Each response earns a score of 1, 2, 3, 4 or 5.

Record your total score on the Progress Chart on page 697.

READING SECTION DIRECTIONS

The Reading section measures your ability to read and understand passages in English. You will read three passages and answer questions about them.

For most questions, you will choose the one best answer of four possible answers. These questions are worth one point each. The last question in each set is worth more than one point. The directions for this question indicate how many points you can receive.

Some passages have one or more words in bold type. For these bolded words, you will see a definition or explanation in a glossary at the end of the passage.

Answer all questions about a passage on the basis of what is stated or implied in that passage.

You have 60 minutes to read the passages and answer all of the questions. Allow approximately 20 minutes to work on each passage.

The Development of Refrigeration

Cold storage, or refrigeration, is keeping food at temperatures between 32 and 45 degrees F in order to delay the growth of microorganisms—bacteria, molds, and yeast—that cause food to spoil. Refrigeration produces few changes in food, so meats, fish, eggs, milk, fruits, and vegetables keep their original flavor, color, and nutrition. Before artificial refrigeration was invented, people stored perishable food with ice or snow to lengthen its storage time. Preserving food by keeping it in an ice–filled pit is a 4,000–year–old art. Cold storage areas were built in basements, cellars, or caves, lined with wood or straw, and packed with ice. The ice was transported from mountains, or harvested from local lakes or rivers, and delivered in large blocks to homes and businesses.

Artificial refrigeration is the process of removing heat from a substance, container, or enclosed area, to lower its temperature. The heat is moved from the inside of the container to the outside. A refrigerator uses the evaporation of a volatile liquid, or refrigerant, to absorb heat. In most types of refrigerators, the refrigerant is compressed, pumped through a pipe, and allowed to vaporize. As the liquid turns to vapor, it absorbs heat because the molecules of vapor use energy to leave the liquid. The molecules left behind have less energy and so the liquid becomes colder. Thus, the air inside the refrigerator is chilled.

Scientists and inventors from around the world developed artificial refrigeration during the eighteenth and nineteenth centuries. William Cullen demonstrated artificial refrigeration in Scotland in 1748, when he let ethyl ether boil into a partial vacuum. In 1805, American inventor Oliver Evans designed the first refrigeration machine that used vapor instead of liquid. In 1842, physician John Gorrie used Evans's design to create an air–cooling apparatus to treat yellow–fever patients in a Florida hospital. Gorrie later left his medical practice and experimented with ice making, and in 1851 he was granted the first U.S. patent for mechanical refrigeration. In the same year, an Australian printer, James Harrison, built an ether refrigerator after noticing that when he cleaned his type with ether it became very cold as the ether evaporated. Five years later, Harrison introduced vapor–compression refrigeration to the brewing and meatpacking industries.

Brewing was the first industry in the United States to use mechanical refrigeration extensively, and in the 1870s, commercial refrigeration was primarily directed at breweries. German–born Adolphus Busch was the first to use artificial refrigeration at his brewery in St. Louis. Before refrigeration, brewers stored their beer in caves, and production was constrained by the amount of available cave space. Brewing was strictly a local business, since beer was highly perishable and shipping it any distance would result in spoilage. Busch solved the storage problem with the commercial vapor–compression refrigerator. He solved the shipping problem with the newly invented refrigerated railcar, which was insulated with ice bunkers in each end. Air came in on the top, passed through the bunkers, and circulated through the car by gravity. In solving Busch's spoilage and storage problems, refrigeration also revolutionized an entire industry. By 1891, nearly every brewery was equipped with mechanical refrigerating machines.

The refrigerators of today rely on the same basic principle of cooling caused by the rapid evaporation and expansion of gases. Until 1929, refrigerators used toxic gases—ammonia, methyl chloride, and sulfur dioxide—as refrigerants. After those gases accidentally killed several people, chlorofluorocarbons (CFCs) became the standard refrigerant. However, they were found to be harmful to the earth's ozone layer, so refrigerators now use a refrigerant called HFC 134a, which is less harmful to the ozone.

1. What is the main reason that people developed methods of refrigeration?

   (A) They wanted to improve the flavor and nutritional value of food.
   (B) They needed to slow the natural processes that cause food to spoil.
   (C) They needed a use for the ice that formed on lakes and rivers.
   (D) They wanted to expand the production of certain industries.

2. The word perishable in paragraph 1 is closest in meaning to

   (A) capable of spoiling
   (B) uncooked
   (C) of animal origin
   (D) highly nutritious

3. What can be inferred from paragraph 1 about cold storage before the invention of artificial refrigeration?

   (A) It kept food cold for only about a week.
   (B) It was dependent on a source of ice or snow.
   (C) It required a container made of metal or wood.
   (D) It was not a safe method of preserving meat.

4. Artificial refrigeration involves all of the following processes EXCEPT

   (A) the pumping of water vapor through a pipe
   (B) the rapid expansion of certain gases
   (C) the evaporation of a volatile liquid
   (D) the transfer of heat from one place to another

5. Which sentence below best expresses the essential information in the highlighted sentence in paragraph 2? Incorrect choices change the meaning in important ways or leave out essential information.

   (A) It takes a lot of energy to transform a liquid into a vapor, especially when the vapor loses heat.
   (B) Some gases expand rapidly and give off energy when they encounter a very cold liquid.
   (C) When kinetic energy is changed to heat energy, liquid molecules turn into vapor molecules.
   (D) During evaporation, the vapor molecules use energy.

6. According to the passage, who was the first person to use artificial refrigeration for a practical purpose?

   (A) William Cullen
   (B) Oliver Evans
   (C) John Gorrie
   (D) Adolphus Busch

7. The word it in paragraph 3 refers to

   (A) printer
   (B) refrigerator
   (C) type
   (D) ether

8. Why does the author discuss the brewing industry in paragraph 4?

   (A) To compare cave storage with mechanical refrigeration
   (B) To describe the unique problems that brewers faced
   (C) To praise the accomplishments of a prominent brewer
   (D) To show how refrigeration changed a whole industry

9. The word constrained in paragraph 4 is closest in meaning to

   (A) restricted
   (B) spoiled
   (C) improved
   (D) alternated

10. According to the passage, the first refrigerated railcar used what material as a cooling agent?

- (A) Ether
- (B) Ice
- (C) Ammonia
- (D) CFCs

11. The word toxic in paragraph 5 is closest in meaning to

- (A) dense
- (B) poisonous
- (C) rare
- (D) expensive

12. Look at the four squares, **A**, **B**, **C**, and **D**, which indicate where the following sentence could be added to the passage. Where would the sentence best fit?

Gorrie's basic principle of compressing a gas, and then sending it through radiating coils to cool it, is the one most often used in refrigerators today.

Scientists and inventors from around the world developed artificial refrigeration during the eighteenth and nineteenth centuries. **A** William Cullen demonstrated artificial refrigeration in Scotland in 1748, when he let ethyl ether boil into a partial vacuum. In 1805, American inventor Oliver Evans designed the first refrigeration machine that used vapor instead of liquid. **B** In 1842, physician John Gorrie used Evans's design to create an air–cooling apparatus to treat yellow–fever patients in a Florida hospital. **C** Gorrie later left his medical practice and experimented with ice making, and in 1851 he was granted the first U.S. patent for mechanical refrigeration. **D** In the same year, an Australian printer, James Harrison, built an ether refrigerator after noticing that when he cleaned his type with ether it became very cold as the ether evaporated. Five years later, Harrison introduced vapor–compression refrigeration to the brewing and meatpacking industries.

13–14. An introductory sentence for a brief summary of the passage is provided below. Complete the summary by selecting the THREE answer choices that express the most important ideas in the passage. Some sentences do not belong in the summary because they express ideas that are not presented in the passage or are minor ideas in the passage. **This question is worth 2 points.**

Methods of refrigeration have changed throughout history.
•
•
•

Answer Choices

(A) A refrigerator has an evaporator that makes the inside of the refrigerator cold.

(B) People used to preserve food by packing it with ice or snow in cold storage areas.

(C) Artificial refrigeration was made possible by the compression and evaporation of a volatile substance.

(D) William Cullen developed a method of artificial refrigeration in 1748.

(E) Practical uses of vapor compression refrigeration were introduced in the nineteenth century.

(F) CFCs have not been used as refrigerants since they were found to damage the earth's ozone layer.

CANADIAN ENGLISH

Canadian English is a regional variety of North American English that spans almost the entire continent. Canadian English became a separate variety of North American English after the American Revolution, when thousands of Loyalists, people who had supported the British, left the United States and fled north to Canada. Many Loyalists settled in southern Ontario in the 1780s, and their speech became the basis for what is called General Canadian, a definition based on the norms of urban middle–class speech.

Modern Canadian English is usually defined by the ways in which it resembles and differs from American or British English. Canadian English has a great deal in common with the English spoken in the United States, yet many Americans identify a Canadian accent as British. Many American visitors to Canada think the Canadian vocabulary sounds British—for example, they notice the British "tap" and "braces" instead of the American "faucet" and "suspenders." On the other hand, many British people identify a Canadian accent as American, and British visitors think the Canadians have become Americanized, saying "gas" and "truck" for "petrol" and "lorry."

People who live outside North America often find it difficult to hear the differences between Canadian and American English. There are many similarities between the two varieties, yet they are far from identical. Canadian English is instantly recognizable to other Canadians, and one Canadian in a crowded room will easily spot the other Canadian among the North Americans.

There is no distinctive Canadian grammar. The differences are mainly in pronunciation, vocabulary, and idioms. Canadian pronunciation reflects the experience of a people struggling for national identity against two strong influences. About 75 percent of Canadians use the British "zed" rather than the American "zee" for the name of the last letter of the alphabet. On the other hand, 75 percent of Canadians use the American pronunciation of "schedule," "tomato," and "missile." The most obvious and distinctive feature of Canadian speech is probably its vowel sound, the **diphthong** "ou." In Canada, "out" is pronounced like "oat" in nearby U.S. accents. There are other identifying features of Canadian vowels; for example, "cot" is pronounced the same as "caught" and "collar" the same as "caller."

An important characteristic of the vocabulary of Canadian English is the use of many words and phrases originating in Canada itself, such as "kerosene" and "chesterfield" ("sofa"). Several words are borrowed from North American Indian languages, for example, "kayak," "caribou," "parka," and "skookum" ("strong"). The name of the country itself has an Indian origin; the Iroquois word "kanata" originally meant "village." A number of terms for ice hockey—"face–off," "blue–line," and "puck"—have become part of World Standard English.

Some features of Canadian English seem to be unique and are often deliberately identified with Canadian speakers in such contexts as dramatic and literary characterizations. Among the original Canadian idioms, perhaps the most famous is the almost universal use of "eh?" as a tag question, as in "That's a good movie, eh?" "Eh" is also used as a filler during a narrative, as in "I'm walking home from work, eh, and I'm thinking about dinner. I finally get home, eh, and the refrigerator is empty."

The traditional view holds that there are no dialects in Canadian English and that Canadians cannot tell where other Canadians are from just by listening to them. The linguists of today disagree with this view. While there is a greater degree of homogeneity in Canadian English compared with American English, several dialect areas do exist across Canada. Linguists have identified distinct dialects for the Maritime Provinces, Newfoundland, the Ottawa Valley, southern Ontario, the Prairie Provinces, the Arctic North, and the West.

Glossary:
   diphthong: a speech sound that begins with one vowel and changes to another vowel

15. According to the passage, how did Canadian English become a distinct variety of North American English?

(A) Linguists noticed that Canadians spoke a unique dialect.
(B) A large group of Loyalists settled in one region at the same time.
(C) Growth of the middle class led to a standard school curriculum.
(D) Canadians declared their language to be different from U.S. English.

16. The word norms in paragraph 1 is closest in meaning to

(A) patterns
(B) history
(C) words
(D) ideas

17. The phrase a great deal in common with in paragraph 2 is closest in meaning to

(A) different words for
(B) the same problems as
(C) many similarities to
(D) easier pronunciation than

18. In paragraph 2, what point does the author make about Canadian English?

(A) Canadian English is more similar to American than to British English.
(B) American and British visitors define Canadian English by their own norms.
(C) Canadian English has many words that are not in other varieties of English.
(D) Canadians speak English with an accent that Americans cannot understand.

19. The phrase the two varieties in paragraph 3 refers to

(A) People who live outside North America
(B) Canadian English and American English
(C) General Canadian and North American
(D) British English and Canadian English

20. The word spot in paragraph 3 is closest in meaning to

(A) describe
(B) ignore
(C) prefer
(D) find

21. Which sentence below best expresses the essential information in the highlighted sentence in paragraph 4? Incorrect choices change the meaning in important ways or leave out essential information.

(A) Canadian English has been strongly influenced by both British and American English.
(B) Canada is the only nation where people can deliberately choose which pronunciation they prefer.
(C) Canadians have tried to distinguish themselves as a nation, and this effort is shown in their pronunciation.
(D) Many newcomers to Canada must work hard to master the national style of pronouncing English.

22. All of the following words originated in North American Indian languages EXCEPT

(A) kerosene
(B) parka
(C) Canada
(D) kayak

23. Which of the following can be inferred from paragraph 5 about vocabulary?

(A) Vocabulary is the most distinctive feature of Canadian English.
(B) World Standard English has a very large vocabulary.
(C) Canadians use more North American Indian words than Americans do.
(D) Much of the vocabulary for ice hockey originated in Canada.

24. The author discusses the expression "eh" in paragraph 6 as an example of

  (A) an idiom that uniquely characterizes Canadian speech
  (B) an expression that few people outside Canada have heard
  (C) a style of Canadian drama and literature
  (D) a word that cannot be translated into other languages

25. The word homogeneity in paragraph 7 is closest in meaning to

  (A) accent
  (B) change
  (C) creativity
  (D) sameness

26. Look at the four squares, **A**, **B**, **C**, and **D**, which indicate where the following sentence could be added to the passage. Where would the sentence best fit?

Thus, "out" rhymes with "boat," so the phrase "out and about in a boat" sounds like "oat and aboat in a boat" to American ears.

There is no distinctive Canadian grammar. The differences are mainly in pronunciation, vocabulary, and idioms. Canadian pronunciation reflects the experience of a people struggling for national identity against two strong influences. About 75 percent of Canadians use the British "zed" rather than the American "zee" for the name of the last letter of the alphabet. On the other hand, 75 percent of Canadians use the American pronunciation of "schedule," "tomato," and "missile." **A** The most obvious and distinctive feature of Canadian speech is probably its vowel sound, the diphthong "ou." **B** In Canada, "out" is pronounced like "oat" in nearby U.S. accents. **C** There are other identifying features of Canadian vowels; for example, "cot" is pronounced the same as "caught" and "collar" the same as "caller." **D**

27–28. An introductory sentence for a brief summary of the passage is provided below. Complete the summary by selecting the THREE answer choices that express the most important ideas in the passage. Some sentences do not belong in the summary because they express ideas that are not presented in the passage or are minor ideas in the passage. *This question is worth 2 points.*

Canadian English is a variety of North American English that contains several distinguishing features.
•
•
•

Answer Choices

(A) Canadian English contains elements of both British and American English.

(B) Several unique varieties of English have evolved in North America.

(C) Canadians pronounce most words the same way as Americans do.

(D) Canadian English asserts its distinctiveness through pronunciation.

(E) Words and idioms originating in Canada also help to define Canadian English.

(F) Most Canadians cannot identify where other Canadians are from.

THE SCIENCE OF ANTHROPOLOGY

Through various methods of research, anthropologists try to fit together the pieces of the human puzzle—to discover how humanity was first achieved, what made it branch out in different directions, and why separate societies behave similarly in some ways but quite differently in other ways. Anthropology, which emerged as an independent science in the late eighteenth century, has two main divisions: physical anthropology and cultural anthropology. *Physical anthropology* focuses on human evolution and variation and uses methods of physiology, genetics, and ecology. *Cultural anthropology* focuses on culture and includes archaeology, social anthropology, and linguistics.

Physical anthropologists are most concerned with human biology. Physical anthropologists are detectives whose mission is to solve the mystery of how humans came to be human. They ask questions about the events that led a tree–dwelling population of animals to evolve into two–legged beings with the power to learn—a power that we call intelligence. Physical anthropologists study the fossils and organic remains of once–living **primates**. They also study the connections between humans and other primates that are still living. Monkeys, apes, and humans have more in common with one another physically than they do with other kinds of animals. In the lab, anthropologists use the methods of physiology and genetics to investigate the composition of blood chemistry for clues to the relationship of humans to various primates. Some study the animals in the wild to find out what behaviors they share with humans. Others speculate about how the behavior of non–human primates might have shaped human bodily needs and habits.

A well–known family of physical anthropologists, the Leakeys, conducted research in East Africa indicating that human evolution centered there rather than Asia. In 1931, Louis Leakey and his wife Mary Leakey began excavating at Olduvai Gorge in Tanzania, where over the next forty years they discovered stone tool and **hominid** evidence that pushed back the dates for early humans to over 3.75 million years ago. Their son, Richard Leakey, discovered yet other types of hominid skulls in Kenya, which he wrote about in *Origins* (1979) and *Origins Reconsidered* (1992).

Like physical anthropologists, cultural anthropologists study clues about human life in the distant past; however, cultural anthropologists also look at the similarities and differences among human communities today. Some cultural anthropologists work in the field, living and working among people in societies that differ from their own. Anthropologists doing fieldwork often produce an ethnography, a written description of the daily activities of men, women, and children that tells the story of the society's community life as a whole. Some cultural anthropologists do not work in the field but rather at research universities and museums doing the comparative and interpretive part of the job. These anthropologists, called ethnologists, sift through the ethnographies written by field anthropologists and try to discover cross–cultural patterns in marriage, child rearing, religious beliefs and practices, warfare—any subject that constitutes the human experience. They often use their findings to argue for or against particular hypotheses about people worldwide.

A cultural anthropologist who achieved worldwide fame was Margaret Mead. In 1923, Mead went to Samoa to pursue her first fieldwork assignment—a study that resulted in her widely read book *Coming of Age in Samoa* (1928). Mead published ten major works during her long career, moving from studies of child rearing in the Pacific to the cultural and biological bases of gender, the nature of cultural change, the structure and functioning of complex societies, and race relations. Mead remained a pioneer in her willingness to tackle subjects of major intellectual consequence, to develop new technologies for research, and to think of new ways that anthropology could serve society.

Glossary:

primates: the order of mammals that includes apes and humans
hominid: the family of primates of which humans are the only living species

29. The phrase branch out in paragraph 1 is closest in meaning to

   (A) separate
   (B) hurry
   (C) look
   (D) originate

30. Which sentence below best expresses the essential information in the highlighted sentence in paragraph 2? Incorrect choices change the meaning in important ways or leave out essential information.

   (A) Physical anthropologists investigate how intelligent human beings evolved from creatures that lived in trees.
   (B) There are unanswered questions about why some tree–dwelling animals have evolved only two legs.
   (C) People want to know more about the behavior of animals and how some animals acquire the ability to learn.
   (D) Some animal populations have the power to ask questions and to learn from the events of the past.

31. The word speculate in paragraph 2 is closest in meaning to

   (A) worry
   (B) forget
   (C) disagree
   (D) think

32. Why does the author discuss the Leakey family in paragraph 3?

   (A) To argue for an increase in the amount of research in Africa
   (B) To contradict earlier theories of human evolution
   (C) To give examples of fieldwork done by physical anthropologists
   (D) To compare hominid evidence from Tanzania with that from Kenya

33. Which of the following is of major interest to both physical and cultural anthropologists?

   (A) Methods of physiology and genetics
   (B) Religious beliefs and practices
   (C) Child rearing in societies around the world
   (D) Clues about human beings who lived long ago

34. According to paragraph 4, cultural anthropologists who do fieldwork usually

   (A) discover hominid evidence indicating when humans evolved
   (B) write an account of the daily life of the people they study
   (C) work at universities and museums interpreting the work of others
   (D) develop new technologies for gathering cultural data

35. The phrase sift through in paragraph 4 is closest in meaning to

   (A) avoid
   (B) sort
   (C) discuss
   (D) contradict

36. The word They in paragraph 4 refers to

   (A) research universities
   (B) ethnologists
   (C) field anthropologists
   (D) museums

37. According to the passage, Margaret Mead wrote about all of the following subjects EXCEPT

   (A) the nature of cultural change
   (B) relations between people of different races
   (C) the biological bases of gender
   (D) economic systems of pioneer women

38. It can be inferred from paragraph 5 that Margaret Mead's work

    (A) made an impact on the field of anthropology
    (B) contradicted that of the Leakey family
    (C) opened Samoa to outside influences
    (D) is not widely read by anthropologists today

39. Look at the four squares, ▣, ▣, ▣, and ▣, which indicate where the following sentence could be added to the passage. Where would the sentence best fit?

Anthropology is the study of the origin, development, and varieties of human beings and their societies.

    ▣ Through various methods of research, anthropologists try to fit together the pieces of the human puzzle—to discover how humanity was first achieved, what made it branch out in different directions, and why separate societies behave similarly in some ways but quite differently in other ways. ▣ Anthropology, which emerged as an independent science in the late eighteenth century, has two main divisions: physical anthropology and cultural anthropology. ▣ *Physical anthropology* focuses on human evolution and variation and uses methods of physiology, genetics, and ecology. *Cultural anthropology* focuses on culture and includes archaeology, social anthropology, and linguistics. ▣

40–42. Select the appropriate sentences from the answer choices and match them to the type of anthropology that they describe. TWO of the answer choices will NOT be used. ***This question is worth 3 points.***

Answer Choices

(A) The focus is on the similarities and differences among cultures.

(B) This field studies life on many different scales of size and time.

(C) Researchers observe similarities between humans and other primates.

(D) Scientists examine the fossils and skulls of early humans.

(E) Researchers live and work in other societies and write ethnographies.

(F) It is the study of the origin, history, and structure of the earth.

(G) The story of humanity's origins is a major topic of investigation.

Type of Anthropology

Physical Anthropology
-
-
-

Cultural Anthropology
-
-

Answers to Test 3 – Reading are on page 605.

Record your score on the Progress Chart on page 697.

How to Score Multiple–Point Questions		
Points Possible	**Answers Correct**	**Points Earned**
2 points	3	2
	2	1
	0 – 1	0
3 points	5	3
	4	2
	3	1
	0 – 2	0
4 points	7	4
	6	3
	5	2
	4	1
	0 – 3	0

TEST 3

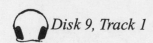

LISTENING SECTION DIRECTIONS

The Listening section measures your ability to understand conversations and lectures in English. You will hear each conversation and lecture only one time. After each conversation or lecture, you will hear some questions about it. Answer all questions based on what the speakers state or imply.

You may take notes while you listen. You may use your notes to help you answer the questions.

Most questions have four possible answers. In some questions, you will see this icon: . This means that you will hear, but not see, part of the question.

Some questions have special directions, which appear in a gray box. Most questions are worth one point. If a question is worth more than one point, special directions will indicate how many points you can receive.

You have approximately 40 minutes to complete the Listening section. This includes the time for listening to the conversations and lectures and for answering the questions.

To make this practice more like the real test, cover the questions and answers during each conversation and lecture. When you hear the first question, uncover the questions and answers.

Disk 9, Track 2

1. What topics do the speakers mainly discuss?

   Click on two answers.

   [A] Their summer plans
   [B] Their mutual acquaintances
   [C] Their musical interests
   [D] Their work experience

2. What does the professor mean when she says this:

   (A) He is one of the best teachers available.
   (B) You should ask for a different teacher.
   (C) Some teachers are more effective than others.
   (D) Students are not allowed to select their teachers.

3. Why does the professor say this: 🎧

   (A) To praise the excellent food at Silverwood
   (B) To comment on the man's summer workload
   (C) To predict which courses the student will like
   (D) To explain why the summer program is popular

4. What does the professor do for relaxation?

   (A) Teach music theory
   (B) Conduct the orchestra
   (C) Play in a jazz band
   (D) Coach voice students

5. What can be inferred from the conversation?

   (A) The professor used to be on the faculty at Silverwood.
   (B) The summer program at Silverwood is not well known.
   (C) The student wants to study music in graduate school.
   (D) The professor recommended the student for a scholarship.

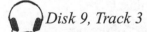 *Disk 9, Track 3*

6. What is the lecture mainly about?

   (A) Media of the twentieth century
   (B) The development of film style
   (C) How film criticism influenced art
   (D) The film techniques of D.W. Griffith

7. Which of the following contribute to the style of a film?

   Click on two answers.

   [A] Theater design
   [B] Acting awards
   [C] Camera framing
   [D] Film cutting

8. According to the professor, why did early film critics dislike films that resembled theater?

   (A) They did not understand the traditions of theater.
   (B) They felt that films should not be shown in theaters.
   (C) They thought that film was a distinct art form.
   (D) They disagreed with the politics of theater owners.

9. Why does the professor discuss cross–cutting?

   (A) To give an example of an early advancement in film style
   (B) To explain why film critics disliked certain types of films
   (C) To describe a technique that confused early film audiences
   (D) To convince students that film should be regarded as high art

10. Listen again to part of the lecture. Then answer the question.

What does the professor mean when he says this:

   (A) D.W. Griffith invented most of the film techniques we use today.
   (B) The actors in Griffith's films always spoke with perfect grammar.
   (C) Critics liked Griffith's films, but audiences did not understand them.
   (D) D.W. Griffith improved film techniques, making film a literary art.

11. Which camera shot would probably best show that a character is frightened?

🎧 *Disk 9, Track 4*

12. What is the talk mainly about?

   (A) The economic importance of bees
   (B) A decline in pollinator populations
   (C) How flowers are pollinated
   (D) Nature's services to farmers

13. According to the professor, what factors have affected pollinator populations?

Click on two answers.

   [A] Parasites
   [B] Air pollution
   [C] Hunting
   [D] Farm chemicals

14. Listen again to part of the talk. Then answer the question.

Why does the professor say this: 🎧

   (A) To show the effect of agriculture on pollinators
   (B) To describe nectar–producing plants
   (C) To show how stones improve a garden
   (D) To describe effects of plant disease

15. Listen again to part of the talk. Then answer the question.

What can be inferred about monarch butterflies?

   (A) They are the most common butterflies in North America.
   (B) Their population has been reduced because of herbicides.
   (C) They have lived on Earth for several million years.
   (D) Their diet consists mainly of other butterflies.

16–17. Based on the information in the talk, indicate whether each sentence below describes the honeybee, the monarch butterfly, or the long–nosed bat.

For each sentence, click in the correct box. This question is worth 2 points.

	Honeybee	Monarch butterfly	Long–nosed bat
It feeds on the nectar of cactus flowers.			
It pollinates four out of five food crops in North America.			
It returns to the same site every year.			
It has been mistaken for a similar animal.			

Disk 9, Track 5

18. What topics does the speaker discuss?

Click on two answers.

- [A] Causes and effects of the agricultural revolution
- [B] A change in the design of human settlements
- [C] The significance of trees in urban spaces
- [D] Why people prefer living in romantic villages

19. How did early rural villages differ from the cities of today?

- (A) Villages grew organically around features of the land.
- (B) Villages were more likely to inspire landscape painters.
- (C) Villages were designed as perfect rectangular grids.
- (D) Villages provided better economic opportunities.

20. What is the "urban forest"?

- (A) The forest surrounding a city
- (B) A park designed by an architect
- (C) The trees cultivated on farms
- (D) All of the trees in an urban area

21. Why does the speaker talk about New York City?

- (A) To give an example of an urban park project
- (B) To recommend places to visit in New York
- (C) To describe urban architecture and culture
- (D) To compare New York to other large cities

22. Listen again to part of the lecture. Then answer the question.

What does the speaker imply about New York's Central Park?

- (A) It is the largest urban forest in the world.
- (B) It was the first park to be designed by architects.
- (C) It contains beautiful buildings of steel and stone.
- (D) It contributes to the quality of life in the city.

23. What is the speaker's opinion of the city?

- (A) The city is better than a traditional village.
- (B) The city is a symbol of human achievement.
- (C) The city is too hard, straight, and unnatural.
- (D) The city is a like an organic machine.

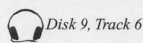

Disk 9, Track 6

24. What is the purpose of the discussion?

    (A) To coordinate methods of library research
    (B) To share ideas for organizing computer files
    (C) To review the different types of computer storage
    (D) To compare human memory and computer memory

25. Where does the computer store information to run programs that are built in?

    (A) Monitor
    (B) ROM
    (C) Floppy disk
    (D) File cabinet

26. Why does the tutor describe doing research at the library?

    (A) To show the student how to be an efficient researcher
    (B) To count how many folders a library table can hold
    (C) To explain the difference between memory and disk storage
    (D) To encourage the student to try a new computer program

27. In the tutor's analogy, what does the library table represent?

    (A) RAM
    (B) ROM
    (C) File folder
    (D) Hard disk

28. The tutor briefly describes what happens during a work session on the computer. Indicate whether each sentence below is a step in the process.

    For each sentence, click in the correct box.

	Yes	No
The files are returned to disk storage.		
The computer loads the files into RAM.		
The librarian lays folders on a table.		
The computer is stored in a briefcase.		

Disk 9, Track 7

29. What is the main idea of the lecture?

    (A) People should protest against war photography.
    (B) Photographers recorded the battle at Antietam.
    (C) The battlefield is too dangerous for photographers.
    (D) Photography changed the nature of war reporting.

30. Listen again to part of the lecture. Then answer the question.

    What does the professor mean by this statement:

    (A) More Americans died on that day than on any other day.
    (B) Antietam was the only battle in which Americans died.
    (C) Deaths were counted for the first time at Antietam.
    (D) Antietam was the shortest battle of the Civil War.

31. Who was Mathew Brady?

  (A) A military leader during the Civil War
  (B) A portrait painter in New York
  (C) The owner of a photography business
  (D) The inventor of photography

32. Listen again to part of the lecture. Then answer the question.

Why does the professor say this:

  (A) To warn students not to look at the pictures
  (B) To encourage students to study photography
  (C) To contrast different photographic styles
  (D) To emphasize the power of photography

33. What were some of the limitations of photography during the Civil War?

  Click on two answers.

  [A] The slow exposure time did not allow action shots.
  [B] Photographers were not permitted on the battlefield.
  [C] Newspapers were not able to reproduce photographs.
  [D] There were only a few schools that taught photography.

34. What does the professor imply about Mathew Brady?

  (A) He was unfairly criticized for his photographs of the dead.
  (B) His work had a lasting effect on photography and journalism.
  (C) He took more photographs during his life than anyone else did.
  (D) His Civil War photographs are worth a lot of money today.

Stop

Answers to Test 3 – Listening are on page 607.

Record your score on the Progress Chart on page 697.

How to Score Multiple–Point Questions		
Points Possible	Answers Correct	Points Earned
2 points	4	2
	3	1
	0 – 2	0

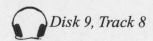
Disk 9, Track 8

SPEAKING SECTION DIRECTIONS

The Speaking section measures your ability to speak in English about a variety of topics. There are six questions in this section. Record your response to each question on a cassette.

Questions 1 and 2 are independent speaking tasks in which you will speak about familiar topics. Your responses will be scored on your ability to speak clearly and coherently about the topics.

Questions 3 and 4 are integrated tasks in which you will read a passage, listen to a conversation or lecture, and then speak in response to a question about what you have read and heard. You will need to combine relevant information from the two sources to answer the question completely. Your responses will be scored on your ability to speak clearly and coherently and on your ability to accurately convey information about what you read and heard.

Questions 5 and 6 are integrated tasks in which you will listen to part of a conversation or lecture, and then speak in response to a question about what you have heard. Your responses will be scored on your ability to speak clearly and coherently and on your ability to accurately convey information about what you heard.

You will hear each conversation and lecture only one time. You may take notes while you listen. You may use your notes to help you answer the questions.

Stop

For questions 1 and 2, you will speak in response to a question about a familiar topic. Use your own personal knowledge and experience to answer each question. After you hear the question, you have 15 seconds to prepare your response and 45 seconds to speak.

QUESTION 1

 Disk 9, Track 9

> Describe an event such as a holiday or other occasion that you enjoy celebrating. Explain why the event is significant to you. Include details and examples to support your explanation.

 Stop

Preparation Time – 15 seconds
Response Time – 45 seconds

QUESTION 2

 Disk 9, Track 10

> Some people keep in touch with friends and family by letter or e–mail. Others keep in touch by telephone. Which method do you prefer to use, and why? Include details and examples in your explanation.

 Stop

Preparation Time – 15 seconds
Response Time – 45 seconds

QUESTION 3

In this question, you will read a short passage about a campus situation, listen to a conversation, and then speak in response to a question about what you have read and heard. After you hear the question, you have 30 seconds to prepare your response and 60 seconds to speak.

Reading Time – 45 seconds

REQUIRED DISCUSSION SECTION

All students who are enrolled in a lecture course in the Social Sciences division must also register for a one–credit discussion section for that course. In the past, this requirement applied only to lecture courses in the History and Political Science departments. However, beginning next quarter, the requirement also applies to lecture courses in Sociology, Anthropology, and Economics. Each discussion section will be taught by a graduate teaching assistant. Students will receive a grade for the discussion section that is separate from their final examination grade for the lecture course.

Now cover the passage and question. Listen to the recording. When you hear the question, uncover the question and begin preparing your response.

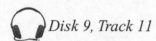 *Disk 9, Track 11*

The man expresses his opinion about the required discussion section. State his opinion and explain the reasons he gives for holding that opinion.

 Stop

Preparation Time – 30 seconds
Response Time – 60 seconds

QUESTION 4

In this question, you will read a short passage on an academic subject, listen to a lecture on the same topic, and then speak in response to a question about what you have read and heard. After you hear the question, you have 30 seconds to prepare your response and 60 seconds to speak.

Reading Time – 45 seconds

HOMEOSTASIS

The concept of homeostasis refers to the regulatory systems that keep an animal's internal environment within acceptable limits, even though the external environment may change. Homeostasis, meaning "steady state," describes the body's tendency toward internal balance. It is the endless balancing and re–balancing of the processes that maintain stability and restore the body's normal state when it has been disturbed. Homeostatic systems protect an animal's internal environment from harmful changes, such as changes in temperature, water level, and the amount of sugar in the blood.

Now cover the passage and question. Listen to the recording. When you hear the question, uncover the question and begin preparing your response.

 Disk 9, Track 12

> The professor describes the large ears of a rabbit. Explain how the rabbit's ears are used in homeostasis.

 Stop

Preparation Time – 30 seconds
Response Time – 60 seconds

QUESTION 5

In this question, you will listen to a conversation. You will then be asked to talk about the information in the conversation and to give your opinion about the ideas presented. To make this practice more like the real test, cover the question during the conversation. After you hear the question, you have 20 seconds to prepare your response and 60 seconds to speak.

 Disk 9, Track 13

> Describe the woman's problem and the suggestions the man makes about how to deal with it. What do you think the woman should do, and why?

 Stop

Preparation Time – 20 seconds
Response Time – 60 seconds

QUESTION 6

In this question, you will listen to part of a lecture. You will then be asked to summarize important information from the lecture. To make this practice more like the real test, cover the question during the lecture. After you hear the question, you have 20 seconds to prepare your response and 60 seconds to speak.

 Disk 9, Track 14

> Using points and examples from the talk, describe the communication between babies and mothers. Explain how this communication is musical in nature.

 Stop

Preparation Time – 20 seconds
Response Time – 60 seconds

Key points for Test 3 – Speaking are on page 609.

Each response earns a score of 1, 2, 3 or 4.

Record your total score on the Progress Chart on page 697.

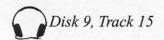 *Disk 9, Track 15*

WRITING SECTION DIRECTIONS

The Writing section measures your ability to use writing to communicate in an academic environment. There are two writing questions.

Question 1 is an integrated writing task. You will read a passage, listen to a lecture, and then answer a question based on what you have read and heard. You have 20 minutes to plan and write your response.

Question 2 is an independent writing task. You will answer a question based on your own knowledge and experience. You have 30 minutes to plan and write your response.

 Stop

QUESTION 1

For this task, you will write a response to a question about a reading passage and a short lecture. The question does not ask you to express your personal opinion.

Read the passage and then listen to the recording. To make this practice more like the real test, cover the passage and question during the lecture. You may take notes, and you may use your notes to help you write your response. When you hear the question, uncover the passage and question. Then allow 20 minutes to plan and write your response.

Typically, an effective response will have 150 to 225 words. Your response will be evaluated on the quality of your writing and on the completeness and accuracy of the content.

Reading Time – 3 minutes

Individuals who are especially talented in solving problems that involve understanding of space are said to have visual–spatial intelligence. Typically, visual–spatial intelligence involves several related capacities, such as the ability to perceive patterns, the ability to create mental imagery and to transform that imagery, and the ability to draw a picture or map of spatial information. These abilities are independent of one another and may develop separately. The use of one visual–spatial ability may reinforce the use of others.

Individuals call upon visual–spatial intelligence in the recognition of objects, both when the objects are seen in their original setting and also when some part of the original setting has changed. Visual–spatial skills are utilized when an individual works with graphic depictions—two–dimensional or three–dimensional versions of real–world scenes—as well as other symbols, such as maps, diagrams, or geometrical forms.

Visual–spatial intelligence is a valuable asset in any society. In some occupations, it is essential—for example, for a sculptor, a chess player, an athlete, or a mathematical topologist.

Individuals with visual–spatial intelligence will notice immediately when a building, painting, or face is not symmetrical. They are skilled at taking things apart and putting them back together again. They love to play games. They have a visual memory, but this memory is abstract rather than pictorial—a kind of geometrical memory. They can mentally rotate complex forms and can draw whatever object they see, usually after seeing the object for only a short time. Visual–spatial intelligence can be seen in the athlete's ability to judge almost perfectly the angle needed to score a goal in hockey or a basket in basketball.

Now cover the passage and question. Listen to the recording. When you hear the question, uncover the passage and question and begin your response.

 Disk 9, Track 16

> Summarize the points made in the lecture, explaining how they illustrate points made in the reading.

 Stop

Writing Time – 20 minutes

QUESTION 2

For this task, you will write an essay in response to a question that asks you to express, explain, and support your opinion on a topic. You have 30 minutes to plan, write, and revise your essay.

Typically, an effective essay will have a minimum of 300 words. Your essay will be evaluated on the quality of your writing, including the organization and development of your ideas and the quality and accuracy of the language you use to express your ideas.

Read the question below and make any notes that will help you plan your response. Then begin typing your essay.

Do you agree or disagree with the following statement?
It is more important to work at a job that you enjoy than it is to earn a lot of money.
Use specific reasons and examples to support your opinion.

Writing Time – 30 minutes

Key points for Test 3 – Writing are on page 609.

Each response earns a score of 1, 2, 3, 4 or 5.

Record your total score on the Progress Chart on page 697.

READING SECTION DIRECTIONS

The Reading section measures your ability to read and understand passages in English. You will read three passages and answer questions about them.

For most questions, you will choose the one best answer of four possible answers. These questions are worth one point each. The last question in each set is worth more than one point. The directions for this question indicate how many points you can receive.

Some passages have one or more words in bold type. For these bolded words, you will see a definition or explanation in a glossary at the end of the passage.

Answer all questions about a passage on the basis of what is stated or implied in that passage.

You have 60 minutes to read the passages and answer all of the questions. Allow approximately 20 minutes to work on each passage.

MUSICAL TALENT

Among all the abilities with which an individual may be endowed, musical talent appears earliest in life. Very young children can exhibit musical precocity for different reasons. Some develop exceptional skill as a result of a well–designed instructional regime, such as the Suzuki method for the violin. Some have the good fortune to be born into a musical family in a household filled with music. In a number of interesting cases, musical talent is part of an otherwise disabling condition such as autism or mental retardation. A musically gifted child has an inborn talent; however, the extent to which the talent is expressed publicly will depend upon the environment in which the child lives.

Musically gifted children master at an early age the principal elements of music, including pitch and rhythm. Pitch—or melody—is more central in certain cultures, for example, in Eastern societies that make use of tiny quarter–tone intervals. Rhythm, sounds produced at certain auditory frequencies and grouped according to a prescribed system, is emphasized in sub–Saharan Africa, where the rhythmic ratios can be very complex.

All children have some aptitude for making music. During infancy, normal children sing as well as babble, and they can produce individual sounds and sound patterns. Infants as young as two months can match their mother's songs in pitch, loudness, and melodic shape, and infants at four months can match rhythmic structure as well. Infants are especially predisposed to acquire these core aspects of music, and they can also engage in sound play that clearly exhibits creativity.

Individual differences begin to emerge in young children as they learn to sing. Some children can match large segments of a song by the age of two or three. Many others can only approximate pitch at this age and may still have difficulty in producing accurate melodies by the age of five or six. However, by the time they reach school age, most children in any culture have a **schema** of what a song should be like and can produce a reasonably accurate imitation of the songs commonly heard in their environment.

The early appearance of superior musical ability in some children provides evidence that musical talent may be a separate and unique form of intelligence. There are numerous tales of young artists who have a remarkable "ear" or extraordinary memory for music and a natural understanding of musical structure. In many of these cases, the child is average in every other way but displays an exceptional ability in music. Even the most gifted child, however, takes about ten years to achieve the levels of performance or composition that would constitute mastery of the musical sphere.

Every generation in music history has had its famous prodigies—individuals with exceptional musical powers that emerge at a young age. In the eighteenth century, Wolfgang Amadeus Mozart began composing and performing at the age of six. As a child, Mozart could play the piano like an adult. He had perfect pitch, and at age nine he was also a master of the art of modulation—transitions from one key to another—which became one of the hallmarks of his style. By the age of eleven, he had composed three symphonies and 30 other major works. Mozart's well–developed talent was preserved into adulthood.

Unusual musical ability is a regular characteristic of certain **anomalies** such as **autism**. In one case, an autistic girl was able to play "Happy Birthday" in the style of various composers, including Mozart, Beethoven, Verdi, and Schubert. When the girl was three, her mother called her by playing incomplete melodies, which the child would complete with the appropriate tone in the proper octave. For the autistic child, music may be the primary mode of communication, and the child may cling to music because it represents a haven in a world that is largely confusing and frightening.

Glossary:

schema: a mental outline or model
anomaly: departure from what is normal; abnormal condition
autism: a developmental disorder involving impaired communication and emotional separation

1. The word precocity in paragraph 1 is closest in meaning to

   (A) strong interest
   (B) good luck
   (C) advanced skill
   (D) personal style

2. Which sentence below best expresses the essential information in the highlighted sentence in paragraph 1? Incorrect choices change the meaning in important ways or leave out essential information.

   (A) Children may be born with superior musical ability, but their environment will determine how this ability is developed.
   (B) Every child is naturally gifted, and it is the responsibility of the public schools to recognize and develop these talents.
   (C) Children with exceptional musical talent will look for the best way to express themselves through music–making.
   (D) Some musically talented children live in an environment surrounded by music, while others have little exposure to music.

3. The author makes the point that musical elements such as pitch and rhythm

   (A) distinguish music from other art forms
   (B) vary in emphasis in different cultures
   (C) make music difficult to learn
   (D) express different human emotions

4. The word predisposed in paragraph 3 is closest in meaning to

   (A) inclined
   (B) gifted
   (C) pushed
   (D) amused

5. According to the passage, when does musical talent usually begin to appear?

   (A) When infants start to babble and produce sound patterns
   (B) Between the ages of two and four months
   (C) When children learn to sing at two or three years old
   (D) Between ten years old and adolescence

6. According to the passage, which of the following suggests that musical talent is a separate form of intelligence?

   (A) Exceptional musical ability in an otherwise average child
   (B) Recognition of the emotional power of music
   (C) The ability of all babies to acquire core elements of music
   (D) Differences between learning music and learning language

7. Why does the author discuss Mozart in paragraph 6?

   (A) To compare past and present views of musical talent
   (B) To give an example of a well–known musical prodigy
   (C) To list musical accomplishments of the eighteenth century
   (D) To describe the development of individual musical skill

8. In music, the change from one key to another is known as

   (A) rhythm
   (B) prodigy
   (C) perfect pitch
   (D) modulation

9. All of the following are given as examples of exceptional musical talent EXCEPT

- (A) a remarkable "ear" or perfect memory for music
- (B) ability to compose major works at a young age
- (C) appreciation for a wide variety of musical styles
- (D) playing a single song in the style of various composers

10. The word haven in paragraph 7 is closest in meaning to

- (A) beautiful art
- (B) safe place
- (C) personal goal
- (D) simple problem

11. Which of the following can be inferred from the passage about exceptional musical ability?

- (A) It occurs more frequently in some cultures than in others.
- (B) It is evidence of a superior level of intelligence in other areas.
- (C) It has been documented and studied but is little understood.
- (D) It is the result of natural talent and a supportive environment.

12. Look at the four squares, **A**, **B**, **C**, and **D**, which indicate where the following sentence could be added to the passage. Where would the sentence best fit?

They can even imitate patterns and tones sung by other people.

All children have some aptitude for making music. **A** During infancy, normal children sing as well as babble, and they can produce individual sounds and sound patterns. **B** Infants as young as two months can match their mother's songs in pitch, loudness, and melodic shape, and infants at four months can match rhythmic structure as well. **C** Infants are especially predisposed to acquire these core aspects of music, and they can also engage in sound play that clearly exhibits creativity. **D**

13–14. An introductory sentence for a brief summary of the passage is provided below. Complete the summary by selecting the THREE answer choices that express the most important ideas in the passage. Some sentences do not belong in the summary because they express ideas that are not presented in the passage or are minor ideas in the passage. ***This question is worth 2 points.***

Musical talent usually appears early in life.
•
•
•

Answer Choices

(A) Very young children can develop exceptional skill in playing the violin by the Suzuki method.

(B) While all children have a basic ability to make music, some exhibit extraordinary skill at a very early age.

(C) Prodigies have a natural understanding of musical structure that enables them to play and compose music with great skill.

(D) Wolfgang Amadeus Mozart had composed several major works and symphonies by the age of eleven.

(E) Autistic children cannot relate to their environment realistically and therefore have difficulty in communicating.

(F) Exceptional musical ability is often part of an otherwise disabling condition such as autism.

CLOTHING AND COSTUME

The ancient Greeks and the Chinese believed that we first clothed our bodies for some physical reason, such as protecting ourselves from the elements. Ethnologists and psychologists have invoked psychological reasons: modesty, taboo, magical influence, or the desire to please. Anthropological research indicates that the function of the earliest clothing was to carry objects. Our hunting–gathering ancestors had to travel great distances to obtain food. For the male hunters, carrying was much easier if they were wearing simple belts or animal skins from which they could hang weapons and tools. For the female gatherers, more elaborate carrying devices were necessary. Women had to transport collected food back to the settlement and also had to carry babies, so they required bags or slings.

Another function of early clothing—providing comfort and protection—probably developed at the same time as utility. As human beings multiplied and spread out from the warm lands in which they evolved, they covered their bodies more and more to maintain body warmth. Today, we still dress to maintain warmth and to carry objects in our clothes. And like our hunting–gathering ancestors, most men still carry things on their person, as if they still needed to keep their arms free for hunting, while women tend to have a separate bag for carrying, as if they were still food–gatherers. But these two functions of clothing are only two of many uses to which we put the garments that we wear today.

There is a clear distinction between attire that constitutes "clothing" and attire that is more aptly termed "costume." We might say that clothing has to do with covering the body, and costume concerns the choice of a particular form of garment for a particular purpose. Clothing depends primarily on such physical conditions as climate, health, and textile, while costume reflects social factors such as personal status, religious beliefs, aesthetics, and the wish to be distinguished from or to emulate others.

Even in early human history, costume fulfilled a function beyond that of simple utility. Costume helped to impose authority or inspire fear. A chieftain's costume embodied attributes expressing his power, while a warrior's costume enhanced his physical superiority and suggested he was superhuman. Costume often had a magical significance such as investing humans with the attributes of other creatures through the addition of ornaments to identify the wearer with animals, gods, or heroes. In more recent times, professional or administrative costume is designed to distinguish the wearer and to express personal or delegated authority. Costume communicates the status of the wearer, and with very few exceptions, the aim is to display as high a status as possible. Costume denotes power, and since power is often equated with wealth, costume has come to be an expression of social class and material prosperity.

A uniform is a type of costume that serves the important function of displaying membership in a group: school, sports team, occupation, or armed force. Military uniform denotes rank and is intended not only to express group membership but also to protect the body and to intimidate. A soldier's uniform says, "I am part of a powerful machine, and when you deal with me, you deal with my whole organization." Uniforms are immediate beacons of power and authority. If a person needs to display power—a police officer, for example—then the body can be virtually transformed. Height can be exaggerated with protective headgear, thick clothing can make the body look broader and stronger, and boots can enhance the power of the legs. Uniforms also convey low social status; at the bottom of the scale, the uniform of the prisoner denotes membership in the society of convicted criminals.

Religious costume signifies spiritual or superhuman authority and possesses a significance that identifies the wearer with a belief or god. A successful clergy has always displayed impressive vestments of one kind or another that clearly demonstrate the religious leader's dominant status.

15. According to the passage, psychological reasons for wearing clothing include

- (A) protection from cold weather
- (B) the availability of materials
- (C) prevention of illness
- (D) the wish to give pleasure

16. According to the passage, what aspect of humanity's hunting–gathering past is reflected in the clothing of today?

- (A) People cover their bodies because of modesty.
- (B) Most men still carry objects on their person.
- (C) Women like clothes that are beautiful and practical.
- (D) Men wear pants, but women wear skirts or pants.

17. The phrase these two functions in paragraph 2 refers to

- (A) hunting and gathering food
- (B) transporting food and carrying babies
- (C) maintaining warmth and carrying objects
- (D) displaying power and social status

18. Which sentence below best expresses the essential information in the highlighted sentence in paragraph 3? Incorrect choices change the meaning in important ways or leave out essential information.

- (A) Clothing serves a physical purpose, while costume has a personal, social, or psychological function.
- (B) We like clothing to fit our body well, but different costumes fit differently depending on the purpose.
- (C) Both clothing and costume are types of attire, but it is often difficult to distinguish between them.
- (D) People spend more time in choosing special costumes than they do in selecting everyday clothing.

19. The word ornaments in paragraph 4 is closest in meaning to

- (A) layers
- (B) words
- (C) feathers
- (D) decorations

20. It can be inferred from paragraph 4 that the author most likely believes which of the following about costume?

- (A) We can learn about a society's social structure by studying costume.
- (B) Costume used to serve a simple function, but now it is very complex.
- (C) The main purpose of costume is to force people to obey their leaders.
- (D) Costume is rarely a reliable indicator of a person's material wealth.

21. The word beacons in paragraph 5 is closest in meaning to

- (A) signals
- (B) lights
- (C) inventions
- (D) reversals

22. Why does the author discuss the police officer's uniform in paragraph 5?

- (A) To describe the aesthetic aspects of costume
- (B) To identify the wearer with a hero
- (C) To suggest that police are superhuman
- (D) To show how costume conveys authority

23. All of the following are likely to be indicated by a person's costume EXCEPT

- (A) playing on a football team
- (B) being a prisoner
- (C) having a heart condition
- (D) leading a religious ceremony

24. Look at the four squares, **A**, **B**, **C**, and **D**, which indicate where the following sentence could be added to the passage. Where would the sentence best fit?

Such power is seen clearly in the judge's robes and the police officer's uniform.

Even in early human history, costume fulfilled a function beyond that of simple utility. **A** Costume helped to impose authority or inspire fear. A chieftain's costume embodied attributes expressing his power, while a warrior's costume enhanced his physical superiority and suggested he was superhuman. Costume often had a magical significance such as investing humans with the attributes of other creatures through the addition of ornaments to identify the wearer with animals, gods, or heroes. **B** In more recent times, professional or administrative costume is designed to distinguish the wearer and to express personal or delegated authority. **C** Costume communicates the status of the wearer, and with very few exceptions, the aim is to display as high a status as possible. Costume denotes power, and since power is often equated with wealth, costume has come to be an expression of social class and material prosperity. **D**

25–28. Select the appropriate phrases from the answer choices and match them to the type of attire that they describe. TWO of the answer choices will NOT be used. *This question is worth 4 points.*

Answer Choices	Type of Attire
(A) Reflects social factors such as personal status or material prosperity	**Clothing**
(B) Makes it legal for people to perform dangerous work	•
(C) Provides comfort, warmth, and protection from the weather	•
	•
(D) Shows that a person is a member of a particular group	
(E) Depends on physical conditions such as climate and health	**Costume**
(F) Conveys personal, administrative, or superhuman authority	•
(G) Enabled early humans to carry the objects needed to obtain food	•
(H) Serves as a symbol that unites all people on the earth	•
(I) Indicates the dominant status of religious leaders	•

THE GREENHOUSE EFFECT AND GLOBAL WARMING

Carbon dioxide and other naturally occurring gases in the earth's atmosphere create a natural greenhouse effect by trapping and absorbing solar radiation. These gases act as a blanket and keep the planet warm enough for life to survive and flourish. The warming of the earth is balanced by some of the heat escaping from the atmosphere back into space. Without this compensating flow of heat out of the system, the temperature of the earth's surface and its atmosphere would rise steadily.

Scientists are increasingly concerned about a human–driven greenhouse effect resulting from a rise in atmospheric levels of carbon dioxide and other heat–trapping greenhouse gases. The man–made greenhouse effect is the exhalation of industrial civilization. A major contributing factor is the burning of large amounts of fossil fuels—coal, petroleum, and natural gas. Another is the destruction of the world's forests, which reduces the amount of carbon dioxide converted to oxygen by plants. Emissions of carbon dioxide, chlorofluorocarbons, nitrous oxide, and methane from human activities will enhance the greenhouse effect, causing the earth's surface to become warmer. The main greenhouse gas, water vapor, will increase in response to global warming and further enhance it.

There is agreement within the scientific community that the buildup of greenhouse gases is already causing the earth's average surface temperature to rise. This is changing global climate at an unusually fast rate. According to the World Meteorological Organization, the earth's average temperature climbed about 1 degree F in the past century, and nine of the ten warmest years on record have occurred since 1990. A United Nations panel has predicted that average global temperatures could rise as much as 10.5 degrees F during the next century as heat–trapping gases from human industry accumulate in the atmosphere.

What are the potential impacts of an enhanced greenhouse effect? According to estimates by an international committee, North American climatic zones could shift northward by as much as 550 kilometers (340 miles). Such a change in climate would likely affect all sectors of society. In some areas, heat and moisture stress would cut crop yields, and traditional farming practices would have to change. For example, in the North American grain belt, higher temperatures and more frequent drought during the growing season might require farmers to switch from corn to wheat and to use more water for irrigation.

Global warming may also cause a rise in sea level by melting polar ice caps. A rise in sea level would accelerate coastal erosion and inundate islands and low–lying coastal plains, some of which are densely populated. Millions of acres of coastal farmlands would be covered by water. Furthermore, the warming of seawater will cause the water to expand, thus adding to the potential danger.

Global warming has already left its fingerprint on the natural world. Two research teams recently reviewed hundreds of published papers that tracked changes in the range and behavior of plant and animal species, and they found ample evidence of plants blooming and birds nesting earlier in the spring. Both teams concluded that rising global temperatures are shifting the ranges of hundreds of species—thus climatic zones—northward. These studies are hard evidence that the natural world is already responding dramatically to climate change, even though the change has just begun. If global warming trends continue, changes in the environment will have an enormous impact on world biology. Birds especially play a critical role in the environment by pollinating plants, dispersing seeds, and controlling insect populations; thus, changes in their populations will reverberate throughout the ecosystems they inhabit.

29. According to the passage, how do carbon dioxide and other greenhouse gases affect the earth–atmosphere system?

  (A) They collect solar radiation that warms the earth's surface.
  (B) They create the conditions for new forms of life to emerge.
  (C) They cause heat to flow from the atmosphere into space.
  (D) They decrease the amount of oxygen in the atmosphere.

30. Which sentence below best expresses the essential information in the highlighted sentence in paragraph 2? Incorrect choices change the meaning in important ways or leave out essential information.

  (A) The greenhouse effect causes breathing problems in industrial workers.
  (B) The growth of industry was made possible by the greenhouse effect.
  (C) Scientists are seeking better ways to manufacture greenhouse gases.
  (D) Industrial activities result in emissions that cause the greenhouse effect.

31. All of the following are contributing factors to global warming EXCEPT

  (A) the burning of coal and petroleum
  (B) the loss of forest lands
  (C) the conversion of carbon dioxide to oxygen
  (D) the buildup of water vapor in the atmosphere

32. The word enhance in paragraph 2 is closest in meaning to

  (A) strengthen
  (B) counteract
  (C) stabilize
  (D) parallel

33. What can be inferred from paragraph 3 about global climate change?

  (A) Climate change will have both positive and negative effects on human society.
  (B) It is difficult to predict the effects of climate change over the next century.
  (C) International organizations have been studying climate change only since 1990.
  (D) Climate change is likely to continue as long as heat–trapping gases accumulate.

34. According to paragraph 4, what is one effect that climate change could have on agriculture in North America?

  (A) Return to more traditional methods of farming
  (B) Movement of farms to the northernmost regions
  (C) Changes in the crops that farmers can grow
  (D) Less water available for irrigating crops

35. The word inundate in paragraph 5 is closest in meaning to

  (A) cover
  (B) reduce
  (C) move
  (D) create

36. Why does the author use the word fingerprint in paragraph 6?

  (A) To show that hundreds of fingerprints were examined
  (B) To introduce conclusive evidence of global warming
  (C) To describe a method used by two research teams
  (D) To suggest that people do not cause global warming

37. The word they in paragraph 6 refers to

  (A) teams
  (B) papers
  (C) species
  (D) birds

38. The word hard in paragraph 6 is closest in meaning to

(A) difficult
(B) real
(C) contradictory
(D) secret

39. What evidence does the author give that climatic zones have shifted northward?

(A) Solar radiation escapes from the atmosphere back into space.
(B) The water in the ocean expands as it gets warmer.
(C) Plants bloom and birds build nests earlier in the spring.
(D) Birds no longer pollinate plants or control insect populations.

40. Look at the four squares, ▬A, ▬B, ▬C, and ▬D, which indicate where the following sentence could be added to the passage. Where would the sentence best fit?

The combination of melting ice caps with the expansion of water could raise the sea level several centimeters by the year 2100.

▬A Global warming may also cause a rise in sea level by melting polar ice caps. A rise in sea level would accelerate coastal erosion and inundate islands and low–lying coastal plains, some of which are densely populated. ▬B Millions of acres of coastal farmlands would be covered by water. ▬C Furthermore, the warming of seawater will cause the water to expand, thus adding to the potential danger. ▬D

41–42. An introductory sentence for a brief summary of the passage is provided below. Complete the summary by selecting the THREE answer choices that express the most important ideas in the passage. Some sentences do not belong in the summary because they express ideas that are not presented in the passage or are minor ideas in the passage. *This question is worth 2 points.*

Scientists are concerned about the greenhouse effect and its role in global warming.
•
•
•

Answer Choices

(A) A rise in atmospheric levels of carbon dioxide and other greenhouse gases is causing the earth's surface to become warmer.

(B) Some scientists think the temperature trend indicates man–made global warming, while others believe it is natural climate variability.

(C) Nine of the ten warmest years on record have occurred since 1990.

(D) A rising sea level and shifts in climatic zones are probable effects of global warming.

(E) Global warming could result in job loss for millions of farmers in coastal areas.

(F) Global warming will alter the range and behavior of plants and animals, changing the balance of ecosystems.

Answers to Test 4 – Reading are on page 610.

Record your score on the Progress Chart on page 697.

How to Score Multiple–Point Questions		
Points Possible	**Answers Correct**	**Points Earned**
2 points	3	2
	2	1
	0 – 1	0
3 points	5	3
	4	2
	3	1
	0 – 2	0
4 points	7	4
	6	3
	5	2
	4	1
	0 – 3	0

TEST 4

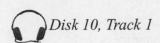

LISTENING SECTION DIRECTIONS

The Listening section measures your ability to understand conversations and lectures in English. You will hear each conversation and lecture only one time. After each conversation or lecture, you will hear some questions about it. Answer all questions based on what the speakers state or imply.

You may take notes while you listen. You may use your notes to help you answer the questions.

Most questions have four possible answers. In some questions, you will see this icon: 🎧. This means that you will hear, but not see, part of the question.

Some questions have special directions, which appear in a gray box. Most questions are worth one point. If a question is worth more than one point, special directions will indicate how many points you can receive.

You have approximately 40 minutes to complete the Listening section. This includes the time for listening to the conversations and lectures and for answering the questions.

To make this practice more like the real test, cover the questions and answers during each conversation and lecture. When you hear the first question, uncover the questions and answers.

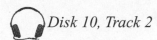 *Disk 10, Track 2*

1. What is the purpose of the conversation?

   (A) The man needs information for a research project.
   (B) The man wants to change his housing situation.
   (C) The man wants to move to a house off campus.
   (D) The man wants to know why his rent was raised.

2. What are some features of the suites in the villages?

   Click on two answers.

   [A] A full refrigerator
   [B] Two study rooms
   [C] A fireplace
   [D] Two to four bedrooms

3. Listen again to part of the conversation. Then answer the question.

   Why does the woman say this:

   (A) To show her concern for the man's situation
   (B) To suggest that she is sad about leaving her suite
   (C) To express regret at not being able to help the man
   (D) To apologize for not answering the man's question

4. What does the man think of the cost of rent in the villages?

   (A) The rent should be lower for such old buildings.
   (B) The rent is reasonable for the features included.
   (C) The rent is higher than he hoped it would be.
   (D) The rent is similar to that of a house off campus.

5. Listen again to part of the conversation. Then answer the question.

   Select the sentence that best expresses how the man probably feels.

   (A) "I don't think I'll be able to get a room in the villages."
   (B) "I'm surprised at the number of people who live there."
   (C) "I don't like the idea of living with 27 people."
   (D) "I'm confused about why there is a waiting list."

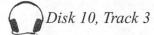 *Disk 10, Track 3*

6. What are the students mainly discussing?

   (A) Characteristics of two design styles
   (B) The relationship of design to architecture
   (C) Popular styles of the 1930s
   (D) Taking photographs of buildings

7. Listen again to part of the conversation. Then answer the question.

   Select the sentence that best expresses how the man probably feels.

   (A) "I'm bored with the designs we are studying."
   (B) "I'm pleased that our professor knows so much."
   (C) "I'm surprised that so many styles exist."
   (D) "I'm concerned about the amount we have to learn."

TEST 4

8. How does the woman help the man?

  (A) She traces the history of architectural design.
  (B) She offers to help him study for an examination.
  (C) She contrasts the details of two design styles.
  (D) She promises to speak to their professor.

9. Indicate whether each sentence below describes Art Deco or Art Moderne.

  For each sentence, click in the correct box.

	Art Deco	Art Moderne
This style has straight lines, slender forms, and geometric patterns.		
This style has rounded corners, smooth walls, and little decoration.		
This is the style of a downtown building that the woman likes.		

10. What can be inferred from the conversation?

  (A) The students' professor is not available for help outside class.
  (B) The man does not care much about the history of design.
  (C) The students are required to do a project for their design class.
  (D) The woman's father is the superintendent of an office building.

Disk 10, Track 4

11. What is the main purpose of the lecture?

  (A) To instruct in the cultivation of wild squash
  (B) To describe how hunter–gatherers found food
  (C) To compare agriculture around the world
  (D) To explain how early people started farming

12. What is probably true about the origins of agriculture?

  (A) The process of gathering wild food led naturally to farming.
  (B) Agriculture and written language developed at the same time.
  (C) People around the world tried similar experiments with squash.
  (D) The cultivation of vegetables occurred before that of grains.

13. The professor explains how the early people of Mexico probably started farming. Summarize the process by putting the events in order.

  Drag each sentence to the space where it belongs.

  (A) The people began to protect the plants.
  (B) The people brought seeds to their camp.
  (C) New plants grew from the fallen seeds.
  (D) Seeds fell to the ground as the people ate.

1	
2	
3	
4	

14. Why did the people begin to use digging sticks?

    (A) They found that water would fill the holes they made.
    (B) They noticed that seeds grew better in turned–over soil.
    (C) They dug trenches around the garden to keep out animals.
    (D) They discovered that food could be stored underground.

15. Listen again to part of the lecture. Then answer the question.

Why does the professor say this:

    (A) To show that people could not work in their gardens at night
    (B) To emphasize the amount of effort it took to protect the plants
    (C) To point out that agriculture developed over a very long time
    (D) To explain why squash was a particularly successful crop

16. What point does the professor make about the transition from hunting–gathering to agriculture?

    (A) The process probably followed a similar pattern around the world.
    (B) The transition to agriculture eliminated the need for hunting.
    (C) Agriculture developed everywhere in the world at the same time.
    (D) The rapid move to agriculture led to environmental devastation.

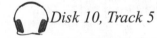 *Disk 10, Track 5*

17. What is the hydrologic cycle?

    (A) The economic issues concerning water
    (B) The movement of water through the earth and atmosphere
    (C) The changes in the amount of rain throughout the year
    (D) The absorption of water vapor into the atmosphere

18. Identify the area in the diagram that mainly concerns climatologists.

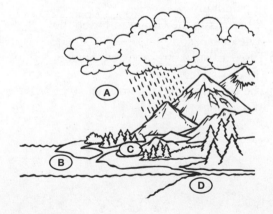

19. What do hydrologists mainly study?

    (A) The role of solar energy in the cycle
    (B) Water movement and storage on land
    (C) Biological reactions that use water
    (D) Atmospheric circulation of water

20. What happens to water that falls to the earth as precipitation?

Click on two answers.

    [A] It is stored in lakes or underground.
    [B] It evaporates before reaching the ground.
    [C] It eventually flows back to the ocean.
    [D] It raises the temperature of the soil.

TEST 4

21. Why does the professor say this: 🎧

    Ⓐ To describe the importance of runoff and groundwater
    Ⓑ To compare the amount of runoff with that of groundwater
    Ⓒ To show similarities between runoff and groundwater
    Ⓓ To explain how runoff eventually becomes groundwater

22. What can be inferred about plants in the hydrologic cycle?

    Ⓐ Plants remove excess water from the cycle.
    Ⓑ Water moves quickly through plants.
    Ⓒ Plants perform the function of water storage.
    Ⓓ Plants recycle more water than animals do.

🎧 Disk 10, Track 6

23. Which of the following best describes the organization of the lecture?

    Ⓐ A list of influential painters
    Ⓑ A history of an art movement
    Ⓒ A comparison of schools of art
    Ⓓ A description of a painting

26. What subjects did the Group of Seven paint?

    Click on two answers.

    Ⓐ Active street scenes
    Ⓑ Jack pine trees
    Ⓒ Sailing ships
    Ⓓ Uninhabited landscapes

24. What is the professor's point of view concerning the Group of Seven?

    Ⓐ They created a distinctive Canadian art inspired by Canada itself.
    Ⓑ They produced a style of painting that was crude and barbaric.
    Ⓒ They deserve more attention than they have received.
    Ⓓ They influenced new trends in Canadian literature and music.

27. What does the professor mean by this statement: 🎧

    Ⓐ Art lovers pay high prices for the Group's paintings.
    Ⓑ Canada has more painters now than at any time in the past.
    Ⓒ Much of the Group's work has come to represent Canada.
    Ⓓ People come from all over the world to study Canadian art.

25. Listen again to part of the lecture. Then answer the question.

    Why does the professor say this: 🎧

    Ⓐ To explain why the Group's work was misunderstood
    Ⓑ To state that the Group earned very little money
    Ⓒ To contrast the methods of different artists in the Group
    Ⓓ To show how one artist inspired the Group's direction

28. Listen again to part of the lecture. Then answer the question.

    What can be concluded about the Group of Seven's style of painting?

    Ⓐ The Group did not share a single style of painting.
    Ⓑ All artists in the Group followed the style of Jackson.
    Ⓒ Three artists are responsible for the Group's style.
    Ⓓ The Group started the abstract style of painting.

Disk 10, Track 7

29. What is the talk mainly about?

   (A) The changing concept of leadership
   (B) Leaders of the restaurant industry
   (C) How leadership and power are related
   (D) Why too much power can lead to evil

30. Why does the professor talk about the headwaiter in a restaurant?

   (A) To show that having power doesn't imply leadership
   (B) To compare the quality of service in two restaurants
   (C) To explain how leaders influence other people
   (D) To give an example of leadership in everyday life

31. Why does the professor say this:

   (A) To explain why dictators have so much power
   (B) To distinguish between leaders and power holders
   (C) To compare qualities of dictators and robbers
   (D) To warn students about the presence of danger

32. According to the professor, how are leadership and power similar?

   (A) Both require the ability to exercise physical force.
   (B) Both are benefits one gets from a university education
   (C) Both are necessary for people who commit crimes.
   (D) Both involve the ability to bring about wanted results.

33. According to the professor, which of the following are sources of power?

   Click on two answers.

   [A] The ability to eat in a restaurant
   [B] The ability to use physical force
   [C] The ability to motivate people
   [D] The ability to follow orders

34. Listen again to part of the talk. Then answer the question.

   What does the professor imply about successful managers?

   (A) They know how and when to use their power.
   (B) Their leadership skills are present from birth.
   (C) They are the only ones who can increase spending.
   (D) Their power comes from the use of physical force.

 Stop

Answers to Test 4 – Listening are on page 612.

Record your score on the Progress Chart on page 697.

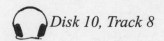

SPEAKING SECTION DIRECTIONS

The Speaking section measures your ability to speak in English about a variety of topics. There are six questions in this section. Record your response to each question on a cassette.

Questions 1 and 2 are independent speaking tasks in which you will speak about familiar topics. Your responses will be scored on your ability to speak clearly and coherently about the topics.

Questions 3 and 4 are integrated tasks in which you will read a passage, listen to a conversation or lecture, and then speak in response to a question about what you have read and heard. You will need to combine relevant information from the two sources to answer the question completely. Your responses will be scored on your ability to speak clearly and coherently and on your ability to accurately convey information about what you read and heard.

Questions 5 and 6 are integrated tasks in which you will listen to part of a conversation or lecture, and then speak in response to a question about what you have heard. Your responses will be scored on your ability to speak clearly and coherently and on your ability to accurately convey information about what you heard.

You will hear each conversation and lecture only one time. You may take notes while you listen. You may use your notes to help you answer the questions.

Stop

For questions 1 and 2, you will speak in response to a question about a familiar topic. Use your own personal knowledge and experience to answer each question. After you hear the question, you have 15 seconds to prepare your response and 45 seconds to speak.

QUESTION 1

 Disk 10, Track 9

> What foreign country would you like to visit? Choose a country and explain why you would like to go there. Include details and examples to support your explanation.

 Stop

Preparation Time – 15 seconds
Response Time – 45 seconds

QUESTION 2

 Disk 10, Track 10

> In some schools, teachers decide what classes students must take. Other schools allow students to select their own classes. Which system do you think is better and why? Include details and examples in your explanation.

 Stop

Preparation Time – 15 seconds
Response Time – 45 seconds

TEST 4

QUESTION 3

In this question, you will read a short passage about a campus situation, listen to a conversation, and then speak in response to a question about what you have read and heard. After you hear the question, you have 30 seconds to prepare your response and 60 seconds to speak.

Reading Time – 45 seconds

NOTICE OF CHANGE TO SWIMMING POOL HOURS

Due to an increase in the number of swimming classes being offered to both university students and the general public, the university must reduce the hours that the pool is open for the personal use of students. The main change is that the pool will be closed to university students on Monday and Wednesday evenings after 3:00 p.m. The pool will be available to university students from 9:00 a.m. to 3:00 p.m. seven days a week, and from 7:00 p.m. to 10:00 p.m. on Tuesday, Thursday, and Friday evenings. The new pool hours will go into effect beginning on January 5.

Now cover the passage and question. Listen to the recording. When you hear the question, uncover the question and begin preparing your response.

 Disk 10, Track 11

> The man expresses his opinion about the change in swimming pool hours. State his opinion and explain the reasons he gives for holding that opinion.

 Stop

Preparation Time – 30 seconds
Response Time – 60 seconds

QUESTION 4

In this question, you will read a short passage on an academic subject, listen to a lecture on the same topic, and then speak in response to a question about what you have read and heard. After you hear the question, you have 30 seconds to prepare your response and 60 seconds to speak.

Reading Time – 45 seconds

CHIROPRACTIC

Chiropractic is a medical practice based on the interactions of the spine and the nervous system. According to chiropractic theory, disease results from a disruption or slowing of nerve function when the vertebrae, the bones that make up the spinal column, are not in their proper position. The method of treatment is to adjust and align the vertebrae. Chiropractors, doctors of chiropractic medicine, use their hands to massage and manipulate the patient's spine in order to relieve pressure on nerves and thus treat disease. Chiropractors typically complete nine years of academic and clinical education.

Now cover the passage and question. Listen to the recording. When you hear the question, uncover the question and begin preparing your response.

 Disk 10, Track 12

> Describe the patient's symptoms, and explain why chiropractic treatment was recommended. Explain how this patient's experience supports the practice of chiropractic.

 Stop

Preparation Time – 30 seconds
Response Time – 60 seconds

QUESTION 5

In this question, you will listen to a conversation. You will then be asked to talk about the information in the conversation and to give your opinion about the ideas presented. To make this practice more like the real test, cover the question during the conversation. After you hear the question, you have 20 seconds to prepare your response and 60 seconds to speak.

 Disk 10, Track 13

> The students discuss two possible solutions to the woman's problem. Describe the problem. Then state which of the two solutions you prefer and explain why.

 Stop

Preparation Time – 20 seconds
Response Time – 60 seconds

QUESTION 6

In this question, you will listen to part of a lecture. You will then be asked to summarize important information from the lecture. To make this practice more like the real test, cover the question during the lecture. After you hear the question, you have 20 seconds to prepare your response and 60 seconds to speak.

 Disk 10, Track 14

> Using points and examples from the lecture, describe fears that young children experience, and explain how these fears help children.

 Stop

Preparation Time – 20 seconds
Response Time – 60 seconds

Key points for Test 4 – Speaking are on page 613.

Each response earns a score of 1, 2, 3 or 4.

Record your total score on the Progress Chart on page 697.

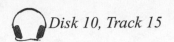 *Disk 10, Track 15*

WRITING SECTION DIRECTIONS

The Writing section measures your ability to use writing to communicate in an academic environment. There are two writing questions.

Question 1 is an integrated writing task. You will read a passage, listen to a lecture, and then answer a question based on what you have read and heard. You have 20 minutes to plan and write your response.

Question 2 is an independent writing task. You will answer a question based on your own knowledge and experience. You have 30 minutes to plan and write your response.

 Stop

TEST 4

QUESTION 1

For this task, you will write a response to a question about a reading passage and a short lecture. The question does not ask you to express your personal opinion.

Read the passage and then listen to the recording. To make this practice more like the real test, cover the passage and question during the lecture. You may take notes, and you may use your notes to help you write your response. When you hear the question, uncover the passage and question. Then allow 20 minutes to plan and write your response.

Typically, an effective response will have 150 to 225 words. Your response will be evaluated on the quality of your writing and on the completeness and accuracy of the content.

Reading Time – 3 minutes

During every season of the year, earthworms and other soil dwellers are continuously at work in forests and gardens. The activities of earthworms have a beneficial effect on the physical and chemical properties of the soil. Earthworms are responsible for mixing forest duff—the decaying organic matter on the forest floor—deeper into the soil. This breaks down the layers of soil and several inches of the hardpan below. Earthworms aerate the soil by their burrowing, and they add mucus that holds the fine soil particles together.

In the garden, earthworms do the same thing: they move organic matter from the surface deeper into the soil. They play an essential role in the compost pile, where they feed on grass clippings and other plant matter and excrete the indigestible portions as castings, which are then eaten by beneficial soil microbes. In this way, earthworms accelerate the decomposition of the compost pile and aid in the production of organic fertilizer.

Among sports fishers who use a hook and line, earthworms are the bait of choice. The most popular bait worms are large night crawlers and the smaller common species known as *Lumbricus rubellus*. Both kinds of worms are readily available in fishing shops or the old–fashioned way: by digging in the back yard.

Several species of earthworms are native to North America, but many of the species that are most abundant today originally came from Asia, Europe, or Africa, having crossed the ocean by hiding among plant roots or other cargo in ships' holds. With the help of gardeners and sports fishers, worm populations continue to spread across the continent, moving at the astonishing speed of five to ten meters a year. Earthworms are an important link in the food web since they are a food source for numerous species of animals.

Now cover the passage and question. Listen to the recording. When you hear the question, uncover the passage and question and begin your response.

 Disk 10, Track 16

> Describe the problems caused by earthworms in forest ecosystems, and explain how these problems contradict information in the reading.

 Stop

Writing Time – 20 minutes

QUESTION 2

For this task, you will write an essay in response to a question that asks you to express, explain, and support your opinion on a topic. You have 30 minutes to plan, write, and revise your essay.

Typically, an effective essay will have a minimum of 300 words. Your essay will be evaluated on the quality of your writing, including the organization and development of your ideas and the quality and accuracy of the language you use to express your ideas.

Read the question below and make any notes that will help you plan your response. Then begin typing your essay.

> Some people think that we learn our most important lessons in school. Others think that the knowledge we acquire outside of school is the most important. Which view do you agree with? Use specific reasons and examples to support your opinion.

Writing Time – 30 minutes

Key points for Test 4 – Writing are on page 614.

Each response earns a score of 1, 2, 3, 4 or 5.

Record your total score on the Progress Chart on page 697.

ANSWER KEY

PART 1 – READING

EXERCISE 1.1.A (p. 20)

1. B Clues: *...the introduction of images—powerful, realistic, moving images—into our everyday communication; ...marriage of words and images....*
2. D Clues: *Computing has spawned new forms of media, such as...the Internet.*
3. D Clues: *...imported exotic animals to sell to traveling showmen...; ...words such as lion or polar bear...; The creatures made such an impression that American English began to acquire new phrases.*
4. B Clues: *To monkey around and monkey business are expressions...to make a monkey out of someone... all being terms based on the increasing number of monkeys seen...; ...big ape...gorilla....*
5. A Clues: *Each tissue system is continuous throughout the plant's body.*
6. C Clues: *The dermal system, or epidermis, is a single layer of cells covering the entire body of the plant.*
7. D Clues: *The third system—the ground tissue—makes up the bulk of a plant, filling all of the spaces between the dermal and vascular tissue systems.*
8. B Clues: *Because of the rising demand for cotton from the mills of England,...the cotton production of the South increased tremendously; ...by the 1850s, output had soared to five million bales.*
9. A Clues: *Northern farmers would boast of... machinery....*
10. C Clues: *...just before the Civil War of the 1860s, the Southern states had developed an economic culture distinct from that of the North; The economic differences between the two regions would ultimately lead to armed conflict....*

EXERCISE 1.1.B (p. 23)

1. D Clues: *The child develops a sense of industry; If the child is encouraged to make and do things, allowed to finish tasks, and praised for trying, a sense of industry is the result.*
2. D Clues: *...if the child's efforts are unsuccessful, or if they are criticized or treated as bothersome, a sense of inferiority is the result.*
3. A Clues: *Erik Erikson believed that personality development is a series of turning points, which he described in terms of the tension between desirable qualities and dangers; ...Erikson called the period from age six to eleven Industry vs. Inferiority.*
4. C Clues: *In the storytelling traditions of West Africa, the tiny rabbit appears frequently as a rascal who teases or plays jokes on bigger animals.*
5. C Clues: *Joel Chandler Harris, a journalist in Georgia...; Harris wrote down and published many of the stories, popularizing them for the general public.*
6. B Clues: *...a trickster rabbit in the character of Brer Rabbit; ...similar versions of the same stories in southern Louisiana, where the rabbit character was known as Compair Lapin...; ...Bugs Bunny—a rascally rabbit who causes trouble, tricks the hunter....*

7. B Clues: *A hot spot is a giant underground caldron of molten rock in one of the world's many volcanically active areas.*
8. B Clues: *Annually, more than 200 geysers erupt in Yellowstone, making this one of the most interesting places in the world for geologists.*
9. C Clues: *The rock heats the water, and the boiling water and steam often make their way back up to the surface in the form of a geyser...; ...pressure builds up, eventually forcing the superheated water to burst to the surface as a geyser.*
10. A Clues: *If the water does not make it all the way to the surface, steam and gases may dissolve rocks and form a bubbling mud pot instead.*

EXERCISE 1.1.C (p. 26)

1. A Clues: *Organic compounds contain atoms of the element carbon, usually combined with itself and with atoms of one or more other elements....*
2. C Clues: *Important organic polymers include carbohydrates, proteins, and nucleic acids.*
3. D Clues: *Most animals, including humans, can manufacture about ten of these amino acids in their cells, but the other ten, called essential amino acids, must be obtained from food in order to prevent protein deficiency.*
4. C Clues: *The oldest of the resource commodities, fish, was traditionally associated with Newfoundland....*
5. D Clues: *...the fur trade was of tremendous value politically because it provided the means for Great Britain to retain its claim over much of Canada....*
6. A Clues: *By the 1840s, British North America had developed a vibrant commercial economy based on its abundant natural resources....; Fish, furs, timber, and grains represented over 90 percent of all economic activity.*
7. B Clues: *...she worked at Johns Hopkins in the laboratories...; Reed's research in pathology....*
8. A Clues: *In 1906, her marriage...took Reed away from the research laboratory; For ten years, she remained at home....*
9. C Clues: *...she concluded that she could not imagine life without her husband and sons, but she hoped for a future when marriage would not have to end a career of laboratory research.*
10. C Clues: *Reed's research in pathology established conclusively that Hodgkin's disease...was a distinct disorder characterized by a specific blood cell, which was named the Reed cell after her.*

EXERCISE 1.2.A (p. 32)

1. C The passage does not mention writing dialogue for characters. All the other answers are mentioned: *Another aspect is costumes...; ...a presentation by performers in front of an audience...; ...drama involves storytelling....*
2. D The passage does not give sun avoidance as a factor that can cause skin cancer; rather, sun avoidance is given as the most effective preventative measure. All the other answers are given: *...exposure to x–rays...; Chronic sun exposure—especially when it causes sunburn or blistering—results in more skin cancer...; ...family history of the disease.*

3. B   Laughter does not increase the body's vulnerability to illness; rather, it is stress hormones that increase vulnerability to illness. All the other answers are given as benefits of laughter: *...boosts brain chemicals that fight pain; ...increase hormones that have been shown to help produce restful sleep; ...diminish feelings of tension, anger....*

4. A   The author does not recommend playing tricks on family and friends. All the other answers are recommended: *...create a weekly fun time to look forward to...; ...spending time with children and animals; ...try keeping a humor journal in which you record some of the amusing things that happen to you.*

5. B   The passage does not state that plants in the *Apiaceae* family are native to one–fourth of the United States. All the other answers describe the *Apiaceae* family: *...3,000 species of the Apiaceae family exist in the Northern Hemisphere; ...aromatic herbs...foods...spices and seasonings...some species are very poisonous; ...small flowers...that are further grouped into a compound cluster.*

6. B   Potatoes are not members of the *Apiaceae* family. All the other answers are given: *carrots, parsnips...parsley....*

7. A   The passage does not state that the films of Satyajit Ray are characterized by adventure. All the other answers are given: *Ray's films are known for their compassion, honesty, and quiet dignity.*

8. C   The third film of the Apu Trilogy does not deal with struggle against poverty—that is a theme of the first film. All the other answers are themes of the third film: *...the young man...fails at his life's ambitions, and then, after losing his wife, he wanders across the country for several years before returning home....*

9. C   The passage does not mention diaries as something studied by archaeologists. All the other answers are mentioned: *...weapons...; ...items used in religious ceremonies...; ...ruins of buildings....*

10. A   Archaeologists do not plan and design more efficient uses for objects and materials. All the other answers are given: *...archaeologists establish the sequence of events that occurred in a given place and time period; ...these objects lie buried in the ground, so our image of the archaeologist is of a scientist who is always digging; ...document how big changes occurred in the way peoples exploited their environment and one another.*

EXERCISE 1.2.B (p. 36)

1. B   Clues: *The enlargement of the electorate...has increased the importance of parties to the point where it is practically impossible for a candidate to get elected without the support of a party organization.* (1.1)

2. D   The passage does not state that voters prefer candidates that express the values of an established party. All the other answers are given: *The job of influencing popular opinion through newspapers, television, the Internet, and other mass media is too complicated...; ...the variety of issues facing nation states has complicated the problem of creating an informed electorate...; Building political support on a nation–wide scale carries a high cost....*

3. B   The passage does not state that coral reefs have caused sea–surface temperatures to rise. All the other answers are given: *Coral reefs are one of the earth's most ancient ecosystems...; The brilliant blue, purple, green, gold, and pink have begun to disappear as a disease called bleaching drains the color and the life from the reefs; The huge cities built by corals provide shelter and food for billions of other marine animals.*

4. D   Rising water level is not given as an effect of the bleaching of coral reefs. All the other answers are given: *...bleaching drains the color...; Millions of aquatic animals that depend directly or indirectly on corals have died as well...; Bleaching has killed more corals....*

5. D   Clues: *...so different from one another...had less to do with their use of plants than with their use of animals; The Native Americans' relationship to the deer, moose, and beaver...was far different from that of the Europeans to the pigs, cows, sheep, and horses....* (1.1)

6. A   European settlers did not raise deer. All the other answers are given: *...Europeans...the pigs...sheep, and horses they owned.*

7. B   Burning the woods was not an agricultural practice of the Europeans; it was a practice of the Native Americans. All the other answers are given: *...the Europeans were responsible for a host of changes in the New England landscape: endless miles of fences...; ...the plow...characteristics of European agricultural practices; ...new fields covered with grass, clover....*

8. C   Landscape architects do not draw or paint scenes from the natural environment. All the other answers are given: *Landscape architects design landscapes in residential areas, public parks, and commercial zones; They usually plan the arrangement of vegetation, walkways, and other natural features of open spaces.*

9. B   The passage does not list building a fence around the construction site as a stage in the landscape design process. All the other answers are listed: *...landscape architects first consider the nature and purpose of the project, the funds available...; ...they prepare working drawings to show all existing and proposed features; They outline the methods of constructing features and draw up lists of building materials.*

10. C   Clues: *Newcomers to the field usually start as junior drafters...doing other simple drafting work for architectural, landscape architectural, or engineering firms.* (1.1)

QUIZ 1 (p. 41)

1. B   Clues: *...small, relatively harmless amounts of ionizing radiation, known as background radiation...; However, other types of ionizing radiation...have the potential to harm the human body.* (1.1)

2. A   Clues: *Most damage occurs in tissues with rapidly dividing cells....* (1.1)

3. A   Genetic defects are not an example of somatic damage; they are an example of genetic damage. All the other answers are examples of somatic damage: *The second type of damage is somatic, which causes victims direct harm in the form of burns...eye cataracts...cancers of the...lung.* (1.2)

4. D Clues: *Exposure to a large dose of ionizing radiation over a short time can be fatal within a few minutes to a few months later.* (1.1)

5. C Clues: *...the populations of most North American canids...have decreased greatly. The coyote, however, has thrived alongside humans, increasing in both numbers and range.* (1.1)

6. B The passage does not state that the coyote uses its distinctive call to trick and catch prey. All the other answers are given: *This call keeps the band alert to the locations of its members; One voice usually prompts others to join in, resulting in the familiar chorus...; ...its scientific name, canis latrans, means "barking dog."* (1.2)

7. D Clues: *In feeding, the coyote is an opportunist, eating rabbits, mice...and carrion—whatever is available.* (1.1)

8. D Clues: *Often a badger serves as involuntary supplier of smaller prey: while it digs for rodents at one end of their burrow, the coyote waits for any that may emerge from an escape hole at the other end.* (1.1)

9. C Clues: *Man is the major enemy....* (1.1)

10. A The passage does not state that the coyote is a serious threat to human activities. All the other answers are given: *The best runner among the canids...a strong swimmer...does not hesitate to enter water after prey; ...the coyote may team up with one or two others, running in relays to tire prey...; ...the coyote population continues to grow, despite efforts at trapping, shooting, and poisoning the animals.* (1.2)

EXERCISE 1.3.A (p. 48)

1. C The referent of *it* is something that is commonly a hare in Asia and Europe. The previous sentence introduces the topic of a favorite imagined figure seen in the moon's surface. Logic tells you that *it* refers to *favorite imagined figure.*

2. D The referent of *another* is the object of *to* in a *from...to* phrase. Logic and sentence structure tell you that *another* refers to *form.*

3. C The referent of *this area* is something in which young people must develop their ability. The previous sentence introduces the topic of *public speaking skills.* Logic tells you that *this area* refers to *public speaking.*

4. B The referent of *Others* is something of which *Stravinsky* is an example. The subject of the previous sentence is *Some composers.* Logic tells you that *Others* refers to *composers.*

5. C The referent of *them* is something that can be identified as being "higher" or "lower." The sentence discusses differences among people. Logic tells you that *them* refers to *people.*

6. C The referent of *they* is something that constitutes a social class. The subject of the sentence's first clause is *large number of families.* Logic tells you that *they* refers to *large number of families.*

7. C The referent of *those* is someone *born in the 1920s.* The sentence discusses current generations of adults. Logic tells you that *those* refers to *adults.*

8. D The referent of *them* is someone of whom one–third are caring for children. The sentence discusses unmarried couples. Logic tells you that *them* refers to *unmarried couples.*

9. A The referent of *them* is something to which insects develop genetic resistance. The subject of the passage is *pesticides.* Logic tells you that *them* refers to *pesticides.*

10. B The referent of *Some* is something that is absorbed from an organism's environment. The subject of the previous sentence is *chemicals.* Logic tells you that *Some* refers to *chemicals.*

EXERCISE 1.3.B (p. 51)

1. B The referent of *These* is something that was promoted in books and magazines. The subject of the previous sentence is *guiding principles.* Logic tells you that *These* refers to *guiding principles.*

2. B The referent of *them* is someone or something that was empowered by art societies and social–reform clubs. The subject of the sentence is *women.* Logic tells you that *them* refers to *women.*

3. C The referent of *one* is something that was planted in mass beddings. The referent is also the object of *to* in a *from...to* phrase. Logic and sentence structure tell you that *one* refers to *flower.*

4. C The referent of *them* is something that the climatic zones of North America did not always suit. The subject of the sentence is *tulips.* Logic tells you that *them* refers to *tulips.*

5. B The referent of *Both* is two things that echo many of the themes of earlier philosophies. The previous sentence discusses the relationship between phenomenology and existentialism. Logic tells you that *Both* refers to *phenomenology and existentialism.*

6. D The referent of *the latter* is someone or something that theorized about the hierarchy of human needs. The referent is also the second of two things mentioned. The previous sentence mentions the thinkers Martin Buber and Abraham Maslow. The second person mentioned is Abraham Maslow, so *the latter* refers to *Abraham Maslow.*

7. D The referent of *they* is something that is incorporated into the bone matrix. The sentence's first clause introduces the idea of adequate amounts of calcium and phosphorus. Logic tells you that *they* refers to *calcium and phosphorus.*

8. A The referent of *it* is something that is exposed to sunlight. The subject of the sentence is *skin.* Logic tells you that *it* refers to *skin.*

9. D The referent of *it* is something that causes bowing of the legs in a child with rickets. The subject of the sentence's first clause is *gravity.* Logic tells you that *it* refers to *gravity.*

10. C The referent of *the disease* is something of which a vitamin D deficiency will increase the severity. The previous two sentences discuss the causes and effects of osteoporosis. Logic tells you that *the disease* refers to *osteoporosis.*

QUIZ 2 (p. 54)

1. B Clues: *...suspects Dr. Caligari, a mountebank...of being responsible for a series of violent crimes. Caligari's instrument of crime is Cesare, a sleepwalker who is under the control of the evil doctor.* (1.1)

2. B The referent of *he* is someone who is the director of an insane asylum. The sentence mentions a search for the doctor. Logic tells you that *he* refers to *Dr. Caligari.* (1.3)

3. D   Clues: *The film's expressionistic sets and lighting reflect the narrator's madness; Walls are slanted and windows triangular; Furniture is distorted and oversized, evoking a nightmare world of insanity.* (1.1)

4. A   Clues: *The so-called expressionistic "street films" dealing with the lives of common people...; Director Fritz Lang's Metropolis....* (1.1)

5. C   The passage does not give luxurious sets and furniture as a characteristic of expressionistic film. All the other answers are given: *Surreal effects of light and shadow...; ...evoking a nightmare world of insanity; Walls are slanted... Furniture is distorted....* (1.2)

6. D   Clues: *However, a more accurate view shows that rural Canadians had access to considerable information.* (1.1)

7. C   The referent of *those* is something of today that the daily newspapers of the period were more substantial than. Logic tells you that *those* refers to *daily newspapers.* (1.3)

8. D   The referent of *them* is something about which rural Canadians held discussions at club meetings. The sentence mentions magazines and books. Logic tells you that *them* refers to *magazines and books.* (1.3)

9. B   The passage does not state that the rural school provided public health clinics. All the other answers are given: *The local school served other functions besides providing formal education...; ...school districts were often the only sign of political organization...; ...one-room schoolhouse as a meeting place...a variety of social and cultural events.* (1.2)

10. C   Clues: *...there was a growing exodus from farms to the city, mainly because smaller farms...were no longer able to support the entire family.* (1.1)

11. A   Clues: *...artists and writers romanticized the family farm. In the novel Anne of Green Gables....* (1.1)

12. D   Clues: *Two conditions are necessary for the formation of ice: the presence of water and temperatures below freezing. Ice in the atmosphere...can assume various forms, depending on the conditions under which water is converted to its solid state.* (1.1)

13. C   Clues: *Ice that forms in the atmosphere can fall to the ground as...hail; Hail consists of rounded or jagged lumps of ice, often in layers....* (1.1)

14. A   Sleet does not form on bodies of water; it forms in the atmosphere. All the other answers are forms of ice that form on bodies of water: *...the first ice to form is a thin surface layer of slush...; ...eventually grows into small floes of pancake ice; If the lake is small enough...the floes may freeze together into a fairly solid sheet of pack ice.* (1.2)

15. B   Clues: *On very large bodies of water, it may not form until late winter because there must be several months of low temperatures to chill such large amounts of water.* (1.1)

16. B   The referent of *it* is something that acts as an insulator. The subject of the sentence's first clause is *ice*. Logic tells you that *it* refers to *ice.* (1.3)

17. D   Clues: *...ice is less dense than liquid water and therefore floats rather than sinks in water; Without the insulating effect of floating ice sheets, surface water would lose heat more rapidly....* (1.1)

18. A   Clues: *Because most people do not volunteer to pay taxes or police their own financial affairs...; To accomplish these things, governments have to pass laws.* (1.1)

19. D   The referent of *This* is something that can be seen in the growth of government taxation and spending. The previous sentence introduces the idea of governments playing an increasing role in economics. Logic tells you that *This* refers to *increasing role in economics.* (1.3)

20. C   Clues: *...large-scale organizations—corporations, labor unions, and government structures—that have grown in importance...; Their presence and growing dominance have shifted capitalist economies... toward government administration of markets.* (1.1)

21. B   Clues: *...laws for the conduct of economic activity that attempt to make it serve the public interest. For instance...laws to shield investors against fraud.* (1.1)

22. C   The referent of *their* is someone or something that chooses representatives. The last part of the sentence lists the rights of workers. Logic tells you that *their* refers to *workers.* (1.3)

23. A   The passage does not give stock ownership as an issue concerning the labor force. All the other answers are given: *...concerns the labor force, such as regulation of work hours...health and safety conditions...and the rights of workers...to strike....* (1.2)

24. D   Clues: *Even governments that are reluctant to regulate commerce directly have undertaken large-scale projects...and other public services.* (1.1)

25. B   The passage does not give small business ownership as an example of government participation in economic activity. All the other answers are given: *...governments...have been playing an increasing role in economics. This can be seen in the growth of government taxation and spending, in the growing share of national income devoted to income-support payments...; Even governments that are reluctant to regulate commerce directly have undertaken... transportation networks....* (1.2)

Exercise 1.4.A (p. 70)

1. D   *Obstructed* means *blocked* in this context. Clues: *...what we consider taste is actually smell. If the sense of smell is -----, as by a head cold, the perception of taste is sharply reduced;* the prefix *ob-* = against; the stem *-struct-* = build.

2. A   *Accounts for* means *explains* in this context. Clues: *...120 degrees—the same angle as the angles of a hexagon —which ----- the characteristic six-sided structure....*

3. B   *Compile* means *put together* in this context. Clues: *...preparing the report...; ...how the report will be used...;* the prefix *com-* = together.

4. A   *Split off* means *separated* in this context. Clues: *...had common origins but then ----- from one another several hundred thousand years ago.*

5. A   *Indulge* means *participate* in this context. Clues: *...travel for pleasure was limited to the wealthy, but since then, improved standards of living and the availability of transportation have allowed more people to -----;* the prefix *in-* = into.

6. B *Exploded* means *expanded rapidly* in this context. Clues: ...*the development of commercial jet airlines enabled fast international travel; Today, airports in nearly every country can accommodate jumbo jets full of tourists...*; the prefix *ex–* = out.

7. A *Grasp* means *understanding* in this context. Clues: ...*must broaden and deepen their understanding...; ...some comprehension of...; ...must gain an understanding of....*

8. D *Pitfalls* means *hazards* in this context. Clues: ...*its negative aspects, such as the sources of human conflict and the ----- of power.*

9. C *Foliage* means *mass of leaves* in this context. Clues: ...*autumn leaves...; Red leaves...; Leaves that appear yellow....*

10. D *Masked* means *concealed* in this context. Clues: *Leaves that appear yellow in autumn are no less yellow in spring and summer. However, in spring and summer the yellow pigments...are ----- by the green pigment chlorophyll....* The yellow pigments do not appear in spring and summer because the green pigment conceals them.

EXERCISE 1.4.B (p. 73)

1. D *Crude* means *simple* in this context. Clues: *The moon with its earthshine acts as a ----- weather satellite by reporting, in a very simple way, the general state of terrestrial cloudiness.*

2. B *Glare* means *bright light* in this context. Clues: *As the phase of the moon progresses beyond a thin crescent...; ...the increasing ----- of the moon's growing crescent...; ...irradiation.*

3. A *Fleeting* means *temporary* in this context. Clues: ...*withstood the ----- nature of most slang; ...has been around a long time. Most slang is temporary, meaning it changes rapidly, but cool has lasted a long time.*

4. C *Carry the same weight* means *have the same importance.* Weight means heaviness or, in this context, importance. Clues: *As long as...Birth of the Cool remains one of the best–selling jazz recordings of all time, cool will stay cool—it will ----- as it did more than 50 years ago.*

5. D *Scouring* means *scraping* in this context. Clues: ...*removing most of the existing soil, and hollowing out countless lakes.*

6. C *Sustained* means *supported* in this context. Clues: ...*attempts to bring them into agricultural use have been largely unsuccessful. However, the region's mineral wealth ----- both temporary and permanent settlements...*; the prefix *sus–* = under.

7. C *Talk over* means *explore* in this context. Clues: ...*small–group discussions allow them to develop healthier ways to think about work; ...ways to make workplaces more ethical and just.*

8. A *In lockstep* means *alike* in this context. Clues: *Groups work best when they consist of people who have similar duties, responsibilities, and missions. This does not mean, however, that everyone in the group must think -----.*

9. B *Fuel* means *stimulate* in this context. Clues: *Finding the right subject matter...; ...several ways to ----- the discussion...; ...the company's mission statement...; ...readings on work and ethics...; ...specific workplace incidents....*

10. A *Overwhelm* means *dominate* in this context. Clues: ...*the dynamics of the group should be balanced...; ...the discussion leader must not be allowed to ----- the conversation or the agenda; ...when the same person is not always in charge*; the prefix *over–* = too much.

EXERCISE 1.4.C (p. 76)

1. A *Wreak havoc on* means *disrupt* in this context. Clues: ...*has a sharp impact on...; ...changes that can ----- precipitation patterns...; ...both delay and stimulate the fall of precipitation....*

2. C *Drenching* means *thoroughly wetting* in this context. Clues: ...*both delay and stimulate the fall of precipitation, depriving some areas of rain while ----- others. While shows contrast between depriving some areas of rain and drenching.*

3. A *Hoisted* means *lifted* in this context. Clues: ...*heavy amounts of heat and pollution rising from cities...; ...up in the sky....*

4. D *Torrential* means *heavy* in this context. Clues: ...*a precipitation shortage...; By contrast...invigorate summer storm activity...allowing clouds to build higher and fuller.... By contrast shows contrast between precipitation shortage and torrential rains.*

5. C *Sentimentality* means *feeling* in this context. Clues: *So much ----- is attached to the rose...emotional excess....*

6. B *Invoked* means *called on* in this context. Clues: ...*symbol of romantic love ----- by every minor poet and painter*; the prefix *in–* = on; the stem *–vok–* = call.

7. C *Decked* means *decorated* in this context. Clues: ...*roses were to be planted on the grave.*

8. D *Plucking* means *picking* in this context. Clues: ...*equated the rose with life, and they believed that when a child died, the figure of death could be seen ----- a rose outside the house.*

9. A *Token* means *symbol* in this context. Clues: ...*association with female beauty; ...a ----- of all that is lovely and good; ...on the other hand, the rose was a symbol not of feminine but of masculine beauty.* The parallel use of *token* and *symbol* shows that they are similar in meaning.

10. C *Sub rosa* means *secretly* in this context. Clues: ...*a sign of secrecy and silence; ...the intention of secrecy.*

EXERCISE 1.4.D (p. 78)

1. A Clues: *When "period" furniture became popular, American furniture factories attempted to duplicate various styles of French and English furniture of the seventeenth and eighteenth centuries.* A reproduction is a duplicate (copy) of something. (1.1)

2. C *Revolt* means *break* in this context. Clues: ...*based not only on individualism but also on a return to simplicity and practicality...; represented a ----- from mass–produced furniture; ...departed greatly from the ornate and pretentious factory–made "period" furniture.... Individualism contrasts with mass–produced, so revolt must indicate a change or break.*

3. D *Primitive* means *simple* in this context. Clues: ...*a return to simplicity and practicality; ...simple, straight lines....*

4. A   *Hallmarks* means *features* in this context. Clues: *...possess the essential qualities of...; ...plain and unornamented...; ...simple, straight lines were the ----- of its construction.*

5. B   Clues: *Craftsman furniture was plain and unornamented...; ...simple, straight lines....* (1.1)

6. B   *Vitality* means *energy* in this context. Clues: *...rhythms of speech...; ...movement, and color of rural black culture;* the stem *–vita–* = life.

7. A   *Calling* means *profession* in this context. Clues: *...continued her fieldwork...but eventually followed her most cherished -----, that of fiction writer.*

8. A   *Autonomy* means *independence* in this context. Clues: *...freedom, -----, and self–realization, while also being...attached to a man;* the prefix *auto–* = self.

9. C   *Out of touch* means that Hurston's opinions differed from those of most other people. Clues: *Hurston was criticized for not writing fiction in the protest tradition. Her conservative views...; ...the temper of the times.*

10. D   *Revere* means *honor* in this context. Clues: *...it was only afterward that later generations...were to rediscover and ----- her celebrations of black culture. It was only afterward* shows contrast with Hurston's dying in poverty and obscurity, indicating that *revere* has a positive meaning.

QUIZ 3 (p. 81)

1. C   *Sparsely populated* means that few people lived in the region. Clues: *...still two years away from becoming the state of Ohio; ...settlers of the Ohio frontier...; ...prepared the way for farms and towns...; When Chapman started his "apple seeding" in 1801, the population of Ohio was 45,000....* (1.4)

2. B   *Pacifist* means *peace advocate* in this context. Clues: *He was a ----- in a time of warfare and brutality against the Indians, treating Indians and settlers alike with respect. Peace advocate* contrasts with *warfare* and *brutality.* (1.4)

3. C   The passage does not state that Johnny Appleseed gave away meat; on the contrary, *He killed no animals and was a vegetarian.* All the other answers are given: *Journeying by foot...; ...constructing simple wooden fences...; ...exchanged knowledge of medicinal plants....* (1.2)

4. B   *Marching* means *advancing* in this context. Clues: *...agricultural development...; ...ever–increasing pace...; ...more than forty percent of the land had been cleared of trees and converted to farms.* (1.4)

5. D   *Subside* means *decrease* in this context. Clues: *Not until 1880 did the cutting of trees -----. By then, three–quarters of Ohio had been cleared, and people were becoming aware of the limits of expansion;* the prefix *sub–* = below, under. (1.4)

6. A   *Primeval* means *original* in this context. Clues: *...the universe began...; ...yet even now...may be present; ...original universe....* (1.4)

7. D   *Transition* means *change* in this context. Clues: *...gradually differentiated it...; ...expanded and cooled...;* the prefix *trans–* = across. (1.4)

8. C   *Uniform* means *consistent* in this context. Clues: *...not completely...; ...some regions that were slightly denser and capable of generating stronger gravitational fields than others;* the prefix *uni–* = one; *uniform* = one form or type. (1.4)

9. B   *Compact* means *dense* in this context. Clues: *Since gravity tends to pull matter together, the denser regions tended to become even more -----; evolved into denser clouds....* Gravity pulled the dense regions together, making them denser than before. (1.4)

10. A   *Luminous* means *light–emitting* in this context. Clues: *...glow...; ...stars...;* the stem *–lum–* = light. (1.4)

QUIZ 4 (p. 84)

1. D   The referent of *those* is something in Great Britain and Ireland that automobile sales in Michigan outnumbered. Logic tells you that *those* refers to *automobile sales.* (1.3)

2. B   *The lifeblood* means *an important part* in this context. Clues: *The growth of roads and the automobile industry made cars ----- of the petroleum industry...; The automobile caused expansions in....* (1.4)

3. A   *Frenzied* means *intense* in this context. Clues: *...automobile industry reached new heights...; ...new roads...; ...road building...; ...largest public works program in history.* (1.4)

4. C   Clues: *After 1945...new roads led out of the city to the suburbs...; The result was a network of federally subsidized highways connecting major urban centers.* (1.1)

5. B   *Scant* means *barely sufficient* in this context. Clues: *...75 percent of federal funds for transportation were spent on highways, while a ----- one percent went to buses, trains, or subways; ...worst public transit system. While* shows contrast between *75 percent* for highways and *one percent* for public transit. (1.4)

6. C   The passage does not state that the growth in the number of cars had a positive impact on subway systems; in fact, there was a negative impact on subways and other forms of public transit. All the other answers are given as positive impacts: *The automobile caused expansions in outdoor recreation, tourism...service stations...; ...two–car families transported children to...shopping malls.* (1.2)

7. A   Clues: *...the American bias was clear, which is why the United States has the world's best road system and nearly its worst public transit system.* (1.1)

8. C   *Range* means *variety* in this context. Clues: *Some species are restricted to a single song...while other species have a ----- of songs and dialects.... While* shows contrast between *single song* and *range.* (1.4)

9. D   Clues: *For all bird species, there is a prescribed path to development of the final song...; This process is similar to the steps through which young children pass as they first babble and then mimic pieces of the songs they hear....* (1.1)

10. A   *Mimic* means *imitate* in this context. Clues: *The most important auditory stimuli for birds are the sounds of other birds...; This process is similar to...young children...as they first babble and then ----- pieces of the songs they hear around them....* (1.4)

11. D   Clues: *...compared to the human larynx, which uses only about two percent of exhaled air, the syrinx is a far more efficient sound–producing mechanism that can create sound from nearly all the air passing through it.* (1.1)

12. B Clues: *Song is a complex activity that young birds must learn, and learning implies that higher–brain activity must be complex in the control of song.* (1.1)

13. A *Lateralized* means *linked to a specific area of the brain.* Clues: *...the song–control centers are located in the left side of the avian brain.* (1.4)

14. D The referent of *there* is someplace where a lesion will destroy bird song. The previous sentence states that the song–control centers are located in the left side of the avian brain. Logic tells you that *there* refers to *the left side of the brain.* (1.3)

15. B The passage does not state that birds are born with the full ability to sing their species song; in fact, birds must learn the species song. All the other answers are given: *The most important auditory stimuli for birds are the sounds of other birds...; Underlying all avian vocal activity is the syrinx, an organ...linked to the brain; Possibly the most interesting aspect of bird song...is its foundation in the central nervous system.* (1.2)

16. A Clues: *Machiavelli was a product of Renaissance Florence, a city–state that was struggling for expansion and survival among a competing group of similar states; Machiavelli came to understand power politics by observing the spectacle around him....* (1.1)

17. B *Illusions* means *false beliefs* in this context. Clues: *...came to understand power politics by observing the spectacle around him without any -----; the prefix il– = not; the stem –lus– = light.* (1.4)

18. C Clues: *In his most famous work, The Prince (1532), Machiavelli described the means by which a leader may gain and maintain power.* (1.1)

19. C The referent of *their* is someone or something with weaknesses that the ideal prince can exploit. The sentence states that the ideal prince studied his fellow men. Logic tells you that *their* refers to *fellow men.* (1.3)

20. A *Pessimistic* means *negative* in this context. Clues: *...all men were brutal, selfish, and cowardly...; ...thought that his own time was too corrupt...; Machiavelli's philosophy arose more from a deeply ----- view of human nature....* (1.4)

21. C Machiavelli's political philosophy did not include the belief that people must organize to fight against evil and corruption in politics. All the other answers are given: *Politics was simply the battle of men in search of power, and since all men were brutal, selfish...; The ideal prince was the man who had studied his fellow men...and was willing to exploit their weaknesses; Machiavelli saw politics as an affair separate from religion and ethics, an activity to be practiced and studied for its own sake.* (1.2)

22. D Clues: *He was, and still is, misunderstood to have promoted...criminality over other means of governing.* (1.1)

23. B *Lucidity* means *clarity* in this context. Clues: *...saw the world more clearly than others...; ...honesty; the stem –luc– = light.* (1.4)

24. A *Monologues* means *speeches* in this context. Clues: *...to comment on his own wickedness...; the prefix mono– = one; the stem –log– = study. Comment* indicates speaking; a monologue is a speech by one person. (1.4)

25. D Complex motivation is not a characteristic of the Machiavel character. All the other answers are given: *...contempt for goodness; The Machiavel had a habit of using humorous monologues to comment on his own wickedness...; ...delight in evil...* (1.2)

EXERCISE 1.5.A (p. 94)

1. B You can infer that people have long been aware of links between music and mathematics. Clues: *In classical and medieval times, the study of music shared many features with the discipline of mathematics....*

2. A You can infer that corvids are a family of birds. Clues: *...stay in their flocks all year round; ...synchronized flight test; ...adaptability and intelligence of this family....*

3. C You can infer that the author believes trees, plants, and organic matter can store solar energy. Clues: *Major indirect forms of solar energy include... biomass—solar energy converted to chemical energy in trees, plants, and other organic matter.*

4. C You can infer that women did not acquire property through inheritance. Clues: *The family members who would not inherit a share in the property were exploited by the laws of inheritance. The system was particularly hard on women, who usually did not share in the ownership of the farm....*

5. B *Embark on* means *begin* in this context. Clues: *When the family's first child is born, the parents ----- a sequence of experiences....* (1.4)

6. D You can infer that the family life cycle shapes several years in the lives of most adults. Clues: *...from infancy and toddlerhood...and eventually, to departure from the nest. Each of these periods in the child's life makes a different set of demands on the parents.*

7. B You can infer that aromatherapy is the use of certain scents to promote health. Clues: *...odors and fragrances affect the body and mind and are capable of healing anxiety, stress, and other sources of disease; Some popular essential oils and their uses in aromatherapy include....*

8. B The passage does not state that jasmine is believed to reduce stress. All the other answers are believed to reduce stress: *...lavender and chamomile, which are reputed to ease stress...; Orange eases anxiety....* (1.2)

9. D You can infer that social interactions related to teaching and learning provide evidence that orangutans have culture. Clues: *Some orangutan parents teach their young...while others demonstrate the technique...; Such social interactions lead researchers to conclude that if orangutans have culture....*

10. C You can infer that primate culture may be older than scientists used to believe. Clues: *The discovery of orangutan culture suggests that early primates... might have developed the ability to invent new behaviors...approximately 6 million years earlier than once believed.*

EXERCISE 1.5.B (p. 98)

1. **A** You can infer that the sources of immigrants shifted to different parts of Europe. Clues: *In the early nineteenth century, most of the Europeans who immigrated to the United States were from northern and western European countries...; However, most of the fifteen million Europeans arriving between 1890 and 1914 came from southern and eastern Europe....*

2. **C** You can infer that the Doukhobors mainly settled in the Canadian prairies. Clues: *The Doukhobors... established communal settlements in Saskatchewan. Together with other immigrants, they arrived in such numbers that...the population of the prairies had increased....*

3. **B** You can infer that David Smith's childhood exposed him to the uses and possibilities of iron. Clues: *His iron sculptures flowed naturally out of the mechanized heart of America, a landscape of railroads and factories. As a child, Smith played on trains and around factories....*

4. **A** The referent of *several* is something that has "heads" or "legs." The subject of the previous sentence is *sculptures*. Logic tells you that *several* refers to *sculptures*. (1.3)

5. **D** You can infer that the *Sentinels* and the *Cubis* each consist of a number of pieces placed in outdoor settings. Clues: *...two series of sculptures...the Sentinels...and the Cubis...; He also began placing his sculptures outdoors...; In the late afternoon sun, the steel planes of the Cubis reflect a golden color....*

6. **C** You can infer that the author believes David Smith's pieces capture the power of industry and the beauty of natural light. Clues: *To Smith, iron spoke of the power, mobility, and vigor of the industrial age; He also began placing his sculptures outdoors, in natural light, where the highly reflective stainless steel could bring sunlight and color into the work.*

7. **A** You can infer that an earned run average is a statistic. Clues: *Baseball fans love statistics; Fans really understand...an earned run average—all those basics....*

8. **B** You can infer that hitting with runners in scoring position is a complex statistic. Clues: *...many new statistics have evolved: hitting with runners in scoring position...; These are the so-called sophisticated statistics.*

9. **D** You can infer that Ty Cobb and Mickey Cochran were great baseball players. Clues: *One "game" is to compare the players of old with the players of today; "Could...have played with Ty Cobb or Mickey Cochran...?"; What they have to argue with is statistics; The statistics are all that remain of the career of that star player of the past.*

10. **B** You can infer that the author believes baseball provides a fascinating way to look at statistics. Clues: *There is absolutely no doubt about it: baseball is the greatest statistics game there is; There is a whole lore of baseball history involving statistics.*

EXERCISE 1.5.C (p. 101)

1. **B** You can infer that the organs for hearing and balance both send nerve impulses to the brain. Clues: *Both organs involve fluid-filled channels containing hair cells that produce electrochemical impulses...; To perform the function of hearing, the ear converts the energy of pressure waves moving through the air into nerve impulses that the brain perceives as sound; When the position of the head changes...the force on the hair cells changes its output of nerve impulses. The brain then interprets these changes....*

2. **A** Hearing does not involve motion of the vocal cords so that they vibrate; this is an aspect of speaking, not hearing. All the other answers are given as part of hearing: *...fluid-filled channels containing hair cells that produce electrochemical impulses when the hairs are stimulated...; ...bones of the middle ear amplify and transmit the vibrations...; the ear converts the energy of pressure waves moving through the air into nerve impulses....* (1.2)

3. **D** You can infer that the cochlea is a part of the inner ear. Clues: *The inner ear is a network of channels containing fluid...; ...the cochlea, the organ of hearing; ...the fluid inside the cochlea. Hair cells in the cochlea convert the energy of the vibrating fluid....*

4. **A** You can infer that gravity has an essential role in the sense of balance. Clues: *Hair cells in the inner ear respond to changes in head position with respect to gravity and movement. Gravity is always pulling down on the hairs, sending a constant series of impulses to the brain.*

5. **C** The referent of *These extraordinary crafts* is something that was fashioned from a single tree trunk and carried as many as forty people. The previous sentence introduces the topic of seagoing dugout canoes. Logic tells you that *These extraordinary crafts* refers to *seagoing dugout canoes*. (1.3)

6. **A** Clues: *...keeping the sections below the waterline thickest and heaviest to help keep the canoe upright in stormy seas.* (1.1)

7. **D** You can infer that canoes were important cultural artifacts of the Haida. Clues: *The canoes were often painted with elaborate designs of cultural significance to the tribe.*

8. **B** *Staunch* means *strong* in this context. Clues: *...the canoe's stability...; ...sturdy wooden thwarts...; ...utility....* (1.4)

9. **D** You can infer that trees provided essential tools for obtaining food. Clues: *...harpoons of yew wood, baited hooks of red cedar, and lines of twisted and braided bark fibers, they fished...and hunted....*

10. **C** You can infer that Haida canoes were of great value in the regional economy. Clues: *...neighboring tribes were willing to exchange quantities of hides, meats, and oils for a Haida canoe. These graceful vessels became the tribe's chief item of export.*

EXERCISE 1.6.A (p. 108)

1. **A** The author's purpose is to point out that financial measurements are not always precise. Clues: *In economics and finance, nothing can be measured with the precision...; ...approximate measurement is often sufficient....*

2. D The author's purpose is to warn potential buyers of the possibility of accounting abuses. Clues: *Accounting scandals occur...; Although the accounting profession and government agencies have attempted to reform some of these abuses....*

3. B The author's purpose is to provide biographical information about the author. Clues: *...Stephen Leacock's masterpiece, Sunshine Sketches of a Little Town...; ...one of the founders of Canadian literature....*

4. A The author's purpose is to describe the tone of the book. Clues: *...a portrait of small–town Canadian life in the early twentieth century; ...a past to be cherished, a pastoral and idyllic town....*

5. C The author's purpose is to illustrate the behavior required of certain social roles. Clues: *...certain types of behavior from people who play certain social roles; Anyone occupying a given position is expected to adopt a specific attitude.*

6. D The author's purpose is to emphasize the value of informal roles to a group. Clues: *...a group's health and happiness....*

7. C Clues: *...the family historian...relays valuable cultural information that maintains both the family and the larger society.* (1.1)

8. C The author's purpose is to compare how various surfaces transfer heat into the atmosphere. Clues: *Thus, the different types of surfaces transfer heat into the atmosphere at different rates.*

9. A Clues: *...we depend on our perceptions of the data...; Human perception must be included if our understanding of climatic processes is to be translated into societal actions.* (1.1)

10. C The author's purpose is to give examples of dangerous effects of climate. Clues: *...the harmful effects of climate—....*

Exercise 1.6.B (p. 112)

1. A The author's purpose is to emphasize his contributions to the field. Clues: *...promoting forestry as a profession. Foremost was Gifford Pinchot...; ...chief of the Forest Service...; ...professor of forestry and founder of the Pinchot School of Forestry....*

2. D The author's purpose is to introduce the types of work done by professional foresters. Clues: *...plan and supervise the growth, protection, and utilization of trees; ...make maps of forest areas...manage timber sales; ...protect the trees...; ...may be responsible for other duties...; ...do research, provide information...teach in colleges and universities.*

3. B The passage does not mention how to select a good school of forestry. All the other answers are mentioned: *Some foresters may be responsible for other duties, ranging from...; Several men have been responsible for promoting forestry as a profession; ...estimate the amount of standing timber and future growth, and manage timber sales.* (1.2)

4. B The passage does not state that fashions serve the purpose of signaling a change in personal beliefs. All the other answers are given: *By keeping up with fashions...members of a group both satisfy their desire for novelty...; ...demonstrating their membership in the group; ...obey the rules....* (1.2)

5. D The author's purpose is to explain how high status may involve an inverted status display. Clues: *Some people...consider themselves of such high status that they do not need to display it with their clothing; ...an inverted status display is most likely to occur where the person's high status....*

6. A The author's purpose is to give an example of an item that conveys one's actual status. Clues: *...a subtle but important signal, such as an expensive -----, will prevail over the message of the casual dress.*

7. A The author's purpose is to show how the war for independence affected the economy. Clues: *The war for independence from Britain was a long and economically costly conflict.*

8. C Clues: *The most serious consequences were felt in the cities, whose existence depended on commercial activity.* (1.1)

9. C The author's purpose is to emphasize the great short–term cost of the war for New York. Clues: *The population...declined from 21,000 in 1774 to less than half that number only nine years later in 1783.*

10. D You can infer that shortages of money and manufactured goods occurred during the years right after the war for independence. Clues: *...the loss of established markets for manufactured goods...the loss of sources of credit...the lack of new investment all created a period of economic stagnation that lasted for the next twenty years.* (1.5)

Quiz 5 (p. 116)

1. B The author's purpose is to identify the freezing point of water. Clues: *Because many foods contain large amounts of water, they freeze solidly at or just below....* (1.6)

2. B The author's purpose is to warn that not blanching will harm the food's nutritional value. Clues: *...avoid this step...; The result would be a product largely devoid of vitamins and minerals.* (1.6)

3. A You can infer that enzyme action in vegetables eventually causes vegetables to spoil. Clues: *...enzyme action, which vegetables require during their growth and ripening but which continues after maturation and will lead to decay....* (1.5)

4. C You can infer that underblanched vegetables would lack vitamins and minerals. Clues: *...to avoid this step would be an expensive mistake. The result would be a product largely devoid of vitamins and minerals; Underblanching is like no blanching at all....* (1.5)

5. D You can infer that the French colonies had fewer people than did other North American colonies. Clues: *...there were never enough French settlers to make French North America a large center of population.* (1.5)

6. A The author's purpose is to emphasize the competition among European groups. Clues: *...the lead...; ... early losses....* (1.6)

7. B You can infer that England was a leading European power. Clues: *England's commercial and political growth at home soon gave it the lead in the colonial race....* (1.5)

8. D   The author's purpose is to illustrate England's growing power in North America. Clues: *England's commercial and political growth at home soon gave it the lead in the colonial race...; ...there were 2,000 in the English colonies; ...the English had absorbed the Dutch colonies; ...the English colonies had a quarter of a million.* (1.6)

9. C   You can infer that the Dutch and the English competed for land, and the English prevailed. Clues: *The Dutch settlements suffered a lot of competition from the English, and eventually the Dutch governor was forced to surrender all Dutch lands to the English; ...the English had absorbed the Dutch colonies.* (1.5)

10. B   Clues: *The conflicts...were mostly over commercial interests and signaled the intense rivalry for control of North American land and resources.* (1.1)

Quiz 6 (p. 119)

1. D   The name is curious because it did not originate in America. Clues: *The name was, in fact, a historical accident, originating with fashionable architects in Victorian England who coined it....* (1.6)

2. B   The referent of *it* is something that was coined by fashionable architects in Victorian England. The subject of the sentence is *name*. Logic tells you that *it* refers to *name*. (1.3)

3. D   *Asymmetrical* means *unbalanced* in this context. Clues: *...how drastically different the right and left sides are....* (1.4)

4. A   The passage does not mention decorative windows as a characteristic of Queen Anne houses. All the other answers are mentioned: *...the wood shingle siding...; ...the inviting wraparound porch...; ...the unusual roof shape—a steeply pitched....* (1.2)

5. C   You can infer that the Queen Anne style was elaborate and ornate. Clues: *...unusual roof shape...; ...the detailing, shown in the wood shingle siding cut into fanciful decorative patterns of scallops, curves, diamonds, or triangles.* (1.5)

6. C   Clues: *Queen Anne houses faded from fashion early in the twentieth century as the public's taste shifted toward the more modern Prairie and Craftsman style houses.* (1.1)

7. A   *Buffs* means *experts* in this context. Clues: *...painstakingly and lovingly restored...; ...reproduced by builders who give faithful attention to the distinctive shapes and detailing....* (1.4)

8. C   The referent of *that* is something connected with sports and games. The subject of the sentence is *type of commentary*. Logic tells you that *that* refers to *commentary*. (1.3)

9. D   Clues: *..."color" commentary provides the audience with pre-event background, during-event interpretation, and post-event evaluation.* (1.1)

10. B   Clues: *Play-by-play commentary...is unlike other kinds of narrative, which are typically reported in past tense. Play-by-play commentary is reported in present tense.* (1.1)

11. A   The author's purpose is to describe the uniqueness of radio play-by-play. Clues: *It is these characteristics that make this kind of commentary unlike any other type of speech situation.* (1.6)

12. A   "He pitched for Chicago" is not an example of play-by-play commentary; rather, it is an example of background information that is part of color commentary. All the other answers are examples of play-by-play commentary: "Junior out of bounds" eliminates the verb; "Straight away it's Owens" has inverted word order and is spoken in present tense; "He can't make the shot" is spoken in present tense. (1.2)

13. D   *Pace* means *speed* in this context. Clues: *...very fluent, keeping up with the ----- of the action. The rate is steady....* (1.4)

14. B   *Crucial* means *important* in this context. Clues: *...informing the listener...; ..."state of play" summary...; ...for listeners or viewers who have just tuned in.* (1.4)

15. C   You can infer that the author believes commentary enhances the excitement and enjoyment of sports. Clues: *"Play-by-play" commentary narrates the sports event, while "color-adding" or "color" commentary provides the audience with... background...interpretation...evaluation; Play-by-play commentary is very fluent, keeping up with the pace of the action.* (1.5)

16. B   Clues: *...the circulatory system, consisting of two cellular pipelines...; One pipeline, called the xylem...; The other, the phloem....* (1.1)

17. C   The referent of *This* is something that is the tree's major growth organ. The subject of the previous sentence is *vascular cambium*. Logic tells you that *This* refers to *vascular cambium*. (1.3)

18. B   You can infer that the xylem is located inside the phloem and the vascular cambium. Clues: *...the vascular cambium produces new phloem cells on its outer surface and new xylem cells on its inner surface.* (1.5)

19. A   You can infer that xylem sap is composed mainly of water. Clues: *Xylem cells in the roots draw water molecules into the tree...; The xylem pipeline transports this life-sustaining mixture upward as xylem sap...; ...bringing xylem sap to thirsty cells. Leaves depend on this delivery system for their water supply....* (1.5)

20. D   *Wilt* means *sag* in this context. Clues: *Unless the transpired water is replaced...the leaves will ----- and eventually die.* The leaves will sag and die because they have lost water. (1.4)

21. C   Clues: *Water moves through the tree because it is driven by negative pressure—tension...; Transpiration, the evaporation of water from leaves, creates the tension that drives long-distance transport up through the xylem pipeline.* (1.1)

22. B   *Adhere to* means *stick to* in this context. Clues: *...cohesion of water due to hydrogen bonding...; ...water molecules ----- each other and are pulled upward...;* the prefix *ad-* = to, toward. (1.4)

23. A   *Gummy* means *sticky* in this context. Clues: *...become clogged...; ...can no longer transport fluids... Gummy* is the adjective form of *gum*, a sticky substance. (1.4)

24. C   The author's purpose is to compare what happens in two aging circulatory systems. Clues: *Over time the innermost xylem cells become clogged with hard or gummy waste products and can no longer transport fluids. A similar situation occurs in the clogging of -----.* (1.6)

25. A   Transporting food from the leaves to the trunk is not a function of the xylem; it is a function of the phloem. All the other answers are functions of the xylem: *Xylem cells in the roots draw water molecules into the tree...carrying chemical nutrients from the soil; ...the dead xylem cells become part of the central column of heartwood, the supportive structure of the tree; ...Within the xylem cells, water molecules...are pulled upward through the trunk.* (1.2)

EXERCISE 1.7.A (p. 128)

1. D   *Some general preparation may be in order* is paraphrased in *As general preparation. Participants may want to take into the conference materials or data that might be useful if a matter comes up* is paraphrased in *participants can bring materials or data that might be a part of the discussion.*

2. A   *This* in the highlighted sentence refers to the fact that *ectotherms heat directly with solar energy,* stated in the previous sentence. *A reptile can survive on less than 10 percent of the calories required by a mammal of equivalent size* is paraphrased in *it requires less than 10 percent of the calories that a mammal of the same size needs.*

3. C   *Sometimes the designer disregards the context* is paraphrased in *they ignore them. The assumption that surrounding structures will later be replaced* is paraphrased in *Architects often believe that nearby structures will not always be there.*

4. B   *They* in the highlighted sentence refers to *folkways* in the previous sentence. *Provided evidence of the everyday life of the people* is paraphrased in *give us a much better description of daily life. Far richer than that in most other historical texts* is paraphrased in *much better...than most histories do.*

5. D   *The ruminant periodically returns the cud to its mouth* is paraphrased in *The cud is sent back to the ruminant's mouth. Chewed at length* is paraphrased in *chewed extensively. To crush the fibers, making them more accessible to further bacterial action* is paraphrased in *so that the fibers can be digested more easily.*

6. B   *Not restricted to city dwellers* is paraphrased in *not just people who live in cities. It can be considered a trait of all modern societies at a high level of technological development* is paraphrased in *Urbanism characterizes all highly developed societies.*

7. C   *Humans drove alligators to near extinction* is paraphrased in *People almost destroyed the native alligator population. Many of their marsh and swamp habitats in North America* is paraphrased in *many North American environments.*

8. A   *It is still protected from excessive harvesting by hunters* is paraphrased in *Alligators are still protected. Limited hunting is allowed* is paraphrased in *hunters are allowed to kill a certain number. To keep the population from growing too large* is paraphrased in *to control their population.*

9. D   *Current archaeological theory holds* is paraphrased in *Archaeologists believe. The first humans in the Americas were bands of advanced Stone Age people* is paraphrased in *groups of Stone Age humans first came to the Americas. Crossed over from what is now Siberia in Asia sometime between 12 and 30 thousand years ago* is paraphrased in *came to the Americas from Asia about 12 to 30 thousand years ago.*

10. C   *In South America, where the glaciers from the ice age melted first* is paraphrased in *The ice age glaciers melted earliest in South America. The migrants took strong root* is paraphrased in *the migrants settled. The fertile soil and warm climate of Patagonia* is paraphrased in *the warm, fertile region of Patagonia.*

EXERCISE 1.7.B (p. 133)

1. D   *Whenever these differences lead to exclusion or discrimination* is paraphrased in *when these people face discrimination. Subcultures develop as a shield to protect members from the negative attitudes of others* is paraphrased in *Subcultures form to protect people who differ from the majority.*

2. A   A desire to join the dominant culture is not given as a characteristic of subcultures. All the other answers are given: *...differ from the mainstream...; ...own special language and customs; ...a "we" feeling among members....* (1.2)

3. C   *These variations are close enough for the subgroup to remain under the societal umbrella* is paraphrased in *A subculture's values...resemble the majority's values enough to keep the subgroup within the larger society. Different enough to reflect the unique experience of subgroup members* is paraphrased in *A subculture's values show its separateness.*

4. B   *Each hemisphere has four discrete lobes* is paraphrased in *The brain's two hemispheres each have four separate parts. Researchers have identified a number of functional areas within each lobe* is paraphrased in *each part controls several functions.*

5. C   Clues: *Without the corpus callosum to function as a switchboard...; The link between sensory input and spoken response was disconnected.* (1.1)

6. A   *Without the corpus callosum to function as a switchboard between the two sides of the brain* is paraphrased in *because the corpus callosum did not provide the link. The subject's knowledge of the size, texture, and function of the key* is paraphrased in *Information about the key. Could not be transferred from the right to the left hemisphere* is paraphrased in *could not travel from one side of the brain to the other.*

7. B   *The microorganisms secrete enzymes* is paraphrased in *microorganisms produce certain enzymes. Break down the cells of the dead vegetation and animal matter* is paraphrased in *Nonliving plant and animal matter is digested.*

8. D   *Cements* means *combines* in this context. Clues: *...the glue that ----- the soil particles into larger, coarser grains.* (1.4)

9. B   You can infer that organic compost relies on the digestive processes of microorganisms. Clues: *The microorganisms secrete enzymes that break down the cells...; This partially digested mixture is compost.* (1.5)

10. A   *The terms "compost" and "humus" are often used interchangeably* is paraphrased in *people sometimes confuse the two words. They are not synonymous* is paraphrased in *Compost and humus are different substances.*

EXERCISE 1.8.A (p. 141)

1. A   In the added sentence, *Most of them* refers to *Kindergartners*, the subject of the previous sentence. The added sentence introduces the idea of talking in front of a group, which the next sentence develops with the example of "sharing time."

2. B   In the added sentence, *However* is a transition that shows contrast between *appear relatively dry* in the previous sentence and *spongy and wet to the touch* in the added sentence.

3. C   In the added sentence, *narrower leaves of trees like willows and mimosa* logically follows *broad leaves of deciduous trees like oaks and maples* in the previous sentence.

4. D   In the added sentence, *This* refers to the oboe's rasping, "sawtooth" sound, mentioned in the previous sentence. The added sentence gives the reason for this sound.

5. C   In the added sentence, *It* refers to *Carbonizing*, the subject of the previous sentence. Also, *method* in the added sentence restates *technique* in the previous sentence. The added sentence gives additional information about carbonizing.

6. D   The added sentence further develops the idea that *no one can find another trade to improve his situation*, mentioned in the previous sentence.

7. C   The added sentence discusses the study mentioned in the previous sentence. The added sentence introduces the idea of bright and dark colors, which the next sentence develops with specific examples.

8. A   In the added sentence, *This irritation* refers to *an inflammation of the bronchial tubes* in the previous sentence.

9. D   The added sentence gives examples of courses in the *curriculum from a variety of ethnic sources* mentioned in the previous sentence.

10. B   The added sentence gives another example of two types of oceanographers, *biological and chemical oceanographers*, that logically follows *physical oceanographers and ocean engineers* given in the previous sentence.

EXERCISE 1.8.B (p. 144)

1. C   *Flourished* means *lived* in this context. Clues: *Their mound construction was especially intensive in this area; ...evidence...; ...five hundred years.* (1.4)

2. B   The referent of *They* is something that includes shell beads, bear and shark teeth, and other items. The subject of the previous sentence is *artifacts*. Logic tells you that *They* refers to *artifacts*. (1.3)

3. C   The added sentence introduces the idea that objects found in particular mounds indicate the status and occupation of the deceased. The next sentence develops this idea with a description of the *pipes found in one mound* that probably belonged *to a chief or priest*.

4. B   You can infer that a 60–centimeter fish can swim faster than a 30–centimeter fish. Clues: *Generally speaking, the larger the fish the faster it can swim.* (1.5)

5. D   *Thrust is used to propel the fish forward* is paraphrased in *Thrust pushes the fish forward. Lateral force tends to make the fish's head deviate from the course in the same direction as the tail* is paraphrased in *lateral force pushes both its head and its tail to the same side.* (1.7)

6. B   The added sentence further describes the undulations mentioned in the previous sentence. The added sentence introduces the idea of the bending of the body, which the next sentence develops with more details.

7. C   The referent of *another* is something for which there is more than one type. The sentence discusses coins. Logic tells you that *another* refers to *type of coin.* (1.3)

8. D   In the added sentence, *However* is a transition that shows contrast between *traders worked out different rates of exchange* in the previous sentence and *this was a long, slow process* in the added sentence. In the added sentence, *this* refers to *rates of exchange* in the previous sentence.

9. B   *The wealthier classes used money for major transactions* is paraphrased in *Rich people used money for important purchases. Ordinary people continued to barter for most things in their daily lives* is paraphrased in *common people traded goods and services directly.* (1.7)

10. A   The added sentence introduces the topic of paper money, which the rest of the paragraph develops with facts and details.

QUIZ 7 (p. 149)

1. C   *In evolutionary history, the development of language* is paraphrased in *The emergence of language. Set humans apart from the rest of the animal kingdom* is paraphrased in *distinguished early humans from other animals.* (1.7)

2. A   The added sentence introduces the topic of written language, which the rest of the paragraph develops with facts and details. (1.8)

3. D   *The expansion of humanity from an oral society to one that also used the written word for communication* is paraphrased in *writing was added to speaking as a form of communication. A defining point in human civilization* is paraphrased in *An important development in human history.* (1.7)

4. B   *It is one of the most important sensations* is paraphrased in *The ability to sense pain is extremely important. Because it is translated into a negative reaction, such as withdrawal from danger* is paraphrased in *because pain signals the body to respond to a threat.* (1.7)

5. A   In the added sentence, *They* refers to *Pain receptors*, the subject of the previous sentence. In the added sentence, *such as* is a transition that introduces examples of *a variety of stimuli*, mentioned in the previous sentence. (1.8)

6. D   In the added sentence, *Thus* is a transition that shows result by linking the idea of *decreasing the perception of pain* in the previous sentence with *natural painkillers* in the added sentence. In the added sentence, *they* refers to *peptides*, the subject of the previous sentence. (1.8)

7. B *Prestige is a valued resource for people at all levels of a society* is paraphrased in *People at all social levels value prestige. This can be seen among inner–city youth* is paraphrased in *for example, among urban youth. To disrespect or "diss" someone has negative consequences* is paraphrased in *to disrespect another is punished.* (1.7)

8. D The added sentence gives the examples of *wisdom, old age, warriors,* and *youth,* which illustrate qualities that are respected in different societies, an idea mentioned in the previous sentence. (1.8)

9. C *Prestige is linked to income, but there are exceptions* is paraphrased in *an exception to the rule that prestige and income are related. College professors, who have high prestige but relatively low salaries compared to physicians and lawyers* is paraphrased in *college professors have high prestige but relatively low incomes.* (1.7)

10. A The added sentence introduces the topic of occupational status, which the rest of the paragraph develops with facts and examples. (1.8)

QUIZ 8 (p. 154)

1. B *Palisades* means *fences* in this context. Clues: *...fortified villages...; ...easy to defend...; Twenty–foot ----- surrounded a group of longhouses and acted as a defensive wall....* (1.4)

2. D The author's purpose is to show that villages varied in population. Clues: *A number of families were housed within each longhouse, which varied in size...; ...huge multiple family structures...; In the more populous villages....* (1.6)

3. D *The longhouse was more than just a shelter* is paraphrased in *The longhouse not only provided housing. The basic unit upon which the entire society was constructed* is paraphrased in *the foundation of the whole society.* (1.7)

4. C Clues: *In building the longhouse, a row of forked wooden poles...; Cross poles were lashed to the forked uprights to form an arched roof; Slender poles or rafters were then secured to the roof frame....* (1.1)

5. A The referent of *dwelling* is something that was compartmentalized (divided into parts) to accommodate each family. The paragraph discusses the longhouse. Logic tells you that *dwelling* refers to *longhouse.* (1.3)

6. A The passage does not state that each longhouse was a separate village. All the other answers are given: *Two families shared the stone–lined hearth... Corn, dried fish, and other foods hung from overhead; A number of families were housed within each longhouse...; ...carved images of clan symbols represented the families living there.* (1.2)

7. C The added sentence gives examples of trees that were sources of bark, which the previous sentence mentions. (1.8)

8. B You can infer that the Harlem Renaissance is the name of a literary movement. Clues: *...African American writers...; ...poetry and storytelling...; ...written form....* (1.5)

9. D *Prolific* means *productive* in this context. Clues: *...literary career...; ...his first book; ...his poetry, plays, screenplays, novels, and short stories;* the prefix *pro–* = forward. (1.4)

10. C Clues: *...the incorporation of the rhythms of black music into his poetry...; ...a collection of poems on African American themes set to rhythms from jazz and blues.* (1.1)

11. A The passage does not state that Langston Hughes taught university courses. All the other answers are given: *His first novel...screenplays...novels...; ...founded African American theaters...; ...The Weary Blues, a collection of poems on African American themes set to rhythms from jazz and blues.* (1.2)

12. A *Sham* means *falsehood* in this context. Clues: *...a wise fool, an honest man who saw through ----- and spoke plainly.* (1.4)

13. D The referent of *those* is something of a younger generation of black poets that overshadowed Hughes's writings. Logic tells you that *those* refers to *writings.* (1.3)

14. B *His poetry and stories remain an enduring legacy of the Harlem Renaissance* is paraphrased in *his writings represent the accomplishments of the Harlem Renaissance. His position in the American canon is secure* is paraphrased in *Hughes attained prominence in American literature.* (1.7)

15. D In the added sentence, *this book* refers to *The Weary Blues* in the previous sentence. (1.8)

16. C The author's purpose is to clarify the distinctions between the two terms. Clues: *...often used interchangeably, but there are actually differences between them. One difference is....* (1.6)

17. D *Submerged* means *underwater* in this context. Clues: *...every part of it is sometimes underwater; ...extends seaward to the edge of the continental shelf...; ...extends down into deep water;* the prefix *sub–* = under. (1.4)

18. B The passage does not state that a coast extends to the continental shelf and a shore extends inland to a highland. All the other answers accurately describe coasts and shores: *A shore is the zone at the edge of an ocean, lake, or river...A coast is the land just inland from the shore...; ..."coast" applies only to oceans, but "shore" can apply to other bodies of water as well; A coast is...beyond the usual reach of high water; The shore is the area between the high–water mark and the low–water mark, and thus every part of it is sometimes underwater.* (1.2)

19. C Clues: *Many coasts are sea bottoms uplifted by earthquakes to become dry land, so they may show some features of shores....* (1.1)

20. A You can infer that the Oregon coast is relatively straight. Clues: *If the grain is mostly parallel to the coast, as along the Oregon coast, the mouths of few rivers will indent the coastline...; Such coastlines...are likely to be smooth, straight, or gently curving.* (1.5)

21. A Clues: *The direction of the structural "grain" of the coastal rock affects the shape of the coastline; If the grain is mostly parallel to the coast...called Pacific type...; ...if the grain of the rock is at an angle to the coast...Atlantic type.* (1.1)

22. C *These forces* in the highlighted sentence refers to *tides, waves, and currents* in the previous sentence. *These forces erode rocky shores* is paraphrased in *Tides, waves, and currents wear away shores. Transport sand and debris from place to place, depleting some beaches* is paraphrased in *wear away shores in some places. Building up others* is paraphrased in *deposit sand and rock elsewhere along the shore.* (1.7)

23. D The referent of *them* is something weakened by waves crashing against sea cliffs during storms. Logic tells you that *them* refers to *cliffs.* (1.3)

24. B *Batter* means *strike* in this context. Clues: *...waves crash against sea cliffs...; Storm waves ----- beaches and...rush beyond them....* (1.4)

25. A The added sentence introduces the idea of the straightness or irregularity of coastlines, which the rest of the paragraph develops with facts and description. (1.8)

EXERCISE 1.9.A (p. 164)

1–2. A, C, F Key information: *Homer was a master of watercolor...understood and exploited the requirements of watercolor...the recording of immediate experience; ...Homer's watercolors of the Adirondack woods...are demonstrations of masterful completeness; In one particular Adirondack painting...all elements come together with perfect unity.* Answers (B) and (D) are not mentioned; answer (E) is a minor idea.

3–4. B, E, F Key information: *The debris transported by a glacier is produced either by erosion of the rock beneath the glacier or by erosion on the slopes rising above the surface of the glacier; ...moraine debris remains unsorted both during its transport and after it has been deposited...; Once the glacial ice has retreated, the moraine deposits are left exposed...The various landforms— moraines....* Answer (A) is not mentioned; answers (C) and (D) are minor ideas.

5–6. B, D, E Key information: *Cultural evolution has occurred in stages...; ...new technology has escalated exponentially, and so has the human impact on the planet; Cultural evolution has enabled us to...shortcut biological evolution. We no longer have to wait to adapt to our environment through natural selection; we simply change the environment to meet our needs.* Answers (A) and (F) are not mentioned; answer (C) is a minor idea.

7–8. A, B, E Key information: *...the central theme of love serves as the trigger for extraordinary adventures...fantastic journeys to exotic lands...; ...and other elements of tragedy...but everything is resolved in the traditional happy ending of comedy; Love is subjected to abnormal strains, often involving separation, jealousy...separation and reunion of loved ones....* Answer (C) is not mentioned; answers (D) and (F) are minor ideas.

9–10. A, C, E Key information: *Humans lose water by evaporation from respiratory and body surfaces and must replenish such losses...; With enough water to drink, the human body can withstand extremely high temperatures...the body's internal environment responds to this change by the evaporative cooling method of sweating; Without water to drink, the body will continue to sweat and lose water...water deficit...collapse occurs...death occurs.* Answers (B) and (D) are minor ideas; answer (F) is not mentioned.

EXERCISE 1.9.B (p. 169)

1. D *Mathematicians are motivated by the belief* is paraphrased in *what motivates mathematicians. They may be able to create a pattern that is entirely new, one that changes forever the way that others think about the mathematical order* is paraphrased in *The idea of establishing a completely new way of understanding mathematics.* (1.7)

2. A Clues: *An extended chain of reasoning may be intuitive...; However, even when guided by intuition, they must eventually work out the solution in exact detail if they are to convince others of its validity.* (1.1)

3. C *Insoluble* means *impossible to solve* in this context. Clues: *...finding the solution to a problem that has long been considered -----;* the prefix *in–* = not. (1.4)

4–5. B, C, E Key information: *At the center of mathematical talent lies the ability to recognize significant problems and then to solve them; ...an exceptional ability to manage long chains of reasoning...develop theories from very simple contexts and then apply them to very complex ones; They must demonstrate the solution without any errors or omissions in definition or in line of reasoning... The mathematician must be rigorous....* Answer (A) is a minor idea; answers (D) and (F) are not mentioned.

6. B The author's purpose is to give an example of a very large case of white–collar crime. Clues: *...there are some very large cases of white–collar crime, such as....* (1.6)

7. C *Line one's pockets* means *take money illegally* in this context. Clues: *White–collar crime...; Government employment... also provides opportunities to -----. For example, building inspectors accept bribes and kickbacks....* (1.4)

8. A *It is likely that there are more criminals in the office suites than in the streets* is paraphrased in *White–collar criminals may be more numerous than street criminals. Yet the nature of white–collar crime makes it difficult to uncover the offenses and pursue the offenders* is paraphrased in *but are difficult to catch because the crimes often go unnoticed.* (1.7)

9–10. A, C, F

Key information: *The majority of cases involve low–level employees…Their crimes are usually never discovered because the amounts of money are small…; White–collar crime is not confined to the business sector. Government employment…also provides opportunities…it involves far more money and harm to the public…; …the nature of white–collar crime makes it difficult to uncover the offenses and pursue the offenders…extremely difficult and expensive to prosecute.* Answers (B) and (E) are minor ideas; answer (D) is not mentioned.

Exercise 1.9.C (p. 173)

1. C — The author's purpose is to give examples of groupings that do not represent social behavior. Clues: *…not all aggregations of animals are social; Clusters of moths…or trout gathering…are groupings of animals responding to environmental signals. Social aggregations, on the other hand….* (1.6)

2. B — A group of turtles sunning on a log is not an example of social behavior; it is a grouping of animals responding to an environmental signal. All the other answers illustrate social behavior: *…an individual fighting to defend a territory; Musk oxen that form a passive defensive circle…; …cooperation in hunting for food….* (1.2)

3. A — *Huddling* means *gathering* in this context. Clues: *…protection from severe weather….* (1.4)

4–5. B, D, E — Key information: *Social behavior includes any interaction that is a consequence of one animal's response to another of its own species…; …not all social to the same degree…reproduction…defense…cooperation in hunting for food…huddling for protection…transmitting information…; One obvious benefit of social organization is defense…from predators.* Answer (A) is inaccurate; answers (C) and (F) are minor ideas.

6. A — You can infer that the best coffee would come from a mountainous region close to the equator. Clues: *The perfect climate for coffee production exists between the latitudes of 25 degrees north and 25 degrees south of the equator; The best–tasting coffees are grown at between five and eight thousand feet in elevation….* (1.5)

7. B — *Bearing* means *influence* in this context. Clues: *Nitrogen in soil gives rise to…; …potassium produces…; …phosphorus, while having no ----- on coffee in the final cup, helps the tree to develop….* (1.4)

8. D — *Caring for the coffee tree* is paraphrased in *the care given to the tree. Critical to the character of the final product* is paraphrased in *The quality of the finished coffee depends on….* (1.7)

9–10. A, D, F — Key information: *The perfect climate for coffee production exists between the latitudes of 25 degrees north and 25 degrees south of the equator…The best–tasting coffees are grown at between five and eight thousand feet in elevation…; …soil chemistry is carefully watched in commercial operations…soil rich in nitrogen, phosphorus, and potassium…the more balanced the soil, the better the coffee; Caring for the coffee tree is critical…seedlings…require careful replanting…transfer from nursery to plantation is a critical part of the process….* Answers (B) and (E) are minor ideas; answer (C) is not mentioned.

Exercise 1.10.A (p. 181)

1–3. B, E — Enlightenment: *…the Enlightenment…dictated that the discipline of formal structure was beneficial to artistic expression; …human society could reach perfection through rational thought….*

A, C, F — Romanticism: *…celebrated emotions and the senses…Romantic philosophy reveled in the beauty and unpredictable power of Nature; Romanticism found inspiration in death as an "other kingdom" and in the supernatural…; Romanticism believed in democracy and the common people, reviving folk traditions…that made heroes of rural characters.* Answers (D) and (G) are not mentioned.

4–6. A, D, F — Rock floor: *The floor of the river channel lies in the bedrock…; As the stream swings across the valley floor, it deposits material on the insides of the bends in the channel; In a rock–floored valley, the valley slopes are undercut and steepened by the sideways erosion.*

C, G — Accumulation floor: *An accumulation valley floor is created by the continuous deposition of gravel and sand…; Both the channel floor and the floodplain…are composed entirely of these gravel and sand deposits.* Answers (B) and (E) are not mentioned.

7–10. B, F, H — Plants: *…construct organic molecules from inorganic chemicals as plants can during photosynthesis; …plants store their food as starch; …two types of tissues that plants do not have. The first is nervous tissue…and the other is muscle tissue.*

A, D, E, I — Animals: *…animals cannot manufacture their own food; Nerves and muscles, which control active behavior, are unique to animals; Animal life began…with the evolution of multi–cellular forms that lived by eating other organisms; Animal cells lack the cell walls….* Answer (C) is not mentioned; answer (G) is inaccurate.

Exercise 1.10.B (p. 184)

1–3. B, D   Arcade: *The Arcade's pitched glass roof sheltered a large open space surrounded by tiered shops; ...the entire focus of large commercial blocks....*

C, E, G   Department store: *...an array of goods were organized under a single management; The origins of the department store...in 1829, a new kind of building...featured a four–story rotunda beneath a huge dome...; ...large plate glass display windows...easily lured in the city's wealthy customers.* Answer (A) is inaccurate; answer (F) is not mentioned.

4–6. D, G   Cross–sectional: *...each subject is tested or interviewed only once; ...groups of subjects at different age levels...Cross–sectional studies...can provide information about possible age differences.*

A, E, F   Longitudinal: *...a relatively small group of subjects who are all about the same age at the beginning of the study and then look at them repeatedly over a period of time; One advantage of longitudinal studies is that any changes found are real changes, not just age–group differences; Longitudinal studies...allow us to look at consistency or change within the same individual.* Answers (B) and (C) are not mentioned.

7. B   *These two types of questions* in the highlighted sentence refers to questions about proximate and ultimate causation, which the paragraph discusses. *Very independent approaches to behavior* is paraphrased in *distinct ways of thinking about behavior.* (1.7)

8–10. B, C, G   Proximate: *The biological sciences that address proximate causes...use the experimental method...; The "how" questions seek to understand the proximate or immediate causes... For example, a biologist might want to explain the singing of a male white–throated sparrow in the spring...; ...the proximate or immediate causes underlying a behavior at a particular time and place.*

A, E   Ultimate: *These are "why" questions that focus on ultimate causation, the evolutionary origin and purpose of behavior; Researchers compare characteristics...among related species to identify patterns of variation.* Answers (D) and (F) are not mentioned.

Quiz 9 (p. 188)

1–2. B, E, F   Key information: *...life expectancy, the average number of years a person can expect to live...rose dramatically, from about 47 years in 1900 to about 76 years in 2000; ...several factors increased life expectancy, most notably improvements in public health...Advances in medical practice...; Large numbers of elderly, many with chronic diseases, become a burden on the health care system and on their families.* Answer (A) is inaccurate; answers (C) and (D) are not mentioned. (1.9)

3–5. C, E, G   Oil paints: *...special manipulative properties of oil colors...smoothly blended tones...; ...the latter remains the standard because the majority of painters find...that in optical quality oil paints surpass all others; ...the principal defect of oil painting is the darkening of the oil over time....*

B, F   Acrylic paints: *Acrylic paints are thinned with water...; ...a painting can be completed in one session that might have taken days in oil because of the drying time required....* Answers (A) and (D) are not mentioned. (1.10)

6–7. A, B, E   Key information: *One major factor determining the uneven patterns of world climates is the variation in the amount of solar energy striking different parts of the earth; ...carrying heat from the equator toward the poles...the warm air becomes cool...cool air masses then flow back toward the equator...This general air circulation pattern...; Two major factors cause seasonal changes in climate. One is the earth's annual orbit around the sun; the other is the earth's daily rotation around its tilted axis....* Answers (C) and (F) are not mentioned; answer (D) is a minor idea. (1.9)

8–10. C, D, F   At the equator: *The large input of heat at and near the equator warms large masses of air; ...near the equator evaporates huge amounts of water from the earth's surface into the troposphere; ...at the equator (zero latitude), where the sun is almost directly overhead....*

A, E   At the poles: *...at the high–latitude poles, where the sun is lower in the sky and strikes the earth at a low angle; At the poles, the warm air becomes cool and falls to the earth.* Answers (B) and (G) are inaccurate for both the equator and the poles. (1.10)

Quiz 10 (p. 192)

1. A   *Fodder* means *material* in this context. Clues: *Black holes have provided endless imaginative ----- for science fiction writers and endless theoretical ----- for astrophysicists.* (1.4)

2. C   Clues: *Outside the event horizon, gravity is strong but finite, and it is possible for objects to break free of its pull. However, once within the event horizon, an object would need to travel faster than light to escape.* (1.1)

3. B   Clues: *...the exclusion principle—the resistance between the molecular particles within the star as they are compressed....* (1.1)

4. C   *Runaway* means *uncontrolled* in this context. Clues: *With no internal force to stop it, the star will simply continue to collapse in on itself.* (1.4)

5. A   The author's purpose is to illustrate the complete disappearance of a collapsing star. Clues: *The star now disappears from the perceivable universe, like...* (1.6)

6. A · *What this process leaves behind is a different kind of hole* is paraphrased in *The collapse of a star creates a black hole. A profound disturbance in space–time* is paraphrased in *a distortion of space and time. Where gravity is so intense that nothing can escape from it* is paraphrased in *with gravity strong enough to pull in any nearby object.* (1.7)

7. B · The passage does not state that astronauts falling into a black hole would travel faster than light. All the other answers are given: *...they would experience acute time distortion...space and time are so warped...; ...would enable them to know, in a few brief seconds, the entire future of the universe; ...intense gravitational forces....* (1.2)

8. D · You can infer that the distance between the event horizon and the singularity is related to the size of the black hole. Clues: *The time it takes to reach the singularity from the event horizon...is proportional to the mass of the black hole.* (1.5)

9. D · The referent of *this point* is something that would mark the end of time itself. The sentence discusses what would happen once astronauts had reached the singularity. Logic tells you that *this point* refers to *the singularity.* (1.3)

10. B · In the added sentence, *A few* refers to *Physicists* in the previous sentence. The added sentence gives another example of what physicists believe would happen to astronauts falling into a black hole. (1.8)

11–12. A, C, F · Key information: *...the formation of a black hole involves the collapse of a large star...the star will simply continue to collapse in on itself...until its entire mass is crushed down to a single point—a point of infinite density and zero volume...; A black hole is very simple in structure: it has a surface—the event horizon—and a center—the singularity. Everything else is gravity; Any object falling within the boundary of a black hole has no choice but to move inward toward the singularity...they would experience acute time distortion...space and time are so warped....* Answer (B) is a minor idea, answer (D) is not mentioned; answer (E) is inaccurate. (1.9)

13. D · *Truth cannot be separated from experience* is paraphrased in *the two are necessarily connected. In order to understand truth, we have to study experience itself* is paraphrased in *We must study experience to know the meaning of truth.* (1.7)

14. A · *Sequential* means *continuous* in this context. Clues: *..."stream" of experience...; ...course of events in our lives;* the stem *–sequ–* = follow. (1.4)

15. A · The author's purpose is to describe how thoughts and feelings flow into each other. Clues: *...a stream of thoughts and feelings...; One wave dissolves into another gradually, like the ripples of water in....* (1.6)

16. C · The referent of *it* is something that is meaningful and can be associated with something already in the person's mind. The subject of the sentence is *incoming thought.* Logic tells you that *it* refers to *incoming thought.* (1.3)

17. B · *Reconstructive* means *creative* in this context. Clues: *...experience and knowledge building on each other;* the stem *–struct–* = build. (1.4)

18. D · Clues: *Dewey believed that experience is an interaction between what a person already knows and the person's present situation.* (1.1)

19. C · Dewey's theory does not include the idea that every experience is educative; in fact, he believed that an experience is miseducative if it distorts the growth of further experience. All the other answers are given: *...experience is an interaction between what a person already knows and the person's present situation; ...together they lead to new knowledge that in turn will influence future experience; Experience is educative only when it contributes to the growth of the individual.* (1.2)

20. D · Clues: *Furthermore, truly progressive education must involve the participation of the learner in directing the learning experience.* (1.1)

21. B · You can infer that William James and John Dewey would probably agree that our life experiences are a very important part of our education. Clues: *In James's theory, thought and experience are connected; James's theory supports later theories of associative learning...; Dewey asserted that experience is central to education...; ...productive experience is both the means and the goal of education.* (1.5)

22. B · The added sentence further develops the idea that incoming thoughts and outgoing thoughts *become associated with each other,* mentioned in the previous sentence. (1.8)

23–25. C, E · William James: *He believed that human consciousness is a stream of thoughts and feelings...waves of bodily sensations... memories of past experiences...; An incoming thought is "workable" only if it is meaningful and can be associated with something already in the person's mind.*

A, D, F · John Dewey: *...learning is more than the amassing and retention of information; learning is learning how to think; Dewey felt that education should be problem–centered and interdisciplinary...productive experience is both the means and the goal of education; Dewey viewed life as a continuously reconstructive process, with experience and knowledge building on each other.* Answers (B) and (G) are not mentioned. (1.10)

PART 2 – LISTENING

EXERCISE 2.1.A (p. 215)

1. C The woman is confused by her professor's response to her paper. She says: *So I'm really confused. This is the first time I ever got a paper back with no grade on it.*

2. C The speakers mainly discuss their plans for spring break, a school vacation. The woman says: *I sure am ready for spring break!* The man asks: *Are you doing anything special?*

3. B The woman is mainly discussing her internship at a children's agency. She says: *I'll be doing an internship...; It's a nonprofit agency that works on children's issues....*

4. A The man has difficulty remembering some terms. He says: *...if only I could remember the difference between xylem and phloem. I can't seem to get it straight....*

5. D The woman suggests that he imagine a tree with key letters on it. She says: *I always think of a tree and imagine a "P" at the top, up in the branches, and an "X" at the bottom.... Now just imagine your tree tomorrow during the quiz!*

EXERCISE 2.1.B (p. 216)

1. B The speaker mainly discusses services of the Safety and Security Office. Key phrases: *The place to go for...is the Safety and Security Office; Safety and Security also provides....*

2. A The speaker mainly discusses traditions of American Indian cultures. Key sentence: *Although the original American Indian cultures were highly diverse, they were similar in many of their traditions.* The speaker then gives examples of traditions.

3. C The speaker mainly gives a classification of insurance. Key phrases: *Each kind of insurance...; Life insurance...; Health insurance...; Another kind, property–liability insurance....*

4. D The speaker mainly discusses how sand dunes shift position. Key phrases: *The dunes of Spirit Sands are constantly changing...; Here's how it works; ...the dune sort of walks downwind; It will reverse direction....*

5. A The speaker mainly discusses research in pain management. Key sentence: *There've been several influential studies in pain management.* The speaker then gives examples of research studies.

EXERCISE 2.1.C (p. 217)

1. A The speaker's main point is that attitudes toward aging can affect how long a person lives. Key phrases: *...the key to a longer life might be the way you think about yourself as you get older...; ...people who view aging positively live longer than people who view it negatively.*

2. C The speaker mainly discusses educational programs for engineers. Key phrases: *...typical four–year engineering program...; ...general engineering curriculum...; ...five–year master's degree programs....*

3. D The speaker mainly gives examples of undergraduate and graduate programs. Key phrases: *...typical four–year engineering program...; ...programs, for example, where a student spends three years in a liberal arts college...; ...five–year master's degree programs...; ...five– or six–year cooperative programs....*

4. B The instructor mainly discusses causes and effects of RSI. Key phrases: *RSI is brought on by...; RSI affects different people differently.*

5. D The instructor describes symptoms of RSI. Key phrases: *...an inflammation of the sheathing around the tendons in the hand...; ...makes your fingers painful and hard to straighten; The swelling causes a numbness or tingling sensation in the hand, and pain shoots up from the wrist....*

EXERCISE 2.2.A (p. 221)

1. A The woman says: *You should check out the job board in the student center.*

2. B The man says: *I'd like a quiet job that would allow me to get some reading done.*

3. C The man says: *...we need extra cashiers...why not volunteer to help us out?* The woman says: *I guess I could spare a few hours; I'll be there around noon.*

4. D The man says: *The library will give you ten dollars in book credit for every hour you work. You have to use the credit at this sale....*

5. B The woman says: *I'll be there around noon.*

6. B The woman says: *Her assignments are challenging but useful. And she has the most interesting stories to illustrate her lectures. She really makes us think; ...I'm starting to figure things out as a result of this class.*

7. D The man says: *We had to write a lot of papers; ...she really makes you work in her class!*

8. B The professor says: *These are all journal articles that I need to go through for my research. It would really help if they were arranged more logically. Can you help me?*

9. A The professor says: *Most are about primate behavior, but a few deal with other mammals or birds, or with behavioral psychology in general.*

10. B The woman says: *I have some free time tomorrow afternoon. Would that be all right?*

EXERCISE 2.2.B (p. 222)

1. C The man says: *The hunting season began in the fall and continued until midwinter.*

2. C, D The man says: *Moose, deer...were the animals sought.*

3. A The man says: *The women often accompanied their husbands on hunting parties. Their job was to take charge of the camps.*

4. B, D Women controlled clan leadership: *...a woman headed each clan, and these women were respected for their role as keepers of the clan.* Women also controlled agriculture: *...women managed all of the agricultural operations.*

5. B, D Talent is an important factor for a career in the arts: *...there are a number of factors to consider. Whether your goal is to be an actor or an animator, a saxophonist or a sculptor, talent is an essential consideration.* Experience is another important factor: *...you also need training, experience...; ...experience is the best way to get a feel for the field.*

6. B   The professor says: *...a career in the arts requires a personal sense of commitment—a calling—because art does have a history of insecure employment.*

7. C   The woman asks: *...how do we get started?* The professor replies: *Experience doesn't have to be formal. It can be part–time or volunteer work; The important thing is getting started—spending time doing something in your chosen medium.*

8. B   The instructor says: *The first step, of course, is to realize the importance of the speech to you.*

9. A, C The speakers mention the purpose of informing others about your subject: *...decide on your purpose. Do you simply want to inform us about your subject?* The speakers also mention making your audience laugh: *Your purpose could be to make your audience laugh.*

10. B   The instructor says: *Why don't you all just take the next few minutes to start brainstorming? Jot down ideas that come to mind....*

EXERCISE 2.2.C (p. 224)

1. B   The professor mainly discusses characteristics of the sea breeze. Key sentences: *The sea breeze is the simplest, most widespread, and most persistent of local winds; The sea breeze results from the heating of land and sea along a coastline in near–calm conditions.* (2.1)

2. D   The professor says: *...a flow of air from sea to land; The airflow forms a circular pattern, from sea to land, upwards, and back out to sea.*

3. A   The professor says: *At the same time as the breeze flows from sea to land, there is a return flow higher up, from land to sea.*

4. B, D The speaker discusses how a horn's sound is produced: *The sound is produced by vibrations from the player's lips.* The speaker also discusses early uses of the horn: *In the Middle Ages in Europe, they were used almost exclusively in hunting and warfare.* (2.1)

5. C   The speaker says: *In the eighteenth century, the horn became a regular member of the orchestra.*

6. B, D The professor describes causes of tsunamis: *Large earthquakes with epicenters under or near the ocean are the cause of most tsunamis. Volcanic eruptions and undersea landslides are also responsible....* The professor also gives examples of tsunamis: *A tsunami was responsible for most of the deaths caused by Krakatoa...; The tsunami that wrecked Hilo, Hawaii, in 1946...; ...a catastrophic tsunami in Japan....* (2.1)

7. D   The professor says: *The term "tidal wave" is often inaccurately used for a tsunami. Tsunamis have nothing to do with the action of tides.*

8. A, C Movement of the ocean floor causes tsunamis: *There has to be a disturbance of the earth's crust to produce a tsunami; ...accompanied by movements of the ocean floor....* Undersea earthquakes also cause tsunamis: *Large earthquakes with epicenters under or near the ocean are the cause of most tsunamis.*

9. B   The professor says: *A tsunami was responsible for most of the deaths caused by Krakatoa, yet this tsunami did not sink any ships. It did wash away several coastal villages and kill more than 36,000 people.*

10. A   The professor says: *This is what happened in 1896 during a catastrophic tsunami in Japan, which was the result of an undersea earthquake.*

EXERCISE 2.2.D (p. 225)

1. A   The students are discussing terms from a lecture. Key phrases: *...history lecture...; ...meant by "partible inheritance"...; ...what's "primogeniture"; ...the word "primogeniture."* (2.1)

2. C   The woman asks: *...what's "primogeniture"?* The man answers: *That's when all the property goes to the eldest son.*

3. D   The professor says: *So, why do so many small businesses fail each year? Well, for one thing, they usually face stiff competition from larger, more established companies. Large companies generally have cash reserves that enable them to absorb losses more easily than small firms can.*

4. D   The professor says: *It's absolutely essential to be a competent manager...; Your primary responsibilities center on planning, management, and marketing, so organizational skills are a must.*

5. B, C One responsibility of a store owner is keeping track of inventory: *To run a store, for example, you need to know how to keep track of your inventory....* Another responsibility is promoting the store's products: *To keep your store in business, you have to adapt to changing market conditions. This means improving services or promoting your products in innovative ways.*

6. C   The woman says: *...I saw something happen—on a hike I did last weekend....*

7. D   The woman says: *I was hiking with my friend—on the desert canyon trail—and we ran into these two guys sitting by the side of the trail. ...it turns out that one of them was sort of having trouble.*

8. A, D The young man received water from the woman: *...we gave them one of our water bottles....* He also received food from his teacher: *We asked if they had water and food, and they said a little, but their teacher went back to get some more; ...the teacher and the ranger were there. The guy was eating saltine crackers.*

9. B   The woman says: *I wondered if his muscle cramps were...because lactic acid ferments when the cell has no oxygen; ...human muscle cells make ATP by lactic acid fermentation when oxygen is scarce; This means lactate collects in the muscle as a waste product, and that causes muscle pain.*

10. A   The teaching assistant says: *Well, Julie, it looks like you saw biology in action!*

EXERCISE 2.2.E (p. 226)

1. C   The instructor says: *...it's the pigment that gives the paint its color.*

2. D   The instructor says: *A pigment should not exert a harmful chemical reaction upon the medium, or upon other color pigments it is mixed with.*

3. A   The instructor says: *Generally, pigments are classified according to their origin, either natural or synthetic.*

4. C   The instructor says: *...Tyrian purple, the imperial purple the Romans prepared from a shellfish native to the Mediterranean.*

5. A, D   Synthetic pigments are superior because they last for a longer time: *Inorganic synthetic colors...are generally the most permanent for all uses. In contrast, pigments from natural sources are less permanent than the average synthetic color.* They also provide stronger, brighter colors: *Synthetic organic pigments provide colors of unmatched intensity and tinting strength. The synthetic counterparts of the yellow and red earths are more brilliant and...are superior in all other respects to the native products.*

6. B   The professor mainly discusses different types of volcanoes. Key phrases: *...several types of volcanoes; ...shield volcanoes...; ...Cinder cone volcanoes...; ...Calderas....* (2.1)

7. A, B   Substances that erupt from volcanoes are hot gases: *...superheated gases;* and liquefied rock: *...hot liquefied rock, or magma, moves to the earth's surface, pouring out as lava.*

8. A   The speaker says: *...gently sloping shield volcanoes. The name "shield volcano" comes from their resemblance to the shields of early Germanic warriors.*

9. C   The speaker says: *Calderas, large basin–like depressions, are formed when a violent eruption blows the top off of an existing cone or when the center of a volcano collapses.*

10. A   The speaker says: *One famous caldera covers much of Yellowstone National Park; Yellowstone's famous geysers and hot springs lie within this giant basin.*

QUIZ 1 (p. 230)

1. B   The speakers mainly discuss health dangers in the workplace. The instructor says: *The computerized workplace can be hazardous to your health...; Today we'll go over what some of these hazards are....* (2.1)

2. B   The instructor says: *A good way to relieve eyestrain is to look away from the screen frequently. Focus your eyes on objects that are far away....* (2.2)

3. D   The instructor says: *Neck and back pain are a big problem for computer people. Always make sure your screen, keyboard, and chair are at the right height for you.* The man says: *...it's important to have a comfortable chair; I put a cushion on my chair, and that really helps my lower back.* (2.2)

4. C   The instructor says: *Photocopy machines aren't a health hazard for people who use them only occasionally. But for people who use them a lot, there can be bad effects. For example, people who handle the toners can get skin rashes.* (2.2)

5. C   The instructor says: *Another problem—if the machines are in an area that's not well ventilated—is ozone; Almost all photocopiers give off some ozone.* (2.2)

6. D   The instructor mainly discusses principles of perspective and related concepts. Key phrases: *Today we'll begin our discussion on perspective...; An understanding of perspective is mandatory...; Everything in perspective is related to the concept of eye level...; Another related concept is the vanishing point.* (2.1)

7. A, D   Architecture and industrial design require an understanding of perspective. The instructor says: *An understanding of perspective is mandatory for anyone who does representational drawing. This includes professionals in a variety of fields...architecture, industrial design....* (2.2)

8. D   Perspective is shown when distant objects appear smaller than close objects. The instructor says: *...objects appear smaller as their distance from the observer increases.* (2.2)

9. B   The instructor says: *The vanishing point is a point at eye level where parallel lines going away from you appear to come together and then vanish.* (2.2)

10. C   The instructor says: *...I advise you to sketch eye level and vanishing points in every drawing, at least temporarily. Eye level and vanishing points will help you convey perspective.* (2.2)

EXERCISE 2.3.A (p. 235)

1. B   The student must leave school for a family emergency. He says: *...I have a problem. My father had to have surgery, and I have to go to Oklahoma. I don't know how long I'll be gone.*

2. A   The professor says: *...you can take a grade of Incomplete. It means you would have six weeks to make up the term paper and the final exam.* (2.2)

3. D   The man would like a different meal arrangement. He says: *I'd like to change my meal plan.*

4. C   The woman's purpose is to emphasize the importance of breakfast because the man says he doesn't have time to eat breakfast in the cafeteria.

5. B   The woman's purpose is to give the man another choice of meal plan in case he would like a plan that would give him lunch and dinner.

6. A   The student wants to take a quiz that she missed. She says: *I was wondering—could I make up the quiz?*

7. C   The professor suggests that the student write about what she learned. The professor says: *...give me a one–page report, summarizing the most important thing you got out of the chapter.* (2.2)

8. C   The speakers are mainly discussing a guest speaker. Key phrases: *...he'd be happy to visit our class; ...assignment to invite a guest speaker....* (2.1)

9. A   The man's purpose is to emphasize the professor's qualifications as a guest speaker in their seminar.

10. B   The man's opinion is that the assignment will help them meet people in their field. He says: *Look at all the professional contacts we're making!*

EXERCISE 2.3.B (p. 236)

1. A The professor is giving a writing assignment. The professor says: *...it would be a good idea if this week's journal theme were along the same lines. What I'd like you to do is think and write about a time....*

2. D The woman finds the assignment boring. She says: *But isn't this the same as last week? I mean, I feel I've already written a lot about it. I had to do something like this in two of my other classes too. Can't we write about something else for a change?; I mean, I'm getting tired of writing about my life.*

3. A The main purpose of the talk is to contrast Native American and European concepts of resources. Key sentences: *...the Native Americans—compared to the European colonists—had a far greater knowledge of what resources in the environment could be eaten or made useful; For the European colonists, on the other hand, resources in the environment were seen more as commodities, as goods that could be exchanged in markets.*

4. C The professor says: *Native Americans used a wide range of resources for economic subsistence....* (2.2)

5. D The professor's purpose is to define the Native American concept of wealth, in response to the student's question.

6. A The professor's purpose is to illustrate the colonists' view of commodities by giving examples of things that could be sold for a profit.

7. D The purpose of the talk is to define what culture is. Key phrases: *What would human life be without culture; ...these aspects of our cultures...; ...what anthropologists call student culture; In a way a culture is like a club...; Culture isn't a thing. It's an idea.*

8. A The professor's purpose is to illustrate how culture involves shared ideas and behaviors. The professor says: *If you could take all the ideas and behaviors, all the tools and technology, all the things that college students share...you'd have what anthropologists call student culture.*

9. C The woman thinks student culture is similar to a club. She says: *So, what you're saying is culture is sort of like a club. College students are a club; This is why—that's what we have in common with other students—it's why our culture makes us feel like part of a club, right?*

10. B The professor thinks that the comparison is imperfect. The professor says: *In a way a culture is like a club...; But the comparison doesn't completely cut it. Think about it. A club has borders that we can define—but we run into trouble if we try to draw borders around a culture.*

EXERCISE 2.3.C (p. 237)

1. D The main purpose of the talk is to discuss ways of dealing with stress. Key phrases: *...managers have to deal with stress. Some handle it by...; Most have some favorite place or pastime...; It's important to have some form of rest and relaxation....*

2. B The professor's opinion is that activity and exercise are forms of rest. The professor says: *It's important to have some form of rest and relaxation—creating art, working with your hands, gardening, playing sports—the list goes on. Rest doesn't always mean inactivity. For some people, exercise is rest.*

3. B The purpose of the lecture is to describe how psychologists diagnose problems. Key phrases: *...the clinical psychologist has to know what causes the client to behave the way he or she does; Identifying the cause is called diagnosis; In diagnosis a psychologist uses two basic tools....*

4. B, C The professor says: *In diagnosis a psychologist uses two basic tools: interviews and psychological tests.* (2.2)

5. A The professor's purpose is to show that a client's past behavior assists in diagnosis. The professor says: *In a diagnostic interview, the psychologist takes the client's case history. This means learning how the client got along with parents, teachers, and friends, as well as how the person handled difficult situations in the past.*

6. D The professor says: *Personality tests can reveal unconscious feelings the person is unable to talk about.* (2.2)

7. C The main purpose of the talk is to give advice about contact with bats. Key phrases: *...if you encounter a bat like that, you should...; If you have bats in your attic or house, contact...; If you should come in physical contact with a bat, it's important to....*

8. C The speaker's purpose is to give an example of how bats benefit us. The speaker says: *Bats are a normal part of our environment and can even be a good thing.*

9. A The speaker says: *To avoid having bats in your house altogether, find all possible entry points into the house and close them by caulking or screening the gap.* (2.2)

10. D The speaker recommends getting medical attention because the bat might be carrying a fatal disease. The speaker says: *Bats are the most likely carriers of rabies in our area, and almost one hundred percent of rabies cases are fatal; If possible, catch the bat so it can be tested for rabies.*

EXERCISE 2.3.D (p. 238)

1. B The professor says: *...a mechanism that releases tension. For most people, a good laugh is welcome—and worth looking for—because it brings pleasure and relief.* (2.2)

2. A The professor's purpose is to give examples of stress that is carefully controlled. The professor says: *This causes the child to experience mild stress, but in a secure setting because the stress is carefully controlled by the parent.*

3. D The professor says: *This element of shock in an otherwise safe situation is a universal characteristic of situations where people laugh.* (2.2)

4. C The professor's purpose is to show that humor is a safe way to bring about social change. The professor says: *Social rules and conventions provide us with a range of situations that we can turn into humor; Humor gives us the power to think about changing the rules. Therefore, comedians...are agents of social change.*

5. B The professor's purpose is to emphasize the importance of humor in managing anxiety. If we had no sense of humor, it would be more difficult to deal with the anxiety of failure, fear, pain, and death.

ANSWER KEY

6. C The instructor discusses an example of a beautification project, the Quinte Wildflower Project. Key sentence: *The Quinte Wildflower Project proves that people can come together to preserve the beauty of the wilderness.* (2.1)

7. A The professor's purpose is to provide an intellectual context for the issue of roadside beautification. The professor says: *Catharine Parr Traill—a botanist who lived in the nineteenth century—she predicted that the natural beauty of Canada's wilderness would disappear because of agricultural development.*

8. D The professor's purpose is to trace the history of roadside beautification efforts. The professor says: *This project continues a trend to beautify North American highways that goes all the way back to the 1960s and the beginning of the Adopt–a–Highway programs...; Since the sixties, beautification programs have been...broadened....*

9. B The professor's purpose is to illustrate the success of the plantings, which produce colorful flowers for several months each year.

10. A The professor thinks that these partnerships have been shown to work successfully. The professor says: *Its greatest success has been in attracting both public interest and private sponsors. It demonstrates that government and citizens can work together... that partnerships between the public and private sectors can and do work.*

Quiz 2 (p. 244)

1. D The students are discussing a report that they are working on. The woman says: *We don't have much time left before our presentation...; Let's talk about what we still need to do.* The man says: *I've got all my data, the graphs and photos of the mountain.* (2.1)

2. B The man's purpose is to inform the woman that he has only a little time now because he must leave soon to go to hockey practice. (2.3)

3. A, C The students will use the history of eruptions in the area: *...I'll give the history of the eruptions in that area.* They will also use a series of pictures of the mountain: *...I'll show them— first the color picture...and then the series of black–and–white photos showing the bulge.* (2.2)

4. C The man's opinion is that the photographs show the mountain's changes very well. The man says: *Aren't they awesome? Some really good shots of the mountain—you can really see how much the bulge has grown.* (2.3)

5. D The man says: *The bulge is forming 'cause a chamber of magma below the surface is growing. Earth's crust is being bent and bent....* (2.2)

6. A The main purpose of the talk is to describe some of the functions of banks. Key phrases: *Banks manage money...; Banks provide a number of important services...; ...banks also lend money; Banks provide these services...; ...their main function is to....* (2.3)

7. C, D Individuals take out bank loans to pay for education: *Ordinary people take out bank loans for a number of reasons—to pay for college... They also take out loans to purchase a home: ...to buy or remodel a home....* (2.2)

8. C The professor says: *For a bank to make a profit, it has to collect more interest than it pays out.* (2.2)

9. D The professor's purpose is to explain how bank failures have occurred. In the past, banks failed because they did not have enough available money to give to people who wanted to withdraw all of their money. The money was not available because the banks had lent it out or invested it. (2.3)

10. B The professor says: *Bank failures...were especially common during the Great Depression of the 1930s. When Franklin Roosevelt became president in 1933, one of the first things he did was close all the banks, so depositors wouldn't panic and try to take all their money out.* (2.2)

Quiz 3 (p. 246)

1. C The student is concerned about his grade for the course. The student says: *...it's about my midterm grade for organizational psychology. I...I'm surprised it's so...low.* (2.3)

2. B The student has spent a lot of time helping a family member, his brother. The student says: *...I've been sort of busy. My younger brother's starting classes here in January, and I have to show him around and help him find a place to live.* (2.2)

3. A The professor says: *...I don't have any record here for the second and third assignments. They were due on October 1st and the 13th.* (2.2)

4. D The professor says the student's work should be his top concern: *After all, your coursework should be your priority.* (2.2)

5. B The student's purpose is to convince his professor that he will complete the work. He suggests that he will get more organized and make up the two papers. (2.3)

6. C The main idea is that television promotes a culture of consumerism. Key phrases: *The American television industry is controlled by people who are more interested in the culture of consumerism...; Television promotes consumerism.* (2.1)

7. D The professor says: *Researchers study television to understand its effects on viewers and to measure its effectiveness in selling products.* (2.2)

8. B The professor says: *The television industry depends on advertising money to survive, and this relationship influences what television offers viewers; This means advertisers have a lot of control over what programs are made and when they are shown.* (2.2)

9. A The professor's purpose is to argue that television images of life lack depth and meaning. The professor suggests that television's images of affluence have less meaning than personal relationships have. (2.3)

10. B The professor's opinion is that television has had a mostly negative effect on society. The professor says: *...I tend to agree with critics of the media; Television promotes consumerism; It encourages greed and envy. Television helps create a wasteful society....* (2.3)

EXERCISE 2.4.A (p. 252)

1. D The student wants to obtain advice about dropping a class. The student says: *…I'm having a hard time keeping up in geometry. I think I'd better get out of the class and try again next quarter.* (2.3)

2. C The adviser says: *…why not drop your history class?* The student says: *Oh, all right. If I drop history, maybe then I'll be able to catch up in geometry.* You can predict that the student will not continue in his history class.

3. B The man has an unpaid charge on his account. The man says: *I ran into a problem when I tried to register by telephone. I got a message that said I had an outstanding charge on my account that needed to be paid….* (2.1)

4. C The woman says: *You'd better go to the accounting office and try to clear it up.* The man says: *Yeah, and I'd better make sure my roommate pays for the damage.* You can predict that the man will speak to someone in the accounting office.

5. B The student will miss the beginning of the summer term. The student says: *I registered for your psychology course for summer session. But I have to go to Vancouver and won't be back until June 25.* (2.3)

6. A The professor says: *…we'll cover the important basics during the first week; Summer session is only six weeks, and you can't afford to get a late start.* The professor implies that it is not acceptable to miss class time.

7. A The student says: *That's OK. I understand. Will you teach this course again in the fall?* You can predict that the student will take the course during the fall.

8. B The students are mainly discussing off–campus apartments for students. The woman says: *I live off campus now, in Forest Glen.* The man says: *Oh, those are the apartments in Glenwood….* (2.1)

9. C The man says: *But how did you manage to get in Forest Glen? I thought it was just for married students.* The woman says: *Three of the buildings are for married people only, but anyone can live in the rest.* You can infer that the woman is not married.

10. D The man says: *Maybe I'll look into that.* You can predict that he will find out more about the apartments.

EXERCISE 2.4.B (p. 253)

1. A The instructor says: *The elements of composition—line, shape, tone, and color—need to be well arranged, need to be ordered. They need to be coherent…just like the words and phrases and sentences in a piece of writing.* The instructor implies that composition in painting is similar to composition in writing.

2. ✓ Disagree: A composition must contain numerous subjects to be interesting: *A composition is better if it says one thing strongly than if it tries to say too many things.*
   ✓ Agree: If a picture is too crowded, it does not possess the element of unity: *A crowded composition is sort of fussy and splintered and lacks unity.*
   ✓ Agree: A successful composition conveys a single, clear message: *The artist's message is strongest when it's clear.*

3. D The main purpose of the talk is to introduce students to the course. Key sentences: *Over the next fifteen weeks, we will be observing the science of biology; This course has something for all of you to discover.* (2.3)

4. A, C Biology studies complex living systems: *In many ways, biology is the most demanding of all sciences. This is partly because living systems are so complex.* Biology also requires knowledge of other sciences: *It requires knowledge of chemistry, physics, and mathematics.* (2.2)

5. D The professor says: *Scientists are people who ask questions about nature and who believe that these questions can be answered. Scientists are explorers who are passionate about discovery.* The professor implies that scientists are enthusiastic in their study of nature.

6. C The professor says: *If you're a biology major or a pre–medical student…; If you're a physical science or engineering major…; And if you're a non–science major….* You can infer that the students in this course are pursuing various fields of study.

7. C The professor says: *A hormone is a chemical signal. …it triggers responses in cells and tissues.* (2.2)

8. B The professor says: *The growth of a plant toward light is called "phototropism."*

9. B, C You can infer that a seedling with the tip cut off would not bend toward light: *The Darwins observed that a grass seedling could bend toward light only if the tip of the shoot was present. If the tip was removed, the shoot would not curve toward light.* You can also infer that a seedling wearing a black cap would not bend toward light: *The seedling would also fail to grow toward light if the tip was covered with an opaque cap.*

10. D The professor says: *The Darwins proposed the hypothesis that some signal was transmitted downward from the tip into the part of the stem that controlled growth; These chemical messengers were hormones.* You can infer that the tip of a plant's stem produces a hormone that affects the stem's growth.

EXERCISE 2.4.C (p. 254)

1. C The man cannot think of a topic for his paper. He says: *I'm having trouble coming up with a good idea.* (2.1)

2. A The woman says: *What about the culture of…your hometown?* The man says: *I grew up in a small town where almost everyone works in the orchards; Well, why not? It's something I know a lot about.* You can predict that the man will describe his hometown culture.

3. C There was a death in the student's family. The student says: *My great aunt passed away and her funeral is tomorrow.* (2.3)

4. A The student asks: *…would it be possible for me to take the test next week?* The professor says: *Of course. Eric handles all make–ups; Can you stop by the office today and make an appointment with him?* You can predict that the student will arrange to take the test next week.

5. C The books that the man needs are a strain on his finances. The man says: *I can't believe how much my books cost this semester; It's a little more than my budget can handle at the moment.* (2.1)

6. D The man says: *And I still need the book for chemistry; I wonder if they'd have my chemistry book.* You can infer that he is taking a chemistry course.

7. A The woman says: *...did you know there's another bookstore...? They carry used copies of most of the textbooks for the university.* The man says: *That's not a bad idea. Where did you say that was again?* You can predict that the man will look for a cheaper copy of the chemistry book.

8. A The man says: *Now, this is a powerful drug, so you need only—no more than two capsules every six hours. And you shouldn't drink alcohol, drive a car, or operate machinery.* The man implies that the medication may be dangerous if taken incorrectly.

9. B The woman says: *Uh oh! I have a big test tomorrow!* You can infer that she is concerned about taking the medication before the test.

10. D The man says: *...you could take two capsules three or four hours before your test.* The woman says: *OK. Well, I guess I have no choice.* You can predict that the woman will take the medicine a few hours before the test.

EXERCISE 2.4.D (p. 255)

1. B The man owes a fee for his lab section. The woman tells him: *The computer shows that you haven't paid the lab fee for your biology class. You'll need to do this before you can attend your lab section.* (2.1)

2. C The woman says: *I'm afraid you'll have to pay it at the cashier's office.* The man says: *OK, I'd better take care of it right away.* You can predict that the man will go to the cashier's office.

3. C The students are discussing birds. Key phrases: *...its song...; ...ate all the fruit in their orchard; ...the black is mixed with a little green, making their feathers look iridescent.* (2.1)

4. A, B You can infer that starlings live in rural and urban areas: *I didn't even know they lived in the city; ...the starlings always ate all the fruit in their orchard.* You can also infer that starlings are a problem for fruit growers: *...the starlings always ate all the fruit in their orchard.*

5. C The student will not attend class today. The student says: *I was going to tell her I wouldn't be in class today....* (2.3)

6. A The secretary says: *...Dr. Owada isn't on campus today because she had a conference to go to. She'll get the message tomorrow.* The secretary implies that Dr. Owada will be absent until the next day.

7. D The secretary says: *...Professor Strong will be giving the lecture today.* The student says: *Oh, it's too bad I'll miss that.* You can predict that the student will miss the lecture by Professor Strong.

8. C The people are discussing a television series. The woman says: *Did anyone happen to catch "The American Metropolis" last night; The program you saw was part of the same series....* (2.1)

9. D The man says: *...there was a huge population explosion that turned America into a nation of cities, all within a decade.* You can infer that the population of the United States grew rapidly.

10. A, D You can infer that New York City was originally five cities: *...the five separate municipalities of New York...; ...those five municipalities were officially united as a single city....* You can also infer that New York has a borough called Brooklyn: *...each borough maintains traces of its original independence; I agree with that. I'm from Brooklyn, and it's definitely different from the rest of New York.*

EXERCISE 2.4.E (p. 256)

1. D The professor says: *Since this is an intro course, you need only a general understanding of the process for now.* You can infer that the course is a general course in life science.

2. B The professor says: *There's a wonderful videotape I'd like you to know about that will help you review for the test next week; I highly recommend it. In fact, you can expect to see examples from it on the test.* The professor implies that the videotape covers material that will be on the next test.

3. C The instructor discusses the origins of jazz. You can infer that the talk is most appropriate for a course titled Music History.

4. C The instructor says: *...the folk music known as the blues, whose origins lay in the work songs...; ...the blues evolved into popular commercial music.* The instructor implies that the blues changed and developed over time.

5. A "St. Louis Blues" combined elements of different musical styles. The instructor says: *Adapting the African–American folk idiom to European conventions of orchestration and harmony, Handy produced a hit song. The "St. Louis Blues" was tremendously influential....* (2.2)

6. ✓ Yes: Jazz was one of the most popular styles of music in the 1920s: *...the music entered the mainstream and even gave its name to the decade of the 1920s.*

   ✓ No: Jazz originated in the electric style of blues from Chicago: Not supported by the information in the talk.

   ✓ Yes: Jazz includes sounds from folk, popular, and classical music: *Jazz, blending African–American folk roots with elements of popular music and European classical traditions....*

7. C The main purpose of the lecture is to describe how various sea animals move. Key sentences: *A sea animal has to push itself through water in order to move; Sea animals use many different ways to swim, creep, or glide through water.* (2.3)

8. A The professor says: *The size of a fish's tail contributes to its swimming speed; Long, pointed tail lobes, like those on the marlin, are found only on fast swimmers.* You can infer that the fastest swimmer is the fish with the longest, most pointed tail fins.

9. B   The professor says: *Because their ancestors lived on the land, they developed tails that moved up and down. Whales and dolphins wave their tails up and down....* You can infer that whales and dolphins move their tails as land mammals do.

10. D   The professor says: *...the creatures that live on the bottom of the sea....creep on a single flat piece of muscle called a foot. Ripples pass along the foot, which allows these animals to glide smoothly forward.* You can infer that creatures that live on the bottom of the ocean move slowly and fluidly.

Quiz 4 (p. 261)

1. D   The speakers mainly discuss an opportunity for the man to work at a television station. The man says: *There's an opening at channel 12 that kind of interests me—an internship. I was kind of thinking of applying for it.* The woman asks: *You mean the television station? What sort of job?* (2.1)

2. B, D The man would like television work in the future: *Some day I'd like to write, or produce.* Also, the man will gain production experience: *It's a part–time internship for production assistant. Production work, general stuff...; It's the experience—the chance to work in television....* (2.2)

3. C   The man says: *I probably don't stand much of a chance....* You can infer that he does not feel confident about getting the internship. (2.4)

4. A   The woman's purpose is to reassure the man about his chance of getting the position. The woman says: *You never know. Sometimes it's not the credentials but the person who matters.* (2.3)

5. D   The woman asks: *You want a recommendation?* The man says: *Uh, yeah, like I said, I need all the help I can get.* You can infer that the man wants the woman to write a letter of recommendation. (2.4)

6. A   The speakers mainly discuss hiking safely in bear habitat. The speakers are a naturalist and members of a hiking club. The naturalist says: *One or two bear attacks occur each year in Glacier Park; In bear country, noise is good for you. Hiking quietly endangers you, the bear, and other hikers; Some trail conditions make it hard for bears to see, hear, or smell approaching hikers.* (2.1)

7. A   The naturalist thinks bear bells are not effective in keeping away bears. The naturalist says: *Most bells—even the so–called bear bells—are not loud enough. Calling out or clapping hands at regular intervals are better ways to make your presence known.* (2.3)

8. C   The naturalist's purpose is to warn that bears many not notice you in certain conditions in which they cannot see, hear, or smell you approaching. (2.3)

9. A   The naturalist says: *They may appear to tolerate you, and then attack without warning.* You can infer that bears may respond to people suddenly. (2.4)

10. B, D Hikers should avoid approaching a bear: *The most important advice I can give you is never to approach a bear intentionally.* Hikers should also avoid hiking when it is dark: *...avoid hiking early in the morning, late in the day, or after dark, when bears are more likely to be active.* (2.2)

Quiz 5 (p. 263)

1. B   The speakers mainly discuss how science and technology are connected. The professor says: *Today we'll focus on science and technology; ...technology often applies the discoveries of science; Science and technology are partners.* (2.1)

2. A   The professor says: *...technology often applies the discoveries of science. Can anyone think of an example; The electron microscope is an excellent example of applied science.* (2.2)

3. D   The professor's purpose is to give examples of technology that came before science. The professor says: *In fact, technology came before science in our prehistory. Technology was driven by inventive humans who built tools, made pottery, designed musical instruments, and so on, all without science....* (2.3)

4. C   The professor means that technology has both helped and harmed us. A double–edged sword cuts both ways, and so does technology. Technology helps us: *It enables us to cure diseases so people can live longer.* It also harms us: *...environmental consequences...; ...nuclear accidents, toxic waste, extinction of species....* (2.4)

5. B   The student says: *I think scientists have a responsibility to educate politicians and the public about the consequences of certain technologies. This is why...I've decided to get a master's degree in public policy.* (2.2)

6. A, C The speakers mainly discuss forestry as a profession: *...professional forester; ...our professional organization...; ...over 700 job categories.* They also discuss where foresters work: *Foresters...do work in the woods...they also work in laboratories, classrooms, planning agencies, corporate offices....* (2.1)

7. A   The forester says: *Managing a forest is both a science and an art, which is why my education included courses in the biological, physical, and social sciences, as well as the humanities.* You can infer that the profession of forestry is a broad field requiring diverse skills. (2.4)

8. B   The student wants to understand how national parks and forests are different. He knows about some similarities between them, but is confused about the differences. (2.3)

9. D   The forester says: *National parks...are set aside and preserved in a near–natural state...; National forests, on the other hand....are managed for their many benefits, including...wood products....* You can infer that national parks do not supply commercial wood products. (2.4)

10. C   The forester's purpose is to show that foresters and biologists have shared interests and often work together to preserve forest habitats. (2.3)

EXERCISE 2.5.A (p. 268)

1. B–C–A The speaker says: *One of the most common tubular drums is the long drum; This drum was carved from a length of tree trunk...; For vessel drums, we have the kettledrum. Kettledrums have a single membrane stretched over a pot or vessel body; The frame is shallow...; A lot of frame drums—like this Turkish tar—have metal jingles attached to the rim.*

2. C–B–A The professor says: *The entrance zone may serve as a place of shelter for animals or people. Prehistoric humans used entrance zones of caves as shelters and burial grounds; The twilight zone is sheltered from direct sunlight and is home to a large, diverse population of animals such as...bats...; In the dark zone live animals that have adapted to the world of darkness, including small shrimp....*

3. ✓ No: Warm temperatures: Not supported by the information in the talk.
   ✓ Yes: Blind animals: *In the dark zone live animals that have adapted to the world of darkness...; These animals are usually blind, and some lack eyes altogether.*
   ✓ Yes: Few air currents: *Perpetually dark, it has...few if any air currents.*
   ✓ No: Green plants: *...no green plants grow in caves....*

4. ✓ Extravert: Prefers looking outward to the world: *Extraverts turn outward—to the world around them....*
   ✓ Introvert: Prefers learning in private, individual ways: *Introverted people usually prefer to learn in private, individual ways.*
   ✓ Extravert: Has a variety of interests: *Extraverts, therefore, usually have a variety of interests....*
   ✓ Introvert: Has fewer interests, but on a deeper level: *Introverts pursue fewer interests, but on a much deeper level.*

5. A The professor says: *Introverts look inward for resources; They sort of take a reflective approach to life; Introverted people usually prefer to learn in private, individual ways.* You can infer that an introverted student would prefer reflective journal writing. (2.4)

6. B The main purpose of the talk is to discuss some effects of inflation. Key phrases: *One of the major problems in our economy is inflation...; Thus, a person has to work more hours...; ...the same money buys fewer things, and everybody's standard of living goes down....* (2.3)

7. B The instructor's purpose is to illustrate the effect of price changes. The instructor says: *For example, let's say that this year a loaf of bread costs $1.00...; That means...; ...the price of the bread goes up to $1.25...; That means...; Inflation means that the same money buys fewer things....* (2.3)

8. D The instructor says: *...inflation, a situation in which prices are going up faster than wages. Thus, a person has to work more hours to pay for the same items.* (2.2)

9–10. ✓ Hyperinflation: People try to get rid of their currency: *And then there is hyperinflation—inflation so severe that people try to get rid of their currency before prices rise further....*
   ✓ Moderate inflation: Incomes and relative prices rise slightly: *Moderate inflation does not distort relative prices or incomes severely.*
   ✓ Galloping inflation: Inflation occurs at a rate of 100 percent in a year: *Galloping inflation happens rapidly, say at a rate of 100 percent or more within a year.*
   ✓ Hyperinflation: There is social and political disorder: *Times of hyperinflation are usually characterized by social and political turmoil.*

EXERCISE 2.5.B (p. 269)

1. C The purpose of the talk is to assist students in career planning. The speaker is a career counselor. Key phrases: *There are a great many careers...; You find these careers in...; It is your job to find out, during your college years, into which of these two job categories you fit, and to plan your career accordingly.* (2.3)

2. A, D Engineers and accountants are likely to be specialists: *There are a great many careers in which the emphasis is on specialization. You find these careers in engineering and in accounting....* (2.2)

3. ✓ Generalist: Skilled in directing other people: *..."generalists" are particularly needed for administrative positions, where it is their job to see that other people do the work....*
   ✓ Specialist: Concerned with tools and technique: *Specialists understand one field; their concern is with technique, tools....*
   ✓ Specialist: Trained in a technical or professional field: *They are "trained" people, and their educational background is technical or professional.*
   ✓ Generalist: Must be able to make overall judgments: *...a demand for people who are capable of seeing the forest rather than the trees, of making overall judgments.*

4. B The speaker says: *..."generalists" are particularly needed for administrative positions, where it is their job to see that other people do the work...; Generalists—and especially administrators—deal with people. Their concern is with leadership, with planning, with direction, and with coordination.* (2.2)

5. D The speaker says: *There are a great many careers in which the emphasis is on specialization; ..."generalists" are particularly needed for administrative positions...; Any organization needs both kinds of people....* You can infer that both specialists and generalists can find jobs. (2.4)

6. D The instructor mainly describes each leaf arrangement and gives an example. Key phrases: *...the one called alternate, each leaf is attached at a different level on the stem. This poppy is a good example; Another type is the opposite arrangement; The bee plant's leaves are paired on opposite sides of the stem; This one's called basal, and our example is the amaryllis.* (2.1)

7. B The instructor says: *...the one called alternate, each leaf is attached at a different level on the stem; ...there's a leaf here, on the right side, and above that a leaf on the left here, and above that, one on the right again...and so on, alternating right and left, all the way up the stem.* (2.2)

8–9. ✓ Opposite: The plant's leaves are paired on the opposite sides of the stem: *The bee plant's leaves are paired on opposite sides of the stem.*

　　　✓ Basal: All the plant's leaves are at ground level: *Notice how all the leaves are at ground level, at the stem's base.*

　　　✓ Alternate: Each leaf is attached at a different level on the stem: *...the one called alternate, each leaf is attached at a different level on the stem.*

　　　✓ Opposite: The leaves are attached at the same level on the stem, but on different sides: *...they're attached at the same level of the stem, but on opposite sides.*

10. B The instructor says: *I have some lovely samples to share with you today. I'd like you all to come up and examine the contents of...these two tables. Many of them are specimens of the sun-flower family....* You can predict that the students will look at flower samples. (2.4)

EXERCISE 2.6.A (p. 275)

1. C The purpose of the talk is to explain how to draw with pen and ink. Key phrases: *If you are unsure of drawing directly in pen and ink, start off with...; ...to allow the ink to flow easily; ...using light and dark strokes of the pen.* (2.3)

2. ✓ Yes: Draw the outline of the violin: *...add contrast by drawing the outline of the violin with gently curved lines.*

　　✓ No: Take a photograph of the subject: Not supported by the information in the talk.

　　✓ Yes: Study the subject for a few minutes: *Take a few minutes to study your subject—this chair and violin.*

　　✓ No: Rub the violin strings with a bow: Not supported by the information in the talk.

3. D The professor says: *The Rogers Pass stretch of the Trans–Canada is at risk of being buried in snow...; ...it's important to control an avalanche when it's small...before it builds up into a serious danger.* (2.2)

4. A, C The natural causes of an avalanche are the weight of the snow and the pull of gravity: *The weight of the snow, together with the force of gravity, is what starts an avalanche.* (2.2)

5. C–A–B–D The professor says: *(1) A team of snow technicians monitors the snowpack. They sort of "read" the snow and try to predict when it's likely to slide; (2) ...they close the road and remove all traffic from the pass; (3) A ten–man artillery crew operates a mobile 105 mm howitzer, firing shells into the slopes; (4) This sends out shock waves that trigger the avalanches.*

6. ✓ No: Salmon compete with eagles for food: Not supported by the information in the discussion.

　　✓ Yes: Young fry swim downstream in rivers: *As fry, the fish then migrate downstream via rivers.*

　　✓ Yes: Adult salmon migrate home to spawn: *When mature, the salmon form into groups of common geographic origin and migrate back toward the river they emerged from as juveniles.*

　　✓ No: Salmon die from pollution in rivers: Not supported by the information in the discussion.

7. B, D Salmon find their way home by seeing the sun's position: *...they navigate by the position of the sun.* They also smell the water: *...their keen sense of smell takes over; The water flowing from each stream carries a unique scent.* (2.2)

8. C The sight of leaping salmon amazed the student. She was surprised to see a fish jump up a waterfall, and then she was amazed to see several others also jump. (2.3)

9. D The professor says: *Salmon provide an important link in the food chain; When they make their return journey, they carry nutrients from the ocean back to the rivers and streams.* (2.2)

10. A You can conclude that baby salmon eat the bodies of dead salmon. After salmon spawn, they die. Their dead bodies, or *carcasses*, become the food source for many organisms, including *their own newly hatched offspring*. (2.4)

EXERCISE 2.6.B (p. 276)

1. D The professor mainly gives a description of a process. Key phrases: *The complex process inside a leaf...; During this process...; First...; Once...; When...; Then...; Finally....* (2.1)

2. A, C Carbon dioxide and water must be present. The professor says: *Carbon dioxide and water—these are the raw materials for photosynthesis. Once carbon dioxide and water are present, photosynthesis can begin.* (2.2)

3. ✓ Yes: Chlorophyll absorbs light from the sun: *When sunlight shines on a leaf..., its energy is absorbed by molecules of chlorophyll.*

　　✓ Yes: The leaves take in water and carbon dioxide: *First, the pores on the leaf's outer skin open up and take in molecules of carbon dioxide. Water...enters the leaf through its stem.*

　　✓ No: The plant pushes roots through the soil: Not supported by the information in the lecture.

　　✓ Yes: Hydrogen combines with carbon dioxide: *...hydrogen from the water combines with carbon dioxide....*

4. B The professor says: *We experimental psychologists are interested in developing laws about human behavior so we'll be able to understand and predict what people do and why they do it.* (2.2)

5. A The professor says: *...to develop laws about human behavior, we must assume there's some regularity to it. We can't be psychologists without making the assumption that behavior follows certain patterns.* (2.2)

6. B — The professor says: *The Law of Effect states that whether or not a person will repeat a behavior depends on the effect that behavior has; If the action is not rewarded, or if it's punished, it's not likely to be repeated.* If a boy stops pulling a cat's tail when the cat bites him, you can infer that it is because of the Law of Effect. The cat's bite punishes the boy's action, so the boy does not repeat the action. (2.4)

7. C–B–D–A — The professor says: *(1) First, using available knowledge, a psychologist makes a hypothesis about behavior; (2) Then, the psychologist tests the hypothesis through an experiment; (3) …many repetitions of the experiment must be conducted under different conditions; (4) Only repeated verification…will result in a law.*

8. B — The professor says: *…marshes usually don't contain trees or shrubs. Marsh vegetation is usually soft–stemmed or herbaceous—for example, grasses….* (2.2)

9. ✓ Yes: Dead plants and animals contribute energy to the food chain: *…an abundance of dead plant and animal material—energy–rich organic matter—enters the food chain each year.*

   ✓ Yes: Acids from decaying vegetation turn the water brown: *The water in marshes may become tea–colored or dark brown because of the organic acids from the decaying vegetation.*

   ✓ No: The marsh is drained for agricultural development: Humans have drained marshes, but this is not a biological process.

   ✓ Yes: Bacteria and fungi break down organic matter in the water: *And much of this energy–rich biomass is broken down by bacteria and water fungi.*

10. C, D — Wetlands have been destroyed because they were thought to cause disease: *In the past, humans have viewed these marshes—and most wetlands—as the source of…disease.* Also, land was needed for agriculture: *Humans have destroyed a lot of wetlands, mostly to make way for agricultural development.* (2.2)

Quiz 6 (p. 279)

1. A, D — Plant life and sunlight characterize the upper zone: *The clear, sunlit waters near the surface are an ideal place for the microscopic plants called plankton to grow.* (2.2)

2. ✓ No: Large fish regulate their body temperature: Not supported by the information in the talk.

   ✓ Yes: Animal plankton eats plant plankton: *The tiny plant plankton provides food for tiny animal plankton….*

   ✓ Yes: Microscopic plants grow in sunlit water: *…an ideal place for the microscopic plants called plankton to grow.*

   ✓ Yes: Large schools of fish feed on plankton: *Huge schools of fish…cruise the upper waters to eat the animal plankton.* (2.6)

3. B–C–A — The professor says: *The clear, sunlit waters near the surface…; About 200 meters below the surface…is a dimly lit twilight world; Utter darkness usually begins at a depth of 1,000 meters….* (2.5)

4. C, D — The worker bee defends the colony and gathers the food. The professor says: *The worker bees…do all the work that is done in the hive. They…gather pollen, feed and rear the brood, and fight all the battles necessary to defend the colony.* (2.2)

5. D–A–B–C — The professor says: *(1) Each egg is laid by the queen bee, who deposits it in the bottom of the worker cell; (2) After three days, the egg hatches into a small white worm called a larva…; (3) The larva then enters the pupa state; (4) When the adult worker emerges from the pupa….* (2.6)

6. C–A–B — The professor says: *Located in the abdomen are the honey sac and the sting, with its highly developed poison sac; On the head are the mandibles, the jaw–like organs which enable the bees to perform the necessary hive duties and to mold the wax and build their combs; The honey bee's four wings and six legs are fastened to the thorax.* (2.5)

7. B, C — The speaker discusses where bread originated: *The first bread was made in the Nile valley about 10,000 years ago.* The speaker also discusses grains that are grown today: *wheat, rye, and oats.* (2.1)

8. ✓ Yes: People discover that yeast makes bread rise: *Leavened breads and cakes, which are made to rise by the action of yeast, were also a discovery of the ancient Egyptians.*

   ✓ No: Beer is commonly used in making bread: Not supported by the information in the talk.

   ✓ Yes: Primitive bread is made on heated stones: *Primitive bread was not like the bread we know today because it was simply flour dough dried on heated stones.*

   ✓ Yes: The Egyptians invent the art of baking: *The Egyptians were the first people to master the art of baking.* (2.6)

9. C — The speaker says: *…many families had to bake their dough in communal bakeries. To identify their loaves, each household would make a distinctive mark on the bread, sometimes with a special stamp bearing the family name.* (2.2)

10. ✓ Oats: Mainly fed to cattle: *Oats are grown in temperate regions and are mainly fed to cattle….*

    ✓ Wheat: Used to make bread and pasta: *The large grains of bread wheat…produce light, airy bread. Another widely cultivated variety of wheat…goes into making pasta.*

    ✓ Wheat: Rich in a protein called gluten: *The large grains of bread wheat are rich in gluten—a kind of protein….* (2.5)

Quiz 7 (p. 281)

1. A, B — Improvisation is difficult to define because there are several kinds: *We hear about the different types of improvisation: "free" improvisation and "controlled" improvisation and "collective" improvisation.* Also, people disagree about what improvisation is: *Every jazz player knows what he or she means by improvisation. And all writers know what they mean by improvisation. The result, of course, is a lot of confusion and disagreement about what improvisation really is.* (2.2)

2. C — The professor discusses the history of improvisation. Key sentence: *Let's try to understand it more by looking at history.* (2.1)

3. C — The professor says: *In the beginning, music was largely improvisational, supplied on the spur of the moment by prehistoric people who "made" music....* (2.2)

4. ✔ — Prehistoric humans: Made music for work, play, and war: *...prehistoric people who "made" music for work, play, war....*
   ✔ — Jazz musicians: Combined their own music with stock melodies: *...the early jazz musicians were very similar to the ancient Greeks in that they were making a music partly their own and partly derived from the "stock melodies" in their environment.*
   ✔ — Prehistoric humans: Used music as a force to show relationships: *...music was a force that communicated the relationship of people to nature, and people to each other.*
   ✔ — Jazz musicians: Improvised on the music of other bands: *...black musicians improvised on the European melodies they heard white bands playing.* (2.5)

5. D — The professor says: *There were a number of musicians who'd played in army bands, and they had training of one kind or another. It was these trained military bandsmen who were responsible for the rise of jazz improvisation.* The professor implies that early jazz improvisation was developed by trained musicians. (2.4)

6. D — The main idea is that children go through stages of mental and social development. Key phrases: *...mental development is related to social development...; ...children gradually acquire...; ...the egocentric stage of social development; ...the multiple role–taking stage.* (2.1)

7. A — The professor says: *...at around four to six years old, they can focus on only one thought at a time; ...don't yet understand that other people may see the same event differently from the way they see it. They don't reflect on the thoughts of others.* (2.2)

8. B — The professor's purpose is to illustrate how children must experience something directly to understand it because they cannot yet think abstractly at six to ten years old. (2.3)

9. A — The professor says: *Children can now manage various social roles...; Because they can play multiple roles, this stage is known as the multiple role–taking stage.* You can infer that children in the multiple role–taking stage know that different social roles require certain behavior. (2.4)

10. ✔ — Yes: The child understands actions as others see them: *...on a social level, children can now understand actions as an outsider might see them.*
   ✔ — No: The child prefers large crayons and paint brushes: Not supported by the information in the lecture.
   ✔ — No: The child is interested in learning about nature: Not supported by the information in the lecture.
   ✔ — Yes: The child can judge actions as they affect all people: *...the young teenager is now able to judge actions by how they might influence all individuals....* (2.6)

Quiz 8 (p. 283)

1. C — The woman wants to talk about ideas for her project. The woman says: *I was hoping...we could talk about the project that's due at the end of May; I have an idea...it's something that interests me.* (2.3)

2. B — The woman asks: *...the project plan...that part's due next week, right?* The professor replies: *Uh...yes, that's right, the first due date—the project plan—is due next week, on Monday, May 3.* (2.2)

3. B — The woman says: *I'm a little—I'm not sure about what you want.* You can infer that she doesn't understand the assignment. (2.4)

4. A, C — You can predict that the woman will write about an economic development organization: *...she works for economic development...; ...a case study of an economic development organization....* You can also predict that she will write about how an organization promotes social change: *...also for social change because it's work that affects women and their role in society; I could do a case study about a group that works for both economic and social change.* (2.4)

5. ✔ — Not include: Photographs of art: Not supported by the information in the conversation.
   ✔ — Include: Information from a Web site: *...information from their Web site.*
   ✔ — Include: An interview with her boss: *...I'd like to interview my boss...; ...combine the interview data....*
   ✔ — Include: A product catalog: *...their product catalog...; ...an analysis and evaluation of their catalog.* (2.4)

6. C — The professor says: *"Mesa" means "table" in Spanish. The Spanish people who explored the area thought these flat–topped hills looked sort of like tables. A mesa is wider than it is high—kind of like a large table.* (2.2)

7. A, D — One reason for the erosion of a mesa is that the rock on the sides is softer than that on the top: *The sides of a mesa are often made of shale or softer sandstone.* Another reason is that the force of water cuts away the softer rock: *The slope of the sides will increase the water's speed and force as it runs down; Debris carried by the running water cuts away the softer surface rock.* (2.2)

ANSWER KEY

8. B   The professor's purpose is to describe the appearance of spires by comparing them to chimneys. (2.3)

9. C–A–D–B   The professor says: *(1) As a mesa is shrunk in size by water, it may be cut into smaller landforms; (2) Further erosion can change a butte into a tower or spire; (3) Further erosion of the softer rock may reduce the spire.... Over time, erosion finally topples these rocks to the ground; (4) ...they might undergo further erosion that completely demolishes them so they disintegrate into pebbles. Finally, these pebbles end up as the sand we walk on....* (2.6)

10. B   The professor says: *On a mesa, conditions are optimal for erosion. With enough time, even the durable top of a mesa will decrease in size; Further erosion can change a butte into a tower or spire; Further erosion of the softer rock may reduce the spire...; Over time, erosion finally topples these rocks to the ground.* You can conclude that erosion continually changes the shape of rock. (2.4)

PART 3 – SPEAKING

EXERCISE 3.5.A (p. 311)
Key points:
- The university is offering a training course for students who want to be tutors.
- The woman thinks that the man should enroll in the course.
- One reason she gives is that the course will give him valuable experience for being a teaching assistant in graduate school.
- Another reason is that he would learn some practical theories about teaching and learning.
- Another reason is that the course might give him skills that could be useful for whatever kind of work he does later.

EXERCISE 3.5.B (p. 312)
Key points:
- The college is considering a proposal that would increase the physical education requirement from one course to two courses.
- The man does not support the proposal to increase the physical education requirement.
- One reason he gives is that students should make the choice to get exercise, and it is not the college's responsibility to require it.
- Another reason is that students' main job is to study and exercise their brains, not their bodies.
- Another reason is that he already gets a lot of exercise outside of school.

EXERCISE 3.5.C (p. 313)
Key points:
- The college is offering a course in theater production to members of the community who are not college students.
- The man's opinion is that the course is not fair because it discriminates against college students who are not in the Theater Arts program.
- One reason he gives is that students pay tuition and fees, so they should be allowed to take any course they want.
- Another reason is that students may want to take the course just to have fun and learn about theater.

EXERCISE 3.5.D (p. 314)
Key points:
- There is an on–campus childcare center for the children of students; however, space at the center is limited.
- The woman's opinion of the childcare center is that the service is not satisfactory.
- One reason she gives is that the center does not have enough space, and many children are on the waiting list for a long time.
- Another reason is that the lack of space prevents a lot of parents from going to college.
- Another reason is that the center closes too early for some parents who take evening classes.

EXERCISE 3.6.A (p. 318)

Key points:
- Emotional intelligence consists of self–awareness, self–control, self–motivation, enthusiasm, and social ability. People with emotional intelligence understand their feelings.
- The young people in the study were extremely intense and enthusiastic, which are qualities of emotional intelligence.
- Emotional intelligence causes young people to experience emotional highs and lows and to feel everything very strongly.
- Emotional intelligence causes young people to think deeply about everything.
- Young people with emotional intelligence often experience problems because they are different from everyone else.

EXERCISE 3.6.B (p. 319)

Key points:
- During a boycott, people refuse to buy, sell, or trade with an individual or business that they believe to be doing something morally wrong.
- According to the lecture, the cause of the grape boycott was the refusal of the grape growers to accept the union of the grape pickers.
- There were several effects of the grape boycott: workers stopped picking grapes; many people marched in support of the pickers; eventually some grape growers signed agreements with the union.
- The lettuce boycott was caused by the lack of union contracts; the effect was that people refused to buy lettuce.
- An effect of both boycotts was the negative attention directed at the growers.

EXERCISE 3.6.C (p. 320)

Key points:
- Role conflict is the stress or tension a person feels because of playing different social roles at home, school, and the workplace.
- Role conflict occurs when there is competition between the expectations of different role partners.
- College students may feel conflict between the role of child and the role of friend.
- Mature adults, especially women, experience role conflict because of the tension between responsibility to an employer and responsibility to family.

EXERCISE 3.6.D (p. 321)

Key points:
- Spatial memory is the ability of animals to remember and recognize objects in the environment.
- Some species of birds use their spatial memory of landscape features to accurately remember where they have hidden food.
- Spatial memory enables some animals to find and investigate new objects in their environment. For example, baboons can quickly find a new object in their pen and will examine the object; they will ignore objects that are not new.

EXERCISE 3.7.A (p. 326)

Key points:
- The woman wants to share a dormitory room on campus with her best friend from high school.
- The man's opinion is that the woman should not share a room with her best friend.
- One reason he gives is that it can destroy a friendship because knowing someone isn't the same as living together.
- Another reason is that having someone else for a roommate will allow her to meet new and interesting people.
- Another reason is that she might benefit by living in a dormitory with other students of her academic major.

EXERCISE 3.7.B (p. 327)

Key points:
- A mild form of depression is linked to changes in the amount of daylight during a certain time of the year, usually fall or winter, when the periods of daylight are shorter.
- The disorder is related to the body's biological clock and to changes in body temperature and hormone levels.
- Symptoms are similar to those of a major depression but usually not as serious; they include lack of energy, a desire to sleep more, and a tendency to gain weight.
- The symptoms usually disappear when the days start getting longer in the spring.
- One treatment involves exposure to a special light that fools the body into thinking that it is getting sunlight.

EXERCISE 3.7.C (p. 328)

Key points:
- The program seminar is the primary mode of instruction for students at the college.
- The woman's opinion is that she will not like seminars.
- One reason she gives is that seminars seem similar to class discussions in her high school, which were boring because a few students always did all the talking.
- Another reason is that she would rather listen to the professor because the professor has all the knowledge, not the students.

EXERCISE 3.7.D (p. 329)

Key points:
- Pollock tried to express his feelings through painting; abstract expressionism emphasized personal expression.
- Pollock was devoted to the process of painting; abstract expressionism valued the act of painting and is also called action painting.
- Pollock painted his huge canvases on the floor; large canvases characterize abstract expressionism.
- Pollock dripped paint onto the canvas in a skillful, controlled gesture; abstract expressionism emphasized surface qualities of paint such as brushstroke and texture.

EXERCISE 3.8.A (p. 334)

1. Key points:
- The man's problem is that his elbow is sore, but he does not want to miss baseball practice because his coach will be angry.
- The woman suggests that he go to the clinic and have someone look at his elbow.
- The woman suggests that he not play baseball and tell his coach about his elbow.
- The woman suggests that he ask his boss for something else to do besides lifting heavy things.
- The woman suggests that he look for a different job.

2. Key points:
- The woman's problem is that she still needs another course in social science, but it appears that nothing will fit into her schedule for Winter Quarter.
- Her adviser suggests that she wait until Spring Quarter to fulfill the social science requirement. However, the woman will be doing a full–time internship in the spring.
- Her adviser suggests that she take an evening course.
- Her adviser suggests that she wait until summer to fulfill the social science requirement.

3. Key points:
- The man's problem is that his learning partner is lazy and has not done any work on a project for which they will be graded together.
- The woman suggests that he have a serious talk with his partner and lay out a plan for completing the project.
- The woman suggests that he let his professor know about the problem.
- The woman suggests that he look around for another group to join in doing the project.

4. Key points:
- The woman's problem is that her car does not always start; she needs to have it checked out, but her regular mechanic is expensive, and she still must pay her tuition.
- The man suggests that she take her car to the community college program in automotive technology, where students can have their cars fixed for less money than it usually would cost.
- The man suggests that she check the bulletin board in the Student Center to find a mechanic that is not expensive.

5. Key points:
- The man's situation is that he will miss an upcoming test, but he has already missed one test and is in danger of not receiving credit for the course (failing).
- His professor suggests that he try not to miss this test and try to do well on it.
- His professor suggests that he do something to raise his grade, such as get a tutor or a study partner to help him.
- His professor suggests that he consider dropping the course.

EXERCISE 3.9.A (p. 343)

1. Key points:
- Hotel managers are responsible for the overall operation of the hotel and for seeing that guests receive good service.
- The general manager is the top executive in a hotel. The general manager directs the work of other managers in the hotel. General managers must be skilled in leadership and financial decision making.
- Hotel controllers are responsible for the management of money. Controllers manage the accounting and payroll departments, find ways to improve efficiency, and interpret financial statements.
- Sales managers market the services of the hotel. Sales managers have constant contact with customers and know what selling points appeal to the public. Sales managers must be skilled in business, marketing, and advertising.

2. Key points:
- Two features of the earth's surface that influence climate are ocean currents and landforms.
- There are two large, circular ocean currents, one in each hemisphere. These currents move warm water from the equator to the north and south.
- Warm and cold ocean currents affect the climates of nearby coastal areas; for example, the Gulf Stream warms the climate of northwestern Europe.
- Landforms such as mountains affect climate. Mountains are cooler, windier, and wetter than valleys; one example is Mount Kilimanjaro, which is near the equator but always covered with snow.
- Mountains interrupt the flow of winds and storms. When moist winds blow toward mountains, the air on the slope facing the wind is cool and moist, causing rain and snow to fall there. The air on the other side of the mountain is warmer and drier.

3. Key points:
- One traditional belief about trees is the concept of a great cosmic tree, or Tree of the World. The Norse and Algonquin people honored the ash tree as the cosmic tree.
- Another belief is that carrying the seeds of the buckeye tree would prevent a disease of the bones.
- Another belief is that a water dowser can find water underground by using a branch from the hazel tree.
- People have thought of trees as special because they provide many of life's necessities, such as food, oils, building materials, medicines, spices, and dyes.

4. Key points:
- One physical difference between water and land is that oxygen is more abundant in air than in water. Land animals can get oxygen more easily than water animals can, but first land animals had to evolve lungs.
- Another physical difference is that air is less dense than water and provides less support against gravity than water does. Therefore, land animals had to develop strong legs and a stronger skeleton for moving in air.
- Another difference is that the temperature of the air on land changes more easily than it does in water. Therefore, land animals had to develop strategies to survive in warm and cold temperatures, such as the ability to maintain a constant body temperature.

5. Key points:
- The Flatiron Building was the first true skyscraper in New York. It is an office tower that stands apart from other buildings on all sides.
- The Flatiron Building is twenty–two stories tall, has a steel frame covered on the outside with stone, and is decorated with geometric patterns, columns, arches, and a crown of carved stone.
- The Flatiron Building is built on an irregular, triangle–shaped site, giving it an unusual shape.
- The building got its name from a joke about its shape. People thought it looked like a flatiron, a triangle–shaped piece of iron used for pressing clothes.

EXERCISE 3.10.A (p. 350)

1. Answers will vary, but may include the following: *Agents of socialization are people...who teach you how to live; Parents take care of you and teach the correct way to behave; Your friends influence you...; Also, teachers are important because they teach you knowledge; Television and the Internet...also influence an individual and teach socialization.*
2. Answers will vary, but may include the following: parents teach you how to live; parents teach you how to behave correctly; parents help you make right choices in life; peers influence how you dress; teachers give you knowledge; television and the Internet teach socialization.
3. Answers will vary, but may include *for example, and, because,* and *also.*
4. Yes.
5. The response would receive a score of 4.

EXERCISE 3.10.B (p. 351)

1. Yes.
2. Answers will vary, but may include the following: her roommate uses her things without permission; her roommate never cleans the bathroom; she should discuss the problem with her roommate, ask the apartment manager to help, or find another apartment.
3. Yes. The student's opinion is *I think the woman should find another apartment.* The reason given is *I think this because I had the same problem.*
4. Answers will vary, but may include *because, but, also, so,* and *another suggestion.*
5. Yes.
6. The response would receive a score of 4.

QUIZ 4 (p. 353)

1. Key points:
   - The university is having a free career workshop for all students.
   - The man's opinion is that the woman should attend the career workshop.
   - One reason he gives is that there will be several people to talk to about working in her field.
   - Another reason is that the university has only one career workshop each year and she shouldn't miss it.
   - Another reason is that the workshop is a good way to start looking for a job after graduation.
2. Key points:
   - The study showed that sleep improved the ability of students to retain knowledge about speech produced by a computer. This supports the belief that sleep has an impact on higher–level learning, such as the ability to learn language.
   - In the study, a group of students was trained in the morning and tested twelve hours later. They had forgotten much of what they had learned; however, when they were allowed a night's sleep and retested the next morning, their test scores had improved.
   - The study supports the belief that sleep protects memories against later interference or loss and also appears to restore memories.

3. Key points:
   - The woman's problem is that she has two midterms on Monday but will have little time to study that weekend because her parents are coming to visit.
   - The man suggests that she join his biology study group to review for the midterm.
   - He suggests that she explain to her parents that she has to study for examinations.
   - He suggests that she give her parents a list of places to go during the afternoon and then spend the evening with them.
4. Key points:
   - Humans have more than one hundred separate gestures and facial expressions that are nonverbal signals in communication.
   - Body language communicates how people perceive a social situation; for example, strangers meeting at a party will lift their eyebrows to communicate friendly feelings.
   - Hand or arm gestures, such as a salute or a handshake, signal involvement.
   - Eye movement and eye contact are used to regulate the rhythm of conversation. In Western society, friends look at each other often during conversation. A speaker looks away to signal his intention to speak; a listener looks at the speaker and nods his head to signal his interest and attention.
   - The smile has a tremendous power to generate friendly feelings. The smile has the same meaning in every culture and is first seen in babies when they are very young.

QUIZ 5 (p. 356)

1. Key points:
   - The man will be taking a writing course that includes a peer feedback group.
   - The man does not want to attend the peer feedback group.
   - One reason he gives is that he was in a student writing group before, but it didn't help with his writing.
   - Another reason is that he can't learn from other students if they don't know how to write.
   - Another reason is that he can learn better from a teacher because a teacher has more education and experience.
2. Key points:
   - A cohort is a group of people who were born within a narrow band of years and move through history together.
   - Historical events influence each cohort differently because each cohort is at a different age.
   - The Great Depression had different effects on people who were young children and teenagers at the time.
   - People who were young children during the Great Depression showed negative effects later in life because they had spent a greater portion of their childhood under economic hardship.
   - People who were teenagers during the Great Depression did not show negative effects later in life.
3. Key points:
   - The woman's problem is that she has to drive to school and needs to park on campus, but the parking lots are not big enough, and a parking permit does not guarantee a space.
   - The man suggests that she register for classes that meet in the afternoon because the parking lots are less full in the afternoon.
   - The man suggests that she park in the park–and–ride lot a mile from campus and ride the free shuttle bus from there to campus.

4. Key points:
- Organizational charts reveal an organization's management structure: who is in charge of what, who reports to whom, and how information flows.
- The pyramid chart shows the formal structure of a company, with the labor force on the bottom and management on the top. The pyramid structure defines the chain of command. Information flows up the chain, and orders flow down.
- The wheel chart shows management as the hub, the departments as the spokes, and the labor force as the rim. Information flows up through the spokes to the hub. The wheel reveals a policy of open communication.

Quiz 6 (p. 359)

1. Key points:
- The university needs students to work as volunteers during an upcoming conference.
- The woman's opinion about volunteering is that it will be a great opportunity to be a part of the conference.
- One reason she gives is that volunteers can go to the reception and meet a lot of prominent scientists from around the world.
- Another reason is to learn how a conference is organized, which interests her because she plans to be involved in environmental issues.
- Another reason is to get a free T–shirt.

2. Key points:
- One variation on the chase film featured a wealthy man who advertises for a wife and ends up being chased by a crowd of women.
- Another variation was the comedy police chase, in which clownish policemen chase villains and bank robbers.
- The chase film was popular because it was humorous, simple to tell, and simple for the audience to follow.
- The chase film was important in the history of film because making the films was a valuable exercise in film style and led to certain filmmaking conventions.

3. Key points:
- The man's problem is that he plans to transfer to the university in the fall, but he still needs a humanities course to complete his basic requirements.
- His adviser suggests that he take a literature course that summer to meet the requirement, but the man wants to go sailing instead.
- His adviser suggests that he decide whether going sailing or going to the university is more important.
- His adviser suggests that he discuss the problem with his family and his friend.

4. Key points:
- Immunization works by strengthening the immune system against a specific disease in a much safer way than the disease process itself.
- Vaccines cause the body to produce antibodies against certain bacteria and viruses.
- Vaccines against bacterial diseases were developed after researchers discovered how to isolate bacteria and grow them in the laboratory; this led to vaccines against typhoid, cholera, tetanus, and tuberculosis.
- Vaccines against viruses were developed for smallpox, rabies, yellow fever, polio, and measles.
- Researchers developed the polio vaccine by cultivating viruses in the laboratory using animal tissues such as eggs.

Quiz 7 (p. 362)

1. Answers will vary.
2. Answers will vary.
3. Key points:
- The dean's office has proposed limiting the student course load to 20 credit hours per semester.
- The woman does not like the idea of limiting students to 20 credits per semester.
- One reason she gives is that twice she has taken more than 20 credits and did not have any problem finishing the work.
- Another reason is that she needs only 21 more credits to graduate and hopes to graduate this spring.
- Another reason is that if she has to take a class this summer, she will have to pay more tuition, and she does not want to ask her family for more money.

4. Key points:
- Forest fires and volcanic eruptions are both factors in climate change.
- Forest fires send chemicals into the air that might affect atmospheric chemistry in a manner similar to the effect of chemicals from volcanic eruptions.
- Like the ash from volcanic eruptions, the smoke from forest fires spreads over large areas and can reach the upper atmosphere.
- Unlike volcanic eruptions, outbreaks of forest fire can be controlled and reduced.

5. Key points:
- The man's problem is that he has trouble remembering the material from class, and he can't understand his notes when he looks at them later.
- The professor suggests that he review his lecture notes as soon as possible after class, when the material is still fresh in his mind.
- The professor suggests that he take a short nap or get a good night's sleep after studying because sleeping will help him remember what he just studied.

6. Key points:
- One way that manufacturers sell goods to consumers is direct sales. Direct sales take place in the customer's home or in a business setting. Examples are door–to–door sales, catalog shopping, telemarketing, and Internet shopping.
- Another way to sell goods is retail sales, which take place in stores. Examples are department stores, discount chains, supermarkets, hardware stores, car dealerships, drugstores, and convenience stores. Retail stores are a convenient way for consumers to buy.
- Another way to sell goods is wholesaling, where goods are sold at lower prices because customers buy in large quantities or in a low overhead setting. Examples are outlet stores and selling to retail stores. Wholesaling is the most practical method for the widespread distribution of goods.

QUIZ 8 (p. 366)

1. Answers will vary.
2. Answers will vary.
3. Key points:
    - One view of the counselor is that if an essay is required for a scholarship application, students should start writing it far in advance of the deadline because they will go crazy if they wait until the last minute.
    - Another view is that if an essay is not required, students should write one anyway because it will help the scholarship committee understand them more and may improve their chance of winning the scholarship.
    - Another view is that students should ask for recommendations from people who know them as an individual because the writers will be able to create a more complete picture of them.
    - Another view is that if recommendations are not required, students should get one or two anyway because they might be useful for future applications.
4. Key points:
    - The emergent quality of crowd behavior is the possibility that several different outcomes could emerge from the situation.
    - Expressive crowds show strong emotions, which can be either positive or negative; when emotions get out of hand, the crowd becomes out of control.
    - Demonstrations have rules of behavior but also an emergent aspect that makes them unpredictable.
    - Crowds have an emergent quality because there is a lack of certainty about what to do, which leads to a particular mood and a breaking of the rules.
5. Key points:
    - The woman's situation is that she has too much work to do. She has forty student papers to grade, and she also has to write a term paper and study for a big test.
    - The man suggests that she ask Doctor Carter for more time to grade the papers.
    - The man suggests that she ask her biology professor for more time to write her term paper.
    - The man suggests that she try her best to get all her work done by grading the student papers first and setting a time limit for each one.
6. Key points:
    - Sunlight provides the energy that drives ecosystems. Plants use sunlight directly in photosynthesis. The length of daylight is a signal for seasonal events such as the flowering of plants and the migration of birds.
    - Rainfall and temperature affect the plant community, which determines the availability of food, nest sites, and shelter for animals. Air temperature affects biological processes and the ability of organisms to regulate their body temperature.
    - Wind increases the effects of air temperature on organisms by increasing heat loss (wind chill). Wind causes water loss in animals and plants.
    - Rocks and soil limit the populations of plants and the animals that eat plants. Rocks and soil contribute to the irregular distribution of plants and animals in ecosystems.

PART 4 – WRITING

EXERCISE 4.1.A (p. 380)
Key points:
- Causes of corneal injuries include being hit in the eye and getting chemicals in the eye.
- Causes of corneal ulcers include injury, chronic dryness, infection, and nutritional deficiency.
- The injury called keratitis can result from wearing hard contact lenses for too long or by overexposure to ultraviolet light.
- Consequences include eye pain, sensitivity to light, bloodshot eyes, inflammation, scar tissue, and vision problems.
- Treatments include antibiotic ointment or drops, artificial tears, and wearing an eye patch.

EXERCISE 4.1.B (p. 381)
Key points:
- Tree topping creates more problems than it solves and is therefore not a good pruning practice.
- Topping speeds up the growth rate of branches; this is not a good pruning practice because it creates many weak branches instead of a few healthy ones.
- Topping is stressful for the tree and increases the risk of infection by diseases and insects; this is not a good pruning practice because the purpose of pruning is to improve the tree's health.
- Topping removes too many leaves, which are the tree's food source; this is not a good pruning practice because the tree might starve.
- Topping destroys the natural shape of the tree; this is not a good pruning practice because the purpose of pruning is to enhance the natural shape and beauty of the tree.

EXERCISE 4.2.A (p. 385)
Key points:
- The International style dominated the architecture of the modern city; this agrees with the points in the reading that the style reshaped the city and was one of the most successful architectural movements in history.
- The International style takes simplicity and "form follows function" to an extreme, leading to office buildings that are ugly, ridiculous, cheap, vulgar, and boring; this disagrees with the point in the reading that utilitarian simplicity is beautiful and elegant.
- The International style received much negative criticism from architects and the public; this disagrees with the point in the reading that the style inspired both architects and ordinary citizens.

EXERCISE 4.2.B (p. 386)
Key points:
- Past uses of geothermal energy include using hot water for bathing and cleansing, to treat disease, to heat buildings, and to generate electricity.
- Present uses of geothermal energy include the generation of electricity and the direct use of hot water for industrial processes, to heat buildings and greenhouses, and to supply heated mineral water for health resorts.
- Some regions have better potential for developing geothermal systems because they are geologically or volcanically active, the concentration of geothermal energy is very high, and geothermal reservoirs exist close to the surface.

EXERCISE 4.3.A (p. 393)

Key points:
- Workers have social and personal needs that go beyond economic concerns; this supports the point in the reading that traditional economic incentives such as pay and promotions are near the bottom of the list of what workers consider important.
- The small work group fills important social and emotional needs of workers; this supports the point in the reading that workers consider social and personal features of the workplace to be important.
- Workers deserve to have a voice in the decisions that affect them; this supports the point in the reading that the most satisfying jobs are those with a high level of autonomy.
- Workers need security and community in the workplace; this supports the point in the reading that workers value social and personal features of the workplace.
- Workers feel angry and alienated when they have no voice; this supports the point in the reading that alienation is a sense of powerlessness.

EXERCISE 4.3.B (p. 394)

Key points:
- Phrenology is no longer thought of as a real science; this refutes the point in the reading that many leading scientists supported its basic principles and attempted to advance it as a science.
- The size and shape of the skull is not a precise measure of a person's intellect or of the function of the brain; this refutes the point in the reading that, according to phrenology, the size and shape of the skull can determine a person's character and intellect.
- Different parts of the brain control distinct functions; this supports the point in the reading that the various mental processes are centered in specific parts of the brain.
- Humans have several different forms of mental powers, or multiple forms of intelligence; this supports the point in the reading where Gall claimed that humans had several different forms of power for each mental process (37 different mental powers).

EXERCISE 4.3.C (p. 395)

Key points:
- Méliès developed the special effect of stop action; this illustrates the point in the reading that Méliès realized that film could be manipulated in countless ways.
- Méliès introduced animation in *A Trip to the Moon*; this illustrates the point in the reading that Méliès saw film's possibilities for trickery and special effects.
- Méliès realized that scenes could be staged for the camera with the aid of scenery and costumes; this illustrates the point in the reading that Méliès transformed the cinema into a storytelling medium.
- Méliès extended the length of films by putting several scenes together; this illustrates the point in the reading that Méliès made longer films.

EXERCISE 4.4.A (p. 399)

1. The speaker talks about a maple tree that was topped. This is not a good pruning practice because topping causes a lot of damage to trees. The first reason is topping causes leaves and branches to grow fast. The growth rate of a tree speeds up when it is topped. Branches become crowded and dangerous and could crush a car. Another reason is topping removes too many leaves, which are the tree's food source. The tree will starve, and it is also more likely to be infected by disease. Topping causes a lot of stress for the tree; therefore, it is not a good pruning practice.

2. In the past, people used geothermal energy in several ways. Some examples are hot springs for bathing, treating disease, and heating buildings. Different tribes in North America called hot springs places of peace, where everybody could share the hot water for bathing. In European history, the Romans also used the water of hot springs for its healing power in eye and skin diseases. Geothermal energy was also used to heat homes in Rome and other places that were geologically active.

3. The professor made many points about the motivation and needs of workers that support points made in the reading. First, the professor said that the small work group, about 3 to 15 people with one leader, is important for workers. The work group fills needs of workers because they can participate and have a sense of respect. The small work group also gives workers the ability to make decisions. This point agrees with the reading, which said the most satisfying jobs are those with a high level of autonomy. This gives workers a voice so they can make their own decisions.

EXERCISE 4.5.A (p. 403)

Response A: Score: 5
The response effectively conveys relevant information from the lecture, including the following key points:
- Bacteria started becoming resistant to antibiotics soon after hospitals started using them regularly, increasing the risk of hospital infections; this differs from the point in the reading that antibiotics are "wonder drugs" that save lives.
- Bacteria became resistant to some antibiotics by evolving weapons against them; this differs from the point in the reading that antibiotics are powerful weapons against disease.
- A few cells of bacteria will survive an antibiotic, leading to new resistant strains; this differs from the point in the reading that antibiotics are "wonder drugs."
- One consequence of antibiotic resistance is the reappearance of dangerous diseases such as tuberculosis; this differs from the point in the reading that antibiotics reduced the number of deaths from tuberculosis.

The response accurately relates information from the lecture to that in the reading. It is well organized and coherent and contains only minor language errors.

Response B: Score: 3
The response contains some relevant information from the lecture, but some points are incomplete, inaccurate, or vague, particularly in the second and third paragraphs. The response contains errors of grammar and usage that result in vagueness of some content.

Response C: Score: 1
The response contains little relevant content from the lecture. It includes some information from the reading, but fails to connect points from the lecture and reading. It contains numerous language errors, such as run–on sentences and incorrect word forms, which greatly obscure meaning.

Response D: Score: 4
The response generally conveys relevant information from the lecture. It is generally good in relating information from the lecture to that in the reading, but some points are vague. The response is generally well organized. The grammar is generally accurate, but some minor language errors result in occasional lack of clarity.

Response E: Score: 2
The response contains some relevant information from the lecture but has significant omissions, such as an explanation of how bacteria became resistant to antibiotics. It contains language errors, such as incomplete sentences and incorrect word forms, which largely obscure the meaning of key ideas.

Quiz 1 (p. 407)
Key points:
- Scientists have always had a problem coming up with a reasonable definition of self–awareness; this contradicts the point in the reading that self–awareness is the same as self–recognition.
- Further use of the mark test with chimpanzees produced results that were inconsistent; this contradicts the point in the reading that the chimpanzees on average touched the marked spots seven times in a half–hour.
- All chimpanzees touch their heads and faces a lot; this contradicts the point in the reading that the chimpanzees touched the marked spots more often when the mirror was present.
- Some of the behaviors we call self–aware are also social responses that chimpanzees show in the presence of another chimpanzee; this contradicts the point in the reading that chimpanzees are self–aware because they are able to recognize the image in the mirror as their own.

Quiz 2 (p. 408)
Key points:
- An advantage of wind power is that it is a clean source of energy; this agrees with the point in the reading that wind power is clean, safe, and environmentally friendly.
- An advantage is that wind power is getting affordable enough to compete with inexpensive coal and oil; this agrees with the point in the reading that wind power is a promising energy resource that can serve as an alternative to electricity generated by fossil fuels.
- A disadvantage is that wind power would require large numbers of wind generators and large amounts of land to produce heat or electricity in useful amounts; this departs from the point in the reading that wind turbines could provide 20 percent of the electricity if they were installed on less than one percent of the land area in the United States.
- A disadvantage is that wind turbines kill a large number of birds; this departs from the point in the reading that wind power is safe and environmentally friendly.

Quiz 3 (p. 409)
Key points:
- Malthus predicted that the amount of food per person would decline as population increased, but his theory had several flaws.
- Malthus never predicted that advances in technology would greatly increase food production; this contradicts the point in the reading that food production tends to increase at an arithmetic rate.
- Malthus overlooked education and birth control as ways to lower population growth; this contradicts the point in the reading that the only checks on population growth are a limited food supply, disease, famine, and war.

Exercise 4.7.A (p. 419)
1. The question has two parts. The first part asks you to state whether you agree or disagree with the given statement. The second part asks you to support your opinion with specific reasons and examples.
2. Yes.
3. The essay is organized into an introduction, a body, and a conclusion. The two body paragraphs develop the two supporting points.
4. In the introduction, the writer states the thesis and previews the supporting points.
5. *It does not cost money to experience the best things in life: enjoying nature and being with our friends and family.*
6. The writer supports the thesis with two supporting points, which are developed in the body paragraphs with examples, reasons, and personal experience.
7. Body paragraph 1: *We can relax and enjoy the beauty of nature without spending money.* Body paragraph 2: *It does not cost money to spend time with our friends and family.*
8. Answers will vary, but may include the following: walking in the park; looking at the leaves; watching the snow falling; listening to the birds; having a garden; visiting friends; going to the library; reading; and spending time with family. Their purpose is to support and develop the thesis.
9. In the conclusion, the writer restates the thesis.
10. Answers will vary.

Exercise 4.8.A (p. 425)
1. The question asks you to do two things: (1) state your position on the given topic, and (2) support your choice with specific reasons and examples.
2. In the introduction, the writer restates the question and states the thesis of the essay.
3. *I prefer to learn by doing things because when I do something myself it becomes more real than when I read about it.*
4. The essay is organized into an introduction, a body, and a conclusion. The three body paragraphs develop the three supporting points.
5. Body paragraph 1: *I learned how to ride a bicycle and drive a car by experience.* Body paragraph 2: *Learning mathematics is another example of learning by doing things.* Body paragraph 3: *Finally, I learned how to use a computer by doing it.*
6. Answers will vary.
7. Answers will vary, but may include *or, because, and, also, similarly, although, another example, therefore, finally, but, however,* and *such as.*
8. Answers will vary.

EXERCISE 4.9.A (p. 430)

1.   I decided not to get married two years ago so I could finish my university studies. My father wanted me to get married, but my parents allowed me to decide. If I had married, I would have had to stay in my husband's home because in my culture, a married woman has a duty to her husband. It is our tradition. I chose to finish my degree instead. I will be a graduate student in Toronto, where I will earn my master's degree in business economics.

2.   I think students should have several short vacations throughout the year instead of one long vacation because they work hard and need breaks often. Students in my country have several short holidays during every season. In contrast, American students have one long vacation in the summer. I read a paper saying that American students forget what they learn because of the long vacation. This is why I believe several short vacations are better than one long vacation.

3.   There are many advantages in having friends that are different from me. For example, my friend from Turkey teaches me a lot about his culture. His family is very big, and my family is not big, so I like to go to his house to visit his family. I enjoy the good food and the conversation because it is really wonderful and interesting. Another friend is an artist who paints pictures and creates other art that is very good. My artist friend is not like me, and I learn interesting things about art from him.

EXERCISE 4.9.B (p. 431)

There are mainly two kinds of occupations. Some occupations require you to work primarily with machines, while others require you to work with other people. My job is working with machines, especially computers, so I prefer this kind of occupation.

Computers are important in our society. I am a computer programmer at a medical university, and I like to solve the problems of the medical record system. Computers have improved business, research, education, and many other fields of study. Many occupations require specialization in computers, so people need specialized training in an area of computer operations.

On the other hand, in some occupations you work mainly with people. This is also necessary for my job because I work on a team with two other people. Therefore, we must help each other solve problems.

In conclusion, I prefer working with machines because machines need people to operate them, and machines improve people's lives. Many occupations, such as computer programmer, require specialization but also the ability to communicate with other people. Therefore, I believe that working with both machines and people is the best kind of job.

EXERCISE 4.10.A (p. 436)

Response A: Score: 5
The essay effectively addresses the task by clearly stating the thesis. It is well organized and well developed with appropriate reasons and examples. The essay has unity and coherence, with appropriate use of transitions. There are only occasional minor language errors.

Response B: Score: 4
The essay addresses the task well, although the point in paragraph 3 is not fully elaborated. The thesis is clearly stated, and the essay is generally well organized and sufficiently developed. The essay has unity and coherence, with appropriate use of transitions, but there are noticeable minor language errors.

Response C: Score: 1
The essay is seriously disorganized and underdeveloped. The thesis is not clear, and the essay contains little detail that is relevant to the task.

Response D: Score: 2
The essay displays limited development in response to the task. The thesis is stated, but there is little organization. There are few connections among ideas to support the thesis. The essay also contains an accumulation of errors in grammar and usage.

Response E: Score: 3
The essay addresses the task by stating a thesis and developing it with some reasons and examples. There is some use of transitions, but connections among ideas are occasionally unclear. The essay contains errors in grammar and a limited range of sentence structures.

QUIZ 7 (p. 442)

Key points:
- A pictorial photograph is one with a successful composition; this illustrates the point in the reading that a pictorial photograph stands on its own as a valuable work of art.
- The important elements of composition are balance, placement, color, and detail; these illustrate the point in the reading that the rules of composition are guidelines that can help the beginning photographer.
- Everything in a photograph is an essential part of the composition, as imagined in a picture of a house on a cliff above the sea. This illustrates the point in the reading that composition is the organization of forms and colors within the frame of the picture.

QUIZ 8 (p. 444)

Key points:
- A child's choice of toys is a natural occurrence, not an example of sexist social conditioning; this disagrees with the point in the reading that boys and girls are taught gender "rules" through social conditioning.
- Younger children of both sexes play with both dolls and trucks; this disagrees with the point in the reading that toys are tools that condition children to learn gender roles and accept these roles as normal.
- Around age five, most children will say that a certain toy is either for girls or for boys; this agrees with the point in the reading that clearly separate classes of toys exist for girls and boys.
- Most boys and girls are naturally drawn to different types of toys, no matter what their parents and society teach them; this disagrees with the point in the reading that children learn their culture's gender rules from adults, media images, and the toys they are given to play with.

TEST 1

READING (p. 447)

1. **C** Clues: *For theater, it is a story performed by actors on a stage; The basic encounter in theater is between the performers and the audience.* (1.1)

2. **B** Clues: *...there is an important difference between the two forms. Unlike a novel, a play is written to be performed, and the script of a play...is an outline for a performance.* (1.1)

3. **D** *This combination of elements* is paraphrased in *the way it joins characters and audience in the telling of a story. Distinguishes theater from other art forms* is paraphrased in *Theater is a distinct art form.* (1.7)

4. **B** The author's purpose is to give an example of a play in which abstract ideas are characters. Clues: *...even when the performers play animals, objects, or abstract ideas. In the medieval play -----, some of the roles are abstract ideas....* (1.6)

5. **B** The referent of *theme* is something that is universal to humans. The sentence introduces the idea of death arriving before we want it to come. Logic tells you that *theme* refers to *death arriving before we want it to come.* (1.3)

6. **C** *Urge* means *motivation* in this context. Clues: *...the impulse toward theater is universal. Every human society has the motivation to create theater.* (1.4)

7. **A** *Realm* means *form* in this context. Clues: *...developed into a separate ----- of theater; ...theater has become a separate art form....* (1.4)

8. **D** You can infer that theater emerged as a distinct art form at different times around the world. Clues: *At various times, these ceremonies and stories developed into a separate realm of theater; In Greece...almost 2,500 years ago; In India...around 2,000 years ago.* (1.5)

9. **A** *Transitory* means *temporary* in this context. Clues: *In the theater, we live in the perpetual present tense; A performance changes from moment to moment...; Theater occurs through time...;* the prefix *trans–* = across. (1.4)

10. **C** Clues: *The performing arts...are not objects but events. Theater occurs through time....* (1.1)

11. **B** The passage does not state that the medium of theater is written language; that is the medium of literature. All the other answers are given: *...theater is universal—there is an impulse toward creating theater in all societies; This combination of elements distinguishes theater from other art forms; The focus of drama is on human beings....* (1.2)

12. **D** In the added sentence, *Thus* is a transition that shows result. It links the idea that *a story...is presented by one group...to another group* in the previous sentence with the idea that *theater is a shared event* that includes *those who perform and those who observe* in the added sentence. (1.8)

13–14. **B, D, F** Key information: *...a story performed by actors on a stage...The basic encounter in theater is between the performers and the audience...the characters are part of a human story...; ...theater is universal— there is an impulse toward creating theater in all societies...The urge to create drama has existed wherever human society has developed...; Theater is a transitory art. A performance changes from moment to moment, and each moment is a direct, immediate adventure for the audience.* Answers (A) and (E) are minor ideas; answer (C) is not mentioned. (1.9)

15. **A** *Suspended* means *hanging* in this context. Clues: *A cloud...in the atmosphere above the earth's surface...;* the prefix *sus–* = below. (1.4)

16. **C** *Laboratory studies have demonstrated* is paraphrased in *Research shows. In clean air—air free of dust and other particles—condensation or deposition of water vapor* is paraphrased in *the formation of clouds in clean air. Requires supersaturated conditions, that is, a relative humidity greater than 100 percent* is paraphrased in *depends on a relative humidity of over 100 percent.* (1.7)

17. **D** Clues: *...dew point, the temperature at which the invisible water vapor in the air condenses....* (1.1)

18. **A** The author's purpose is to identify the inventor of our system for classifying clouds. Clues: *...among the first to devise a system for grouping clouds; ...the essentials of Howard's classification scheme are still in use today.* (1.6)

19. **B** The referent of *Those* is something that has vertical development. The subject of the previous two sentences is *clouds*. Logic tells you that *Those* refers to *clouds.* (1.3)

20. **C** Cumulus clouds are not characterized by stable air; that is a characteristic of stratus clouds. All the other answers are characteristics of cumulus clouds: *...the base is...roughly horizontal; ...capped with a cauliflower–like dome...; Low–level cumulus clouds....* (1.2)

21. **A** *Sharp* means *distinct* in this context. Clues: *...detached from one another...; ...well–defined bases....* (1.4)

22. **D** You can infer that stratus clouds differ from cumulus clouds in appearance. Clues: *Cumulus clouds occur as heaps or puffs, stratus clouds are layered...; Stratus, or layered, clouds grow from top to bottom in wide sheets...; ...like a formless blanket....* (1.5)

23. **B** Clues: *...cirrus clouds look like threads; Cirrus clouds are detached clouds that take the form of delicate white filaments, strands, or hooks; ...bands of threadlike cirrus clouds...spread across the entire sky.* (1.1)

24. **C** *Fibrous* means *threadlike* in this context. Clues: *...cirrus clouds look like threads; ....take the form of delicate white filaments, strands...; ...bands of threadlike cirrus clouds...; ...streamers....* (1.4)

25. **D** In the added sentence, *These strands* refers to *feathery strands called "mares' tails"* in the previous sentence. (1.8)

26–28. C, E, G Heaped clouds: *...they often develop vertically in the form of rising puffs, mounds, domes, or towers; ...heaped clouds, resulting from rising unstable air currents...; ...white, heaped clouds capped with a cauliflower–like dome...The sunlit parts are brilliant white; the base is relatively dark and roughly horizontal.*

A, F Layered clouds: *...layered clouds, resulting from stable air...The air is stable, with little or no convection present; These clouds spread laterally to form layers that sometimes cover the entire sky...like a formless blanket.* Answer (B) describes raindrops; answer (D) describes cirrus clouds. (1.10)

29. A *Shoals* means *shallows* in this context. Clues: *...a series of shallow areas....* (1.4)

30. B Clues: *...the Grand Banks...where the warm waters of the Gulf Stream meet the cold waters of the Labrador Current. As the currents brush each other....* (1.1)

31. B *This rich environment* is paraphrased in *The Grand Banks...favorable natural conditions. Has produced cod by the millions and once had a greater density of cod than anywhere else on Earth* is paraphrased in *used to have the world's largest concentration of cod.* (1.7)

32. D The referent of *the region* is someplace where settlers used to think the only sea creature worth talking about was cod. The previous two sentences and the following sentence discuss the cod fishery in Newfoundland. Logic tells you that *the region* refers to *Newfoundland.* (1.3)

33. C The author's purpose is to stress the economic and cultural significance of cod. Clues: *...the entire Newfoundland economy was based on...catching fish...; ...the only sea creature worth talking about was cod...; ...a pudding whose main ingredient was cod.* (1.6)

34. C The passage does not state that fishers competed with farmers for natural resources. All the other answers are given: *...controlled by merchants based in the capital...This system kept the fishers in a continuous state of debt and dependence on the merchants; ...the entire Newfoundland economy was based on Europeans arriving, catching fish... and then taking fish back to European markets; Cod laid out to dry on wooden "flakes"....* (1.2)

35. C *Replenish* means *restock* in this context. Clues: *...fishers believed in the cod's ability to ----- itself and thought that overfishing was impossible;* the prefix *re–* = again. (1.4)

36. A Clues: *Until the twentieth century, fishers...thought that overfishing was impossible. However, Newfoundland's cod fishery began to show signs of trouble during the 1930s, when cod failed to support the fishers and thousands were unemployed.* (1.1)

37. A Clues: *...when an international agreement in 1977 established the 200–mile offshore fishing limit, the Canadian government decided to build up the modern Grand Banks fleet and make fishing a viable economic base for Newfoundland again.* (1.1)

38. D *Commanding* means *receiving* in this context. Clues: *...the conglomerate was prospering, and cod were ----- excellent prices in the market.* (1.4)

39. B You can infer that the author believes it may be a long time before cod stocks recover from overfishing. Clues: *Today, cod stocks are at historically low levels and show no signs of imminent recovery...; ...no one can predict whether and when the cod will return to the Grand Banks.* (1.5)

40. A In the added sentence, *They* refers to *inshore fishermen*, the main subject of the previous sentence. The added sentence develops the idea of *catches dropping off*, mentioned in the previous sentence, by discussing a possible reason for this. (1.8)

41–42. A, C, E Key information: *This rich environment has produced cod by the millions and once had a greater density of cod than anywhere else on Earth; Until the twentieth century, fishers believed in the cod's ability to replenish itself and thought that overfishing was impossible...Newfoundland's cod fishery began to show signs of trouble...when cod failed to support the fishers...; Today, cod stocks are at historically low levels and show no signs of imminent recovery, even after drastic conservation measures and severely limited fishing.* Answers (B) and (D) are minor ideas; answer (F) is not mentioned. (1.9)

LISTENING (p. 460)

1. D The woman is requesting an interview with the dean. The woman says: *Our class is doing a radio program, and we'll have interviews with a lot of people from all parts of campus life. We'd like to interview the new Dean of Students, if he's willing.* (2.3)

2. C The man's purpose is to let the woman know that the dean is very busy and that his schedule is already full. (2.3)

3. A The woman says: *I hope Dean Evans will agree to meet with us.... It would be a way for the whole community to get to know him, get to know his ideas and everything...like the kind of vision he has for the university.* (2.2)

4. B The woman says: *This will be a great way for everyone to learn about our new dean.* You can infer that the dean has been dean for only a short time. (2.4)

5. C The meeting will take place in two weeks, the week after next week. The man says: *...it looks like he's got a lot of meetings this week, and, well, most of next week, too. What about the week after that?* The woman says: *Um, yeah, I think so.* (2.2)

6. B The students are mainly discussing the concept of opportunity cost. The woman says: *Let's start with "opportunity cost."* The man says: *Opportunity cost—that's when...; You have an opportunity cost when....; This is the opportunity cost....* (2.1)

7. A The man illustrates the concept with an example. The man says: *Say you want to have your own business, so you, so you open a restaurant.* He then explains how the concept of opportunity cost applies in the restaurant example. (2.1)

8. C The man's purpose is to suggest that the restaurant's profit is less than it seems because of the opportunity cost. (2.3)

9. D   The man says: *...an economist tries to look at all the factors, all the costs; An economist's definition of costs is broader than an accountant's.* (2.2)

10. A   The woman says: *...it's more than what we pay for tuition and books! We have to subtract the income we lose by not working full time.* You can infer that the true cost of a college education includes the cost of lost income. (2.4)

11. A   The professor says: *The eruption cycle had sort of a harmless beginning. In March of 1980, seismologists picked up signs of earthquake activity below the mountain. And during the next week, the earthquakes increased rapidly, causing several avalanches.* (2.2)

12. C   The professor's purpose is to show that the eruptions interested a lot of people, including tourists and hikers who were not scientists. (2.3)

13. D   The professor means that the small eruptions paused briefly just before the major eruption. There were a few days with no volcanic activity, and then the major eruption occurred. (2.4)

14. ✓   Yes: An earthquake caused a huge landslide: *The earthquake triggered a massive landslide that carried away huge quantities of rock.*
   ✓   No: The mountain gained sixty feet in height: Not supported by the information in the lecture.
   ✓   Yes: Ash and steam rose from the mountain: *...pouring out more ash, steam....*
   ✓   Yes: The mountain's side and top exploded: *...the north side of the mountain was blown away. Then, the top of the mountain went too....* (2.6)

15. B, C   One effect of the eruption was that large numbers of animals and people were killed: *The blast killed the mountain's goats, millions of fish and birds, thousands of deer and elk—and around sixty people.* Another effect was that an ash cloud affected weather around the world: *The ash cloud drifted around the world, disrupting global weather patterns.* (2.2)

16. D   The professor says: *...geologists who've studied the mountain believe she won't stay asleep forever. The Cascade Range is volcanically active. Future eruptions are certain and—unfortunately—we can't prevent them.* You can conclude that Mount St. Helens is likely to erupt in the future. (2.4)

17. C   The speaker says: *When European explorers first approached the coast of North America, ...the first thing they noticed was the pungent aroma...; ...the agreeable smells didn't come from spices; they came from the lush vegetation of the North American forests.* (2.2)

18. A   The speaker says: *Pine sap was a valuable commodity to the sailors who explored the coast; ...what were known as naval stores—pitch and pine tar; Sailors used naval stores for caulking and waterproofing their wooden ships, which kept them seaworthy.* (2.2)

19. C   The speaker says: *The Native Americans already knew about the medicinal properties of the dogwood, and they used its bark and roots to treat malaria and other fevers; European settlers also used the dogwood to relieve attacks of malaria.* (2.2)

20. C   The speaker wants the students to smell a piece of wood after scraping it with their thumbnail to release the scent. The speaker says: *I have a sassafras twig with me here, which I'll pass around so you can all enjoy its smell.* (2.3)

21. D   The speaker says: *Other Native American tribes used sassafras tonic as a cure for everything from fever to stomachache; For centuries, sassafras enjoyed a fantastic reputation as a cure for almost every disease.* (2.2)

22. B   The speaker says: *...sassafras has been banned for human consumption.* The speaker implies that sassafras is no longer a legal medicine. (2.4)

23. D   The professor mainly discusses Plato's views on education. Key sentences: *Plato believed the state should take an active role in education...the state should create a curriculum that leads students from thinking about concrete information toward thinking about abstract ideas; Plato believed our most important goal was the search for truth.* (2.1)

24. B   The professor's purpose is to give an example of a lasting truth. The professor says: *Plato believed the only true reality consists of ideas; For instance, the mathematical concept of two plus two equals four— this is an idea that's always existed.* (2.3)

25. A, C   Idealists believe that higher-level thinking develops a person's character and benefits the whole society: *Higher-level thinking would develop the individual student's character, and thus ultimately benefit the larger society.* (2.2)

26. A   The woman thinks that the idealist view of education does not give students useful knowledge. The woman says: *But isn't that kind of impractical? I mean, most of us go to college because we want knowledge about certain subjects, not the whole universe.* (2.3)

27. C   The professor means that idealism has diminished in influence. The professor says: *...it's questions like this that have led to a weakening of idealism today. He says that developments in science and technology have changed our way of thinking about what is true.* (2.4)

28. B   The professor says: *Critics of idealism would agree with you that "character development" comes at the expense of creativity, and that too much emphasis on traditional values can be harmful—if it makes students stop questioning what they're being taught.* (2.2)

29. D   The professor says: *In physics, work means moving an object when there is some resistance to its movement. Every time we lift an object, push it, pull it, or carry it, we are doing work.* (2.2)

30. B   The professor's purpose is to explain what happens when a moving object meets resistance. The plow meets resistance in the soil, requiring the tractor's engine to use more energy. (2.3)

31. ✓   Yes: Electricity can be converted to heat or light: *Energy comes in several different forms. It can take the form of heat, light, motion, electricity, chemical energy, nuclear energy, and so on. Energy can change forms....*
   ✓   Yes: The amount of energy in any system stays the same: *The law of conservation of energy tells us that the energy of any system...must balance out in the end. The amount of energy in the system is conserved....*
   ✓   No: Nuclear energy is regulated by international law: Not supported by the information in the talk. (2.4)

32. A, C   A car changing chemical energy to motion illustrates the conversion of energy from one form to another: *Machines do work by converting one form of energy to another. For example, a car converts the chemical energy in gasoline to kinetic energy—to motion.* An electric stove converting electricity to heat is another illustration: *A stove converts electrical energy or chemical energy into heat energy that cooks our food.* (2.2)

33. D   The professor's purpose is to show that both machines and living things need energy. Both must convert one form of energy to another in order to work. If there is no energy, the machine stops or the organism dies. (2.3)

34. C   The professor says: *The first law of thermodynamics—conservation of energy—says the earth must end up with the same amount of energy it started out with. The energy changes forms, but no energy is lost or gained.* You can infer that in the earth as a whole system, no new energy is created, and no energy is destroyed. (2.4)

SPEAKING (p. 466)

1. Answers will vary.
2. Answers will vary.
3. Key points:
   • The man is thinking of registering for an online course.
   • The adviser's opinion about online courses is that they are not right for all students.
   • One reason she gives is that online courses require students to be self–motivated and able to learn on their own, mainly by reading.
   • Another reason is that online courses have a fairly high dropout rate.
   • Another reason is that some students prefer going to class and interacting face–to–face with the professor and other students.
4. Key points:
   • Corporations are similar to any other culture because they have values, norms, rituals, symbols, and texts.
   • Corporate culture gives meaning to the daily activities of the company.
   • Corporations have norms that regulate behavior, maintain order, and establish conventions such as clothing styles and business hours.
   • Well–established companies have traditional corporate cultures.
   • Many new technology firms have very informal cultures with no fixed traditions to follow.
5. Key points:
   • The man's problem is that he is concerned about his grade for his geology course, but he does not have enough time to study because he has to work more hours at his job.
   • The woman suggests that he get a tutor.
   • The woman suggests that he quit his job or look for a different job.
   • The woman suggests that he drop the geology course and take it again next quarter.

6. Key points:
   • Ocean water is clear when there are no particles suspended in it, so light is able to pass through.
   • Some water is green because of a mixture of blue light from scattered sunlight and yellow pigment from phytoplankton, the floating plant life.
   • Some water is brown or brownish–red because of the presence of large quantities of brown algae, which contain brown pigments.
   • Some water is blue because of the scattering of sunlight by tiny particles in the water; blue light is distributed easily because it has a short wavelength.

WRITING (p. 471)

1. Key points:
   • The reasons for traveling have changed; in the past, peopled traveled for political or economic purposes; in modern times, people travel for personal enrichment and adventure. This is similar to the point in the reading that the earliest tourists traveled in search of resources, while later tourists traveled for cultural, educational, and scientific purposes.
   • Hemingway illustrates the conquest ideal in tourism and was very influential. This is similar to the point in the reading that Hemingway exposed people to the possibilities of journeying to faraway lands for adventure.
   • Ethnic tourism is a new kind of cultural tourism in which tourists learn about aboriginal cultures. This is similar to the point in the reading that young Europeans took "grand tours" to expand their cultural horizons; it also differs because the European example occurred in the seventeenth century rather than in the present.
   • Environmental tourism is traveling to wilderness areas to observe, photograph, and learn about nature. This is similar to the point in the reading that people traveled to observe and preserve the natural world; it also differs from the point in the reading that people traveled to hunt and kill big game.

TEST 2

READING (p. 475)

1. **B** *Abolish* means *end* in this context. Clues: *...objected to slavery...; ...wanted to ----- the institution; ...Canada passed a law abolishing slavery and declared that any escaped slaves who came to Canada would be free citizens*; the prefix *ab–* = away. (1.4)

2. **D** Clues: *In 1793, Canada passed a law abolishing slavery and declared that any escaped slaves who came to Canada would be free citizens.* (1.1)

3. **C** The referent of *The term* is something that was first used in the 1830s. The previous sentence introduces the topic of the Underground Railroad and defines its meaning. Logic tells you that *The term* refers to *Underground Railroad*. (1.3)

4. **D** *Because the Underground Railroad was so secret* is paraphrased in *it was a secret organization. Few records exist that would reveal the true number of people who traveled it to freedom* is paraphrased in *We do not know exactly how many slaves escaped on the Underground Railroad.* (1.7)

5. **C** *Fugitives* means *runaways* in this context. Clues: *Runaway slaves...; ...hid in wagons...; ...traveled on foot...; ...escaped...* (1.4)

6. **C** The passage does not mention riding in a railcar as a method of escape on the Underground Railroad. All the other answers are mentioned: *The fugitives hid in wagons under loads of hay...; Boys disguised themselves as girls, and girls dressed as boys; ...twenty–eight slaves escaped by walking in a funeral procession....* (1.2)

7. **B** The author's purpose is to illustrate the secret nature of the escape network. Clues: *...the Underground Railroad was so secret...; ...developed its own language; ...elude the slave hunters; ...hiding places...; ...slaves who dared to run away and break for liberty.* (1.6)

8. **A** *Elude* means *avoid* in this context. Clues: *...backcountry roads that were used to ----- the slave hunters; ...hiding places....* The runaway slaves had to avoid being caught by the slave hunters. (1.4)

9. **A** Clues: *...the Underground Railroad, a loosely organized system whereby runaway slaves were passed from safe house to safe house as they fled northwards to free states or Canada.* (1.1)

10. **C** Clues: *...Harriet Tubman, a former slave who dedicated her life to helping other runaways. Tubman made 19 trips into the South to guide 300 relatives, friends, and strangers to freedom.* (1.1)

11. **D** You can infer that the author believes the railroad represented a psychological victory for abolitionists. Clues: *...the few thousand slaves who made their way to freedom in this way each year had a symbolic significance...; ...slavery in the United States was finally abolished in 1865.* (1.5)

12. **A** The added sentence adds the example of women and children escaping, which logically follows the example of young men given in the previous sentence. (1.8)

13–14. **B, D, E** Key information: *The abolitionist movement...objected to slavery on moral grounds...The American antislavery movement was at the height of its activity during the 1800s, when abolitionists developed the Underground Railroad...; ...a loosely organized system whereby runaway slaves were passed from safe house to safe house as they fled northwards to free states or Canada...hiding places where the slaves were fed and cared for...; The "agents" were the people who planned the escape routes..."conductors" were the fearless men and women who led the slaves toward freedom..."passengers" were the slaves who dared to run away and break for liberty.* Answer (A) is not mentioned; answers (C) and (F) are minor ideas. (1.9)

15. **A** *Recurrent* means *repeating* in this context. Clues: *...the alternating rise and fall...; ...cycle of the tides*; the prefix *re–* = again. (1.4)

16. **D** Clues: *The force that generates tides results from the interaction of two forces: the centrifugal force...and the gravitational attraction of the moon acting upon the earth's waters.* (1.1)

17. **D** Clues: *...the moon's closer distance outranks its much smaller mass, and thus the moon's tide–raising force is more than twice that of the sun.* (1.1)

18. **C** *Bulges* means *increases* in this context. Clues: *...a maximum accumulation of the waters of the oceans at two opposite positions on the earth's surface.* The increase in water level in two opposite positions on the earth results in high tides in those places. (1.4)

19. **B** You can infer that when it is high tide in some places, it is low tide in other places. Clues: *...a maximum accumulation of the waters of the oceans at two opposite positions on the earth's surface. At the same time, compensating amounts of water are drawn from all points 90 degrees away....* (1.5)

20. **A** Clues: *A spring tide occurs...when the moon and earth are lined up with the sun, and thus the moon's pull is reinforced by the sun's pull.* (1.1)

21. **C** *Counteract* means *oppose* in this context. Clues: *...the gravitational forces of the moon and sun ----- each other; thus, the moon's pull is at minimum strength...*; the prefix *counter–* = against; the prefix *op–* = against. (1.4)

22. **A** *Spring...tides...have a range of about 20 percent more* is paraphrased in *Spring tides are 20 percent more. Neap tides...have a range of about 20 percent...less, respectively, than the average high tide* is paraphrased in *neap tides 20 percent less, than the average high tide. At any given location* is paraphrased in *in a particular place.* (1.7)

23. **C** The author's purpose is to give the most extreme example of a tidal range. Clues: *The vertical range of tides...varies according to the size, surface shape, and bottom topography...; Along the narrow channel of the ----- in Nova Scotia, the difference between high and low tides may reach 45 feet under spring tide conditions—the world's widest tidal range.* (1.6)

24. **A** *Prolonged* means *extended* in this context. Clues: *...periods...*; the prefix *pro–* = forward. (1.4)

25. C The passage does not mention increasing levels of pollution in the oceans as an influence on the vertical range of tides. All the other answers are mentioned: *The vertical range of tides…varies according to the size, surface shape…of the basin in which tidal movement occurs; Several factors affect tidal ranges, including abrupt changes in atmospheric pressure…; They are also influenced by…the growing or shrinking of the world's glaciers.* (1.2)

26. B In the added sentence, *yet another factor* is a transition that adds an example of factors that affect tidal ranges, which the previous two sentences discuss. (1.8)

27–28. C, D, F Key information: *Tides…caused by the gravitational pull of the moon and the sun. The combination of these two variable forces produces the complex recurrent cycle of the tides; The highest and lowest levels of high tide, called spring tide and neap tide, each occur twice in every lunar month…; The vertical range of tides…varies according to the size, surface shape, and bottom topography of the basin… Several factors affect tidal ranges, including abrupt changes in atmospheric pressure… the density and volume of seawater, variations in ocean–current velocities, earthquakes, and the growing or shrinking of the world's glaciers.* Answers (A) and (E) are minor ideas; answer (B) is not mentioned. (1.9)

29. A *Thrust* means *movement* in this context. Clues: *…toward a style…; …endorsing an American architecture…; …developed regional styles….* (1.4)

30. D Clues: *Her Lookout Studio…appears to rise straight from the rim of the Grand Canyon…; …she wanted the building to be a part of its environment…; Like Mary Colter, Frank Lloyd Wright believed that architecture was an extension of the natural environment; Wright's own studio–residence in Wisconsin was completely integrated with the surrounding landscape.* (1.1)

31. C Clues: *Colter created a uniquely Southwestern idiom…; She preferred to use materials indigenous to the region, such as Kaibab limestone and yellow pine.* (1.1)

32. A *She took great stock in materials and setting* is paraphrased in *Colter valued materials and location. Gathering many of her materials on–site* is paraphrased in *many natural materials collected from the building site. Incorporating them in their natural state into her projects* is paraphrased in *she blended into her works many natural materials.* (1.7)

33. C The referent of *them* is something that Mary Colter merged seamlessly. The sentence states that Colter treated building and site as integral halves of a single composition. Logic tells you that *them* refers to *building and site.* (1.3)

34. B Clues: *The ancient Round Tower at Mesa Verde became the direct inspiration for the form and proportions of the Watchtower.* (1.1)

35. B You can infer that the Watchtower's purpose was to help people appreciate the desert scenery. Clues: *Her magnificent Watchtower, overlooking the Grand Canyon in Arizona, was built to suggest an ancient Native American ruin preserved for the delight of the present–day traveler; …enhancing the view of the surrounding desert and the canyon and river below.* (1.5)

36. B The passage does not state that a direct reference to the region's history characterizes the Prairie style of architecture. All the other answers are given: *Every element of the design corresponded to the surrounding landscape; …the Prairie style of residential architecture, whose emphasis on horizontal elements…; The eaves of the low–pitched roof extend well beyond the walls, enhancing the structure's horizontality.* (1.2)

37. A *Nestled* means *set comfortably* in this context. Clues: *…integrated with the surrounding landscape; …in the brow of a hill….* (1.4)

38. D The author's purpose is to show that Wright did not work in just one style. Clues: *…yet it departs from the Prairie philosophy….* (1.6)

39. B The added sentence develops the topic of Taliesin, mentioned in the previous sentence. The added sentence discusses the idea of blurring the distinction between the manmade and the natural, which the rest of the paragraph develops with examples. (1.8)

40–42. C, E, G Mary Colter: *Colter created a uniquely Southwestern idiom incorporating desert landscapes with Native American arts… Colter's integration of history, architecture, and landscape in a unified work of art; She decided to recreate a Native American watchtower… The ancient Round Tower at Mesa Verde became the direct inspiration…; She treated building and site as integral halves of a single composition and merged them seamlessly. Her Lookout Studio…appears to rise straight from the rim of the Grand Canyon….*

A, D Frank Lloyd Wright: *Wright and his followers in Chicago developed the Prairie style of domestic architecture that reflected the natural landscape of the Midwest; …his favorite commissions were for homes, usually in the country.* Answer (B) is not mentioned; answer (F) is inaccurate for both Mary Colter and Frank Lloyd Wright. (1.10)

Listening (p. 488)

1. C The students are mainly discussing the woman's interest in an internship. The woman says: *I'm hoping to do something in the arts, maybe some sort of work experience or internship.* The man says: *What do you have in mind; It sounds like you need to be a theater intern.* (2.1)

2. D The woman says: *It's the whole atmosphere of theater that I find exciting.* (2.2)

3. C The woman thinks she is not very skilled at acting. She says: *…I took drama in high school, but I was awful on stage.* (2.3)

4. B The man's purpose is to learn more about the woman's interests in theater, specifically whether directing or lighting interests her. (2.3)

5. A, D   The man suggests that the woman talk to her adviser: *Better go see your adviser about this.* He also suggests that she write to the theater: *...what I did—how I got started was, ...just sent formal letters of introduction; It's worth a try, isn't it?* (2.4)

6. B   The student wants to discuss an idea for a paper. The student says: *...just an idea I have. I've been thinking—um, I was reading about what's been going on with those houses on Fox Point; ...I was sort of thinking I could write a paper on it.* (2.3)

7. A   The man is mainly interested in some houses that are sliding. The man says: *...I was reading about what's been going on with those houses on Fox Point; ...I was sort of thinking I could write a paper on it.* (2.1)

8. B   The student thinks the local slide may have a similar cause to that of the Leaning Tower of Pisa, which was caused by settlement. The student says: *I thought maybe...the slide on Fox Point was a case of subsidence...when the earth sinks 'cause there's a weakening of support. I was thinking this might be an example of settlement.* (2.3)

9. B   The professor says: *Mudslides are most common on intermediate slopes—27 to 45 degrees....* (2.2)

10. C, D   You can predict that the man will include in his research a study of the area's geology: *One suggestion I have is to take a look at the county's Web site. There's a page on the geology of the region.* You can also predict that he will include a search for other mudslides in the area: *This area has a history of slides. There was one on Johnson Island about ten, twelve years ago.* (2.4)

11. B, C   The class discusses the organs of a flower: *...its four organs are arranged in four whorls...; ...let's quickly go over the four parts of the flower.* The class also discusses the composite family of flowers: *The large composite family, for example...; ...in the composite family, there are about 19,000 different species worldwide.* (2.1)

12. B   The student says: *The petals, the colorful part of the flower. It's the petals that make the flower attractive to insects and birds....* (2.2)

13. D   The professor's purpose is to imply that the student will see examples of this type of flower in the lab, and that seeing the flowers will help clarify the point. (2.3)

14. B   The professor says: *The large composite family...have flower heads that form a central disk; The flower head—the center part of the plant—actually consists of many tiny, tightly packed complete flowers that stand upright on a flat disk; The petals—what look like petals—are actually larger flowers called rays that extend from the rim of the disk.* (2.2)

15. ✓   True: Incomplete flowers do not have all four basic flower organs: *...incomplete flowers—those lacking one or more of the four floral parts.*
   ✓   Not true: The sunflower has one large symmetrical flower on its stalk: *...a single sunflower is really hundreds of flowers put together.*
   ✓   Not true: All varieties of the English daisy are white with a yellow center: *The English daisy comes in lots of colors—rose, lavender, pink, and white.*
   ✓   True: The arrangement of flowers on the stalk can help identify the plant's family: *One important element in plant classification is the arrangement of flowers on their stalks.* (2.4)

16. B   The professor says: *The word "daisy" means "day's eye" and comes from an older Anglo–Saxon word. The English daisy folds up its rays at night and unfolds them again at dawn—the "eye of the day" or "day's eye."* (2.2)

17. C   The main idea is that sports contain many elements of hunting. Key phrases: *...the ancient pattern of killing prey is kept alive...; Think of how many Olympic sports there are that involve aiming, throwing, and running—which are all hunting skills; In some sports, there's still a strong symbolic element of the kill.* (2.1)

18. D   The professor's purpose is to encourage the student to elaborate, to give a more detailed answer. (2.3)

19. A   The professor says: *The ancient Romans brought the hunt to the people by confining it to an arena—the Coliseum. The Coliseum made the hunting field smaller, and this sort of intensified the activity for the entertainment of the spectators.* (2.2)

20. D   The professor says: *Take track and field sports. These don't involve animals, but they did originate in hunting; Think of how many Olympic sports there are that involve aiming, throwing, and running—which are all hunting skills.* (2.2)

21. A, D   Fencing and boxing contain a symbolic element of the kill. The professor says: *In some sports, there's still a strong symbolic element of the kill. Wrestling, boxing, fencing, martial arts—all these are examples of ritualized fighting.* (2.2)

22. B   The professor says: *Because sports contain such a powerful negative element, most have an ideal of acceptable behavior—something we call "sportsmanship."* The professor implies that the concept of sportsmanship makes sports less negative. (2.4)

23. C   The speaker mainly discusses how epidemiologists gather data. Key phrases: *We use statistical analyses, field investigations, and a range of laboratory techniques; We gather data in a variety of ways. One way is through what we call descriptive epidemiology...; A second approach is observational epidemiology...; A third approach is experimental epidemiology....* (2.1)

24. A, C   Epidemiologists study what causes outbreaks of a disease: *We try to determine the cause and distribution of a disease.* They also study how diseases spread through populations: *We also look at how quickly the disease spreads—and by what method....* (2.2)

25–26. ✓ Descriptive: Statistics are used to describe the trend of a disease over time: ...*descriptive epidemiology, or looking at the trends of diseases over time...; Statistics are important in descriptive epidemiology....*

✓ Experimental: Researchers intervene to test a hypothesis about cause and effect: ...*experimental epidemiology, sometimes called an intervention study. Experimental research is the best way to establish cause–and–effect relationships...; ...a way to test a hypothesis about cause and effect.*

✓ Observational: Researchers examine the eating habits of sick and well people: ...*observational epidemiology, where we observe what people do. We take a group of people who have a disease and a group of people who don't have a disease. We look at their patterns of eating....*

✓ Experimental: A treatment group is compared with a non–treatment group: ...*experimental studies...we study treatment and non–treatment groups and then compare the outcomes.* (2.5)

27. A The speaker says: *We take a group of people who have a disease and a group of people who don't have a disease; We also take a group of people who've been exposed to something...and a group of people who haven't, and then observe them over time to see whether they develop a disease or not.* (2.2)

28. A The speaker's purpose is to show how one organization uses various approaches to epidemiology. The speaker says: *From these different approaches— descriptive, observational, and experimental—we can judge whether a particular factor causes or prevents the disease that we're looking at.* (2.3)

29. D The professor says: *A child's first experience with playing an instrument should be by ear, without the distraction of printed music.* (2.2)

30. B The professor's purpose is to introduce the main point he wants to make about when and how children should learn to read music. (2.3)

31. B, C The professor says children should learn to read musical notation when a group of children play music together: *A good time to teach notation is when a group of children play together. The printed score is a way to help them sort of keep track of who plays what and when.* Also, they should learn how to read when the music is too complex to learn by ear: *Another good time is when the child wants to play music that's so complex it would be difficult to learn by ear.* (2.2)

32. A The professor says: *The teacher should play the score for the child the first time through, and demonstrate how the notes on the page are transformed into music.* (2.2)

33. B–C–A The professor says: *(1) Playing by ear is the natural beginning for children; (2) ...a natural first step toward reading music is playing by chord symbols; (3) After children can play by ear, and then by chord symbols, the next step is to read standard music notation.* (2.6)

34. A The professor says: *The three methods of playing music...are all valuable in their own way. Some children will always prefer...; Others will like...; And still others will find their musical home....* The professor implies that each method of playing music is appropriate for some students. (2.4)

Speaking (p. 494)

1. Answers will vary.
2. Answers will vary.
3. Key points:
   - The man says he is going to miss the first day of biology class, although attendance is mandatory on the first day.
   - The woman's opinion about the attendance policy is that it is fair and justified.
   - One reason she gives is that the instructor has the right to set the attendance policy.
   - Another reason is that the instructor has to be there every day, and so should the students.
   - Another reason is that participating in class is an important part of learning.
   - Another reason is that students need to go to class because they can't always understand everything on their own.
4. Key points:
   - The ethical problem in the study of fast–food workers was that the researcher had to lie about her background to get the job in the fast–food restaurant.
   - Also, the researcher was using other people without their knowledge or permission to advance her own career by writing a book about the experience.
   - To solve the problem, the researcher told her co–workers that she was writing a book about them. This was acceptable because she was able to get their approval to tell their stories.
5. Key points:
   - The man's problem is that his parents want him to do an internship at a bank, but he would rather work as an intern on a population study.
   - The woman suggests that he do the internship on the population study because it will help him know if he wants a career in pure research.
   - The woman suggests that he tell his father why he wants to work on the population study and explain what a great opportunity it is.
6. Key points:
   - Direct competition is when a bird actively excludes others from getting resources. Examples of direct competition are stealing food, establishing territories, and fighting.
   - Indirect competition is when birds simply use up a resource so that other birds cannot use that resource. An example is a flock of geese eating all the food in an area.
   - Competition and population size are related because when a population increases, the likelihood of competition also increases. Competition may limit the population size because there are not enough resources for more birds.

WRITING (p. 499)

Key points:
- The Robbers Cave Experiment points to the more troubling aspects of peer groups; this casts doubt on the point in the reading that peers play an important positive role in children's socialization.
- The first stage of the experiment discouraged competition, yet the groups began to show signs of feeling competitive; this contradicts the point in the reading that peer groups build friendship, tolerance, and cooperation.
- The second stage of the experiment encouraged competition in a series of contests, resulting in insults and negative attitudes between the groups; this casts doubt on the point in the reading that competitive strategies are healthy and necessary in a competitive society.
- The third stage of the experiment involved a cooperative task, which greatly reduced prejudice in just a few days; this casts doubt on the point in the reading that peers can tease and tolerate each other without the intervention of adults.
- The experiment shows that, in peer groups, competition comes more naturally than cooperation; this contradicts the point in the reading that peer groups promote both cooperation and the learning of competitive strategies.

TEST 3

READING (p. 503)

1. **B** Clues: *Cold storage, or refrigeration...in order to delay the growth of microorganisms—bacteria, molds, and yeast—that cause food to spoil.* (1.1)

2. **A** *Perishable* means *capable of spoiling* in this context. Clues: *...delay the growth of microorganisms...that cause food to spoil; ...lengthen its storage time.* (1.4)

3. **B** You can infer that cold storage was dependent on a source of ice or snow. Clues: *Before artificial refrigeration was invented, people stored perishable food with ice or snow to lengthen its storage time; ...keeping it in an ice–filled pit...; ...ice was transported from mountains, or harvested from local lakes or rivers....* (1.5)

4. **A** Artificial refrigeration does not involve the pumping of water vapor through a pipe; rather, a refrigerant is pumped through a pipe. All the other answers are given: *The refrigerators of today rely on the same basic principle of cooling caused by the rapid evaporation and expansion of gases; A refrigerator uses the evaporation of a volatile liquid...; The heat is moved from the inside of the container to the outside.* (1.2)

5. **D** *As the liquid turns to vapor* is paraphrased in *During evaporation. It absorbs heat because the molecules of vapor use energy to leave the liquid* is paraphrased in *the vapor molecules use energy.* (1.7)

6. **C** Clues: *In 1842, physician John Gorrie used Evans's design to create an air–cooling apparatus to treat yellow–fever patients in a Florida hospital.* (1.1)

7. **C** The referent of *it* is something that became very cold as the ether evaporated. The sentence states that printer James Harrison cleaned his type with ether. Logic tells you that *it* refers to *type.* (1.3)

8. **D** The author's purpose is to show how refrigeration changed a whole industry. Clues: *In solving Busch's spoilage and storage problems, refrigeration also revolutionized an entire industry.* (1.6)

9. **A** *Constrained* means *restricted* in this context. Clues: *...stored their beer in caves, and production was ----- by the amount of available cave space.* (1.4)

10. **B** Clues: *...the newly invented refrigerated railcar, which was insulated with ice bunkers in each end.* (1.1)

11. **B** *Toxic* means *poisonous* in this context. Clues: *...ammonia, methyl chloride, and sulfur dioxide...; After those gases accidentally killed several people....* (1.4)

12. **C** The added sentence discusses the work of Gorrie, whom the previous sentence introduces. Answer (D) is incorrect because adding the sentence there would interrupt the logical link between *in 1851* and *In the same year* in consecutive sentences. (1.8)

ANSWER KEY

13–14. B, C, E   Key information: *Before artificial refrigeration was invented, people stored perishable food with ice or snow to lengthen its storage time; A refrigerator uses the evaporation of a volatile liquid, or refrigerant, to absorb heat. ...the refrigerant is compressed, pumped through a pipe, and allowed to vaporize; In 1842...an air–cooling apparatus to treat yellow–fever patients... ...vapor–compression refrigeration to the brewing and meatpacking industries.* Answers (A), (D), and (F) are minor ideas. (1.9)

15. B   Clues: *Canadian English became a separate variety of North American English...when thousands of Loyalists...fled north to Canada. Many Loyalists settled in southern Ontario in the 1780s....* (1.1)

16. A   *Norms* means *patterns* in this context. Clues: *...their speech became the basis...; ...a definition based on the ----- of urban middle–class speech.* (1.4)

17. C   *A great deal in common with* means *many similarities to* in this context. Clues: *...the ways in which it resembles....* (1.4)

18. B   Clues: *Modern Canadian English is usually defined by the ways in which it resembles and differs from American or British English; ...many Americans identify a Canadian accent as British; ...many British people identify a Canadian accent as American....* (1.1)

19. B   The referent of *the two varieties* is two things that have many similarities. The previous sentence discusses Canadian and American English. Logic tells you that *the two varieties* refers to *Canadian English and American English.* (1.3)

20. D   *Spot* means *find* in this context. Clues: *...instantly recognizable...; ...one Canadian in a crowded room will easily ----- the other Canadian among the North Americans.* (1.4)

21. C   *Canadian pronunciation reflects the experience of a people struggling* is paraphrased in *this effort is shown in their pronunciation. Struggling for national identity against two strong influences* is paraphrased in *have tried to distinguish themselves as a nation.* (1.7)

22. A   *Kerosene* did not originate in a North American Indian language. All the other answers did originate in Indian languages: *Several words are borrowed from North American Indian languages, for example, "kayak,"... "parka,"...; The name of the country itself has an Indian origin; the Iroquois word "kanata" originally meant "village."* (1.2)

23. D   You can infer that much of the vocabulary for ice hockey originated in Canada. Clues: *...many words and phrases originating in Canada itself...; A number of terms for ice hockey...have become part of World Standard English.* (1.5)

24. A   Clues: *Some features of Canadian English...are often deliberately identified with Canadian speakers...; Among the original Canadian idioms, perhaps the most famous is the almost universal use of "eh?"....* (1.1)

25. D   *Homogeneity* means *sameness* in this context. Clues: *While there is a greater degree of ----- in Canadian English...several dialect areas do exist across Canada. Linguists have identified distinct dialects....* (1.4)

26. C   In the added sentence, *Thus* is a transition that shows result by linking *"out" is pronounced like "oat"* in the previous sentence with *"out" rhymes with "boat"* in the added sentence. (1.8)

27–28. A, D, E   Key information: *Canadian English has a great deal in common with the English spoken in the United States... About 75 percent of Canadians use the British "zed"... ...75 percent of Canadians use the American pronunciation of...; The differences are mainly in pronunciation... Canadian pronunciation reflects the experience of a people struggling for national identity...; An important characteristic of the vocabulary of Canadian English is the use of many words and phrases originating in Canada itself....* Answers (B), (C), and (F) are minor ideas. (1.9)

29. A   *Branch out* means *separate* in this context. Clues: *...in different directions...; ...separate societies....* (1.4)

30. A   *They* in the highlighted sentence refers to *physical anthropologists,* the subject of the previous sentence. *They ask questions* is paraphrased in *Physical anthropologists investigate. The events that led a tree–dwelling population of animals to evolve into two–legged beings with the power to learn—a power that we call intelligence* is paraphrased in *how intelligent human beings evolved from creatures that lived in trees.* (1.7)

31. D   *Speculate* means *think* in this context. Clues: *...investigate...; ...study...; ...find out...;* the stem *–spec–* = see, observe. (1.4)

32. C   The author's purpose is to give examples of fieldwork done by physical anthropologists. Clues: *...excavating at Olduvai Gorge in Tanzania...; ...discovered stone tool and hominid evidence...; ...discovered yet other types of hominid skulls in Kenya....* (1.6)

33. D   Clues: *Like physical anthropologists, cultural anthropologists study clues about human life in the distant past....* (1.1)

34. B   Clues: *Anthropologists doing fieldwork often produce an ethnography, a written description of the daily activities of men, women, and children....* (1.1)

35. B   *Sift through* means *sort* in this context. Clues: *...try to discover cross–cultural patterns....* (1.4)

36. B   The referent of *They* is someone or something that uses findings to argue for or against particular hypotheses. The subject of the previous sentence is *ethnologists.* Logic tells you that *They* refers to *ethnologists.* (1.3)

37. D   The passage does not state that Margaret Mead wrote about economic systems of pioneer women. All the other answers are given: *Mead published t major works...studies of...the cultural and biologic bases of gender, the nature of cultural change...and race relations.* (1.2)

38. A   You can infer that Margaret Mead's work made an impact on the field of anthropology. Clues: *A cultural anthropologist who achieved worldwide fame was Margaret Mead; ...published ten major works...; ...subjects of major intellectual consequence...; ...new technologies for research...; new ways that anthropology could serve society.* (1.5)

39. A The added sentence introduces and defines the field of anthropology, which the rest of the paragraph develops with facts and examples. (1.8)

40–42. C, D, G Physical anthropology: ...study the connections between humans and other primates that are still living. ...clues to the relationship of humans to various primates; Physical anthropologists study the fossils and organic remains of once–living primates. ...hominid evidence... ...hominid skulls...; Physical anthropology focuses on human evolution... ...detectives whose mission is to solve the mystery of how humans came to be human.

A, E Cultural anthropology: Cultural anthropology focuses on culture... ...cultural anthropologists also look at the similarities and differences among human communities today; Some cultural anthropologists work in the field, living and working among people in societies that differ from their own. ...often produce an ethnography, a written description.... Answers (B) and (F) are inaccurate for both physical anthropology and cultural anthropology. (1.10)

LISTENING (p. 516)

1. A, C The speakers discuss their summer plans. The professor asks: So are you ready for summer? The student then describes his plans for the summer program at Silverwood. The student asks: What will you be doing this summer? The professor then discusses her teaching. The speakers also discuss their musical interests. The student says: I'll be studying oboe with him, and also orchestra...and I'm hoping to do the French horn, too, and maybe take up the krummhorn.... The professor says: I'll be teaching Theory I and II, and coaching voice; I play piano and sing. (2.1)

2. A The professor means that he is one of the best teachers available. Couldn't ask for a better teacher means that there is no better teacher to ask for. (2.4)

3. B The professor's purpose is to comment on the man's summer workload. A full plate is a busy schedule with a lot of activities. (2.3)

4. C The professor says: Yes, I am—a jazz quintet. We do mostly standards. I play piano and sing. For me, that's fun and relaxation time. (2.2)

5. D The professor says: I heard you got the scholarship for the summer program at Silverwood. The student says: ...I'm sure your recommendation helped me a lot; And thanks again for the recommendation. You can infer that the professor recommended the student for a scholarship. (2.4)

6. B The professor mainly discusses the development of film style. Key phrases: ...film was developing its own style...; ...the editing technique of cutting; ...stylistic camera work and editing...; ...elements of film "grammar" and the art of the story film. (2.1)

7. C, D Camera framing contributes to the style of a film: ...style is the texture of a film's images and sounds; ...the filmmaker's systematic use of the techniques of the medium—for example... camera framing.... Film cutting also contributes to style: A few filmmakers of the silent era were already developing film style, most notably in the editing technique of cutting. (2.2)

8. C The professor says: ...film was something new...it was an art form that owed its birth to the technology of the moving picture camera. The critics preferred to see stylistic camera work and editing—the techniques that set film apart from theater. (2.2)

9. A The professor's purpose is to give an example of an early advancement in film style. The professor says: Another film technique—called cross–cutting—made it possible to tell two stories at the same time. Cross–cutting—it's also called parallel action—it involves showing segments from two different sequences, moving back and forth from one to the other so the two stories appear to be taking place at the same time. (2.3)

10. D The professor means that D.W. Griffith improved film techniques, making film a literary art. Griffith redefined the innovations of other filmmakers. His films were recognized as a unique narrative form because he improved the "grammar" and storytelling of film. (2.4)

11. C The professor says: ...closer views of people's faces or gestures. These closely framed shots are known as close–ups. The close–up conveys a character's emotions through subtle changes in the eyes, mouth, and brow. You can infer that the close–up camera shot would best show that a character is frightened. (2.4)

12. B The professor mainly discusses a decline in pollinator populations. Key phrases: ...pollinator scarcity; ...the worst pollinator crisis in history; ...a steep decline in North American populations of honeybees. (2.1)

13. A, D Parasites have affected pollinator populations: An outbreak of parasitic mites has caused a steep decline in North American populations of honeybees. Farm chemicals have also affected pollinator populations: In California, farm chemicals are killing around ten percent of all the honeybee colonies. (2.2)

14. A The professor's purpose is to show the effect of agriculture on pollinators. Large–scale agriculture has reduced the areas of nectar–producing plants that pollinators depend on. (2.3)

15. B The professor says: Unfortunately, the herbicides used on the milkweed in the Great Plains are taking a toll on monarchs, and fewer of them are reaching their winter grounds in Mexico. You can infer that the population of monarch butterflies has been reduced because of herbicides. (2.4)

16–17. ✓ Long–nosed bat: It feeds on the nectar of cactus flowers: *...the long–nosed bat. These amazing animals feed on cactus flowers.*
✓ Honeybee: It pollinates four out of five food crops in North America: *...honeybees are the dominant pollinator because they play a role in pollinating four out of five food crops in North America.*
✓ Monarch butterfly: It returns to the same site every year: *The monarch is the only butterfly that returns to a specific site year after year.*
✓ Long–nosed bat: It has been mistaken for a similar animal: *But the long–nosed bat is having a tough time, too. Some desert ranchers mistake them for vampire bats....* (2.5)

18. B, C The speaker discusses a change in the design of human settlements: *As human settlements evolved from simple groups of huts to larger villages, and then to towns and cities, their basic pattern changed.* He also discusses the significance of trees in urban spaces: *The rest is covered by trees and grass—foresters call it the "urban forest"...; The extent of this forest is sort of amazing—two–thirds of our urban space.* (2.1)

19. A The speaker says: *The early rural villages grew naturally—sort of organically...; ...buildings were clustered near water sources...; Our city planners and architects have converted the organic pattern of the village into a geometrically perfect grid.* (2.2)

20. D The speaker says: *...foresters call it the "urban forest"—meaning all the trees in city parks, the trees planted along streets and highways, and the trees in people's yards.* (2.2)

21. A The speaker's purpose is to give an example of an urban park project. The speaker says: *...one of North America's first public parks—that was sort of created as a unified project—was Central Park in New York City.* (2.3)

22. D The speaker says: *...an oasis in the middle of steel and stone. Central Park has been called "the city's lung" because of its purifying effect on the air, not to mention its effect on the human psyche.* The speaker implies that New York's Central Park contributes to the quality of life in the city. (2.4)

23. B The speaker's opinion is that the city is a symbol of human achievement. The speaker says: *...the city is our most spectacular creation...; ...the finest evidence of our civilization is the city. The city is a symbol of experimentation and creation....* (2.3)

24. C The purpose of the discussion is to review the different types of computer storage. Key phrases: *...can we go over memory again; ...memory can be either of two things...; ...two kinds of memory. I need to be able to explain them. Now, what's the difference between RAM and ROM?* (2.3)

25. B The tutor says: *ROM—read–only memory—stores the information your computer needs to perform basic functions and run programs that are built into your computer....* (2.2)

26. C The tutor's purpose is to explain the difference between memory and disk storage because the student doesn't understand the difference between them. The tutor says: *That's a really good question. I'll answer it with an analogy. Imagine you're at the library, doing research....* (2.3)

27. A The tutor says: *Now, which part of your computer's memory is sort of like the library table; That's right. RAM.* (2.2)

28. ✓ Yes: The files are returned to disk storage: *When you finish your work session on the computer, all the files are returned to disk storage.*
✓ Yes: The computer loads the files into RAM: *...when I ask for another file, the computer gets it from the disk...and loads it into RAM.*
✓ No: The librarian lays folders on a table: Not part of a computer work session.
✓ No: The computer is stored in a briefcase: Not part of a computer work session. (2.6)

29. D The main idea is that photography changed the nature of war reporting. Key phrases: *...a series of photographs that ushered in a new era in the visual documentation of war; ...the first time most people had ever seen the carnage of the war; ...the battlefield was no longer comfortably distant—the camera was bringing it closer...; ...photography made a huge impact, and media coverage of war—and public opinion about war—would never be the same again.* (2.1)

30. A The professor means that more Americans died on that day than on any other day in American history. Several thousand men died or were wounded in one day, and there has never been another day like that. (2.4)

31. C The professor says: *...Mathew Brady, a leading portrait photographer of the time. Brady owned studios in New York and in Washington....* (2.2)

32. D The professor's purpose is to emphasize the power of photography in making people aware of the effects of the war. (2.3)

33. A, C One limitation of photography was that the slow exposure time did not allow action shots: *...the exposure time of the camera was slow...; ...it was not possible for photographers to take action pictures.* Another limitation was that newspapers were not able to reproduce photographs: *...newspapers couldn't yet reproduce photographs.* (2.2)

34. B The professor says: *Mathew Brady's work was the first instance of the comprehensive photo–documentation of a war—the Civil War—which as a result became the first media war; ...media coverage of war—and public opinion about war—would never be the same again.* The professor implies that Mathew Brady's work had a lasting effect on photography and journalism. (2.4)

SPEAKING (p. 522)

1. Answers will vary.
2. Answers will vary.
3. Key points:
   - A new policy requires that students who take a lecture course in social science also take a discussion section for that course.
   - The man's opinion about the required discussion section is favorable.
   - One reason he gives is that three hours of lecture time is not long enough for the professor to cover all the material they need to know for the examination.
   - Another reason is that the discussion section will give students a chance to talk to the teacher and other students and thus to learn more.
   - Another reason is that it is easy to get a high grade in the discussion section.
4. Key points:
   - The rabbit's large ears are part of a homeostatic system by which the rabbit can maintain a constant internal body temperature.
   - The rabbit regulates the amount of blood flowing through the blood vessels of its ears to adjust heat loss to the surroundings.
   - When the rabbit's body temperature increases, the rabbit's brain turns on the body's cooling system. The blood vessels in the ears expand and fill with warm blood; heat escapes from the ears, causing the body temperature to drop.
   - When the rabbit's body temperature decreases, the brain turns on the body's warming system. Blood vessels in the ears constrict and send blood away from the skin, which reduces heat loss from the ears.
5. Key points:
   - The woman's problem is that she needs an official copy of her transcript right away, but she cannot get one because there is an unpaid charge on her student account that was mistakenly charged to her instead of her roommate.
   - The man suggests that she pay the charge to clear her account, and then have her roommate pay her back.
   - The man suggests that she send her roommate in to pay the charge.
   - The man suggests that she talk to the dean's secretary about releasing the transcript.
6. Key points:
   - The communication between babies and mothers is musical because there is a shared sense of timing.
   - A baby will often lead the earliest "conversations" with his mother, just as one musician will lead another in a performance.
   - A baby's sounds connect two people in an exchange of sounds. A baby can make sounds with a musical inflection when "talking" with his mother.
   - Babies and mothers create a special musical language called baby talk.
   - Babies learn to make a large vocabulary of meaningful sounds; different meanings are expressed by changes in intonation, rhythm, and timing—all characteristics of music.

WRITING (p. 527)

1. Key points:
   - Chess players have the ability to plan ahead and predict moves; this illustrates the point in the reading that visual–spatial intelligence involves the ability to create mental imagery and to transform that imagery.
   - Blindfolded chess players must remember the positions of the chess pieces because they cannot see the board; this illustrates the point in the reading that visual–spatial intelligence involves having a visual memory.
   - The chess player's memory stores patterns, plans, ideas, and strategies rather than a rote list of moves; this illustrates the point in the reading that visual–spatial intelligence involves a memory that is abstract rather than pictorial—a kind of geometrical memory.
   - Chess masters have the ability to reconstruct a chessboard they have seen for just a few seconds; this illustrates the point in the reading that people with visual–spatial intelligence can draw whatever object they see, usually after seeing the object for only a short time.

TEST 4

READING (p. 531)

1. C   *Precocity* means *advanced skill* in this context. Clues: *...abilities...; ...talent...; ...exceptional skill...; gifted....* (1.4)

2. A   *A musically gifted child has an inborn talent* is paraphrased in *Children may be born with superior musical ability. The extent to which the talent is expressed publicly* is paraphrased in *how this ability is developed. Will depend upon the environment in which the child lives* is paraphrased in *their environment will determine.* (1.7)

3. B   Clues: *Pitch—or melody—is more central in certain cultures...; Rhythm ...is emphasized in sub–Saharan Africa....* (1.1)

4. A   *Predisposed* means *inclined* in this context. Clues: *All children have some aptitude for making music; Infants are especially ----- to acquire these core aspects of music...;* the prefix *pre–* = before; the stem *–pos–* = put. (1.4)

5. C   Clues: *Individual differences begin to emerge in young children as they learn to sing. Some children can match large segments of a song by the age of two or three. Many others can only approximate pitch at this age....* (1.1)

6. A   Clues: *The appearance of superior musical ability in some children provides evidence that musical talent may be a separate and unique form of intelligence; In many of these cases, the child is average in every other way but displays an exceptional ability in music.* (1.1)

7. B   The author's purpose is to give an example of a well–known musical prodigy. Clues: *Every generation in music history has had its famous prodigies...; In the eighteenth century, Wolfgang Amadeus Mozart began composing and performing at the age of six.* (1.6)

8. D   Clues: *...modulation—transitions from one key to another....* (1.1)

9. C   Appreciation for a wide variety of musical styles is not given as an example of exceptional musical talent. All the other answers are given: *...a remarkable "ear" or extraordinary memory for music...; By the age of eleven, he had composed three symphonies and 30 other major works; ...able to play "Happy Birthday" in the style of various composers....* (1.2)

10. B   *Haven* means *safe place* in this context. Clues: *...the child may cling to music because it represents a ----- in a world that is largely confusing and frightening.* (1.4)

11. D   You can infer that exceptional musical ability is the result of natural talent and a supportive environment. Clues: *...exceptional skill as a result of a well–designed instructional regime...; ...the good fortune to be born into a musical family in a household filled with music; A musically gifted child has an inborn talent; however, the extent to which the talent is expressed publicly will depend upon the environment in which the child lives.* (1.5)

12. B   In the added sentence, *They* refers to *normal children*, the subject of the previous sentence. The added sentence develops the idea that children *can produce individual sounds and sound patterns*, mentioned in the previous sentence. The added sentence introduces *patterns and tones sung by other people*, which the next sentence develops with *their mother's songs.* (1.8)

13–14. B, C, F   Key information: *Musically gifted children master at an early age the principal elements of music...All children have some aptitude for making music... The early appearance of superior musical ability in some children...; ...a natural understanding of musical structure. ...prodigies—individuals with exceptional musical powers... ...began composing and performing at the age of six; ...musical talent is part of an otherwise disabling condition such as autism... Unusual musical ability is a regular characteristic of certain anomalies such as autism.* Answers (A) and (D) are minor ideas; answer (E) is not mentioned. (1.9)

15. D   Clues: *...psychological reasons: modesty, taboo, magical influence, or the desire to please.* (1.1)

16. B   Clues: *And like our hunting–gathering ancestors, most men still carry things on their person....* (1.1)

17. C   The referent of *these two functions* is two uses for the garments that we wear today. The paragraph discusses using clothing to maintain warmth and to carry objects. Logic tells you that *these two functions* refers to *maintaining warmth and carrying objects.* (1.3)

18. A   *We might say that clothing has to do with covering the body* is paraphrased in *Clothing serves a physical purpose. Costume concerns the choice of a particular form of garment for a particular purpose* is paraphrased in *costume has a personal, social, or psychological function.* (1.7)

19. D   *Ornaments* means *decorations* in this context. Clues: *...a function beyond that of simple utility; ...the addition of....* (1.4)

20. A   You can infer that the author believes we can learn about a society's social structure by studying costume. Clues: *...costume fulfilled a function beyond that of simple utility; Costume communicates the status of the wearer...; Costume denotes power...; ...costume has come to be an expression of social class and material prosperity.* (1.5)

21. A   *Beacons* means *signals* in this context. Clues: *...uniform says, "I am part of a powerful machine..."; Uniforms are immediate ----- of power and authority. If a person needs to display power....* (1.4)

22. D   The author's purpose is to show how costume conveys authority. Clues: *Uniforms are immediate beacons of power and authority. If a person needs to display power—a police officer, for example...; Height can be exaggerated...thick clothing can make the body look broader and stronger, and boots can enhance the power of the legs.* (1.6)

23. C The passage does not state that having a heart condition is likely to be indicated by a person's costume. All the other answers are given: *A uniform is a type of costume that serves the important function of displaying membership in a group... sports team...; ...the uniform of the prisoner...; Religious costume signifies spiritual or superhuman authority....* (1.2)

24. C The added sentence gives examples of *professional or administrative costume*, mentioned in the previous sentence; *the judge's robes and the police officer's uniform* are examples that express authority and power. (1.8)

25–28. C, E, G Clothing: *Another function of early clothing—providing comfort and protection... ...covered their bodies more and more to maintain body warmth; ...we first clothed our bodies for some physical reason, such as protecting ourselves from the elements; ...the function of the earliest clothing was to carry objects. ...carrying was much easier if they were wearing simple belts or animal skins from which they could hang weapons and tools. ...transport collected food back to the settlement....*

A, D, F, I Costume: *...costume reflects social factors such as personal status, religious beliefs...; A uniform is a type of costume that serves the important function of displaying membership in a group...; Costume helped to impose authority... ...enhanced his physical superiority and suggested he was superhuman. ...professional or administrative costume is designed to distinguish the wearer and to express personal or delegated authority; Religious costume signifies spiritual or superhuman authority....* Answers (B) and (H) are not mentioned. (1.10)

29. A Clues: *Carbon dioxide and other naturally occurring gases in the earth's atmosphere create a natural greenhouse effect by trapping and absorbing solar radiation. These gases act as a blanket and keep the planet warm....* (1.1)

30. D *The man–made greenhouse effect* is paraphrased in *emissions that cause the greenhouse effect. The exhalation of industrial civilization* is paraphrased in *Industrial activities result in emissions.* (1.7)

31. C The passage does not give the conversion of carbon dioxide to oxygen as a contributing factor to global warming. All the other answers are given: *A major contributing factor is the burning of large amounts of fossil fuels—coal, petroleum...; Another is the destruction of the world's forests...; The main greenhouse gas, water vapor, will increase in response to global warming and further enhance it.* (1.2)

32. A *Enhance* means *strengthen* in this context. Clues: *...causing the earth's surface to become warmer; ...will increase in response to...; ...further....* (1.4)

33. D You can infer that climate change is likely to continue as long as heat–trapping gases accumulate. Clues: *This is changing global climate at an unusually fast rate; ...global temperatures could rise as much as 10.5 degrees F during the next century as heat–trapping gases from human industry accumulate in the atmosphere.* (1.5)

34. C Clues: *...higher temperatures and more frequent drought during the growing season might require farmers to switch from corn to wheat....* (1.1)

35. A *Inundate* means *cover* in this context. Clues: *A rise in sea level...; ...islands and low–lying coastal plains...; Millions of acres of coastal farmlands would be covered by water.* (1.4)

36. B The author's purpose is to introduce conclusive evidence of global warming. Clues: *Global warming has already...; ...ample evidence...; Both teams concluded...; These studies are hard evidence....* (1.6)

37. A The referent of *they* is something or someone that found ample evidence of plants blooming and birds nesting earlier in the spring. The subject of the sentence is *research teams*. Logic tells you that *they* refers to *teams*. (1.3)

38. B *Hard* means *real* in this context. Clues: *...hundreds of published papers...; ample evidence...; These studies are ----- evidence that the natural world is already responding dramatically to climate change....* (1.4)

39. C Clues: *...ample evidence of plants blooming and birds nesting earlier in the spring. Both teams concluded that rising global temperatures are shifting the ranges of hundreds of species—thus climatic zones—northward.* (1.1)

40. D The added sentence summarizes the two ideas discussed in the paragraph, melting ice caps and the expansion of water. The first three sentences discuss the effect of melting polar ice caps. The fourth sentence mentions the expansion of water in the clause *the warming of seawater will cause the water to expand*, which the added sentence logically follows. (1.8)

41–42. A, D, F Key information: *...a rise in atmospheric levels of carbon dioxide and other heat–trapping greenhouse gases. ...buildup of greenhouse gases is already causing the earth's average surface temperature to rise; Global warming may also cause a rise in sea level... ...rising global temperatures are shifting the ranges of hundreds of species—thus climatic zones—northward; ...changes in the range and behavior of plant and animal species... If global warming trends continue, changes in the environment will have an enormous impact on world biology.* Answer (B) is not mentioned; answers (C) and (E) are minor ideas. (1.9)

Listening (p. 544)

1. B The man wants to change his housing situation. He says: *I'd kind of like to live in a smaller building. I'm thinking of moving next semester.* (2.3)

2. A, D A full refrigerator and two to four bedrooms are features of the suites. The woman says: *The suites have two to four bedrooms...and a full refrigerator.* (2.2)

3. D The woman's purpose is to apologize for not answering the man's question. The man asks about the rent more than once before the woman answers him. (2.3)

4. C The man thinks the rent in the villages is higher than he hoped it would be. He says: *Wow. That's more than I expected; ...I was hoping it'd be a lot less.* (2.3)

5. A The man says: *Number twenty–seven...oh...wow.* He is the 27th person on the waiting list. You can infer that he doesn't think he will be able to get a room in the villages. (2.4)

6. A The students mainly discuss characteristics of two design styles, Art Deco and Art Moderne. The man says: *...it seems to me that Art Deco and Art Moderne are the same thing.* The woman says: *...Art Deco came a little before Moderne; Art Deco has more decoration than Art Moderne; Art Moderne is simpler than Deco.* (2.1)

7. D The man says: *There's a lot we have to remember; ...there's Art Nouveau, and Art Deco, and Art Moderne...I have a hard time keeping it all straight.* You can infer that he is concerned about the amount they have to learn. (2.4)

8. C The woman contrasts the details of two design styles. She says: *Art Deco has more decoration than Art Moderne; Art Deco uses a lot of straight lines and slender forms; Art Moderne is simpler than Deco. It has...things like more rounded corners, flat roofs, and...the walls are smooth and don't have any decoration. It's more streamlined than Deco.* (2.1)

9. ✓ Art Deco: This style has straight lines, slender forms, and geometric patterns: *...geometric designs.... Art Deco uses a lot of straight lines and slender forms.*

   ✓ Art Moderne: This style has rounded corners, smooth walls, and little decoration: *Art Moderne is simpler than Deco. It has...things like more rounded corners, ...the walls are smooth and don't have any decoration.*

   ✓ Art Deco: This is the style of a downtown building that the woman likes: *My favorite building is the Maritime Building. It's downtown, right across from my father's office. It's Art Deco....* (2.5)

10. C The man says: *...this is an idea for our project. We could take pictures of the buildings and do a slide show in class; Let's talk to Professor Vargas and see what he thinks.* You can infer that the students are required to do a project for their design class. (2.4)

11. D The main purpose of the lecture is to explain how early people started farming. Key sentences: *What led these people to invent agriculture, a completely different way of life; ...ancient people changed from hunters and gatherers to farmers when they began to domesticate wild plants and animals.* (2.3)

12. A The professor says: *The people brought the squash seeds back to their camp. As they ate the seeds, some seeds fell to the ground all around the camp. Later, some of these seeds germinated and produced new plants. Thus, the hunter–gatherers became farmers sort of by accident.* You can infer that the process of gathering wild food led naturally to farming. (2.4)

13. B–D–C–A The professor says: *(1) The people brought the squash seeds back to their camp; (2) As they ate the seeds, some seeds fell to the ground...; (3) Later, some of these seeds germinated and produced new plants; (4) ...they started to take more of an interest in the plants. They tried to protect the plants in practical ways.* (2.6)

14. B The professor says: *Eventually, the people realized that seeds grew better when they were planted in earth that was turned over. So they began to scratch the earth with a digging stick....* (2.2)

15. C The professor's purpose is to point out that agriculture developed over a very long time. When something doesn't happen overnight, it takes a long time. The professor says: *The process probably took thousands of years.* (2.3)

16. A The professor says: *...it's very likely that the change from a hunting–gathering society to an agricultural society followed a similar pattern in different regions of the world.* (2.2)

17. B The hydrologic cycle is the movement of water through the earth and atmosphere. Key sentences: *Water continuously circulates from the ocean to the atmosphere, to the land, and back to the ocean, providing us with a renewable supply of purified water. This complex cycle—known as the hydrologic cycle—balances the amount of water in the ocean, in the atmosphere, and on the land.* (2.1)

18. A The professor says: *Climatologists study the role of solar energy in the cycle. They're mainly concerned with the atmospheric phase of the cycle—how solar energy drives the cycle through the...processes of evaporation, atmospheric circulation, and precipitation.* (2.2)

19. B The professor says: *The land phase of the cycle is the concern of hydrologists. Hydrologists study the vast quantities of water in the land phase of the cycle, how water moves over and through the land, and how it's stored on or within the earth.* (2.2)

20. A, C Water that falls to the earth as precipitation is stored in lakes or underground: *The water that falls to earth is stored on the surface in lakes, or it penetrates the surface....* The water eventually flows back to the ocean: *Eventually, all of the water falling on land makes its way back to the ocean.* (2.2)

21. A The professor's purpose is to describe the importance of runoff and groundwater. The amount of runoff and groundwater equals the amount of water from the ocean that falls on the land as precipitation. (2.3)

22. C The professor says: *Trees and plants circulate and store water...; ...plants...are also part of the cycle, since water is a large part of the mass of most organisms. Living organisms store and use water....* You can infer that plants perform the function of water storage. (2.4)

23. B The professor mainly gives a history of an art movement. Key phrases: *The Group's origins date back to the 1911 showing...; ...a new direction for Canadian art, a distinctly Canadian style of painting; Their 1920 exhibition was an important moment in Canadian art.* (2.1)

24. A The professor's view is that the Group of Seven created a distinctive Canadian art inspired by Canada itself. The professor says: *...a generation of artists set out to create a school of painting that would record the Canadian scene and reinforce a distinctive Canadian identity; Their 1920 exhibition was an important moment in Canadian art. It proclaimed that Canadian art must be inspired by Canada itself.* (2.3)

25. D The professor's purpose is to show how one artist, Tom Thomson, inspired the Group's direction in seeking a distinctly Canadian art. (2.3)

26. B, D The Group of Seven painted jack pine trees and uninhabited landscapes: *... "The Jack Pine," one of the nation's best-loved pictures; ...a bleak, somber, incredibly beautiful landscape of rock outcroppings, storm-driven lakes, and jack pine trees—a land totally uninhabited by people.* (2.2)

27. C The professor means that much of the Group's work has come to represent Canada. An *icon* is a symbol, a representation of something else. (2.4)

28. A The professor says: *A.Y. Jackson was influential for his...; Arthur Lismer's work has an intensity all its own...; Lawren Harris went further than the rest....* You can conclude that the Group did not share a single style of painting. (2.4)

29. C The professor mainly discusses how leadership and power are related. Key phrases: *...leaders always have some degree of power; Both leadership and power involve the ability to...; Although leadership and power are different things, they're related in important ways.* (2.1)

30. A The professor's purpose is to show that having power doesn't imply leadership. The professor says: *The headwaiter has power to some degree—for example, the power to seat you at the best table by the window—but he doesn't necessarily have the qualities we associate with leadership.* (2.3)

31. B The professor's purpose is to distinguish between leaders and power holders. A military dictator and a robber have power, but they may lack leadership skills. (2.3)

32. D The professor says: *Leadership and power are not the same thing, although they are similar in this one way. Both leadership and power involve the ability to...bring about the results you want....* (2.2)

33. B, C The ability to use physical force is a source of power: *Probably the oldest source of power is the ability to use physical force.... The ability to motivate people is another source of power: ...the ability to motivate—all of these are sources of power.* (2.2)

34. A The professor says: *Remember, both leadership and power involve the ability to accomplish the results you want, and successful managers understand how the two work together to make this happen.* The professor implies that successful managers know how and when to use their power. (2.4)

SPEAKING (p. 550)

1. Answers will vary.
2. Answers will vary.
3. Key points:
   - Because of an increase in the number of swimming classes, the university will reduce the hours that the swimming pool is open for students' personal use.
   - The man does not like the change in swimming pool hours.
   - One reason he gives is that the change will eliminate late afternoon hours, when he likes to swim.
   - Another reason is that swimming classes don't take up the whole pool; he suggests keeping half of the pool open for other people.
   - Another reason is that it is not fair for the university to take away pool time; he suggests extending the morning hours to make up for the loss.
4. Key points:
   - The patient's symptoms included tremors of the head, headaches, stiff neck, sore back, clicking jaw, and inability to open her mouth.
   - Chiropractic treatment was recommended because the symptoms had been present for 20 years and painkilling medication did not help; the patient was very frustrated and willing to try anything.
   - This patient's experience supports the practice of chiropractic because it was successful. Patient success stories help increase the acceptance of chiropractic in the medical establishment.
5. Key points:
   - The woman's problem is that she wants to take statistics, but that course is full, so she may have to take calculus instead.
   - The man suggests that she register for both courses, get on the waiting list for statistics, and if she gets into statistics, then she can drop calculus.
   - The man suggests that she talk to the statistics instructor and try to persuade the instructor to let her in the class.
6. Key points:
   - Fears in young children are normal. Fears help children solve issues of change and development, and get attention and help from parents when needed.
   - The fear of falling is shown as a clasping motion that the baby makes when he is uncovered, surprised, or dropped. The baby cries out, which attracts a parent's attention and gets help.
   - The fear of strangers alerts the child to a new situation.
   - Fears appear during periods of new and rapid learning, such as when children learn to walk. New independence brings new things to fear, such as dogs, loud noises, and strange places.
   - By overcoming fears, children acquire confidence in their own new abilities.

WRITING (p. 555)

1. Key points:
- Earthworms are causing significant damage to some forest ecosystems by destroying the soil cover; this contradicts the point in the reading that earthworms have a beneficial effect on the soil in forests.
- There is evidence of earthworm damage near the shoreline of a lake, where the duff layer and wildflowers are disappearing; this contradicts the point in the reading that earthworms have a beneficial effect on the soil.
- Worms are eating the forest floor right out from under the plants, which also has a negative effect on animals; this contradicts the points in the reading that earthworms have a beneficial effect and are an important link in the food web.

PART 2 – LISTENING

Disk 1, Track 1

2.1 IDENTIFYING THE TOPIC AND MAIN IDEA

Focus (p. 213)

Listen to a conversation in a university office.

W: Good afternoon. May I help you?
M: Hello. I'm thinking of taking Dr. Perry's class this summer—Intro to Political Science. And I was wondering … uh … is there a … do you happen to have a book list for that class?
W: I can check the computer to see if she submitted it yet.
M: Thanks. I'd appreciate it.
W: Did you say Introduction to Political Science?
M: Yes. For summer session.
W: Here it is, I found it. Oh … and it sure looks like a substantial amount of reading!
M: Really? Is it long?
W: Would you like me to print out a copy for you?
M: Yeah, that would be great!
W: All right. This will only take a few minutes.
M: Thank you. I really appreciate it.

What is the subject of the conversation?

Disk 1, Track 2

Exercise 2.1.A (p. 215)

Question 1. Listen to a conversation between two students.

M: Hi, Kelsey! How's it going?
W: Well, I don't know. I just got my history paper back, and my professor didn't grade it. He just wrote on it, "Come and talk to me about this."
M: Really? Is that all he said? Didn't he make any other comments?
W: No. So I'm really confused. This is the first time I ever got a paper back with no grade on it.
M: That is strange, isn't it?
W: Sure is. I did everything I was supposed to. I mean, I followed the instructions of the assignment.
M: You'd better go talk to him. You need to find out what he's thinking.
W: Yeah, I will. I hope he doesn't ask me to rewrite the paper.

What is the woman's problem?

Question 2. Listen to a conversation between two students.

W: I don't know about you, but I sure am ready for spring break!
M: Are you doing anything special?
W: I'm going to Mexico to hang out on the beach! Four of us will be staying at a resort owned by Maria's family. How about you?

M: I wish I could do the same. Unfortunately, I told my brother I would help him move. But, I don't mind. It's my turn. He's done so much for me in the past.
W: Well, I'll be thinking of you as I bask in the sun.
M: Gee, thanks. I'll repay the favor some day!

What is the conversation mainly about?

Question 3. Listen to a conversation between two students.

M: What courses will you be taking next semester?
W: I won't be taking any courses. I'll be doing an internship instead.
M: Oh, really? Where?
W: At the Children's Union. It's a nonprofit agency that works on children's issues, like education, nutrition, crime, family issues—even music and the arts.
M: That sounds like a great experience because you want to work in that area.
W: Yes, I do, and I'm really excited. The position is actually very political. I'll be traveling all over the state, helping to organize events in a lot of different places. I may even get to spend some time in the state capital.
M: Excellent! I'm sure you'll learn a lot. Good luck!
W: Thanks. I hope this will lead to a job after graduation.

What is the woman mainly discussing?

Questions 4 through 5. Listen to part of a discussion between two students.

W: Are you ready for our first quiz in botany?
M: I guess so, if only I could remember the difference between xylem and phloem. I can't seem to get it straight on which one goes up and which one goes down.
W: I always think of a tree and imagine a "P" at the top, up in the branches, and an "X" at the bottom, down in the roots. "P" is above "X" in the tree, just as "P" comes before "X" in alphabetical order.
M: OK, now what?
W: Well, if "P" is up in the branches, it has to go down.
M: OK, then it's phloem that goes down.
W: Right. And "X" is down in the roots, so it has to go up.
M: Xylem is down, so it must go up. Xylem up, phloem down.
W: Right! Now just imagine your tree tomorrow during the quiz!

4. What problem does the man have?
5. How does the woman help the man?

Disk 1, Track 3

Exercise 2.1.B (p. 216)

Question 1. Listen to part of a talk given to first–year university students.

The place to go for parking permits is the Safety and Security Office on the first floor of the University Services Building. Parking permits are required for all on–campus parking. Special permits are available for students who carpool. You can also get passes for the Fourth Avenue Garage, bus passes, and maps there. The hours are 8:00 a.m. to 7:00 p.m. Monday to Thursday, and 8:00 to 4:00 on Fridays.

Safety and Security also provides special services 24 hours a day. These include escort service to and from your car, criminal incident reporting and investigation, lost and found, and battery jumper service.

What is the talk mainly about?

Question 2. Listen to part of a lecture in an American studies class.

Although the original American Indian cultures were highly diverse, they were similar in many of their traditions. Religious beliefs and rituals permeated every aspect of Indian life. Southwest tribes such as the Hopi and the Apaches had a rich and elaborate year–round sequence of ceremonials including songs, dances, and poetry. The Hopi performed dances to bring rain. The Apaches engaged in special dances and ceremonies to gain the support of the spirits before undertaking raids or going into war. The Plains tribes often sought contact with the spirits by going on a vision quest.

What is the topic of the lecture?

Question 3. Listen to part of a talk in a business class.

Each kind of insurance protects its policyholder against possible financial loss. Life insurance pays your family a certain sum upon your death. The purpose of life insurance is to provide your family with financial security, an immediate estate that will allow them to maintain the household after you die. Health insurance protects you against large medical expenses. When you pay premiums to your insurance company, you can ensure payment of your medical bills. Another kind, property–liability insurance, is sometimes called casualty insurance because it covers the cost of accidents—like automobile accidents, fire, and theft. If you're like most people, your home is the largest single investment you make in your life. This is why most homeowners have some type of property–liability insurance.

Which of the following best describes the organization of the talk?

Question 4. Listen to part of a lecture in a geography class.

The dunes called Spirit Sands make up the Manitoba Desert—Canada's only desert. These five kilometers of dunes were formed 10,000 years ago, when an ancient river dumped billions of tons of sand and gravel at the edge of a glacial lake.

The dunes of Spirit Sands are constantly changing … they are truly "rolling" dunes. Here's how it works. The sand in each dune becomes progressively finer toward the top. The heavier particles tend to settle at the base on the windward side. The wind blows the finer particles up the slope, and eventually they kind of trickle down the other side. Thus, the dune sort of walks downwind. It will reverse direction when the wind changes. Each dune is covered with tiny, rolling waves, and each wave itself is a tiny dune.

What is the lecture mainly about?

Question 5. Listen to part of a lecture in a biochemistry class.

There've been several influential studies in pain management. Some of the most interesting of these study endorphins, the body's own natural painkillers. For example, we now know that exercise stimulates the production of endorphins. Lack of exercise, on the other hand, not only shuts down endorphin production, but can also lead to muscle deterioration. This is why you see a lot of pain specialists prescribing exercise for patients with chronic pain.

Another interesting area involves the power of the placebo effect. We've known for some time that a sugar pill or other inactive placebo can sometimes make a sick person feel better. Somehow, the power of suggestion … or faith in the doctor, or the drug … will start a process of healing. We now think a neurochemical component—what may actually happen is the placebo effect allows some people to sort of tap into the supply of endorphins in their own brains.

What is the lecture mainly about?

Disk 1, Track 4

Exercise 2.1.C (p. 217)

Question 1. Listen to part of a lecture in a psychology class.

One study on aging suggests that the key to a longer life might be the way you think about yourself as you get older, that is, how you see your own aging. The researchers found that people who view aging positively live longer than people who view it negatively.

This study began 26 years ago and took place in a small town in the Midwest. The participants were 640 men and women who were 50 to 90 years old at the time. The subjects were asked to agree or disagree with statements about aging … for example, statements like "As you get older, you become less useful" and "Older people can't learn new skills." The data showed that respondents with the most positive attitudes survived a median of 22 years after their initial interview, while those with negative views lived just 15 years—a difference of seven years.

What is the speaker's main point?

Questions 2 through 3. Listen to part of a talk given by an academic adviser.

A bachelor's degree in engineering is the generally accepted educational requirement for most entry–level engineering jobs. In a typical four–year engineering program, the first two years are spent studying basic sciences—mathematics, physics, chemistry, and introductory engineering—and the humanities, social sciences, and English. The last two years are devoted to specialized engineering courses. Some programs offer a general engineering curriculum, letting students choose a specialty in graduate school or to acquire one later on the job.

Several engineering schools have formal arrangements with liberal arts colleges … programs, for example, where a student spends three years in a liberal arts college studying pre–engineering subjects and a couple years in an engineering school, and then … uh … receives a bachelor's degree from each school.

Now most engineers have some training beyond the bachelor's degree. An advanced degree is desirable for promotion, or is necessary to keep up with new technology. Graduate training is essential for most teaching and research positions.

Now a number of colleges and universities offer five–year master's degree programs offering an accelerated, intensive program of study. Some schools—particularly the state technical schools—have five– or six–year cooperative programs where students coordinate classroom study with practical work experience. These programs are popular because, in addition to gaining useful job experience, students can finance part of their education.

2. What is the speaker mainly discussing?
3. How does the speaker organize the information that he presents?

Questions 4 through 5. Listen to part of a talk in a health class.

W: RSI—repetitive strain injury—is probably the fastest–growing job–related illness. We hear about RSI so much today because of high–speed keyboard technology. Repetitive strain injury—also called repetitive motion syndrome—is a real problem for people who sit at the computer all day. RSI is brought on by doing the same movements with the arms and hands over and over again, all day long. This type of injury … RSI … it's … uh … been a problem for a long time for violinists, typists, mechanics, construction workers—anyone whose job involves repeated wrist movements.

M: My mother used to work in the lab at St. Peter's, and she got something like that. She worked there for around fifteen years—and it got to the point where she couldn't handle the instruments anymore. You could hear her fingers crack and pop when she moved them.

W: Hmm. Your mother may have had RSI—a serious case, from the sound of it. RSI affects different people differently. Some people get an inflammation of the sheathing around the tendons in the hand called tendonitis. The inflammation makes your fingers painful and hard to straighten. It's possible your mother's problem was tendonitis. A more serious condition that a lot of workers develop is carpal tunnel syndrome. That's when the nerves that go through the wrist to the hand are pinched by swollen tissue. The swelling causes a numbness or tingling sensation in the hand, and pain shoots up from the wrist—either up the arm or down into the hand. The pain can be so bad at night it wakes you up.

4. What aspect of RSI does the instructor mainly discuss?
5. How does the instructor develop the topic of RSI?

Disk 1, Track 5

2.2 LISTENING FOR DETAILS

Focus (p. 219)

Listen to a professor talk about hearing loss.

Long–term exposure to noise can lead to loss of hearing. The relative loudness of sounds is measured in decibels. Just to give you an idea of what this means, the sound of a whisper is 30 decibels, while a normal conversation is 60 decibels. The noise a vacuum cleaner makes is around 85 decibels.

The danger zone—the risk of injury—begins at around 90. Continual exposure to sounds above 90 decibels can damage your hearing. Loud noises—especially when they come at you every day—all this noise can damage the delicate hair cells in your inner ear. Lots of everyday noises are bad for us in the long run. For example, a car horn sounds at around 100 decibels. A rock band at close range is 125 decibels. A jet engine at close range is one of the worst culprits at an ear–busting 140 decibels.

The first thing to go is your high–frequency hearing, where you detect the consonant sounds in words. That's why a person with hearing loss can hear voices, but has trouble understanding what's being said.

Now choose the best answer to each question.

1. At what decibel level does the risk of hearing loss begin?
2. Which sounds could contribute to hearing loss?

Disk 1, Track 6

Exercise 2.2.A (p. 221)

Questions 1 through 2. Listen to a conversation between two students.

M: I had a lot of expenses this quarter, and the money my parents sent didn't last very long. I may have to get some kind of job.

W: You can probably find something right here on campus. You should check out the job board in the student center.

M: Where is that exactly?

W: In the student center, on the first floor, next to counseling. In fact, I think it's part of the counseling center. You can ask one of the counselors if you want more information about any of the jobs listed.

M: My problem is that I need the money but I don't have a lot of spare time. I'd like a quiet job that would allow me to get some reading done.

W: Then go on over there. Maybe there's an opening for night watchman.

1. What does the woman suggest the man do?
2. What type of job does the man want?

Questions 3 through 5. Listen to a conversation on a college campus.

M: Hey, Lorrie, are you doing anything on Wednesday afternoon?

W: I usually either go to the computer lab or go home after I get out of class. Why?

M: Well, we're having our annual book sale at the library, and we need extra cashiers.

W: When is the sale?

M: All day Wednesday, from ten until six. The busiest time will be from around noon to three. If you're free in the afternoon, why not volunteer to help us out? The library will give you ten dollars in book credit for every hour you work. You have to use the credit at this sale, but that will get you a lot of books. Most are priced around one or two dollars.

W: Why are you selling books from the library?

M: The sale includes mostly books people have donated to the library. There are a lot of paperbacks and things like encyclopedias.

W: Oh, I see. I guess I could spare a few hours.

M: Great! I can put your name down then?

W: Sure. I'll be there around noon.

M: Thanks, Lorrie!

3. What does the woman agree to do?
4. How are book sale workers compensated?
5. When will the woman arrive at the book sale?

Questions 6 through 7. Listen to a conversation between two students.

M: How do you like your classes this term?

W: All of my classes are really good. I especially like political science with Professor Hahn.

M: Oh, I had Professor Hahn for American history. We had to write a lot of papers. But one time we had a debate, and I'll never forget that.

W: Her assignments are challenging but useful. And she has the most interesting stories to illustrate her lectures. She really makes us think.

M: And she really makes you work in her class!

W: I know. But I'm starting to figure things out as a result of this class.

M: Great!

6. Why does the woman like her class with Professor Hahn?
7. What does the man say about Professor Hahn?

Questions 8 through 10. Listen to a conversation between a student and a professor.

W: Professor Abraham, did you want to see me?

M: Yes, please come in Nina, I have a job here that I hope you can help me with.

W: I'd like to, if I can.

M: Well, see this stack of paper? These are all journal articles that I need to go through for my research. It would really help if they were arranged more logically. Can you help me? I imagine it will take a few hours of your time.

W: Yes, of course I can. How do you want them organized?

M: Well, primarily by subject, and then by date. There are articles from the past four or five years. Most are about primate behavior, but a few deal with other mammals or birds, or with behavioral psychology in general.

W: This will be interesting. I have some free time tomorrow afternoon. Would that be all right?

M: That sounds perfect.

8. What does the professor want the woman to do?
9. What is the subject of the professor's research?
10. When will the woman do the work?

Disk 1, Track 7

Exercise 2.2.B (p. 222)

Questions 1 through 4. Listen to part of a discussion in an anthropology class.

M: The men of the northwoods tribes were the hunters. The hunting season began in the fall and continued until midwinter. These expeditions frequently took the hunters away from the village for long periods of time. Moose, deer, beaver, bear, and elk were the animals sought. Large deer drives were common, and small animals were taken with snares or the bow and arrow.

W: Did the women ever go hunting with the men?

M: The women often accompanied their husbands on hunting parties. Their job was to take charge of the camps.

W: Do you mean they just cooked for the men? I thought the Native Americans had more of a system of equality.

M: Overall, men and women shared the labor. On hunting expeditions, women basically supported the men, whose job was to procure the game. On the other hand, women controlled other realms of life. For example, women managed all of the agricultural operations. Also, a woman headed each clan, and these women were respected for their role as keepers of the clan.

1. When did the hunting season take place?
2. What animals did the northwoods tribes hunt?
3. According to the man, how did women participate in hunting?
4. Which activities did women control?

Questions 5 through 7. Listen to part of a talk in an introductory art class. The professor is talking about choosing a career in the arts.

M: Before you undertake a career in the arts, there are a number of factors to consider. Whether your goal is to be an actor or an animator, a saxophonist or a sculptor, talent is an essential consideration. But talent alone won't guarantee a successful career in the arts; you also need training, experience, and self-discipline. Most importantly, however, you should realize that a career in the arts requires a personal sense of commitment—a calling—because art does have a history of insecure employment. A lot of artists find it difficult—even impossible—to live on the money they make from their art. Most have to supplement their income by teaching, or by working behind the scenes, or by doing other work not related to the arts.

W: In your opinion, what's the best way for us to know if we really have a calling to art?

M: Well … those of you who are interested in art as a career should talk with arts professionals, or work in the arts yourselves. Professionals can give good firsthand advice, but experience is the best way to get a feel for the field.

W: What kind of experience? I mean … how do we get started?

M: Experience doesn't have to be formal. It can be part–time or volunteer work. For example, if you want to be a photographer or graphic designer, you could work for your school newspaper. Or if your interest is acting, you could start out in community theater. The important thing is getting started— spending time doing something in your chosen medium.

5.   According to the professor, what factors are important in choosing a career in the arts?
6.   According to the professor, why does a career in the arts require a special calling?
7.   How does the professor suggest one get started in a career in the arts?

Questions 8 through 10. Listen to a discussion in a speech communications class.

W: For your speaking assignment, you will want to follow a logical series of steps in preparing for your speech. The first step, of course, is to realize the importance of the speech to you.

M1: But isn't that always the same in this class? After all, you give us an assignment and we want to get a good grade for it.

W: Yes, that's true, but the grade isn't the only thing that's important.

M2: Yeah, Paul, think of us, your listeners! We want you to believe in what you're saying!

W: Next, of course, you select your subject. Then, decide on your purpose. Do you simply want to inform us about your subject? Or do you want to influence us in some way? Write down a statement of exactly what you wish to accomplish in the speech. This is the first step in organizing your thoughts.

M1: Is entertainment a purpose?

W: It could be, yes. Your purpose could be to make your audience laugh.

M2: I expect you to be really funny, Paul!

W: After you decide on your purpose and organize your ideas, you are ready to develop your ideas interestingly and soundly. Why don't you all just take the next few minutes to start brainstorming? Jot down ideas that come to mind—things that matter to you, things you feel strongly about.

8.   According to the instructor, what is the first step in preparing a speech?
9.   What examples of purpose are mentioned in the discussion?
10. What does the instructor want the students to do next?

Disk 1, Track 8

Exercise 2.2.C (p. 224)

Questions 1 through 3. Listen to part of a talk in a geography class.

Now we'll turn our attention to a type of local wind known as the sea breeze. The sea breeze is the simplest, most widespread, and most persistent of local winds. The sea breeze results from the heating of land and sea along a coastline in near–calm conditions.

The more rapid heating of the land during the daytime results in the development of a temperature gradient across the coast. This leads to ascent over the land and descent over the sea. Thus, a pressure gradient causes a flow of air from sea to land.

At the same time as the breeze flows from sea to land, there is a return flow higher up, from land to sea. The airflow forms a circular pattern, from sea to land, upwards, and back out to sea. The flow develops through the day, and by the middle of the afternoon, may extend several kilometers inland.

At night, the situation is reversed and the flow is from the colder land to the warmer sea, as a land breeze.

1.   What is the main topic of the talk?
2.   Select the diagram that represents the sea breeze.
3.   Identify the part of the diagram that shows the sea breeze's return flow.

Questions 4 through 5. Listen to part of a talk in a music history class.

The simplest type of horn is made from an animal horn, and animal horns are the model for other primitive horns made of shells, wood, animal hide, or clay. The sound is produced by vibrations from the player's lips. Now some horns are blown at the end, and some are blown on the side. Most primitive horns are end–blown. Unless the horn has finger holes, it will have a limited melodic range.

Horns have been around since very early times. In the Middle Ages in Europe, they were used almost exclusively in hunting and warfare. From about the fourteenth century onward, metal horns with special mouthpieces were developed, and this increased the horn's versatility. In the eighteenth century, the horn became a regular member of the orchestra.

Various types of horns are still widely used for signaling and ritual. The bugle is a simple horn dating from the Middle Ages that was first used for hunting and signaling. Starting in the nineteenth century, it became standard in military bands.

4.   What topics does the speaker discuss?
5.   When did the horn become a standard part of the orchestra?

Questions 6 through 10. Listen to a talk in an earth science class. The professor is talking about tsunamis.

The term "tidal wave" is often inaccurately used for a tsunami. Tsunamis have nothing to do with the action of tides. A more accurate term is "seismic sea wave." There has to be a disturbance of the earth's crust to produce a tsunami.

Large earthquakes with epicenters under or near the ocean are the cause of most tsunamis. Volcanic eruptions and undersea landslides are also responsible, but unless accompanied by movements of the ocean floor, their effects are usually localized. Possibly this was true about the eruption of Krakatoa in 1883. A tsunami was responsible for most of the deaths caused by Krakatoa, yet this tsunami did not sink any ships. It did wash away several coastal villages and kill more than 36,000 people.

Tsunamis work in complex ways. Some pounce on coastal settlements like large breakers. Others produce a gentle wave that floats buildings off their foundations. But then a violent backwash may sweep buildings and people out to sea. The tsunami that wrecked Hilo, Hawaii, in 1946 was so forceful it folded parking meters. It caused needless deaths when people returned to save their belongings and got caught between waves.

The deeper the water, the lower the tsunami and the faster it moves. In the open ocean, it travels at about 700 kilometers per hour, but being sometimes no more than a meter in height, a tsunami often passes a ship unnoticed. This is what happened in 1896 during a catastrophic tsunami in Japan, which was the result of an undersea earthquake. Thousands of people were drowned onshore, while fishermen far out at sea didn't notice the waves passing beneath their boats. But when they went home, they found their villages destroyed.

6. How does the professor develop the topic of tsunamis?
7. Why is the term "tidal wave" inaccurate for a tsunami?
8. What causes tsunamis?
9. What point does the professor make about the eruption of the volcano Krakatoa?
10. What is true of the tsunami that struck Japan in 1896?

Disk 1, Track 9

Exercise 2.2.D (p. 225)

Questions 1 through 2. Listen to a discussion between two students.

M: That was a pretty good history lecture, don't you think?
W: Well, to be honest, I didn't understand what Dr. Marquez meant by "partible inheritance," and it seems like that's an important thing to know.
M: Partible inheritance means that a man's property would be divided equally among all his children. After the man died, that is.
W: Oh. Then what's "primogeniture"?
M: That's when all the property goes to the eldest son. Just think about the word "primogeniture." "Primo" means "one" or "first," right?
W: Right. Oh, I get it! "Primogeniture" is when the first son gets everything.
M: That's right.
W: Now it's starting to make sense.

1. What are the students discussing?
2. What does "primogeniture" mean?

Questions 3 through 5. Listen to part of a discussion in a business class. The professor is talking about small businesses.

W: Small business owners usually consider themselves successful when they can support themselves solely from the profits of their business. So, why do so many small businesses fail each year? Well, for one thing, they usually face stiff competition from larger, more established companies. Large companies generally have cash reserves that enable them to absorb losses more easily than small firms can. Still, with the right combination of factors, a small business can do quite well.
M: My friend has a bicycle shop, and he runs the entire operation by himself. He buys the inventory, repairs bicycles, and sells to customers. He also builds the displays and cleans the shop—he does everything! And he manages to stay in business!
W: It is possible to make it—with hard work, good management, and a product or service for which there's a demand. A small business owner performs

a lot of different tasks. It's absolutely essential to be a competent manager, as I'm sure your friend is. You also need to have a thorough knowledge of your field—a combination of formal education and practical training suited to your kind of business. To run a store, for example, you need to know how to keep track of your inventory—what you have to sell—and your accounts, so you need courses in accounting and business. Experience in retailing is helpful, too. Your primary responsibilities center on planning, management, and marketing, so organizational skills are a must. To keep your store in business, you have to adapt to changing market conditions. This means improving services or promoting your products in innovative ways.

3. According to the professor, why do many small businesses fail?
4. According to the professor, what is essential for success as a small business owner?
5. What are two responsibilities of a store owner?

Questions 6 through 10. Listen to a discussion between a student and a biology teaching assistant.

W: Hi, Gordon.
M: Hello, Julie. How are you?
W: Fine. I wonder if I could ask you a few questions.
M: Sure. What's on your mind?
W: Well, something happened—I mean I saw something happen—on a hike I did last weekend, and I was wondering if it sort of fit what we learned about muscle cells.
M: This sounds like it might be interesting. What did you see?
W: Well, I was hiking with my friend—on the desert canyon trail—and we ran into these two guys sitting by the side of the trail. It turns out they were part of a high school group. My friend and I stopped to talk to them, and it turns out that one of them was sort of having trouble. He said he'd been having leg cramps for about five hours.
M: Oh. That's not good on the canyon trail.
W: I know. We asked if they had water and food, and they said a little, but their teacher went back to get some more. The guy with the cramps said he didn't feel like eating. So, we gave them one of our water bottles, and we just went on. Later on, on the way back, we ran into them again. This time the teacher and the ranger were there. The guy was eating saltine crackers. It turns out he'd skipped breakfast that day.
M: Well that was a dumb thing to do! A strenuous hike in the desert is not the time to diet.
W: So, I wondered if his muscle cramps were because of what we talked about in class, because lactic acid ferments when the cell has no oxygen.
M: I'd say that's what happened with this young man. Do you remember why it happens?
W: Well, I know that human muscle cells make ATP by lactic acid fermentation when oxygen is scarce. It's what happens when … during exercise, when ATP production needs more oxygen than the muscles can supply. The cells then have to switch from aerobic respiration to fermentation. This means lactate collects in the muscle as a waste product, and that causes muscle pain.

M: That's absolutely correct. And the young man made his problem worse by not eating after he first experienced cramps. He was simply out of fuel. His teacher did the right thing by getting him to eat something salty.

W: I guess it's important to balance food and water intake.

M: That's right. Well, Julie, it looks like you saw biology in action!

W: Yeah! It's cool. I can really understand what happened.

6. What does the woman want to discuss with the teaching assistant?
7. Where did the woman meet the young man who had a problem?
8. What help did the young man receive?
9. Why did the young man experience muscle cramps?
10. What point does the teaching assistant make about what the woman saw?

Disk 1, Track 10

Exercise 2.2.E (p. 226)

Questions 1 through 5. Listen to a talk in an art class. The instructor is talking about pigments.

Whether you're working with oil, tempera, or watercolor, it's the pigment that gives the paint its color. A pigment can either be mixed with another material or applied over its surface in a thin layer. When a pigment is mixed or ground in a liquid vehicle to form paint, it does not dissolve but remains suspended in the liquid.

A paint pigment should be a smooth, finely divided powder. It should withstand the action of sunlight without changing color. A pigment should not exert a harmful chemical reaction upon the medium, or upon other color pigments it is mixed with.

Generally, pigments are classified according to their origin, either natural or synthetic. Natural inorganic pigments, also known as mineral pigments, include the native "earths" such as ochre—yellow iron oxide—and raw umber—brown iron oxide. Natural organic pigments come from vegetable and animal sources. Some examples are indigo, from the indigo plant, and Tyrian purple, the imperial purple the Romans prepared from a shellfish native to the Mediterranean.

Today, many pigments are synthetic varieties of traditional inorganic and organic pigments. Synthetic organic pigments provide colors of unmatched intensity and tinting strength. The synthetic counterparts of the yellow and red earths are more brilliant and, if well prepared, are superior in all other respects to the native products. Inorganic synthetic colors made with the aid of strong heat are generally the most permanent for all uses. In contrast, pigments from natural sources are less permanent than the average synthetic color.

1. What is a pigment?
2. According to the instructor, what characteristic should a pigment have?
3. How are pigments generally classified?
4. Which natural pigment did the Romans obtain from a shellfish?
5. According to the instructor, why are synthetic pigments superior to natural pigments?

Questions 6 through 10. Listen to part of a lecture in a geology class. The professor is talking about volcanoes.

A volcano is a vent in the earth which erupts when hot liquefied rock, or magma, moves to the earth's surface, pouring out as lava. The lava may flow out as a liquid, or it may explode from the vent as solid or liquid particles accompanied by superheated gases. Ash and cinders form a cone around the vent.

There are several types of volcanoes. The most fluid magmas erupt quietly and flow from the vent to form gently sloping shield volcanoes. The name "shield volcano" comes from their resemblance to the shields of early Germanic warriors. The lava flows from shield volcanoes are usually only one to ten meters thick but may extend for great distances from the vent. The volcanoes of Hawaii and Iceland are typical volcanoes of this type.

Cinder cone volcanoes are formed when magmas with high gas contents and high viscosity are blown high into the air during an eruption. The magma falls as volcanic bombs which accumulate around the vent and form steep-sided cones.

Calderas, large basin-like depressions, are formed when a violent eruption blows the top off of an existing cone or when the center of a volcano collapses. One famous caldera covers much of Yellowstone National Park. Six hundred thousand years ago there was a huge volcanic explosion which devastated the landscape. At the center there remained only a smoldering caldera, a collapsed crater more than forty miles wide. Yellowstone's famous geysers and hot springs lie within this giant basin.

6. What aspect of volcanoes does the professor mainly discuss?
7. Identify the types of substances that erupt from volcanoes.
8. Select the picture that is most like a shield volcano.
9. Select the picture that is most like a caldera.
10. Which type of volcano is associated with the geysers in Yellowstone National Park?

Disk 1, Track 11

Quiz 1 (p. 230)

Questions 1 through 5. Listen to a discussion in a business class.

M1: The computerized workplace can be hazardous to your health if you don't take preventative measures. Today we'll go over what some of these hazards are, and more importantly, what can be done about them. One major complaint—maybe the biggest complaint—of people who spend time at the computer is eyestrain. To help ease the strain on the eyes, the computer screen should be about two feet from your eyes. The entire screen should be in focus. The brightness and contrast should be adjusted for best readability. A good way to relieve eyestrain is to look away from the screen frequently. Focus your eyes on objects that are far away, like something outside—the building across the street or the tree in the parking lot.

W: But what if your office doesn't have a window? I mean, I've worked in lots of places where there's no window.

M1: Then in that case, you need to get up and walk around. You should never sit for more than 30 minutes at a time anyway. This is important for the rest of your body as well, namely your back. Neck and back pain are a big problem for computer people. Always make sure your screen, keyboard, and chair are at the right height for you.

M2: I think it's important to have a comfortable chair, one that sort of shifts your weight a little bit forward. I put a cushion on my chair, and that really helps my lower back.

M1: That's not a bad idea. The right chair is a must, the right posture as well. Remember what your mother told you—sit up straight, with your feet on the floor. Another thing I wanted to talk about is air pollution in the workplace—sorry, did you have a question, Martha?

W: I've heard that copy machines are bad for you. Is there anything to this?

M1: Photocopy machines aren't a health hazard for people who use them only occasionally. But for people who use them a lot, there can be bad effects. For example, people who handle the toners can get skin rashes. If you handle the toner, you should pour it in slowly, to avoid spreading the dust, and always wash your hands afterward. Another problem—if the machines are in an area that's not well ventilated—is ozone.

W: Ozone! No kidding!

M1: It's true. Almost all photocopiers give off some ozone. However, the amount is usually less than what's considered hazardous. Most machines have an ozone filter, but this can still leak if the machine's not properly maintained. If you can smell a sort of electrical odor coming from the machine, it's a sign that it's giving off too much ozone.

1. What is the discussion mainly about?
2. What does the instructor recommend for relieving eyestrain?
3. According to the discussion, why is it important to have the right chair?
4. According to the instructor, what health problem is associated with copy machines?
5. Where in the workplace might ozone be a problem?

Questions 6 through 10. Listen to a talk in a drawing class.

Today we'll begin our discussion on perspective, or how to represent three–dimensional forms on a two–dimensional surface. The basic rules of perspective date back to the early Renaissance and are still used today. Perspective can be challenging when you're first learning to draw from observation, but it's essential to grasp if you want your drawings to represent the visual world as you see it. An understanding of perspective is mandatory for anyone who does representational drawing. This includes professionals in a variety of fields—interior design, illustration, architecture, industrial design, and fine arts, to name a few.

Simply put, perspective allows us to differentiate between objects of different sizes and at different distances from the viewer. It enables us to see immediately what the relationships are. The fundamental principle is that objects appear smaller as their distance from the observer increases. For instance, someone across the street appears smaller than the person standing next to you. Someone down the street looks even smaller, someone farther away looks smaller still, and so on.

Think of buildings in a landscape … the cross–ties of railroad tracks … the cars on a train. These are just a few things we know are approximately equal in size, yet seem to diminish with distance because of perspective.

Everything in perspective is related to the concept of eye level—the horizontal line at the level of your eyes as you turn your head from side to side. Another related concept is the vanishing point. The vanishing point is a point at eye level where parallel lines going away from you appear to come together and then vanish. When you draw a building, for example, the vanishing point makes the building sort of recede in space and grow smaller. Yet, in reality, you know the sides of the building are parallel. If lines are drawn along these sides, they will converge at a distant point—the vanishing point.

In real life, the eye level is rarely visible, and vanishing points virtually never are. Yet you should—it's important for you to always work with an awareness of them. This is why I advise you to sketch eye level and vanishing points in every drawing, at least temporarily. Eye level and vanishing points will help you convey perspective. As you gain an understanding of perspective, you'll find that your work is more confident and you're better able to create a finished drawing from your sketches.

6. What aspect of perspective does the instructor mainly discuss?
7. According to the instructor, which fields require an understanding of perspective?
8. Select the drawing that illustrates the concept of perspective.
9. Identify the part of the drawing that represents the vanishing point.
10. What does the instructor advise the students to do?

Disk 2, Track 1

2.3   DETERMINING ATTITUDE AND PURPOSE

Focus (p. 232)

Listen to part of a conversation between a student and an academic adviser.

W: Hi, Greg. Um…do you have a minute?

M: Nicole. Hello. I have … uh … about twenty minutes. Come in and sit down.

W: Thanks. I wanted to talk about the school psychology program. I've been thinking about this for a while, and I've decided to change my major to counseling.

M: Really? It's quite a change from being an accountant to being a counselor!

W: I know. It's funny, isn't it? All my life I thought I wanted to run my own business someday. But this year I've been working as a volunteer tutor—at Garfield Elementary—and I'm just so impressed with what the counselors are doing there.

M: Did you say Garfield?

W: Yes, where those kids in the accident went to school. That was terrible, that accident. It was such a shock to the whole school. But it was eye opening for me. I had a chance to observe some of the counselors talking to the kids, helping them deal with the tragedy. They—the counselors, that is—they were so, so … they were really amazing. It really got me thinking about … about how to make … how to help people heal. I started thinking, "This is something I'd like to do."

Now choose the best answer to each question.

1. Why does the student go to see her adviser?
2. What is the student's attitude toward the school counselors that she observed?

Disk 2, Track 2

Exercise 2.3 A (p. 235)

Questions 1 through 2. Listen to a conversation between a student and a professor.

M: Professor Park?
W: Hello, Tony. How can I help you?
M: Professor Park, I have a problem. My father had to have surgery, and I have to go to Oklahoma. I don't know how long I'll be gone. I was wondering if I could take an Incomplete for your class.
W: I'm so sorry to hear about your father. Of course you can take a grade of Incomplete. It means you would have six weeks to make up the term paper and the final exam. There is also a form that you need to fill out that I have to sign.
M: I've got the form right here.
W: Oh, then why don't we take care of it right now?

1. Why does the student go to see his professor?
2. What is required for an Incomplete?

Questions 3 through 5. Listen to part of a conversation that takes place in the student services office of a university.

M: Excuse me, I'm looking for Janice.
W: I'm Janice. What can I do for you?
M: The cashier in the cafeteria sent me here. I'd like to change my meal plan.
W: What plan do you have now?
M: Two meals a day, breakfast and dinner. But I have an early morning class three days a week, and I don't have time to eat breakfast in the cafeteria.
W: What, no breakfast? That's not good!
M: Oh, I still eat! We take turns bringing doughnuts or bagels to have at the break.
W: Glad to hear it. So … uh … what you have now is Plan B. And what did you want to do?
M: Well, I was thinking of switching to dinner only, if I can do that, and get a refund for the breakfast I don't eat.
W: Do you know about Plan C?
M: Plan C?
W: It's for lunch and dinner, and costs only $20 more than Plan B.
M: Oh, really? Hmm. That sounds like a good deal.

3. What is the purpose of the conversation?
4. Why does the woman say this:
"What, no breakfast? That's not good!"
5. Why does the woman tell the man about Plan C?

Questions 6 through 7. Listen to a conversation between a student and a professor.

W: Professor Curtis, may I ask you something?
M: Of course.
W: My daughter was sick yesterday, and I had to stay home with her. I was wondering—could I make up the quiz?
M: I usually don't do that for quizzes, only for tests.
W: But I'm concerned this will affect my grade. I need to do well in this class.
M: Then I've got an idea. If you want to show me what you've learned, give me a one–page report, summarizing the most important thing you got out of the chapter.
W: Oh, I can do that. That's even better than a quiz. Thank you, Professor Curtis.

6. Why does the student speak to the professor?
7. What does the professor suggest the student do?

Questions 8 through 10. Listen to a telephone conversation between two graduate students.

W: Hello.
M: Leona? This is Jaspar.
W: Hi! I've been waiting for you to call. Could you get Dr. Bryant for next week?
M: Dr. Bryant is on sabbatical, but Professor Slocum says he'd be happy to visit our class.
W: I don't know Professor Slocum.
M: He's an expert on the natural history of the region and has written several books on the topic. I think he'll be an excellent addition to our seminar.
W: Good work, Jaspar! This assignment to invite a guest speaker has turned out to be harder than I thought.
M: But it's a great assignment, and besides, everyone has to do it. Look at all the professional contacts we're making!
W: You're right, it's very useful. Thanks, again, and I'll see you tomorrow!

8. What are the speakers mainly discussing?
9. Why does the man say this:
"He's an expert on the natural history of the region and has written several books on the topic. I think he'll be an excellent addition to our seminar."
10. What is the man's opinion of the assignment?

Disk 2, Track 3

Exercise 2.3.B (p. 236)

Questions 1 through 2. Listen to part of a discussion in a writing class.

M: You probably noticed in your reading for this week that all the stories involved cases of miscommunication between people. You probably also noticed that a lot of this miscommunication was due to cultural differences. This is all good stuff, and so I thought it would be a good idea if this week's journal theme were along the same lines. What I'd like you to do is think and write about a time when you—or someone you know—experienced some type of miscommunication. It could be any kind of problem in conveying or in understanding a … Yes?
W: But isn't this the same as last week? I mean, I feel I've already written a lot about it. I had to do something like this in two of my other classes too. Can't we write about something else for a change?
M: What did you have in mind?

W: I mean, I'm getting tired of writing about my life. And I don't feel qualified to write about any of my friends' problems.

M: Then why not focus on someone you don't know personally? For example, a scene in a movie or a television show.

W: Oh. I can do that?

M: Of course. What's important is your awareness of—that you can recognize instances of miscommunication.

1. What is the main purpose of the discussion?
2. What is the woman's attitude toward the assignment?

Questions 3 through 6. Listen to part of a talk in a United States history class. The professor is talking about economics in colonial New England.

W: We know that in colonial New England, the Native Americans—compared to the European colonists—had a far greater knowledge of what resources in the environment could be eaten or made useful. Native Americans used a wide range of resources for economic subsistence, and these resources were simply used by the family that acquired them. Only a few resources were accumulated for the purpose of showing a person's social status—for example, shells, furs, and ornaments of the hunt.

M: Excuse me, Dr. Singer, but did they … um … did the Native Americans have a concept of wealth?

W: The Native Americans believed a person's status came more from kinship and personal alliances than from stores of wealth. Their definition of "need" was what they needed to survive. So if they had food, clothing, and shelter, they considered themselves wealthy. For the European colonists, on the other hand, resources in the environment were seen more as commodities, as goods that could be exchanged in markets. European economies measured commodities in terms of money values—abstract equivalencies that could be accumulated and could function as indicators of wealth and social status. So, for the colonists, "need" was defined by the markets that bought New England goods. So the Europeans perceived few resources in New England ecosystems, but they saw many commodities—fur, fish, timber—which could be sold in the marketplace for profit.

3. What is the main purpose of the talk?
4. What does the professor say about the Native Americans' use of resources?
5. Listen again to part of the discussion. Then answer the question.
   "Excuse me, Dr. Singer, but did they … um … did the Native Americans have a concept of wealth?"
   "The Native Americans believed a person's status came more from kinship and personal alliances than from stores of wealth. Their definition of "need" was what they needed to survive. So if they had food, clothing, and shelter, they considered themselves wealthy."
   Why does the professor say this:
   "So if they had food, clothing, and shelter, they considered themselves wealthy."
6. Why does the professor say this:
   "So the Europeans perceived few resources in New England ecosystems, but they saw many commodities—fur, fish, timber—which could be sold in the marketplace for profit."

Questions 7 through 10. Listen to part of a talk in an anthropology class. The professor is discussing culture.

M: What would human life be without culture? It's impossible for us to imagine what we'd be like without language, without art or religion or technology. Over hundreds of thousands of years of evolution, these aspects of our cultures have become as much a part of us as our anatomy and physiology. We have a lot in common with the people around us. In fact, the number of ideas we have in common with nearby people is very large. A complete list of shared ideas—for example, ideas we share with our own—the people around us—this list would include our ideas about what's right and wrong, what's beautiful and ugly, and so on … also our ideas about food, work, love, marriage—every aspect of our lives—even our rules about how to behave toward strangers, friends, animals, and the earth. Think of a particular group of people—any group—say, for example, college students. If you could take all the ideas and behaviors, all the tools and technology, all the things that college students share as a result of being in contact with each other, you'd have what anthropologists call student culture.

W: So, what you're saying is culture is sort of like a club. College students are a club. It's because our experience is … like, we go to class, we do homework, we have our computers and cell phones, we hang out with other students. Sometimes we forget what the outside world is like. This is why—that's what we have in common with other students—it's why our culture makes us feel like part of a club, right?

M: Hmmm. In a way a culture is like a club—neighboring cultures might share the same ideas and rules, like neighboring clubs do. But the comparison doesn't completely cut it. Think about it. A club has borders that we can define—but we run into trouble if we try to draw borders around a culture. Culture isn't a thing. It's an idea. Still—even though the idea of culture is problematic—some of us believe that by continuing to study cultures, we will eventually be able to explain the similarities and differences among us.

7. What is the purpose of the talk?
8. Why does the professor mention student culture?
9. What is the woman's attitude toward student culture?
10. What does the professor think of comparing a culture to a club?

Disk 2, Track 4

Exercise 2.3.C (p. 237)

Questions 1 through 2. Listen to part of a talk in a business management class.

Management requires a great deal of energy and effort—more than most people care to make. One factor that affects managers and inhibits their capacity to provide leadership is stress. Stress has lots of causes—work overload, criticism from workers—and can have negative health effects, including loss of sleep.

It's a fact: managers have to deal with stress. Some handle it by making time to be by themselves. Most have some favorite place or pastime—a beach to walk on, maybe a stream to fish in, or a game to play with the kids. It's important to have some form of rest and relaxation—creating art, working with your hands, gardening, playing sports—the list goes on. Rest doesn't always mean inactivity. For some people, exercise is rest.

1. What is the main purpose of the talk?
2. What is the professor's opinion of rest?

Questions 3 through 6. Listen to part of a lecture in a psychology class. The professor is talking about clinical psychology.

In order to know how behavior patterns can be changed, the clinical psychologist has to know what causes the client to behave the way he or she does. Identifying the cause is called diagnosis. In diagnosis a psychologist uses two basic tools: interviews and psychological tests. Through interviews and tests, the psychologist tries to classify the problem to see if it falls into any known categories.

A psychologist may also attempt to describe the client's personality in terms of how he or she deals with life. For example, some people like to lead, and some prefer to follow the lead of others. Some people are active and outgoing, while others are quiet and reflective.

In a diagnostic interview, the psychologist takes the client's case history. This means learning how the client got along with parents, teachers, and friends, as well as how the person handled difficult situations in the past.

Psychological testing is the other way that a psychologist tries to diagnose the client's problems. Clinical psychologists have developed tests that can help them learn about a person's intelligence and personality, as well as tests that show whether a person's behavior or perception is influenced by emotions, disabilities, or other factors.

Personality testing is useful in discovering how the client tries to adjust to life. Personality tests can reveal unconscious feelings the person is unable to talk about. This information can be important and could help shorten the length of treatment required.

3. What is the purpose of the lecture?
4. How do clinical psychologists diagnose a client's problems?
5. Why does the professor discuss taking a client's case history?
6. According to the professor, why are personality tests useful?

Questions 7 through 10. A public health officer has been invited to speak to a biology class. She will be discussing bats. Listen to the beginning of the talk.

Now that the warmer weather and longer days are here, we aren't the only ones spending more time outdoors. This is an active time for bats as well. Migratory bats are now returning to the area, and young bats are starting to explore their environment. Young bats go off course, and this is when most people come into contact with them.

Bats are a normal part of our environment and can even be a good thing. Bats help keep down the insect population, especially mosquitoes. Normal bat activity includes sleeping during the daytime and becoming active and flying around in search of food at night, starting at dusk. It's unusual to see a bat during the day. Normal bats don't fly around in the daytime, or lie or crawl on the ground, so if you encounter a bat like that, you should call the health department immediately.

If you have bats in your attic or house, contact a pest control agency. They do not kill the bats, but make recommendations on how to get the bats out of your home. You'll want to create a one–way valve from your house to outside so they can get out but can't come in. To avoid having bats in your house altogether, find all possible entry points into the house and close them by caulking or screening the gap. Bats can squeeze through a gap of one–half inch.

Bats are the most likely carriers of rabies in our area, and almost one hundred percent of rabies cases are fatal. Make sure your dogs and cats are vaccinated against rabies. If you should come in physical contact with a bat, it's important to get in touch with the health department or a doctor immediately. If possible, catch the bat so it can be tested for rabies.

7. What is the main purpose of the talk?
8. Why does the speaker say this:
   "Bats help keep down the insect population, especially mosquitoes."
9. How can you prevent bats from entering your house?
10. Why does the speaker recommend getting medical advice if you come in physical contact with a bat?

Disk 2, Track 5

Exercise 2.3.D (p. 238)

Questions 1 through 5. Listen to part of a lecture in an anthropology class. The professor is discussing humor and laughter.

Being amused is a condition we're all familiar with, but what exactly is a sense of humor? Well, it's something very personal, and yet we communicate it to others by laughing. Laughter is a universal human expression. All normal human beings can laugh. Children as young as one month old will laugh. People often laugh together, and people laugh louder and more frequently when other people around them are also laughing. Every comedian knows this, and research has confirmed it.

Physically, laughter is an involuntary tensing of the chest muscles, followed by a rapid inhalation and exhalation of breath—a mechanism that releases tension. For most people, a good laugh is welcome—and worth looking for—because it brings pleasure and relief.

Human adults everywhere in the world enjoy making their children laugh. Adults make playful attacks on their children, tickling, teasing, and even pretending to bite them. Adults will throw small children up in the air and catch them again. This causes the child to experience mild stress, but in a secure setting because the stress is carefully controlled by the parent. And when the child laughs, it's a signal that he or she has successfully dealt with mild feelings of insecurity. This teaches the child about the shocks and fears that are part of human life, and which every human eventually has to deal with. This element of shock in an otherwise safe situation is a universal characteristic of situations where people laugh.

Our sense of humor allows us to tell stories about situations we haven't experienced firsthand. We call these little stories "jokes." We tell jokes to show our frustration with the society we live in, especially its … well, its rules. Social rules and conventions provide us with a range of situations that we can turn into humor. And the things we joke about—the conventions and rules we live by—are sort of tense areas in our society, they're areas where we can see the need for change. Humor gives us the power to think about changing the rules. Making jokes and laughing are safe ways to change our social rules and conventions. Therefore, comedians—whether they know it or not—are agents of social change.

The ability to laugh is a vital part of being human. People who laugh together—or laugh at each other's jokes—feel close to each other. Laughter creates a sense of connection. Humor can also help us deal with anxieties that we can't escape. Failure, fear, pain, and death—they're all real to us, as they are to no other animal on Earth. And without a sense of humor, it would be difficult for us to live with everything we that know about the world.

1. According to the professor, why do most people welcome laughter?
2. Why does the professor say this:
   "Adults make playful attacks on their children, tickling, teasing, and even pretending to bite them. Adults will throw small children up in the air and catch them again."
3. Which of the following is a universal characteristic of situations where people laugh?
4. Why does the professor talk about social rules and conventions?
5. Listen again to part of the lecture. Then answer the question.
   "The ability to laugh is a vital part of being human. People who laugh together—or laugh at each other's jokes—feel close to each other. Laughter creates a sense of connection. Humor can also help us deal with anxieties that we can't escape. Failure, fear, pain, and death—they're all real to us, as they are to no other animal on Earth. And without a sense of humor, it would be difficult for us to live with everything that we know about the world."
   Why does the professor say this:
   "And without a sense of humor, it would be difficult for us to live with everything that we know about the world."

Questions 6 through 10. Listen to part of a lecture in a horticulture class. The professor is talking about roadside beautification.

There's always been tension—throughout our history—a kind of tension between private development and government regulation, especially when it comes to development of land for agriculture.

Catherine Parr Traill—a botanist who lived in the nineteenth century—she predicted that the natural beauty of Canada's wilderness would disappear because of agricultural development. She wrote in 1868 that the wilderness was, quote, "destined to be swept away, as the onward march of civilization clears away the primeval forest … and turns the waste places into fruitful field," unquote.

But, fortunately for us, Catherine Parr Traill's prediction turned out to be not entirely true. The Quinte Wildflower Project proves that people can come together to preserve the beauty of the wilderness. This project continues a trend to beautify North American highways that goes all the way back to the 1960s and the beginning of the Adopt-a-Highway programs, the programs that use volunteers to clean up the litter along roadsides. Since the sixties, beautification programs have been … um … broadened to include the planting of native flowers and shrubs.

In Canada, a lot of time and money were being spent mowing the grass on roadsides. Weeds and wildflowers alike—all were sprayed with herbicides to kill them off. Eventually, the high cost forced the government to stop spraying and mowing. Since the 1980s, Ontario has turned to volunteers and private sponsors for roadside beautification.

The Quinte Wildflower Project is the largest roadside planting of wildflowers in Ontario. The project was born in 1996, with the help of private sponsors and government horticulturists. Areas along an 18–kilometer stretch of Highway 401—from Trenton to Belleville—were … um … most of the sites were planted with one of two native wildflower seed mixtures. Both seed mixtures produce flowers that require little maintenance and are hardy enough to survive roadside conditions. Each seed mixture contains several different species, so wildflowers bloom, so there's a steady show of colors from June to October.

The Quinte Wildflower Project has been a huge success. Its greatest success has been in attracting both public interest and private sponsors. It demonstrates that government and citizens can work together … that partnerships between the public and private sectors can and do work.

6. How does the instructor develop the topic of roadside beautification?
7. Why does the professor quote botanist Catherine Parr Traill?
8. Why does the professor mention the Adopt-a-Highway programs that began in the 1960s?
9. Why does the professor say this:
   "Each seed mixture contains several different species, so wildflowers bloom, so there's a steady show of colors from June to October."
10. What does the professor think of partnerships between government and private citizens?

Disk 2, Track 6

Quiz 2 (p. 244)

Questions 1 through 5. Listen to a conversation between two students.

W: Am I ever glad to see you! We don't have much time left before our presentation—only the rest of this week. Let's talk about what we still need to do.
M: Do we have that much left to do? I was under the impression we're just about ready. I've got all my data, the graphs and photos of the mountain.
W: Let's—we'd better go over what we have.
M: Oh, sure, but I have hockey practice in half an hour.
W: This won't take long, I hope. Now, I'll do the introduction. First, I'll talk about how the geologists at Volcano Watch detected another tiny earthquake on Stone Peak two weeks ago. The quake registered only point 8, but they think it could be part of a series of small quakes that precede an eruption. Then I'll give the history of the eruptions in that area.
M: How far are you going to go back?
W: Two thousand years. That's the last time Stone Peak erupted. I won't go over every little eruption, just the six or seven major ones in the range. Then … I guess at that point I'll turn it over to you.
M: And I'll show my graphs—no, maybe the pictures first, at least this one of the bulge. George Davidson at the observatory gave me all these photographs. I

still have to make slides out of 'em, and of my graphs, too, but that won't take long. Aren't they awesome? Some are really good shots of the mountain—you can really see how much the bulge has grown.

W: It's grown … how much, a few inches?

M: A few inches a year, for the past six years. The bulge is forming 'cause a chamber of magma below the surface is growing. Earth's crust is being bent and bent—a few inches a year is a lot of bending—and sooner or later, it'll start to break open. Then there'll be a show! First I'll show them—first the color picture, then the graphs showing the eruptions over the past six years … and then the series of black–and–white photos showing the bulge. It shows up better in black and white.

W: Then … when you're through with the slides, we should probably allow enough time for questions.

M: Yeah, that sounds good. That should about wrap it up. See? We're all set to go.

1. What are the students discussing?
2. Listen again to part of the conversation. Then answer the question.
   "Let's—we'd better go over what we have."
   "Oh, sure, but I have hockey practice in half an hour."
   Why does the man say this:
   "Oh, sure, but I have hockey practice in half an hour."
3. What types of data will the students use in their presentation?
4. What is the man's opinion of the photographs?
5. According to the man, why is a bulge forming on the mountain?

Questions 6 through 10. Listen to part of a talk in an economics class.

One very important institution in our economy is the bank. Banks manage money for individual people, corporations, and the government. Banks provide a number of important services for you and your family. Most importantly, they're a safe place to store your money. They also provide an easy way for you to transfer money from one place to another. When you write a personal check, the check authorizes the bank to give your money to the person or business whose name is on the check.

Of course, banks also lend money. Ordinary people take out bank loans for a number of reasons—to pay for college, to buy or remodel a home, to start or expand a business, and so forth. Banks provide these services to individuals; however, their main function is to lend large sums of money, for example, to corporations. When people or corporations borrow money from a bank, they must, of course, pay interest—a percentage of the money they borrowed.

Banks pay interest on the money they hold, and charge interest on the money they lend. For a bank to make a profit, it has to collect more interest than it pays out.

Sometimes banks invest money as well as lend it. To invest money means to put it into a corporation or some other project—for example, building a housing complex or doing medical research—in exchange for a share of the profits. Most businesses need loans and investments at some time, and banks are an important source of both.

You might wonder what would happen if all the people with money in a bank wanted to take their money out at the same time. I mean, how would the bank be able to give everyone their money, if it had lent out or invested most of it? In fact, this can be a serious problem for banks. They count on the fact that most people won't want their money for a long time once it's deposited. That leaves the bank free to lend or invest the money. If every person—or even lots of people—tried to withdraw their money at the same time, the bank might not be able to honor all of its deposits. This causes some banks to fail, or go bankrupt.

Bank failures used to be common during times of recession or depression. They were especially common during the Great Depression of the 1930s. When Franklin Roosevelt became president in 1933, one of the first things he did was close all the banks, so depositors wouldn't panic and try to take all their money out.

6. What is the main purpose of the talk?
7. For what reasons do individuals take out bank loans?
8. How do banks make a profit?
9. Why does the professor say this:
   "If every person—or even lots of people—tried to withdraw their money at the same time, the bank might not be able to honor all of its deposits."
10. Why were banks closed during the Great Depression of the 1930s?

Disk 2, Track 7

Quiz 3 (p. 246)

Questions 1 through 5. Listen to a conversation between a student and a professor.

M: Excuse me, Dr. Kilmer. Do you have a minute?

W: Hello, Darren. Come on in, have a seat. What can I do for you?

M: Well, it's about my midterm grade for organizational psychology. I … I'm surprised it's so … low. I feel like I've been working pretty hard in this class.

W: I see. Well, let's go back and have another look at each of your assignments … here we go. OK, I've pulled up your record. Hmm … you had a "C" on the midterm exam and a "B" on your first assignment.

M: Yeah, that was the paper about the interview. I talked to a woman at a bio–research firm.

W: Yes, I remember that paper. You must have learned some useful things. But unfortunately, Darren, I don't have any record here for the second and third assignments. They were due on October 1st and the 13th.

M: I know … but I've been sort of busy. My younger brother's starting classes here in January, and I have to show him around and help him find a place to live. He's staying with me for now, but he doesn't have a car, so I have to drive him.

W: Can't your brother take the bus some of the time? After all, your coursework should be your priority.

M: Uh, it's really hard. He is my brother, and he's had some problems in the past. My parents want me to help him get settled. They live two thousand miles away.

W: I see. That does make it tough.

M: I'd like to … Would it be all right if I made up those two papers? I started the first one, but I just didn't get everything typed up.

W: Yes, of course you can make up the work, but it would be best if you did that as soon as possible. Remember, these short papers, together with the long term paper, count for 50 percent of your final grade.

M: I know. And I need my final grade to be better than my midterm grade. Don't worry. I'll get it together. I really like this class … I just have to get more organized.

W: Well, good luck, Darren. I'm glad you came to talk to me.

M: Thanks, Dr. Kilmer. I appreciate your time.

1. Why does the student speak to his professor?
2. What reason does the student give for not completing his assignments?
3. When were the assignments due?
4. What point does the professor make about the student's work?
5. Why does the student say this:
"Don't worry. I'll get it together."

Questions 6 through 10. Listen to part of a lecture in a communications class.

Researchers study television to understand its effects on viewers and to measure its effectiveness in selling products. Much of the research on TV audiences is market research, paid for by corporations with something to sell. Let me repeat: research on television is funded largely by advertisers.

The television industry depends on advertising money to survive, and this relationship influences what television offers viewers. Advertisers aim to reach mass audiences and specific social groups. In turn, the television industry tries to meet the needs of advertisers, because pleasing the advertisers is nearly as important as pleasing the public. This means advertisers have a lot of control over what programs are made and when they are shown.

The American television industry is controlled by people who are more interested in the culture of consumerism than in preserving cultures or natural resources. I mean, for the first time in history, most of the stories children learn don't come from their parents or schools; they come from a small number of large corporations with something to sell. And this culture of consumerism is exported to other countries.

Television is the most effective marketing tool ever created. Many advertisements apply basic psychology by sort of appealing to our insecurities and desires. Ads convince us that the things we once thought were luxuries are now necessities. Television is highly skilled at creating images of affluence, not just in the ads, but in the programs as well. Using sophisticated market research, programmers and advertisers sort of paint a picture of life centered on material possessions. This kind of life may look glamorous and desirable, but it's all at the expense of personal relationships.

As you probably can tell, I tend to agree with critics of the media. Advertising does create false needs, and products we really need don't require advertising. Television promotes consumerism. It shows us things, things, and more things. It encourages greed and envy. Television helps create a wasteful society, where things are thrown out long before they are worn out.

6. What is the main idea of the lecture?
7. According to the professor, why do researchers study television?
8. According to the professor, why do advertisers have control over television programming?
9. Listen again to part of the lecture. Then answer the question.
"Television is highly skilled at creating images of affluence, not just in the ads, but in the programs as well. Using sophisticated market research, programmers and advertisers sort of paint a picture of life centered on material possessions. This kind of life may look glamorous and desirable, but it's all at the expense of personal relationships."
Why does the professor say this:
"This kind of life may look glamorous and desirable, but it's all at the expense of personal relationships."
10. What is the professor's opinion of television?

Disk 3, Track 1

2.4 MAKING INFERENCES AND PREDICTIONS

Focus (p. 248)

Listen to a conversation between a student and a professor.

W: Professor Elliott, did you read the draft of my paper yet?

M: Why hello, Amy. Uh, yes, I did read it. As a matter of fact, I wanted to talk to you about it. I'm glad you stopped by. I think I have your paper … here we go, I have it right here.

W: Is there something wrong with it?

M: No, not terribly, but … I can't tell where you're going with it.

W: Oh. I'm not sure I understand.

M: Let me put it like this. You start out strong. In fact, your introduction is done quite well. You really get your teacher interested in technology and society and how they're related and all. The middle part, too— where you interview the engineer—that, that's very engaging. Lots of good and original ideas. But after that … well, I'm lost. What does it all mean? It just gets a little vague.

W: Oh, I think I see what you mean. Do you mean my conclusion's not clear?

M: Well, it's a little too open. You need to tie it all together … leave your reader with one clear thought, one new way of thinking about technology.

W: Oh well, I see. Um … maybe I'd better work on that part some more. I really appreciate your comments. This helps me a lot. Thanks, Professor Elliott.

M: My pleasure. Any time.

Now choose the best answer to each question.

1. What does the professor imply about the student's paper?
2. What will the student probably do?

Disk 3, Track 2

Exercise 2.4.A (p. 252)

Questions 1 through 2. Listen to a conversation between a student and his adviser.

M: Excuse me, Mrs. Lyons, do you have a minute?
W: Yes, how are you, Bruce?
M: Fine, I guess. But I'm having a hard time keeping up in geometry. I think I'd better get out of the class and try again next quarter.
W: Let's have a look at the preliminary list for next quarter. Hmm. I'm afraid geometry won't be offered again in the spring.
M: Oh, no.
W: If you feel your workload is too heavy now, why not drop your history class? You could easily get that course again. It's offered every quarter.
M: Oh, all right. If I drop history, maybe then I'll be able to catch up in geometry. Thanks, Mrs. Lyons.
W: You're welcome, Bruce. Good luck!

1. Why does the student go to see his adviser?
2. What will the student probably do?

Questions 3 through 4. Listen to a conversation between two students.

M: I ran into a problem when I tried to register by telephone. I got a message that said I had an outstanding charge on my account that needed to be paid before I could complete my registration.
W: What does that mean?
M: I'm not sure. A recorded voice just said I had to go to the Student Accounts Office.
W: Do you have any idea what it could be about?
M: The only thing I can think of is last quarter my roommate broke the shower door in our suite, and maybe they billed me by mistake.
W: Oh, I'll bet that's expensive. You'd better go to the accounting office and try to clear it up.
M: Yeah, and I'd better make sure my roommate pays for the damage. I do need to register for next quarter.

3. What is the man's problem?
4. What will the man probably do?

Questions 5 through 7. Listen to a conversation between a student and a professor.

W: Professor Pollard?
M: Yes?
W: I've ... um ... I registered for your psychology course for summer session. But I have to go to Vancouver and won't be back until June 25.
M: Oh. That means you'll miss the first week.
W: I know. Could I ... um ... make up the work when I get back?
M: That would be kind of a problem. It's like this ... we'll cover the important basics during the first week. And you'll be forming study groups and starting to plan your research projects. The first group report is due on the 25th.
W: Would I still be able to join a group?
M: I don't think that would be fair to the others in your group. Summer session is only six weeks, and you

can't afford to get a late start.
W: That's OK. I understand. Will you teach this course again in the fall?
M: Yes. In fact, in fall semester there'll be two, maybe three sections.

5. Why does the student go to see her professor?
6. What does the professor imply?
7. What will the student probably do?

Questions 8 through 10. Listen to a conversation between two students.

M: I haven't seen you around lately. Where have you been hiding yourself?
W: I live off campus now, in Forest Glen.
M: Oh, those are the apartments in Glenwood that the university owns, right?
W: Right, and would you believe they don't cost much more than the dormitories?
M: I didn't realize that. But how did you manage to get in Forest Glen? I thought it was just for married students.
W: Three of the buildings are for married people only, but anyone can live in the rest. And the best part of it is I can ride the city bus for free! All I had to do was show my rent receipt to the transit company, and they gave me a bus pass that's good for the whole semester!
M: Maybe I'll look into that. I might save some money on parking.
W: Why not? The apartments are nice and spacious, and you wouldn't even need your car.

8. What are the students mainly discussing?
9. What can be inferred about the woman?
10. What will the man probably do?

Disk 3, Track 3

Exercise 2.4.B (p. 253)

Questions 1 through 2. Listen to an art instructor talk about composition.

Composition is the organization of shapes and forms into a whole—an expressive whole. The elements of composition—line, shape, tone, and color—need to be well arranged, need to be ordered. They need to be coherent ... just like the words and phrases and sentences in a piece of writing.

All paintings have a compositional element. Successful paintings sort of suggest the third dimension, the sense that the design goes beyond the picture frame. A picture's unity—which includes the shapes, tones and colors—is linked to what the artist has to say. The artist's message is strongest when it's clear. A composition is better if it says one thing strongly than if it tries to say too many things. A crowded composition is sort of fussy and splintered and lacks unity. Even a painting of a single object needs thoughtful composition so the character of the object is present in every shape.

1. What does the instructor imply about composition?
2. Would the instructor most likely agree or disagree with each statement below?

Questions 3 through 6. Listen to part of a talk in a biology class.

Biology is considered one of the natural sciences. It is the science of life and life's processes. And like life, science is better understood by observing it than by trying to create a precise definition. Over the next fifteen weeks, we will be observing the science of biology.

In many ways, biology is the most demanding of all sciences. This is partly because living systems are so complex. Biology is also a multidisciplinary science. It requires knowledge of chemistry, physics, and mathematics. And of all the sciences, biology is the most linked to the social sciences and humanities.

The word "science" comes from a Latin verb meaning "to know." Science is a way of knowing. It emerges from our curiosity about ourselves and our world. Striving to understand is one of our basic drives.

Who are scientists? Scientists are people who ask questions about nature and who believe that these questions can be answered. Scientists are explorers who are passionate about discovery.

This course has something for all of you to discover. If you're a biology major or a pre–medical student, you'll discover ways to become a better scientist. If you're a physical science or engineering major, you'll discover in biology many applications for what you've learned in your other science courses. And if you're a non–science major, you've chosen a course in which you can sample many disciplines of discovery.

3. What is the main purpose of the talk?
4. According to the professor, why is biology the most demanding of all sciences?
5. What does the professor imply about scientists?
6. What is probably true about the students in this course?

Questions 7 through 10. Listen to a lecture in a botany class. The professor is talking about plant hormones.

The word "hormone" is derived from a Greek verb that means "to excite." Hormones are found in all multi–cellular organisms and function to coordinate the parts of the organism. A hormone is a chemical signal. It's produced by one part of the body and is then transported to other parts of the body, where it triggers responses in cells and tissues.

The concept of chemical messengers in plants first emerged from a series of classic experiments on how plant stems respond to light.

Think about this. A houseplant on a windowsill grows toward light. If you rotate the plant, it will soon reorient its growth until its leaves again face the window.

The growth of a plant toward light is called "phototropism." In a forest or other natural ecosystem where plants may be crowded, phototropism directs growing seedlings toward the sunlight that powers photosynthesis.

Some of the earliest experiments on phototropism were conducted in the late nineteenth century by Charles Darwin and his son, Francis. The Darwins observed that a grass seedling could bend toward light only if the tip of the shoot was present. If the tip was removed, the shoot would not curve toward light. The seedling would also fail to grow toward light if the tip was covered with an opaque cap.

The Darwins proposed the hypothesis that some signal was transmitted downward from the tip into the part of the stem that controlled growth. Later experiments by other scientists studying phototropism led to the discovery of chemical messengers that stimulated growth in the stem. These chemical messengers were hormones.

7. What do plant hormones do?
8. Which picture illustrates phototropism?
9. Which grass seedlings would probably NOT bend toward light?
10. What can be inferred about the tip of a plant's stem?

Disk 3, Track 4

Exercise 2.4.C (p. 254)

Questions 1 through 2. Listen to a conversation between two students.

W: Have you finished your paper for anthropology yet?
M: No, I haven't even started. I'm having trouble coming up with a good idea. We're supposed to describe the cultural characteristics of a group, but any group I can think of would seem too artificial. I don't know much about any one cultural group.
W: Of course you do. Write about your own culture!
M: But that's my problem. I don't really have a culture.
W: That's ridiculous! Everyone has a culture. What about the culture of your family? Or your high school? Or your hometown?
M: I grew up in a small town where almost everyone works in the orchards.
W: Bingo! Write about the culture of the orchard community.
M: I never thought of that. Well, why not? It's something I know a lot about.

1. What is the man's problem?
2. What will the man probably do?

Questions 3 through 4. Listen to a conversation between a student and a professor.

M: Professor Martin, I will have to miss class tomorrow. My great aunt passed away and her funeral is tomorrow.
W: Oh, let me offer my condolences to you and your family.
M: Thank you. My aunt was a wonderful lady. Ah, so would it be possible for me to take the test next week?
W: Of course. Eric handles all make–ups. He's the instructional aide for our department. Can you stop by the office today and make an appointment with him?
M: Sure. Would he be there now?
W: He should be. He works every day.
M: Then I'll do it right now. Thank you, Professor Martin.
W: You're welcome, Jerry. Take care.

3. Why does the professor say this:
   "Oh, let me offer my condolences to you and your family."
4. What will the student probably do next?

Questions 5 through 7. Listen to a conversation between two students.

M: I can't believe how much my books cost this semester! I just spent over one hundred dollars in the university bookstore, for only four books! And I still need the book for chemistry. That one costs fifty–five dollars! It's a little more than my budget can handle at the moment.

W: Science books are always out of sight. But did you know there's another bookstore in the Pioneer District? They carry used copies of most of the textbooks for the university.

M: I wonder if they'd have my chemistry book. I need the third edition.

W: I found all of my books there. You can sell any kind of book, too, not just textbooks.

M: That's not a bad idea. Where did you say that was again?

5. What is the man's problem?
6. What can be inferred about the man?
7. What will the man probably do?

Questions 8 through 10. Listen to a conversation in a campus pharmacy.

W: Hello. I'm here for an allergy medication. The nurse sent me—I think her name was Margaret—in the student clinic. She said I didn't need a prescription, and that you would know the right medication. It's for allergies, for my itchy nose and burning eyes. I've been having sneezing fits, and it's driving me crazy.

M: All right. I think she means the new product, the really strong one.

W: Maybe that's the one. She says it really works for allergies.

M: All right. We have—you have a choice actually of capsules or tablets. There's no difference in price.

W: It doesn't matter. Hmm … capsules, I guess.

M: All right. Now, this is a powerful drug, so you need only—no more than two capsules every six hours. And you shouldn't drink alcohol, drive a car, or operate machinery.

W: Uh oh! I have a big test tomorrow! I don't know … if this is going to make me drowsy … Do you have anything else that's effective but won't knock me out?

M: Nothing that will relieve your symptoms like this drug. Why don't you—you could take two capsules three or four hours before your test. That way, the drug's still working, but the drowsiness has mostly worn off when you take your test.

W: OK. Well, I guess I have no choice. I can't start sneezing during the test.

8. What does the man imply about the medication?
9. Listen again to part of the conversation. Then answer the question.
"Uh oh! I have a big test tomorrow! I don't know … if this is going to make me drowsy … Do you have anything else that's effective but won't knock me out?"
Select the sentence that best expresses how the woman probably feels.
10. What will the woman probably do?

Disk 3, Track 5
Exercise 2.4.D (p. 255)

Questions 1 through 2. Listen to a conversation in a university office.

W: Hello. May I help you?

M: Yes, I hope so. My name is Harry Burke. I got a message from someone in this office saying I still needed to pay a lab fee.

W: Let me check. Harry Burke. Oh, yes. The computer shows that you haven't paid the lab fee for your biology class. You'll need to do this before you can attend your lab section.

M: I didn't know there was a lab fee. I don't remember seeing it on my bill.

W: Did you register after September 15?

M: Uh, I think so.

W: The fee probably didn't show up on your bill because you registered late. I'm afraid you'll have to pay it at the cashier's office.

M: OK, I'd better take care of it right away. Thanks for letting me know.

1. What problem does the man have?
2. What will the man probably do next?

Questions 3 through 4. Listen to a conversation between two students on a field trip.

W: Look! Isn't that a house finch?

M: No, I think it's just a little brown sparrow.

W: It seems reddish to me. And its song is like a recording we heard of a house finch. Professor Flynn said we'd probably see a lot of red finches today.

M: Well, maybe you're right. We'd better write it down anyway. But I still say it's too brown to be a house finch. I'll put a question mark by it.

W: We've sure seen enough starlings. I didn't even know they lived in the city. I can remember hearing my cousin complain about how the starlings always ate all the fruit in their orchard.

M: They are kind of pretty, though, don't you think? Look at how the black is mixed with a little green, making their feathers look iridescent.

3. What are the students discussing?
4. What can be inferred about starlings?

Questions 5 through 7. Listen to a conversation between a student and the physics department secretary.

M: Hello. May I leave a message here for Dr. Owada?

W: Yes. I can give her a message, or if you've written her a note, you can put it in her mailbox over there.

M: I didn't write her a note, but I can. May I sit here and write it?

W: Sure. Oh, I just realized that Dr. Owada isn't on campus today because she had a conference to go to. She'll get the message tomorrow. Would that be all right?

M: I was going to tell her I wouldn't be in class today, but maybe I don't need to now. Is her two o'clock class canceled?

W: No, Professor Strong will be giving the lecture today.

M: Oh, it's too bad I'll miss that. He's a great speaker. Well, thank you for your help.

W: It's OK. Have a nice day.

5. Why does the student want to leave a message for Dr. Owada?

6. What does the secretary imply about Dr. Owada?

7. What will the student probably do?

Questions 8 through 10. Listen to a discussion in a history class.

W: Did anyone happen to catch "The American Metropolis" last night? It was about the growth of cities.

M: I didn't see that, but I did see part of a documentary last week that told about a guy—I think he was a visitor from another country—who wrote a book about the growth of industry and so on—the things we've just studied. I remember he said there was a huge population explosion that turned America into a nation of cities, all within a decade. He was talking mostly about Baltimore.

W: Baltimore then or now?

M: In the nineteenth century, right after the Civil War.

W: The program you saw was part of the same series as the one I want to tell you about. Last night the topic was New York City. As early as 1880, the federal government wrote a report on how the five separate municipalities of New York actually constituted one vast metropolitan area. It was a progressive way of thinking at the time. And within twenty years, those five municipalities were officially united as a single city, by a vote of the people. To this day, however, each borough maintains traces of its original independence.

M: I agree with that. I'm from Brooklyn, and it's definitely different from the rest of New York.

8. What are the people discussing?

9. What can be inferred about the United States in the nineteenth century?

10. What can be inferred about New York City?

Disk 3, Track 6

Exercise 2.4.E (p. 256)

Questions 1 through 2. Listen to part of a talk in a science class.

As you recall from our previous discussion, the chemistry of life is organized into metabolic pathways. Next year, in your organic chemistry lab, you'll go into this—into metabolism—in more depth. Since this is an intro course, you need only a general understanding of the process for now.

There's a wonderful videotape I'd like you to know about that will help you review for the test next week. It's part of the "Transformations" series that was on television about a year ago. The episode you should watch is called "The Industry of a Cell." I strongly urge you to see it. I believe our library has more than one copy.

It shows lots of examples—the many ways that cells use energy for metabolism. For example, it shows how bacteria in the "headlight" of a certain fish—how these bacteria take the energy stored in food and convert it into light, in a process

called bioluminescence. You should all try to see this program before next week. I highly recommend it. In fact, you can expect to see examples from it on the test.

1. What can be inferred about the course in which the talk is given?

2. What does the professor imply about the videotape?

Questions 3 through 6. Listen to an instructor give a talk about jazz.

The origins of jazz are as richly textured as the music itself. The term "jazz" really covers many different kinds of music. In the late nineteenth century, African Americans began performing the folk music known as the blues, whose origins lay in the work songs of slavery days. Within the African–American community, the blues evolved into popular commercial music.

In 1914, a black orchestra leader named W.C. Handy wrote the "St. Louis Blues." Adapting the African–American folk idiom to European conventions of orchestration and harmony, Handy produced a hit song. The "St. Louis Blues" was tremendously influential among black and white musicians, and Handy's style of music became famous under the name of "jazz."

Early jazz musicians were active in many cities and towns throughout the southern United States. It was New Orleans—with its long tradition of African–American music—that was the home of many "fathers" of jazz. After World War One, the musicians of New Orleans joined the general northward migration of African Americans. The first great national center of jazz was Chicago. From there, the music entered the mainstream and even gave its name to the decade of the 1920s.

Jazz, blending African–American folk roots with elements of popular music and European classical traditions, has been called "America's classical music."

3. For which course would the talk be most appropriate?

4. What does the instructor imply about the style of music known as the blues?

5. According to the instructor, why is the song "St. Louis Blues" significant?

6. Based on the information in the talk, indicate whether each statement below accurately describes jazz.

Questions 7 through 10. Listen to part of a lecture in a marine biology class.

Land animals move easily through air, because air does not slow them down. Sea creatures, on the other hand, have to move through water, which is hundreds of times thicker than air. A sea animal has to push itself through water in order to move.

Sea animals use many different ways to swim, creep, or glide through water.

Fish are able to swim by bending their bodies into waves. They have flattened fins and tails that push against the water like oar blades, converting their body waves into forward movement. The size of a fish's tail contributes to its swimming speed. Small tail fins are found in slow swimmers like the eel. The medium size tail of the bass is linked with a medium–to–fast swimming speed. Long, pointed tail lobes, like those on the marlin, are found only on fast swimmers.

Sea mammals like whales and dolphins swim in a very fish–like way, except for one important difference. Because their ancestors lived on the land, they developed tails that moved up and down. Whales and dolphins wave their tails up and down rather than side to side like fish do.

The seahorse is a fish whose tail is not used for swimming at all. The seahorse uses its thin, coiled tail to attach itself to seaweed, like a monkey's tail holds onto a tree branch.

Squids and octopuses move in a completely different way. They use a type of jet propulsion—shooting water out through a nozzle to force themselves along.

And then there are the creatures that live on the bottom of the sea. Sea slugs, limpets, and whelks creep on a single flat piece of muscle called a foot. Ripples pass along the foot, which allows these animals to glide smoothly forward.

7. What is the main purpose of the lecture?
8. Select the drawing of the creature that is probably the fastest swimmer.
9. Listen again to part of the lecture. Then answer the question.
"Sea mammals like whales and dolphins swim in a very fish–like way, except for one important difference. Because their ancestors lived on the land, they developed tails that moved up and down. Whales and dolphins wave their tails up and down rather than side to side like fish do."
What is probably true about whales and dolphins?
10. What can be inferred about creatures that live on the bottom of the ocean?

Disk 3, Track 7

QUIZ 4 (p. 261)

Questions 1 through 5. Listen to a conversation in a university office.

M: Jackie, I wonder if I could talk to you about something.
W: Sure. What's on your mind?
M: There's an opening at channel 12 that kind of interests me—an internship. I was kind of thinking of applying for it.
W: You mean the television station? What sort of job? Oh, I hope that doesn't mean you'll have to leave us!
M: No, no, I wouldn't quit my job. It's a part–time internship for production assistant. Production work, general stuff … probably mostly I'd be a gofer.
W: I see.
M: Anyway, it'd be a way in the door. Unfortunately, it's not a paid internship, but that doesn't matter. It's the experience—the chance to work in television—that's more important to me right now. Some day I'd like to write, or produce. I probably don't stand much of a chance, though. I'm sure there'll be lots of other people who apply, with more qualifications than me.
W: Don't be so sure about that. You never know. Sometimes it's not the credentials but the person who matters. My friend got a really good job in the mayor's office—public relations, a power position—and before that the only work she'd done was emergency rescue—evacuating people in helicopters! Flood victims, accidents and the like. And then she goes and lands this glamour job in the mayor's office, with no experience in politics whatsoever!
M: Wow!
W: Yeah. So you can never tell.

M: Still, I'm going to need all the help I can get. If only I could … uh … convince them of how much—I need them to know how much this would mean to me. I was wondering, Jackie, if you….
W: You want a recommendation?
M: Uh, yeah, like I said, I need all the help I can get.
W: I'd be happy to do what I can. I feel I know your work pretty well. Here in the lab you've always been good at troubleshooting, and helping people figure out their e–mail. I can emphasize that in the letter. When do you need this?
M: Um … by the end of the week? The application is due next Tuesday.
W: All right, Alex. I hope this will work out for you.
M: If not this, then something else.
W: There you go. That's the spirit!

1. What is the conversation mainly about?
2. Why does the man want to get the internship?
3. Listen again to part of the conversation. Then answer the question.
"I probably don't stand much of a chance, though. I'm sure there'll be lots of other people who apply, with more qualifications than me."
Select the sentence that best expresses how the man probably feels.
4. Why does the woman tell a story about her friend?
5. What does the man want the woman to do?

Questions 6 through 10. A naturalist has been invited to speak to the members of a college hiking club. Listen to part of the discussion.

W1: Because of their protected status, a lot of bears have lost their fear of people. This may make them appear tame, but they're still potentially very dangerous. Bears are wild animals. One or two bear attacks occur each year in Glacier Park. The majority of attacks occur because people have surprised the bear.
M: What should we do if we surprise a bear?
W1: You should try to avoid encounters in the first place by being alert. And make noise. Talk loud. Holler. Bears will usually move out of the way if they hear people approaching.
W2: Some people say to carry bells, or put bells on your pack.
W1: Most bells—even the so–called bear bells—are not loud enough. Calling out or clapping hands at regular intervals are better ways to make your presence known.
M: But isn't it kind of rude to make a lot of noise in the woods? I mean, people go there for peace and quiet.
W1: In bear country, noise is good for you. Hiking quietly endangers you, the bear, and other hikers. People sometimes assume they don't have to make noise while hiking on a well–used trail. Some of the most frequently used trails in Glacier Park are surrounded by excellent bear habitat. You can't predict when and where bears might appear along a trail.
M: That's for sure. I remember my surprise when a black bear charged me. It must have been running away from hikers who surprised it on the trail ahead of me.
W1: Don't assume a bear's hearing is any better than your own. Some trail conditions make it hard for bears to see, hear, or smell approaching hikers. You should be especially careful near streams, against the wind, or in dense vegetation. Stay with your group and, if

possible, avoid hiking early in the morning, late in the day, or after dark, when bears are more likely to be active. Bears spend a lot of time eating, so avoid hiking in areas like berry patches or fields of glacier lilies.

W2: How will the bear act if we surprise it?

W1: Bears react differently to each situation. They may appear to tolerate you, and then attack without warning. The most important advice I can give you is never to approach a bear intentionally. Each bear will react differently, and its behavior can't be predicted. All bears are dangerous and should be respected equally.

6. What is the discussion mainly about?
7. What does the naturalist think of bear bells?
8. Listen again to part of the discussion. Then answer the question.
   "Don't assume a bear's hearing is any better than your own. Some trail conditions make it hard for bears to see, hear, or smell approaching hikers. You should be especially careful near streams, against the wind, or in dense vegetation."
   Why does the naturalist say this:
   "You should be especially careful near streams, against the wind, or in dense vegetation."
9. What can be inferred about the behavior of bears?
10. Which situations should hikers avoid?

Disk 3, Track 8

Quiz 5 (p. 263)

Questions 1 through 5. Listen to a professor lead a discussion in a biology class.

W1: In our last meeting we discussed how science is a process. Science involves the formation of a hypothesis and the testing of that hypothesis through observation and experimentation. We use this process to answer our questions about nature. Today we'll focus on science and technology. Technology, especially in the form of new instruments, can extend our ability to observe. Technology enables us to work on questions that were previously unapproachable. In turn, technology often applies the discoveries of science. Can anyone think of an example? Yes, Rosa?

W2: The inventors of the electron microscope used electromagnetic theory from physics.

W1: The electron microscope is an excellent example of applied science. But not all technology can be described as applied science. In fact, technology came before science in our prehistory. Technology was driven by inventive humans who built tools, made pottery, designed musical instruments, and so on, all without science—that is, without people necessarily understanding why their inventions worked.

M1: Technology might not be science, but I think technology mostly helps us. It enables us to cure diseases so people can live longer.

W2: But look at the environmental consequences, like global warming and holes in the ozone.

M2: Not to mention nuclear accidents, toxic waste, extinction of species—technology can't save us from ourselves.

W1: You're all raising some very important issues. Technology has improved our standard of living in many ways, but technology is a double–edged sword. Science and technology are partners. Science can help us identify problems and provide insight about what course of action may prevent further damage. But solutions to these problems have as much to do with politics, economics, and culture as with science and technology.

M1: I think scientists have a responsibility to educate politicians and the public about the consequences of certain technologies. This is why I'm a science major now, but I've decided to get a master's degree in public policy.

W1: And a decision like that is important. Scientists should try to influence how technology applies the discoveries of science.

1. What is the discussion mainly about?
2. What does the electron microscope provide an example of?
3. Why does the professor mention tools, pottery, and musical instruments?
4. Listen again to part of the discussion. Then answer the question.
   "You're all raising some very important issues. Technology has improved our standard of living in many ways, but technology is a double–edged sword."
   What does the professor mean by this statement:
   "…technology is a double–edged sword"?
5. Why does one of the students plan to get a master's degree in public policy?

Questions 6 through 10. A forester has been invited to speak to a group of students. Listen to part of the talk.

M1: No matter whether we live in the country, the suburbs, or the city, we come in contact with forests every day. A combination of trees, other plants, insects, wildlife, soil, water, air, and people is a forest. I'm a professional forester. That means I've been trained in the management of forests. Managing a forest is both a science and an art, which is why my education included courses in the biological, physical, and social sciences, as well as the humanities.

W: Doesn't being a forester mean you always work in the woods?

M1: Foresters, of course, do work in the woods. More and more, however, they also work in laboratories, classrooms, planning agencies, corporate offices, and so forth. In fact, our professional organization, the Society of American Foresters, lists over 700 job categories.

M2: I've always been confused about the difference between a national park and a national forest. In a lot of ways they're similar. For example, we can camp and hike in both.

M1: There is a difference between them. National parks, such as Yellowstone, are set aside and preserved in a near–natural state, mainly for the recreational enjoyment of the public. Our parks are administered by the Department of the Interior. National forests, on the other hand, are administered by the Department of Agriculture. Our forests are managed for their many benefits, including recreation, wood products, wildlife, and water.

M2: That means there's a difference between a forester and a park ranger, right?

M1: Yes, there are differences. A forester manages an area of forest for forest products, water quality, wildlife, recreation, and so on. A park ranger, on the other hand, manages an area in a national or state park, mainly for recreation. Another difference is who owns the land. A forester can work on federal, state, or private land, while a park ranger is almost always a government employee.

W: My major is biology, but I'd like to work in the woods in the area of wildlife preservation. Would that make me a forester or a biologist?

M1: Some foresters are primarily biologists. But most foresters majored in forestry management. Foresters and wildlife biologists often work together as a team. Both foresters and biologists want to see that various types of habitat flourish. Deer, for example, require a different habitat than wolves—yet the forest can accommodate them both.

6. What is the talk mainly about?
7. What can be inferred about the profession of forestry?
8. Why does the student say this:
"I've always been confused about the difference between a national park and a national forest. In a lot of ways they're similar. For example, we can camp and hike in both."
9. Listen again to part of the talk. Then answer the question.
"National parks, such as Yellowstone, are set aside and preserved in a near–natural state, mainly for the recreational enjoyment of the public. Our parks are administered by the Department of the Interior. National forests, on the other hand, are administered by the Department of Agriculture. Our forests are managed for their many benefits, including recreation, wood products, wildlife, and water."
What can be inferred about national parks?
10. Listen again to part of the talk. Then answer the question.
"My major is biology, but I'd like to work in the woods in the area of wildlife preservation. Would that make me a forester or a biologist?"
"Some foresters are primarily biologists. But most foresters majored in forestry management. Foresters and wildlife biologists often work together as a team. Both foresters and biologists want to see that various types of habitat flourish."
Why does the forester say this:
"Both foresters and biologists want to see that various types of habitat flourish."

Disk 4, Track 1

2.5   CATEGORIZING INFORMATION

Focus (p. 265)

Listen to part of a talk in a geography class.

Each biome is characterized chiefly by the dominant forms of plant life and the prevailing climate. The largest biome on Earth is the taiga. The taiga—also known as boreal or evergreen forest—is a broad band across North America, Europe, and Asia. Winters are long and cold, and summers are short, wet, and sometimes warm. Precipitation here is mostly in the form of snow.

Moving northward, we have the arctic tundra here, which extends northward from the taiga and circles the North Pole. The tundra is the northernmost … uh … limit … for plants to grow. The vegetation is mostly … uh … sort of shrubby, low, mat–like plant forms. And about 20 percent of Earth's land surface is tundra.

We also have alpine tundra, a biome found on high mountaintops. Alpine tundra occurs in all latitudes. That means even in the tropics, anywhere the elevation is high enough. Here, above the tree line, strong winds and cold temperatures create plant communities similar to those of the arctic tundra.

Match each biome with the correct description.

Disk 4, Track 2

Exercise 2.5.A (p. 268)

Question 1. Listen to a musicologist talk about drums.

Drums can be divided according to shape. Some of the types are tubular, vessel, and frame drums.

One of the most common tubular drums is the long drum. A lot of long drums are cylindrical—they have the same diameter from top to bottom—like this Polynesian drum. This drum was carved from a length of tree trunk and has a single–skin head.

For vessel drums, we have the kettledrum. Kettledrums have a single membrane stretched over a pot or vessel body. Vessel drums come in a variety of sizes, from the very large drums of Africa to the very compact and portable drums like this one from Hawaii.

The third type I want you to see is the frame drum. A frame drum consists of one or two membranes stretched over a simple frame, which is usually made of thin wood. The frame is shallow, which adds little resonance when the skin is beaten. A lot of frame drums—like this Turkish tar—have metal jingles attached to the rim.

Match each type of drum with the correct picture.

Questions 2 through 3. Listen to a biology professor talk about caves.

The interior of a cave is divided into three zones. The entrance zone may serve as a place of shelter for animals or people. Prehistoric humans used entrance zones of caves as shelters and burial grounds. Therefore, such zones are of interest to archaeologists, as they provide clues to the habitat of early human beings.

The next zone is called the twilight zone. The twilight zone is sheltered from direct sunlight and is home to a large, diverse population of animals such as salamanders, bats, and during severe winters, bears.

The third zone, the dark zone, is the true cave environment. Perpetually dark, it has only slight seasonal changes in temperature, few if any air currents, and a constant relative humidity of nearly 100 percent. In the dark zone live animals that have adapted to the world of darkness, including small shrimp, beetles, spiders, and fish. These animals are usually blind, and some lack eyes altogether. Since no green plants grow in caves, these animals depend largely on food that is washed in by streams or mud.

2. Which creatures have lived in each cave zone?
3. Indicate whether each item below characterizes the dark zone of a cave.

Questions 4 through 5. Listen to a psychology professor talk about personality types.

The theory of personality types suggests there are pairs of what are known as "type preferences." Type preferences are not the same as character traits that can be worked on and changed. Rather, they're preferred ways of being in the world, different ... uh ... different ways of ...uh ... experiencing daily life. One well–known pair of type preferences is extraversion–introversion. Some people are extraverts and some are introverts.

Extraverted people are—by nature—continuously aware of events outside of themselves. Extraverts turn outward—to the world around them—to pick up ... uh ... ideas, values, and interests. Extraverts, therefore, usually have a variety of interests and sort of take an active approach to life.

Introversion is the just the opposite. Introverts look inward for resources. Introverts pursue fewer interests, but on a much deeper level. They sort of take a reflective approach to life. What I mean is, they involve themselves in inner events, ideas, and impressions. Introverted people usually prefer to learn in private, individual ways.

4. Indicate whether each phrase below describes an extravert or an introvert.
5. What type of assignment would an introverted student probably prefer?

Questions 6 through 10. Listen to a talk given by an economics instructor.

One of the major problems in our economy is inflation, a situation in which prices are going up faster than wages. Thus, a person has to work more hours to pay for the same items.

For example, let's say that this year a loaf of bread costs $1.00 and the average salary in the United States is $10.00 per hour. That means a person could earn enough money to buy a loaf of bread in one–tenth of an hour, or six minutes. Then, halfway through the year, the price of the bread goes up to $1.25, while wages stay the same. That means that a person now has to work one–eighth of an hour—seven and a half minutes—to buy the same loaf of bread.

Now let's say that at the end of the year, wages go up to $11.00 per hour, but the price of bread goes up to $1.50. Now a person has to work more than one–seventh of an hour—over eight minutes—to buy the same loaf of bread. As you can see, if more and more work time is spent earning money to buy loaves of bread, employees will have less money left over to buy other things. Inflation means that the same money buys fewer things, and everybody's standard of living goes down, even if salaries are going up.

Some kinds of inflation are worse than others. Moderate inflation does not distort relative prices or incomes severely. Galloping inflation happens rapidly, say at a rate of 100 percent or more within a year. And then there is hyperinflation—inflation so severe that people try to get rid of their currency before prices rise further and render the money worthless. Times of hyperinflation are usually characterized by social and political turmoil.

6. What is the main purpose of the talk?
7. Why does the instructor talk about a loaf of bread?
8. What happens when prices go up but salaries remain the same?
9–10. Based on the information in the talk, indicate whether each sentence below describes moderate inflation, galloping inflation, or hyperinflation.

Disk 4, Track 3

Exercise 2.5.B (p. 269)

Questions 1 through 5. Listen to a career counselor talk about two different types of employees.

Are you going to be more effective and happy as a specialist or as a generalist? Do you find real satisfaction in the precision, order, and system of a clearly laid–out job? Or are you one of those people who tend to grow impatient with anything that looks like a "routine" job?

There are a great many careers in which the emphasis is on specialization. You find these careers in engineering and in accounting, in production, in statistical work, and in teaching. But there is an increasing demand for people who are able to take in a great area at a glance. There is, in other words, a demand for people who are capable of seeing the forest rather than the trees, of making overall judgments. And these "generalists" are particularly needed for administrative positions, where it is their job to see that other people do the work, where they have to plan for other people, to organize other people's work, to initiate it and appraise it.

Specialists understand one field; their concern is with technique, tools, media. They are "trained" people, and their educational background is technical or professional. Generalists—and especially administrators—deal with people. Their concern is with leadership, with planning, with direction, and with coordination. They are "educated" people, and the humanities are their strongest foundation.

Any organization needs both kinds of people, although different organizations need them in different ratios. It is your job to find out, during your college years, into which of these two job categories you fit, and to plan your career accordingly.

1. What is the purpose of the talk?
2. According to the speaker, which people are likely to be specialists?
3. Based on the information in the talk, indicate whether each characteristic below more accurately describes a specialist or a generalist.
4. According to the speaker, why are generalists needed in administrative positions?
5. What can be inferred from the talk?

Questions 6 through 10. Listen to part of a talk in a botany class.

There are several common leaf arrangements in wildflowers. In the usual arrangement, the one called alternate, each leaf is attached at a different level on the stem. This poppy is a good example. See how ... uh ... there's a leaf here, on the right side, and above that a leaf on the left here, and above that, one on the right again ... and so on, alternating right and left, all the way up the stem.

Another type is the opposite arrangement. Notice the difference between the alternate leaves on the poppy and the opposite leaves on this bee plant. The bee plant's leaves are paired on opposite sides of the stem. See how they're attached at the same level of the stem, but on opposite sides.

And here we have yet another kind. This one's called basal, and our example is the amaryllis. Notice how all the leaves are at ground level, at the stem's base. The amaryllis ... this particular plant, and all other members of the amaryllis family ... uh ... it has narrow basal leaves and a long, leafless stalk.

I have some lovely samples to share with you today. I'd like you all to come up and examine the contents of ... uh ... these two tables. Many of them are specimens of the sunflower family, which includes several species with alternate and opposite leaves. Take a good look and see if you can identify the three types of arrangements. It's OK to handle … but let me ask you to please handle with care, as some of them are quite delicate.

6. How does the instructor organize the information that she presents?
7. Select the drawing that best shows the alternate leaf arrangement.
8–9. Based on the information in the talk, indicate whether each sentence below describes the alternate, opposite, or basal leaf arrangement.
10. What will the students probably do next?

Disk 4, Track 4

2.6 SUMMARIZING A PROCESS

Focus (p. 272)

Listen to part of a talk in a film class.

The part of filmmaking that most people know about is the production phase—when the film is actually being shot. But a lot of the real work is done before and after the filming. The film's producers are in charge of the whole project. The producer hires a director to make the creative decisions. The producer and the director work together to plan the film. They hire writers to develop a script for the film. Then, from the script comes the storyboard, an important step in the planning. The storyboard is like a picture book, with a small picture for each camera shot. Under each picture, there's a summary of the action and sometimes a bit of dialogue.

Then comes the production, when the filming takes place. During production, the director and crew concentrate on getting the perfect camera shot. The director may ask for several takes of the same shot, sometimes changing the script for each take.

After the filming is done, there's still a lot to do. This is the post–production phase, and includes editing the film. The editor's job is to cut up the various film sequences and then put them together in the right order so the story is told in the best way. The editor works closely with the director, as well as various artists and technicians. This is when the sound and special effects are added—the final result being the finished movie you see in the theater.

The professor explains how a film is made. Summarize the process by putting the steps in the correct order.

Disk 4, Track 5

Exercise 2.6.A (p. 275)

Questions 1 through 2. Listen to part of a talk in an art class.

If you are unsure of drawing directly in pen and ink, start off with a light pencil sketch. This will allow you to make sure that your proportions are correct and that you are happy with the composition.

Take a few minutes to study your subject—this chair and violin. Notice how the straight lines of the chair differ from the curves of the violin. Once you are ready to begin drawing, define the shape of the chair with clean straight lines. Then add

contrast by drawing the outline of the violin with gently curved lines. You may have to apply more pressure to the nib when drawing curved lines to allow the ink to flow easily.

When you have drawn the outlines of both objects, add in the finer details, such as the seat of the chair and the violin strings. Suggest the texture of the woven seat by using light and dark strokes of the pen.

1. What is the purpose of the talk?
2. The instructor briefly explains how to draw the subject. Indicate whether each sentence below is a step in the process.

Questions 3 through 5. Listen to a geography professor talk about avalanche control.

Avalanches are a constant threat on mountain highways. The Rogers Pass stretch of the Trans–Canada is at risk of being buried in snow from November to April every year. This is why the highway now has a sophisticated defense system. The best way … it's important to control an avalanche when it's small … so a slide is set off while it's still small, before it builds up into a serious danger.

A team of snow technicians monitors the snowpack. They sort of "read" the snow and try to predict when it's likely to slide. They study data from the weather stations in the mountains. As the danger increases, they drop explosives onto test slopes to see if the snow can be made to slide.

It's kind of tricky trying to decide just when the snow will slide. The weight of the snow, together with the force of gravity, is what starts an avalanche. The technicians don't want to wait till it's too late, but if they're too early, before conditions are just right, the snow won't release.

When the time is right, they close the road and remove all traffic from the pass. Most closures last two to four hours. Then the army comes in. A ten–man artillery crew operates a mobile 105 mm howitzer, firing shells into the slopes. This sends out shock waves that trigger the avalanches. Slides are set off, one by one. The technicians direct the action, telling the troops where to aim the gun. Visibility can be awful. Then they have to check and see if the avalanche has released well enough. Sometimes they drive their trucks below the slide path—kind of dangerous work—and they listen to the snow come down. Sometimes, if the slide is bigger than they expected, they might have to make a speedy getaway.

3. According to the professor, why is it important to control an avalanche when it is small?
4. What are the natural causes of an avalanche?
5. The professor explains how a controlled avalanche is achieved. Summarize the process by putting the steps in the correct order.

Questions 6 through 10. Listen to a discussion in an ecology class. The class is talking about the salmon's run.

W1: Various species of Pacific salmon make a round trip from the small streams where they are born, to the sea, and then back to the stream of their origin, where they spawn and die. This round trip is known as the salmon's run. The end of the salmon's run is the beginning of the next generation. Pacific salmon hatch in the headwaters of a stream. As fry, the fish then migrate downstream via rivers, and eventually to the ocean, where they require several years to mature. While in the sea, salmon from many river systems school and feed together. When mature, the salmon form into groups of common geographic origin and migrate back toward the river they emerged from as juveniles.

M: Is it true that they find their way home by their sense of smell?

W1: During the first stage of their return, they navigate by the position of the sun. But later, when they reach the river leading to their home stream, their keen sense of smell takes over.

M: Just what is it they can smell? The other fish?

W1: The water flowing from each stream carries a unique scent. This scent comes from the types of plants, soil, and other components of that stream. This scent is apparently imprinted in the memory of a salmon fry before it migrates to the sea.

W2: I remember having a real shock when I was hiking once. I was looking at a waterfall, and I saw a salmon jump up, about ten feet! At first, I couldn't believe my eyes. But then I saw another one do it! And then several more! It was an awesome sight.

M: They must have an incredibly powerful instinct.

W1: The survival of their species depends on their ability to get home and reproduce. And, of course, other species depend on the survival of the salmon. Salmon provide an important link in the food chain. They spend 90 percent of their lives in the ocean, where they feed on plankton, shrimp, and small fish. When they make their return journey, they carry nutrients from the ocean back to the rivers and streams.

M: Up north, where I used to live in the river valley, the eagles would gather for the salmon run every year. They'd gorge themselves on all the salmon that had just spawned.

W1: Nothing is wasted in nature. After the salmon spawn, their carcasses feed birds, mammals, and vegetation—and even their own newly hatched offspring.

6. The professor explains what happens during the salmon's run. Indicate whether each sentence below is a step in the process.

7. How do salmon find their way to their home stream?

8. Listen again to part of the discussion. Then answer the question.
"I remember having a real shock when I was hiking once. I was looking at a waterfall, and I saw a salmon jump up, about ten feet! At first, I couldn't believe my eyes. But then I saw another one do it! And then several more! It was an awesome sight."
Why does the student say this:
"At first, I couldn't believe my eyes."

9. According to the professor, why are salmon an important link in the food chain?

10. What can be concluded from this statement:
"Nothing is wasted in nature. After the salmon spawn, their carcasses feed birds, mammals, and vegetation—and even their own newly hatched offspring."

Disk 4, Track 6

Exercise 2.6.B (p. 276)

Questions 1 through 3. Listen to part of a lecture in a botany class. The professor is discussing photosynthesis.

The complex process inside a leaf takes energy from the sun and uses it to convert water and carbon dioxide into sugars. During this process—photosynthesis—plants convert light energy into chemical energy.

All leaves carry out photosynthesis in basically the same way. First, the pores on the leaf's outer skin open up and take in molecules of carbon dioxide. Water absorbed by the roots is transported upward through the plant, and it enters the leaf through its stem. Carbon dioxide and water—these are the raw materials for photosynthesis. Once carbon dioxide and water are present, photosynthesis can begin.

The chemical reactions of photosynthesis take place in two stages: the light–dependent reactions and the light–independent reactions. When sunlight shines on a leaf during the light–dependent stage, its energy is absorbed by molecules of chlorophyll, which you all know is the pigment giving a leaf its green color. The light energy absorbed by the chlorophyll is used to split the hydrogen and oxygen in the water. Then, during the light–independent reactions, hydrogen from the water combines with carbon dioxide ... and forms carbohydrates, including the sugar glucose, but also other molecules that are rich in food energy for the plant. In the process, excess oxygen is released to the outside air through the leaf's pores.

Finally, the plant transports the products of photosynthesis. Microscopic veins in the leaf carry the food out through the stem and into the cells of the plant. This process continues all throughout the growing season, that is, as long as the leaves remain green.

1. Which of the following best describes the organization of the lecture?
2. What must be present for photosynthesis to begin?
3. The professor briefly explains what happens during photosynthesis. Indicate whether each sentence below is a step in the process.

Questions 4 through 7. Listen to part of a lecture in a psychology class. The professor is talking about stating laws in the science of psychology.

Psychology is a relatively new science. Like other sciences, psychology must be able to state laws. A law is a way of organizing knowledge about something so that we can make predictions. When enough knowledge is gained about a subject, a scientist can state precisely what will happen under certain conditions.

We experimental psychologists are interested in developing laws about human behavior so we'll be able to understand and predict what people do and why they do it. Of course, to develop laws about human behavior, we must assume there's some regularity to it. We can't be psychologists without making the assumption that behavior follows certain patterns.

One of the major laws psychologists have discovered is called the Law of Effect. The Law of Effect states that whether or not a person will repeat a behavior depends on the effect that behavior has. If an action is rewarded, it's likely to be repeated. If the action is not rewarded, or if it's punished, it's not likely to be repeated.

How do psychologists state laws? First, using available knowledge, a psychologist makes a hypothesis about behavior. Then, the psychologist tests the hypothesis through an experiment. But even if the experiment proves the hypothesis was correct, it's not yet a law. It's just the beginning of the work. To arrive at a law that will apply to all humans, many repetitions of the experiment must be conducted under different conditions. Only repeated verification, especially proof that the behavior can be predicted, will result in a law.

4. According to the professor, why are psychologists interested in developing laws?
5. According to the professor, what assumption do psychologists make?
6. Which behavior illustrates the Law of Effect?
7. The professor explains how psychologists develop laws. Summarize the process by putting the steps in the correct order.

Questions 8 through 10. Listen to part of a lecture in a biology class.

There are lots of different wetlands—from marshes to swamps to bogs. The flow of water through a wetland determines the types of plants that grow there. A marsh is a wetland where the soil is regularly or permanently saturated with water. Because of the continuous presence of water, marshes usually don't contain trees or shrubs. Marsh vegetation is usually soft–stemmed or herbaceous—for example, grasses, sedges, and mosses.

Wetlands are among the richest of all biomes. Animal life is highly diverse and includes an array of insects, amphibians, reptiles, and birds. Because marshes are so biologically productive, an abundance of dead plant and animal material—energy–rich organic matter—enters the food chain each year. And much of this energy–rich biomass is broken down by bacteria and water fungi. The water in marshes may become tea–colored or dark brown because of the organic acids from the decaying vegetation.

In the past, humans have viewed these marshes—and most wetlands—as the source of mosquitoes, bad odors, and disease. Humans have destroyed a lot of wetlands, mostly to make way for agricultural development. Now, however, we recognize the ecological importance of wetlands and we're putting a lot of research into figuring out how wetlands can be restored.

8. According to the professor, which type of vegetation grows in marshes?
9. The professor briefly describes a biological process that occurs in a marsh. Indicate whether each sentence below is a step in the process.
10. Why have so many wetlands been destroyed?

Disk 4, Track 7

QUIZ 6 (p. 279)

Questions 1 through 3. Listen to part of a talk in a marine biology class.

An ocean's waters are not the same all the way through. They are divided up like a building with several stories, where life is very different at the top, middle, and bottom stories.

The upper layer of the ocean is warmer than the layers underneath. The clear, sunlit waters near the surface are an ideal place for the microscopic plants called plankton to grow.

The tiny plant plankton provides food for tiny animal plankton, and so they start off the food chain for everything else in the sea. Huge schools of fish, like herring and sardines, cruise the upper waters to eat the animal plankton. Big, fast–swimming fish, like tuna and swordfish, swim through the same levels to capture the smaller fish.

About 200 meters below the surface, the temperature suddenly drops. This is a dimly lit twilight world. From there to the ocean's bottom, it is very cold.

Utter darkness usually begins at a depth of 1,000 meters. Down in the bottom zone, no plants can survive, and all that can be found there are animals hunting and feeding on other animals.

1. According to the professor, what characterizes the ocean's upper zone?
2. The professor briefly describes the ocean's food chain. Indicate whether each sentence below is a step in the process.
3. How does the professor describe each layer of the ocean's waters?

Questions 4 through 6. Listen to part of a talk in a zoology class. The professor is talking about bees.

The worker bees, underdeveloped females, do all the work that is done in the hive. They secrete the wax, build the comb, gather pollen, feed and rear the brood, and fight all the battles necessary to defend the colony. The worker bees possess the whole ruling power of the colony and regulate its economy.

The worker develops from the egg into a perfect adult bee in twenty–one days. Each egg is laid by the queen bee, who deposits it in the bottom of the worker cell. After three days, the egg hatches into a small white worm called a larva, which, being fed by the adult bees, increases rapidly in size. When the cell is nearly filled by the growing larva, it is closed up by the bees. The larva then enters the pupa state.

When the adult worker emerges from the pupa, she usually does not leave the hive until about eight days later. Then, accompanied by other young workers, she takes her first flight in the warmth of the afternoon.

The body of the worker bee is divided into three segments—head, thorax, and abdomen. On the head are the mandibles, the jaw–like organs which enable the bees to perform the necessary hive duties and to mold the wax and build their combs. The honey bee's four wings and six legs are fastened to the thorax. Located in the abdomen are the honey sac and the sting, with its highly developed poison sac. The sting is used by the workers for self–defense and for the protection of their colony. The worker uses her sting only once, for in doing so, she loses her life.

4. What tasks does the worker bee perform?
5. The professor describes the stages of a worker bee's development. Summarize the process by putting the events in the correct order.
6. What segment of the bee's body contains the feature necessary for each activity?

Questions 7 through 10. A student is giving an oral report in a world history class. She is talking about bread and cereals.

Bread and cereals have a long history. The first bread was made in the Nile valley about 10,000 years ago. The people used stones to crush the grain into coarse flour, and then they made the flour into primitive forms of bread. Primitive bread was not like the bread we know today because it was simply flour dough dried on heated stones. The invention of ovens came later.

Leavened breads and cakes, which are made to rise by the action of yeast, were also a discovery of the ancient Egyptians. The Egyptians were the first people to master the art of baking. News of this new wonder food spread to other places in the Middle East. Soon other people were collecting seed, cultivating land, and inventing ways to turn grain into flour.

Baking used to be a social activity. While some homes had their own ovens, many families had to bake their dough in communal bakeries. To identify their loaves, each household would make a distinctive mark on the bread, sometimes with a special stamp bearing the family name.

Modern cereals descended from the cereals grown long ago. These grains now supply the world with everything from bread and breakfast cereal to pasta, and even candy and beer.

The most important grain crop in the temperate regions of the world today is wheat. Bread wheat is the most widely planted variety. The large grains of bread wheat are rich in gluten—a kind of protein—and produce light, airy bread. Another widely cultivated variety of wheat is durum, which goes into making pasta.

Other important cereal crops are rye and oats. Rye is the hardiest cereal and is more resistant to cold, pests, and disease than wheat. Oats are grown in temperate regions and are mainly fed to cattle, but the best quality oats are made into oatmeal and other breakfast foods.

7. What topics does the speaker discuss?
8. The speaker traces the history of bread. Indicate whether each sentence below describes an event in the history.
9. Why did people stamp their bread with the family name?
10. Based on the information in the talk, indicate whether each phrase below describes wheat or oats.

Disk 4, Track 8

Quiz 7 (p. 281)

Questions 1 through 5. Listen to a discussion in a music history class. The class is studying improvisation.

M1: Every jazz player knows what he or she means by improvisation. And all writers know what they mean by improvisation. The result, of course, is a lot of confusion and disagreement about what improvisation really is. We hear about the different types of improvisation: "free" improvisation and "controlled" improvisation and "collective" improvisation. What does it all mean? Yes, Mary?

W: My dictionary says "improvise" means "to compose or recite without preparation."

M1: That's true, but it tells us only part of the story. As we know, musicians learn how to play their instruments before they can improvise. So they do have some preparation. Yes, Arthur?

M2: Maybe a better definition is "composing and performing at the same time."

M1: That tells us another part of the story. Let's try to understand it more by looking at history. Improvisation is as old as music itself. In the beginning, music was largely improvisational, supplied on the spur of the moment by prehistoric people who "made" music for work, play, war, love, worship, and so on. Music was not separate from everyday life. Rather, music was a force that communicated the relationship of people to nature, and people to each other. Two thousand years ago, the practice of improvisation was widespread among the ancient Greeks. The Greeks based their improvisations on what we might call "stock melodies"—a collection of tunes known by all musicians. In sixteenth–century Italy, organists had contests for improvising. The ability to improvise in a fugal style—several melodies going at the same time—was a standard requirement for all appointments to organ positions. So, these "cutting" contests were like job interviews.

M2: Didn't some of the early jazz musicians have those kinds of contests, too?

M1: Actually, the early jazz musicians were very similar to the ancient Greeks in that they were making a music partly their own and partly derived from the "stock melodies" in their environment. In most cases, black musicians improvised on the European melodies they heard white bands playing.

W: Were they really just creating music, without any preparation except hearing other musicians?

M1: I'm glad you asked that, Mary. There were a number of musicians who'd played in army bands, and they had training of one kind or another. It was these trained military bandsmen who were responsible for the rise of jazz improvisation.

1. Why is improvisation difficult to define?
2. How does the professor develop the topic of improvisation?
3. Who first improvised when playing music?
4. Based on the information in the discussion, indicate whether each phrase below describes prehistoric humans or jazz musicians.
5. What does the professor imply about early jazz improvisation?

Questions 6 through 10. A professor of education is giving a lecture about child development. Listen to part of the lecture.

In some ways, mental development is related to social development in school–aged children. Between the ages of six and twelve, children move from being able to think only on a concrete level—that is, about real objects they can touch—to being capable of abstract thought. In their social development, children gradually acquire interpersonal reasoning skills. They learn to understand the feelings of other people, and also learn that a person's actions or words don't always reflect their inner feelings.

When children first start school, at around four to six years old, they can focus on only one thought at a time. Socially, they can understand only their own perspective, and don't yet understand that other people may see the same event differently from the way they see it. They don't reflect on the thoughts of others. What I mean is, children at this age are self–centered, and for this reason it's known as the egocentric stage of social development.

Children six to ten years old solve problems by sort of generalizing from their own experiences. What I mean is, they can understand only what they've experienced for themselves. They can't think theoretically or abstractly. They have to handle real objects in order to solve problems. But socially, children are learning to distinguish between the way they understand social interactions and how other people interpret them.

From ten to twelve years old, children's mental processes are still sort of tied to direct experience. But on a social level, children can now understand actions as an outsider might see them. This permits children to understand the expectations people have of them in a variety of situations. Children can now manage various social roles—for example, son or daughter, older or younger brother or sister, fifth grader, classmate, friend, teammate, and so on. Because they can play multiple roles, this stage is known as the multiple role–taking stage.

Beginning around age twelve, children can start dealing with abstractions. What I mean is, they can form hypotheses, solve problems systematically, and not have to handle real objects. And the social perspective is also expanding, because in this stage children can now take a more analytical view of their own behavior, as well as the behavior of other people. Sometime between twelve and fifteen years old, a societal perspective begins to develop. I mean, the young teenager is now able to judge actions by how they might influence all individuals, not just the people who are immediately concerned.

6. What is the main idea of the lecture?
7. At what age is a child least able to recognize the thoughts of other people?
8. Listen again to part of the lecture. Then answer the question.
"Children six to ten years old solve problems by sort of generalizing from their own experiences. What I mean is, they can understand only what they've experienced for themselves. They can't think theoretically or abstractly. They have to handle real objects in order to solve problems."
Why does the professor say this:
"They have to handle real objects in order to solve problems."
9. What can be inferred about children in the multiple role–taking stage?
10. The professor briefly explains the stages of social development in children. Indicate whether each sentence below is a stage in the process.

Disk 4, Track 9

Quiz 8 (p. 283)

Questions 1 through 5. Listen to a conversation between a student and a professor.

W: Dr. Zarelli?
M: Hello, Karen. How are you?
W: Pretty good, thanks. I was hoping … um … we could talk about the project that's due at the end of May.
M: Of course. What can I do for you?
W: Well … the project plan … that part's due next week, right?
M: Uh … I believe that's right. Let me look at the syllabus. I tend to forget dates unless I have them right in front of me! Uh … yes, that's right, the first due date—the project plan—is due next week, on Monday, May 3.
W: I'm a little—I'm not sure about what you want. Do you just … uh … what exactly should the plan look like?
M: Well, a description—a summary of your project. A short description of the topic and a summary of your materials and methods and what you hope to accomplish.
W: I have an idea … um … it's something that interests

me. But I'm not sure if—I don't know whether it fits the assignment. It's not about marketing as much as—it has more to do with social change.
M: Let's try it on for size. Tell me your idea.
W: Well, my boss—I work part–time at a credit union—and my boss is a person who's done a lot of different things. She used to be the president of an organization that helped set up cooperatives for women artisans in India. They make clothes mostly, and things like tablecloths and toys. She's really interesting—my boss, I mean—and so are the stories about her work. I guess you could say she works for economic development, but also for social change because it's work that affects women and their role in society.
M: Can you tell me more about the organization?
W: Sure. They're called Hearts and Hands. I looked at their Web site. They have a motto, "Changing views, changing lives," and their mission statement is "To empower artisans by providing economic opportunities and exposure to new ideas." My boss was the president for five years, and she's still on their board of directors.
M: Hmm. And what would you like to do with all this?
W: Well, I'd like to interview my boss—a more formal interview—and write about her work with Hearts and Hands.
M: OK, and …?
W: I could do a case study about a group that works for both economic and social change. I could combine the interview data with information from their Web site.
M: It would also be a good idea to link some of your findings with the theories and models we've discussed in class.
W: Oh, like, for example, their product catalog? They have a printed catalog, and it's also online.
M: Great idea! You could include an analysis and evaluation of their catalog. I have to say, Karen, you've got a fairly solid plan here. Your idea of a case study of an economic development organization is a good one, and it fits right in with our course content. All you need to do now is put down your plan on paper.
W: Really? I'm so glad to hear you say that! I'll do it then. I'll write it up for next week. Thank you, Dr. Zarelli. You've been a great help!
M: It's my pleasure. Glad you stopped by.

1. Why does the woman go to see her professor?
2. When is the project plan due?
3. Listen again to part of the conversation. Then answer the question.
"I'm a little—I'm not sure about what you want. Do you just … uh … what exactly should the plan look like?"
Select the sentence that best expresses how the woman probably feels.
4. What topics will the woman write about?
5. What information will the woman include in her project?

Questions 6 through 10. Listen to a talk in a geology class. The professor is discussing rock formations.

Now that you know how sedimentary rocks are formed, the next step is to look at various shapes and learn to read them. On our next field trip, we'll see several of the formations called "mesas." This landform gets its name from its flat top. "Mesa" means "table" in Spanish. The Spanish people who explored the area thought these flat–topped hills looked sort of like tables. A mesa is wider than it is high—kind of like a large table.

We'll also see a variety of other formations, such as buttes, spires, and pillars. All of these spectacular forms are the result of the erosion of rocks of differing hardness. Water erodes rocks both mechanically and chemically. The fast–moving water of rivers carries silt, gravel, and rock debris, and this scours the rock underneath. Slow–moving standing water also erodes when it enters tiny rock pores and dissolves the cements holding the rock together.

On a mesa, conditions are optimal for erosion. With enough time, even the durable top of a mesa will decrease in size. The sides of a mesa are often made of shale or softer sandstone. The slope of the sides will increase the water's speed and force as it runs down. Freezing and thawing loosen the surface rock. Debris carried by the running water cuts away the softer surface rock. As the softer base of the mesa recedes, the edge of the top is weakened, and it eventually cracks, splits, and falls.

As a mesa is shrunk in size by water, it may be cut into smaller landforms. If these smaller remnants are at least as high as they are wide, they are called "buttes." The great buttes we'll see were all created by water—rather than wind—erosion.

Further erosion can change a butte into a tower or spire. This is because the shaft of the spire is usually harder than the base on which it stands, and—and like a mesa or butte—it's capped with a rim of even harder rock. The spires you'll see were left standing after the sandstone around them eroded away. You can see why they're also called "chimneys." I mean, they sort of jut up from the sandstone floor.

Further erosion of the softer rock may reduce the spire to some interesting and really weird forms. We'll see some hourglass–shaped rocks, mushroom–shaped rocks, and a sort of strangely eroded pillar. Over time, erosion finally topples these rocks to the ground. They might remain there as boulders, or they might undergo further erosion that completely demolishes them so they disintegrate into pebbles. Finally, these pebbles end up as the sand we walk on as we explore the surface of the plateau.

6. Which picture represents a mesa?
7. What reasons are given for the erosion of a mesa?
8. Listen again to part of the talk. Then answer the question.
   "The spires you'll see were left standing after the sandstone around them eroded away. You can see why they're also called "chimneys." I mean, they sort of jut up from the sandstone floor."
   Why does the professor say this:
   "I mean, they sort of jut up from the sandstone floor."
9. The professor briefly explains how erosion changes landforms. Summarize the process by putting the stages in the correct order.
10. What can be concluded about erosion?

PART 3 – SPEAKING

QUIZ 1 (p. 305)

Disk 5, Track 1

What is the most interesting class you have ever taken? Explain the aspects of the class that made it interesting. Include details and examples in your explanation.

Disk 5, Track 2

Some people like to read classic works of literature. Others prefer watching film versions of the same stories. Which do you prefer and why? Include details and examples in your explanation.

QUIZ 2 (p. 306)

Disk 5, Track 3

Describe a city or town where you have lived. Explain why this place is either a good place or not a good place to live. Include details and examples in your explanation.

Disk 5, Track 4

Some students take one long examination at the end of a course. Others have several shorter tests throughout the course. Which situation do you think is better for students, and why? Include details and examples in your explanation.

QUIZ 3 (p. 307)

Disk 5, Track 5

Describe your idea of the perfect job. Explain why this job would be appealing to you. Include details and examples in your explanation.

Disk 5, Track 6

Some people like taking their vacation in a city. Others prefer spending their vacation in the countryside. Which do you prefer and why? Include details and examples in your explanation.

**3.5   INTEGRATED SPEAKING:
        CONNECTING INFORMATION FROM TWO SOURCES**

Do You Know (p. 310)

Disk 5, Track 7

Now listen to two students as they discuss the campus food service.

W: Have you voted on the food service yet?
M: No, but I intend to. I'm going to vote for the second option.
W: That's the one that closes the main cafeteria, isn't it?
M: Right.

W: But the main cafeteria is in the Student Center. That's where everyone goes at lunchtime. Doesn't it make sense to have food there?

M: But it's always so crowded in there at lunchtime. You have to wait a long time in the food line. And there are never enough places to sit.

W: That's true, but they say they'll add more tables.

M: There aren't enough bike racks outside either. I have no place to put my bike. Most of the time I eat at one of the snack bars. Besides, I like the idea of having several smaller eating places all over campus. That seems a lot more convenient, since we have classes all over campus anyway. It also means less crowding, and you don't have to wait as long to get your food. More food choices, too—I kind of like the idea of barbecue on campus.

W: Yeah, that does sound good, doesn't it?

The man expresses his opinion about the campus food service. State his opinion and explain the reasons he gives for holding that opinion.

Exercise 3.5.A (p. 311)

Disk 5, Track 8

Now listen to two students as they discuss the course for tutors.

W: Hey, Gavin, you should enroll in this course for tutors.

M: Me? I'm not a tutor.

W: But you want to go to graduate school, right?

M: Right.

W: And in graduate school you'll be a teaching assistant, right?

M: Probably.

W: Then this training course is just what you need. It will give you a head start on learning how to teach. Some of the universities don't give their TAs much training. They just expect you to know how to do it, so this course might be really useful for the future.

M: Maybe. I could at least get a job as a math tutor.

W: And you'd learn how to do it right. You'd learn some practical theories about teaching and learning.

M: True.

W: Anyway, it might give you skills that could be useful later—no matter what kind of work you end up doing.

The woman expresses her opinion about the training course for tutors. State her opinion and explain the reasons she gives for holding that opinion.

Exercise 3.5.B (p. 312)

Disk 5, Track 9

Now listen to two students as they discuss the proposal.

W: I just heard the college is increasing the phys. ed. requirement to two courses.

M: Well, that's what they want to do, but I don't think it will happen. Everybody I know hates the idea.

W: Why? Phys. ed. is good for us! Most students need to get more exercise. That's why we have a new phys. ed. building.

M: But it's not up to the college to require us to get more exercise. We have a responsibility to make that choice on our own. I don't think there should be any phys. ed. requirement in college—high school, yes, but not college. Our main job in college is to study. We need to exercise our brains, not our bodies. Besides, I already get a lot of exercise. I'm on my neighborhood basketball team and I also go hiking and rock climbing.

W: Well, obviously you don't need physical education, but other people do.

The man expresses his opinion about the physical education requirement. State his opinion and explain the reasons he gives for holding that opinion.

Exercise 3.5.C (p. 313)

Disk 5, Track 10

Now listen to two students as they discuss the theater course.

M: This course isn't open to students! That means we can't take it. Don't you think that's strange?

W: Well, yeah, kind of … but students have to be enrolled in the Theater Arts program if they want to be in any of the plays. This course is for people who live in town.

M: I don't think that's right. We pay tuition and fees, so we should be able to take any course we want at this school.

W: But this is a chance for other people to work with the theater students. It's a community class.

M: But it's not fair. What if I want to learn about theater, too? I'm a full–time student. I'm not enrolled in the Theater Arts program, but I'd love the chance to work on a play. The instructor is the director of the Theater program. I would enjoy taking this course just for fun. But I can't because I'm a student! It doesn't make sense!

W: Maybe you should go talk to the dean.

M: I think I will. Maybe I can convince him that this rule discriminates against students.

The man expresses his opinion about the theater course. State his opinion and explain the reasons he gives for holding that opinion.

Exercise 3.5.D (p. 314)

Disk 5, Track 11

Now listen to a student as she speaks to other students who are parents.

My two sons have been enrolled at the campus childcare for a semester now. However, I have to say our experience has been less than satisfactory. For one thing, there really isn't enough space there. There's room for only 20 children at a time, which means a lot of people can't get their children in. My children were on the waiting list for three months before getting in. This is a real problem because it prevents a lot of parents from going to college. The college really needs to find a bigger space so there'll be more room for children, don't you think?

Another thing is, they need to extend the evening hours past nine o'clock because some of the classes don't end until 9:30. So if you have a class that lasts till 9:30, you have to leave early to pick up your children. This isn't fair to the parents who need those night classes because they miss important information in class.

The woman expresses her opinion on the on–campus childcare. State her opinion and explain the reasons she gives for holding that opinion.

3.6   INTEGRATED SPEAKING: TAKING NOTES

Focus (p. 315)

Disk 5, Track 12

Because a fungus can survive for years in the soil, the best way to control such a disease is to remove and destroy the infected plants, as well as six centimeters of soil around them. Avoid spreading disease by washing off your tools and your shoes when you go from an infected area to a healthy part of your garden. At the end of the gardening season, do a complete cleanup.

Do You Know (p. 317)

Disk 5, Track 13

Now listen to part of a lecture in a botany class.

Because a fungus can survive for years in the soil, the best way to control such a disease is to remove and destroy the infected plants, as well as six centimeters of soil around them. Avoid spreading disease by washing off your tools and your shoes when you go from an infected area to a healthy part of your garden. At the end of the gardening season, do a complete cleanup.

You can also keep disease away by rotating crops. Crop rotation can be effective in preventing soil–borne disease, especially when the disease is caused by a fungus that likes specific plants. For example, the fungus that causes southern blight is attracted to tomatoes. Once this fungus is present, it will thrive in the soil from year to year, attacking the tomato plants.

With crop rotation, you don't grow the same plant in the same place for at least three consecutive years. So, for example, if you grow tomatoes one year, the next year you shouldn't plant tomatoes in the same place. By planting something else the second and third years, any tomato–loving fungus that survived the winter wouldn't have any tomato plants to feed on. With three years between planting tomatoes, the fungus will die off from lack of a host plant.

Explain ways that a gardener can control plant disease caused by a fungus, and explain why these methods work.

Exercise 3.6.A (p. 318)

Disk 5, Track 14

Now listen to part of a talk on this topic in a psychology class.

A recent study on emotional intelligence looked at the mental health of young people with high intellectual and artistic abilities. The researcher interviewed gifted students from 12 to 17 years old. He asked them questions like "Do you ever think about your own thinking?" and "If you ask yourself, 'Who am I?', what is the answer?"

So the researcher found all of his subjects to be extremely intense and enthusiastic young people. The subjects experienced emotional highs and lows that caused intense happiness, but also conflict, pain, and a tendency to get overexcited.

For example, one 16–year–old said, "I am a very misunderstood person. People think that my life is easy because I am talented, but I have a lot of problems of my own just because of these talents. I am a very sensitive and emotional person. I get angered or saddened very easily."

What the student said shows us that people with emotional intelligence understand their feelings. However, when young people think deeply about everything and feel everything very strongly, they often experience problems. They're criticized and teased, and they start to believe that something is wrong with them. They feel embarrassed and guilty for being "different" from everyone else.

The professor discusses a study on emotional intelligence. Explain how emotional intelligence affects the experiences of young people like those in the study.

Exercise 3.6.B (p. 319)

Disk 5, Track 15

Now listen to part of a lecture in a history class.

A name often associated with boycotts is Cesar Chavez. Chavez was a labor union organizer who used nonviolent action to achieve the goals of fair pay and better working conditions for farm workers.

Chavez organized a union of grape pickers in California. When the farm owners who grew table grapes refused to accept the union, Chavez organized a nationwide boycott of grapes. The workers stopped picking grapes, and the grapes began to rot on the vines.

The boycott got a lot of attention. Lots of people from all across the country—public officials, religious leaders, and ordinary citizens—all went to California to march in support of the farm workers. As a result of the boycott, some grape growers signed agreements with the union. So the union ended the boycott, and the workers began to pick grapes again.

Chavez also called for a boycott of lettuce produced by growers without union contracts. People from all parts of the country refused to buy lettuce. Some even protested in front of supermarkets.

The power of boycotts is the negative attention they direct at the people responsible for an offense. In the case of the grape and lettuce boycotts, the growers were the offenders. The boycotts hurt the grape and lettuce growers economically because people stopped buying their products. But even more importantly, the boycotts hurt their reputation.

Explain what happens during a boycott, and explain the causes and effects of the boycotts discussed in the lecture.

Exercise 3.6.C (p. 320)

Disk 5, Track 16

Now listen to part of a lecture on this topic in a sociology class.

OK … I want to say a couple of things about social roles and role partners. Because relationships exist among various social roles, we can't study one role all by itself. We have to look at a role in relation to its role partners. For example, a man can't be a father without a child, so father and child are role partners.

When there's competition between the expectations of different role partners, we have something called role conflict. For example, as a college student, you've probably noticed that your parents and your friends—both role partners to you— often expect different behavior from you. Your parents want you to stay home and study hard, while your friends say, "you've studied enough, let's go out and party." This is a case of role conflict, and you feel stress of the conflict between your role as a child and your role as a friend.

Mature adults experience the most severe role conflicts. The main conflict is the tension between responsibility to an employer and responsibility to spouse and children. The conflict between work and family roles is especially difficult for women, who feel a great amount of stress because in our society women are still expected to make their family role primary.

Explain the concept of role conflict, and explain when and why a person experiences role conflict.

Exercise 3.6.D (p. 321)

Disk 5, Track 17

Now listen to part of a lecture on this topic in a zoology class.

A few species of birds will store food in hiding places for later use. For example, nutcrackers bury food and are able to remember the locations of the hiding places with great accuracy. They use landscape features—like distinctive rocks, logs, and other landmarks—as spatial cues to where the food is buried. Spatial memory allows the birds to return and dig up most of the food. Even when an object such as a log or rock has been moved, the birds appear to search in a particular spatial relationship to the object.

Experiments show that animals in familiar landscapes are very skilled at finding and investigating new objects. For example, a group of fourteen baboons were put into their outdoor pen after a new object had been placed there each day

when they were absent. The baboons generally took less than three minutes to find the new object. The new objects included both artificial things, like drinking cups and balls, and natural things, like coconut shells and branches. The baboons clearly reacted differently to the new objects. For example, they were much more likely to touch and handle today's new object. But they quickly paid little attention to yesterday's new object. Similar experiments with other animals show that moving familiar objects will cause animals to examine the objects; otherwise, the animals will ignore them.

Explain how the skill of spatial memory influences the behavior of specific animals.

3.7 INTEGRATED SPEAKING: DEVELOPING A TOPIC

Focus (p. 323)

Disk 5, Track 18

You can also keep disease away by rotating crops. Crop rotation can be effective in preventing soil-borne disease, especially when the disease is caused by a fungus that likes specific plants. For example, the fungus that causes southern blight is attracted to tomatoes. Once this fungus is present, it will thrive in the soil from year to year, attacking the tomato plants.

With crop rotation, you don't grow the same plant in the same place for at least three consecutive years. So, for example, if you grow tomatoes one year, the next year you shouldn't plant tomatoes in the same place. By planting something else the second and third years, any tomato-loving fungus that survived the winter wouldn't have any tomato plants to feed on. With three years between planting tomatoes, the fungus will die off from lack of a host plant.

Exercise 3.7.A (p. 326)

Disk 5, Track 19

Now listen to a student as she discusses campus housing with an adviser in the Housing Office.

W: Next semester, I'd like to move on-campus. My best friend from high school will also start school here, and the two of us want to share a room in a dormitory.
M: OK … but are you sure you want to room with your friend from high school?
W: Of course. We were best friends last year.
M: You know, this might sound strange, but generally we don't recommend that you share a room with your best friend.
W: Really?
M: It could work out, but a lot of times it can destroy a friendship. The reason is that knowing someone— even being best friends—isn't the same as living together. A better idea might be to live on the same floor as your friend—in the same "neighborhood," so to speak—but have someone else for a roommate. This way, you'll preserve your friendship and also get to know new and interesting people.
W: That does sort of make sense.
M: Or you could live in a dorm with others of your academic major. You'll meet people with similar

interests and develop relationships that can benefit you later, in your professional life.

W: I need to think about this. Thanks for your advice.

The man expresses his opinion about the woman's desire to live on campus. State his opinion and explain the reasons he gives for holding that opinion.

Exercise 3.7.B (p. 327)

Disk 5, Track 20

Now listen to part of a lecture in a psychology class.

There's growing evidence that several types of depression are linked to biological and environmental factors. For example, one mild form of depression is linked to the changes in the amount of daylight.

People with seasonal affective disorder—or SAD—have repeated bouts of depression during a particular time of the year, usually fall or winter, when the periods of daylight are shorter. Research suggests that the disorder is related to the body's biological clock and to changes in body temperature and hormone levels. So, when your body doesn't get enough sunshine, the result is symptoms that are similar to those of a major depression but usually not as serious. Usually, you have no energy and just want to sleep more, or you eat more carbohydrates and gain weight. The symptoms usually disappear when the days start getting longer in the spring. So, just as in most other types of mild depression, the symptoms go away when the underlying problem goes away in the spring.

However, some people with the disorder can't wait for spring. So they get relief from a treatment that involves exposure to light from a special fluorescent tube for a certain number of hours each day. Since they can't get real sunlight, they spend a few hours in a room with this special light that fools the body into thinking it's getting sunlight.

Describe the form of depression discussed in the lecture, explaining its causes, symptoms, and treatment.

Exercise 3.7.C (p. 328)

Disk 5, Track 21

Now listen to two students as they discuss seminars.

W: I just transferred here from another college, and we didn't have seminars there. I don't think I'll like seminars.

M: How do you know you won't like seminars, if you've never had one before?

W: Well, the program seminar reminds me of the class discussions we had in high school. I didn't like those discussions because two or three students always did all the talking. Everyone else in the class had to listen to what the big talkers had to say. There was never a chance for the shy or quiet people to speak up and say what they were thinking. So, most of the discussions were pretty boring.

M: But the seminars at this school aren't like that. Sometimes one or two students lead the discussion, but usually everyone participates.

W: I'd rather listen to what the professor has to say. After

all, it's the professor who has the knowledge. It's the professor who's supposed to teach us, not the students.

M: I think you'll change your mind about seminars after you see what they're really like.

The woman expresses her opinion about seminars. State her opinion and explain the reasons she gives for holding that opinion.

Exercise 3.7.D (p. 329)

Disk 5, Track 22

Now listen to part of a lecture in an art history class.

One of the leading artists of abstract expressionism was a painter by the name of Jackson Pollock. Like other artists of the movement, Pollock tried to express his feelings through painting. He developed an abstract style of painting where he vigorously "dripped" complicated patterns onto enormous canvases. His devotion to the act of painting led to the term "action painting."

Pollock was influential not just for his art but for the process of making it. He painted his huge canvases on the floor so he could work around and over the canvas. He felt more at ease on the floor. He could walk around the painting, work from all four sides, and literally be in the painting. He sort of danced around the borders of the canvas. He spattered the canvas with sprays and drips of paint.

Pollock gave the drip a special character. His technique was to hold the brush or stick a foot above the canvas, and then to throw lines of paint in the air so the paint would fall on the canvas. He controlled this gesture skillfully, and thus, the painting grew from his control of the drip.

A lot of Pollock's paintings were called "all-over" paintings because the paint fills the entire canvas. In these paintings, the canvas is filled with a series of lines, curves, and loops—twisting forms of color that suggest movement—an effect entirely given by the skillful gestures of the artist's brush.

The professor describes the painting style of Jackson Pollock. Explain how Pollock's style made him a leading artist of the movement called abstract expressionism.

3.8 INTEGRATED SPEAKING: SUMMARIZING A PROBLEM AND SOLUTIONS

Focus (p. 331)

Disk 5, Track 23

W: Say, Lenny, do you know anyone who wants a cat?

M: A cat? No. Why?

W: Well, this poor little cat showed up outside my apartment one day. He was hungry and cold, so I gave him some cheese, and now he's still hanging around. My landlord found out and said I have to get rid of it because pets aren't allowed.

M: You shouldn't be feeding it. If you stop giving it food, it will go away.

W: I know, I know, but he's so hungry. I like the cat, and I want him to have a good home. Actually, I'd like to keep him myself.

M: Well, if that's the case, then you'd better look for another apartment—one that allows pets.
W: I hate to do that. My apartment is so close to campus.
M: Why don't you give the cat to your mother? She likes animals.
W: My mother already has two cats, so I don't know…
M: Well, you'd better do something fast, or your landlord will throw you out.

Do You Know (p. 333)

Disk 5, Track 24

Listen to a conversation between two students.

W: Say, Lenny, do you know anyone who wants a cat?
M: A cat? No. Why?
W: Well, this poor little cat showed up outside my apartment one day. He was hungry and cold, so I gave him some cheese, and now he's still hanging around. My landlord found out and said I have to get rid of it because pets aren't allowed.
M: You shouldn't be feeding it. If you stop giving it food, it will go away.
W: I know, I know, but he's so hungry. I like the cat, and I want him to have a good home. Actually, I'd like to keep him myself.
M: Well, if that's the case, then you'd better look for another apartment—one that allows pets.
W: I hate to do that. My apartment is so close to campus.
M: Why don't you give the cat to your mother? She likes animals.
W: My mother already has two cats, so I don't know…
M: Well, you'd better do something fast, or your landlord will throw you out.

Describe the woman's problem and the suggestions the man makes about how to solve it. What do you think the woman should do, and why?

Exercise 3.8.A (p. 334)

Disk 5, Track 25

Number 1. Listen to a conversation between two students.

W: Is something wrong with your arm?
M: Oh, not really, it's just that my elbow is bothering me.
W: What happened to it?
M: It's been a little sore lately. I think I lift too many heavy boxes at my job.
W: Well, you'd better go to the clinic and have someone look at your elbow. Are you free right now?
M: Yes, for a little while.
W: Well, come on then. I'll walk over there with you. I'm already heading that way.
M: I can't go to the clinic right now. I have baseball practice at three o'clock.
W: Baseball practice! You shouldn't play baseball if your elbow hurts.
M: I know, but I can't afford to miss any more practice. I've missed a lot already, and my coach will be angry.
W: You need to tell your coach about your elbow. And ask your boss for something else to do besides lifting heavy things.
M: There isn't anything else to do at my job.

W: Well, then you'd better look for a different job. You could really hurt yourself if you're not careful.
M: I know, I know.

Describe the man's problem and the suggestions the woman makes about what he should do. What do you think the man should do, and why?

Disk 5, Track 26

Number 2. Listen to part of a conversation between a student and her academic adviser.

W: I need help with my registration for Winter Quarter.
M: OK. What can I do for you?
W: I still need to take another course in social science, but it doesn't look like anything will fit into my schedule.
M: Hmm. I see what you mean. You've already got a full schedule. Why don't you wait until Spring Quarter to fulfill the social science requirement?
W: Because I'll be doing an internship in the spring that will be full–time.
M: Hmm. Well … you could take an evening course. There are lots of evening classes in the social sciences, in both Winter and Spring Quarters.
W: An evening course … ugh … I don't like going to class at night.
M: Well, with your schedule, this may be your only choice. Another possibility, of course, is to wait until summer, and fulfill the social science requirement then. Will you be around this summer?
W: I hope to graduate, and then go home for the summer. So this is kind of a problem for me.

Describe the woman's problem and the suggestions her adviser makes about how to solve it. What do you think the woman should do, and why?

Disk 5, Track 27

Number 3. Listen to a conversation between two students.

W: How are your classes going?
M: All right mostly, that is, except for environmental science. The class is fine, but my learning partner—the guy I'm supposed to do my project with—well, to be honest, he's lazy. I've done all the work so far, but we're being graded together.
W: That's not good. You need to have a serious talk with your partner. You can't let him ruin your grade. You need to lay out a plan for who does what and when. He has to take responsibility for his part of the project.
M: That's for sure. He's hard to get a hold of, too. I've left several messages on his answering machine.
W: You'd better let your professor know about this. Maybe he'll let you do the project with someone else.
M: It's kind of late for that. Besides, I've already started working on it, and so has everyone else.
W: You never know. Maybe you could sort of look around for another group to join. But I would see what your professor says first.

Describe the man's problem and the suggestions the woman makes about how he should deal with it. What do you think the man should do, and why?

Disk 5, Track 28

Number 4. Listen to a conversation between two students.

M: Hi, Nicole. How's it going?

W: My classes are going well. I wish I could say the same for my car.

M: What's wrong with your car?

W: I'm not sure, exactly. It just won't start up sometimes. It gave me a lot of trouble this morning. It took me ten minutes to get it running, and then I was late for class. I need to have it checked out, but my regular mechanic is expensive, and I still have to pay my tuition.

M: You could take your car to the community college. They have a program in automotive technology, and they fix students' cars for less than a regular mechanic would charge.

W: But I'm not a student at the community college.

M: Check it out anyway. Maybe you don't have to be a student at that school. Just tell them you're a student.

W: Well, maybe.

M: Another place you could try is the bulletin board in the Student Center. People sometimes advertise services like this. Maybe you can find a mechanic that's not too expensive.

W: Hmm. Maybe. Thanks for the tips.

M: No problem. Good luck.

The students discuss two possible solutions to the woman's problem. Describe the problem. Then state which of the two solutions you prefer and explain why.

Disk 5, Track 29

Number 5. Listen to a conversation between a student and a professor.

M: Professor Fisher, I'm not going to be in class on Monday, so I'll miss the test. I was wondering if I could make it up later.

W: Well, you know my policy is not to give make–up tests. If you miss one test, then you can try to earn extra points on the other tests. But … haven't you already missed a test?

M: Um … yeah, I missed one a few weeks ago.

W: Then try not to miss this test, and try to do well on it too. Your test scores so far have not been strong. You could be in danger of not receiving credit for the course.

M: Do you mean I might fail?

W: At this point, you need to do something to raise your grade. Why don't you get a tutor to help you, or get a classmate to be your study partner?

M: Well, I guess I could. But, to tell the truth, I don't have the extra time for a tutor or a study partner.

W: Then, in that case, you need to think about whether or not you should stay enrolled in this course. If you're too busy to study and come to class, you should consider dropping it.

Describe the man's situation and the suggestions his professor makes about what he should do. What do you think the man should do, and why?

3.9 INTEGRATED SPEAKING: SUMMARIZING IMPORTANT IDEAS

Do You Know (p. 342)

Disk 5, Track 30

Listen to part of a lecture in a world history class. The professor is talking about mass migrations of people.

In the nineteenth century, there were several periods when large numbers of people moved from one place to another around the world. In many cases, people moved to another continent. These mass migrations were on a much larger scale than any previous migrations in history. One major movement was from Europe to the Americas, Australia, and Africa. This migration of Europeans involved around 60 million people over one hundred years. Another mass migration was from Russia to Siberia and Central Asia. Another was from China, India, and Japan to Southeast Asia.

These large movements of people were made possible by the new cheap and fast means of transportation, specifically railroads and steamships. Another important factor was the rapid growth in banking and capital, by which large investors financed a lot of the settlement. In some places, immigrants were given free land and other benefits if they settled there. This is what encouraged a lot of people—both immigrant and native–born—to move westward in the United States and Canada. Thus, most regions of the U.S. and Canada were populated by the end of the nineteenth century.

The majority of the people in these mass migrations came from the lower social and economic classes of society. The immigrants were motivated mainly by the hope of a better life for themselves and their children. Since most of the immigrants were unskilled workers, their main contribution to their new countries was the labor they supplied. It was the hard work and high hopes of the immigrants that contributed to the economic growth of their new countries.

Using points and examples from the lecture, describe the mass migrations of people in the nineteenth century, and explain why these migrations occurred.

Exercise 3.9.A (p. 343)

Disk 5, Track 31

Number 1. Listen to part of a talk in a hotel management class.

Hotel managers are responsible for the overall operation of their establishment. They see that guests receive good service so they will come back to that hotel. Managers are also in charge of finances and see that the hotel earns a profit without sacrificing service.

The top executive in a hotel is the general manager. In a small hotel the general manager may also be the owner. In large establishments with many facilities, the general manager directs the work of department managers such as executive housekeepers, personnel managers, and food and beverage managers. General managers need to be skilled in areas of leadership and financial decision making. They must be able to judge when to make budget cuts and when to spend money for advertising or remodeling in order to earn profits in the future.

Another type of manager is the controller. Hotel controllers usually work in large hotels, where they are responsible for the management of money. They manage the accounting and payroll departments and find ways to improve efficiency. The controller is an expert at interpreting financial statements, so the general manager and other top managers in the hotel consult with the controller on all financial matters.

Large hotels rely heavily on advertising and public relations to sell their services. Such hotels have sales managers to market the services of the hotel. Sales managers have constant contact with customers and know what selling points appeal to the public. Sales managers need courses in business, marketing, and advertising in addition to hotel management.

Using points and examples from the talk, describe the duties of different types of managers in large hotels.

Disk 5, Track 32

Number 2. Listen to part of a lecture in a meteorology class. The professor is discussing climate.

Several features on the earth's surface influence climate. Two of these features are ocean currents and landforms.

Ocean currents are formed when the earth's rotation and prevailing winds work together. The prevailing winds push the ocean waters westward in the Atlantic, Pacific, and Indian oceans until these waters bounce off the nearest continent. This causes two large, circular ocean currents, one in each hemisphere. The current in the Northern Hemisphere turns clockwise, and the one in the Southern Hemisphere turns counterclockwise. These currents move warm water from the equator to the north and south.

Warm and cold currents in the world's oceans affect the climates of nearby coastal areas. For example, the warm Gulf Stream in the Atlantic Ocean warms the coast of northwestern Europe. Without the Gulf Stream, the climate of northwestern Europe would be more like that of the cold sub–Arctic.

Landforms such as mountains also affect climate. Because of their higher elevation, mountains tend to be cooler, windier, and wetter than valleys. For example, even though Mount Kilimanjaro, Africa's highest peak, stands near the equator, its summit is always covered with snow. Another thing mountains do is interrupt the flow of winds and storms. When moist winds blow from the ocean toward land, then hit a mountain range, the moist air becomes cooler as it's forced to rise. This causes the air to lose its moisture as rain and snow on mountain slopes that face the wind. The air on the other side of the mountain will be warmer and drier.

Using points and examples from the lecture, explain how two features of the earth's surface influence climate.

Disk 5, Track 33

Number 3. Listen to part of a talk in a cultural history class. The professor is discussing traditional beliefs about trees.

Throughout the world, there is an extensive mythology about trees. For example, the concept of a great cosmic tree—a Tree of the World—appears in numerous traditions. We find the Tree of the World in Norse mythology. The Norse people, the ancestors of present–day Scandinavians, honored the ash tree as the cosmic tree because it was much larger in size than all other trees in northern Europe. In southeastern Canada, the Algonquin people also believed the ash was the cosmic tree. According to their tradition, the world's first human beings came from the ash tree.

The Europeans who settled in North America also had special beliefs about trees. One belief is that by carrying the seeds of the buckeye tree in their pockets, people would avoid getting a disease of the bones. Another tradition is the water dowser—a person who is said to have the ability to find water underground by using a branch from the hazel tree. I have a personal story about water dowsers because my uncle used one for digging a well on his land. My uncle hired this old man—a dowser—to help him locate the best spot to put the well, and the guy used a hazel branch to do it! He walked back and forth across the property until the branch signaled where the water was. So, you can see that some people still hold this tradition.

So why have trees been so respected in world mythology? For one thing, people have always depended on trees for many of life's necessities: food, oils, building materials, medicines, spices, and dyes. So it's really no wonder that trees are thought of as special … and why there are so many traditions about trees.

Using points and examples from the talk, describe traditional beliefs about trees, and explain why people have thought of trees as special.

Disk 5, Track 34

Number 4. Listen to part of a talk in a biology class. The professor is discussing animal life in water and on land.

Animal life began in water. When some animals moved from water to land, it was a dramatic event in animal evolution because land is an environment that is very different from water. There were several important physical differences that animals had to adapt to.

The first difference between water and land is the oxygen content. Oxygen is at least 20 times more abundant in air than in water, and it spreads much more quickly through air than through water. Consequently, land animals can get oxygen much more easily than water animals can—that is, once land animals evolved the appropriate organs, such as lungs.

A second difference is in the density of water and air. Air is much less dense than water, and because of this, air provides less support against gravity than water does. This means that land animals had to develop strong legs to support themselves. They also needed a stronger skeleton with better structural support—a skeleton and bones designed for standing and moving in air rather than in water.

And a third difference between life in water and on land is, on land, the temperature of the air changes more easily than it does in water. This means that land environments experience severe and sometimes unpredictable cycles of freezing, thawing, drying, and flooding. Therefore, land animals need to protect themselves from temperature extremes. Land animals had to develop behavioral and physiological strategies to survive in warm and cold temperatures. And one important strategy is being able to maintain a constant body temperature—a physiological strategy that birds and mammals possess.

Using points and details from the talk, describe the physical differences that animals had to adapt to when they moved from water to land.

Disk 5, Track 35

Number 5. Listen to part of a lecture in an architecture class.

In the late nineteenth century, New York's early "skyscrapers" were steel–framed stone buildings that were only eight or nine stories tall. Then, in 1902, the city got its first true skyscraper. It was called the Flatiron Building, and it was the first structure to come close to being the ideal skyscraper—that is, an office tower that stood apart, forever free on all sides.

The Flatiron Building is twenty–two stories tall. It has a steel frame that's covered on the outside with stone. The first three stories give a sense of heaviness to the lower part of the building. The next thirteen stories have windows grouped in pairs, with carved geometric patterns between them. The top stories are even more decorated with columns and arches, and the top is a heavy crown of carved stone.

The Flatiron Building is different from most other skyscrapers because of the shape of the site it's built on. The irregular, triangle–shaped site was the result of three streets coming together. Because the site is surrounded by streets, the Flatiron Building will always stand alone, separate from other buildings on all three sides.

The building's name—actually its nickname—was a joke about its flatiron shape. At that time, electric irons hadn't been invented, so clothing was pressed with a flatiron, a heavy triangle–shaped piece of iron that was heated on top of a stove. People joked that the building looked like a flatiron, and the name stuck.

Because the Flatiron Building was so narrow, a famous photographer said it looked like the front end of a huge steamship. We can honestly say that this bold design, this strange, tall, thin building, changed the design of the office building forever.

Using points and details from the lecture, describe the Flatiron Building and explain how it got its name.

3.10 EVALUATING INTEGRATED SPEAKING

Exercise 3.10.A (p. 350)

Disk 5, Track 36

Now listen to part of a talk in a sociology class.

Agents of socialization are the people and institutions that teach you about the culture you live in, including its rules. The first agents of socialization are your parents or other adults who take care of you when you're a baby. Your parents give you the first important lessons in how to behave in society.

When you're a teenager, your peers—your friends and classmates—are important agents of socialization. Your peers support you and help you grow up and out of your family's nest. Your parents and peers are important in different ways. Your parents give you guidance on long–term goals, like career choice, but your peers are more likely to influence your immediate lifestyle choices, like how you dress and what you do for fun.

And since you spend so many years in school under the guidance of teachers, teachers are also agents of socialization. Teachers give you knowledge and also serve as models for responsible adulthood. Institutions—like clubs and religious organizations—are also agents of socialization. So are the mass media—television, magazines, popular music, and the Internet.

Define agents of socialization, and explain how specific agents of socialization influence an individual.

Exercise 3.10.B (p. 351)

Disk 5, Track 37

Listen to part of a conversation between two students.

M: How do you like living in the campus apartments?
W: Well … it's OK. I mean, I like the apartment, but my roommate is kind of a problem. Sometimes she uses my things without asking—mostly little things, like paper and toothpaste, but once it was my favorite sweater. And she never cleans the bathroom when it's her turn.
M: Have you sat down with her and had a good talk about these things?
W: Maybe if I saw her more often. The problem is, she's hardly ever home.
M: Try leaving her a note.
W: I did, but it didn't help.
M: Isn't there an apartment manager, someone who will help you sort out problems like this? I don't know … like set up a meeting with your roommate?
W: I didn't know the manager does that kind of thing. I guess I could find out.
M: And if that doesn't work … if talking it over doesn't help, then you should probably just move out, find another place. There's always someone looking for a roommate.

Describe the woman's problem with her roommate and the suggestions the man makes about how she could deal with it. What do you think the woman should do, and why?

QUIZ 4 (p. 353)

Disk 5, Track 38

Now listen to two students as they discuss the career workshop.

M: Are you going to the career workshop on Saturday?
W: Um. I don't know. I don't think so. I have a lot of studying to do this weekend.
M: You should go. It's supposed to be really good.
W: Oh, yeah? How?
M: My professor recommended it. He owns a small business downtown, and he'll be there. He says that talking to the business people who'll be there is one of the best ways to find out what's happening.
W: But my major isn't business; it's nursing.
M: Oh. But you should go anyway. There'll be a lot of people to talk to, people in health services. You should talk to people working in the field to find out more about what it's like. Some of them are graduates of this university.
W: But I have a test on Monday. I really need to study all day.
M: Study on Sunday instead. This is more important. The university has only one of these workshops each year. You shouldn't miss it. It's a good way to start looking for a job after graduation.
W: Hmm. Maybe you're right.

The man expresses his opinion about the career workshop. State his opinion and explain the reasons he gives for holding that opinion.

Disk 5, Track 39

Now listen to part of a lecture in a psychology class.

We have new evidence that sleep improves our ability to learn language. Researchers have found that sleep improves the ability of students to retain knowledge about computer speech—even when the students forget part of what they've learned.

The researchers tested college students' understanding of a series of common words produced by a computer that made the words difficult to understand. They first measured the students' ability to recognize the words. After that, they trained the students to recognize the words and then tested them again to measure the effectiveness of the training.

One group of students was trained in the morning and tested twelve hours later, at night. During that 12–hour period, the students had lost much of their learning. The students were then allowed a night's sleep, and were retested the next morning. When they were tested again in the morning, their scores had improved significantly from the night before.

The researchers were amazed by the loss of learning the students experienced during the day and then recovered after sleeping. The students forgot what they learned during the day because they listened to other speech or thought about other things. The results of the study are fairly clear: a good night's sleep is good for learning. Even if information is forgotten, sleep helps restore a memory.

The professor describes a study about the effects of sleep. Explain how the study supports the connections between sleep and learning.

Disk 5, Track 40

Now listen to a conversation between two students.

W: This weekend is going to be crazy! I have two midterm exams on Monday, and I should study all weekend, but my parents are coming to visit. They'll want to spend time with me and want me show them around town. I look forward to seeing them, but I don't know when I'll have time to study for my exams!

M: Why don't you join our biology group tonight? There are three of us so far. We're reviewing for the midterm, starting at six o'clock.

W: Tonight? Uh … I'd have to get the night off from work.

M: Well, if you can make it, then please come. We meet at Mark's house at six o'clock.

W: Uh … OK, but I'll have to talk to my boss.

M: Another thing you could do is just explain to your parents that you have to study for examinations. I'm sure they'll understand. You don't have to spend the entire weekend with them. Just give them a list of places to go during the afternoon and then spend the evening with them.

W: Hmm. I could at least try that. I've got to do something to get ready for exams.

The students discuss possible solutions to the woman's problem. Describe the problem. Then state which of the solutions you prefer and explain why.

Disk 5, Track 41

Now listen to part of a talk in a communications class.

Communicating with other human beings relies heavily on what is called body language—all the nonverbal signals that people send to each other. Humans have more than one hundred separate gestures and facial expressions. This makes us the biggest communicators in the animal world, even without our spoken language.

Body language communicates a great deal about how people perceive a social situation. When strangers first meet in a social situation, such as a meeting or a party, they often will lift their eyebrows to communicate friendly feelings. Also, they may make some hand or arm gesture, such as a salute or a handshake, to signal involvement.

The human face is extremely expressive. Eye movement, for example, has an important role in regulating the rhythm of conversation. In Western society, eye contact is usually held between people about one third of the time they are talking together. The closer and more friendly they are, the more often they look at each other. Often a speaker will signal his intention to speak by looking away from the other person and then continuing to look away while speaking. The listener signals his interest and attention by looking at the speaker and nodding his head slightly.

Most important is the smile, the very human gesture that recognizes the other person as a fellow social being. Even though a lot of body language varies in meaning across cultures, the meaning of the smile is the same in every culture. The smile has a tremendous power to generate friendly feelings. The smile is first seen in human babies as early as four or five weeks old, and a baby can be made to smile by any smiling human face, or even by any stimulus that resembles a face, such as a simple drawing.

Using points and examples from the talk, describe the uses of gestures and facial expressions in human communication.

QUIZ 5 (p. 356)

Disk 5, Track 42

Now listen to a student and a professor as they discuss the writing course.

M: Professor Olson, I'll be in your writing course next session, and I … uh … I was wondering if I could skip the peer feedback group and just come to the lecture and writing workshop.

W: Oh?

M: It's like this … I … uh … you see, I was in a student writing group before, but it didn't help at all with my writing. The other students were not good writers, so it was a waste of time. I can't learn from other students if they don't know how to write.

W: Learning how to write with other students, responding to the writing of others, expressing yourself in a small group—these are important steps in the learning process.

M: But I can learn better from a teacher because a teacher has more education and experience. The other students don't know how to teach writing. Isn't that the teacher's job?

W: I promise that you'll learn from the teacher, but you'll also learn more than you think from your peers.

The man expresses his opinion about the peer feedback group. State his opinion and explain the reasons he gives for holding that opinion.

Disk 5, Track 43

Now listen to part of a talk on this topic in a sociology class.

The concept of cohort helps us understand the similarities and differences in the lives of adults of different ages. If we look at times of major social change—like the Great Depression of the 1930s—we can see how variations in experience affected successive cohorts. Everyone who was alive during that period was affected in some way, but because events hit each cohort at a different age, the effects are different for each cohort.

The timing of events interacts with developmental issues, and this produces unique patterns of influence for each cohort. For example, one study showed that people who were teenagers during the Great Depression showed fewer long–term effects than people who were younger children at the time. The younger cohort spent a greater portion of their childhood under conditions of economic hardship, and that affected their family life and their educational opportunities. The negative effects of the Depression on the children's personalities could still be seen in adulthood.

In contrast, people who were teenagers during the Depression didn't show negative effects later in life. In fact, some of them showed more independence and initiative. Thus, you can see how two cohorts that were close in age experienced the same circumstances differently because they were different ages at the time.

Describe the effect of historical events on different cohorts, and explain how the Great Depression influenced two cohorts that were close in age.

Disk 5, Track 44

Now listen to a conversation between a student and a college administrator.

W: How much does it cost for a permit to park my car on campus?

M: A parking permit is $45 for the quarter. But I'm required to tell you that a parking permit does not guarantee a parking space on campus.

W: What? It takes me an hour to drive here, and I have to park my car somewhere.

M: We know it's a problem. Our parking lots just aren't big enough for all the students we have this year. That's why I'm required to warn you about the situation.

W: What am I supposed to do? I have to drive to school.

M: One thing you can do, if possible, is register for classes that meet in the afternoon. The parking lots are usually full in the morning, but less full in the afternoon.

W: OK.

M: Another thing you can do is park in our park–and–ride lot on Western Avenue, a mile from here. Your parking permit is good there, and you can usually find a parking space. You catch a free shuttle bus to campus from there. They run every 20 minutes.

W: OK, thanks. I appreciate your advice.

Describe the woman's problem and the two suggestions the man makes about how to deal with it. What do you think the woman should do, and why?

Disk 5, Track 45

Now listen to part of a talk given by the president of a company to students in a business class. The speaker is discussing organizational charts.

No matter what size a business is, its organizational chart tells who is in charge of what, and who reports to whom. Organizational charts facilitate the free flow of information so people can communicate with one another in an orderly way.

The formal structure of many companies is designed in the shape of a pyramid. In the pyramid scheme, the labor force on the bottom supports the whole structure. In the middle are the various layers of management, one on top of the other, on up to the top. The pyramid structure defines the chain of command. Information flows up the chain, and orders flow down. Everyone knows his or her place in the hierarchy.

Although the pyramid is logical, this system never satisfied me. Decision–making can take a long time. Everything must work its way up and down the chain of command. I've seen companies with this structure stagnate when the managers become as rigid as the management structure. But without a formal structure and chain of command, there would be chaos.

In my company, the organizational chart looks more like a wheel than a pyramid. Management is the hub, and all the departments are the spokes giving the wheel its shape. The labor force is the rim. Information flows up through the spokes to the hub.

My company has a policy of open communication throughout the organization. This means that any staff member can go anywhere in the company to ask questions and get answers. I believe that anyone with an idea for improving the company's performance should be able to send it up to my office. I do insist, however, that every report be signed by the person who wrote it. This is so I can contact that person directly if I have questions.

Using points and examples from the talk, describe two types of organizational charts, and explain what they reveal about an organization.

QUIZ 6 (p. 359)

Disk 5, Track 46

Now listen to two students as they discuss the request for volunteers.

W: What do you think? Are you going to volunteer for the conference?

M: Oh, I don't know. It's difficult for me to plan that far ahead. It's over a month away.

W: I know, but this conference is going to be great. There'll be a lot of prominent speakers from this country and all over the world, including a couple of scientists who won the Nobel Prize.

M: Really?

W: Yeah, and if we work for just two hours, we get to go to the reception and meet lots of experts on global warming. It's a great opportunity—kind of exciting for our school, isn't it? I mean, this conference is a really big event for us, and volunteering is a way to be a part of it.

M: That's true. But you have to work! Isn't it better to just attend the conference?

W: Ah, but this is one way to learn how a conference is organized. I'm really interested in knowing how to do this sort of thing since I plan to be involved in environmental issues.

M: And you want the free T–shirt.

W: Right!

The woman expresses her opinion about volunteering for the conference. State her opinion and explain the reasons she gives for holding that opinion.

Disk 5, Track 47

Now listen to part of a talk on the same topic in a film history class.

There were lots of variations on the chase film. One of the most popular chase films was a comedy called *Personal*. This movie told the story of a wealthy man who advertises for a wife in a personal ad. He announces that he'll meet any potential wives at a famous landmark, but when he goes there, he ends up being chased by a crowd of eager women. This variation was such a hit that other filmmakers quickly copied it.

Another variation was the slapstick police chase made famous by the Keystone Kops. The Keystone Kops were the kings of early silent comedy. The seven clownish Kops created confusion and silliness as they chased villains and bank robbers. The actors performed all their own stunts. And a lot of these stunts involved moving cars, tall buildings, and of course, somebody getting a cream pie in the face.

The chase film was not only popular but also important in the history of film. Making chase films was a valuable exercise in film style. The movement of the chase provided its own visual excitement and led to certain filmmaking conventions. For example, it was common to have the person being chased and the people who were chasing all running forward, past the camera.

Describe two variations on the chase film, and explain why the chase film was significant in the history of film.

Disk 5, Track 48

Now listen to a conversation between a student and his college adviser.

W: I'm glad to see you, Alan. I want to discuss your plan to transfer to the university in the fall.

M: OK.

W: It turns out that you still need a humanities course to complete your basic requirements.

M: I do?

W: Yes. Remember that philosophy class you dropped a while back? You never made it up, so you'll need to do that this summer.

M: This summer?

W: Yes. I suggest you take a literature course to meet the requirement.

M: Oh, no ... I can't do it this summer. My best friend is taking his sailboat to Hawaii, and he wants me to go with him. We'll be gone all summer, so that means I can't go to school. Besides, I need the vacation.

W: Well ... you want to go to the university, right? You need one more course to be able to transfer this fall.

M: But the sailing trip is a once–in–a–lifetime opportunity! And I've already promised my friend that I'd go with him.

W: Then you'll have to decide what's more important to you: going sailing or going to the university. I suggest you discuss this with your family, and with your friend. Perhaps they will help you decide.

Describe the man's problem and the suggestions his adviser makes about what to do. What do you think the man should do, and why?

Disk 5, Track 49

Now listen to part of a talk in a nursing class. The professor is discussing immunization.

Before we had immunizations, thousands of children and adults died or were disabled from diseases that are now almost completely eliminated. The results of worldwide immunization programs are amazing, making this the greatest success story in medical history.

Immunization works by strengthening the immune system against a specific disease in a much safer way than the disease process itself. In order to control a disease, we have to immunize at least 80 percent of the population. If we fall below 80 percent, the disease will find enough human hosts where it can live and flourish. Immunizing an entire population can eliminate bacteria or viruses that survive only if they have a human host.

The methods for developing vaccines against bacterial diseases were available in the early 1900s. Researchers had discovered how to isolate bacteria and grow them in the laboratory. This led to experiments with vaccines that caused the body to produce antibodies against certain bacteria. Soon we had safe vaccines against the typhoid, cholera, tetanus, and tuberculosis bacteria.

For diseases caused by viruses, some of the first successful immunizations were for smallpox, rabies, and yellow fever. The polio vaccine took a long time to develop because this virus couldn't be grown outside the living human body. Efforts to isolate the poliovirus and develop a vaccine were finally successful in 1955. By this time, we had methods for cultivating viruses in the laboratory using animal tissues such as eggs. We could then develop vaccines against other viruses such as measles.

Using points and examples from the talk, explain how immunization works and how vaccines were developed against various diseases.

QUIZ 7 (p. 362)

Disk 6, Track 1

What book have you read that you would recommend to others? Explain why you think other people should read this book. Include details and examples to support your explanation.

Disk 6, Track 2

Some people have a few favorite foods that they eat most of the time. Others are always trying new dishes and styles of cooking. Which do you prefer and why? Include details and examples in your explanation.

Disk 6, Track 3

Now listen to two students as they discuss the proposal.

W: Have you heard about the proposal to limit our course load?

M: Yeah. But I don't really see why it's necessary.

W: I don't either. So what if people want to take more than 20 credits? I've done it twice already, and I never had any problem finishing the work. It's hard, I mean you're working all the time, but if you manage your time well, you can do it.

M: It's not something I'd want to do, but I can see your point.

W: Actually, this proposal is kind of a problem for me because I need only 21 more credits to graduate. I was hoping to graduate this spring. If I'm only allowed to take 20 credits, that makes it impossible for me to graduate. I'd have to go to summer school.

M: Oh, that's too bad.

W: And if I take a class this summer, that's more tuition I have to pay. I don't want to ask my family for any more money. So this new policy causes a financial problem for me. I think I'll go hear the dean speak, but I also have some tough questions to ask her.

The woman expresses her opinion about the proposal. State her opinion and explain the reasons she gives for holding that opinion.

Disk 6, Track 4

Now listen to part of a talk in a meteorology class.

Now we have evidence that forest fires are a factor in climate change. Forest fires send chemicals into the air, and these chemicals might affect atmospheric chemistry in a manner similar to—and on the same scale as—the effect of chemicals from volcanic eruptions.

Like the ash from volcanic eruptions, the smoke from forest fires spreads over large areas and goes very high. New data show that smoke can reach the upper levels of the atmosphere. The smoke from a forest fire in Canada reached into the stratosphere. And sulfurous chemicals from the fire caused effects similar to what we see after a volcanic eruption.

What happens is, powerful, rising air currents in the thunderstorms carry fire debris up into the upper atmosphere, where the sulfur and other chemicals can affect conditions. Some of the effects are cloud formation and climate change.

We're still in the early stages of understanding the role of forest fires in climate change. Yet these two points are clear. First, the effect of fires on climate is likely to grow as warming temperatures cause more fire outbreaks in northern latitudes. Second, there's an important difference between volcanoes and forest fire. We can't control volcanic eruptions, but we can control and reduce the number of wildfires.

Explain how forest fires are related to climate change, and compare this to the effect of volcanic eruptions.

Disk 6, Track 5

Now listen to a conversation between a student and a professor.

M: Hi, Professor Hogan, do you have a minute?

W: Of course, Dustin. What can I do for you?

M: I have trouble remembering the material from class. When I listen to your lectures, I understand everything, but then I always forget it during the tests.

W: Do you take notes in class?

M: Yes, but sometimes I can't understand my notes when I look at them later.

W: Hmm. I can suggest a couple of things. First, you should review your lecture notes as soon as possible after class, when the material is still fresh in your mind. Our class ends at noon. If you can, look over your notes while you're eating lunch. That's a good time to underline things, and make notes to yourself about things to look up later or ask about in class.

M: OK.

W: And the other thing is to get enough sleep. Take a short nap, not in class, but after you've been studying for a few hours.

M: But won't I forget what I just studied?

W: Believe it or not, sleeping helps you remember what you just studied. So, it's a good idea to study in the evening and then get a good night's sleep.

Describe the man's problem and the two suggestions the professor makes about how to solve it. What do you think the man should do, and why?

Disk 6, Track 6

Now listen to part of a lecture in a marketing class.

Manufacturers choose different ways to present their goods for sale. The three main ways of selling goods are direct sales, retail sales, and wholesaling.

Direct sales take place away from a store. Direct sales usually take place in the customer's home, although sometimes it's in a business setting. Direct sales include the activities of door–to–door salespeople and real estate agents. Other examples are catalog shopping, telemarketing, and at–home Internet shopping.

The second type of sales—retail sales—take place in stores. Department stores, discount chains, supermarkets, hardware stores, car dealerships, drugstores, convenience stores—all of these are retail stores, where consumers directly purchase small quantities of goods. Most manufacturers choose to sell their products through retail stores because they're a convenient way for consumers to buy. Consumers can inspect merchandise and take their purchases with them. They can exchange or return things easily. They can ask sales clerks for advice about products, or about how something works.

The third type of sales is wholesaling—where goods are sold below the retail or direct–sale price. Wholesale prices are lower because customers are buying in large quantities or in a low overhead setting. Wholesalers operate in a variety of ways. Some have their own outlet stores where they sell directly to consumers. Others send sales representatives to retail stores that buy goods at wholesale prices and then mark them up for resale. Because it's difficult for a manufacturer to contact every buyer directly, wholesaling is the most practical method for the widespread distribution of goods.

Using points and examples from the lecture, explain the three main ways that manufacturers sell goods to consumers.

QUIZ 8 (p. 366)

Disk 6, Track 7

What is the best gift you have ever received? Describe this gift and explain its importance to you. Include details and examples in your explanation.

Disk 6, Track 8

Some students like to study for a long period of hours at a time. Others divide their study time into many shorter sessions. Which method do you think is better for studying and why? Include details and examples in your explanation.

Disk 6, Track 9

Now listen to a college counselor as he speaks to prospective students about scholarship applications.

If an essay is required for your scholarship application, start writing it far in advance of the deadline. You'll go crazy if you wait until the last minute to write different essays for each scholarship you apply for. If an essay is not required, write one anyway and attach it to your application. Compose a general statement that tells why you want to follow a particular program of study, and then explain how your talents and interests match what the program has to offer. Doing this will let the scholarship committee understand more about you and your goals, and may boost your chance of winning the scholarship.

Regarding letters of recommendation, ask people for recommendations early, before they're flooded with other requests. Ask teachers, counselors, and employers who know you as an individual. This personal touch will help the writers create a more complete picture of you. If recommendations are not required, get one or two anyway—they might be useful for future applications.

The counselor expresses his views on scholarship applications. State his views and explain the reasons he gives for holding them.

Disk 6, Track 10

Now listen to part of a talk on this topic in a psychology class.

One fascinating thing about crowd behavior is, how a crowd ends up isn't always clear at the beginning. Crowds have what's known as an emergent quality—the possibility of several different outcomes emerging from the situation. For example, the crowd could just break up, or it could turn angry, or the police could break it up, or it could become a riot.

An expressive crowd shows strong emotions, and these feelings can be either positive or negative. You've probably been at events, for example, when the musicians at a concert were drowned in cheers, or, on the other hand, maybe they were booed off stage. This sort of thing is an emergent quality. And maybe you've even been in crowds where emotions got out of hand, and everyone stormed the stage, or tore down the goal-posts. When this happens, the crowd becomes out of control.

But not all expressive crowds are out of control. Some are organized into demonstrations for or against a specific goal. Demonstrations usually have their own rules of behavior, such as marching and chanting—although they, too, can become unpredictable. That's their emergent aspect. Some elements of crowd behavior that lead to emergent possibilities include a lack of certainty about what to do next and the spread of a feeling that something should be done. This leads to a particular mood based on that uncertainty, and finally, to a breaking of the rules.

Describe the emergent quality of crowd behavior, and explain why some crowds behave in certain ways.

Disk 6, Track 11

Now listen to a conversation between two teaching assistants.

M: Hi, Molly. How are you?
W: I was afraid you'd ask. Things couldn't be much worse. Dr. Carter just gave me about forty student papers to grade, and she wants them all done by the end of this week! And I also have to write my term paper for biology by Friday. And I have a big test in another class! I don't see how I can get it all done. If I finish grading all the papers, I'll never have time to do my own work.
M: Wow. You'd better ask Dr. Carter for more time to grade the papers.
W: Hmm. I could, I suppose, but she said she really needs these papers done.
M: Oh. Well, why don't you talk to your biology professor and ask for more time to write your paper? Professors understand. They know how overworked we are.
W: I already know what he'll say: No late papers. He's very strict about that.
M: Well, then just try your best to get it all done. If I were you, I'd grade the student papers first. Set a time limit for each one, and don't spend any more time than that. I wish you luck
W: Thanks. It looks like I won't be getting much sleep this week.

Describe the woman's situation and the suggestions the man makes about how to manage it. What do you think the woman should do, and why?

Disk 6, Track 12

Now listen to part of a lecture in an ecology class. The professor is discussing abiotic factors in ecosystems.

Ecosystems are made up of both living and nonliving components. The nonliving—or abiotic—components of ecosystems include various physical factors such as sunlight, rainfall, temperature, and wind, as well as chemical nutrients in the water, rocks, and soil that living things need to survive.

Sunlight provides the energy that drives ecosystems, and almost all forms of life get their energy from sunlight. Plants use sunlight directly in photosynthesis. Light is important to the development and behavior of many plants and animals that are sensitive to the relative lengths of day and night. The length of daylight is a signal for seasonal events, such as the flowering of plants and the migration of birds.

Rainfall and temperature affect habitats and food supplies in several ways. Climate greatly influences the plant community, which then determines the availability of food, nest sites, and shelter for animals. Air temperature is an important factor because of its effect on biological processes and the ability or inability of organisms to regulate their body temperature. Only some plants and animals can maintain an active metabolism at very low or very high temperatures.

The abiotic factor of wind increases the effects of air temperature on organisms by increasing heat loss—what we call the wind chill factor. Wind also causes water loss in organisms by increasing the rate of evaporation in animals and transpiration in plants.

Rocks and soil are important abiotic components of ecosystems. Their physical structure and chemical composition limit the populations of plants, and also the animals that feed upon plants. Thus, rocks and soil contribute to the irregular distribution of plants and animals in ecosystems.

Using points and examples from the lecture, explain how various abiotic factors in ecosystems affect plants and animals.

PART 4 – WRITING

4.1 INTEGRATED WRITING: CONNECTING INFORMATION FROM TWO SOURCES

Do You Know (p. 379)

Disk 6, Track 13

Now listen to part of a lecture on the same topic.

One thing that really concerns water resource analysts is how much water agriculture uses. Agriculture uses a lot of water, more than all other water–using sectors of society. One of our greatest concerns is the very high use of water by irrigation. This is because, in most cases, the water used for irrigation can't be used afterward for other purposes, such as water supply for homes or industry.

Some forms of irrigation use water more efficiently than others. The efficiency of water use varies by region, crop, agricultural practice, and technology. The least efficient types of irrigation are the surface methods. Your reading really didn't go into this, but think of how much water it takes for a traditional surface method like field flooding. It takes a lot of water to flood a field. The water collects into ponds or basins, but then most of it either evaporates into the air or passes down through the soil into groundwater. This means that, in lots of places, less than half of all the water applied to a field is actually used by the crop. The rest is lost to evaporation or to groundwater. All of the flooding methods generally waste a lot of water—water that could otherwise be used for other purposes.

Fortunately, there are several irrigation technologies that are more efficient than the poorly controlled and highly wasteful flooding methods. They range from sprinkler systems to drip irrigation. In sprinkler systems, water is sprayed over crops, and this provides an even distribution of water. New precision sprinkler technologies have greatly improved our ability to deliver water exactly when and where it's needed. However, sprinkler systems are also a form of surface irrigation, and just as in other surface methods, some of the water is still lost to evaporation.

Summarize the points made in the lecture, explaining how they cast doubt on points made in the reading.

Exercise 4.1.A (p. 380)

Disk 6, Track 14

Now listen to a professor talk about corneal injuries.

Your cornea can be injured by any number of causes. If something hits you in the face—like a ball, a fist, or the dashboard of your car during a traffic accident—your cornea can be injured, and so can the other sensitive tissues around your eye. Any flying debris can be a cause of corneal injury. If you're working with a table saw or … any other machine that creates flying debris, one or more small pieces could fly into your eye. Another cause is getting certain chemicals in the eye. A lot of chemicals—like ammonia or chlorine—can injure corneas. So can ill–fitted or poorly cleaned contact lenses. Even ordinary dust can scratch your cornea if you rub your eye when there's dust in it.

Dryness or allergies can cause your cornea to become inflamed. Corneal ulcers can result from injury or chronic dryness, or from infection with a virus, bacteria, fungus, or protozoa, or—this is rare—from a nutritional deficiency.

You can get the corneal injury known as keratitis if you wear hard contact lenses for too long, or if your eyes are exposed to too much ultraviolet light. If you have keratitis, it means the cells on the outer layer of your cornea die. A common cause of keratitis is overexposure to ultraviolet light—which can come from the sun, a sunlamp, or even a welding arc. If the cause is exposure to ultraviolet light, the symptoms might not show up until a couple of hours after the exposure stops. Keratitis can be treated. Your eye doctor might prescribe antibiotic ointment or drops … or artificial tears, and you might have to wear an eye patch until your cornea can heal.

Describe the causes and consequences of corneal injuries and ulcers, and explain how these problems are treated.

Exercise 4.1.B (p. 381)

Disk 6, Track 15

Now listen to an urban forester talk about pruning trees.

One of my clients has a silver maple in the front yard. The tree is diseased and hazardous because it was the innocent victim of tree topping. Topping—the cutting off the top and the ends of major branches—usually creates more problems than it solves. My client's silver maple was first topped about 15 years ago and then again a few years back. Because of the bad pruning it received in the past, the tree now has seven gangly, 300-pound limbs. The big limbs stretch out over the house and the driveway, and any one of them could crush a car. This tree is dangerous and has to be removed.

This tree should have one main trunk with three or four sturdy main branches. Instead, it has seven weak limbs. It should have been left alone to grow, with an occasional light pruning, not the chainsaw topping it got. In most cases, tree topping is done because people just don't know any better. They don't understand pruning. They think that cutting off the big branches at the ends will solve their problems. Instead, it causes new problems and hurts the tree.

How does topping hurt trees? Well … first of all, topping won't keep a tree small. The growth rate of a tree speeds up once it's topped, and within a few years, the tree is close to its original size. Second, topping is very stressful for the tree. The tree is more likely to be infected by diseases and insects. Topping removes too many of the leaves, which are the tree's food factories, and so large-scale removal of leaves will starve the tree. Also, trees that are badly pruned can become a hazard—like my client's silver maple. The shoots that grow back after topping are weak limbs that break off easily in wind and snowstorms. And finally, topping a tree destroys its natural shape. It turns a beautiful branching tree into an ugly eyesore.

Of course, there are times when tree topping has to be done. But usually topping creates more problems than it solves, and it's the perfect example of bad pruning.

Summarize the points made in the talk, explaining how they depart from good pruning practices.

4.2 INTEGRATED WRITING: TAKING NOTES

Focus (p. 383)

Disk 6, Track 16

One thing that really concerns water resource analysts is how much water agriculture uses. Agriculture uses a lot of water, more than all other water–using sectors of society. One of our greatest concerns is the very high use of water by irrigation. This is because, in most cases, the water used for irrigation can't be used afterward for other purposes, such as water supply for homes or industry.

Exercise 4.2.A (p. 385)

Disk 6, Track 17

Now listen to part of a lecture on the topic you just read about.

The International style dominated commercial architecture for most of the twentieth century. The International style was the style of the modern city. We can see the results in New York City today. Most of New York's skyline is made up of tall, straight, severe, glass–and–steel towers. These towers so completely dominate the cityscape that they shade the city streets. A person walking on the street is completely overpowered.

Strict simplicity is the defining feature of the International style, but it takes the idea that "form must follow function"—it takes this idea to an extreme. In the hands of a true master, the style has creative potential. However, there aren't that many true masters. And starting almost immediately, what we saw was the uglification of the office building … to the point where the glass box became not only ugly but also ridiculous.

The International style started an explosion of cheap imitations. Take the UN Secretariat building. It's a beautiful building on its own. It has an elegance that commands respect. But this type of beauty was turned into something cheap and vulgar because we saw too much of it. It lost its elegance and became, well, a little boring.

The philosophy of the International style is summed up in the familiar phrase "less is more." But is less really more? "Less is more" inspired thousands of starkly simple buildings. In large numbers, and especially when they dominate a city's skyline, these buildings can be ugly and uninspiring, even cold and unfriendly—more machine than human.

Critics of the International style saw its ugliness very early on. The glass box received a great deal of negative criticism—not only from the public but also from professional architects. One of the greatest architects, Frank Lloyd Wright, said, "Less is more … where more is no good." Robert Venturi was even harsher when he said, "Less is a bore."

Summarize the points made in the lecture, explaining how they agree or disagree with points made in the reading.

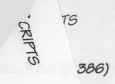

...a geology professor talk about geothermal
...gy.

The first use of geothermal energy in North America
probably took place more than ten thousand years ago. This is
when aboriginal people settled around mineral hot springs. The
hot springs served as a source of warmth, also cleansing and
healing. Hot springs were so important to aboriginal North
Americans that they were considered neutral zones—places
where members of warring tribes could bathe together in peace.
In European history, people also valued hot springs for their
healing powers. For example, the Romans used geothermal
water to treat eye and skin disease and also to heat buildings at
Pompeii.

Today, humans benefit in a much different way from this
important natural resource. Ever since the world's first
geothermal–generated electricity was produced in Italy in 1904,
we've tapped geothermal heat as a power source. Geothermal
heat can generate electricity without the harmful fossil–fuel
emissions that cause pollution and climate change. In
geothermal power plants, the physical force that spins turbine
blades is steam, heat, or hot water from within the earth.

Another use of geothermal energy today is direct use of hot
water. Direct use involves taking heated water—without a heat
pump or power plant—and using it for industrial processes, or
to heat buildings and greenhouses, or to supply heated mineral
water for health resorts.

The concentration of geothermal energy has to be very
high in order to make heat extraction economical for a nation.
Geothermal sites around the world aren't all equal in their
power potential. The best places for developing geothermal
energy systems are regions that are volcanically active, like
places around the Pacific Rim and in certain parts of Europe.
For example, Iceland is a geologic hot spot, where geothermal
energy is used to heat almost every home in the nation.

Describe past and present uses of geothermal energy, and
explain why some regions have better potential than others for
developing geothermal systems.

4.3 INTEGRATED WRITING: DEVELOPING IDEAS

Exercise 4.3.A (p. 393)

Disk 6, Track 19

Now listen to part of a talk in a business management class.

Research has taught us a lot about the motivation of
workers. We've learned that workers have needs and
expectations that go beyond economic concerns. We know,
for example, that an informal social organization among
workers is important. If you ask ten people what they like or
don't like about their job, around eight will mention the people
they work with.

The small work group fills important social and emotional
needs of workers. By definition, the small work group—I mean
a group of usually around three to fifteen people with one lead
person. And what takes place within that group affects
attitudes, motivation, productivity, and the quality of the
company's product or service.

Managers have to face this reality if we want to have a
highly motivated workforce. We have to accept that workers
deserve to have a voice in the decisions that affect them. For
example, workers should be able to participate in the setting
of goals and the evaluation of results. If workers have a say—
especially within the work group—they feel a greater sense of
pride in their work.

Workers need a sense of security and community in the
workplace. Security comes from confidence in the system that
they're part of, the quality of the product or service they
provide, and the reputation of the company. A sense of
community grows when workers get recognition for their
accomplishments and when they believe their skills are being
well used.

A lot of people resent the big, impersonal systems that
dominate their lives. They feel angry at the unseen power
holders in management, at the administrators who make
decisions about them but don't actually know them. And people
feel alienated when they have no voice. Anything that managers
can do to help workers feel they have some control over what
happens during the work day—anything to promote worker
satisfaction—will be good for the company.

Summarize the points the professor made in the talk, explaining how they support points made in the reading.

Exercise 4.3.B (p. 394)

Disk 6, Track 20

Now listen to part of a lecture on this topic in a psychology
class.

Today, phrenology is no longer thought of as a real science.
We can easily see the mistakes in Gall's doctrine. We know,
for example, that the sheer size of the brain has no clear
connection to an individual's intellect. In fact, people with very
small brains have achieved great success, just as people with
very large brains are sometimes mentally retarded. Moreover,
we've come to understand that the size and shape of the skull
isn't a precise measure of the function of the human brain.

But even though we can see the flaws in Gall's claims, we
shouldn't dismiss his ideas completely. After all, Gall was
among the first modern scientists to state that different parts
of the brain control different functions. The fact that we still
don't know the specific relationship between size, shape, and
function of the brain doesn't mean we won't ever be able to
figure it out.

Other scientists have demonstrated a clear relationship
between specific types of brain injury and specific mental
impairments. One showed that damage to a certain area in
the left side of the brain causes a person to lose the ability to
speak. Others showed that one kind of injury affects reading
ability, while another kind of injury affects the person's ability
to name things, or to repeat words and phrases. So, we can see
that Gall was wrong about the shape of human skulls, but right
about the fact that different parts of the brain serve distinct
functions.

Gall was right about other things too. For example, he
claimed that we don't ...uh ... have general mental powers ...
but instead we have several different forms of power for each
of our mental abilities. What he meant was, each of us has
many separate skills for memory, language, music, vision, et
cetera. And in the 200 years since Gall, there've been several
other theories of multiple forms of intelligence.

Summarize the points made in the lecture, explaining how they either support or refute points made in the reading.

Exercise 4.3.C (p. 395)

Disk 6, Track 21

Now listen to part of a talk on this topic in a film history class.

George Méliès invented several techniques that have now become basics of filmmaking. One of these is the special effect of stop–action photography. Méliès discovered stop action almost by accident. He bought a camera and started filming everything in sight—crowds, traffic, fire engines—anything that moved. One day, while he was filming a truck moving down the street, his camera jammed. By the time he got the camera working again, there was a hearse where the truck had been before. Later, when he watched the film, what he saw was a truck turning magically into a hearse. So, it was by chance—a camera jamming—that he invented stop action.

Another technique Méliès introduced was animation, which we can see in his most famous film, *A Trip to the Moon*. In the animated sequence, we see the moon in the distance and a spaceship moving toward it. As the spaceship moves closer, the moon becomes larger and larger until it's giant–sized. The moon gradually takes on the shape of a living, grotesque, smiling face. Suddenly the spaceship lands in one of the moon's eyes. The animated face frowns and grimaces, and then huge tears flow from the eye. It's really an amazing sequence, especially when you realize it was made over a hundred years ago!

Méliès realized very early on that films were stories told in scenes, and scenes could be staged for the camera with the aid of painted scenery and elaborately designed costumes. One of his most important contributions was to extend the length of films to tell a story. Before this, a film was a single shot, complete in itself, and usually ran for only a minute or less. But Méliès put several scenes together into a single story for the first time in 1899 in *Cinderella*. The various scenes in *Cinderella* were linked by dissolves—a technique where one scene fades out while the next scene appears behind it and grows clearer as the first one disappears. This technique is also called overlap dissolve because one scene overlaps another.

Summarize the points made in the talk, explaining how they illustrate points made in the reading.

4.5 EVALUATING THE RESPONSE

Exercise 4.5.A (p. 403)

Disk 6, Track 22

Now listen to part of a lecture in a biology class.

As soon as we developed antibiotics, new strains of bacteria appeared that were resistant to some or all of the drugs. Hospitals started using antibiotics regularly in the 1950s, but resistance started appearing within a few years. Today, one–third of the patients in hospitals are on antibiotics, but antibiotic resistance is increasing the danger of hospital infections—to the point where people are almost safer staying home than going to a hospital.

In the forties, penicillin really was a wonder drug. Back then, you could give a patient with bacterial pneumonia ten thousand units of penicillin four times a day and cure the disease. Today, you could give 24 million units of penicillin a day, but the patient might still die. Why? Well, in a way, bacteria are smarter than us. They evolve to counteract any drug we attack them with. A lot of bacteria are now completely resistant to penicillin.

Bacteria can evolve very effective weapons against antibiotics. Some of them develop enzymes to match every antibiotic we throw at them. All these weapons and counter–weapons match one another—just like the weapons in real military warfare. So, no matter what antibiotic we use, the bacteria will come up with a way to make it useless.

How does this happen? Well, if you douse a colony of bacteria with an antibiotic, the colony will be killed—that is, all except for a few cells. A few cells will survive because they carry a resistance gene for that particular antibiotic. The surviving cells quickly multiply, and they pass along this lucky gene to their offspring. And soon you have a new strain of bacteria that's resistant to that drug.

One consequence of antibiotic resistance is the reappearance of tuberculosis as a major illness. Twenty years ago, doctors thought tuberculosis was a defeated disease. Since then, however, new cases of tuberculosis have increased by 20 percent. And several strains of the disease are resistant to any drug we can attack them with.

Summarize the main points made in the lecture, explaining how they differ from points made in the reading.

QUIZ 1 (p. 407)

Disk 6, Track 23

Now listen to a psychology professor talk about the reading.

Scientists who study animal behavior have always had a problem coming up with a reasonable definition of self–awareness. Is self–awareness the same as self–recognition? If an animal recognizes itself in a mirror, does that mean the animal is self–aware?

The mark test has been repeated on many different species. The results of experiments on other animals at first seem consistent with the idea that self–recognition is a higher mental ability that only humans and the great apes possess. But further testing with chimpanzees produced results that were inconsistent. For example, one study with eleven chimpanzees found only one who touched the mark during the test. Why were those results so different from others that showed a high rate of chimps touching the mark?

There are some basic problems in interpreting the results of all these experiments. One is that chimpanzees perform these very same behaviors routinely, whether there's a mirror there or not. All chimpanzees touch their heads and faces a lot. In the experiment with the eleven chimpanzees, one chimp rubbed his head while coming out of the sleeping drug. He rubbed the mark off even before he had the chance to see it in the mirror—thus confounding the test results and making it impossible to conclude anything.

Another problem is that some of the behaviors we call self–aware are also social responses that chimpanzees show in the presence of other chimpanzees. Self–grooming in many primates is a social behavior. For example, when monkeys are put in a cage with a mirror along one wall, they show an increase in the amount of self–grooming. But so do monkeys in a cage next to another of the same species—when they can see the other monkey through a window.

So … what does this mean? It means that we can't always tell from an animal's behavior whether the animal is reacting in a "self–aware" manner to a mirror image as an image of itself, or whether it's reacting "socially" to the image as that of another animal.

Summarize the points made in the talk, explaining how they cast doubt on points made in the reading.

QUIZ 2 (p. 408)

Disk 6, Track 24

Now listen to part of a lecture on the same topic.

The main advantage of wind power is that it's a clean source of energy. Wind power can decrease our dependence on fossil fuels, which is critical to the health of all living things. Using wind power instead of coal, oil, and gas means fewer emissions of greenhouse gases like carbon dioxide. It also means lower emissions of sulfur and other gases that cause smog and acid rain. So, more wind power means less smog and soot, less acid rain, and fewer emissions that contribute to global warming.

Wind power is also getting affordable enough to compete with inexpensive coal and oil. This is because better turbine technology has helped reduce the cost of wind energy by more than 80 percent since the 1980s. In several places around the world, energy companies offer wind–generated electricity at a cost that's almost half the cost for coal power, and around one–fifth the cost for nuclear power. And where coal and nuclear power both threaten the environment, wind power is clean.

However, even though wind energy is now more affordable, more available, and pollution–free, it does have some disadvantages. One is that wind power has the same lack of energy density as direct solar radiation. Wind as a source of power is very spread out, and this means it would take large numbers of wind generators—and thus large amounts of land—to produce heat and electricity in useful amounts. We can't build wind turbines everywhere, simply because lots of places aren't windy enough to generate power.

Another disadvantage is the high number of birds killed by the blades on wind turbines. One study found 182 dead birds on a wind farm in California. The wind industry is responding by modifying the equipment so it's safer for birds. They're coming up with solutions like reducing the number of places for birds to sit on turbines, spacing the turbines farther apart, and painting patterns on the blades that contrast with the surrounding landscape, so the birds can see the blades and will avoid flying into them.

Summarize the advantages and disadvantages of wind power discussed in the lecture, explaining how they agree with or depart from points made in the reading.

QUIZ 3 (p. 409)

Disk 6, Track 25

Now listen to part of a lecture given by an economics professor.

The gloomy theory of Thomas Malthus caused economics to be called "the dismal science." Malthus said that food production can't keep up with the growth of population. He predicted that the amount of food per person would decline as population increased. But the statistics of economic history reveal that Malthus was dead wrong. Just as he was making his prediction of gloom and doom, the countries of Europe and North America were beginning their century and a half of tremendous growth in real wages, life expectancies, and living standards.

Malthus said that as population keeps doubling, it's like the globe keeps shrinking to half its size—until finally it shrinks so much that food production falls below the level necessary for life. There are several flaws in this theory. One problem is that, despite his careful use of statistics, Malthus left out important factors. For example, he never predicted the advances in technology during the Industrial Revolution. In the century after Malthus, new technology increased food production tremendously in Europe and North America. This rapid change allowed food output to far exceed population growth. And this led to an increase in real wages and a higher standard of living. And Malthus didn't predict that … in most Western nations, living standards and real wages would grow most rapidly, just at the same time that population growth began to decline.

Most economists today disagree with the Malthusian idea that population would shoot up quickly if the negative checks of disease, famine, and war declined. The history of developed countries proved Malthus was wrong. Because of improvements in education and birth control, population growth has stabilized in most developed countries. Malthus and his followers have been criticized on several grounds, but especially for ignoring the possibility of technical advance and for overlooking the importance of education and birth control as a way to lower population growth.

Summarize the points made in the lecture, explaining how they contradict points made in the reading.

QUIZ 7 (p. 442)

Disk 6, Track 26

Now listen to a photography instructor talk about pictorial photography.

Since the pictorial awards are usually the most desired in the photography contest, I thought I'd say a word about composition. A pictorial photograph is one with a successful composition. You can have the most interesting subject in the world, but unless the subject is well composed it won't have the impact of good composition. For example, you can have a shot of a beautiful child sitting on a bench in the park, but if the signpost behind her looks like it's growing out of her head, it's not a good composition.

Let's go over the elements of composition. First, balance—remember that a photograph is balanced if it has similar amounts of light and dark areas, or if one interesting detail balances another.

Another important element is placement—the location of the main focal point of the picture. The best placement is generally not right in the center of the frame. Instead, the four points just above and below, both to the right and left of center—these are the strongest choices for the main point of interest.

Color is important to composition. Generally, warm colors are stronger than cool colors. A small amount of red—a warm color—will balance a larger area of green or blue, which are cool colors.

Finally, concerning detail, remember that a few bold masses balancing each other are more satisfying than a large number of details spread evenly throughout the composition. Now, I ask you to imagine this scene: a white house stands on a cliff, a few seabirds soar in a vast blue sky overhead, a few clouds float high on the left, a tiny wave breaks at the bottom of the cliff, down in the right corner. All objects of the composition—the house, the cliff, the sky, the clouds, the birds, the waves, and the spaces between the objects—all combine to create a mood. The composition is balanced and complete. You can see that everything in the photograph is an essential part of the composition. This is a pictorial photograph.

Summarize the points made by the instructor, explaining how they illustrate points made in the reading.

QUIZ 8 (p. 444)

Disk 6, Track 27

Now listen to a psychology professor's response to the reading.

So … when children grab for their favorite toys, what's guiding them? Is it social conditioning, or is it nature?

Research shows that two–year–old boys like to play with dolls and kitchen sets as much as little girls do. Still, by age five or so, most will tell you those toys are for girls. The older they get, the more children will say that a certain toy is either for girls or for boys. How do they learn this? Are they really conditioned by society in a sexist scheme, as the reading suggests?

I believe—and research supports this—that a child's choice of toys is a natural occurrence, not a sexist plot by society. Studies show that monkeys, like children, pick their toys based on gender. When male and female monkeys were given a wide choice of toys to play with, male monkeys spent more time playing with cars and balls, and females spent more time with dolls and pots.

In one study of human children, researchers observed children playing with toys in a preschool class. There were eight boys and three girls in the class. During the hour for free play, two of the girls usually went straight to the kitchen area and stayed there most of the hour. One girl usually sat at the table, coloring and drawing pictures. The boys usually spent most of the hour with blocks—building towers and then knocking them down.

I'll briefly summarize the rest of their findings. First, they observed that younger children of both sexes play with both dolls and trucks, with no apparent thought of being a boy or girl. But around age five, the boys start moving away from kitchen play, and the girls start ignoring cars and trucks. Older kids of both sexes like blocks. And … sometimes kids will hear that they shouldn't play with something because it's a boy or girl toy. Sometimes an older kid tells them; sometimes it's a parent.

So, it seems that parents and older children do reinforce the gender stereotypes to some extent. But still, despite some minor evidence of social conditioning, the research supports the idea that most boys and girls are naturally drawn to different types of toys, and it doesn't matter what their parents and society teach them.

Summarize the points made in the talk, explaining how they agree or disagree with points made in the reading.

TEST 1

Disk 7, Track 1

LISTENING SECTION DIRECTIONS (p. 460)

The Listening section measures your ability to understand conversations and lectures in English. You will hear each conversation and lecture only one time. After each conversation or lecture, you will hear some questions about it. Answer all questions based on what the speakers state or imply.

You may take notes while you listen. You may use your notes to help you answer the questions.

Most questions have four possible answers. In some questions, you will see this icon: 🎧. This means that you will hear, but not see, part of the question.

Some questions have special directions, which appear in a gray box. Most questions are worth one point. If a question is worth more than one point, special directions will indicate how many points you can receive.

You have approximately 40 minutes to complete the Listening section. This includes the time for listening to the conversations and lectures and for answering the questions.

To make this practice more like the real test, cover the questions and answers during each conversation and lecture. When you hear the first question, uncover the questions and answers.

Disk 7, Track 2

Questions 1 through 5. Listen to a conversation in a university office.

M: Good afternoon. May I help you?
W: Yes, I hope so. My name is Jennifer Taylor, and I'm in the communications program. Our class is doing a radio program, and we'll have interviews with a lot of people from all parts of campus life. We'd like to interview the new Dean of Students, if he's willing.
M: Hmm. That sounds interesting.
W: I hope Dean Evans will agree to meet with us, and let us tape the conversation for the radio. It would be a way for the whole community to get to know him, get to know his ideas and everything … like the kind of vision he has for the university.
M: How much time would you need?
W: Oh, probably about an hour, no more than that.
M: Hmm. I'm sure the dean would like to participate, but … uh … you know, his schedule is pretty tight.
W: Oh, I was afraid of that. Um …
M: He's tied up all this week. Everybody wants to, you know, get acquainted. But we can probably work something in. When would you like to do the interview?
W: The radio station can air the show on either the 16th or the 23rd, so we'd have to work around that.
M: Let me look at the dean's schedule … Let's see … it looks like he's got a lot of meetings this week, and, well, most of next week, too. What about the week after that? He doesn't have anything scheduled on Tuesday or Wednesday afternoon. Would either of those days work for you?

W: Um, yeah, I think so. How about Tuesday afternoon?
M: On Tuesday, he's free from two o'clock till four–thirty.
W: Let's see. I'll be in class until two–thirty, so how about three?
M: All right. Three o'clock, Tuesday, April 15.
W: OK, that will be great. Thank you so much. This will be a great way for everyone to learn about our new dean. We really appreciate the opportunity to do this.
M: You're really quite welcome. It's our pleasure. In fact, I've put it on the dean's calendar, and we will see you on the 15th.
W: The 15th. OK. Thank you very much.

1. What is the purpose of the conversation?
2. Why does the man say this:
"I'm sure the dean would like to participate, but … uh … you know, his schedule is pretty tight."
3. Why does the woman want to meet with the dean?
4. What can be inferred about the dean?
5. When will the meeting with the dean take place?

Disk 7, Track 3

Questions 6 through 10. Listen to part of a conversation between two students. They are studying for an economics test.

M: OK … so what do we do next?
W: Why don't we go over the chapter on analysis of costs? That'll be on the test.
M: OK.
W: Let's start with "opportunity cost." That part's still confusing to me. I understand fixed cost and variable cost, and marginal cost, the cost of producing one more unit of something. I'm sure there'll be a question about that on the test. But I don't get "opportunity cost."
M: Opportunity cost—that's when you have to consider the things you give up when you make a certain decision. You have an opportunity cost when you're forced to choose between different alternatives.
W: OK. That sort of makes sense.
M: Say you want to have your own business, so you, so you open a restaurant. You put in 60 hours a week, but you don't pay yourself wages. At the end of the first year, your restaurant shows a profit of … um … say, 30 thousand dollars—looks pretty good for a small business. But is it really that good? An economist would say no, because you have to count your own labor as a cost, even if you don't get paid. You have to consider that you had alternative opportunities for work, and you have to count that lost opportunity as a cost. You could have taken a job at, say, an accounting firm and earned 50 thousand a year. This is the opportunity cost—the earnings you gave up—because you decided to open your own business instead.
W: OK. So what that means is … um … if I lost 50 thousand dollars by not taking an accounting job, then … my restaurant's profit of 30 thousand isn't that great after all—at least in an economic sense. Maybe I had more enjoyment, though—I mean the enjoyment of being my own boss.
M: Right. But your enjoyment comes with a cost. An economist would say the real profit of your restaurant isn't 30 thousand dollars. You'd have to subtract the 50 thousand opportunity cost of your own labor.

When you subtract 50 thousand from 30 thousand, you find you have a net loss of 20 thousand dollars!
W: Wow! That means the enjoyment of having my own business cost me 20 thousand dollars!
M: Yeah. Something like that.
W: This is really different from what we learned about costs in my accounting class. I think an accountant would say my 30 thousand–dollar profit made me a viable business. But an economist—if I understand it correctly—an economist would say my business is a loser!
M: Right. And that's because an economist tries to look at all the factors, all the costs. An economist would count the opportunity cost.
W: An economist looks at the big picture.
M: Right. An economist's definition of costs is broader than an accountant's. Opportunity cost is actually a very broad concept. It takes into account the cost of the choices we make. When we choose one thing, we have to give up something else.
W: That's right. We chose to go to college, so that means we had to give up full–time employment, for the time being.
M: Right! So, how do you measure the true cost of a college education?
W: Well, it's more than what we pay for tuition and books! We have to subtract the income we lose by not working full time.
M: Yeah, and that's why college is really more expensive than it seems.

6. What are the students mainly discussing?
7. How does the man help the woman understand a concept that she finds difficult?
8. Listen again to part of the conversation. Then answer the question.
"Say you want to have your own business, so you, so you open a restaurant. You put in 60 hours a week, but you don't pay yourself wages. At the end of the first year, your restaurant shows a profit of … um … say, 30 thousand dollars—looks pretty good for a small business. But is it really that good?"
Why does the man ask this:
"But is it really that good?"
9. According to the man, how does an economist's view of costs differ from that of an accountant?
10. What can be inferred about the true cost of a college education?

Disk 7, Track 4

Questions 11 through 16. Listen to part of a lecture in a geology class.

Mount St. Helens is in the Cascade Range, a chain of volcanoes running from southern Canada to northern California. Most of the peaks are dormant—what I mean is, they're sleeping now, but are potentially active. Mount St. Helens has a long history of volcanic activity, so the eruptions of 1980 weren't a surprise to geologists. The geologists who were familiar with the mountain had predicted she would erupt.

The eruption cycle had sort of a harmless beginning. In March of 1980, seismologists picked up signs of earthquake activity below the mountain. And during the next week, the earthquakes increased rapidly, causing several avalanches. These tremors and quakes were signs that large amounts of magma were moving deep within the mountain. Then, suddenly one day there was a loud boom, a small crater opened on the summit. St. Helens was waking up.

The vibrations and tremors continued. All during April, there were occasional eruptions of steam and ash. This attracted tourists and hikers to come and watch the show. It also attracted seismologists, geologists, and—of course—the news media.

By early May, the north side of the mountain had swelled out into a huge and growing bulge. The steam and ash eruptions became even more frequent. Scientists could see that the top of the volcano was sort of coming apart. Then there were a few days of quiet, but it didn't last long. It was the quiet before the storm.

On the morning of May 18—a Sunday—at around eight o'clock, a large earthquake broke loose the bulge that had developed on the north face of the mountain. The earthquake triggered a massive landslide that carried away huge quantities of rock. Much of the north face sort of swept down the mountain.

The landslide released a tremendous sideways blast. Super-heated water in the magma chamber exploded, and a jet of steam and gas blew out of the mountain's side with tremendous force. Then came the magma, sending up a cloud of super-heated ash. In only 25 seconds, the north side of the mountain was blown away. Then, the top of the mountain went too, pouring out more ash, steam, and magma. The ash cloud went up over 60,000 feet in the air, blocking the sunlight.

Altogether, the eruptions blew away three cubic kilometers of the mountain and devastated more than 500 kilometers of land. The energy of the blast was equivalent to a hydrogen bomb of about 25 megatons. It leveled all trees directly to the northeast and blew all the water out of some lakes. The blast killed the mountain's goats, millions of fish and birds, thousands of deer and elk—and around sixty people. The ash cloud drifted around the world, disrupting global weather patterns.

For over twenty years now, Mount St. Helens has been dormant. However, geologists who've studied the mountain believe she won't stay asleep forever. The Cascade Range is volcanically active. Future eruptions are certain and—unfortunately—we can't prevent them.

11. According to the professor, how did the cycle of volcanic eruptions begin?
12. Why does the professor say this:
"This attracted tourists and hikers to come and watch the show. It also attracted seismologists, geologists, and—of course—the news media."
13. Listen again to part of the lecture. Then answer the question.
"By early May, the north side of the mountain had swelled out into a huge and growing bulge. The steam and ash eruptions became even more frequent. Scientists could see that the top of the volcano was sort of coming apart. Then there were a few days of quiet, but it didn't last long. It was the quiet before the storm."
What does the professor mean when he says this:
"Then there were a few days of quiet, but it didn't last long."
14. The professor explains what happened when Mount St. Helens erupted. Indicate whether each sentence below was part of the event.
15. What were some effects of the eruption?
16. What can be concluded about Mount St. Helens?

Disk 7, Track 5

Questions 17 through 22. A botanist has been invited to speak to a geography class. She will be discussing aromatic trees of North America. Listen to part of the talk.

When European explorers first approached the coast of North America, even before their ships landed, the first thing they noticed was the pungent aroma carried to the ships by the offshore breezes. Some sea captains thought this aroma was the scent of the valuable Oriental spices that had prompted their voyages of exploration. But in fact, the agreeable smells didn't come from spices; they came from the lush vegetation of the North American forests.

The fragrance came from the blossoms of numerous trees and from the volatile oils in pine sap. Pine sap is a resinous fluid that pine trees put out to heal wounds caused by wind, fire, and lightning, and also to protect the pine tree's seeds. Pine sap was a valuable commodity to the sailors who explored the coast. The smell of pine meant there was an abundant supply of what were known as naval stores—pitch and pine tar. Pitch and pine tar were thick, sticky, semi-solid substances that were made by distilling pinewood. Sailors used naval stores for caulking and waterproofing their wooden ships, which kept them seaworthy.

The Europeans found fragrant trees all along the Atlantic coast, from Massachusetts in the north to Florida in the south. Everywhere along the coast, the air was filled with the strong perfume of the flowering dogwood. The Native Americans already knew about the medicinal properties of the dogwood, and they used its bark and roots to treat malaria and other fevers. They brewed the aromatic bark into a bitter, astringent tea. European settlers also used the dogwood to relieve attacks of malaria. They soaked the dogwood bark in whiskey and drank the strong infusion. This was before they knew about quinine from South America, and before quinine became available.

In the south, probably the best-known aromatic tree was the sassafras. The sassafras is a fast-growing tree, a member of the laurel family. Like the other fragrant laurels—cinnamon, bay, and camphor—sassafras is noted for its aromatic bark, leaves, roots, flowers, and fruit. I have a sassafras twig with me here, which I'll pass around so you can all enjoy its smell. Just give it a small scrape with your thumbnail to release the scent. I think you'll find it strong but pleasant.

The Choctaw Indians used powdered sassafras leaves as a spice. Other Native American tribes used sassafras tonic as a cure for everything from fever to stomachache. News of this wonder tree reached Europe in the sixteenth century by way of the French and the Spanish, and sassafras was one of the first exports from North America to Europe. It sold for a high price on the London market, which sort of inspired other English explorers to … um … seek their fortunes in the North American colonies.

For centuries, sassafras enjoyed a fantastic reputation as a cure for almost every disease. Maybe you've heard of the medicinal spring tonic of the old days. Well, sassafras was a main ingredient in spring tonic—the stuff pioneer parents gave their kids. My grandmother had to take the spring tonic that her grandmother made from sassafras.

Sassafras leaves, bark, and roots used to provide the flavoring for root beer and chewing gum. Sassafras was also used in soaps and perfumes. However, in the 1960s, the United States Food and Drug Administration found sassafras oil to be a potential carcinogen for humans because it caused cancer in rats. Since that time, sassafras has been banned for human consumption. No one really knows just how harmful it is to human beings, but some studies show that one cup of strong sassafras tea contains more than four times the amount of the volatile oil safrole that is hazardous to humans if consumed on a regular basis.

17. According to the speaker, what did European explorers notice as they sailed toward the shores of North America?
18. According to the speaker, why was pine sap a valuable commodity?
19. How was the flowering dogwood used?
20. Why does the speaker say this:
"Just give it a small scrape with your thumbnail to release the scent. I think you'll find it strong but pleasant."
21. Why was sassafras once considered a wonder tree?
22. Listen again to part of the talk. Then answer the question.
"However, in the 1960s, the United States Food and Drug Administration found sassafras oil to be a potential carcinogen for humans because it caused cancer in rats. Since that time, sassafras has been banned for human consumption. No one really knows just how harmful it is to human beings, but some studies show that one cup of strong sassafras tea contains more than four times the amount of the volatile oil safrole that is hazardous to humans if consumed on a regular basis."
What does the speaker imply about sassafras?

Disk 7, Track 6

Questions 23 through 28. Listen to part of a discussion in a philosophy class. The class is studying Plato.

M1: Plato believed the only true reality consists of ideas. Thus, we often refer to his philosophy as "idealism." He didn't think people could create ideas; rather, we discovered them. For instance, the mathematical concept of two plus two equals four—this is an idea that's always existed. It's always been true that two plus two equals four—even before people discovered it. Plato's ideas were—and still are—valuable because they've stimulated a great deal of thinking about the meaning and purpose of humanity, society, and education. The ideas of Plato survive in our thinking today, and survive in our educational system. Another important principle—yes?

W: Excuse me, Dr. MacDonald, but could you ... like ... uh ... say more about how Plato's ideas are in education today?

M1: Sure. Plato believed the state should take an active role in education—most governments today agree—and the state should create a curriculum that leads students from thinking about concrete information toward thinking about abstract ideas. Higher–level thinking would develop the individual student's character, and thus ultimately benefit the larger society. Plato believed our most important goal was the search for truth. The idealists of today generally agree that a major focus of education should be on the search for knowledge, but some feel it's not truth per se that's important as much as the search for truth. Idealists favor learning that's holistic over learning that's specialized. For instance, idealists consider subjects like chemistry and physics useful, but they're of real value only when they help us to see the whole picture of our universe. Idealists aren't concerned with turning out graduates with specific technical skills as much as giving students a broad

understanding of the world they live in.

W: But isn't that kind of impractical? I mean, most of us go to college because we want knowledge about certain subjects, not the whole universe.

M1: Idealists believe that education should teach students to think—not what to think, but how to think. Thinking is the skill that develops character. If you develop the ability to think, you—and all of humanity—will become more noble and rational.

M2: The philosophy of idealism seems kind of conservative.

M1: Idealism is often criticized as being a conservative philosophy because so much of its emphasis is on character development and preserving traditions. Idealists care about ultimate truths, so their notion of education is largely a matter of passing on knowledge.

M2: But what's the ultimate truth? Who gets to decide what's true?

M1: Who gets to decide what's true? Excellent question ... and it's questions like this that have led to a weakening of idealism today. Developments in science and technology have changed what we've thought of as true. Our contemporary emphasis on relevance, usefulness, and innovation—as opposed to lasting values—all of these trends have cut idealism down to size.

W: I think all the concern with character development is kind of old–fashioned. Doesn't that make people ... uh ... doesn't it just lead to conformity?

M1: Good point. Critics of idealism would agree with you that "character development" comes at the expense of creativity, and that too much emphasis on traditional values can be harmful—if it makes students stop questioning what they're being taught.

23. What aspect of Plato's philosophy does the professor mainly discuss?
24. Why does the professor mention the mathematical concept of 2 + 2 = 4?
25. What do idealists believe about higher–level thinking?
26. Listen again to part of the discussion. Then answer the question.
"Idealists aren't concerned with turning out graduates with specific technical skills as much as giving students a broad understanding of the world they live in."
"But isn't that kind of impractical? I mean, most of us go to college because we want knowledge about certain subjects, not the whole universe. "
What is the woman's attitude toward the idealist view of education?
27. Listen again to part of the discussion. Then answer the question.
"Who gets to decide what's true? Excellent question ... and it's questions like this that have led to a weakening of idealism today. Developments in science and technology have changed what we've thought of as true. Our contemporary emphasis on relevance, usefulness, and innovation—as opposed to lasting values—all of these trends have cut idealism down to size."
What does the professor mean when he says this:
"...all of these trends have cut idealism down to size."
28. According to the professor, what do critics say about idealism?

Disk 7, Track 7

Questions 29 through 34. Listen to part of a lecture in a physics class. The professor is discussing energy and work.

In physics, energy is defined as the ability to do work. And in physics, work doesn't refer to what you do at your job. In physics, work means moving an object when there is some resistance to its movement. Every time we lift an object, push it, pull it, or carry it, we are doing work.

Two things are necessary for work to occur. First, force—or energy—must be applied to the object. If no energy is used, no work has been done. Second, the object must be moved a distance. If the object is pushed or pulled but it doesn't move, no work has been done.

When we move an object, there's always some resistance, or opposition to movement. Resistance is a force that tends to oppose or slow down movement. Whenever an object meets resistance, more energy is needed to do the work. A good example is what happens when a farmer's plow moves through the soil. The plow encounters resistance if it gets too deep into the soil, or if rocks and roots in the soil make the soil hard to turn. When this happens, the tractor's engine has to work harder. The engine strains under the load and uses more fuel.

Each time we do work, we use energy. If our muscles do the work, energy in the form of food is required. If a machine does the work, energy in the form of oil, gas, coal, electricity, or some other source is required. Without energy, no work can be done.

Energy comes in several different forms. It can take the form of heat, light, motion, electricity, chemical energy, nuclear energy, and so on. Energy can change forms, but it cannot be created or destroyed. Energy is always conserved—that is a law of nature. This law is known as the law of conservation of energy, or the first law of thermodynamics. The law states that energy can be converted from any form to any other form, but no matter what form it takes, it's still energy, and none of the energy disappears when it changes form.

Machines do work by converting one form of energy to another. For example, a car converts the chemical energy in gasoline to kinetic energy—to motion. A stove converts electrical energy or chemical energy into heat energy that cooks our food. The law of conservation of energy tells us that a machine needs to have a source of energy. And a machine can't supply more power than it gets from its energy source. When the fuel runs out, the machine stops. The same rule applies to living organisms: if the organism doesn't have food, it dies.

The law of conservation of energy tells us that the energy of any system—whether the system is a machine, a living organism, or an ecosystem—that the energy must balance out in the end. The amount of energy in the system is conserved, even though the energy changes forms.

The earth as a whole is a complex system that receives almost all its energy from the sun in the form of light. Some of the solar energy converts to heat, which warms the earth. Some of it evaporates water, forms clouds, and produces rain. Some energy is captured by plants, and is turned into chemical energy during photosynthesis. The first law of thermodynamics—conservation of energy—says the earth must end up with the same amount of energy it started out with. The energy changes forms, but no energy is lost or gained.

29. How does the field of physics define "work"?
30. Listen again to part of the lecture. Then answer the question.

"Whenever an object meets resistance, more energy is needed to do the work. A good example is what happens when a farmer's plow moves through the soil. The plow encounters resistance if it gets too deep into the soil, or if rocks and roots in the soil make the soil hard to turn. When this happens, the tractor's engine has to work harder. The engine strains under the load and uses more fuel."
Why does the professor talk about a plow?
31. Based on the information in the lecture, indicate whether each statement below reflects the first law of thermodynamics.
32. Which two sentences illustrate the conversion of energy from one form to another?
33. Listen again to part of the lecture. Then answer the question.
"The law of conservation of energy tells us that a machine needs to have a source of energy. And a machine can't supply more power than it gets from its energy source. When the fuel runs out, the machine stops. The same rule applies to living organisms: if the organism doesn't have food, it dies."
Why does the professor say this:
"The same rule applies to living organisms: if the organism doesn't have food, it dies."
34. What can be inferred about the energy in the earth as a whole system?

Disk 7, Track 8

SPEAKING SECTION DIRECTIONS (p. 466)

The Speaking section measures your ability to speak in English about a variety of topics. There are six questions in this section. Record your response to each question on a cassette.

Questions 1 and 2 are independent speaking tasks in which you will speak about familiar topics. Your responses will be scored on your ability to speak clearly and coherently about the topics.

Questions 3 and 4 are integrated tasks in which you will read a passage, listen to a conversation or lecture, and then speak in response to a question about what you have read and heard. You will need to combine relevant information from the two sources to answer the question completely. Your responses will be scored on your ability to speak clearly and coherently and on your ability to accurately convey information about what you read and heard.

Questions 5 and 6 are integrated tasks in which you will listen to part of a conversation or lecture, and then speak in response to a question about what you have heard. Your responses will be scored on your ability to speak clearly and coherently and on your ability to accurately convey information about what you heard.

You will hear each conversation and lecture only one time. You may take notes while you listen. You may use your notes to help you answer the questions.

Disk 7, Track 9

What game do you enjoy playing? Describe the game, and explain why you like to play it. Include details and examples in your explanation.

Disk 7, Track 10

Some people drive their own car to school or work. Others ride a bus, train, or other form of public transportation. Which do you think is better and why? Include details and examples in your explanation.

Disk 7, Track 11

Now listen to a student as he discusses online courses with his academic adviser.

M: I want to take astronomy next quarter, and I was thinking of registering for the online course.

W: Have you ever taken an online course before?

M: No. But I have a computer, and it seems fairly easy to take a course this way.

W: Let me just point out a couple of things. First, you have to be able to learn on your own, mainly by reading. So you have to be self–motivated. There are a few online lectures, but mainly you have to read the information on a computer. You also have to keep up with a schedule, just as in any other class. So unless you're self–motivated, online courses are generally not a good idea. In fact, there's a fairly high dropout rate for online courses.

M: Hmmm. I didn't know that. It seems like it would be so easy because you don't have to be in class at a specific time.

W: Believe it or not, the main reason that students drop out is they miss going to class. They miss the face–to–face contact with the professor. So, if interacting with the professor and other students is important to you, then you should consider taking a regular classroom course.

The adviser expresses her opinion about online courses. State her opinion and explain the reasons she gives for holding that opinion.

Disk 7, Track 12

Now listen to part of a talk in a business class.

When you think about it, corporations have all the familiar elements of other types of culture. Corporations have values, norms, rituals, symbols, and so forth. As in any society, these things define the whole group.

Corporate culture gives meaning to the daily activities of the company. The company logo and colors are like the flag of any nation. In a lot of corporations, your rank is signified by the suit you wear and the size and location of your office. Corporations have rituals, like the employee picnic or the executive fishing trip. These rituals bring people together to celebrate corporate unity. There are also corporate texts, such as the sayings of the founder or president.

Generally speaking, well–established companies have traditional corporate cultures. For example, new employees may learn the company song or may wear the corporate uniform of dark suit, white shirt, and striped tie. Business hours are standard and office conduct is formal.

In contrast, many new technology firms have a very informal culture. Employees go to work in blue jeans, T–shirts, and sneakers. They may come and go at will; they may bring their pets to work. In informal cultures like this, there are often no fixed traditions to follow.

Explain how corporations are similar to any other culture, and explain how corporate culture varies in different companies.

Disk 7, Track 13

Now listen to a conversation between two students.

W: Hi, Jim. How's it going this quarter?

M: Well, to be honest, not very well. I just got my geology test back and I'm afraid my grade was not good. I'm disappointed, too, because I like the professor and the class.

W: Oh. Well, would it help if you got a tutor?

M: I don't know. The main problem is I don't have enough time to study. My boss has asked me to work more hours at my job, and that leaves me less time for geology.

W: Oh, I see. Well, what if you quit your job?

M: I can't afford to do that.

W: But maybe you could look for a different job, here on campus. The campus jobs are posted in the Career Center.

M: Well, maybe … if I could find a job that pays as well as the one I have. I just wish I had more time to study. I need to pass my geology course.

W: You know … you could drop the class now and take it again next quarter. You already have the textbook, and you could read ahead on your own.

M: Well, I need to do something fast because I can't fail the course.

Describe the man's problem and the suggestions the woman makes about how to solve it. What do you think the man should do, and why?

Disk 7, Track 14

Now listen to part of a lecture in a marine biology class.

Ocean scientists study several physical properties of water, including transparency—or water clarity—and color. Clear water indicates an absence of particles suspended in the water that would affect the ability of light to pass through it. Water clarity determines how much plant growth there may be in an ocean region. Plant growth usually depends on how deep the sunlight will reach: the clearer the water, the deeper the light will penetrate.

The color of seawater varies a lot from place to place. For example, the water of the Gulf Stream in the Atlantic Ocean is a deep indigo blue, while a similar current in the Pacific off Japan is called the Black Stream because of the very dark color of its water. Along many coasts, the water is green. The green color is a mixture of blue—due to the scattering of sunlight in the water—and the soluble yellow pigment associated with phytoplankton, the floating plant life.

In some places, the water is brown or brownish red. Brown or brownish red water gets its color from large quantities of certain types of microscopic brown algae. Brown algae are common along temperate coasts, where the water is cool. Their brown color comes from the brown pigments they contain. A bucket of water scooped from the surface of the sea may contain millions of microscopic brown algae.

In tropical or subtropical regions, various shades of blue are common. The blue color results from the scattering of sunlight by tiny particles suspended in the water, or by molecules of the water itself. Blue light has a short wave length, and because of this, blue light is more readily distributed than light of longer wavelengths. Therefore, the ocean appears blue for the same reason that the sky does.

Using points and examples from the lecture, explain why some ocean water is clear and why some water is a certain color.

Disk 7, Track 15

WRITING SECTION DIRECTIONS (p. 471)

The Writing section measures your ability to use writing to communicate in an academic environment. There are two writing questions.

Question 1 is an integrated writing task. You will read a passage, listen to a lecture, and then answer a question based on what you have read and heard. You have 20 minutes to plan and write your response.

Question 2 is an independent writing task. You will answer a question based on your own knowledge and experience. You have 30 minutes to plan and write your response.

Disk 7, Track 16

Now listen to a professor's response to the reading.

Why do people travel to distant lands? Centuries ago, their reasons were primarily political or economic, for conquest or colonization. The idea of traveling for personal enrichment is fairly modern, only a few centuries old, and traveling just for adventure is even newer.

It's interesting that the reading mentions Ernest Hemingway's big game hunts in Africa as an example of traveling for adventure. Actually, Hemingway illustrates the conquest ideal in tourism. Hemingway was an adventurer who traveled to so–called "savage" lands to hunt wild animals and bring back trophies. Of course, only a few people at the time could afford his style of travel—with servants to make the trip more comfortable—yet Hemingway was very influential, and his writings were very popular. You can still see his influence in tourism today, especially in sports that involve the control and conquest of nature, like hunting and fishing.

The tourists of today take trips purely for pleasure, recreation, adventure, and, of course, personal growth. More travelers seek out the most distant places as well as the most unusual cultures. We can see this in ethnic tourism, a new kind of cultural tourism that includes visits to traditional villages and people's homes to observe social customs, and see native arts and crafts, and watch local ceremonies, and so on. Ethnic tourism helps preserve aboriginal cultures that might otherwise be endangered by assimilation into the larger society. In fact, ethnic tourism allows us to enjoy folk dances, songs, costumes, and ceremonies that might otherwise be lost.

Another growing area of tourism is environmental tourism, which is kind of related to ethnic tourism. Environmental tourism is traveling to pristine wilderness areas where few people have gone before. The goal is to observe and learn about nature. The African safaris of today, for example, are for the purpose of observing and photographing wildlife—not killing it.

Summarize the points made in the lecture, and explain how they are similar to or different from points made in the reading.

TEST 2

Disk 8, Track 1

LISTENING SECTION DIRECTIONS (p. 488)

The Listening section measures your ability to understand conversations and lectures in English. You will hear each conversation and lecture only one time. After each conversation or lecture, you will hear some questions about it. Answer all questions based on what the speakers state or imply.

You may take notes while you listen. You may use your notes to help you answer the questions.

Most questions have four possible answers. In some questions, you will see this icon: 🎧. This means that you will hear, but not see, part of the question.

Some questions have special directions, which appear in a gray box. Most questions are worth one point. If a question is worth more than one point, special directions will indicate how many points you can receive.

You have approximately 40 minutes to complete the Listening section. This includes the time for listening to the conversations and lectures and for answering the questions.

To make this practice more like the real test, cover the questions and answers during each conversation and lecture. When you hear the first question, uncover the questions and answers.

Disk 8, Track 2

Questions 1 through 5. Listen to part of a conversation between two students.

M: Oh, hi! It's good to see you. What's happening?
W: I'm busy with my classes. The quarter's going by really quickly. How about you? What have you been up to?
M: Busy with school and work. Hey, what are you taking spring quarter?
W: Literature, sociology … botany, and … uh … I'm hoping to do something in the arts, maybe some sort of work experience or internship.
M: No kidding! I didn't know you were artistic. What do you have in mind?
W: Well, there's this theater group I just found out about in Chester. I went to a couple of their plays. They're an interesting company. They perform a lot of new works, and they also do older plays that aren't very well known, and … well … I'm really impressed and would love to work with them in some way.
M: No kidding! I didn't know you were into theater. Do you act?
W: Not really … I took drama in high school, but I was awful on stage. No … it's not acting that interests me as much as … all the other stuff.
M: Like what? Directing? Lighting?
W: All of it, actually. This theater I told you about—they have the best sets! I'd like to build sets. Or make costumes, find props—I don't know, even work in the office. It's the whole atmosphere of theater that I find exciting.

M: It sounds like you need to be a theater intern.

W: But, as far as that goes … my problem is I don't know anything about setting it up.

M: What, the internship?

W: Yeah.

M: Do you know anyone who works there?

W: No, I only found out about it 'cause I went to a couple of plays.

M: Better go see your adviser about this. Doesn't the advising department post a list of internships that are available?

W: Yeah, there's a list. I already checked it, and there was nothing in theater. But I'll talk to Sherry, of course. She's my adviser.

M: You know what you could do? When I had to do an observation last year for my psychology class—we had to observe a work group for two weeks—what I did—how I got started was, I picked out a couple of law firms and then just sent formal letters of introduction. I told them I was a student, and had to do a report for one of my classes, and asked if I could meet with them to arrange an observation in their workplace.

W: Oh … really? And what happened?

M: I said I'd call them, and the first firm I called said I could do it there.

W: Wow! You make it sound so easy. I wonder if that'd work with the theater.

M: It's worth a try, isn't it?

W: It's worth a try. Hey, I'm glad I ran into you!

1. What are the students mainly discussing?
2. What does the woman like about theater?
3. What is the woman's opinion of her own acting ability?
4. Why does the man say this:
   "Like what? Directing? Lighting?"
5. What does the man suggest the woman do?

Disk 8, Track 3

Questions 6 through 10. Listen to a conversation between a student and a professor.

M: Hi, Professor Reynolds.

W: Oh, hi, Jeff. I just read your note. You wanted to talk about something?

M: Uh, yeah, just an idea I have. I've been thinking— um, I was reading about what's been going on with those houses on Fox Point.

W: You mean the slide?

M: Yeah, that's right. The paper said a few days ago there was only one house that was affected, but this morning there was another article saying there were lots more houses involved than they previously thought, maybe as many as fifteen or twenty homes. A couple of houses have big cracks in the foundation.

W: I read the article too. It seems like nothing but bad news for the homeowners.

M: Yeah. My old boss lives out there on Fox Point. I don't know if his house is one that's affected. Anyway … I was … um … I was sort of thinking I could write a paper on it. I remember how in your Intro to Geology course we studied gravity movements. I thought maybe … um … the slide on Fox Point was a case of subsidence … um … when the earth sinks 'cause there's a weakening of support. I was thinking this might be an example of settlement.

W: Settlement happens from the more or less gradual compacting of underlying material—for example, when wet soil at the surface dries and shrinks, and creates a depression. It can also happen when frozen ground melts.

M: In class you talked about the Leaning Tower of Pisa.

W: Yes. The settlement that's caused the Tower of Pisa to lean is due to the failure of a clay layer beneath it. Engineers have been working on it for decades, but still haven't been able to stop the process.

M: There was another kind of settlement you talked about … um … when groundwater's removed.

W: Yes, that's what happened in the San Joaquin Valley in California. Part of the valley floor sank 30 feet because of the removal of groundwater for irrigation. But the problem on Fox Point may not be subsidence at all. This probably has more to do with the slope, and with the amount of rain we've been having lately.

M: So … it's just a regular old mudslide, not like the Leaning Tower?

W: It's probably not like the Leaning Tower.

M: The article did say the houses were on a slope, but it's only slight, it's not steep at all.

W: Mudslides are most common on intermediate slopes—27 to 45 degrees—because these slopes are gentle enough for sediment to accumulate and steep enough for sliding. One suggestion I have is to take a look at the county's Web site. There's a page on the geology of the region. This area has a history of slides. There was one on Johnson Island about ten, twelve years ago.

M: Oh, really? I didn't know that. Maybe there's a connection.

W: Possibly. It's an idea to work on.

M: Well, this gives me a place to start. Thanks, Professor Reynolds. I appreciate your input.

6. Why does the student go to see the professor?
7. What topic is the man mainly interested in?
8. Why does the student say this:
   "In class you talked about the Leaning Tower of Pisa."
9. According to the professor, where are mudslides most common?
10. What will the man probably include in his research?

Disk 8, Track 4

Questions 11 through 16. Listen to part of a discussion in a botany class. The class is talking about flowers.

W1: In a perfect, idealized flower, its four organs are arranged in four whorls, all attached to the receptacle at the end of the stem. Before we go on, let's quickly go over the four parts of the flower. First, let's start from the outside and work in. Which organ is on the outside, closest to the stem?

M: The sepal. That's the part that kind of looks like a leaf 'cause it's usually green. The sepal protects the flower bud before it opens up.

W1: Right. Then what comes next?

W2: The petals, the colorful part of the flower. It's the petals that make the flower attractive to insects and birds … and people, too.

W1: Right. And inside the petal layers we have …?

M: The flower's reproductive parts—the stamens and carpels.

W1: That's right. So we have the four parts of a flower: sepals, petals, stamens, and carpels. Now, during the millions of years in the history of flowering plants, numerous variations evolved. In certain flowers, one or more of the four basic floral organs—sepals, petals, stamens, and carpels—have been eliminated. Plant biologists distinguish between complete flowers—those with all four organs—and incomplete flowers—those lacking one or more of the four floral parts. For example, most grasses have incomplete flowers that lack petals.

There are many variations in the size, shape, and color of flowers. One important element in plant classification is the arrangement of flowers on their stalks. The large composite family, for example, which includes asters, daisies, and sunflowers, have flower heads that form a central disk. What appears to be a single flower is actually a collection of hundreds of flowers. The central disk consists of tiny, complete flowers. And what appear to be petals surrounding the central disk are actually imperfect flowers called ray flowers.

M: I'm not sure I got that. Could you say that again?

W1: Sure. The flower head—the center part of the plant—actually consists of many tiny, tightly packed complete flowers that stand upright on a flat disk. The whole arrangement looks like a single, symmetrical flower, but it's actually a collection of hundreds of separate flowers. The petals—what look like petals—are actually larger flowers called rays that extend from the rim of the disk. Does that help?

M: Uh, yeah, I guess so. What you're saying is, a single sunflower is really hundreds of flowers put together.

W1: That's right. This will make more sense in the lab this afternoon.

So … in the composite family, there are about 19,000 different species worldwide. Many are grown as ornamentals—cosmos, zinnia, dahlia, marigold, and aster. Probably the most–recognized composite flower is the English daisy. The daisy was introduced from Europe and now is a wildflower found on lawns, in fields, and at roadsides throughout North America. The name of the daisy has an interesting origin. The word "daisy" means "day's eye" and comes from an older Anglo–Saxon word. The English daisy folds up its rays at night and unfolds them again at dawn—the "eye of the day" or "day's eye." Several cultivated varieties of English daisy are popular as edging plants or in rock gardens. The English daisy comes in lots of colors—rose, lavender, pink, and white. It has a long bloom time, from April to September. The plants are compact and attractive, with flower heads up to two inches across. In the lab, we'll be looking at some different varieties of the daisy, and you'll see for yourself why they're so popular.

11. What aspects of flowers does the class mainly discuss?
12. Which part of the flower attracts insects and birds?
13. Listen again to part of the discussion. Then answer the question.
    "The whole arrangement looks like a single, symmetrical flower, but it's actually a collection of hundreds of separate flowers. The petals—what look like petals—are actually larger flowers called rays that extend from the rim of the disk. Does that help?"
    "Uh, yeah, I guess so. What you're saying is, a single sunflower is really hundreds of flowers put together."

"That's right. This will make more sense in the lab this afternoon."
Why does the professor say this:
"This will make more sense in the lab this afternoon."
14. Select the drawing that is most likely a member of the composite family.
15. Based on the information in the discussion, indicate whether each statement below is true or not true.
16. According to the professor, how did the daisy get its name?

Disk 8, Track 5

Questions 17 through 22. Listen to part of a lecture in an anthropology class.

M: Every human society has developed some interest in activities that could be considered sports. The more complex the culture, the more various the range of sporting behavior. There are certain elements in all human sports that are clues to the common underlying structure of sports. Sports tell us a great deal about the kinds of behavior that our prehistoric ancestors evolved—activities that were basic survival skills. Now, let me ask you—what skills were most important to the survival of our ancestors? Yes, Lynne?

W: The ability to find food?

M: Yeah …. But what skills were necessary to find food?

W: Um … good eyesight?

M: OK. What else?

W: Well, if they were hunters, they also had to be fast runners … and they had to have good eyes and a good arm—I mean a good aim—so they could kill game.

M: Yes! And isn't it interesting that you just used the word "game"? Our prehistoric ancestors were gamers—they hunted game animals to survive. Look at the number of sports that originated in hunting. First, hunting itself. But for some societies, the ancient pattern of killing prey is kept alive in the form of blood sports—these are sports that involve the killing of an animal. Even in places where the killing is no longer a matter of survival, it still survives as a sport. The animals—like ducks or pheasant, certain fish—are often eaten as luxury foods. It's the personal sense of mastery, the sort of delight in the skills of the hunter … these are more important than the food itself. For our prehistoric ancestors, the climax of the hunt was always a group celebration, with songs of praise for the hunters. As hunting sort of became more symbolic, spectators became more important. The ancient Romans brought the hunt to the people by confining it to an arena—the Coliseum. The Coliseum made the hunting field smaller, and this sort of intensified the activity for the entertainment of the spectators. The systematic killing of animals for sport still survives in parts of the world today—think of bullfights and cock fights. But animal sports are only part of the picture. Today, people find human competition more satisfying than competition involving just animals. Take track and field sports. These don't involve animals, but they did originate in hunting. The earliest sports meetings—or meets, as we call them—were probably ritualized competitions of important skills. Think of how many Olympic sports there are that involve aiming, throwing, and running—which are all hunting skills.

The difference is that now the hunting has become totally symbolic. In some sports, there's still a strong symbolic element of the kill. Wrestling, boxing, fencing, martial arts—all these are examples of ritualized fighting. Even tennis is kind of a fight—of course, an abstract one. There are lots of direct references to fighting in the language of sports, too. For example, what do soccer and chess players do? They "attack" or "defend."

Today, even the most violent fighting sports have strict rules that are designed to prevent serious injury. There's also some kind of referee to make sure that the rules are observed. In sports, the objective is victory, not the actual destruction of your opponent. Another objective is to impress and entertain the spectators—not to shock or offend them. Because sports contain such a powerful negative element, most have an ideal of acceptable behavior—something we call "sportsmanship." There's also a universal convention in sports where the winner honors the defeated opponent—with a handshake, with words of praise, or some token of respect.

17. What is the main idea of the lecture?
18. Listen again to part of the discussion. Then answer the question.
   "Now, let me ask you—what skills were most important to the survival of our ancestors? Yes, Lynne?"
   "The ability to find food?"
   "Yeah …. But what skills were necessary to find food?"
   Why does the professor say this:
   "Yeah …. But what skills were necessary to find food?"
19. According to the professor, why did the ancient Romans build the Coliseum?
20. What point does the professor make about track and field sports?
21. Which sports contain a symbolic element of the kill?
22. What does the professor imply about the negative element of sports?

Disk 8, Track 6

Questions 23 through 28. An epidemiologist has been invited to speak to students in a public health class. Listen to part of the talk.

Epidemiology is the field of medicine that deals with epidemics—outbreaks of disease that affect large numbers of people. As an epidemiologist, I look at factors involved in the distribution and frequency of disease in human populations. For example, what is it about what we do, or what we eat, or what our environment is, that leads one group of people to be more likely—or less likely—to develop a disease than another group of people? It's these factors that we try to identify.

We use statistical analyses, field investigations, and a range of laboratory techniques. We try to determine the cause and distribution of a disease. We also look at how quickly the disease spreads—and by what method—so we can implement measures to control and prevent the disease. Some epidemiologists concentrate on communicable diseases, like tuberculosis and AIDS. Others focus on the growing epidemics in cancer, diabetes, and heart disease.

We gather data in a variety of ways. One way is through what we call descriptive epidemiology, or looking at the trends of diseases over time, as well as … uh … trends of diseases in one population relative to another. Statistics are important in descriptive epidemiology, because numbers are a useful way to simplify information.

A second approach is observational epidemiology, where we observe what people do. We take a group of people who have a disease and a group of people who don't have a disease. We look at their patterns of eating or drinking and their medical history. We also take a group of people who've been exposed to something—for example, smoking—and a group of people who haven't, and then observe them over time to see whether they develop a disease or not. In observational epidemiology, we don't interfere in the process. We just observe it.

A third approach is experimental epidemiology, sometimes called an intervention study. Experimental research is the best way to establish cause–and–effect relationships between variables. A typical experiment studies two groups of subjects. One group receives a treatment, and the other group—the control group—does not. Thus, the effectiveness of the treatment can be determined. Experimental research is the only type of research that directly attempts to influence a particular variable—called the treatment variable—as a way to test a hypothesis about cause and effect. Some examples of treatments that can be varied include the amount of iron or potassium in the diet, the amount or type of exercise one engages in per week, and the minutes of sunlight one is exposed to per day.

The Health Research Institute, of which I am the director, is mostly involved in experimental studies—I say mostly because we study treatment and non–treatment groups and then compare the outcomes. However, we do collect and study various types of data in any given year. From these different approaches—descriptive, observational, and experimental—we can judge whether a particular factor causes or prevents the disease that we're looking at.

23. What is the talk mainly about?
24. What factors do epidemiologists study?
25–26. Based on the information in the talk, indicate whether each sentence below describes descriptive, observational, or experimental epidemiology.
27. Why do epidemiologists often study two groups of people?
28. Listen again to part of the talk. Then answer the question.
   "The Health Research Institute, of which I am the director, is mostly involved in experimental studies—I say mostly because we study treatment and non–treatment groups and then compare the outcomes. However, we do collect and study various types of data in any given year. From these different approaches—descriptive, observational, and experimental—we can judge whether a particular factor causes or prevents the disease that we're looking at."
   Why does the speaker talk about her own work?

Disk 8, Track 7

Questions 29 through 34. Listen to part of a talk in a music education class.

Learning to play a musical instrument is one of the best experiences that a young child can have. Learning to play music begins with listening to others play music. A child's first experience with playing an instrument should be by ear, without the distraction of printed music. Playing by ear is the natural beginning for children. The ability to play by ear will help them throughout their lives, and it also enriches the experience of music making. But children should eventually learn to read music. So, when is the right time? And what's the best way for a child to learn how to read music?

A lot of children start playing an instrument at the age of eight or nine. It's best for them to spend a couple of years playing by ear before the teacher introduces notation—printed music. Children should first be able to feel that their instrument is a part of them. Playing by ear is the best way for children to become comfortable with their instrument.

The teacher should introduce notation only when the child is ready. The right time is when the child feels a need for notation. This might be when the child has learned so many pieces it's sort of difficult to remember them all. Then the teacher can present the printed music as a memory aid, so learning to read music has a practical purpose and isn't just a meaningless task.

A good time to teach notation is when a group of children play together. The printed score is a way to help them sort of keep track of who plays what and when. The score will organize their cooperative effort in a way that makes sense to them.

Another good time is when the child wants to play music that's so complex it would be difficult to learn by ear. In this case, learning to read music is a natural step toward playing the music the child wants to play. The teacher should play the score for the child the first time through, and demonstrate how the notes on the page are transformed into music. The child listens as he or she looks at the printed notes. This way, the child can begin to see how the notes represent sound and a printed score becomes a piece of music. As the child listens—and maybe plays along—he or she begins to understand the shape of the new piece.

For students who play a chord–producing instrument—the guitar, for example—a natural first step toward reading music is playing by chord symbols. Chord symbols are found in a lot of different styles of music—like pop and jazz—and at various levels of difficulty. Chord symbols are a simple form of written music—they're kind of a halfway point between playing by ear and reading a standard musical score.

After children can play by ear, and then by chord symbols, the next step is to read standard music notation. Although that's the natural order for children to learn, it doesn't mean that each successive step is better than the one that came before. The three methods of playing music—playing by ear, playing chords, and playing by standard notation—are all valuable in their own way. Some children will always prefer to play by ear. Others will like chord playing and have no desire to learn another method. And still others will find their musical home in the tradition of note reading. It's the job of the music teacher to fit the method to the needs of the students.

29. What is playing by ear?
30. Listen again to part of the talk. Then answer the question.
    "Playing by ear is the natural beginning for children. The ability to play by ear will help them throughout their lives, and it also enriches the experience of music making. But children should eventually learn to read music. So, when is the right time? And what's the best way for a child to learn how to read music?"
    Why does the professor ask this:
    "So, when is the right time? And what's the best way for a child to learn how to read music?"
31. According to the professor, when should children learn to read musical notation?
32. According to the professor, why should a music teacher play the score for a child the first time?
33. According to the professor, what is the natural order for children to learn music?
34. What does the professor imply about the three methods of playing music?

Disk 8, Track 8

SPEAKING SECTION DIRECTIONS (p. 494)

The Speaking section measures your ability to speak in English about a variety of topics. There are six questions in this section. Record your response to each question on a cassette.

Questions 1 and 2 are independent speaking tasks in which you will speak about familiar topics. Your responses will be scored on your ability to speak clearly and coherently about the topics.

Questions 3 and 4 are integrated tasks in which you will read a passage, listen to a conversation or lecture, and then speak in response to a question about what you have read and heard. You will need to combine relevant information from the two sources to answer the question completely. Your responses will be scored on your ability to speak clearly and coherently and on your ability to accurately convey information about what you read and heard.

Questions 5 and 6 are integrated tasks in which you will listen to part of a conversation or lecture, and then speak in response to a question about what you have heard. Your responses will be scored on your ability to speak clearly and coherently and on your ability to accurately convey information about what you heard.

You will hear each conversation and lecture only one time. You may take notes while you listen. You may use your notes to help you answer the questions.

Disk 8, Track 9

Describe a person who has influenced you in an important way. Explain why this person has had an effect on your life. Include details and examples in your explanation.

Disk 8, Track 10

Some people get most of their news from the radio or television. Others read the newspaper. Which source of news do you think is better and why? Include details and examples in your explanation.

Disk 8, Track 11

Now listen to two students as they discuss the attendance policy.

M: It looks like we'll be in the same biology class. I'm going to miss the first day because I won't be back from vacation yet, so I'll ask you for the lecture notes.
W: But you can't miss the first day! Attendance is mandatory on the first day.
M: Oh, I don't agree with that. It will be all right. That policy is unfair anyway.
W: It's not unfair! The instructor has the right to set the attendance policy, and the right to kick you out of class if you don't follow it. The way I look at it, if the instructor has to be there every day, then so should the students. That seems fair to me.
M: Oh, but the students can read and study on their own. It's not important to go to class. The only thing that's important is the examinations.

W: I disagree. I think it's important to participate in class. That's an important part of learning.

M: But you can learn what you need to know by studying on your own!

W: But how do you know you won't miss something important? You can't always understand everything on your own. That's why you need to go to class. And that's why there's an attendance policy.

The woman expresses her opinion about the attendance policy. State her opinion and explain the reasons she gives for holding that opinion.

Disk 8, Track 12

Now listen to part of a lecture on the same topic in a sociology class.

One ethical problem with participant observation is that researchers usually come from social backgrounds very different from those of the people they're studying, so they have to be dishonest about their reason for being there. They may have to lie about who they are. For example, in one study, a researcher wanted to study fast–food workers, so she got a job in a fast–food restaurant. She changed her name and lied about her work history, and pretended not to have a university education. This is where the ethical problem starts.

To complicate matters, the researcher used other people's acceptance of her lies in order to advance her own career. She was pretending to be someone else, a fast–food worker, to write a book about the experience. So she was basically using other people without their knowledge or permission.

One solution to the problem is to be honest about who you really are. However, this might influence the results of the study because people might not act naturally if they know they're being observed. Another acceptable solution is to tell everyone as soon as possible after the project is completed. That's what our fast–food researcher did. At the end of the study, she told the other workers that she was writing a book about them in order to get their approval to tell their stories.

Explain the ethical problem in the participant observation study discussed in the lecture. State what the researcher did to solve the problem, and explain why this was acceptable.

Disk 8, Track 13

Now listen to a conversation between two students.

W: So, are you doing the internship at the bank next semester?

M: Maybe. I'll be doing an internship anyway. My parents want me to take the bank internship because they want me to go into banking. But Dr. Kim has asked me to be her intern. She's doing a study of population growth and wants me to help her. I'd rather work on the population study, but I don't want to disappoint my parents either.

W: Do you want your career to be in banking?

M: At one time I thought I did. But now I'm much more excited about the idea of working with statistics, you know, doing pure research.

W: Then you should do the internship with Dr. Kim on the population study. That way you'll know for sure if pure research is what you want to do with your life.

M: My father won't be happy about that.

W: How do you know? Talk to him. Tell him why the population project excites you. Tell him it's a great opportunity to work with Dr. Kim, and quite an honor for a professor to ask you like this. That might actually please your father. But in the end, you have to do what makes you happy.

Describe the man's problem and the suggestions the woman makes about what he should do. What do you think the man should do, and why?

Disk 8, Track 14

Now listen to part of a talk in a biology class. The professor is discussing competition in bird populations.

Competition is the struggle among birds for resources. Whenever there's a limited supply of a resource—such as food, nest sites, or mates—there'll be competition. Competition can take place between birds of the same species or between birds of different species.

There are a couple of forms of competition: direct and indirect. Direct competition is when a bird actively excludes others from getting resources. A common example is stealing; a bird may simply take food from another. Another example is territories. Especially during the breeding season, birds maintain and defend some sort of territory. They form territories to defend resources like food, or to maintain access to good nest sites, or to attract mates. Some birds compete directly by fighting, for example, when they compete for mates. Others fight over food; you can see this if you watch gulls feeding on the garbage at the local garbage dump.

And the second type of competition is indirect competition, when birds simply use up a resource. When one species eats all the seeds or berries or grubs, this will prevent other species from using that resource. Indirect competition is less open than direct competition, but it can have just as great an influence on populations. For example, a flock of geese grazing in a field will gradually decrease the amount of food there. The larger the flock, the faster the food will be used up, and this reduces the amount of food available to other species.

Competition determines the size of bird populations. As the population of a species increases in a particular area, the likelihood of competition also increases. Eventually, competition may limit the size of the population because there's simply not enough food and nest sites for more birds.

Using points and examples from the talk, explain the two types of competition in bird populations. Then explain how population size and competition are related.

Disk 8, Track 15

WRITING SECTION DIRECTIONS (p. 499)

The Writing section measures your ability to use writing to communicate in an academic environment. There are two writing questions.

Question 1 is an integrated writing task. You will read a passage, listen to a lecture, and then answer a question based on what you have read and heard. You have 20 minutes to plan and write your response.

Question 2 is an independent writing task. You will answer a question based on your own knowledge and experience. You have 30 minutes to plan and write your response.

Disk 8, Track 16

Now listen to part of a lecture in an anthropology class.

Now I'd like to tell you about a famous study that points to some of the more troubling aspects of same–age peer groups. It's known as the Robbers Cave Experiment, and it looked at a group of 22 normal eleven–year–old boys. All of the boys had similar social, economic, and educational backgrounds. The boys were taken to a summer camp in Robbers Cave State Park in Oklahoma.

The study took place in three stages. In the first stage, which lasted one week, the boys were randomly divided into two groups. In this stage, competition was discouraged, and there were joint activities. But the two groups nevertheless began to show signs of feeling competitive. For example, they named themselves the Eagles and the Rattlers, and they began to tease and belittle each other.

In the second stage, a series of contests was set up between the two groups: baseball, tug–of–war, skits, treasure hunts, and even cabin inspections. There were prizes for the winners, like medals and camp knives. After the second day, there was an increase in name–calling and insults between the two groups, to the point that the negative attitudes became very clearly defined.

Then, in the third stage of the study, the two groups were put back together again. They were given important goals to reach together, such as fixing the water tank … so all the boys would have water to drink. This project greatly reduced prejudice in just a few days. By the end of stage three, most of the conflict between the groups had disappeared.

So … what does this experiment tell us? Well, for one thing, dividing boys into two groups can easily lead to prejudice and insults between the groups. Also, when the two rival groups are given a cooperative task, like fixing the water tank, they can put away their differences and get the job done. The experiment shows that, in peer groups, competition comes more naturally than cooperation. And—we have to wonder— without the supervision of adults, would competition, teasing, and negative attitudes get even more extreme?

Summarize the points made by the professor about same–age peer groups, explaining how they cast doubt on points made in the reading.

TEST 3

Disk 9, Track 1

LISTENING SECTION DIRECTIONS (p. 516)

The Listening section measures your ability to understand conversations and lectures in English. You will hear each conversation and lecture only one time. After each conversation or lecture, you will hear some questions about it. Answer all questions based on what the speakers state or imply.

You may take notes while you listen. You may use your notes to help you answer the questions.

Most questions have four possible answers. In some questions, you will see this icon: 🎧. This means that you will hear, but not see, part of the question.

Some questions have special directions, which appear in a gray box. Most questions are worth one point. If a question is worth more than one point, special directions will indicate how many points you can receive.

You have approximately 40 minutes to complete the Listening section. This includes the time for listening to the conversations and lectures and for answering the questions.

To make this practice more like the real test, cover the questions and answers during each conversation and lecture. When you hear the first question, uncover the questions and answers.

Disk 9, Track 2

Questions 1 through 5. Listen to a conversation between a student and a music professor.

M: Hi, Professor Casey. How are you?

W: Fine, thanks, Michael. I heard you got the scholarship for the summer program at Silverwood. Congratulations!

M: Thank you. I mean, thank you very much—I'm sure your recommendation helped me a lot.

W: I was happy to do it. So are you ready for summer?

M: I wish it was next week, but I … uh … still have a lot to do before exams. But I'm looking forward to it. I'll be studying oboe with Peter Stanley—he heads the woodwind ensemble there.

W: I know him. You couldn't ask for a better teacher. That's great. I'm really happy for you.

M: Thanks. I'm looking forward to it. He was on the panel for my interview. I'll be studying oboe with him, and also orchestra—Dr. Fine is the conductor— and I'm hoping to do the French horn, too, and maybe take up the krummhorn—it has such a cool sound. They're supposed to have an early music specialist there, but I forgot her name.

W: The krummhorn!

M: Yeah.

W: That's right. You did tell me of your interest in medieval and Renaissance music. I hope you get a chance to pursue that. There's been a revival of interest there. Well, Michael, it looks like you'll have a full plate this summer.

M: I know. I'm sure I'll be working hard! But it'll be great.

W: So what comes after that? What are your plans for next year? You'll be a sophomore, right?

M: Right. I'll be coming back here, so I'm sure I'll be seeing you. You'll still be teaching theory and composition, right?

W: Of course I will. And I look forward to having you in class.

M: What will you be doing this summer?

W: I'll be teaching Theory I and II, and coaching voice.

M: Uh–huh. You're also in a band, aren't you? I mean, outside of school?

W: Yes, I am—a jazz quintet. We do mostly standards. I play piano and sing. For me, that's fun and relaxation time.

M: My girlfriend said she heard you at the Back Alley.

W: Yes, we play there every Wednesday night. You should come hear us sometime.

M: I'd like that. I'll bring my girlfriend. She says you were really good.

W: Well then, I hope to see you some Wednesday night.

M: I'll be there. Well … I gotta go now. I'm supposed to meet my German teacher in fifteen minutes. And thanks again for the recommendation.

W: It's my pleasure, Michael. You'll make the most of it, I'm certain. Good luck!

1. What topics do the speakers mainly discuss?
2. What does the professor mean when she says this: "I know him. You couldn't ask for a better teacher."
3. Why does the professor say this: "Well, Michael, it looks like you'll have a full plate this summer."
4. What does the professor do for relaxation?
5. What can be inferred from the conversation?

Disk 9, Track 3

Questions 6 through 11. Listen to part of a lecture in a film studies class.

In the first two decades of the twentieth century, cinema established itself as a powerful mass medium. Movies were a popular entertainment for working people, but they were more than just entertainment. Movies were also regarded as high art by the intellectuals of the day. Many people believed that cinema—or film—would be the defining art form of the new century.

Even in its earliest years, film was developing its own style—a style that was distinct from that of the theater. But what do we mean when we speak of film style? To put it simply, style is the texture of a film's images and sounds. It's the filmmaker's systematic use of the techniques of the medium—for example, staging, lighting, performance, camera framing and focus. Editing and sound also contribute to style.

A few filmmakers of the silent era were already developing film style, most notably in the editing technique of cutting. Cutting is when the action is broken up into separate shots, or pieces of film, and then the shots are recombined to tell the story in a coherent way. Before cutting, the action in films was like it was in the theater. The action took place far away from us, and it was continuous—it wasn't interrupted by any closer views of the actors.

Early film critics didn't like films that looked too much like theater. Theater was a well recognized art form with its own traditions and methods. However, film was something new, and well, it was an art form that owed its birth to the technology of the moving picture camera. The critics preferred

to see stylistic camera work and editing—the techniques that set film apart from theater. A lot of critics felt that editing was the most important film technique. Cutting—the change from shot to shot—was regarded as the key to film artistry.

Another film technique—called cross–cutting—made it possible to tell two stories at the same time. Cross–cutting—it's also called parallel action—it involves showing segments from two different sequences, moving back and forth from one to the other so the two stories appear to be taking place at the same time. Cross–cutting was used in the 1903 film *The Great Train Robbery*. The film shows bandits escaping from the scene of their crime, and then it cross–cuts to a scene where the townspeople are dancing at a party, unaware the robbery has taken place. The audience easily understands that the two scenes are going on at the same time.

The person who usually receives the credit for inventing most film techniques is D.W. Griffith. While Griffith didn't invent everything about film—actually he defined and redefined the innovations of other filmmakers—he created movies that critics and audiences recognized as a unique narrative form. This is because he perfected the elements of film "grammar" and the art of the story film.

Instead of having one camera shoot a scene from one position, D.W. Griffith filmed each scene from many angles, and then he pieced together the sequences in the editing room. He used editing to heighten and control the dramatic impact of a scene. He introduced analytical editing, that is, breaking down a scene into shots that show closer views of people's faces or gestures. These closely framed shots are known as close–ups. The close–up conveys a character's emotions through subtle changes in the eyes, mouth, and brow. After D.W. Griffith, the close–up became a standard tool in the language of film.

6. What is the lecture mainly about?
7. Which of the following contribute to the style of a film?
8. According to the professor, why did early film critics dislike films that resembled theater?
9. Why does the professor discuss cross–cutting?
10. Listen again to part of the lecture. Then answer the question.
"The person who usually receives the credit for inventing most film techniques is D.W. Griffith. While Griffith didn't invent everything about film—actually he defined and redefined the innovations of other filmmakers—he created movies that critics and audiences recognized as a unique narrative form. This is because he perfected the elements of film 'grammar' and the art of the story film."
What does the professor mean when he says this:
"This is because he perfected the elements of film 'grammar' and the art of the story film."
11. Which camera shot would probably best show that a character is frightened?

Disk 9, Track 4

Questions 12 through 17. Listen to part of a talk in a biology class.

M: Until recently, we knew almost nothing about how important bees are in maintaining natural diversity. Now we know more about them. We know, for example, that honeybees are the dominant pollinators because they play a role in pollinating four out of five food crops in North America. We also know that honeybees—along with the other insects, bats, and birds that transfer pollen between flowers—all together they contribute more than ten billion dollars a year to fruit and seed production on North American farms. Pollination is one of nature's services to farmers. So think about this: if you eliminated the pollinators, it would take the food right out of our mouths. We biologists never imagined we'd see the day when wild plants or crops suffered from pollinator scarcity. But, unfortunately, that day has come. In fact, farmers in Mexico and the U.S. are suffering the worst pollinator crisis in history. So … what happened? Any ideas? Alicia?

W: Is it … um … because of natural enemies? I read something about a kind of parasite that's killed lots of bees.

M: It's true. An outbreak of parasitic mites has caused a steep decline in North American populations of honeybees. But parasites aren't the only factor.

W: What about the pesticides used on farms? All those chemicals must have an effect.

M: Most definitely, yes. Pesticides are a major factor. Both wild and domesticated bees are in serious trouble because of pesticides. In California, farm chemicals are killing around ten percent of all the honeybee colonies. Agriculture in general is part of the problem. Think about this for a minute: the North American continent is a vast collection of "nectar corridors" made up of flowering plants. These corridors stretch for thousands of miles, from Mexico to as far north as Alaska. And every year, there's an array of migratory pollinators flying north and south with the seasons, following the flowers. The migratory corridors—the flyways—are like … uh … something like a path of stepping-stones for the pollinators, with each "stone" being a collection of flowering plants. But our system of large-scale agriculture has interfered. During the past fifty years, millions of acres of desert in western Mexico and the southwestern United States have been turned into chemically intensive farms, planted with exotic grasses, creating huge stretches of flyway that are devoid of nectar-producing plants for migratory pollinators. What we have now are huge gaps between the stepping-stones—patches of plants here and there. A couple of migratory pollinators are worth noting. One is the lesser long-nosed bat, and another is the most famous pollinator—what is our most famous pollinator? Or I should say our most beautiful pollinator.

W: Oh, I know. It's the monarch butterfly!

M: The monarch butterfly—yes. Millions of monarchs from all over the U.S. and southern Canada fly south every year in late summer. The monarch is the only butterfly that returns to a specific site year after year. Unfortunately, the herbicides used on the milkweed in the Great Plains are taking a toll on monarchs, and fewer of them are reaching their winter grounds in Mexico. Another important pollinator is the long-nosed bat. These amazing animals feed on cactus flowers. What they do is, they lap up the nectar at the bottom of the flower, and then when the bat flies off to another cactus, the pollen stuck to its head is transferred to that plant's flower. But the long-nosed bat is having a tough time, too. Some desert ranchers mistake them for vampire bats, and they've tried to poison them, or dynamite the caves where they roost.

12. What is the talk mainly about?

13. According to the professor, what factors have affected pollinator populations?

14. Listen again to part of the talk. Then answer the question.
"But our system of large-scale agriculture has interfered. During the past fifty years, millions of acres of desert in western Mexico and the southwestern United States have been turned into chemically intensive farms, planted with exotic grasses, creating huge stretches of flyway that are devoid of nectar-producing plants for migratory pollinators. What we have now are huge gaps between the stepping-stones—patches of plants here and there."
Why does the professor say this:
"What we have now are huge gaps between the stepping-stones—patches of plants here and there."

15. Listen again to part of the talk. Then answer the question.
"Millions of monarchs from all over the U.S. and southern Canada fly south every year in late summer. The monarch is the only butterfly that returns to a specific site year after year. Unfortunately, the herbicides used on the milkweed in the Great Plains are taking a toll on monarchs, and fewer of them are reaching their winter grounds in Mexico."
What can be inferred about monarch butterflies?

16–17. Based on the information in the talk, indicate whether each sentence below describes the honeybee, the monarch butterfly, or the long-nosed bat.

Disk 9, Track 5

Questions 18 through 23. A cultural historian has been invited to speak to an urban studies class. Listen to part of the lecture.

The agricultural revolution of ten thousand years ago started the great shift from rural to urban living. As human settlements evolved from simple groups of huts to larger villages, and then to towns and cities, their basic pattern changed.

The early rural villages grew naturally—sort of organically—as if they were plants or bushes, and buildings were clustered near water sources, and around village gardens, with trees for shade and pastures for animals.

A lot of us yearn to escape to these simpler, more romantic settlements of the past. But there are probably more of us who have a powerful urge to explore new ideas and to build bigger and better structures. We now have super-settlements called cities. Our city planners and architects have converted the organic pattern of the village into a geometrically perfect grid. Our natural habitat has been transformed into an expanse of hard, straight surfaces, with stone and metal and concrete and glass.

Of course, the city is still a wonderful place for stimulation, for opportunity, and for cultural interaction. In fact, you could say the city is our most spectacular creation. And, believe it or not, it still has elements of the rural past.

In the average North American city, about one-third of the surface is given to streets and buildings. The rest is covered by trees and grass—foresters call it the "urban forest"—meaning all the trees in city parks, the trees planted along streets and highways, and the trees in people's yards. The extent of this forest is sort of amazing—two-thirds of our urban space.

The concept of a tree-lined village green has a long history, but one of North America's first public parks—that was sort of created as a unified project—was Central Park in New York City. Central Park was designed by landscape architects Olmsted and Vaux in the late nineteenth century. They took their inspiration from the gardens of European estates and the romantic landscape paintings from that period.

Central Park was set in a rectangular site covering over 800 acres in the middle of Manhattan Island. By the nineteenth century, the original forest was long gone. The area had been used as a common pasture for farm animals, but eventually it deteriorated into a kind of urban wasteland, dotted with garbage dumps.

Olmsted and Vaux transformed this wasteland into something like its original appearance, with rolling hills, grassy meadows, and woody thickets with thousands of trees. The result is sort of an oasis in the middle of steel and stone. Central Park has been called "the city's lung" because of its purifying effect on the air, not to mention its effect on the human psyche. It remains one of the best examples of what we can do with the open spaces of our cities.

When you look at how far we've come as humans, when you consider that we've developed something called civilization, you come to realize that the finest evidence of our civilization is the city. The city is a symbol of experimentation and creation, a place where we can come together for work and entertainment, for art and culture, for wonder and opportunity. And, like the rural villages of the past, the city is where we come together to share cultural experiences with other humans—indeed, to define what it is to be human.

18. What topics does the speaker discuss?
19. How did early rural villages differ from the cities of today?
20. What is the "urban forest"?
21. Why does the speaker talk about New York City?
22. Listen again to part of the lecture. Then answer the question.
"Olmsted and Vaux transformed this wasteland into something like its original appearance, with rolling hills, grassy meadows, and woody thickets with thousands of trees. The result is sort of an oasis in the middle of steel and stone. Central Park has been called 'the city's lung' because of its purifying effect on the air, not to mention its effect on the human psyche. It remains one of the best examples of what we can do with the open spaces of our cities."
What does the speaker imply about New York's Central Park?
23. What is the speaker's opinion of the city?

Disk 9, Track 6

Questions 24 through 28. Listen to a discussion between a student and her tutor.

W: My first test in computer science is on Monday, and I'm sure there'll be a question about memory. So, can we go over memory again?
M: Sure. Just remember the term "memory" is used a bit loosely. It describes an important element inside the system unit—the part of your computer where information is stored. Technically, memory can be either of two things: RAM or ROM.
W: RAM and ROM—two kinds of memory. I need to be able to explain them. Now, what's the difference between RAM and ROM?
M: RAM—or random–access memory—stores the programs and data you're using in your current work session. When you turn off the computer, the information in RAM is lost. ROM—read–only memory—stores the information your computer needs to perform basic functions and run programs that are

built into your computer … like the program to start up the computer. ROM is permanent memory.
W: OK. You said RAM stores the programs and the data. OK, then what does the hard disk store? I guess I don't understand the difference between the memory and the disk storage.
M: That's a really good question. I'll answer it with an analogy. Imagine you're at the library, doing research for a new product your company wants to make. You've found a cabinet of one hundred file folders with all the information you need. You also have five sheets of instructions from your boss on how to use the information. So, what do you do? You sit down at a table, open several folders, and lay out only the instruction sheet you need for this part of the research. After all, the library table is only so big. When you finish gathering data from the first set of folders, you put them back and get another bunch. Similarly, when you complete the first page of your boss's instructions, you put that page back in your briefcase and pull out another page. Now, which part of your computer's memory is sort of like the library table?
W: RAM?
M: That's right. RAM. Why is that?
W: Because RAM stores only the program and data I need for this part of my work. RAM is sort of my work area—the tabletop—it's what I use when I work with files in a program.
M: That's right. And what are the one hundred file folders?
W: I get it now. The file folders are the disk storage. In a program, when I ask for another file, the computer gets it from the disk—the file cabinet—and loads it into RAM. What I mean is, it sort of puts the file on my work table.
M: That's right! And by keeping in RAM only the files needed for your current work session, you can work much faster and more efficiently. When you're finished, before you leave the library, you clear the table and return all the folders to the cabinet. It's exactly like what the computer does. When you finish your work session on the computer, all the files are returned to disk storage.

24. What is the purpose of the discussion?
25. Where does the computer store information to run programs that are built in?
26. Why does the tutor describe doing research at the library?
27. In the tutor's analogy, what does the library table represent?
28. The tutor briefly describes what happens during a work session on the computer. Indicate whether each sentence below is a step in the process.

Disk 9, Track 7

Questions 29 through 34. Listen to part of a lecture in a United States history class.

The battle at Antietam Creek in 1862 was the bloodiest twenty–four hours of the Civil War. Nearly 8,000 men lost their lives and another 15,000 were severely wounded. No single day in American history has been as tragic. Antietam was memorable in another way, too—it saw the advent of the war photographer.

The best known pictorial records of the Civil War are the

photographs commissioned by Mathew Brady, a leading portrait photographer of the time. Brady owned studios in New York and in Washington, and was known for his portraits of political leaders and celebrities. At the outbreak of the Civil War, he turned his attention to the conflict. He wanted to document the war on a grand scale, so he hired twenty photographers and sent them into the field with the troops. The battlefield carried dangers and financial risks, but Brady was persistent.

Brady himself did not actually shoot many of the photographs that bore his name. His company of photographers took the vast majority of the pictures—images of camp life, artillery, fortifications, railroads, bridges, battlefields, officers, and ordinary soldiers. Brady was more of a project manager. He spent his time supervising his photographers, preserving their negatives, and buying negatives from other photographers.

Two days after the battle at Antietam, two photographers from Brady's New York gallery took a series of photographs that ushered in a new era in the visual documentation of war. This was the first time that cameras had been allowed near the action before the fallen bodies of the dead were removed. Within a month of the battle, the images of battlefield corpses from Antietam were on display at Brady's gallery in New York. A sign on the door said simply, "The Dead of Antietam." America was shocked. The exhibition marked the first time most people had ever seen the carnage of the war. The photographs had a sensational impact, opening people's eyes as no woodcuts or lithographs had ever done.

The New York Times wrote, "If Mr. Brady has not brought bodies and laid them in our door–yards, he has done something very like it." Thousands of people, especially mothers and wives of men serving in the Union forces, flocked to look at these first dramatic images of death and destruction. Suddenly the battlefield was no longer comfortably distant—the camera was bringing it closer, erasing romantic notions about war.

Mathew Brady's work was the first instance of the comprehensive photo–documentation of a war—the Civil War—which as a result became the first media war. Photography had come of age, although it was still a relatively new technology with several limitations. For example, the exposure time of the camera was slow, and negatives had to be prepared minutes before a shot and developed immediately afterwards. This meant that it was not possible for photographers to take action pictures. They were limited to taking pictures of the battlefield after the fighting was over. Another limitation was that newspapers couldn't yet reproduce photographs. They could print only artists' drawings of the scene. Nevertheless, photography made a huge impact, and media coverage of war—and public opinion about war—would never be the same again.

29. What is the main idea of the lecture?
30. Listen again to part of the lecture. Then answer the question.
    "The battle at Antietam Creek in 1862 was the bloodiest twenty–four hours of the Civil War. Nearly 8,000 men lost their lives and another 15,000 were severely wounded. No single day in American history has been as tragic."
    What does the professor mean by this statement:
    "No single day in American history has been as tragic."
31. Who was Mathew Brady?
32. Listen again to part of the lecture. Then answer the question.
    "Within a month of the battle, the images of battlefield corpses from Antietam were on display at Brady's gallery in New York. A sign on the door said simply, 'The Dead of Antietam.' America was shocked. The exhibition marked

the first time most people had ever seen the carnage of the war. The photographs had a sensational impact, opening people's eyes as no woodcuts or lithographs had ever done."
Why does the professor say this:
"The photographs had a sensational impact, opening people's eyes as no woodcuts or lithographs had ever done."
33. What were some of the limitations of photography during the Civil War?
34. What does the professor imply about Mathew Brady?

Disk 9, Track 8

SPEAKING SECTION DIRECTIONS (p. 522)

The Speaking section measures your ability to speak in English about a variety of topics. There are six questions in this section. Record your response to each question on a cassette.

Questions 1 and 2 are independent speaking tasks in which you will speak about familiar topics. Your responses will be scored on your ability to speak clearly and coherently about the topics.

Questions 3 and 4 are integrated tasks in which you will read a passage, listen to a conversation or lecture, and then speak in response to a question about what you have read and heard. You will need to combine relevant information from the two sources to answer the question completely. Your responses will be scored on your ability to speak clearly and coherently and on your ability to accurately convey information about what you read and heard.

Questions 5 and 6 are integrated tasks in which you will listen to part of a conversation or lecture, and then speak in response to a question about what you have heard. Your responses will be scored on your ability to speak clearly and coherently and on your ability to accurately convey information about what you heard.

You will hear each conversation and lecture only one time. You may take notes while you listen. You may use your notes to help you answer the questions.

Disk 9, Track 9

Describe an event such as a holiday or other occasion that you enjoy celebrating. Explain why the event is significant to you. Include details and examples to support your explanation.

Disk 9, Track 10

Some people keep in touch with friends and family by letter or e–mail. Others keep in touch by telephone. Which method do you prefer to use, and why? Include details and examples in your explanation.

Disk 9, Track 11

Now listen to two students as they discuss the required discussion section.

W: What do you think of the new requirement? Starting next quarter, we need a discussion section for every lecture course we take.
M: It sounds like something I'm OK with.

W: Oh, I think it's just a bother. We already have three hours of lecture every week.

M: But that's not enough. The professor never covers everything we need to know for the examination. And there's hardly any time to ask questions.

W: Oh, but you can ask the professor questions during office hours.

M: Have you ever actually tried to do that? Some professors are never in their office, and the ones who are, well … they're usually too busy to talk to students. I like the idea of a discussion section. It gives us more of a chance to talk to the teacher, and other students too. Lecture classes are so big that you never get to know your classmates. Discussion classes have only around 20 or 25 people, and that's really nice. It's a lot more personal and informal, and you can learn so much more. Besides, it's easy to get a high grade in the discussion section.

The man expresses his opinion about the required discussion section. State his opinion and explain the reasons he gives for holding that opinion.

Disk 9, Track 12

Now listen to part of a lecture in a zoology class.

One example of a homeostatic system is temperature control, by which some animals can maintain a constant internal body temperature. The large ears of a rabbit are an amazing device in homeostasis. The rabbit can regulate the amount of blood flowing through blood vessels of its big ears. This adjusts heat loss to the rabbit's surroundings and maintains the stability of the rabbit's body temperature.

The control center for body temperature is the brain, and nerve cells in the skin do much of the work. Here's what happens. When the rabbit's body temperature increases, because of exercise or hot surroundings, the rabbit's brain notices the change and it sets out to bring the temperature back to normal. So the brain turns on the body's cooling system. In the rabbit's ears, the blood vessels expand and fill with warm blood. Heat is then able to escape from the surface of the skin on the ears. This causes the rabbit's body temperature to drop, and the brain can then turn off the cooling system.

On the other hand, when the rabbit's body temperature decreases because of cold surroundings, the brain turns on the body's warming system. Blood vessels in the ears constrict and get narrow, and send blood from the skin to deeper parts of the rabbit's body. And this reduces heat loss from the ears.

The professor describes the large ears of a rabbit. Explain how the rabbit's ears are used in homeostasis.

Disk 9, Track 13

Now listen to a conversation between a student and a college administrator.

M: May I help you?

W: I hope so. I need to get an official copy of my transcript, but it seems I can't do that because there's an unpaid charge in my student account. The charge is a mistake—it's for a window my roommate broke in our dormitory room. Somehow the charge ended up on my account instead of hers. The problem is, I need my transcript right away because I'm applying for a scholarship.

M: I see. Well, the fastest thing would be for you to just pay the charge to clear your account, and then have your roommate pay you back. Or you could send your roommate in to pay it.

W: Can't you just remove the charge from my account? After all, it's the university's mistake.

M: I can't do that until I get approval from the Housing Office, and that could take a while. But here's what you can do. Go down the hall right now and talk to the dean's secretary. Tell her what you've told me. She might let us release your transcript now, and then we can worry about the problem on your account later.

Describe the woman's problem and the suggestions the man makes about how to deal with it. What do you think the woman should do, and why?

Disk 9, Track 14

Now listen to part of a talk in a linguistics class.

The communication between a baby and a parent—especially the mother—has many of the same features as communication in music. One feature is timing. A mother and a child have a shared sense of timing, both before and after the child is born. It's like the mother and child kind of "swing" together in a common rhythm.

Just as one musician will lead another in a performance, a child will often lead the earliest "conversations" with his mother. A baby's sounds are conversational in the way that they connect two people in an exchange of sounds. This interplay between mother and child suggests that a child has, from the very beginning, an ability to communicate with his mother. The child recognizes his mother's voice. He also learns very quickly how to use his own voice in various ways. By the time he's two months old, a baby can make sounds with a musical inflection when he's "talking" with his mother.

The communication between babies and mothers develops from the intense daily contact between them. The mother creates a special language for the child—baby talk—a very special, very musical language. Several studies show that babies understand the patterns of baby talk, and will respond appropriately—by using facial expressions, movements, and their voice.

Babies quickly develop a large vocabulary of sounds. They learn to make meaningful sounds, long before any of these sounds become real words. The meaning lies in the music of the sounds—different meanings expressed by changes in intonation, rhythm, and timing. Babies learn to adjust their voice to match their mother's voice. They will imitate their mother's speech, even after Mother has stopped talking.

Using points and examples from the talk, describe the communication between babies and mothers. Explain how this communication is musical in nature.

Disk 9, Track 15

WRITING SECTION DIRECTIONS (p. 527)

The Writing section measures your ability to use writing to communicate in an academic environment. There are two writing questions.

Question 1 is an integrated writing task. You will read a passage, listen to a lecture, and then answer a question based on what you have read and heard. You have 20 minutes to plan and write your response.

Question 2 is an independent writing task. You will answer a question based on your own knowledge and experience. You have 30 minutes to plan and write your response.

Disk 9, Track 16

Now listen to part of a lecture on this topic in a psychology class.

One area that illustrates the importance of visual–spatial intelligence is the game of chess. An important skill for a chess player to have is the ability to predict moves and their consequences before they're made. This ability to plan ahead is closely tied to having a superior visual sense, or visual imagination, as chess players call it.

In a form of chess called blindfold chess, a person plays several games at the same time. So, for example, a blindfolded chess player might be playing ten games against ten different opponents, moving from table to table around a room. His opponents can see the chessboard, but the blindfolded chess player can't. The blindfolded player's only information about the chessboard is from someone announcing his opponent's last move. So, you can see why a strong visual memory is necessary.

For most chess players, each chess game has its own character, its own shape, and this makes an impression on the player. The blindfolded player has to remember the positions of the chess pieces, since he can't actually see the chessboard. As he tries to recall a given position, he remembers his reasoning at an earlier time, and he remembers a specific move—not all by itself, but ... uh ... instead, he remembers his specific strategy and why that move was necessary.

Chess players have strong visual memories of important games they've played in the past. This memory isn't just simple, rote recall. It's really the memory of the game's patterns of reasoning. The chess player's memory stores plans and ideas and strategies—not just a rote list of moves.

Chess masters have an amazing ability to reconstruct a chessboard they've seen for just a few seconds—if the pieces on the board are set in meaningful positions, as they are in the middle of a real game. But if the chess pieces are randomly located, then they don't have any real meaning, and the chess master may or may not be able to reconstruct the board.

Summarize the points made in the lecture, explaining how they illustrate points made in the reading.

TEST 4

Disk 10, Track 1

LISTENING SECTION DIRECTIONS (p. 544)

The Listening section measures your ability to understand conversations and lectures in English. You will hear each conversation and lecture only one time. After each conversation or lecture, you will hear some questions about it. Answer all questions based on what the speakers state or imply.

You may take notes while you listen. You may use your notes to help you answer the questions.

Most questions have four possible answers. In some questions, you will see this icon: 🎧. This means that you will hear, but not see, part of the question.

Some questions have special directions, which appear in a gray box. Most questions are worth one point. If a question is worth more than one point, special directions will indicate how many points you can receive.

You have approximately 40 minutes to complete the Listening section. This includes the time for listening to the conversations and lectures and for answering the questions.

To make this practice more like the real test, cover the questions and answers during each conversation and lecture. When you hear the first question, uncover the questions and answers.

Disk 10, Track 2

Questions 1 through 5. Listen to a conversation in a university housing office.

M: Hi. Um ... I live in Tower One ... and I was ... um ... I'd kind of like to live in a smaller building. I'm thinking of moving next semester.

W: Do you know about the villages? They're on the other side of campus from the towers.

M: Uh huh. I've seen them—I mean, from the outside. What's the rent like? I mean, compared to the towers.

W: The rent depends on the situation, like how many people are in the suite.

M: Suite? What's that?

W: It's a unit for either four, six, or eight people. They're like apartments.

M: Oh. Aren't there any private rooms?

W: No, not in the villages. It's all suites. The bedrooms are for two people—that part's kind of like in the dormitories. You have to share a bedroom with another student. The suites have two to four bedrooms, one or two bathrooms, and a kitchen with a stove and a microwave, and a full refrigerator. Some of them also have a big living room.

M: Oh, that sounds kind of nice. So ... what's the rent like?

W: I've just been checking in the computer. It looks like there's going to be a couple of openings next semester, but there's also a waiting list with about twenty–something people on it.

M: Oh.

W: Yeah. A lot of people want to live in the villages. I lived there for two years myself, before I moved to a house off campus.

M: Uh huh. So what is the rent?

W: Oh, sorry. Um … OK, the buildings in Swanson Village all have four–person suites. Those are 900 dollars a semester.

W: Wow.

M: And the other villages … let me see … they're anywhere from eight–fifty to a thousand. It depends. The six– and eight–person units are usually a little less. The ones with living rooms are a little more.

M: Wow. That's more than I expected.

W: The cheaper ones are less than the dorms in the towers.

M: Yeah, but I was hoping it'd be a lot less. But still … I'd kind of like to get out of the towers. Um … how do I get on the waiting list?

W: I can add your name now, if you like.

M: OK. It's Ian Jacobs.

W: Ian Jacobs. OK, Ian, I've added you to the waiting list. What we'll do is send you a notice by e–mail if something opens up in the villages. Your name is uh … number twenty–seven on the list.

M: Number twenty–seven … oh … wow.

W: You'd be surprised. Sometimes people change their minds, so people further down the list get a chance. You'll get in the villages eventually, maybe next semester.

M: OK. Thanks for your help.

W: No problem. Have a nice day!

1. What is the purpose of the conversation?
2. What are some features of the suites in the villages?
3. Listen again to part of the conversation. Then answer the question.
   "Oh, that sounds kind of nice. So … what's the rent like?"
   "I've just been checking in the computer. It looks like there's going to be a couple of openings next semester, but there's also a waiting list with about twenty–something people on it."
   "Oh."
   "Yeah. A lot of people want to live in the villages. I lived there for two years myself, before I moved to a house off campus."
   "Uh huh. So what is the rent?"
   "Oh, sorry."
   Why does the woman say this:
   "Oh, sorry."
4. What does the man think of the cost of rent in the villages?
5. Listen again to part of the conversation. Then answer the question.
   "Ian Jacobs. OK, Ian, I've added you to the waiting list. What we'll do is send you a notice by e–mail if something opens up in the villages. Your name is uh … number twenty–seven on the list."
   "Number twenty–seven … oh … wow."
   Select the sentence that best expresses how the man probably feels.

Disk 10, Track 3

Questions 6 through 10. Listen to a conversation between two students.

W: Our design class is getting really interesting, don't you think?

M: Yeah, I like Professor Vargas, but sometimes he goes too fast, and I feel like I'm missing something. There's a lot we have to remember.

W: True. There are a lot of details about all the different styles.

M: Yeah, there's Art Nouveau, and Art Deco, and Art Moderne … I have a hard time keeping it all straight.

W: I know what you mean.

M: For example, it seems to me that Art Deco and Art Moderne are the same thing.

W: Well, there is some overlap. They were both popular in the 1930s, although Art Deco came a little before Moderne. I think Professor Vargas said Art Deco started at an exhibition in Paris in 1925.

M: So, they were about the same time. That's one thing that gets confusing. Another thing is, they seem so similar it's hard to see why they're considered different styles.

W: Art Deco has more decoration than Art Moderne. Art Deco is the style you see in a lot of movie theaters and hotels that were built in the twenties and thirties. It has facades with geometric designs … and uh … strips of windows with decorative spandrels. Art Deco uses a lot of straight lines and slender forms. "Sleekness" is the word that comes to mind. At the time, it was considered "modernistic."

M: But that's what gets confusing! Doesn't "modernistic" also apply to Art Moderne?

W: Art Moderne is simpler than Deco. It has … uh … things like more rounded corners, flat roofs, and … the walls are smooth and don't have any decoration. It's more streamlined than Deco. Art Moderne buildings remind me of boats. The walls are smooth, and the trim is usually stainless steel. A lot of the windows are round, kind of like the portholes on a boat.

M: Oh … I know a building like that. It's right here in town, on Second Avenue. It has a rounded corner and round windows. It used to be a gas station, but now it's a restaurant. We should go there sometime.

W: Yeah, I'd like to see that. My favorite building is the Maritime Building. It's downtown, right across from my father's office. It's Art Deco—built in 1927—I know that from the cornerstone. You should see the lobby! It's just beautiful. There's a geometric pattern in the tile on the floor—kind of a big circle with lots of triangles. And you should see the elevator doors. They're gorgeous.

M: You know, we should go around and look at some of these buildings.

W: Yeah, that would be fun.

M: And … you know what else … this is an idea for our project. We could take pictures of the buildings and do a slide show in class.

W: Oh, that's a cool idea! But don't we need to get permission to take photographs? Especially of the interior … we need pictures of the lobby of the Maritime Building.

M: We could ask for permission. That shouldn't be a problem. Let's talk to Professor Vargas and see what he thinks.

W: OK. Why don't you do that, and I'll go down to the Maritime Building and see if there's anyone there—like a building superintendent—who can give us permission. I'll let you know. Why don't we meet again on Thursday?

M: OK. Fine with me.

6. What are the students mainly discussing?
7. Listen again to part of the conversation. Then answer the question.
   "Yeah, I like Professor Vargas, but sometimes he goes too fast, and I feel like I'm missing something. There's a lot we have to remember."
   "True. There are a lot of details about all the different styles."
   "Yeah, there's Art Nouveau, and Art Deco, and Art Moderne … I have a hard time keeping it all straight."
   Select the sentence that best expresses how the man probably feels.
8. How does the woman help the man?
9. Indicate whether each sentence below describes Art Deco or Art Moderne.
10. What can be inferred from the conversation?

Disk 10, Track 4

Questions 11 through 16. Listen to part of a lecture in a world history class.

For thousands of years, early peoples found their food in nature. They hunted and fished, and ate plants and fruits that grew wild. What led these people to invent agriculture, a completely different way of life?

We know that ancient people changed from hunters and gatherers to farmers when they began to domesticate wild plants and animals. The first farmers on each continent did not have other farmers to observe, so they could not have chosen farming consciously. However, once agriculture had started in one part of a continent, neighboring people could see the result and make the conscious decision to farm.

We have no written records about prehistoric agriculture in the Americas, and very few artifacts or physical clues. We do have evidence that early people used sharp sticks to dig furrows for planting seeds. Those sticks were probably the first agricultural tools. We think the first Americans began to grow crops around ten thousand years ago. The evidence comes from a cave in Mexico, where cultivated squash seeds have been found. These seeds are evidence of the early domestication of plants.

Hunting–gathering people selected wild plants for domestication for various reasons. Some plants had tasty fruit, some had fleshy or seedless fruit, and some had fruit with oily or tasty seeds. In a certain part of prehistoric Mexico, there was a kind of squash that grew in abundance on hillsides. The flesh of this squash was bitter, so the people didn't eat it, but the seeds were tasty and nourishing, and the people liked to gather them. The people brought the squash seeds back to their camp. As they ate the seeds, some seeds fell to the ground all around the camp. Later, some of these seeds germinated and produced new plants. Thus, the hunter–gatherers became farmers sort of by accident. It was probably not a conscious decision to plant squash in their camp, yet that was the result.

Now the people had a wild garden of squash plants at their campsite. This was fortunate, so they started to take more of an interest in the plants. They tried to protect the plants in practical ways. They cut back and cleared out the less healthy–looking plants. They pulled up other types of plants that were weeds. They gave the plants water during long dry spells. Eventually, the people realized that seeds grew better when they were planted in earth that was turned over. So they began to scratch the earth with a digging stick and to plant seeds systematically in rows. They realized that a tilled, watered, weeded garden provided larger, better, more numerous squash plants than those that grew naturally on a dry hillside. Thus, with a series of conscious decisions, the people started cultivating a new breed of squash plants. Because of their success with squash, they started to experiment with other kinds of plants. In time, they built a fence around the garden to protect it from animals. At this point, agriculture was firmly established in their culture.

Of course, all of this didn't happen overnight. The process probably took thousands of years. Different peoples acquired agriculture at different times in prehistory. In some areas, crops and agricultural technology spread as ancient peoples conquered and traded with one another. In other places, agricultural technology developed in isolation. Even so, it's very likely that the change from a hunting–gathering society to an agricultural society followed a similar pattern in different regions of the world.

11. What is the main purpose of the lecture?
12. What is probably true about the origins of agriculture?
13. The professor explains how the early people of Mexico probably started farming. Summarize the process by putting the events in order.
14. Why did the people begin to use digging sticks?
15. Listen again to part of the lecture. Then answer the question.
    "Because of their success with squash, they started to experiment with other kinds of plants. In time, they built a fence around the garden to protect it from animals. At this point, agriculture was firmly established in their culture. Of course, all of this didn't happen overnight."
    Why does the professor say this:
    "Of course, all of this didn't happen overnight."
16. What point does the professor make about the transition from hunting–gathering to agriculture?

Disk 10, Track 5

Questions 17 through 22. Listen to part of a discussion in an ecology class. The class is studying the hydrologic cycle.

W1: Water is essential for life, and in parts of the world, it's a precious commodity. Water continuously circulates from the ocean to the atmosphere, to the land, and back to the ocean, providing us with a renewable supply of purified water. This complex cycle—known as the hydrologic cycle—balances the amount of water in the ocean, in the atmosphere, and on the land. We get our understanding of how the cycle operates from research in climatology and hydrology. So … who can tell me what climatology is?

M: It's the study of climate … and … uh … the causes and effects of different climates.

W1: That right. And what is hydrology? Sarah?

W2: Well, "hydro" means "water," so it's something to do with water … like the study of water.

W1: Yes, the prefix "hydro" does refer to water. The hydrologic cycle is the water cycle. And hydrology is the study of the water—the distribution and effect of the water—on the earth's surface and in the soil and layers of rock. Think of climatology as the atmospheric phase, and hydrology as the land phase of the water cycle. Climatologists study the role of solar energy in the cycle. They're mainly concerned with the atmospheric phase of the cycle—how solar energy drives the cycle through the … uh … processes of evaporation, atmospheric circulation, and precipitation. Water is continuously absorbed into the atmosphere as vapor—evaporation—and returned to the earth as rain, hail, or snow—precipitation. The amount of water evaporating from oceans exceeds precipitation over oceans, and the excess water vapor is moved by wind to the land.

The land phase of the cycle is the concern of hydrologists. Hydrologists study the vast quantities of water in the land phase of the cycle, how water moves over and through the land, and how it's stored on or within the earth. Over land surfaces—of the precipitation that falls over land, small amounts evaporate while still in the air and … uh … reenter the atmosphere directly. The rest of it reaches the surface of the land. The water that falls to earth is stored on the surface in lakes, or it penetrates the surface, or it runs off over the surface and flows in rivers to the ocean. Some of the water is stored temporarily in the upper soil layers and used later by trees and plants. When it rains—yes?

M: I was … um … I wondered if that makes trees and plants part of the hydrologic cycle. I mean, they take in water, and the water moves through them, and then later on … um … the water evaporates from their leaves.

W1: I'm glad you mentioned that, Justin. Plants do play an important role in the land phase of the cycle and are therefore part of the cycle. Trees and plants circulate and store water—they draw it up through their roots and return it to the atmosphere through their leaves during evapotranspiration.

When it rains, if the soil is already saturated, water will seep downward through the upper soil layers, and possibly reach the water table. When it reaches the water table, it passes into groundwater storage. Most of the groundwater later returns to the surface, either as springs or as stream flow, supplying water to plants.

Eventually, all of the water falling on land makes its way back to the ocean. The movement of water from land to the ocean is called runoff. Runoff and groundwater together balance the amount of water that moves from the ocean to the land.

Every molecule of water in the natural system eventually circulates through the hydrologic cycle. Tremendous quantities of water are cycled annually. And, as Justin pointed out, living organisms—plants, and animals as well—are also part of the cycle, since water is a large part of the mass of most organisms. Living organisms store and use water, since water is the … uh … solvent for most biological reactions.

17. What is the hydrologic cycle?
18. Identify the area in the diagram that mainly concerns climatologists.
19. What do hydrologists mainly study?

20. What happens to water that falls to the earth as precipitation?
21. Why does the professor say this:
"Eventually, all of the water falling on land makes its way back to the ocean. The movement of water from land to the ocean is called runoff. Runoff and groundwater together balance the amount of water that moves from the ocean to the land."
22. What can be inferred about plants in the hydrologic cycle?

Disk 10, Track 6

Questions 23 through 28. Listen to part of a lecture in a Canadian studies class. The professor is talking about art.

The painter Arthur Lismer wrote, "Most creative people, whether in painting, writing or music, began to have a guilty feeling that Canada was as yet unwritten, unpainted, unsung." According to Lismer, there was a job to be done, and so a generation of artists set out to create a school of painting that would record the Canadian scene and reinforce a distinctive Canadian identity. Calling themselves the Group of Seven, they proclaimed that—quote, "Art must grow and flower in the land before the country will be a real home for its people."

The Group's origins date back to the 1911 showing in Toronto of the painting "At the Edge of the Maple Wood" by A.Y. Jackson of Montreal. This painting's vibrant color and texture made a deep impression on local artists. They persuaded Jackson to come to Toronto and share a studio with them. Jackson began to accompany another painter, Tom Thomson, on sketching trips to Algonquin Park, north of the city.

Several of the artists worked at the same Toronto commercial design firm, and it was here that they met and discovered their common artistic interests. After work, they socialized together at the Arts and Letters Club. They talked about finding a new direction for Canadian art, a distinctly Canadian style of painting. It was a romantic quest—mainly fueled by the restless spirit of Tom Thomson, who led the others to the Canadian wilderness to sketch and paint.

A patron gave the artists the famous Studio Building in Toronto. It was here that Thomson did some of his finest paintings from sketches made in the wild. Among them was "The Jack Pine," one of the nation's best–loved pictures. But then, suddenly and tragically, Thomson died in 1917—drowning in a canoe accident—shocking his fellow painters and Canadian art lovers.

The other artists continued their sketching trips to the vast wilderness of northern Ontario. It was there that they found inspiration for some of their greatest paintings. Each artist had his own vision and his own technique, but they all captured the essence of wilderness Canada—a bleak, somber, incredibly beautiful landscape of rock outcroppings, storm–driven lakes, and jack pine trees—a land totally uninhabited by people.

After a 1919 trip to the wilderness, the artists decided to organize an exhibition and to formally call themselves the Group of Seven. The seven founding artists were Jackson, Lismer, Harris, MacDonald, Varley, Johnston, and Carmichael.

Their 1920 exhibition was an important moment in Canadian art. It proclaimed that Canadian art must be inspired by Canada itself. However, the initial response was less than favorable. Several major art critics ignored the show, while others called the paintings crude and barbaric. Yet, when British critics praised the Group's distinctly Canadian vision, the Canadian public took another look. Later exhibitions drew increasing acceptance for the Group's work, establishing them as the "national school." Before long, they were the most influential painters in the country, and several of their paintings have become icons of Canada.

A.Y. Jackson was influential for his analysis of light and shadow. Arthur Lismer's work has an intensity all its own—particularly his painting of the "Canadian Jungle," the violently colored forest in the fall. Lawren Harris went further than the rest in simplifying the forms of nature into sculptural shapes, organizing an entire scene into a single, unified image, and eventually into abstraction.

23. Which of the following best describes the organization of the lecture?
24. What is the professor's point of view concerning the Group of Seven?
25. Listen again to part of the lecture. Then answer the question.
"After work, they socialized together at the Arts and Letters Club. They talked about finding a new direction for Canadian art, a distinctly Canadian style of painting. It was a romantic quest—mainly fueled by the restless spirit of Tom Thomson, who led the others to the Canadian wilderness to sketch and paint."
Why does the professor say this:
"It was a romantic quest—mainly fueled by the restless spirit of Tom Thomson, who led the others to the Canadian wilderness to sketch and paint."
26. What subjects did the Group of Seven paint?
27. What does the professor mean by this statement:
"Before long, they were the most influential painters in the country, and several of their paintings have become icons of Canada."
28. Listen again to part of the lecture. Then answer the question.
"A.Y. Jackson was influential for his analysis of light and shadow. Arthur Lismer's work has an intensity all its own—particularly his painting of the "Canadian Jungle," the violently colored forest in the fall. Lawren Harris went further than the rest in simplifying the forms of nature into sculptural shapes, organizing an entire scene into a single, unified image, and eventually into abstraction."
What can be concluded about the Group of Seven's style of painting?

Disk 10, Track 7

Questions 29 through 34. Listen to part of a talk in a business management class.

What do we mean when we talk about leadership? First, it's important not to confuse leadership with power. It's true that—by definition—leaders always have some degree of power. Leaders have power because of their ability to influence other people. However, many power holders do not have the qualities of leadership. Consider the headwaiter in your favorite restaurant. The headwaiter has power to some degree—for example, the power to seat you at the best table by the window—but he doesn't necessarily have the qualities we associate with leadership.

We have to distinguish between leaders and power holders. There are a lot of powerful people who lack leadership skills. A military dictator has power. So does the robber who sticks a gun in your face and demands your wallet. Leadership is something else.

Leadership and power are not the same thing, although they are similar in this one way. Both leadership and power involve the ability to … bring about the results you want, and to … prevent the results that you don't want to happen.

Here's another way to think of it. In sociological terms, … uh … power is simply the ability to bring about certain behavior in other people. For example, parents have power over their children, and they use it to get their children to behave in acceptable ways. Teachers have power, and so do mid–level managers—all as a result of their position.

Where does power come from? The sources are varied. Probably the oldest source of power is the ability to use physical force—a source available to both the military and the biggest kid on the playground. The power that comes from physical might is not the same as leadership. Just think of the military dictator … or the school bully. We don't usually think of these power holders as leaders—despite the brute force they use to control others.

Wealth, position, the ability to motivate—all of these are sources of power. Being close to others with power is a source of power. That's why people gravitate toward political leaders. Some power comes from qualities people were born with—like physical beauty, or the ability to influence friends. Science and technology are also sources of power. Corporations understand this and spend huge amounts of money on research, information systems, and consultants.

Although leadership and power are different things, they're related in important ways. Consider, for example, a chief executive officer who has the ability to motivate people, a CEO with vision, who can lift the spirit of his or her employees and bring about a rise in productivity—that is leadership. But consider this scenario. The company realizes they're sort of falling behind in the technology race, so the CEO responds by increasing the amount of money available to the company's research division. That is the exercise of power. Authorizing a spending increase could have been made only by a chief executive with the power to do so. Remember, both leadership and power involve the ability to accomplish the results you want, and successful managers understand how the two work together to make this happen.

29. What is the talk mainly about?
30. Why does the professor talk about the headwaiter in a restaurant?
31. Why does the professor say this:
"A military dictator has power. So does the robber who sticks a gun in your face and demands your wallet. Leadership is something else."
32. According to the professor, how are leadership and power similar?
33. According to the professor, which of the following are sources of power?
34. Listen again to part of the talk. Then answer the question.
"Authorizing a spending increase could have been made only by a chief executive with the power to do so. Remember, both leadership and power involve the ability to accomplish the results you want, and successful managers understand how the two work together to make this happen."
What does the professor imply about successful managers?

Disk 10, Track 8

Speaking Section Directions (p. 550)

The Speaking section measures your ability to speak in English about a variety of topics. There are six questions in this section. Record your response to each question on a cassette.

Questions 1 and 2 are independent speaking tasks in which you will speak about familiar topics. Your responses will be scored on your ability to speak clearly and coherently about the topics.

Questions 3 and 4 are integrated tasks in which you will read a passage, listen to a conversation or lecture, and then speak in response to a question about what you have read and heard. You will need to combine relevant information from the two sources to answer the question completely. Your responses will be scored on your ability to speak clearly and coherently and on your ability to accurately convey information about what you read and heard.

Questions 5 and 6 are integrated tasks in which you will listen to part of a conversation or lecture, and then speak in response to a question about what you have heard. Your responses will be scored on your ability to speak clearly and coherently and on your ability to accurately convey information about what you heard.

You will hear each conversation and lecture only one time. You may take notes while you listen. You may use your notes to help you answer the questions.

Disk 10, Track 9

What foreign country would you like to visit? Choose a country and explain why you would like to go there. Include details and examples to support your explanation.

Disk 10, Track 10

In some schools, teachers decide what classes students must take. Other schools allow students to select their own classes. Which system do you think is better and why? Include details and examples in your explanation.

Disk 10, Track 11

Now listen to two students as they discuss the swimming pool hours.

M: What do you think about the new pool hours?
W: It doesn't affect me much, since I only swim on weekends, and those times aren't changing. What about you?
M: Well, it's kind of a big change to the pool schedule. They're completely eliminating times in the late afternoon, after three o'clock. That's when I like to swim—right after my last class.
W: It looks like they're adding more swimming classes in the afternoon and evening.
M: Yeah, but I don't see why they have to close the pool to everyone else. A class doesn't usually take up the whole pool. I don't see why they can't leave half of the pool open for people who just want to swim laps. It's not fair to just take away our pool time like this. The least they could do is extend the morning hours. They should open the pool at seven instead of nine in

the morning. That would make up for the time they cut in the afternoon.
W: You would go swimming at seven o'clock in the morning?
M: Sure. I'm a morning person—and what a way to start the day!

The man expresses his opinion about the change in swimming pool hours. State his opinion and explain the reasons he gives for holding that opinion.

Disk 10, Track 12

Now listen to part of a talk in a biology class for pre–medical students.

Recently in the clinic we had a patient who had been suffering from tremors of the head that caused headaches. These headaches left her neck stiff and her back sore. In addition, her jaw clicked when she opened and closed her mouth. Sometimes her jaw locked up while she was eating, and she couldn't even open her mouth. Doctors had been treating her symptoms with painkilling medication for 20 years, with little success. The patient felt very frustrated and was willing to try anything to relieve her head, neck, and jaw problems. Finally, we referred her to the chiropractic clinic.

After her third visit to the chiropractor, the patient noticed a huge difference. Her headaches and lockjaw were gone, and the head tremors greatly reduced. She was able to stop taking painkillers. Patient success stories like this one are a big reason why chiropractic is becoming more accepted in the medical establishment. Research findings are also helping to increase acceptance. In a survey of doctors taken two years ago, for example, 62 percent of the physicians said that chiropractic treatment helped their patients.

Describe the patient's symptoms, and explain why chiropractic treatment was recommended. Explain how this patient's experience supports the practice of chiropractic.

Disk 10, Track 13

Now listen to a conversation between two students.

M: So, have you registered for the next semester yet?
W: Not yet. I want to take statistics, but the course is already full. So it looks like I have to take a different math course, like maybe calculus. But I'd much rather take statistics.
M: If you want statistics, why don't you register to get on the waiting list? Then if someone drops it, you might get in.
W: Do you think so? I didn't think of that.
M: You could register for both courses. Get on the waiting list for statistics, and also register for calculus— that way you'll be sure to get one of the classes. If you get in statistics, you can drop calculus.
W: I guess I could try that.
M: Another thing you could do is talk to the instructor that teaches statistics. If you can convince the instructor that you really want the class, maybe they'll let you in anyway, even though the class is full. It's worth a try.

The students discuss two possible solutions to the woman's problem. Describe the problem. Then state which of the two solutions you prefer and explain why.

Disk 10, Track 14

Now listen to part of a lecture in a psychology class. The professor is discussing children's fears.

All children experience periods of fear. Fears are normal, and they help children solve issues of change and development. Fears also call parents' attention to a child's situation so the parent will provide extra support when the child needs it.

The fear of falling is built into each newborn baby in the form of a clasping motion. A baby will make this motion when he is uncovered or surprised, or when he is dropped suddenly. His arms shoot out sideways and then come together as if to grab anything or anyone nearby. The baby usually cries out when he makes this motion. The startled cry attracts a parent's attention. Thus, even from birth, a baby is able to use this natural fear of falling to get help.

Another fear that babies have is the fear of strangers, a natural fear that alerts the child to a new situation. Anxiety around strangers is one of the earliest signs of fear in babies. In studies that filmed babies as they played with adults, it was shown that even at one month old, the babies could distinguish between their mother, father, and strangers, and they showed this with clear differences in their own responses.

Fears appear during periods of new and rapid learning. At one year old, and all through the second year, a whole new world opens up when children learn to walk. They will both value and fear their new independence. At the same time they learn to run away from their parents, children also find new things to be afraid of—dogs, loud noises, strange people and places. Fears help children adjust to their new independence. By overcoming their fears, children acquire confidence in their own new abilities.

Using points and examples from the lecture, describe fears that young children experience, and explain how these fears help children.

Disk 10, Track 15

WRITING SECTION DIRECTIONS (p. 555)

The Writing section measures your ability to use writing to communicate in an academic environment. There are two writing questions.

Question 1 is an integrated writing task. You will read a passage, listen to a lecture, and then answer a question based on what you have read and heard. You have 20 minutes to plan and write your response.

Question 2 is an independent writing task. You will answer a question based on your own knowledge and experience. You have 30 minutes to plan and write your response.

Disk 10, Track 16

Now listen to part of a talk on this topic in an ecology class.

Nothing is more dependable than the lowly earthworm … right? Well, not exactly. We now know that earthworms are causing significant damage to some forests. The problem is, they're destroying the soil cover. Native plant communities are disappearing, and so is the habitat for a lot of different animals. It's because earthworms change the structure of the soil, and change how nutrients are cycled … it's because of this that they have such a huge, rippling effect on forest ecosystems.

The idea that worms are suddenly a problem isn't easy for us to grasp, but now we have evidence of their damage. There's a forest ecologist in Minnesota who's studying the soil near a popular fishing lake. She noticed that the forest floor was changing rapidly near the shoreline of the lake, where fishers dump their unused bait worms. A thick layer of spongy duff was disappearing, and so were the native wildflowers. When she took a shovel and looked at the soil, she could see that earthworms were present in large numbers wherever the duff was disappearing.

The worms are doing just what gardeners like them to do. They're taking organic matter from the surface—in this case, the leaf litter and decaying branches—and they're moving it down deeper into the soil. Except that here, by the lakeshore, they're cleaning the forest floor so well that fallen leaves disappear in just a few weeks.

The decaying leaves in the duff are of vital importance to the forest ecosystem. Duff contains the nutrients that are slowly released into the soil—the nutrients that plants need to sprout. But worms are literally eating the forest floor right out from under the plants. And the disappearance of the duff has an effect beyond the native plants. The duff also gives shelter to salamanders, insects, and spiders … so when the duff disappears, so do these animals and the other animals that feed on them.

Describe the problems caused by earthworms in forest ecosystems, and explain how these problems contradict information in the reading.

DELTA'S KEY TO THE NEXT GENERATION TOEFL® TEST

INDEX

PROGRESS CHARTS

Record your quiz and test scores on Progress Charts 1 through 6. Use the charts to monitor your achievement and set goals for future study. You can remove the charts from the book and put them in a portfolio of your work to show your instructor.

The left column of each chart shows the percentage correct on quizzes and tests. The bottom row of Progress Charts 1 through 4 refers to relevant units to study for each quiz.

Example of Progress Chart 1 – Reading Quizzes

Example of Progress Chart 5 – Tests

PROGRESS CHART 1

Reading Quizzes

Circle the number correct on each quiz. Draw a line to connect the circles.

% Correct	Quiz 1	Quiz 2	Quiz 3	Quiz 4	Quiz 5	Quiz 6	Quiz 7	Quiz 8	Quiz 9	Quiz 10
100%	10	25	10	25	10	25	10	25	10	25
		24		24		24		24		24
90%	9	23	9	23	9	23	9	23	9	23
		22		22		22		22		22
		21		21		21		21		21
80%	8	20	8	20	8	20	8	20	8	20
		19		19		19		19		19
70%	7	18	7	18	7	18	7	18	7	18
		17		17		17		17		17
		16		16		16		16		16
60%	6	15	6	15	6	15	6	15	6	15
		14		14		14		14		14
50%	5	13	5	13	5	13	5	13	5	13
		12		12		12		12		12
		11		11		11		11		11
40%	4	10	4	10	4	10	4	10	4	10
		9		9		9		9		9
30%	3	8	3	8	3	8	3	8	3	8
		7		7		7		7		7
		6		6		6		6		6
20%	1	5	1	5	1	5	1	5	1	5
Units to Study	1.1 thru 1.2	1.1 thru 1.3	1.4	1.1 thru 1.4	1.5 thru 1.6	1.1 thru 1.6	1.7 thru 1.8	1.1 thru 1.8	1.9 thru 1.10	1.1 thru 1.10

PROGRESS CHART 2

Listening Quizzes

Circle the number correct on each quiz. Draw a line to connect the circles.

% Correct	Quiz 1	Quiz 2	Quiz 3	Quiz 4	Quiz 5	Quiz 6	Quiz 7	Quiz 8
100%	10	10	10	10	10	10	10	10
90%	9	9	9	9	9	9	9	9
80%	8	8	8	8	8	8	8	8
70%	7	7	7	7	7	7	7	7
60%	6	6	6	6	6	6	6	6
50%	5	5	5	5	5	5	5	5
40%	4	4	4	4	4	4	4	4
30%	3	3	3	3	3	3	3	3
20%	2	2	2	2	2	2	2	2
Units to Study	2.1 thru 2.2	2.1 thru 2.3	2.1 thru 2.3	2.1 thru 2.4	2.1 thru 2.4	2.5 thru 2.6	2.1 thru 2.6	2.1 thru 2.6

PROGRESS CHART 3

Speaking Quizzes

Circle the points earned on each quiz. Draw a line to connect the circles.

% Correct	Quiz 1	Quiz 2	Quiz 3	Quiz 4	Quiz 5	Quiz 6	Quiz 7	Quiz 8
100%	8	8	8	16	16	16	24	24
				15	15	15	23	23
90%							22	22
	7	7	7	14	14	14	21	21
80%				13	13	13	20	20
							19	19
	6	6	6	12	12	12	18	18
70%				11	11	11	17	17
							16	16
				10	10	10	15	15
60%	5	5	5	9	9	9	14	14
							13	13
50%				8	8	8	12	12
	4	4	4	7	7	7	11	11
40%							10	10
				6	6	6	9	9
	3	3	3	5	5	5	8	8
30%							7	7
				4	4	4	6	6
20%	2	2	2	3	3	3	5	5
Units to Study	3.1 thru 3.4	3.1 thru 3.4	3.1 thru 3.4	3.5 thru 3.10	3.5 thru 3.10	3.5 thru 3.10	3.1 thru 3.10	3.1 thru 3.10

PROGRESS CHART 4

Writing Quizzes

Circle the points earned on each quiz. Draw a line to connect the circles.

% Correct	Quiz 1	Quiz 2	Quiz 3	Quiz 4	Quiz 5	Quiz 6	Quiz 7	Quiz 8
100%	5	5	5	5	5	5	10	10
90%							9	9
80%	4	4	4	4	4	4	8	8
70%							7	7
60%	3	3	3	3	3	3	6	6
50%							5	5
40%	2	2	2	2	2	2	4	4
30%							3	3
20%	1	1	1	1	1	1	2	2
Units to Study	4.1 thru 4.5	4.1 thru 4.5	4.1 thru 4.5	4.6 thru 4.10	4.6 thru 4.10	4.6 thru 4.10	4.1 thru 4.10	4.1 thru 4.10

PROGRESS CHART 5

Tests

Circle the number correct in each test section. Draw four separate lines to connect the circles for Reading, Listening, Speaking, and Writing. See the example on page 692.

% Correct	Test 1				Test 2				Test 3				Test 4			
	R	L	S	W	R	L	S	W	R	L	S	W	R	L	S	W
100%	42	34	24	10	42	34	24	10	42	34	24	10	42	34	24	10
	41	33			41	33			41	33			41	33		
	40		23		40		23		40		23		40		23	
	39	32			39	32			39	32			39	32		
90%	38	31	22	9	38	31	22	9	38	31	22	9	38	31	22	9
	37	30	21		37	30	21		37	30	21		37	30	21	
	36	29			36	29			36	29			36	29		
	35		20		35		20		35		20		35		20	
	34	28			34	28			34	28			34	28		
80%	33	27	19	8	33	27	19	8	33	27	19	8	33	27	19	8
	32	26			32	26			32	26			32	26		
	31		18		31		18		31		18		31		18	
	30	25			30	25			30	25			30	25		
70%	29	24	17	7	29	24	17	7	29	24	17	7	29	24	17	7
	28	23			28	23			28	23			28	23		
	27	22	16		27	22	16		27	22	16		27	22	16	
	26	21	15		26	21	15		26	21	15		26	21	15	
60%	25			6	25			6	25			6	25			6
	24	20	14		24	20	14		24	20	14		24	20	14	
	23	19			23	19			23	19			23	19		
	22	18	13		22	18	13		22	18	13		22	18	13	
50%	21	17	12	5	21	17	12	5	21	17	12	5	21	17	12	5
	20				20				20				20			
	19	16	11		19	16	11		19	16	11		19	16	11	
	18	15			18	15			18	15			18	15		
40%	17	14	10	4	17	14	10	4	17	14	10	4	17	14	10	4
	16				16				16				16			
	15	13	9		15	13	9		15	13	9		15	13	9	
	14	12			14	12			14	12			14	12		
	13	11	8		13	11	8		13	11	8		13	11	8	
30%	12	10	7	3	12	10	7	3	12	10	7	3	12	10	7	3
	11				11				11				11			
	10	9	6		10	9	6		10	9	6		10	9	6	
	9	8			9	8			9	8			9	8		
20%	8	7	5	2	8	7	5	2	8	7	5	2	8	7	5	2

PROGRESS CHART 6

TOEFL® Scores for Tests

Use the TOEFL Score Conversion Tables on the next page to find your TOEFL scores for each test section. Write each section score below in the correct box for each test. To calculate the total test score, add the four section scores.

Section/Test	Test 1	Test 2	Test 3	Test 4
Reading				
Listening				
Speaking				
Writing				
Total Test				

Example

Reading, number correct: 28   TOEFL section score: 20
Listening, number correct: 26   TOEFL section score: 19
Speaking, points earned: 15   TOEFL section score: 19
Writing, points earned: 7   TOEFL section score: 22

Total test score: 20 + 19 + 19 + 22 = 80

TOEFL® SCORE CONVERSION TABLES

To find your approximate TOEFL scores for Test 1 through Test 4, use the tables below. For each test section, look on the correct line for the number of points you earned, and then find your TOEFL section score on the same line. Record your scores on Progress Chart 6 on page 698.

Reading		**Listening**		**Speaking**		**Writing**	
Points Earned	TOEFL® Section Score	Points Earned	TOEFL® Section Score	Points Earned	TOEFL® Section Score	Points Earned	TOEFL® Section Score
42	30	34	30	24	30	10	30
41	30	33	29	23	29	9	28
40	29	32	27	22	28	8	25
39	28	31	26	21	27	7	22
38	27	30	25	20	26	6	20
37	27	29	23	19	24	5	17
36	26	28	22	18	23	4	14
35	25	27	21	17	22	3	11
34	24	26	19	16	20	2	8
33	24	25	18	15	19	1	5
32	23	24	17	14	18		
31	22	23	15	13	17		
30	21	22	14	12	15		
29	20	21	14	11	14		
28	20	20	12	10	13		
27	19	19	11	9	11		
26	18	18	10	8	10		
25	18	17	9	7	9		
24	17	16	8	6	8		
23	16	15	8	5	6		
22	15	14	7	4	5		
21	14	13	6	3	4		
20	13	12	5	2	3		
19	13	11	4	1	1		
18	12	10	4				
17	10	9	3				
16	10	8	2				
15	9	7	2				
14	7	6	1				
13	6						
12	5						
11	4						
10	3						
9	2						
8	1